Teen Health Resources

health.glencoe.com

New Student Edition Includes

- The latest health information
- Guide to Reading and Graphic Organizers
- TIME health news
- Spanish Edition

Activities to Build Reading & Writing Skills

- Building Vocabulary
- Quick Write
- Reading Checks
- Write About It

Online Learning Center

- Online Student Edition
- Chapter Summaries in English and Spanish
- Interactive Study Guides
- eFlashcards
- Crossword Puzzles
- Health Inventories
- Building Health Skills
- Student Web Activities
- Career Corner

Teen Health
COURSE 3

Mary H. Bronson, Ph.D.

Michael J. Cleary, Ed.D., C.H.E.S.

Betty M. Hubbard, Ed.D., C.H.E.S.

Contributing Authors

Dinah Zike, M.Ed.

TIME®

McGraw Hill **Glencoe**

New York, New York   Columbus, Ohio   Chicago, Illinois   Peoria, Illinois   Woodland Hills, California

Meet the Authors

Mary H. Bronson, Ph.D., recently retired after teaching for 30 years in Texas public schools. Dr. Bronson taught health education in grades K–12, as well as health education methods classes at the undergraduate and graduate levels. As Health Education Specialist for the Dallas School District, Dr. Bronson developed and implemented a district-wide health education program. She has been honored as Texas Health Educator of the Year by the Texas Association for Health, Physical Education, Recreation, and Dance and selected Teacher of the Year twice, by her colleagues. Dr. Bronson has assisted school districts throughout the country in developing local health education programs. She is also the coauthor of the *Glencoe Health* textbook.

Betty M. Hubbard, Ed.D., C.H.E.S., has taught science and health education in grades 6–12, as well as undergraduate- and graduate-level courses. She is a professor at the University of Central Arkansas, where, in addition to teaching, she conducts in-service training for health education teachers in school districts throughout Arkansas. In 1991, Dr. Hubbard received the university's teaching excellence award. Her publications, grants, and presentations focus on research-based, comprehensive health instruction. Dr. Hubbard is a fellow of the American Association for Health Education and serves as the contributing editor for the Teaching Ideas feature of the *American Journal of Health Education*.

Michael J. Cleary, Ed.D., C.H.E.S., is a professor at Slippery Rock University, where he teaches methods courses and supervises field experiences. Dr. Cleary taught health education at Evanston Township High School in Illinois and later served as the Lead Teacher Specialist at the McMillen Center for Health Education in Fort Wayne, Indiana. Dr. Cleary has published widely on curriculum development and assessment in K–12 and college health education. Dr. Cleary is also coauthor of the *Glencoe Health* textbook.

Contributing Authors

Dinah Zike, M.Ed., is an international curriculum consultant and inventor who has designed and developed educational products and three-dimensional, interactive graphic organizers for over thirty years. As president and founder of Dinah-Might Adventures, L.P., Dinah is author of over 100 award-winning educational publications. Dinah has a B.S. and an M.S. in educational curriculum and instruction from Texas A&M University. Dinah Zike's *Foldables*™ are an exclusive feature of McGraw-Hill textbooks.

TIME is the nation's leading news and information magazine. With over 80 years of experience, TIME provides an authoritative voice in the analysis of the issues of the day, from politics to pop culture, from history-making decisions to healthy living. TIME Learning Ventures brings the strength of TIME and TIME For Kids' editorial and photographic excellence to educational resources for school and home.

The *McGraw-Hill* Companies

Send all inquiries to:
Glencoe/McGraw-Hill
21600 Oxnard Street, Suite 500
Woodland Hills, California 91367

ISBN-13: 978-0-07-869762-3   (Course 3 Student Edition)
ISBN-10: 0-07-869762-X   (Course 3 Student Edition)

ISBN-13: 978-0-07-869765-4   (Course 3 Teacher Wraparound Edition)
ISBN-10: 0-07-869765-4   (Course 3 Teacher Wraparound Edition

7 8 9 10 11 12   079   12 11 10 09 08 07

Health Consultants

Alia Antoon, M.D.
Chief of Pediatrics
Shriners Hospital for Children
Assistant Clinical Professor, Pediatrics
Harvard Medical School
Boston, Massachusetts

Elissa M. Barr, Ph.D., C.H.E.S.
Assistant Professor of Public Health
University of North Florida
Jacksonville, Florida

Beverly Bradley, Ph.D., R.N., C.H.E.S.
School Health Consultant
Retired Assistant Clinical Professor
University of California, San Diego
San Diego, California

Roberta L. Duyff, M.S., R.D., C.F.C.S.
Food and Nutrition Consultant/President
Duyff Associates
St. Louis, Missouri

Kristin Danielson Fink, M.A.
National Director
Community of Caring
Salt Lake City, Utah

Kathryn J. Gust, M.A.
Instructional Technology Specialist
Freedom High School
Morganton, North Carolina

Christine A. Hayashi, M.A. Ed., J.D.
Attorney at Law, Special Education Law
Adjunct Faculty, Educational Leadership
and Policy Studies Development
California State University, Northridge
Northridge, California

Tinker D. Murray, Ph.D., FACSM
Professor of Health, Physical Education, and Recreation
Texas State University
San Marcos, Texas

Don Rainey, M.S., C.S.C.S.
Director, Physical Fitness and Wellness
Texas State University
San Marcos, Texas

Michael Rulon, M.S.
Instructional Coach
Health Instructor
Albuquerque Public Schools
Albuquerque, New Mexico

Robin Scarcella, Ph.D.
Director, Academic English/ESL
University of California, Irvine
Irvine, California

Peter T. Whelley, M.S., N.C.S.P.
School Psychologist
Moultonborough School District
Adjunct Faculty
Plymouth State University
Plymouth, New Hampshire

David C. Wiley, Ph.D.
Professor of Health Education
Texas State University
San Marcos, Texas

Reviewers

Kathy Bowman-Harrow

Supervisor, Health Education
Orange County Public Schools
Orlando, Florida

Pamela Rizzo Connolly, M.E.

*Curriculum Coordinator for Health
and Physical Education*
North Catholic High School
Diocese of Pittsburgh
Pittsburgh, Pennsylvania

Audrey Maria Diamond

Science Teacher
Ellis G. Arnall Middle School
Newnan, Georgia

Allison Duckworth, M.A.

Physical Education Teacher
Head Athletic Trainer
Freedom High School
Morganton, North Carolina

Valerie Hernandez, R.N., M.S.

School Nurse/Health Educator
Escambia County School District
Pensacola, Florida

Norma H. Lee, M.A.

Wellness Instructor
Jefferson County High School
Dandridge, Tennessee

Bobby Jean Moore, M.A.T.

Health Education Specialist
Creekside Middle School
Lawrenceville, Georgia

Joan Gilger Stear, M.Ed

Health Education Instructor
West Clermont Institute of Performing Arts
Glen Este High School
Cincinnati, Ohio

Stacia K. Tatum

Physical Education Teacher
Westridge Middle School
Orlando, Florida

Jeanne Title

County Coordinator
Office of Safety and Wellness
Napa County Office of Education
Napa, California

Robert T. Wieselberg

Health Educator
Westridge Middle School
Orlando, Florida

Understanding Your Health

CHAPTER 2 Skills for a Healthy Life

CHAPTER 3 Mental and Emotional Health

CHAPTER 14

Drugs

CHAPTER 15

Personal Care and Consumer Choices

CHAPTER 18

Common Communicable Diseases

CHAPTER 19

Noncommunicable Diseases

Getting the most out of

Making healthy and responsible choices is easy with Teen Health. Follow the guidelines below to make the most out of each lesson.

Lesson 4

Your Respiratory System

Guide to Reading

Building Vocabulary
Read each of the words below. If the word is familiar, write down what you think its meaning is. If it's not, guess at its meaning.
- respiratory system (p. 418)
- respiration (p. 418)
- bronchi (p. 420)
- alveoli (p. 420)
- diaphragm (p. 420)
- asthma (p. 420)
- Air Quality Index (AQI) (p. 421)

Focusing on the Main Ideas
In this lesson, you will learn to
- **explain** how your body uses the air you breathe.
- **identify** the parts and functions of the respiratory system.
- **describe** ways to maintain the health of your respiratory system.
- **analyze** the role of posture on respiratory health.

Reading Strategy
Organizing Information Create an outline using the major and minor headings in the lesson. As you read, take notes under each heading on your outline.

Quick Write
Write about a time when you felt out of breath. Tell what caused this and what, if anything, you did to get your breath back.

Breathing

While reading this paragraph you will breathe in and out four or five times. This will happen without you even thinking about it. Breathing is a function of your body's **respiratory system**—*a system that consists of organs that supply the body with constant oxygen and rid the body of carbon dioxide.* Your body needs oxygen to survive. In fact, a person can live only a few minutes without oxygen.

Functions of the Respiratory System

The respiratory system's main job, as its name suggests, is **respiration.** This is *the exchange of gases between your body and the air.* There are two major types of respiration: external and internal.

- **External respiration.** This is the exchange of oxygen and carbon dioxide between the blood and the air in the lungs. As you inhale, you breathe oxygen-rich air into your lungs. The oxygen exchanges with carbon dioxide inside your lungs. When you exhale, you release carbon dioxide into the air.

418 Chapter 16: Your Body Systems

Review Key Terms
Complete the Building Vocabulary activity to become familiar with the key terms before you read the lesson. Vocabulary terms are highlighted in yellow to make them easy to find.

Do the Quick Write
This feature will help you start thinking about the information in the lesson.

Preview the Lesson
Get a preview of what's coming by reading the lesson objectives in Focusing on the Main Ideas. You can also use this feature to prepare for quizzes and tests.

Strengthen Your Reading Skills
Complete the Reading Strategy activity to help you understand the information in the lesson.

Health Online

Use Glencoe's Online Learning Center to Boost Your Health Smarts!

- Rate your health by taking the Health Inventories for each chapter. Jump-start your goals by filling out a Personal Wellness Contract.
- Check out Student Web Activities for fun and interactive learning.
- Learn about different health-related careers at Career Corner.
- Get ready for tests by using the different Online Study Tools to review vocabulary terms and chapter content. E-flashcards, crossword puzzles, review questions, and online quizzes make studying fun!
- Building Health Skills features give you another chance to master important skills for good health.

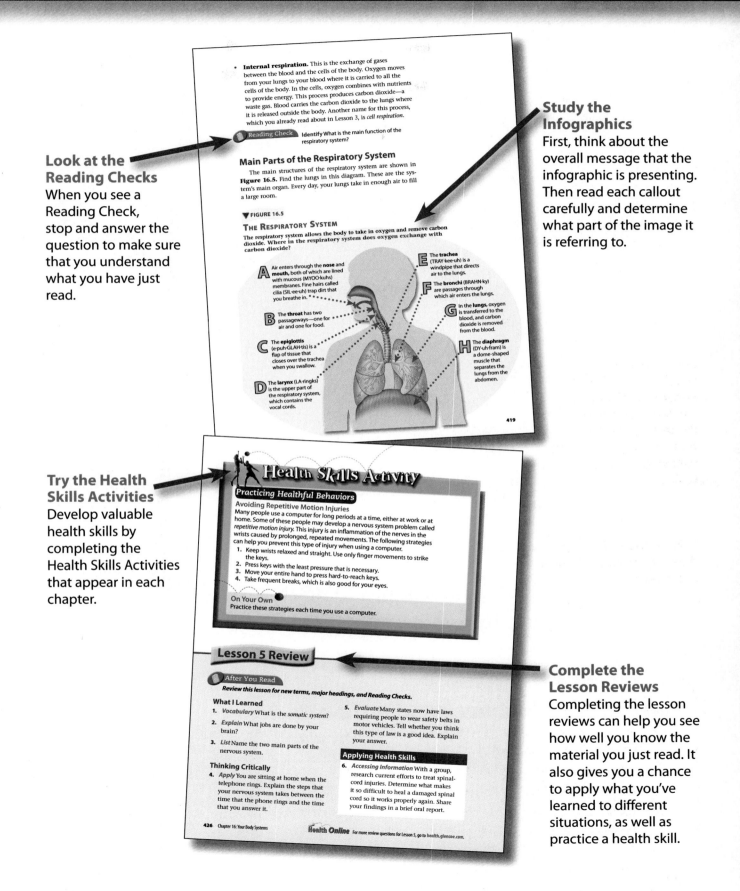

Look at the Reading Checks
When you see a Reading Check, stop and answer the question to make sure that you understand what you have just read.

Study the Infographics
First, think about the overall message that the infographic is presenting. Then read each callout carefully and determine what part of the image it is referring to.

Try the Health Skills Activities
Develop valuable health skills by completing the Health Skills Activities that appear in each chapter.

Complete the Lesson Reviews
Completing the lesson reviews can help you see how well you know the material you just read. It also gives you a chance to apply what you've learned to different situations, as well as practice a health skill.

Within the infographic image:

- **Internal respiration.** This is the exchange of gases between the blood and the cells of the body. Oxygen moves from your lungs to your blood where it is carried to all the cells of the body. In the cells, oxygen combines with nutrients to provide energy. This process produces carbon dioxide—a waste gas. Blood carries the carbon dioxide to the lungs where it is released outside the body. Another name for this process, which you already read about in Lesson 3, is *cell respiration*.

Reading Check Identify What is the main function of the respiratory system?

Main Parts of the Respiratory System
The main structures of the respiratory system are shown in **Figure 16.5.** Find the lungs in this diagram. These are the system's main organ. Every day, your lungs take in enough air to fill a large room.

▼ FIGURE 16.5

THE RESPIRATORY SYSTEM
The respiratory system allows the body to take in oxygen and remove carbon dioxide. Where in the respiratory system does oxygen exchange with carbon dioxide?

A. Air enters through the **nose** and **mouth**, both of which are lined with mucous (MYOO-kuhs) membranes. Fine hairs called cilia (SIL-ee-uh) trap dirt that you breathe in.

B. The **throat** has two passageways—one for air and one for food.

C. The **epiglottis** (e-puh-GLAH-tis) is a flap of tissue that closes over the trachea when you swallow.

D. The **larynx** (LA-ringks) is the upper part of the respiratory system, which contains the vocal cords.

E. The **trachea** (TRAY-kee-uh) is a windpipe that directs air to the lungs.

F. The **bronchi** (BRAHN-ky) are passages through which air enters the lungs.

G. In the **lungs**, oxygen is transferred to the blood, and carbon dioxide is removed from the blood.

H. The **diaphragm** (DY-uh-fram) is a dome-shaped muscle that separates the lungs from the abdomen.

419

Health Skills Activity

Practicing Healthful Behaviors

Avoiding Repetitive Motion Injuries
Many people use a computer for long periods at a time, either at work or at home. Some of these people may develop a nervous system problem called *repetitive motion injury*. This injury is an inflammation of the nerves in the wrists caused by prolonged, repeated movements. The following strategies can help you prevent this type of injury when using a computer.
1. Keep wrists relaxed and straight. Use only finger movements to strike the keys.
2. Press keys with the least pressure that is necessary.
3. Move your entire hand to press hard-to-reach keys.
4. Take frequent breaks, which is also good for your eyes.

On Your Own
Practice these strategies each time you use a computer.

Lesson 5 Review

After You Read
Review this lesson for new terms, major headings, and Reading Checks.

What I Learned
1. *Vocabulary* What is the *somatic system*?
2. *Explain* What jobs are done by your brain?
3. *List* Name the two main parts of the nervous system.

Thinking Critically
4. *Apply* You are sitting at home when the telephone rings. Explain the steps that your nervous system takes between the time that the phone rings and the time that you answer it.

5. *Evaluate* Many states now have laws requiring people to wear safety belts in motor vehicles. Tell whether you think this type of law is a good idea. Explain your answer.

Applying Health Skills
6. *Accessing Information* With a group, research current efforts to treat spinal-cord injuries. Determine what makes it so difficult to heal a damaged spinal cord so it works properly again. Share your findings in a brief oral report.

Health Online For more review questions for Lesson 5, go to health.glencoe.com.

1 Understanding Your Health

Chapter Preview

▲ *Working With the Photo*

Good health includes being physically active, but there is more to it than just that. **What other sides of the health triangle are these teens working on?**

Start-Up Activities

Before You Read Do you practice good health habits? Take the short health inventory on this page. Keep a record of your answers.

HEALTH INVENTORY

1. I try to stay physically active.
(a) always   (b) sometimes   (c) never

2. I try to get along well with others.
(a) always   (b) sometimes   (c) never

3. I eat well-balanced meals.
(a) always   (b) sometimes   (c) never

4. I avoid high-risk activities.
(a) always   (b) sometimes   (c) never

FOLDABLES™ Study Organizer

As You Read Make this Foldable™ to record what you learn about health and wellness in Lesson 1. Begin with a plain sheet of 11" × 17" paper.

1 Fold the short sides of the sheet of paper inward so that they meet in the middle.

2 Draw two circles—one that covers both sides of the Foldable, and one that covers only one side of the Foldable. Label as shown.

3 On the back of each panel of your Foldable, take notes, define terms, and record examples of health and wellness. In the middle section, draw your personal health triangle.

Health Online Visit **health.glencoe.com** and use the e-flashcards to preview vocabulary terms for Chapter 1.

What Is Health and Wellness?

Guide to Reading

● Building Vocabulary
As you read this lesson, write each new highlighted term and its definition in your notebook.

- health (p. 4)
- wellness (p. 6)

● Focusing on the Main Ideas
In this lesson, you will learn to

- **define** *health*.
- **identify** the three sides of the health triangle.
- **explain** how health habits affect wellness.

● Reading Strategy
Classifying Using the health triangle to the right as a guide, create a concept map that gives examples of each of the three types of health.

Physical   Mental/Emotional   Social

FOLDABLES Study Organizer Use the Foldable™ on p. 3 as you read this lesson.

◯uick Write
Make a list of three healthful behaviors that you can practice. List which side of the triangle each would be associated with.

What Is Health?

Do you know someone who you would describe as "healthy"? What kinds of healthy traits do they demonstrate? Maybe they are involved in sports. Perhaps they just "look" healthy. Looking fit and feeling well are important, but good health does not stop there. Good health includes getting along well with others. It also means feeling good about yourself. An accurate definition of *health* includes all these traits. **Health** is *a combination of physical, mental/emotional, and social well-being.* Your physical health, mental/emotional health, and social health all relate and make up your total health.

▶ Your physical health is one aspect of your total health. **What are some positive ways of improving your physical health?**

The choices you make and actions you take every day shape your health. Look back at the short health inventory that opened this chapter on page 3. Your answers provide a first glimpse of your behaviors and decisions. In the pages ahead you will learn how your behaviors have an influence on your health. You will also learn steps for making good decisions and ways of practicing good health habits.

Your Health Triangle

Total health is sometimes pictured as a triangle (see **Figure 1.1**). This shape best reflects the three sides of health. These sides are physical health, mental/emotional health, and social health.

Physical Health

Connie plays on the basketball team, while her sister, Danielle, walks to and from school. Both girls make regular physical activity part of their daily routine. How about you? Do you take part in behaviors that promote good physical health?

▶ FIGURE 1.1

THE HEALTH TRIANGLE

Each picture shows a different side of health. The health triangle has three equally important sides. **Which side deals with managing stress?**

MediaWatch

Being "In the Know"

This health book will provide you with a foundation of health knowledge. There are, however, many other sources available that offer health information. You can use resources from your home, school, and community that provide valid health information. Being able to find this information will keep you up-to-date on current health issues.

Examine newspapers and magazines. What are some of the current health topics? How many different health articles can you find?

MENTAL/EMOTIONAL

SOCIAL

PHYSICAL

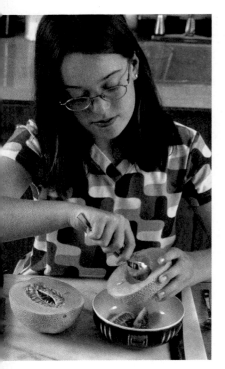

Eating healthful foods for breakfast is one extremely important health habit during your growth years. **What are some other health habits important to teens?**

Visit **health.glencoe.com** and complete the Interactive Study Guide for Lesson 1.

You can improve your physical health in different ways. One way is by eating nutritious meals and snacks. Another way is to get regular checkups from a doctor and a dentist. You can also maintain good physical health by avoiding harmful behaviors. This includes avoiding alcohol, tobacco, and other drugs.

Mental/Emotional Health

Do you like and accept yourself? Are you able to handle challenges that come your way? Do you find positive solutions to problems? These actions are part of good mental/emotional health.

Your mental/emotional health also involves how you handle your feelings, thoughts, and the situations you face each day. You can improve your mental/emotional health by expressing yourself in a healthy way. This includes sharing your thoughts and feelings with a friend or with your family, and having a positive attitude.

Social Health

Do you get along well with friends, classmates, and teachers? Do you spend time with your family? Good social health includes supporting the people we care about. It also includes communicating with, respecting, and valuing people. The ability to keep and make friends is another mark of good social health. Spending quality time with your family and friends is one way to improve your social health.

Reading Check **List** Name one way you can build good physical health. Do the same for mental/emotional health and social health.

Achieving a Healthy Balance

Like a triangle, the three sides of health are connected. When one side changes, the other two are affected. For example, Sean awoke late for school this morning and did not have time for breakfast. Now it is mid-morning and Sean is having trouble paying attention in class. He also feels tired. His choice to skip breakfast is negatively affecting his mental and physical health. Over time, ignoring any side of your health triangle can affect your total health. Being healthy means balancing the three sides of your health triangle.

Wellness and Total Health

When your health is in balance, you are more likely to have a high level of wellness. **Wellness** is *a state of well-being, or total health.* It is an indication of your current health habits and behaviors. All the decisions you make can affect your wellness.

Wellness is sometimes represented by a *continuum,* or scale, such as the one in **Figure 1.2.** Wellness, in this way, provides a picture of your health triangle at any given time. It lets you know if you are taking good care of your health, or if you need to improve your health habits. The pages ahead will give you ideas and suggestions for maintaining wellness. These ideas will help you achieve good total health now and in the future.

Reading Check **Define** What is *wellness*?

▶ **FIGURE 1.2**

THE WELLNESS CONTINUUM

Personal health varies. Where would you place your health currently on the wellness continuum?

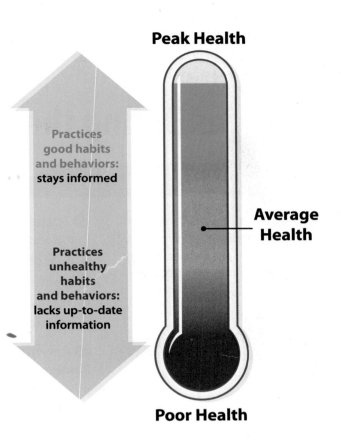

Peak Health

Practices good habits and behaviors: **stays informed**

Practices unhealthy habits and behaviors: **lacks up-to-date information**

Average Health

Poor Health

Lesson 1 Review

After You Read

Review this lesson for new terms, major headings, and Reading Checks.

What I Learned

1. *Vocabulary* Define *health.*

2. *List* Name the three sides of the health triangle.

3. *Describe* What role do decisions play in wellness? What other factors affect a person's wellness?

Thinking Critically

4. *Evaluate* Kathy spends a lot of time with her friends. They watch movies, listen to CDs, and go shopping. Kathy gets good grades except in her physical education class. Evaluate which part of her total health could be out of balance. What could Kathy do to improve this area of wellness?

5. *Apply* Masaki rarely catches a cold. Does this mean he has a high level of wellness? Why or why not?

Applying Health Skills

6. *Practicing Health Behaviors* Look back at your behaviors over the past week. What behaviors help you improve your wellness? What behaviors bring down your wellness? What changes can you make to improve your total health? How important is it for you to assume responsibility for your personal health behaviors?

Changes During the Teen Years

Guide to Reading

Building Vocabulary
Write definitions for terms you think you may know. As you read, make any corrections.

- adolescence (p. 8)
- puberty (p. 9)
- hormones (p. 9)
- peers (p. 11)
- community service (p. 12)

Focusing on the Main Ideas
In this lesson, you will learn to

- **describe** physical changes that occur during the teen years.
- **identify** the mental and emotional changes hormones cause.
- **explain** how your relationships may change.
- **practice** healthful behaviors to improve total health.

Reading Strategy
Finding the Main Idea For each of the main headings in this lesson, write one sentence that states the main idea.

Quick Write

Write a paragraph about the ways in which your relationships with family and peers have changed over the past year.

Adolescence: Time of Change and Challenge

Next to infancy, the fastest period of physical growth is during **adolescence.** Also known as the teen years, this is *the stage of life between childhood and adulthood.* It is a time when you begin to form your own beliefs and values. Adolescence is a period of discovery. The object of discovery is *you.* Maybe without realizing it, you begin seeking answers to the question "Who am I?" As

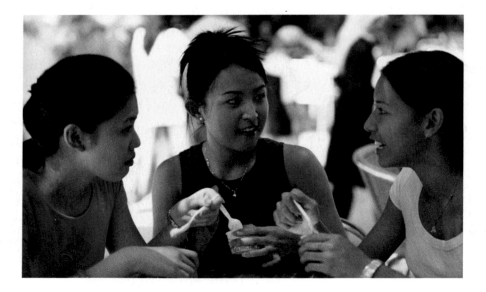

► Your teen years connect your childhood with your adult years. **What are some changes that take place during adolescence?**

a result of this search, you learn more about yourself and your abilities. You meet new people and have new experiences. You gain greater independence and take on new responsibilities.

These changes in life can be very exciting, but they can also be challenging, and even a little scary. The changes you experience during adolescence affect all three sides of your health triangle. You might grow a few inches, make some new friends, discover new interests, and experience mood swings—all within a short period of time. Knowing what to expect can make this a smoother transition.

▲ Growth spurts are common during puberty. **What are some other physical changes that can occur?**

Physical Changes

Josh couldn't believe his eyes the first day of school. His classmate, Marty, had grown much taller over the summer. Growth spurts are a normal part of adolescence. Some, like Marty's, can be quite dramatic.

In addition to growing taller, some of the changes that occur during adolescence include the growth of body hair and changes to the shape of your body. Boys may also notice that their voices are getting deeper. These and other changes that occur during adolescence are the result of **puberty** (PYOO·buhr·tee). This is *the time when you start developing physical characteristics of adults of your gender.* Puberty begins at different ages for different people. For girls, puberty usually begins between ages 8 and 14. For boys, puberty usually begins between ages 11 and 14.

The changes that occur during puberty are all related to the release of **hormones.** These are *chemical substances, produced in glands, that help regulate many body functions.* The changes hormones cause can make some teens feel uncomfortable or awkward. This is because the rapid growth during adolescence is sometimes uneven. Your hands and feet sometimes grow first, which may make them feel too big for the rest of your body. It is important to remember that puberty is a normal part of the growth process. It is something that everyone goes through. If you have concerns, talk with a parent or other trusted adult.

Reading Check

Define What are *hormones*? How do they relate to physical changes during adolescence?

Your Growing Responsibility

The responsibilities you take on during adolescence prepare you for your adult years. Your current responsibilities may include helping with household chores, such as washing the dishes or mowing the lawn. You may also be responsible for looking after a younger brother or sister, or for walking the dog.

List responsibilities that you believe lie ahead. What responsibilities are you looking forward to?

Mental/Emotional Changes

Another change that occurs during adolescence is in the way you think and reason. You are able to face problems that are more complex. You are able to imagine the possible consequences of your actions. You begin to understand different points of view and to think of different solutions to a problem. You begin realizing that your choices affect others. Many teens also begin developing their own values and beliefs.

Adolescence brings emotional changes as well. Many teens experience mood swings. You may feel happy one minute and sad the next. These sudden emotional changes are caused by the release of hormones. Although mood swings can be confusing and even challenging, they are normal. It is important that you know how to use resources from home, school, and the community that provide valid information when you need it. If you are feeling alone, angry, or sad, talking to a friend, family member, or trusted adult can help.

Another emotional development that occurs during adolescence is feelings of attraction toward others. These feelings lead some, though not all, teens to think about dating. These feelings develop at different times for different people. Some teens simply are not ready or do not feel interested in dating, but others are.

An increased awareness in what is important to you is another emotional change experienced during adolescence. You may begin to understand how important your family, friends, and physical activity are to you. You might also realize that setting and achieving goals is important to you. You may also become aware of the importance of assuming responsibility for your personal health behaviors.

▲ Your emotional growth helps you better understand what others are going through. This enables you to become a source of support for them. **How could you help a friend who is feeling sad?**

Reading Check **Describe** Tell how a teen's thinking is likely to change during adolescence.

Social Changes

Another change that occurs in adolescence is in your *relationships*. These are social connections you have with other people and groups. Healthy relationships are important to good social health. During adolescence you are likely to experience changes in your relationships with family, peers, and the community.

Health Skills Activity

Practicing Healthful Behaviors

Making Health a Habit as You Grow

Changes that occur during your teen years affect all three sides of your health triangle. Therefore, you need to develop good health habits for all three areas of your health. The health habits you develop now will have positive long-term effects on your health and wellness. Here are some examples of good health habits for each side of your health triangle:

PHYSICAL HEALTH
- Make physical activity part of your daily routine.
- Eat well-balanced meals and healthy snacks.
- Get plenty of sleep so you will have enough energy during the day.

MENTAL/EMOTIONAL HEALTH
- Think about possible consequences of your actions and behaviors.
- Talk to a friend or trusted adult when you are feeling sad or overwhelmed.
- Keep a positive attitude.

SOCIAL HEALTH
- Ask family members what you can do to help them instead of waiting to be asked.
- Be a good friend by listening and giving encouragement.
- Help out at a community event.

On Your Own

What are some strategies for improving and maintaining your personal health? What new health habits can you develop to improve your total health? Name at least one example for each side of your health triangle.

Family Relationships

You may no longer depend as much on parents or other family members as you once did. Now you are learning to act independently and to make decisions for yourself. Sometimes this can cause differences between you and your family members. For example, differences over how late you are allowed to stay up may occur. Despite your differences, keeping a positive relationship with your family is important to having good social health.

Peer Relationships

During adolescence, your friends and peers take on a greater importance. **Peers** are *people in your age group.* You may begin

Health Online

Visit **health.glencoe.com** and complete the Interactive Study Guide for Lesson 2.

spending more time with your friends. Your opinions and behaviors will often be influenced by your peers. You may feel pressure to think and act like them. Peer pressure can influence healthful choices. Good social health includes learning to benefit from positive peer influence while resisting negative influences. Helping a friend with homework, volunteering with a friend, or simply listening to a friend are examples of positive peer influence.

Relationships with the Community

When you think of the word *community,* you probably think of your neighborhood. However, your community also includes your school and the city you live in. Social growth includes making positive contributions to your community. You might become involved, for example, in a neighborhood cleanup or park project. Many schools have begun sponsoring **community service** programs to get teens involved. These are *volunteer programs whose goal is to improve the community and the life of its residents.* These programs allow teens to help at different community events or help others in need. Many teens find community service to be a rewarding experience. It is also great preparation for the adult years ahead.

Reading Check

Explain In what ways can peer pressure be a positive influence?

Lesson 2 Review

After You Read

Review this lesson for new terms, major headings, and Reading Checks.

What I Learned

1. **Vocabulary** Define *puberty*.

2. **Identify** What are mood swings? What causes them?

3. **Recall** What are some physical changes that occur during the teen years?

Thinking Critically

4. **Analyze** Regi's cousin told her she is upset about differences she is having with her parents. What advice would you give this teen if you were in Regi's place?

5. **Apply** What are two ways that you could become involved in your own community?

Applying Health Skills

6. **Analyzing Influences** Give two examples of how peer influence can positively affect a teen's decisions.

12 Chapter 1: Understanding Your Health

Health Online For more review questions for Lesson 2, go to health.glencoe.com.

Taking Responsibility for Your Health

Guide to Reading

Building Vocabulary
As you read this lesson, write each new highlighted term and its definition in your notebook.

- lifestyle factors (p. 13)
- risk behaviors (p. 14)
- sedentary lifestyle (p. 15)
- cumulative risks (p. 15)
- precautions (p. 15)
- prevention (p. 15)
- abstinence (p. 16)
- attitude (p. 17)

Focusing on the Main Ideas
In this lesson, you will learn to

- **explain** the role of lifestyle factors in a person's health.
- **identify** ways to reduce risks in your life.
- **tell** how abstinence benefits the three sides of your health triangle.
- **evaluate** a source of health information

Reading Strategy
Predicting Quickly look at the main headings, figures, and captions before you read this lesson. Write down the sort of information you think this lesson will provide.

Quick Write

What does the word *responsibility* mean to you? Write a brief definition. Then list the ways you show that you are responsible.

Choosing to Live Healthfully

Do you protect your skin from the sun's harmful rays? Do you get enough sleep so you are not tired in class? If a friend approached you with a problem, would you stop to listen? How you answer these questions reflects your personal **lifestyle factors.** These are *behaviors and habits that help determine a person's level of health and wellness.* These factors are related to the cause or prevention of disease and other health problems. Positive lifestyle factors promote good health. Negative lifestyle factors do the opposite. **Figure 1.3** lists some positive lifestyle factors.

▶ Protective gear is one type of safety precaution that can help you reduce the risk of injury. **What are some others?**

► FIGURE 1.3

POSITIVE LIFESTYLE FACTORS

Lifestyle factors affect your total health. **Which of these lifestyle factors do you currently practice?**

	Eating well-balanced meals, starting with a good breakfast.
	Getting at least 60 minutes of physical activity daily.
	Sleeping at least eight hours every night.
	Doing your best in school and other activities.
	Avoiding tobacco, alcohol, and other drugs.
	Following safety rules and wearing protective gear.
	Relating well to family, friends, and classmates.

Risks and Your Health

"Dangerous intersection. Proceed with caution." "Don't walk." "No lifeguard on duty." You have probably seen these signs or ones like them. They are there to alert you to possible risks or dangers and to ensure your safety.

Risks are an unavoidable part of life. Everyday tasks such as preparing food with a sharp knife or crossing a busy street both carry a degree of risk. Even when there are no signs to warn you, you have some awareness of risks. For example, you know that stairways carry a risk of falls. If you hurry or push through people on stairs, you increase your own and others' risk of getting hurt. Taking responsibility for your personal health behaviors is a part of growing into a responsible adult.

Risk Behaviors

Risk behaviors are *actions or behaviors that might cause injury or harm to yourself or others.* Some of these behaviors are obvious. Walking out on a street from between parked cars is an example. Other risk behaviors are less obvious because the effects are not immediate. For example, smoking is a risk behavior. Even though you may not notice any immediate damaging effect, unhealthful lifestyle behaviors may have a lasting negative impact on your health. When you understand the short-term and long-term

DEVELOPING

Good Character

Self-Discipline

Developing a healthy lifestyle takes commitment. For example, you may need to remind yourself to turn off the TV or computer, and participate in activities that build good physical health.

What are some other ways you can show self-discipline?

consequences of safe, risky, or harmful behavior, you will probably stop to consider the impact your behavior can have on your health.

Another risk behavior is a **sedentary lifestyle.**This is *a way of life that includes little physical activity.* Sitting in front of the TV or a computer is a sedentary behavior. Either becomes a risk factor when it continually replaces sports or other physical activities.

Reading Check **Explain** What role do positive lifestyle factors play in a person's health?

Risks and Consequences

All risk behaviors have consequences. Some consequences are minor or short-term. For example, eating a candy bar too close to mealtime may prevent you from eating more of the healthy foods your body needs for proper growth.

Other risk behaviors carry serious and sometimes life-threatening consequences. These are long-term consequences. Experimenting with alcohol, tobacco, or other drugs is an example. These types of risk behaviors can seriously damage your health. Using these substances can affect all three sides of your health triangle. They can lead to dangerous *addictions*—physical and mental dependencies. These substances can cloud the user's judgment, increasing the risks he or she takes. Using these substances can also lead to problems with family and friends, and problems at school.

Risks that affect your health are further complicated when they are cumulative. **Cumulative risks** are *related risks that increase in effect with each added risk.* **Figure 1.4** shows an example of a cumulative risk that could be prevented.

Reading Check **Define** What are *cumulative risks*?

▼ The Internet is a good source for current health information. **How can staying informed help you maintain your health?**

Reducing Risks

Taking precautions can minimize the possibility of harm. **Precautions** are *planned actions taken before an event to increase the chances of a safe outcome.* You can use positive health behaviors to reduce some risks. Examples include checking the depth of water before diving and wearing a safety helmet when bike riding. Another strategy for reducing risks is **prevention.** This means *taking steps to keep something from happening or getting worse.* Prevention includes getting regular medical and dental checkups. Checkups can detect health or dental problems early, thus preventing the problems from getting worse.

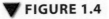

▼ FIGURE 1.4

CUMULATIVE RISKS ADD UP

Notice that each added risk brings about a result that is more severe.
What precautions could this person take to avoid a bad outcome?

 + **+** **=**

Blind intersection   Bad weather   Not wearing a helmet

Choosing Abstinence

One of the most effective forms of prevention is **abstinence.** This is *the conscious, active choice not to participate in high-risk behaviors.* Often, the word *abstinence* is used in connection with avoiding sexual activity. As a preventive strategy, however, abstinence extends to any high-risk behavior. This includes the use of tobacco, alcohol, and other drugs.

Abstinence benefits all sides of your health triangle. It promotes your physical health by helping you avoid injury and illness. It protects your mental/emotional health by giving you peace of mind. When you avoid taking risks, you also avoid the pressure and worries that go along with these actions. Abstinence is a smart choice because it maintains your family's trust in you. It also benefits your relationships with peers and friends. Practicing abstinence shows that you are assuming responsibility for your personal health behaviors and that you respect yourself and others.

Health Online

Visit **health.glencoe.com** and complete the Interactive Study Guide for Lesson 3.

Reading Check **List** Identify three benefits of abstinence.

Taking Responsibility For Your Health

Are you eager to take on more responsibility in your life? Many teens are. You can now begin by accepting responsibility for your health. You can choose behaviors that promote good health.

Staying informed is one way of taking responsibility for your health. Learning about developments and breakthroughs in health is an important part of maintaining your own health.

▼ Getting regular medical checkups is one form of prevention.

You will also have greater success in taking responsibility for your health if you keep a positive attitude. An **attitude** is *a personal feeling or belief.* Teens who have a positive attitude about their health are more likely to practice good health habits.

Taking responsibility for your health means more than just recognizing healthy choices and risk factors. It means *believing* that good health habits can have a positive effect.

Lesson 3 Review

After You Read

Review this lesson for new terms, major headings, and Reading Checks.

What I Learned

1. *Vocabulary* What are *lifestyle factors*?

2. *List* What are some ways teens can reduce risks related to health problems?

3. *Explain* How does abstinence benefit all sides of your health triangle?

Thinking Critically

4. *Compare* Steve and Michael are brothers who both play on the school basketball team. Before practice, Michael takes a few minutes to stretch and warm up, but Steve does not. Compare and contrast the teens' methods for preventing injuries.

5. *Apply* Give an example of a cumulative risk that affects all three sides of your health triangle. Identify each risk.

Applying Health Skills

6. *Practicing Healthful Behaviors* Identify a positive lifestyle factor you would like to start practicing. Develop a plan for making this behavior a regular part of your life.

Analyzing Influences

DIRECTIONS

Analyzing Influences involves recognizing the ways in which internal and external factors affect your health choices. This activity will give you the opportunity to develop and master this important health skill. Here's a guide to the different parts of this activity:

❶ In the **Model** section, you will read about a teen who performs the health skill successfully. This "model" scenario will show you how the skill is done.

❷ The **Practice** section will help guide you in practicing the skill.

❸ In the **Apply** section, you will have a chance to perform the skill on your own. You can use the Self-Check to check your work.

To complete this activity, first read the scenario presented in the Model. Then move on to the Practice. Finally, go ahead and try the Apply.

❶ Model

Many factors influence your choices. Some, including your personal likes and dislikes, are *internal;* they come from within you. Others are *external.* Your friends, family, environment, culture, and the media are all external influences.

When Sebastian decided to try out for a junior varsity sport, he got some suggestions. His older brother said he should continue a family tradition and try out for track. He had been on the track team and so had their father. However, Coach Walker felt Sebastian would be a natural at volleyball because of his ability to jump high. Sebastian's friends were encouraging him to try out for basketball.

Sebastian made a chart to help him decide what to do.

Decision: Which sport should I try out for?

Influences affecting me most	Influences I value most right now, and why
Personal likes/dislikes	I've always liked playing volleyball.
Friends	My friends want me to play basketball.
Family	It would be nice to keep a family tradition, but I don't enjoy track that much.
Coach	Coach Walker thinks I would be really good at volleyball.

Sebastian realized his personal likes/dislikes affected his decision the most. He would try out for volleyball!

② Practice

Sebastian used the skill of analyzing influences again to help him plan a training program to prepare for volleyball tryouts. He wants to run two miles every day to strengthen his heart and lungs. He lives in a part of the country that gets a lot of snow. This makes running outdoors difficult. He also needs to allow time for two other school clubs he belongs to. These clubs meet after school three days a week. Plus, his father does not want him running after dark.

1. What factors have an influence on Sebastian's choice to run?

2. In your opinion, which influences would affect Sebastian the most?

Skill Summary
ANALYZING INFLUENCES

There are many influences on your health behaviors and decisions, some internal, some external. They include:

Internal
- knowledge
- likes and dislikes
- values
- curiosity
- fears

External
- family
- friends and peers
- environment
- culture
- media and technology
- role models

③ Apply

What activities do you participate in? Do you belong to any clubs or community groups? Do you take music lessons or play sports? Think about what influences you to choose your activities. Maybe it is your friends or family, or perhaps your own interests. Make a list of your own external and internal influences and how they influence your choice of activities. Identify which influence affects you most.

Self-Check

- Did I analyze the internal and external influences on my choice of activities?
- Did I show which influence affects me the most?

Your Personal Health

The personal health inventory that follows will help you find out if your health triangle is balanced.

What You Will Need

- pencil or pen
- paper

What You Will Do

Make three columns with the name of each side of the health triangle listed at the top of each column. Number the paper 1–5 for each health area. Think about each of the following statements and respond with a *yes* or *no* answer.

Physical Health

1. I eat well-balanced meals each day.
2. I get at least 60 minutes of physical activity daily.
3. I sleep at least eight hours a night.
4. I avoid the use of tobacco, alcohol, and drugs.
5. I have good personal hygiene.

Mental/Emotional Health

1. I feel good about who I am.
2. I can name several things that I can do well.
3. I generally keep a positive attitude.
4. I ask for help when I need it.
5. I try to improve myself.

Social Health

1. I relate well to family, friends, and classmates.
2. I try to work out any differences I have with others.
3. I express my feelings in positive ways.
4. I treat others with respect.
5. I can say no to risky behaviors.

Wrapping It Up

Give yourself 1 point for each yes answer. A score of 5 in any area reflects excellent health. A score of 3–4 shows good health, meaning some changes need to be made. If you score 0–2 in any area, make a plan to improve that part of your health triangle by talking to a parent or a trusted adult.

Reading Review

Lesson 1 What Is Health and Wellness?

Key Ideas

- Health is defined as a combination of physical, mental/emotional, and social well-being.
- The three sides of the health triangle are physical health, mental/emotional health, and social health.
- The behaviors and decisions you make will affect one or more of the three sides of your health triangle, which will in turn determine your degree of wellness.

Vocabulary

- health (p. 4)
- wellness (p. 6)

Lesson 2 Changes During the Teen Years

Key Ideas

- Physical changes that occur during the teen years include growth spurts, changes in body shape, the growth of body hair, and the release of hormones.
- During adolescence you develop a greater ability to solve more complex problems. You are able to recognize the consequences of your actions. You may experience mood swings. Also, you may develop feelings of attraction toward others.

- Relationships with family, peers, and friends may change. Adolescence is a time when you are learning to act more independently.

Vocabulary

- adolescence (p. 8)
- hormones (p. 9)
- puberty (p. 9)
- peers (p. 11)
- community service (p. 12)

Lesson 3 Taking Responsibility for Your Health

Key Ideas

- Positive lifestyle factors promote good health, while negative lifestyle factors do the opposite.
- Ways to reduce risks in your life include taking precautions, practicing prevention, and choosing abstinence.
- Abstinence is avoiding participation in high-risk behaviors. Abstinence promotes all sides of the health triangle: physical health by helping you avoid injury and illness; mental/emotional health by giving you peace of mind; and social health by maintaining your family's trust in you.

Vocabulary

- lifestyle factors (p. 13)
- risk behaviors (p. 14)
- sedentary lifestyle (p. 15)
- cumulative risks (p. 15)
- precautions (p. 15)
- prevention (p. 15)
- abstinence (p. 16)
- attitude (p. 17)

Reviewing Vocabulary and Main Ideas

On a sheet of paper, write the numbers 1–6. After each number, write the term from the list that best completes each sentence.

- adolescence
- health
- hormones
- peers
- puberty
- wellness

Lesson 1 What Is Health and Wellness?

1. _____ is a combination of physical, mental/emotional, and social well-being.
2. _____ is a state of well-being, or total health.

Lesson 2 Changes During the Teen Years

3. The stage of life between childhood and adulthood is known as _____.
4. Your _____ are people in your age group.
5. Chemical substances, produced in glands, that help to regulate many body functions are called _____.

6. _____ is the time when you start developing physical characteristics of adults of your gender.

Lesson 3 Taking Responsibility for Your Health

On a sheet of paper, write the numbers 7–10. After each number, write the letter of the answer that best completes each statement.

7. A way of life that includes little physical activity is called a(n)
   a. cumulative risk.   **c.** attitude.
   b. sedentary lifestyle.   **d.** prevention.

8. Behaviors and habits that help determine a person's level of health are known as
   a. cumulative risks.
   b. sedentary lifestyles.
   c. lifestyle factors.
   d. risk behaviors.

9. You can reduce risks in your life by doing all of the following *except*
   a. becoming sedentary.
   b. practicing prevention.
   c. taking precautions.
   d. choosing abstinence.

10. All of the following statements are true of abstinence *except*
   a. It helps you avoid injury and illness.
   b. It applies only to avoiding sexual activity.
   c. It is a preventive strategy.
   d. It helps you maintain your family's trust in you.

Health Online Visit **health.glencoe.com** and take the Online Quiz for Chapter 1.

Thinking Critically

Using complete sentences, answer the following questions on a sheet of paper.

11. **Analyze** Why is it important to recognize that health is more than just looking good or feeling fit?

12. **Apply** What advice might you have for a friend who is concerned over mood swings she or he has been experiencing?

Write About It

13. **Communication Skills** Write a private journal entry describing some of the physical, mental/emotional, and social changes you are experiencing.

14. **Accessing Information** Read a health-related article from a newspaper, magazine, or the Internet. Write a brief description of the article. Explain whether or not you think the information is accurate and comes from a reliable source, and why.

Standardized Test Practice

Math

The Centers for Disease Control and Prevention gathers data on teen risk behaviors. This table shows trends in several risk behaviors over a six-year period. Use the table to answer the questions that follow.

Selected Risk Behaviors Among Teens, 1999–2003			
Risk Behavior	1999	2001	2003
Rarely or never wore seatbelts	16.4%	14.1%	18.2%
Rarely or never wore bicycle helmets	85.3%	84.7%	85.9%
Rode with a driver who had been drinking alcohol	33.1%	30.7%	30.2%

TEST-TAKING TIP

Make sure you understand the parts of a table. Read the title of the table. This will help you figure out its subject. Read each column heading and the label of each row.

1. Which risk behavior steadily decreased over the time span shown?
   A. Rarely or never wore seatbelts.
   B. Rarely or never wore bicycle helmets.
   C. Rode with a driver who had been drinking alcohol.
   D. None of the above.

2. Which risk behavior is the most common among teens?
   A. Rarely or never wore seatbelts.
   B. Rarely or never wore bicycle helmets.
   C. Rode with a driver who had been drinking alcohol.
   D. None of the above.

2 Skills for a Healthy Life

Chapter Preview

▲ **Working With the Photo**

Achieving a goal can be very rewarding. **Have you ever set and reached a goal? How did you go about reaching your goal?**

Start-Up Activities

Before You Read Do you know how to make good decisions? Do you know how to set and reach goals in your life? Take the short quiz on this page. Keep a record of your answers.

HEALTH QUIZ Choose the best answer for each of the following questions:

1. All of the following are steps in making informed decisions *except*
   a. listing your options.
   b. weighing the possible outcomes.
   c. avoiding tough decisions.
   d. evaluating a past decision.

2. Setting goals helps you
   a. identify what you want out of life.
   b. use your time, energy, and other resources wisely.
   c. select goals that are realistic.
   d. all of the above.

3. All of the following are steps to take when setting a goal *except*
   a. set up checkpoints to evaluate your progress.
   b. make excuses for yourself if you do not achieve your goal.
   c. identify a specific goal and write it down.
   d. give yourself a reward once you have achieved your goal.

ANSWERS: 1. c.; 2. d.; 3. b.

FOLDABLES™ Study Organizer

As You Read Make this Foldable™ to help you progress through the six steps of the decision-making process. Begin with a plain sheet of notebook paper.

1 Fold the sheet of paper from side to side, leaving a ½" tab along the side.

2 Turn the paper and fold it into thirds.

3 Unfold and cut the top layer along both folds. Then cut each tab in half to make six tabs.

4 Label the tabs as shown.

Under the appropriate tab, define terms and record information about each step in the decision-making process.

Health Online Visit **health.glencoe.com** and complete the Chapter 2 crossword puzzle.

Making Decisions and Setting Goals

Guide to Reading

● Building Vocabulary
As you read this lesson, write each new highlighted term and its definition in your notebook.

- decision making (p. 27)
- values (p. 28)
- goal setting (p. 29)

● Focusing on the Main Ideas
In this lesson, you will learn to

- **describe** how decisions affect your health and the health of others.
- **develop** decision-making skills to make healthful choices.
- **identify** the benefits of setting goals.
- **practice** the goal-setting process to work toward an accomplishment.

● Reading Strategy
Comparing and Contrasting Create a chart to compare and contrast the steps used in decision making and goal setting.

FOLDABLES Study Organizer Use the Foldable™ on p. 25 as you read this lesson.

Quick Write
Identify an important decision you made in the last month. Explain what factors influenced your decision and whether you were pleased with the outcome.

Decisions and Goals

Do you have privileges now that you did not have a few years ago? Maybe you are able to stay up—or out—later. Perhaps you make more of your own decisions, such as which clothes to buy. You might even have more say in how you spend your time and who you spend it with. As you grow older, you gain more freedom, but with it comes more responsibility. For example, you will be challenged to make decisions that are sometimes tough. You will need to understand the short-term and long-term consequences of decisions you make. Another responsibility is setting goals for yourself and planning how to reach those goals. Making decisions and setting goals will help give you purpose and direction in your life. These skills will allow you to focus on the future as well as the

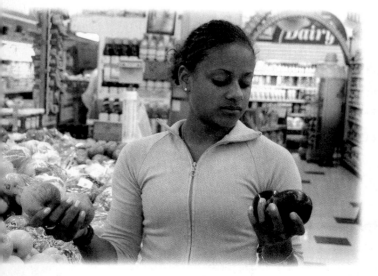

◀ Making good decisions is a skill you can learn. **What are some decisions you have made in the last week?**

present. In this lesson, you will learn healthful skills for making decisions and setting goals that will benefit you now and in the future.

Making Responsible Decisions

Life is filled with decisions. You make plenty of them every day. Some decisions are small, like what to wear or what to eat for breakfast. Even minor decisions, however, can have major consequences. So major that they could permanently change your life and the lives of others. One example is whether or not to fasten your safety belt while riding in a car. This is a small choice, but the consequences could be great if you were involved in a car accident.

Kevin's story is another example. He began riding his bike toward his friend's garage, where their band was practicing. After he had gone one block, he realized he had forgotten his safety helmet. Even though it was inconvenient, Kevin decided to return home for his helmet. On the way back to his friend's garage, he was forced to swerve to avoid a car and his bike went down. His decision to wear a helmet prevented a possible head injury.

▲ The decision-making process can help you make responsible decisions. **Why is it helpful to write down the steps you take to reach a decision?**

Reading Check **Give Examples** Give an example of a minor decision that can affect your health.

The Decision-Making Process

When faced with a decision, whether big or small, you want to make the best one you can. It is helpful if you are aware of steps you can take that will guide you in making a good decision. **Decision making** is *the process of making a choice or finding a solution.* It involves a series of six steps.

Step 1: State the Situation

The first step in making any decision is to identify the situation. What choice do you need to make? One useful approach is to ask yourself questions. Ask yourself what the facts are and who else, if anyone, is involved. Kevin, for example, wants to meet with his friends for band practice.

Step 2: List the Options

Next, make a list of your options. Try to be as complete as you can. It may be helpful to ask other people for suggestions. Since Kevin does not drive yet, his options are walking, taking the bus, or riding his bike.

Respect

Liking and respecting yourself is important to good mental health. However, it is hard to do this when you make a decision that goes against your values. When you are faced with a difficult choice, you want to earn the respect of others, but more importantly, you want to respect yourself. Making healthy decisions shows that you respect yourself and your health.

What are some other ways of showing respect for yourself?

Step 3: Weigh the Possible Outcomes

The third step is to consider the possible outcomes, or consequences, of each option. One possible outcome of riding your bike without a helmet could be serious injury in the event of an accident. When weighing your choices, you might use the *H.E.L.P.* formula. The first letters spell out the word *HELP*:

- **H (Healthful)** Will my choice affect my well-being or the well-being of those around me?
- **E (Ethical)** Will my choice show respect for myself and other people?
- **L (Legal)** Will I be breaking the law? Is it legal for someone my age?
- **P (Parent Approval)** Would my parents approve of my decision?

Step 4: Considering Values

When making a decision, always consider your values. **Values** are *the beliefs and principles that guide the way a person lives.* Kevin wore his safety helmet because he valued his health and safety. Many values, such as *honesty,* are important to people everywhere. Respecting yourself and others, and gaining the trust of family and friends are also important values to many people. Considering your values will guide you in the right direction as you make decisions.

Step 5: Make a Decision and Act

Once you have weighed your options and considered the risks and consequences, you are ready to take action. Choose the course that seems best and that supports your values. Make sure you are comfortable with your decision and how it may affect others as well as yourself. If you are uncomfortable with your decision, reconsider your options or ask a parent or trusted adult for help. Looking at the example of Kevin, he chose to go back for his helmet.

Step 6: Evaluate Your Decision

After you have taken action, you should evaluate the outcome of your decision. Did you expect the outcome to turn out the way it did? How did your decision affect others? Do you think you made the right decision? How did your decision make you feel about yourself? If the outcome was not what you had expected, use the decision-making process and try again. Think about what you could do differently. Kevin felt good about his decision because he knew he was protecting his health and safety.

Reading Check

List What are the six steps in the decision-making process?

Setting Realistic Goals

Achieving a realistic goal can be very rewarding. A realistic goal is one that you can reach. What are your personal goals? What do you plan to do after you finish school? Goal setting is a skill that helps you identify what you want out of life. **Goal setting** is *the process of working toward something you want to accomplish.* This process can help you set and achieve goals. Health-related goals help you improve your physical, mental/emotional, or social health. What health-related goals can you set for yourself?

Types of Goals

There are two basic types of goals—*short-term* and *long-term.* Short-term goals are just that: goals you plan to accomplish in a short period of time. This might be a period of hours, days, or weeks. Short term goals may include doing well on a test or writing an e-mail to a friend. Long-term goals are those you plan to achieve within a period of months or years. These may include learning how to play an instrument or becoming a professional athlete. Often, long- and short-term goals are connected. Many short-term goals are stepping stones to achieving long-term goals.

Reading Check　**Identify** What are the two types of goals? How are they related?

The Goal-Setting Process

Like the skill of decision making, goal setting is a process. This process might be viewed as a road map to your accomplishments. It provides a well-defined plan you can follow. Another benefit of the process is that it helps you focus on achievable goals. Finally, this process helps you to make the best use of your time, energy, and other resources.

Step 1: Identify a Specific Goal and Write It Down

Instead of saying "I want to be a better baseball player," try to make your goal more specific. Chris's goal is to make the school's baseball team.

▶ Chris wants to eventually become a starter on the school's baseball team. **What are some short- and long-term goals of your own?**

▲ Often, just reaching your goal is the best reward of all. **How can reaching a goal be rewarding?**

Step 2: List the Steps You Will Take to Reach Your Goal

Achieving big goals can be easier when you break them down into smaller tasks. To achieve his long-term goal, Chris began by setting a short-term goal to improve his throwing and batting skills. He practices for one hour each weekday.

Step 3: Get Help and Support from Others

Identify people who can help you achieve your goals. Possibilities include your friends, parents, teachers, or other trusted adults. Chris's adult neighbor, Royce, who used to be on the school baseball team, is helping Chris train. Chris's teammates are also supportive.

Step 4: Identify and Overcome Specific Obstacles

Sometimes, you may run into a specific obstacle that prevents you from moving forward. Before continuing, you should identify this obstacle and consider ways to overcome it. If you cannot move past this obstacle, you may have to change your goal. Chris, for example, needs a baseball glove in order to practice his catching skills. He will need to borrow a glove from someone until he can save enough money to buy one.

Step 5: Evaluate Your Progress

Regularly check to see how well you are progressing toward your goal. Chris was able to measure his progress at the plate by keeping a record of his batting average. Evaluating your progress allows you to measure your success and adjust your plan to better reach your goal.

Step 6: Give Yourself a Reward

Celebrate your accomplishments. When you reach a goal, reward yourself. When Chris succeeded in making the baseball team, he rewarded himself by buying a new glove.

Health Online

Visit **health.glencoe.com** and complete the Interactive Study Guide for Lesson 1.

Reading Check

List Name two steps in the goal-setting process.

Health Skills Activity

Goal Setting

Achieving Group Goals

Reaching group goals can be challenging. That is because groups are made up of individuals with different personalities, ideas, and skills. Reaching a goal as a group requires effective communication, respect, and teamwork. Imagine that your health class wants to raise money for an important cause. Use the goal-setting process to help you develop a plan to achieve this goal.

- **Identify a specific goal.**
- **List the steps to reach your goal.**
- **Get help from others.**
- **Identify and overcome specific obstacles**
- **Evaluate your progress.**
- **Reward yourself.**

With a Group

Decide on a worthy cause you might raise funds for. Then, use the six-step process to map out a way of reaching your goal.

Lesson 1 Review

After You Read

Review this lesson for new terms, major headings, and Reading Checks.

What I Learned

1. *Vocabulary* Define *values*. Use the word in an original sentence.

2. *Recall* What are the steps of the decision-making process?

3. *Identify* What are the benefits of using the goal-setting process?

Thinking Critically

4. *Analyze* How are the skills of decision making and goal setting related?

5. *Hypothesize* Sometimes goals need to be changed. What are some possible reasons for this?

Applying Health Skills

6. *Decision Making* You have to study for a big test. A friend calls to invite you to a party. Use the decision-making process to help you make a choice. Consider the short-term and long-term consequences of your decision.

Building Your Character

Guide to Reading

● Building Vocabulary
Define the terms you think you know. As you read, revise your definitions as needed.

- character (p. 32)
- integrity (p. 33)
- tolerance (p. 34)
- prejudice (p. 34)
- accountability (p. 35)
- empathy (p. 36)

● Focusing on the Main Ideas
In this lesson, you will learn to

- **identify** the traits of good character.
- **explain** the role of tolerance in social health.
- **describe** qualities found in a good citizen.

● Reading Strategy
Predicting Quickly look at the main headings, figures, and captions before you read this lesson. Predict the kinds of information you think this lesson will provide.

*Q*uick Write

Make a list of the good deeds you did this month. Which of these do you think reveal good character?

What is Character?

How would you describe someone you know? You would probably mention what the person looks like—their physical appearance. You might also mention other qualities, such as what the person says and does. These qualities reveal a person's character. **Character** is *the way in which a person thinks, feels, and acts.*

Character involves understanding, caring about, and acting upon certain values. Most people around the world respect certain ethical values, such as trust, respect, responsibility, and fairness. **Figure 2.1** shows different factors that influence character.

Character in Action

Good character is not something you show only once in a while. It is part of who you are and how you live. By having good character, you promote not only your own health but the health of others. Having good character builds good social health. It strengthens your relationships with others. For example, if you are honest, people will trust you. You also set a good example for others to follow.

There are six main traits of good character. These are *trustworthiness, respect, responsibility, fairness, caring,* and *citizenship.*

▼ FIGURE 2.1

WHAT INFLUENCES CHARACTER?

There are many factors that can influence a person's character. Can you think of other factors that are not shown here?

Parents or Guardian	Stories
The earliest influence on your character was likely a parent or guardian. Parents or guardians are our first teachers of character.	Stories have morals. These are lessons that teach about values or character traits.

Life Experiences	Examples Set by Others
Experience is often a great teacher. Think about sports and games that build and reinforce character and values.	Role models inspire us to act or think in a certain way. They set good examples. What people do you look up to for inspiration?

Trustworthiness

At the beginning of this school year, Keith was given a key to his house. His parents explained that, as a teen, he was becoming more independent. They felt he could be *trusted* with this responsibility.

People who are trustworthy are reliable. They follow through with what they promise they will do. Suppose you agree to meet a friend after school to work on a project. If you are trustworthy, you show up at the agreed-upon location—on time. If you cannot make it, you let the other person know.

Trustworthy people are also honest, or truthful. This is a quality that cannot be compromised. You cannot be "a little honest" or "truthful some of the time." Honest people do not lie or give false impressions. They do not steal or cheat.

Trustworthy people have integrity. **Integrity** is *the quality of doing what you know is right.* Imagine seeing a wallet lying on the street outside your school. Would you keep it for yourself or return it to its owner? Even though it may be difficult, a person with integrity would make the second choice. At the very least, he or

► Loyalty is one quality of a trustworthy person. **Do you show loyalty to your school's teams? Describe an action you have taken that shows your loyalty to your school or community.**

she would take the wallet to the school office or lost-and-found. A trustworthy person is also loyal, or *faithful*. A loyal friend will not allow others to say untrue or mean things about you.

 Reading Check **List** Name two qualities displayed by trustworthy people.

Respect

What does *respect* mean to you? You might say it means being polite, but respect is much more than that. When you respect people, you consider their feelings. For example, when you disagree with friends or family members, you listen to what they have to say without criticizing them. You also respect their wishes and never ask them to do things that are unhealthy or unsafe.

Showing respect also applies to yourself. When you respect yourself, you avoid dangerous situations and high-risk behaviors. You abstain from sexual activity and from using alcohol, tobacco, or other drugs. Respecting yourself means respecting your body. It means keeping yourself physically active and giving your body the rest it needs.

One element of respect that is especially critical in today's world is **tolerance.** This is *the ability to accept other people as they are*. We live in a society made up of people who come from different cultures and backgrounds. Learning about these groups and their customs can enrich your life. Tolerance can also be a tool for fighting prejudice. **Prejudice** is *an opinion or fear formed without having facts or firsthand knowledge*. Examples include negative opinions formed for no good reason, usually against a different racial, religious, or cultural group.

DEVELOPING
Good Character

Being a "Good Winner"

It is just as important to be a "good winner" as it is to be a "good loser." Good winners do not taunt or tease their opponents. Instead, they look for ways to show them appreciation and respect.

What are some positive ways of behaving when you win?

Responsibility

Think about some of the things you are responsible for now. You may be responsible for helping out with family chores. Maybe you are responsible for watering the plants, setting the table, or doing your own laundry. As you grow older, your responsibilities will increase even more.

With responsibility comes **accountability.** This is *a willingness to answer for your actions and decisions.* When you are accountable, you do not blame others for your mistakes. You accept the consequences for your actions.

Reading Check **Give Examples** What are some behaviors that demonstrate trustworthiness, respect, and responsibility? Give an example for each trait.

Fairness

Fairness is a character trait learned early in life. You may recall being taught the importance of sharing at an early age. In sports, being fair means obeying a set of rules. It also extends to the larger world around us. If you are fair, you keep an open mind. You are willing to listen to people whose opinions differ from yours.

Another quality shared by fair people is good sportsmanship. Life is filled with contests and competitions. Whenever two people compete, someone loses. A good sport is able to accept defeat gracefully. A fair person is a good sport, on and off the playing field.

▼ Responsibility includes following through with assigned tasks. **In which of these two scenes is the teen acting responsibly?**

▶ This teen volunteers his time tutoring other students. **What are some ways in which you could demonstrate the spirit of giving?**

Health *Online*

Topic: Making a Difference

Visit **health.glencoe.com** for Student Web Activities to learn about how teens can make a difference by taking action on issues that are important to them.

Activity: Using the information provided at the link above, interview other teens about an issue at your school. Then, post the results where other students can view them (with the permission of school officials).

Caring

When you care about others, you are kind to them. You consider their feelings by showing **empathy.** This is *the ability to understand and show concern for another person's feelings.*

Caring people do not try to take revenge when they feel mistreated. They do not think about ways to get even. Instead, they forgive—or at least *try* to forgive—those who hurt them.

One quality found in caring people is the spirit of giving. This does not mean giving material objects, such as *gifts.* Rather, it means giving of yourself, by sharing your time and talents. Rochelle helps out at a local homeless shelter on weekends by making sandwiches. Sal shares his knowledge of Spanish by tutoring other students at school.

Reading Check **Define** What is the meaning of *empathy*?

Citizenship

Citizenship is the way you conduct yourself as a member of a community. Good citizens look for ways to improve their surroundings. They respect their community and its members. A "community" includes a neighborhood, a school, or a whole city.

As a good citizen, you also have a responsibility to protect your environment. You can do this by keeping your environment clean, conserving natural resources, and recycling. You can also encourage others to do the same. Picking up litter you see on the ground is one way to help.

Good citizens work at making the community a better place, not only for themselves, but also for future generations. One way to achieve this goal is to become active in your community. You can speak out, or look for ways to improve your community.

Health Online

Visit **health.glencoe.com** and complete the Interactive Study Guide for Lesson 2.

◄ Showing concern for the environment is one way of demonstrating good citizenship. **What are some other ways of showing this character trait?**

Lesson 2 Review

After You Read

Review this lesson for new terms, major headings, and Reading Checks.

What I Learned

1. *Vocabulary* What is *character*?

2. *Recall* Name the six traits of good character.

3. *Identify* How is giving related to the character trait of caring?

Thinking Critically

4. *Synthesize* Why do you think tolerance is important to good social health?

5. *Apply* Larry sometimes leaves garbage on top of the lunch tables at school and assumes the janitor will pick it up. Does this action show good citizenship? Explain your answer.

Applying Health Skills

6. *Analyzing Influences* Many professional athletes try to be a positive influence on young people. As a group, research one such athlete. Be prepared to discuss your professional athlete's sportsmanship on and, if possible, off the field. What other character traits does this athlete demonstrate?

Developing Other Health Skills

Guide to Reading

● Building Vocabulary
Some of the terms below may seem familiar. Using a pencil, write the definition of words you think you know.

- communication (p. 39)
- refusal skills (p. 40)
- conflict resolution (p. 40)
- media (p. 41)
- stress (p. 43)
- advocacy (p. 43)

● Focusing on the Main Ideas
In this lesson, you will learn to

- **describe** ten important health skills.
- **explain** how to find reliable information.
- **identify** influences on your health.
- **develop** refusal skills to avoid certain situations.

● Reading Strategy
Organizing Information Arrange the health skills from this lesson in two lists. One list should contain skills that have to do with information and how it is passed along. The other should be a list of skills dealing with managing your health.

Quick Write

Write a paragraph about a skill or talent you have learned. Identify how this skill or talent has benefited you.

Skills for a Healthy Life

In Lesson 1, you learned about two important *health skills:* decision making and goal setting. In this lesson, you will learn about eight others. All ten of these skills appear in **Figure 2.2.** They are sometimes called life skills. That is because they can help you maintain good health now and in the future.

Developing good health skills will help you maintain your physical, mental/emotional, and social health. Health skills will help you develop positive health behaviors to prevent injury, illness, disease, and other health problems. Health skills will also help you communicate effectively and develop healthy relationships.

◀ Good communication is important to healthy relationships. **What are two types of communication?**

THE HEALTH SKILLS

These ten skills affect your physical, mental/emotional, and social health. These skills can help you, not just during your teen years, but throughout your entire life. **How do refusal skills protect your health?**

Health Skills	What It Means to You
Accessing Information	You know how to find valid and reliable health information and health-promoting products and services.
Practicing Healthful Behaviors	You take action to reduce risks and protect yourself against illness and injury.
Stress Management	You find healthy ways to reduce and manage stress in your life.
Analyzing Influences	You recognize the many factors that influence your health, including culture, media, and technology.
Communication Skills	You express your ideas and feelings and listen when others express theirs.
Refusal Skills	You can say no to risky behaviors.
Conflict-Resolution Skills	You can work out problems with others in healthful ways.
Decision Making	You think through problems and find healthy solutions.
Goal Setting	You plan for the future and work to make your plans come true.
Advocacy	You take a stand for the common good and make a difference in your home, school, and community.

Communication Skills

The idea of communicating may seem obvious to you. You may be saying to yourself "I already know how to communicate." To understand communication skills, consider the difference between *hearing* and *listening*. Imagine that someone is speaking to you while your attention is elsewhere. Maybe you are in the middle of watching a TV show, or perhaps your mind is just wandering. In such cases, you may have *heard* the speaker's words without really listening to what is being said.

Communication is *the clear exchange of ideas and information*. Verbal communication involves a speaker or writer on one end, and a listener or reader on the other. Good communication involves speaking clearly and carefully. It also involves good listening skills. A speaker's message has meaning only if the listener receives it.

Communication also has nonverbal aspects, such as tone of voice. Often, how you say something is more important than what

▲ Resolving conflicts requires one or both parties to give a little. **What are some conflicts you have been involved in? Were these major or minor disagreements? How did you resolve them?**

you say. Body language is also a form of communication. Body language includes facial expressions and gestures.

Refusal Skills

Two other related communication skills are *refusal skills* and *conflict-resolution skills*. The first of these, **refusal skills,** are *communication strategies that help you say no to others effectively.* This skill is especially useful during your teen years. There may be occasions when you are asked to do something you do not want to do or that you are unable to do. Maybe you are not interested. Maybe the activity costs money and you are low on cash. Maybe it is an activity that goes against your values—something you feel is wrong or unhealthy. Even though using refusal skills can sometimes be challenging, they can help you stay true to yourself and to your beliefs. Also, other people will respect you for being honest about your needs and wants.

The steps for practicing refusal skills are based on the letters in the word *STOP.* This makes it easy to remember.

- **S**ay no in a firm voice.
- **T**ell why not.
- **O**ffer another idea.
- **P**romptly leave.

When you use refusal skills, show that you mean what you say by using strong body language. Strong body language includes eye contact, crossed arms, and a serious expression.

Conflict Resolution

Conflict resolution involves *solving a disagreement in a way that satisfies both sides.* Conflicts, or disagreements with others, are part of life. Learning to deal with them in a healthy way is important. Imagine that your favorite TV show is about to begin when a family member comes along and changes the channel. At such times, conflict-resolution skills can help you find a solution that satisfies everyone involved. Also, by using this positive health behavior, you can prevent conflicts from getting out of hand. Maybe the solution to this conflict is turning off the television and doing something else the family enjoys.

Reading Check

Compare How do refusal skills differ from conflict-resolution skills?

Accessing Information

Being informed means having correct, up-to-date information. Much of the health information you get comes from the media. The **media** are *the various methods for communicating information*. The media include newspapers, magazines, radio, television, and the Internet. Before you accept a report from any of these sources, you need to find out if the health information you receive is valid. Is the report based on research done by a respected institution? Or is it simply one person's opinion, unsupported by evidence or facts?

When you check the reliability of a source, you might ask your health teacher, school nurse, family doctor, or other trusted adult about the source. Any media source that sells products should be considered with caution.

Analyzing Influences

Analyzing influences involves recognizing factors that affect or influence your health. Some of these factors are internal—they come from inside you. Others are external—they come from outside sources. **Figure 2.3** shows many of these sources.

▼ **FIGURE 2.3**

INFLUENCES ON YOUR HEALTH

Both internal and external factors affect your health. Which sources have the most influence on your health decisions?

Internal	External
Personal Likes and Dislikes • Tastes in food • Values • Skills and talents	**Your Family and Culture** • Beliefs, behaviors, and habits • Family traditions • Food served at home
Desires and Ambitions • Plans for the future • Goals • Dreams and hopes	**Media and Technology** • TV and movies • Magazines • Internet
Curiosity • Things I wonder about • Things I want to do or try	**Friends and Peers** • Behaviors and opinions of my friends and classmates
Fears • Things that scare or frighten me • Things I *never* want to try	**Environment** • Place where I live • School I attend • Air quality • Sources of recreation

Practicing Healthful Behaviors

The skill of *practicing healthful behaviors* can help you balance your health triangle. This skill involves taking care of yourself and avoiding risks. It includes developing health-promoting habits. The checklist in **Figure 2.4** explores some of these habits and behaviors. How many of these are part of *your* personal checklist? How does practicing health-promoting behaviors help you prevent diseases and other health problems?

▶ **FIGURE 2.4**

HEALTH BEHAVIORS CHECKLIST

Habits are things you do regularly and almost without even thinking about them. Establishing good habits are key elements for good health. **Which of these health habits do you practice every day?**

✔ I eat well-balanced meals, including breakfast, and choose healthful snacks.

✔ I get regular daily physical activity and at least 8 hours of sleep each night.

✔ I avoid using tobacco, alcohol, and other drugs.

✔ I understand the health benefits of brushing and flossing my teeth regularly.

✔ I understand the benefit of wearing a safety belt every time I ride in a car.

✔ I stay within 5 pounds of my healthy weight.

✔ I practice good personal hygiene habits.

✔ I get regular physical checkups.

✔ I can name several things I do well.

✔ I generally keep a positive attitude.

✔ I express my emotions in healthy ways.

✔ I ask for help when I need it.

✔ I take responsibility for my actions.

✔ I take on new challenges to improve myself.

✔ I relate well to family, friends, and peers.

✔ I have several close friends.

✔ I can disagree with others without becoming rude.

✔ I treat others with respect.

✔ I use refusal skills to avoid risk behaviors.

✔ I get along with all kinds of people.

Stress Management

Do you get nervous just before a big test? How about when you have to speak in front of an audience? Do you get stage fright? These are symptoms of **stress**—*your body's response to change.* Stress is a normal part of life.

The health skill of *stress management* can help you develop strategies for managing stress. Some ways of positively managing stress include relaxation and managing one's time efficiently. You will examine this skill more closely in Chapter 3. You will learn coping techniques and ways to better manage your time.

Advocacy

To advocate for something means "to support it or speak out in favor of it." The health skill of **advocacy** means *informing others about health practices and encouraging healthful behaviors.* Some people choose careers as advocates. Their job is to raise the community's awareness of health issues and concerns. Advocacy includes warning people about possible risks and sharing knowledge of positive health behaviors. As you will discover, health advocacy goes hand in hand with citizenship. Advocating on behalf of others is part of growing into a mature, responsible adult.

Reading Check **Define** What does *advocacy* mean?

Health Online

Visit **health.glencoe.com** and complete the Interactive Study Guide for Lesson 3.

Lesson 3 Review

After You Read

Review this lesson for new terms, major headings, and Reading Checks.

What I Learned

1. *Vocabulary* Define *communication* when used as a health skill.

2. *Recall* Give two examples of internal and external influences when making health decisions.

3. *Identify* What are two kinds of stress?

Thinking Critically

4. *Explain* Why is it important to practice refusal skills?

5. *Apply* Suppose you discovered that a factory in your community was dumping waste products into a local river. Explain how you could use the skill of advocacy to help put an end to this behavior. How could eliminating this risk factor prevent disease and other health problems?

Applying Health Skills

6. *Advocacy* Identify a problem in your school or city. Write an article for your school newspaper that will raise readers' awareness of this problem.

Saying No to Unhealthy Choices

DIRECTIONS

Refusal Skills involve saying no to behavior that is unhealthy or unsafe. This activity will give you the opportunity to develop and master this important health skill. Here's a guide to the different parts of this activity:

❶ In the **Model** section, you will read about a teen who performs the health skill successfully. This "model" scenario will show you how the skill is done.

❷ The **Practice** section will help guide you in practicing the skill.

❸ In the **Apply** section, you will have a chance to perform the skill on your own. You can use the Self-Check to check your work.

To complete this activity, first read the scenario presented in the Model. Then move on to the Practice. Finally, go ahead and try the Apply activity.

❶ Model

James told his friends he had managed to get three tickets to the home opener for the town's professional baseball team. Sam, however, wondered where the tickets came from. He also realized that the game started at 1:30. He knew that going would mean cutting class. He didn't think that was the right thing to do.

Sam uses the S.T.O.P. strategy to help him say no effectively.

JAMES: Listen, Sam. Time is running out, we've gotta get going. Are you coming?

SAM: No. I'll pass. **(Say no in a firm voice)**

LOUIS: What *is* your problem?

SAM: I don't want to cut class. **(Tell why not)**

JAMES: Would you stop being so uptight? If we don't leave now, we'll be late.

SAM: If you're willing to wait for the weekend, I'll go to that game with you. **(Offer another idea)**

LOUIS: You are really weird sometimes.

SAM: Later, guys. **(Promptly leave)**

② Practice

Form a group with two or three classmates, and read the situation below. Then write lines of dialogue for each of the boys. Use the S.T.O.P. strategy to show how James refuses pressure to do something wrong.

James is with friends at the mall. One of his friends dares him to take some magazines without paying for them. Show how James can refuse by using the S.T.O.P. strategy.

Your conversation should be guided by the following questions:

1. Does your dialogue follow the steps in the S.T.O.P. strategy?

2. Does your dialogue show an effective way to resist pressure to do something wrong?

Skill Summary
REFUSAL SKILLS

When a situation arises that goes against your values, use refusal skills:

- Say no in a firm voice.
- Tell why not.
- Offer another idea.
- Promptly leave.

③ Apply

Choose one of the following situations. Working with a partner, write a skit that shows refusal skills in action. Use each of the four steps in the S.T.O.P. strategy. Perform your skit for the class.

Situation 1: *Someone offers you the answers to a test. The test begins in a few minutes.*

Situation 2: *You get a phone call inviting you to a party at a classmate's home. You are told that there will be beer at the party.*

Self-Check

- Did our skit follow the steps in the S.T.O.P. strategy?
- Did our skit show an effective way to resist pressure to do something wrong?

Sending "I" Messages

Communicating effectively is especially important when there is a disagreement. When you use "I" messages, you express your feelings. "I" messages are unlike "you" messages, which place blame on the other person. To see the difference, compare these two statements:

- **"You" message:** You always get your way! You're selfish!
- **"I" message:** Sometimes I would like to have a say in what we do.

This activity will give you the opportunity to practice sending "I" messages. If you practice this skill, you will become a better communicator.

What You Will Need

- pencil or pen
- paper

What You Will Do

1 Working in pairs, imagine an everyday situation in which "you" messages might occur. Think of your own "you" message. Write the situation across the top of the paper. Then write the "you" message below on the left. Change that same message into an "I" message, writing the "I" version on the right.

2 Here are three sample situations:
- Your older brother kept you waiting at the mall. He arrived an hour late and had no excuse.
- A classmate told a lie about you.
- Your sister borrowed something of yours and returned it in damaged condition.

3 Read each "you" message to the class. Then read the corresponding "I" message.

Wrapping It Up

Was the "you" message or "I" message most effective? Explain why.

Think of a recent disagreement you had with a family member or friend. How could using "I" messages have helped resolve the conflict? How does practicing positive health behaviors, such as "I" messages, benefit your health?

2 Reading Review

Foldables™ and Other Study Aids Take out the Foldable™ that you created for Lesson 1 and any graphic organizers that you created for Lessons 1–3. Find a partner and quiz each other using these study aids.

Lesson 1 Making Desicions and Setting Goals

Key Ideas

- The steps in making healthful decisions include stating the situation, listing the options, weighing the possible outcomes, considering your values, making a decision, taking action, and evaluating your decision.

- Goal-setting skills enable you to have a well-defined plan to follow. It allows you to focus on realistic, achievable goals. It also lets you make the best use of your time, energy, and other resources.

Vocabulary

- decision making (p. 27)
- values (p.28)
- goal setting (p. 29)

Lesson 2 Building Good Character

Key Ideas

- Traits of good character are trustworthiness, respect, responsibility, fairness, caring, and citizenship.

- Tolerance is important to social health. It helps us accept people who are different from ourselves. Being tolerant helps us get along better with others.

- Good citizens obey the community's rules and laws, respect authority, protect their environment, and work to make the community a better place.

Vocabulary

- character (p. 32)
- integrity (p. 33)
- tolerance (p. 34)
- prejudice (p. 34)
- accountability (p. 35)
- empathy (p. 36)

Lesson 3 Developing Other Health Skills

Key Ideas

- Health skills can help you stay healthy now and in the future. They can improve and maintain your physical, mental/emotional, and social health.

- Ten important health skills are accessing information, practicing healthful behaviors, stress management, analyzing influences, communication skills, refusal skills, conflict resolution, decision making, goal setting, and advocacy.

- Influences on a person's health include personal likes and dislikes, desires and ambitions, curiosity, fears, family, culture, friends and peers, environment, media, and technology.

Vocabulary

- communication (p. 39)
- refusal skills (p. 40)
- conflict resolution (p. 40)
- media (p. 41)
- stress (p. 43)
- advocacy (p. 43)

2 Assessment

After You Read

HEALTH QUIZ

Now that you have read the chapter, look back at your answers to the Health Quiz on the chapter opener. Would you change any of them? What would your answers be now?

Reviewing Vocabulary and Main Ideas

On a sheet of paper, write the numbers 1–6. After each number, write the term from the list that best completes each sentence.

- accountability
- character
- communication
- decision making
- goal setting
- integrity
- values
- media

Lesson 1 Making Decisions and Setting Goals

1. _____ is the process of making a choice or finding a solution.
2. _____ is the process of working toward something you want to accomplish.
3. The beliefs and ideals that guide the way a person lives are that person's _____.

Lesson 2 Building Good Character

4. The way a person thinks, feels, and acts is known as _____.
5. The quality of always doing what you know is right is _____
6. _____ is a willingness to answer for your actions and decisions.

Lesson 3 Developing Other Health Skills

On a sheet of paper, write the numbers 7–9. After each number, write the letter of the answer that best completes each statement.

7. Good communication involves all of the following *except:*
   a. speaking and listening.
   b. clearly exchanging ideas and information.
   c. shouting at those who do not agree with you.
   d. facial expressions and gestures.

8. When you analyze influences, you should:
   a. pay attention to both internal and external factors.
   b. pay attention to external factors but ignore internal factors.
   c. pay attention to internal factors but ignore external factors.
   d. give the most attention to aspects of your physical environment.

9. Effective refusal skills include all of the following *except:*
   a. saying no in a firm voice.
   b. arguing with the other person
   c. offering another idea.
   d. promptly leaving.

Thinking Critically

Using complete sentences, answer the following questions on a sheet of paper.

10. Apply Laurie just made plans to go to a concert with friends this weekend. She forgot that her cousin is coming in from out of town to visit her. What are some options Laurie might consider before making a decision?

11. Analyze How might the skill of analyzing influences benefit your health?

Write About It

12. Decision Making Write a short story in which a teen must make a decision related to his or her health.

13. Advocacy Write a paragraph describing how you could demonstrate good citizenship.

Standardized Test Practice

Reading

Read the passage below and then answer the questions that follow.

You are a citizen of many different communities. The largest community you belong to is the world. Sadly, not all members of this global community share its resources equally. Did you know one in seven of your neighbors in the world goes to bed hungry every night? Others suffer from diseases that were stamped out in our own country a long time ago.

As a health advocate, you can help suffering communities. One way is to tell others. Another is to become and stay informed. The World Health Organization is currently taking action to help people in need. You can visit their Web site for further information.

TEST-TAKING TIP

Read the passage carefully once to find out what information it contains. After you read each question, look back at the passage to find the answer.

1. Which statement best sums up the main point of the passage?

  A. We all live in many different communities.

  B. The health skill of advocacy can be used to help nations in need.

  C. Other countries are suffering from diseases that we have already overcome.

2. The passage notes that "not all members of this global community share its resources equally." Of the following quotes, which is *not* a detail that supports that comment?

  A. "One in seven of your neighbors in the world goes to bed hungry every night."

  B. "Others suffer from diseases that were stamped out in our own country a long time ago."

  C. "You are a citizen of many different communities."

3 Mental and Emotional Health

Chapter Preview

▲ Working With the Photo

Emotions are part of being human. What emotions are these teens experiencing? What are some other emotions?

Start-Up Activities

Before You Read — Look at the Instant Message below. What would you say to your friend if you were "katrosa"? Keep a record of your answer.

IM Express

katrosa: What'd you think of the invitation to Allyson's party? Looks like fun, huh?

ami_j81: Allyson sent out invites? I didn't get one.

FOLDABLES™ Study Organizer

As You Read — Make this Foldable™ to help you organize the main ideas on mental and emotional health in Lesson 1. Begin with a plain sheet of 8½" × 11" paper.

1 Line up one of the short edges of a sheet of paper with one of the long edges to form a triangle. Fold and cut off the leftover rectangle.

2 Fold the triangle in half, then unfold. The folds will form an X dividing four equal sections.

3 Cut up one fold line, and stop at the middle. This forms two triangular flaps. Draw an X on one tab, and label the other three as shown.

4 Fold the X flap under the other flap, and glue together to make a three-sided pyramid.

Write the main ideas on mental and emotional health on the back of the appropriate side of the pyramid.

Health Online — Visit **health.glencoe.com** and complete the Health Inventory for Chapter 3.

Your Mental and Emotional Health

Guide to Reading

● Building Vocabulary
As you read this lesson, write each new highlighted term and its definition in your notebook.
- adapt (p. 52)
- personality (p. 53)
- self-concept (p. 54)
- self-esteem (p. 55)
- resilience (p. 55)

● Focusing on the Main Ideas
In this lesson, you will learn to
- **recognize** traits of good mental and emotional health.
- **identify** factors that influence your self-concept.
- **develop** skills to build your self-esteem.
- **practice** communication skills to improve your mental and emotional health.

● Reading Strategy
Finding the Main Idea Copy each of the main headings from the lesson into your notebook. For each, write one sentence that states the main idea.

FOLDABLES Study Organizer Use the Foldable™ on p. 51 as you read this lesson.

Quick Write

In a short paragraph or poem, describe your personality. Use descriptive words and give examples.

Mental and Emotional Health

Do you have a positive outlook on life? Do you deal effectively with challenges when they arise? If you answered yes to these questions, you probably have good mental and emotional health. People with good mental and emotional health are able to accept themselves and others. They also know how to **adapt,** or *adjust to new situations.*

Other traits of people who are mentally and emotionally healthy appear in **Figure 3.1.** Which of these traits do you have?

► Your mental/emotional health affects every aspect of your life. **What strategies can you use to improve your mental/emotional health?**

✓ You accept the fact that situations and events will not always go the way you plan.

✓ You set and achieve goals.

✓ You understand and cope with your feelings in healthy ways.

✓ You accept constructive criticism.

✓ You express your feelings through your words and creative outlets.

◀ FIGURE 3.1

MENTAL AND EMOTIONAL HEALTH CHECKLIST

Copy this checklist onto a sheet of paper. Place a check mark next to those traits that currently describe your mental/emotional health. Be as honest as you can. **Can you think of any other traits that describe good mental/emotional health?**

What Makes You Who You Are?

Have you ever thought about what makes you unique? You have a number of qualities that make you who you are. The teen years are a time to develop these qualities and learn more about yourself. You develop your physical and mental abilities. You discover the kinds of people you want to build relationships with and the kinds of activities you enjoy. You also begin to form your own values and to understand the importance of standing behind them. All of these things help shape the unique and special person that you are.

Personality and self-concept also play a big role in shaping who you are. Both of these factors are especially influential during your teen years. Therefore, it is important to develop your personality and self-concept in positive and healthy ways. This can help you develop good mental and emotional health.

Your Personality

Are you outgoing and friendly? Are you shy? Are you someone who takes charge of a situation, or do you wait to be told what to do? These are a few of the many qualities that define your personality. **Personality** is *the unique combination of feelings, thoughts, and behaviors*

▼ Your personality and self-concept are two factors that determine your mental and emotional health. **How would you describe your personality? How do you view yourself?**

Learning from Mistakes

What do Thomas Edison, Alexander Graham Bell, and Booker T. Washington have in common? They were all inventors who failed many times before they succeeded in making a discovery. They all learned from their own mistakes and those of others to advance their ideas.

Use outside resources to learn about a person who invented something. List the challenges he or she faced before finally succeeding.

that make you different from everyone else. Your personality affects how you handle problems and new situations. How would you feel about moving to a new school, for example? Would you be excited and confident, or scared and nervous? Different people react in different ways to the same situation.

Your Self-Concept

When you see your reflection in the mirror, who do you see looking back at you? How do you believe others see you? Your answers to these questions reveal your **self-concept.** This is *the view you have of yourself.* The environment in which you live affects your personal health. It influences your self-concept.

Self-concept begins to form in early childhood. It grows out of your experiences and relationships with those around you. The earliest influence on self-concept is family. Members of a loving family support and care for each other. Children brought up in this kind of environment are more likely to develop a positive self-concept.

As you grow older and begin school, your peers and teachers influence your self-concept through their words and actions. Praise from a teacher or coach for a job well done promotes a positive self-concept. Being ignored or teased by peers can have the opposite effect.

When a teen with a positive self-concept makes a mistake, the teen learns from the mistake and moves on. Those with a negative self-concept might feel like one mistake means that everything they do is wrong. This type of attitude can stand in the way of achieving your goals. It is important to remember that everyone makes mistakes. If everyone let a single mistake hold them back, nobody would accomplish anything.

Working toward a positive self-concept is an important part of good mental and emotional health. It can help you form a view of yourself that allows you to work toward and achieve your goals. A positive self-concept will give you confidence and make you feel good about yourself.

Reading Check **Identify** What two factors influence your self-concept?

◀ Part of this teen's self-concept is "musician." **What are some ways that you define yourself? What are some of your skills and talents?**

Self-Esteem

Your personality and self-concept affect the way you feel about yourself. They affect your **self-esteem.** This is *the way you feel about yourself, and how you value yourself.* When you have high self-esteem, you feel appreciated and valued as a person. You have a high degree of confidence in your abilities, and you meet new challenges with a "can-do" attitude. When things go wrong, you are resilient. **Resilience** is *the ability to bounce back from disappointment.* Resilience is an important personality trait to develop. It enables you to get back on your feet after a disappointment and keep moving forward.

Maria is an example of a resilient teen. Maria spent months practicing to try out for the cheerleading squad. On the day of tryouts, she felt ready, and was sure she would make the team. Maria was disappointed when she was not chosen, but she did not let that stop her. She still practiced cheerleading in her free time because she loved it, and she hoped it would help her make the team next year. She also decided to join the school choir. She wanted to focus on her other strengths as well as get involved in a school activity. She used strategies for improving and maintaining her personal health as a way to develop her self-esteem.

Reading Check   **Define** What is *resilience*?

Building Self-Esteem

Whether your self-esteem is high or low, it can always be improved upon. You can develop skills to build your self-esteem and feel good about yourself. These skills can increase your overall level of mental/emotional health. The skills you can practice include:

- **List your strengths.** Identify your talents and abilities. Everyone has special talents and skills. Make a list of them. For example, you may be a loyal friend or a good listener.

Health *Online*

Topic: Body Image and Self-Esteem

Visit **health.glencoe.com** for Student Web Activities to learn about how the image you have of your body can affect your self-esteem.

Activity: Using the information provided at the link above, create a questionnaire that tests for self-esteem and body image.

▶ Recognizing your talents is one way of building your self-esteem. **How does a high self-esteem benefit your health?**

- **Remember that everyone makes mistakes.** No one is perfect. Making mistakes is part of being human. When you get something wrong, learn and grow from the experience.
- **Motivate yourself.** Identify your goals and what you need to do to reach them. Make a plan for getting from where you are to where you want to be. Achieving a goal you set for yourself will give you a sense of accomplishment.

Understanding and Managing Your Feelings

An important part of your mental and emotional health is managing your feelings. Like mental and emotional health itself, feelings can be complicated. Sometimes it is difficult to understand why you feel the way you do. In the next lesson, you will examine the subject of feelings more closely. You will learn skills for managing your feelings.

Health Online

Visit health.glencoe.com and complete the Interactive Study Guide for Lesson 1.

Reading Check **Give Examples** What are three ways to build your self-esteem?

Lesson 1 Review

After You Read

Review this lesson for new terms, major headings, and Reading Checks.

What I Learned

1. *Vocabulary* Define *self-esteem*. Use the term in an original sentence.

2. *Recall* What are traits of good mental and emotional health?

3. *Explain* How does your personality affect how you handle problems and new situations?

Thinking Critically

4. *Evaluate* Review the traits of good mental and emotional health described at the beginning of the lesson and in Figure 3.1. Which of these traits do you think is the most important, and why?

5. *Hypothesize* Shawn was hoping to make the gymnastics team but was turned down. Now he feels terrible and has vowed never to do gymnastics again. How can Shawn build his self-esteem?

Applying Health Skills

6. *Communication Skills* Like other areas of health, mental and emotional health is better on some days than others. Think about messages that would help you feel better when your mental and emotional health is "down." Make a list of these. Remember your list when you are having a down day.

 Health Online For more review questions for Lesson 1 go to health.glencoe.com.

Understanding Your Emotions

Guide to Reading

● Building Vocabulary
Some of the terms below may seem familiar. Write these terms in your notebook, adding definitions in pencil. As you come across them in your reading, finalize the definitions in pen.

- emotions (p. 57)
- anxiety (p. 58)
- panic (p. 59)
- emotional needs (p. 61)

● Focusing on the Main Ideas
In this lesson, you will learn to

- **identify** common emotions.
- **express** emotions in healthy ways.
- **recognize** healthy ways to meet emotional needs.
- **practice** healthful behaviors to manage anger.

● Reading Strategy
Classifying Make a chart that shows some common emotions and healthy ways to express them.

What are Emotions?

Terri had worked hard over the past several months campaigning to be the student council president. Today, she stood side by side with her opponents on the stage of the school auditorium. The results of the vote were about to be announced.

Have you ever been in a situation like Terri's? Even if you have not, you can probably imagine her emotions at this moment. **Emotions** are *feelings created in response to thoughts, remarks, and events*. Some common emotions are shown in **Figure 3.2.**

Quick Write

Think about times when you have been upset or angry over something. Try to recall how you dealt with these feelings.

◀ It is healthy to express happiness about an achievement. **How do you celebrate your accomplishments?**

This table lists several emotions that most people experience regularly. **Which of these emotions have you experienced?**

Emotion	Description
Anger	Strong feeling of displeasure that results from being harmed or hurt
Empathy	Ability to understand and share another person's feelings
Fear	An emotion that can help keep you safe from danger
Happiness	A sense of well-being, of feeling good about life in general
Jealousy	Resentment or unhappiness at another's good fortune
Love	A combination of caring and affection that binds one person to another
Sadness	A normal, healthy reaction to an unhappy event or disappointment
Sympathy	Ability to understand and share another's problems or sorrow

Expressing Emotions

There are many ways to express how you feel. When you look around you, you can see people expressing emotions in different ways. No emotion is either good or bad by itself. What is important is how you *express* your emotions. The way you express emotions affects your mental/emotional, social, and physical health. Therefore, learning to express emotions in healthy ways is important to maintaining good health. Some basic emotions that you can learn to express in healthy ways include anxiety, fear, and anger.

Expressing Anxiety

Have you ever had "pre-game jitters" or waited backstage for your entrance in a performance? At these times, your heart beats faster and your stomach may churn. These physical responses are typical of anxiety. **Anxiety** is *a state of uneasiness, usually associated with a future uncertainty.*

Mild anxiety can actually be helpful. It gets your body ready for action and increases your energy levels. This energy can improve your performance. When anxiety builds up, however, it is not helpful. It can interfere with normal and necessary functions like sleeping and eating. To help you deal with feelings of anxiety, you can use resources from your home, school, and community. For example, talking through a problem with a family member, friend, or counselor can help you express your anxiety in a positive way. Sharing your feelings of anxiety with others may give you the reassurance and encouragement you need. When you do overcome anxiety, you build resilience. Another way to manage anxiety is to meet challenges "head on." Escaping from or avoiding situations is not helpful. When you meet a challenge, the anxiety may not be as bad the next time you face a similar challenge.

A heightened state of anxiety produces **panic,** *a feeling of sudden, intense fear.* Symptoms of panic include dizziness and a pounding heart. You will read more about extreme anxiety and panic in the next chapter.

Expressing Fear

An emotion related to anxiety is fear. Have you ever jumped at a sudden loud noise? This reaction is an ex-pression of fear. Fear is your mind and body's alert system. It prepares you for quick action in case a real threat exists. Therefore, expressing fear can be positive because it can help keep you safe from danger.

▲ Anxiety is uneasiness, usually over something that is about to occur. **Name a school-related event that has caused you to feel anxious.**

However, some fears, such as the fear of failure, may keep you from doing things you want or need to do. Fear stops being a protective force when it becomes a central focus in your life. Being afraid all the time is emotionally and physically draining. A positive way of expressing fear is to talk about it with a family member or friend. Support from family and friends can sometimes help you overcome your fears.

Reading Check **Explain** In what way is fear a helpful emotion?

Expressing Anger

Everyone feels angry sometimes. A younger brother or sister scribbles all over your homework. A friend you were supposed to meet shows up late and has no excuse. Showing anger is not only normal, it is also an important emotional release. Keeping this emotion bottled up inside can be physically and emotionally harmful.

Although it is good to express anger, you need to express it in a healthful way. Assuming responsibility for expressing anger in appropriate ways is a positive health behavior. The Health Skills Activity on page 60 gives specific suggestions for expressing anger appropriately. Yelling at the cause of your anger is not a good solution. Neither is using threats, sarcasm, or other negative forms of behavior. These actions will only worsen the problem.

Health Skills Activity

Practicing Healthful Behaviors

Anger Management

When emotions are running high, they can be difficult to control. It is at these times, though, that self-control is most important. The next time you feel angry, try these steps:

1. Take a deep breath. Try to relax.
2. Identify the specific cause of your anger. If necessary, leave the room so that you can collect your thoughts.
3. When you are calm enough to speak, tell the other person how you feel and what action has caused you to feel this way.
4. Write down your thoughts in a journal.
5. Practice the relaxation skills that are described in the next lesson.
6. Do a physical activity. A positive way to manage stress is to keep physically active.
7. Look for opportunities to laugh. Keeping a sense of humor is also a positive skill for managing anger.

With a Group

Role-play a situation in which one or both of you is upset over something. Use anger management skills to express your anger in a healthy way. Be prepared to perform your role-play for classmates.

Mixed Emotions

Sometimes, identifying what you are feeling is difficult. This is especially true when you have *mixed emotions*. These are opposite or different feelings that occur at once. Suppose you and your best friend both applied for the same after-school job. If your friend gets the job, you feel happy for her or him. At the same time, you feel disappointed that you were not chosen.

Mixed emotions can be confusing, but they are perfectly natural. When you feel mixed emotions, talk with someone who is not directly involved in the situation. Often, such a person can help you gain a better perspective. A new perspective can help you look at your feelings differently and deal with each one in a healthful way.

Reading Check **Identify** What are mixed emotions?

Recognizing Emotional Needs

Just as everyone has emotions, everyone has emotional needs. These needs can be as important as physical needs such as water, food, and sleep. **Emotional needs** are *needs that affect your feelings and sense of well-being.*

Mental health experts recognize three main emotional needs.

- **The need to love and be loved.** Love—caring for others and feeling cared about—is a basic human need. It directs many of the decisions we make and the actions we take. Your need to be loved—to feel special—is met by your family and friends.

- **The need to belong.** This need is also met by your family and friends. Think about all the different groups you belong to. You are a member of your family and your class. You may belong to clubs or teams in or outside your school. This sense of belonging is essential. It lets you know there are others who accept and respect you for who you are.

- **The need to make a difference.** You need to feel that you are making a contribution, that your life has meaning, and that you are accomplishing something.

▲ When anxiety builds up, it can affect your overall health. **What are some healthy ways to express feelings of anxiety?**

Healthy Ways to Meet Emotional Needs

As with emotions, there are healthy and unhealthy ways of meeting emotional needs. How you meet these needs is largely a matter of choice. You will want to assume responsibility for personal health behavior, including fulfilling your emotional needs in a healthy way. For example, one way to meet your need for love is to show others that you care about them. Offer to help out at home without being asked. Ask a friend how his or her day went. Encourage others when they feel down. When you show others that you care about them, they are more likely to show you the same caring.

As for your need to belong, think about your favorite hobbies or activities. What do you enjoy doing in your free time? Perhaps there is already a group or club devoted to it. Membership in this type of group will help satisfy your need to belong. It will also promote your social health by putting you in contact with others with similar interests. You may discover it is easier to build a friendship when you share a common interest.

► Joining a group or team can meet your emotional need to belong. **What are some healthy ways to meet your emotional need to make a difference?**

To meet your need to feel you are making a difference, you could try volunteering. Find out some ways that you can help your community. Offer the gift of your time or talents. Accomplishing short- and long-term goals will also help you meet this emotional need. Having a positive influence on others will give you a sense that you are making a difference.

Health Online

Visit health.glencoe.com and complete the Interactive Study Guide for Lesson 2.

Reading Check

Identify Which emotional need can be met by friends and family members?

Lesson 2 Review

 After You Read

Review this lesson for new terms, major headings, and Reading Checks.

What I Learned

1. *Vocabulary* Define *panic*. Which emotion does panic grow out of?

2. *Recall* What are mixed emotions?

3. *Explain* What are the basic human emotional needs?

Thinking Critically

4. *Analyze* Rick is annoyed at a teammate whose mistake on the field caused the team to lose the game. What emotions is Rick probably feeling? Explain.

5. *Synthesize* Certain character traits such as caring and respect help meet emotional needs. For example, a person who feels cared for will feel secure and loved. Give another example of a character trait and the emotional need it can meet.

Applying Health Skills

6. *Advocacy* Create a flyer that informs students of volunteer opportunities for teens in your community.

Managing Stress

Guide to Reading

Building Vocabulary
As you read this lesson, try to identify which terms below are causes of other terms. Which are effects?

- stress (p. 63)
- stressor (p. 64)
- fight-or-flight response (p. 64)
- adrenaline (p. 65)
- time management (p. 67)

Focusing on the Main Ideas
In this lesson, you will learn to

- **identify** the causes of stress.
- **describe** how your body responds to stress.
- **develop** skills to manage stress in your life.

Reading Strategy
Organizing Information
Look at Figure 3.4. List each body part in the chart. Tell how each is affected by stress.

What Is Stress?

As Scott waited for the midterm exam to start, his heart raced. His palms sweated, and his stomach felt like it had been tied in knots. What Scott was experiencing was a common form of anxiety called stress. **Stress** is *the body's response to change*. It is a normal reaction to certain situations or events in your life. The long-term physical effects of stress include nervous habits and problems sleeping or eating. Biting or picking your fingernails is an example of a stress-related habit.

Not all stress is bad. In fact, some stress is necessary. Positive stress can motivate you to do your best. For example, a small amount of stress can get you ready for a big game. Stress can also make you more alert and improve your concentration. This type of stress can help you perform to your fullest when faced with a big exam.

Quick Write

Identify some causes of stress in your life that you have experienced more than once. Choose one, and write about steps you could take to lessen the effects of stress.

▶ Stress is a normal part of life. **What are some healthy ways of coping with stress?**

Causes of Stress

Anything that causes stress is called a **stressor.** A stressor ranges from everyday annoyances to serious personal problems. They can be positive or negative. Have you ever been too excited to sleep? Maybe you feel this way the night before your birthday or at the start of a vacation. The symptoms you experience are similar to those caused by negative stress, even when the stressor itself is a pleasant event.

Negative stressors can be minor events or major life-changing events. Some common stressors among teens appear in **Figure 3.3.** Not all people respond the same way to a given stressor. For example, doing a presentation in front of the entire class may be stressful to one student but not to another. What are some common stressors in your life?

Reading Check   **Define** What are *stressors*?

The Body's Response to Stress

Although stress is an emotional reaction to events, your body is also affected. You have already read about some of the physical effects of stress. All of these are part of the **fight-or-flight response.** This response is *the process by which the body prepares to deal with a stressor.* Fighting or fleeing is the body's natural response to threats of harm. Imagine a situation in which you feel afraid. For example, you are walking past a yard when a large dog starts barking at you. Your body undergoes changes that prepare

► FIGURE 3.3

SOME COMMON TEEN STRESSORS

Different people respond to stressors differently. If you were to rank these stressors in terms of most to least stressful, which would come first? Which would you put last?

Extremely Stressful	Somewhat Stressful
Separation or divorce of parents	Arguing with a sibling or friend
Family member's alcohol or drug problem	Moving to a new home
Getting arrested	Going to a new school
Failing classes at school	Getting glasses or braces
Being suspended from school	Arguing with a parent
Starting to use alcohol or other drugs	Worrying over height, weight, or acne
Loss or death of a pet	Getting a lead role in the school play
Family member having a serious illness	Being sick or injured

it to act. One is the release of **adrenaline.** This is *a hormone that gives the body extra energy.* In the example of the dog, your response might be to back away. **Figure 3.4** shows how various body parts respond to stress.

Reading Check **List** Name several parts of the body involved in the fight-or-flight response.

Excess Stress

Although some stress can be useful, your body can handle only so much. When stress—positive *or* negative—is intense, your health suffers. Excessive stress can affect all sides of your health triangle:

- **Physical Health:** People with too much stress may have headaches, digestive problems, and high blood pressure. Ongoing stress can tire you out physically and reduce your body's ability to fight infection.

- **Mental and Emotional Health:** Excessive stress can make you feel anxious, moody, and irritable. It can interfere with your schoolwork and take away your desire to have fun.

▼ FIGURE 3.4

THE BODY'S RESPONSES TO STRESS

Many parts of your body respond to stress. How do the lungs respond?

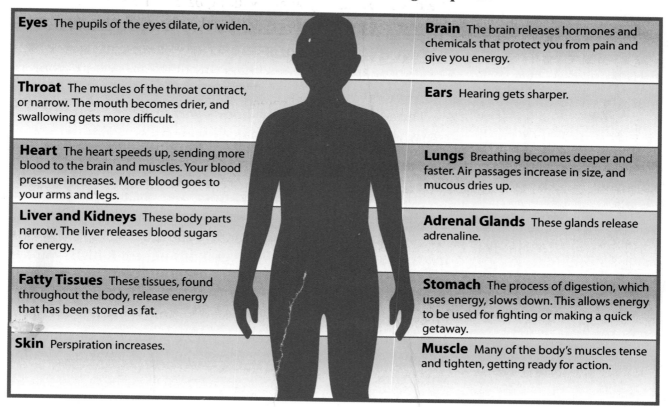

Eyes The pupils of the eyes dilate, or widen.

Throat The muscles of the throat contract, or narrow. The mouth becomes drier, and swallowing gets more difficult.

Heart The heart speeds up, sending more blood to the brain and muscles. Your blood pressure increases. More blood goes to your arms and legs.

Liver and Kidneys These body parts narrow. The liver releases blood sugars for energy.

Fatty Tissues These tissues, found throughout the body, release energy that has been stored as fat.

Skin Perspiration increases.

Brain The brain releases hormones and chemicals that protect you from pain and give you energy.

Ears Hearing gets sharper.

Lungs Breathing becomes deeper and faster. Air passages increase in size, and mucous dries up.

Adrenal Glands These glands release adrenaline.

Stomach The process of digestion, which uses energy, slows down. This allows energy to be used for fighting or making a quick getaway.

Muscle Many of the body's muscles tense and tighten, getting ready for action.

Health Skills Activity

Stress Management

Stress Chasers

When you are feeling tense, doing some simple exercises can reduce stress. Practice the exercises below. Remember them for those stressful times when you need them.

- **Shoulder Lift.** Hunch your shoulders up to your ears for a few seconds, then release. Repeat.
- **Elastic Jaw.** Take a few deep relaxing breaths. Open your mouth, and shift your jaw to the right as far as you can without discomfort. Hold for a count of three. Repeat on the left side.
- **Fist Clench.** Make a fist. Tense the muscles in your hand and forearm, then release. Repeat this with your other hand.

On Your Own

Estimate your current level of body tension or stress. Use a scale of 1 to 5, where 1 is *Totally Calm* and 5 is *Very Stressed*. Then perform one of the exercises listed here. When you are done, write down your estimated level of body tension. Repeat for each of the other exercises. How did each exercise affect your tension level? Compare your results with those of classmates.

- **Social Health:** Some people under extreme stress will yell at those around them. Others withdraw, or back off, from social contacts.

These reactions are your body's way of telling you that it is overwhelmed. You need to manage your stress.

Skills for Managing Stress

You cannot remove stressors from your life, but you can manage the stress they cause. One way is to practice good health habits. This includes eating well and getting enough rest, especially during the teen years. When your level of wellness is high, you feel good and are better able to handle problems.

Specific skills can also help you deal with stress. These include relaxing, laughing, and maintaining a positive outlook. In addition, staying physically active, managing your time, and socializing with family and friends are great ways for dealing with stress.

Relaxation

Did you know you have the ability to slow down your heart rate? This ability is part of the stress-management skill known as *relaxation*. Relaxation makes you feel less tense. It helps you sleep better at night, which is an effective stress-reducing tool. Other relaxation skills include taking deep, even breaths and doing exercises that relax your muscles. Even quiet activities, such as reading a book or magazine, can help you relax and reduce stress.

▲ When you are feeling overwhelmed, having a good sense of humor can be a great help. **What are some other actions you could take that would bring a smile to your face?**

Reading Check **List** What are three specific skills for managing stress?

Laughter and a Positive Outlook

One of the great stress relievers is a good laugh. If you can find a way to laugh when you are tense, you will find that it redirects the energy that stress creates. Think of a funny situation the next time you feel tense, or remind yourself of a good joke.

Even if you cannot laugh, try to maintain a positive outlook. Think positive thoughts. Remind yourself to look at the big picture and keep things in perspective. Ask for help if you need it.

Physical Activity

One of the healthiest ways to manage stress is to do something physical. Run around the block or a track at school. Shoot baskets. When you are physically active, your brain releases chemicals that positively affect your mood. You tend to feel happier and more relaxed.

Time Management

One of the biggest causes of stress for teens is scheduling. Do you have trouble finding enough time for activities, chores, and homework? A skill that can help is **time management,** *strategies for using time efficiently.* The key to time management is arranging the hours in your day. One way of doing this is by making a day planner like the one in **Figure 3.5.** A day planner is an organized list of daily activities. Using a day planner can help you identify priorities and stay organized.

Reading Check **Explain** What information goes in a day planner?

PLANNER FOR TYPICAL WEEKDAY

Highlighting certain activities can help you identify priorities. On this schedule, school activities are highlighted in yellow. **Which activities are shown in light blue?**

```
12:30 P.M.  Lunch
1:15 P.M.  Math
2:00 P.M.  Social Studies
2:45 P.M.  End of school; quick snack
3:00 P.M.  Field hockey practice
4:00 P.M.  Cello lesson
4:45 P.M.  Go home; start homework
6:00 P.M.  Dinner
7:00 P.M.  TV
8:00 P.M.  Finish homework
8:30 P.M.  Work briefly on poster for
group project due next week
8:50 P.M.  Call Frannie
9:00 P.M.  Ready for bed
```

Health Online

Visit **health.glencoe.com** and complete the Interactive Study Guide for Lesson 3.

Lesson 3 Review

After You Read

Review this lesson for new terms, major headings, and Reading Checks.

What I Learned

1. *Recall* What causes stress? Give several examples.

2. *Identify* What are three ways that your body responds to stress?

3. *Vocabulary* Define *time management.* Use the term in a sentence that describes how it reduces stress.

Thinking Critically

4. *Evaluate* Which stressor mentioned in the chapter affects you most? Explain why.

5. *Apply* As soon as Lisa came to class, she discovered that a report assigned two weeks earlier was due. Lisa had forgotten about it and was now feeling stress. How could using a planner have helped her?

Applying Health Skills

6. *Practicing Healthful Behaviors* One way to reduce stress is to prepare for it. Make a list of personal health behaviors that will prevent or reduce stress in your life. For example, identify physical activities you enjoy doing. Keep your list handy.

Health Online For more review questions for Lesson 3, go to **health.glencoe.com**.

Coping with Loss

Guide to Reading

● **Building Vocabulary**
As you read this lesson, write each new highlighted term and its definition in your notebook.

- grief (p. 69)
- grief reaction (p. 69)
- coping strategies (p. 70)

● **Focusing on the Main Ideas**
In this lesson, you will learn to

- **identify** stages in the grief reaction.
- **recognize** strategies for coping with personal loss.
- **provide** emotional support to someone who is grieving.

● **Reading Strategy**
Predicting Quickly look at the main headings, figures, and captions before reading the lesson. Based on previous knowledge, tell what you think you might learn.

Loss

Loss is unfortunately an unavoidable part of life. Perhaps your team loses a game. Maybe your neighbor loses a bracelet that belonged to her grandmother. Losses can be very painful. Emotional pain can sometimes be more intense than physical pain.

One of the most painful types of loss is when someone close to you dies. This loss can be a relative, a friend, or even a family pet. At such times, it is normal for those who suffer the loss to experience grief. **Grief** is *the sorrow caused by loss of a loved one.* How long grief lasts after a death depends on the individual.

The Grief Reaction

Any loss or serious disappointment can lead to a grief reaction. A **grief reaction** is *the process of dealing with strong feelings following any loss.* Major stressors in a person's life can cause a grief reaction. The stressor might be the breakup of a friendship following a big argument. It might be disappointment over getting turned down by a club or team. When it comes to grieving, judgments of *right* or *wrong* do not apply. People feel sad for different reasons.

Quick Write

Write a paragraph describing how you would help a friend who has lost a loved one.

▼ Friends can be a source of comfort when you are grieving. **What are some other ways of coping with loss?**

▲ During the acceptance stage of the grief reaction, a person becomes ready to move on. **What are some ways that we remember loved ones whom we have lost?**

The grief reaction usually occurs in stages. Each stage has a different emotional state. These stages usually happen in the order shown below, but there are no hard and fast rules. Not all people go through all the stages.

Shock. Shock is usually the first stage you go through after a major loss. People at this stage frequently feel numb. The full emotional impact of the loss or disappointment has not yet set in.

Anger. At this stage, you may feel intense bitterness or anger. In the case of a death, the feelings may be toward the person who died. They can even be directed at other family members or friends.

Yearning. In the yearning stage, you begin to appreciate the *scope,* or size, of the loss. Some people describe this stage as a big "emotional hole" in their heart. When the loss is a death, this empty space represents the place in your life that your loved one once occupied.

Depression. Deep sadness sets in at this stage. The reality of the loss begins to sink in. You begin to acknowledge, maybe for the first time, that the loss is permanent.

Acceptance. This stage, which often comes last, is one where you feel ready to move on with your life. The pain lessens. If the loss was a death, the person now becomes the subject of memories that you can always have with you.

Reading Check **Compare** Explain the difference between grief and the grief reaction.

Coping with Grief

As everyone knows, there is no way to undo a loss. Fortunately, there are ways of coping with the grief that loss creates. These **coping strategies** are *ways of dealing with the sense of loss people feel at the death of someone close.* These strategies may help you during a very difficult time.

Coping with grief includes confronting your feelings head-on. When you suffer a loss, sadness and crying are normal reactions. Shedding tears is a way that your body deals physically with strong emotions. Instead of keeping your emotions bottled up inside, share them with others. Sometimes just talking about it helps. Some people find that religious traditions help them cope with loss, especially the loss of a loved one.

Helping Others Who Are Grieving

When someone close to you, such as a friend, suffers a loss, you can be a great help to that person. It is important, however, to understand the person's needs. Different people have different emotional needs. Here are some suggestions:

- Let the person decide how you can be a source of comfort. Do not insist on talking or giving advice. Sometimes you can be a big source of comfort just by being there. Ask the person what you can do to help.

- Respect the person's feelings. Remember that feeling sad is not wrong or immature. The loss a person feels may not seem important to you, but it may cause great pain to the other person.

- Allow the person to decide how much time they need to recover. Some people get over losses faster than others. It is up to each individual to decide how long to grieve.

Reading Check **Define** What are *coping strategies*?

Health Online

Visit **health.glencoe.com** and complete the Interactive Study Guide for Lesson 4.

Lesson 4 Review

After You Read

Review this lesson for new terms, major headings, and Reading Checks.

What I Learned

1. **Vocabulary** What is *grief*?

2. **Recall** Name the five stages in the grief reaction.

3. **List** What are three ways of showing emotional support for someone who is grieving?

4. **Explain** What are some coping strategies for dealing with grief?

Thinking Critically

5. **Synthesize** How might coping with a personal loss be said to be both emotional and physical?

6. **Evaluate** Trish just found out her best friend is moving away. Trish is feeling sad and upset. Trish's sister Brittany told her she needs to "get over it." Do you think Brittany's words show emotional support? Explain your answer.

Applying Health Skills

7. **Managing Stress** The death of a loved one can be a very stressful experience. Talk with a grandparent or other older adult about strategies for managing this stress. Share your findings with classmates.

Building Health Skills

Putting Stress in Its Place

DIRECTIONS

Stress Management involves learning how to handle stress in healthy ways. This activity will give you the opportunity to develop and master this important health skill. Here's a guide to the different parts of this activity:

1 In the **Model** section, you will read about a teen who performs the health skill successfully. This "model" scenario will show you how the skill is done.

2 The **Practice** section will help guide you in practicing the skill.

3 In the **Apply** section, you will have a chance to perform the skill on your own. You can use the Self-Check to check your work.

To complete this activity, first read the scenario presented in the Model. Then move on to the Practice. Finally, go ahead and try the Apply.

1 Model

Alex has a busy schedule. He works on the school newspaper and plays on two school sports teams. Lately, Alex has been having trouble sleeping.

His teacher, Mrs. Grace, explained that Alex's hectic schedule could be causing his stress. She showed Alex a strategy for managing his stress.

- **Identify Sources of Stress:** Besides his packed schedule, Alex was feeling anxious about his upcoming performance in the school play.

- **Set Priorities:** First he decided which after-school activities were most important to him. He decided to eliminate one after-school sport.

- **Manage Your Time Wisely:** After reducing his activities, Alex made a day planner to help him stay organized.

The plan worked! Before long, Alex found himself falling asleep the minute his head hit the pillow.

② Practice

Alex's success with the stress-management strategy gave him confidence. He decided to try applying it to another situation. He and his sister shared a computer at home. Each of them felt the other "hogged" the computer after school. Alex was sometimes up late at night doing his homework as a result of this problem. Use the three-step stress-management strategy to solve the problem as you think Alex might. Use these questions to guide your work:

1. What is the source of the stress?

2. What priorities could Alex and his sister set?

3. How could time management apply to this situation?

Skill Summary
STRESS MANAGEMENT

Stress-management strategies include the following:

- Identify sources of stress.
- Set priorities.
- Manage your time wisely.

③ Apply

With a group, write an article for a school newspaper about stress. In your article, explain the effects of stress. Then, choose one source of teen stress. Give examples that show how to set priorities and manage time to reduce this source of stress. Share your article with the rest of the class.

Self-Check

- Did we explain the effects of stress?
- Did we describe a source of stress for teens?
- Did we show how to set priorities and manage time to reduce stress?

Looking for ways to manage stress in your life? The tips on this page can help!

STRESS STOPPERS

Whether it's from schoolwork or issues with friends, pressure has a way of popping up all over the place. Keep a handle on the stress in your life by…

HAVING FUN

After-school activities are a great way to blow off steam. Just make sure they make life more fun—not more stressful! Here's how:

1. Follow your heart. Don't think about whether other kids think a club is cool or not. You'll enjoy yourself more if the activity is something that interests you.

2. Don't let extracurriculars run your life. Limit yourself to a few clubs or teams at a time. You can always try a new one next semester.

3. Make it a bonding experience. Sometimes extracurriculars are less about the actual activity and more about the chance to make friends.

GETTING TO KNOW YOUR TEACHER

Prevent stressful situations in the classroom by building a good relationship with your teacher.

1. Figure out what kind of teacher you have. Is your teacher strict or laid back? The answer will tell you how to work in class. Really listen to your teacher about grading and class participation so you know what to expect.

2. Communicate after class. Even if you're just double-checking the details of an assignment, log some one-on-one face time with your teacher. It shows you're taking responsibility for your class performance.

TAKING A BREATH

To get rid of stress, try pausing for five minutes to focus on your breathing.

• Sit down and close your eyes.

• Take slow, deep breaths.

• If your mind wanders to the stress of your day, reign in your thoughts by concentrating on your breathing.

• Inhale slowly and hold the breath in for a few seconds.

• Now exhale, imagining you're exhaling any stress or tension.

• Keep at it for three to five minutes and you'll feel more calm and relaxed.

Reading Review

Lesson 1 Your Mental and Emotional Health

Key Ideas

- Traits of good mental and emotional health include having a healthy outlook on life, dealing effectively with problems, bouncing back from disappointment, and accepting yourself and others.

- Ways to improve your self-esteem include listing your strengths, learning from your mistakes, and motivating yourself.

Vocabulary

- adapt (p. 52)
- personality (p. 53)
- self-concept (p. 54)
- self-esteem (p. 55)
- resilience (p. 55)

Lesson 2 Understanding Your Emotions

Key Ideas

- Common human emotions include anxiety, fear, and anger.

- The basic human emotional needs are the need to love and be loved, the need to belong, and the need to make a difference.

Vocabulary

- emotions (p. 57)
- anxiety (p. 58)
- panic (p. 59)
- emotional needs (p. 61)

Lesson 3 Managing Stress

Key Ideas

- Stress is caused by positive or negative stressors.

- Positive ways to manage stress include relaxing, laughing, maintaining a positive outlook, staying physically active, and managing your time.

Vocabulary

- stress (p. 63)
- stressor (p. 64)
- fight-or-flight response (p. 64)
- adrenaline (p. 65)
- time management (p. 67)

Lesson 4 Coping with Loss

Key Ideas

- Stages in the grief reaction include shock, anger, yearning, depression, and acceptance.

- Strategies for coping with personal loss include confronting your feelings, allowing yourself to cry, and letting others know how you feel.

Vocabulary

- grief (p. 69)
- grief reaction (p. 69)
- coping strategies (p. 70)

Reviewing Vocabulary and Main Ideas

On a sheet of paper, write the numbers 1–6. After each number, write the term from the list that best completes each sentence.

- anxiety
- coping strategies
- emotional needs
- emotions
- personality
- self-concept
- self-esteem
- stress

Lesson 1 Your Mental and Emotional Health

1. Your _____ is the unique combination of feelings, thoughts, and behavior that makes you different from everyone else.

2. The view you have of yourself is your _____.

3. Your _____ is the way you feel about yourself, and how you value yourself.

Lesson 2 Understanding Your Emotions

4. _____ are feelings created in response to thoughts, remarks, and events.

5. A state of uneasiness, that usually relates to being uncertain about something in the future, is called _____.

6. Needs that affect your feelings and sense of well-being are your _____.

*On a sheet of paper, write the numbers 7–11. Write **True** or **False** for each statement below. If the statement is false, change the underlined word or phrase to make it true.*

Lesson 3 Managing Stress

7. <u>Stress</u> is the body's response to change.

8. The process by which the body prepares to deal with a stressor is called <u>adrenaline</u>.

9. Physical activity and <u>laughter</u> are two skills for managing stress.

Lesson 4 Coping with Loss

10. The grief reaction includes shock, anger, <u>time management</u>, depression, and acceptance.

11. One important <u>grief</u> strategy that can help you deal with sorrow over a loss is confronting your feelings head-on.

Thinking Critically

Using complete sentences, answer the following questions on a sheet of paper.

12. **Compare and Contrast** Kris and Tom are both on the hockey team. A big game is coming up. Kris is unable to eat or think about anything else. Tom, meanwhile, cannot wait for the day of the big game. Compare and contrast the teens' levels of anxiety.

13. **Analyze** Felicia was very upset by the death of her cat. Her brother offered to get her a new cat, but this made Felicia feel worse. Explain what Felicia is going through. Also, explain her brother's attempt to make her feel better.

14. **Synthesize** What are some time management strategies a teen could use to reduce stress?

Write About It

15. **Stress Management** Write a short story about a teen who is having a stressful day. In your story, identify the cause of the teen's stress. Show how the teen manages stress in healthy ways.

Career Corner

Mental Health Counselor Do you enjoy helping others solve personal problems? Then you might consider a career as a mental health counselor. This profession requires that you have a four-year college degree and a two-year advanced degree in counseling. You must also have supervised counseling experience to become licensed. Learn more by clicking on *Career Corner* at **health.glencoe.com**.

16. **Communication Skills** Imagine that a good friend of yours has recently lost a close relative. Write a letter of support to your friend to let him or her know that you care.

Standardized Test Practice

Math

One way of analyzing how you spend your time is by making a time pie chart like the sample chart shown. Use the sample chart to answer the questions that follow.

Other — 2.75 hours
After-School Activities — 2 hours
Classes — 5.75 hours
Homework — 3 hours
2.5 hours — Meals and Snacks
8 hours — Sleep

TEST TAKING TIP

Make sure you understand the different kinds of graphs and what each shows. Read the title of a graph for added information about what it contains.

1. Based on the number of hours per day this teen spends sleeping, it can be concluded that
   A. the teen gets too little sleep.
   B. the teen sleeps ¼ of the day.
   C. the teen sleeps ⅓ of the day.
   D. the teen spends too much time sleeping.

2. The percentage of the day this teen spends on homework is
   A. 12.5%
   B. 30%
   C. 3%
   D. 8.33%

4 Mental and Emotional Problems

Chapter Preview

▲ Working With the Photo

People with mental or emotional problems sometimes feel very alone. They can feel this way even in a room full of people. **What comes to your mind when you hear the term *mental/ emotional problem*?**

Start-Up Activities

Before You Read Do you handle mental and emotional problems in healthful ways? Find out by taking the short health inventory on this page. Keep a record of your answers.

HEALTH INVENTORY

1. I deal with my problems in healthful ways.
(a) always   (b) sometimes   (c) never

2. I ask for help when a problem arises.
(a) always   (b) sometimes   (c) never

3. I am able to help a friend with an emotional problem.
(a) always   (b) sometimes   (c) never

FOLDABLES™ Study Organizer

As You Read Make this Foldable™ to help you learn about mental and emotional problems. Begin with a plain sheet of 11″ × 17″ paper.

1 Fold a sheet of paper along the long axis. Leave a 1/2″ tab along the side.

2 Turn the paper. Fold in half, then fold again.

3 Unfold and cut the top layer along the three fold lines. This makes four tabs.

4 Turn the paper vertically and label the tabs as shown. Write down the definitions of each type of mental and emotional disorder. Also, list characteristics of each type of mental and emotional disorder under the appropriate tab.

Anxiety Disorders

Personality Disorders

Schizophrenia

Mood Disorders

Health Online Visit **health.glencoe.com** and use the e-flashcards to preview Chapter 4 vocabulary terms.

Mental and Emotional Disorders

Guide to Reading

● **Building Vocabulary**
As you read this lesson, write each new highlighted term and its definition in your notebook.

- disorder (p. 80)
- anxiety disorder (p. 81)
- phobia (p. 81)
- personality disorder (p. 82)
- mood disorder (p. 83)
- major depression (p. 83)
- schizophrenia (p. 85)

● **Focusing on the Main Ideas**
In this lesson, you will learn to

- **identify** types of anxiety disorders.
- **describe** two mood disorders.
- **identify** signs of major depression.

● **Reading Strategy**
Comparing and Contrasting Create a diagram that shows similarities and differences among mental and emotional health disorders described in the lesson.

FOLDABLES Study Organizer Use the Foldable™ on p. 79 as you read this lesson.

Quick Write

Think about a time when you were very upset. Tell what you did to overcome these feelings.

◀ Some anxiety is normal. **When does being anxious suggest a larger problem?**

Kinds of Mental and Emotional Disorders

Many myths surround the subject of mental and emotional problems. One myth is that these conditions are not true illnesses, like heart disease or diabetes. Another myth is that people can just "snap out of" these problems if they try hard enough.

The truth is that mental and emotional problems are as real as physical problems. They can affect people of any age. Studies released by the National Mental Health Information Center show that mental disorders affect at least one in five children and adolescents. Like other diseases they can be treated. Treatment can include medication, counseling, or both. Getting help can reduce the risks related to health problems in adolescence.

In this lesson you will learn about several common mental and emotional disorders. A **disorder** is *a disturbance in the normal function of a part of the body.*

Anxiety Disorders

Everyone feels anxious at one time or another. For example, you might be worried the night before a big test. Problems at home or at school can also be a source of anxiety. It is normal to feel this way when you are faced with a challenge. Some people, however, become frequently and unreasonably worried. They might have an **anxiety disorder.** This is *a disorder in which intense anxiety or fear keeps a person from functioning normally.* The five types of anxiety disorders and their symptoms are listed in **Figure 4.1.**

One type of mental and emotional disorder is a **phobia,** or *an exaggerated fear of a specific situation or object.* You have probably heard of certain phobias, such as fear of flying or of spiders. **Figure 4.2** on the next page shows some common phobias. Some fears are not only normal, but necessary. For example, concern over walking down a dark, deserted street in an unsafe neighborhood is understandable. It shows that you have a healthy awareness of risk, not that you have a phobia.

Anxiety disorders may first become apparent during the teen years or young adulthood. Treatments are available that can help people with these disorders lead full, productive lives.

Reading Check **List** Identify three anxiety disorders and their symptoms.

▼ FIGURE 4.1

TYPES OF ANXIETY DISORDERS

Anxiety disorders are grouped into the five categories shown here. **What are the symptoms of obsessive-compulsive disorder?**

Disorder	Symptoms
Generalized Anxiety Disorder	Restlessness, tiredness, difficulty concentrating, irritability, muscle tension, sleep disturbances
Panic Disorder	Pounding heart, sweating, trembling, shortness of breath, nausea, fear of losing control
Phobia	An intense or exaggerated fear of a specific situation or object
Obsessive-Compulsive Disorder	A need to perform behaviors over and over again, such as handwashing, counting, hoarding, or arranging possessions
Post-Traumatic Stress Disorder	Withdrawal or depression after a distressing experience such as sexual abuse, natural disaster, accident, or witnessing violence

SOME COMMON PHOBIAS FROM A TO Z

The table lists several different types of phobias. **What is an acrophobia?**

Some Common Phobias from A to Z	
Acrophobia	Fear of heights
Agoraphobia	Fear of crowded places or open areas
Astraphobia	Fear of thunder and lightning
Claustrophobia	Fear of enclosed spaces
Ecophobia	Fear of home
Hydrophobia	Fear of water
Kenophobia	Fear of empty spaces
Noctiphobia	Fear of night
Phasmophobia	Fear of ghosts
Socialphobia	Fear of people
Tachophobia	Fear of speed
Zoophobia	Fear of animals

Personality Disorders

People have a basic need to belong and be accepted by others. Some people, however, have a lot of trouble relating to others. They may suffer from a personality disorder. A **personality disorder** is *a psychological condition that affects a person's ability to interact normally with others.*

One example is *passive-aggressive personality disorder.* People with this disorder can have a hard time cooperating with others. They do not like being told what to do, and can become very angry when they feel like they do not have control over a situation. In these cases, they show their anger in unhealthy and inappropriate ways. For example, in a group activity if a passive-aggressive person becomes angry, he or she might respond passively—by not participating at all. He or she may also respond aggressively—by yelling or being mean to others in the group.

Another personality disorder is *borderline personality disorder.* People with this disorder have trouble in close relationships with others. This is because when they are involved in a close relationship with someone, they tend to idealize that person. If they become disappointed in that person, they might lash out in anger or even violence. People with this disorder also tend to engage in high-risk behaviors, have poor self-esteem, and have an intense fear of abandonment.

▼ Arachnophobia, a fear of spiders, is a common phobia. **What are some other phobias that you have heard of?**

Mood Disorders

People who feel sad over a long period of time and for no explainable reason may have a **mood disorder.** This is *a disorder in which a person undergoes changes in mood that seem inappropriate or extreme.* Being overly happy, giddy, or energetic for no apparent reason can also be a sign of a mood disorder.

One mood disorder, previously known as manic-depressive disorder, is *bipolar disorder.* This illness is known for its mood "cycles." A person with bipolar disorder may experience alternating high and low periods. During the high—or *manic*—periods, the person can have increased energy. In the low—or *depressive*—periods, energy slows down drastically. Sometimes these mood cycles are rapid, but most often they are gradual.

The symptoms that come with the depressive side of bipolar disorder also occur in **major depression.** This is *a very serious mood disorder in which people lose interest in life and can no longer find enjoyment in anything.*

Everyone feels sad from time to time. Having occasional brief periods of sadness does not mean you have a mental or emotional disorder. Sharing your feelings with a parent or trusted adult can help.

Reading Check **Define** What is a *mood disorder*?

◀ Receiving bad news can make you feel down. **How is this type of sadness different from major depression?**

Depression Among Teens

The teen years can be a difficult time in life. Friendships may suddenly seem more complicated. Your relationship with parents and other family members are changing. During this time of life, some teens become depressed.

Some studies suggest that as many as 20 percent of teens suffer from major depression. Teens who are depressed may appear moody, angry, hostile, aggressive, and irritable. Depressed teens may turn to alcohol or other drugs. Other common signs of depression are shown in **Figure 4.3.**

When left untreated, depression can become worse. If you know someone who seems depressed, encourage that person to talk to a parent or other trusted adult. If he or she says that talking to someone will not help, you should tell a trusted adult about your concerns.

▼ **FIGURE 4.3**

WARNING SIGNS OF DEPRESSION

A teen showing three or more of these warning signs for more than two weeks may be suffering from depression. **What can you do if you suspect someone you know is depressed?**

1. Irritability, anger, or anxiety
2. Lack of energy; feeling tired all the time
3. Significant change in sleep patterns; an inability to fall asleep, stay asleep, or get up in the morning
4. Inability to concentrate
5. Putting blame on other people for their problems, especially adults
6. Feelings of worthlessness or guilt
7. Indifference to things that used to bring pleasure
8. Pessimism
9. Physical problems, like stomachaches or headaches, that can't be explained
10. Thoughts of death or suicide

▶ One characteristic of schizophrenia is a withdrawal from others. **Why might a person who suffers from schizophrenia want to withdraw from interacting with others?**

Schizophrenia

Schizophrenia (skit·zoh·FREE·nee·uh) is *a severe mental disorder in which people lose contact with reality.* They may have hallucinations in which they see or hear things that are not actually there. Schizophrenics are often unable to tell the difference between real events and ones they are imagining. For example, people in this state might think they are historical figures or that they have special powers.

One common aspect of schizophrenia is a withdrawal from others and from society. Schizophrenics tend to function in their own worlds, in which they develop a fear and mistrust of others.

Today, there is medication available to treat schizophrenia. Schizophrenics can lead relatively functional lives if they take these medicines properly.

Health Online

Visit **health.glencoe.com** and complete the Interactive Study Guide for Lesson 1.

Lesson 1 Review

After You Read

Review this lesson for new terms, major headings, and Reading Checks.

What I Learned

1. *Vocabulary* What is a *disorder*? Use this term in an original sentence.

2. *List* Name two mood disorders, and describe each.

3. *Recall* What are the five types of anxiety disorders?

Thinking Critically

4. *Synthesize* Look back at the myths about mental illness that opened the lesson. What do you think is a negative consequence of spreading these myths?

5. *Evaluate* Carl had worked hard on his entry for the school science fair. He was sad when he did not win an award for his project. Do you think Carl was experiencing major depression? Explain your answer.

Applying Health Skills

6. *Accessing Information* With a group, investigate one of the disorders described in the lesson. Use a variety of reliable sources. Make notes about the kinds of help available.

Suicide Prevention

Guide to Reading

● Building Vocabulary
Find the term below where it appears highlighted in the lesson. Write the term and its definition in your notebook.

- suicide (p. 86)

● Focusing on the Main Ideas
In this lesson, you will learn to

- **identify** causes of teen suicide.
- **identify** warning signs of suicide.
- **demonstrate** effective communication skills to help someone with mental and emotional problems.

● Reading Strategy
Finding the Main Idea For each of the main headings in this lesson, write one sentence that states the main idea.

Quick Write

Write a paragraph describing what you could do to help a friend who is talking about suicide.

Suicide

When depression lasts for weeks or months, the emotional pain can be overwhelming. Life may begin to seem hopeless for some individuals. Some teens may begin having thoughts of **suicide.** This is *the intentional taking of one's own life*. It is important to recognize the warning signs of suicide and seek help if you or someone you know is suffering from severe depression.

Causes of Teen Suicide

During the teen years, you will begin to accept new responsibilities and challenges within your family and at school. Accepting new challenges and responsibilities can cause stress. Life-changing events such as a family breakup or the death of someone close can feel overwhelming. Alcoholism or other drug dependencies within the family can cause a teen to become depressed. So can witnessing domestic violence or being a victim of physical or sexual abuse. In some instances, teens consider suicide because they cannot handle the pressures they face at home or at school. If a teen feels that his or her family is not supportive, he or she may become depressed. Being depressed can lead to thoughts of suicide.

Not all causes of teen suicide involve the home or family. Some teens consider suicide because they feel disconnected from or rejected by peers. Because these teens may have few friends, their sadness can sometimes go unnoticed.

Warning Signs of Suicide

Teens thinking about suicide often share their plans openly. Many drop hints through their words and actions. They may say things like, "I can't take it anymore" or "No one cares if I live or die." Comments like these are warning signs. Never assume that a person who makes these kinds of remarks does not really mean it. Talk to a trusted adult immediately about what you heard. You might try suggesting that a person who needs help use resources in home, school, and community that provide valid health information.

Other warning signs of suicide include:

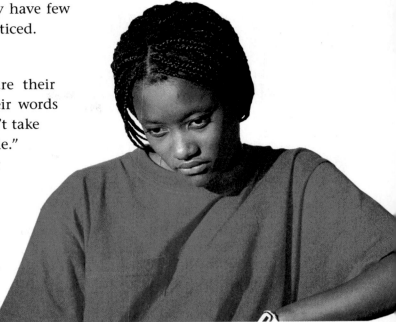

▲ Teens who are feeling depressed should seek help and support from others. **Who can teens turn to for help during a difficult time?**

- **A sudden fascination with the topic of death.** The person may talk about different ways of dying. He or she may start reading or writing poems and stories about death.

- **Dramatic changes in the person's appearance.** The person may no longer take an interest in his or her appearance.

- **Self-destructive behavior.** The person may do reckless things. She or he may also suddenly decide to become sexually active or use drugs.

- **Withdrawal from friends, family, and regular activities.** Withdrawal is also a symptom of depression, and it shows that the person is letting go of things that were once important. He or she may also begin giving away valued possessions.

- **A sudden change in mood.** After weeks or months of being depressed, the person suddenly appears cheerful. This may look like a positive change, but sometimes it is not. Sometimes it means that the person has made up his or her mind to commit suicide.

 Reading Check **List** Name two causes of teen suicide.

Providing Support

People who think about or attempt suicide usually do not want to die. Rather, their actions are a plea for help.

Health Skills Activity

Communication Skills

Giving "Emotional First Aid"

People who are severely depressed have an emotional injury. Eventually, they will need professional treatment for their "wounds." Before they can get that help, they require "emotional first aid." This can come from anyone with good communication skills, including you. Perhaps you can influence the person to make healthful choices. Here are some tips:

- Let them speak and express their negative emotions.
- Don't challenge or dare the person.
- Remind the person of past successes. Recall challenges that she or he overcame.
- Tell the person how important he or she is to you and others. Provide the person with reasons for living.

With a Group

Make a pamphlet with suggestions for helping troubled teens. Pass out copies of your pamphlet.

You can provide this help and support. If someone you know shows warning signs of suicide, talk to the person. Just showing interest in the person's problem can be a positive first step. It shows the person that they are not alone. Do not be afraid to ask whether the individual is planning to harm him or herself. Urge the person to share her or his feelings and thoughts with a trusted adult. Finally, never promise to keep suicide plans a secret. This is one secret a true friend will never agree to keep.

Reading Check

Explain What are some ways to give emotional support to someone who is depressed?

Health Online

Visit health.glencoe.com and complete the Interactive Study Guide for Lesson 2.

Dealing with Depression

Depression can feel like a heavy weight. Sometimes, people feel that they cannot get out from under it. This hopelessness is what leads some people to think about taking their own lives. However, you can assume responsibility for your personal health behaviors. If you ever find yourself thinking about suicide, remember:

- Suicide is *never* a solution to depression. Solutions do exist for every problem, but this is not one of them.

- Feelings of depression do not go on forever. There are people who can help you get through a difficult time. If you feel hopeless, remember that there is always a light at the end of the tunnel.

- You are not alone. There are people who love and want to help you. If you are feeling low, talk to someone close. Do this even if you do not think it will help. You may be surprised by the power of words.

There are organizations you can contact that help teens deal with suicidal thoughts. One is SPAN USA. The letters in *SPAN* stand for "Suicide Prevention Action Network." Another is the National Youth Violence Prevention Resource Center. Each of these organizations has a Web site and a telephone hot line.

▲ Group counseling is one way a person who is feeling depressed can receive emotional support. **What are some other ways someone who is experiencing depression can receive emotional support?**

Lesson 2 Review

After You Read

Review this lesson for new terms, major headings, and Reading Checks.

What I Learned

1. *Vocabulary* What is *suicide*? Use this term in an original sentence.

2. *Give Examples* Give two examples of actions or behaviors that suggest that a teen might be thinking about suicide.

3. *Recall* What are some causes of teen suicide?

Thinking Critically

4. *Synthesize* Barbara's parents are getting divorced and selling the home she has lived in all her life. Barbara feels like her life is crumbling. What kind of support can you give Barbara?

5. *Apply* Larry's friend Pete has been very down since his father's death. Lately, Pete seems to be better. However, he has offered Larry his skateboard and his best jacket. Should Larry be concerned about his friend?

Applying Health Skills

6. *Communication Skills* With a partner, perform a role-play about a friend helping another who is feeling down. Use skills from the Health Skills Activity and the lesson as a whole.

Help for Mental and Emotional Disorders

Guide to Reading

● Building Vocabulary

Several of the terms below share a common word part. Look up this word part in a dictionary, and write its meaning.

- therapy (p. 91)
- family therapy (p. 92)
- psychologist (p. 93)
- clinical social worker (CSW) (p. 93)
- psychiatrist (p. 93)

● Focusing on the Main Ideas

In this lesson, you will learn to

- **determine** if you or someone you know needs professional help.
- **describe** the kinds of therapies used to treat mental and emotional disorders.
- **identify** kinds of professionals who help people with mental health problems.

● Reading Strategy

Comparing and Contrasting Create a chart that lists the different types of mental health professionals and the treatments they provide.

Quick Write

Create an outline on treatment options for people with emotional problems. Use the terms and headings from the lesson as a guide.

What to Do If You Need Help

It is not always easy to determine whether a mental health problem is serious. However, there are certain symptoms you should be aware of as possible signs of a serious problem. If you have been experiencing any, they should not be ignored. It is important that you know ways to reduce risks related to adolescent health problems.

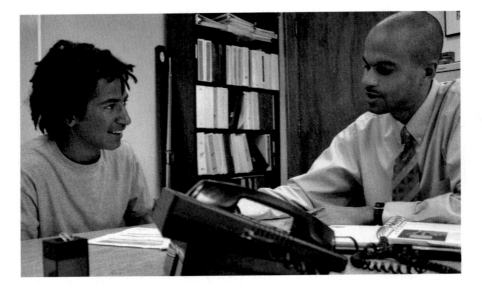

▶ Admitting that help is needed is a first step in dealing with a mental or emotional disorder. **Why do some people avoid seeking the help they need?**

If you have been feeling sad or angry for two weeks or longer it is likely an indicator of a problem that will not disappear on its own. Wanting to spend all your time alone is another possible indicator. If your feelings begin to affect your sleep, eating habits, schoolwork, or relationships with family and peers, help is most likely needed. Other factors include feeling "out of control", or feeling worried or nervous all the time.

If you feel that you need help, talk to a parent or guardian, the school nurse, a counselor at school, or other trusted adult. Tell someone what you are feeling and how long you have been experiencing those feelings. They may be able to provide the help you need or point you toward someone who can, such as a mental health professional.

Reading Check **Identify** What are some steps to take if you think you need help?

Kinds of Help

Help for mental and emotional problems almost always includes some form of counseling. This is a process of talking through your problems with someone trained to listen. For teens, the first step toward this process is talking with a trusted adult. A parent, guardian, or even an older brother or sister can sometimes be a great source of comfort. So can a teacher or coach to whom you feel close.

Once the problem is out in the open, steps toward emotional healing may begin. For many emotional problems, professional counseling, or therapy, is often needed. **Therapy** is *an approach that teaches you different ways of thinking or behaving.* Therapy gets to the root of your emotional and mental problems and helps you work to find a solution.

Connect To... Science

The Brain's Chemical Messengers

Have you ever banged an elbow or knee and then rubbed it to make it feel better? Scientists believe that rubbing a sore spot activates chemical messengers in the brain called neurotransmitters. Some of these reduce pain, while others affect your mood. Incorrect amounts of these messengers in a person's brain can cause emotional problems.

Using online or print resources, find information on neurotransmitters. Identify the name of one and tell what it does.

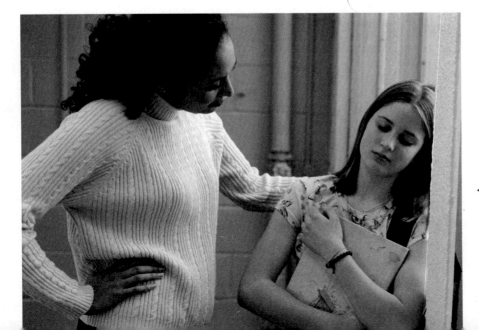

◀ When you have a problem, talking to a trusted adult can help. **Who are some people you could talk to if you had a problem?**

▶ Family therapy can help families cope with problems that threaten the health of the family. **How do therapists help?**

Therapy Settings

Different settings for therapy are available, depending on the problem and the person's needs. Some possibilities include individual therapy, group therapy, and family therapy.

In *individual therapy*, the individual and therapist meet alone for sessions. This is the setting most often used with people entering therapy for the first time. The privacy of individual therapy allows some patients to open up more freely and talk about their problems.

In *group therapy*, the therapist meets with several people who all have the same or similar problems. Group members are taught to support and show empathy toward one another. It can be reassuring for patients to know they are not alone, and that others share the same difficulties.

A special form of group therapy is **family therapy.** This is *counseling that seeks to improve troubled family relationships*. The therapist does not act as a judge or say who is at fault. Instead, he or she helps the family to help itself. This often includes teaching family members to communicate better.

Drug Treatment Therapy

In the last several decades, effective new medicines for treating emotional disorders have been produced. Many of these work at correcting chemical imbalances in the brain. These medicines can provide relief for depression and other mental disorders.

It is important to be aware that these medicines are not right for everyone. Also, they do not treat every mental and emotional problem. Finally, these medicines are not meant as a replacement for therapy. In fact, they are generally only given to patients who have received, or are currently in, therapy.

Mental Health Providers

Different types of mental health professionals provide therapy. All of these professionals have gone through special training to treat people with mental and emotional problems. Often, people with emotional problems will see a **psychologist** (sy·KAH·luh·jist). This is *a mental health professional who is trained and licensed by the state to perform therapy.* Psychologists have a doctoral degree and often specialize in a specific area, such as child psychology.

A **clinical social worker (CSW)** is *a licensed, certified mental health professional with a master's degree in social work.* CSWs can also provide therapy, but they are not usually as specialized as psychologists. Some schools have CSWs on their staff.

A third type of mental health professional is a **psychiatrist** (sy·KY·uh·trist). This is *a medical doctor with a specialty in the treatment of mental health problems.* In most states, a psychiatrist is the only mental health professional who can prescribe medications. Various mental health professionals often work as a team in treating a single patient in order to provide the patient with the best possible care.

Reading Check

List Name three types of mental health providers.

Health Online

Visit health.glencoe.com and complete the Interactive Study Guide for Lesson 3.

Lesson 3 Review

After You Read

Review this lesson for new terms, major headings, and Reading Checks.

What I Learned

1. *Vocabulary* Define *family therapy.*

2. *Identify* Name several different types of therapy settings used in treating mental and emotional problems.

3. *Recall* How do current medications work to treat mental and emotional problems?

Thinking Critically

4. *Evaluate* Ernesto has been feeling sad every day for the last two weeks and he doesn't know why. What should he do?

5. *Analyze* What factors might influence which type of mental health provider a person chooses?

Applying Health Skills

6. *Advocacy* With classmates, create posters that address the importance of seeking help for mental and emotional problems. Include some of the possible signs and symptoms that can indicate a serious problem.

Listen Up!

DIRECTIONS

Communication Skills involves learning how to effectively express yourself and understand others. This activity will give you the opportunity to develop and master this important health skill. Here's a guide to the different parts of this activity:

1. In the **Model** section, you will read about a teen who performs the health skill successfully. This "model" scenario will show you how the skill is done.

2. The **Practice** section will help guide you in practicing the skill.

3. In the **Apply** section, you will have a chance to perform the skill on your own. You can use the Self-Check to check your work.

To complete this activity, first read the scenario presented in the Model. Then move on to the Practice. Finally, go ahead and try the Apply.

1 Model

Being a good listener is a health skill for life, and one that plays a big part in the development of your social health. Read about how one teen was able to help a friend in need just by listening.

Christa noticed that her friend Susan seemed very depressed lately. Christa approached Susan and asked her what was wrong. Finally, Susan told Christa she had been feeling sad but didn't know why. As she spoke, Christa sat down next to Susan. She listened quietly as Susan continued to express how she had been feeling. While Susan spoke, Christa just looked at Susan reassuringly and listened.

Christa's ability to listen to her friend helped. Susan felt better after expressing her feelings. When Christa finally spoke, she suggested that Susan also talk to her parents or the school counselor. They could help, too.

② Practice

Christa had another chance to use her listening skills several days later. She arrived home from school to find her older sister sitting in front of the TV, obviously in a bad mood. The angry look on Jan's face told Christa much about her feelings. Christa knew from experience that at times like this Jan needed her space. Choosing not to disturb her sister, Christa went to get a snack. She knew that when Jan was ready to speak, she would. An hour later that is exactly what happened. Again, Christa listened carefully as her sister described the events of an awful day at school.

1. What did Christa learn from Jan's body language?
2. What did both Christa and Jan gain from Christa's waiting until Jan was ready to speak?
3. How did Christa let her actions speak for her?

Skill Summary
COMMUNICATION SKILLS

When another person has an emotional problem, good listening skills include the following:

- Waiting for the person to speak
- Paying attention to body language
- Letting your actions "speak" for you by using gestures

③ Apply

With a partner, write and perform a skit that shows the effective use of listening skills to help someone who is having a difficult time. Don't reveal the problem by name in your skit. Instead, show the problem through the emotions of the characters. Perform your finished skit for your classmates. Challenge them to identify the problem highlighted in your skit.

Self-Check

- Did we show one character using effective listening skills?
- Did we portray emotions effectively?
- Were our classmates able to identify the emotional problem in our skit?

HANDS-ON HEALTH

Interpreting Vocal Stress

Sometimes the way in which you say something is more revealing than the words themselves. To better understand this concept, consider this ordinary sentence: "Is he a good catcher?" Read the sentence aloud. Did you notice the sound of your voice rising at the end? This rise in pitch is part of the *intonation pattern* of speech. Different kinds of sentences—statements, questions, and commands—have different intonation patterns.

This activity will give you a chance to work with another aspect of vocal intonation. This time you will be working with *vocal stress*. Also known as "emphasis," vocal stress is saying one word slightly louder than the rest of the words in a sentence. On paper, vocal stress is shown by *italics* or underlining. Changing the word that is stressed in a sentence can change the sentence's meaning.

What You Will Need

- pencil or pen
- paper

What You Will Do

1. Work as part of a small group. Think up and write five ordinary sentences on separate sheets of paper. Try reading each sentence aloud, each time stressing a different word. Notice how the meaning of the sentence changes each time. Consider these examples:

   a. "I told *Ed* to give me the book." (Meaning: I told Ed—not someone else—to give me the book.)

   b. "I told Ed to give me the *book*." (Meaning: I told Ed what to give me—the book, not something else.)

2. Exchange sentences with another group. Try reading each sentence with the stress on different words. See how many different meanings you can come up with.

Wrapping It Up

After each group has exchanged sentences, discuss these questions as a class:

How does changing the vocal stress in a sentence change its meaning? Do you think changes in vocal stress reveal differences in the speaker's feelings? Explain your answer.

Reading Review

FOLDABLES | Study Organizer

Foldables™ and Other Study Aids Take out the Foldable™ that you created for Lesson 1 and any graphic organizers that you created for Lessons 1–3. Find a partner and quiz each other using these study aids.

Lesson 1 Mental and Emotional Disorders

Key Ideas

- Types of anxiety disorders include obsessive-compulsive disorder, panic disorder, post-traumatic stress disorder, social phobia disorder, and generalized anxiety disorder.

- Two mood disorders include bipolar disorder and major depression.

- Signs of major depression include irritability, anger, anxiety, or lack of energy; significant change in sleep patterns; inability to concentrate; blaming one's problems on other people; feelings of worthlessness or guilt; pessimism; thoughts of death or suicide.

Vocabulary

- disorder (p. 80)
- anxiety disorder (p. 81)
- phobia (p. 81)
- personality disorder (p. 82)
- mood disorder (p. 83)
- major depression (p. 83)
- schizophrenia (p. 85)

Lesson 2 Suicide Prevention

Key Ideas

- Factors in teen suicide include a family breakup or parent's death, alcoholism or drug dependency, witnessing domestic violence, experiencing physical or sexual abuse, feeling rejected by peers.

- Warning signs of suicide include talking, reading, or writing about death; reckless behavior; impulsively becoming sexually active or using drugs.

Vocabulary

- suicide (p. 86)

Lesson 3 Help for Mental and Emotional Disorders

Key Ideas

- If you are concerned about your mental health, talk to a trusted adult.

- Therapy settings include individual therapy, group therapy, and family therapy.

- Professionals who help people with mental health problems include psychologists, clinical social workers, and psychiatrists.

Vocabulary

- therapy (p. 91)
- family therapy (p. 92)
- psychologist (p. 93)
- clinical social worker (CSW) (p. 93)
- psychiatrist (p. 93)

Assessment

After You Read

HEALTH INVENTORY

Now that you have read the chapter, look back at your answers to the Health Inventory in the chapter opener. Is there anything that you should do differently?

Reviewing Vocabulary and Main Ideas

On a sheet of paper, write the numbers 1–4. After each number, choose a term from the list that best completes each sentence.

- mood disorder
- personality disorder
- phobia
- self-destructive behaviors
- suicide

Lesson 1 Mental and Emotional Disorders

1. An anxiety disorder characterized by an exaggerated fear of a specific situation or object is a(n) _____.

2. A psychological condition that affects a person's ability to interact normally with others is called a _____.

Lesson 2 Suicide Prevention

3. _____, the intentional taking of one's own life, is a leading cause of death among teens.

4. Doing reckless or impulsive things and other _____ may be a warning sign of suicide.

Lesson 3 Help for Mental and Emotional Disorders

On a sheet of paper, write the numbers 5–6. After each number, write the letter of the answer that best completes each statement.

5. All of the following are signs that a person may need help with an emotional problem *except*:
   a. feeling sad or angry for no apparent reason.
   b. having aches or pains that cannot be explained.
   c. treating an injury at home with items from the medicine cabinet.
   d. sleeping too much or waking up too early.

6. Which statement is true of therapy?
   a. It uses the same techniques for everyone.
   b. It may be provided only by psychiatrists.
   c. It is an approach that teaches different ways of thinking or behaving.

Thinking Critically

Using complete sentences, answer the following questions on a sheet of paper.

7. **Synthesize** Do mood swings make teens more likely to become depressed? Explain.

8. **Apply** A friend who is depressed considers seeking help a sign of weakness. What do you tell your friend?

Health *Online* Visit health.glencoe.com and take the Online Quiz for Chapter 4.

Write About It

9. **Advocacy** Write a paragraph persuading others that people who are mentally ill deserve the same level of respect and care as those who are physically ill.

10. **Communication Skills** Write an article describing the warning signs of suicide. What are some ways to provide support to someone who may be considering suicide?

11. **Decision Making** Write a short story about a teen who is depressed. Explain how the teen makes a decision to get help and who the teen goes to for help.

Career Corner

Psychiatrist Psychiatrists are medical doctors who diagnose and treat people with emotional problems and mental health disorders. Some psychiatrists specialize in problems older adults face, and others specialize in problems children face. Psychiatrists must have a four-year college degree and attend medical school to become a licensed physician. The person must then do a minimum of four years of specialized work, or residency, in psychiatry. Learn more by clicking on *Career Corner* at **health.glencoe.com**.

Standardized Test Practice

Reading

Read the passage and then answer the questions.

One of the first people to closely study the human mind was an Austrian doctor, Sigmund Freud. Freud was especially interested in how the mind operated.

In 1893, Freud published a study on what he called *hysteria*. Freud used this term to mean uncontrollable emotion, such as panic or fear. In the study, he claimed that hysteria was unspent emotional energy connected to forgotten disturbing events. By 1899, Freud had become convinced that dreams were a window to the inner workings of the mind. That year he published what many consider to be his most important work, *The Interpretation of Dreams*.

Over the next thirty years, Freud revised and added to his theory. Later, other researchers with different ideas came along. Though many disagreed with Freud's theory, few disagreed with his reputation as the "father of modern psychology."

1. Which sentence from the biography states an opinion, rather than a fact?
   A. One of the first people to study the human mind was Sigmund Freud.
   B. In 1899, Freud published *The Interpretation of Dreams*.
   C. In 1893, Freud published a study on what he called hysteria.
   D. Dreams are a window to the inner workings of the mind.

2. Which statement best captures the theme of the biography?
   A. Different people find different topics interesting.
   B. Freud's investigations led to the founding of the field of modern psychology.
   C. Today, no one disagrees with the ideas Freud developed so long ago.
   D. Sigmund Freud was a doctor from Austria.

5 Relationships: The Teen Years

Chapter Preview

Working With the Photo

Friendships take on a greater importance during adolescence. **What are some things you have in common with your friends? What qualities in your friends do you most admire?**

Start-Up Activities

HEALTH QUIZ Answer *true* or *false* for each of the following statements.

1. Good friends show support for each other when needed.
2. Active listening can get in the way of good communication.
3. Refusal skills should be used whenever you feel peer pressure, even if it is positive pressure.
4. Abstinence from harmful behaviors is an important factor in maintaining good health.

ANSWERS: 1. true; 2. false; 3. false; 4. true

FOLDABLES™ Study Organizer

As You Read Make this Foldable™ to help you organize the information about friendships in Lesson 1. Begin with a plain sheet of 11″ × 17″ paper.

1 Fold the short sides of a sheet of paper inward so that they meet in the middle.

3 Open and cut along the inside fold lines to form four tabs.

2 Fold the top to the bottom.

4 Label the tabs as shown.

Write down the qualities of a good friendship on the back of the Foldable. Then describe the Who, What, When, and Why of a close friend under the appropriate tab.

Friendships During Adolescence

Guide to Reading

● **Building Vocabulary**

As you read this lesson, write each new highlighted term and its definition in your notebook.

- relationships (p. 102)
- sympathetic (p. 103)
- clique (p. 105)
- peer pressure (p. 105)

● **Focusing on the Main Ideas**

In this lesson, you will learn to

- **explain** changes that occur in friendships during adolescence.
- **identify** the qualities of a good friend.
- **develop** communication skills to make new friends.

● **Reading Strategy**

Classifying Using the diagram as a guide, create a concept map that shows the qualities of a good friend.

FOLDABLES | Study Organizer Use the Foldable™ on p. 101 as you read this lesson.

Quick Write

Write a short paragraph that completes this sentence opener with a definition and examples: "A friend is _____."

Friendships

If you ask a group of people what they like most about their closest friend, you will probably get many different answers. One person might respond, "She makes me laugh." Another might say, "We have a great time together."

Unlike other types of relationships, friendships are relationships people choose to have. **Relationships** are *connections you have with other people and groups in your life.* Friendships form as a result of common interests and shared values. They are an important part of good social health.

Reading Check **Define** What are *relationships*?

◀ We tend to make friends with people who share similar interests. **What are some things you and your friends enjoy doing together?**

Changes in Friendships During Adolescence

Your teen years are a bridge between childhood and adulthood. During these years, friendships take on a greater importance than they once did. They grow and mature, just as you yourself do. You still share good times and have fun with your friends, but you also begin seeking deeper qualities in the people you choose as friends. Such qualities may include loyalty and trust. Your group of friends may also begin to include more members of the opposite gender.

During this transitional period, some teens outgrow the friendships they formed when they were younger. New interests in and out of school may cause old friends to drift apart. Differences in growth and emotional maturity also lead some friends in separate directions.

Sometimes, however, a friend may not be ready for a friendship to end. Although it can be painful, saying goodbye to old friends is a normal part of growing up. The healthiest thing you can do when a friend moves on is to do the same. Eventually, you will find another person or people who share your interests, values, and goals.

Qualities of a Good Friend

What makes a friend a *good* friend? Several qualities define strong friendships. One of these is trustworthiness. Trustworthy friends are honest and reliable. You can share private thoughts and feelings with them because they respect you. They also keep their promises to you. You can trust that they mean what they say.

Good friends are **sympathetic** (simp·uh·THET·ik), meaning they are *aware of how you may be feeling at a given moment.* Any friend will be willing to share your happy times. Only a good friend will stand by you during the bad or rough ones. During such times, it is encouraging to have a friend who understands how you feel.

Good friends care about and respect each other. Caring friends value each other's feelings as much as they do their own. They respect each other's decisions, differences, and opinions.

One of the most important qualities of a real friend is forgiveness. True friends understand that neither person in a relationship is perfect. They are willing to forgive mistakes and say "I'm sorry" for their own.

▶ Good friends are loyal. They stay with you through thick and thin. **What are some other qualities of a good friend?**

DEVELOPING
Good Character

You may have noticed that many qualities of good friends happen to be traits of good character. That is no accident. Friendships provide an opportunity to develop and practice good character traits. Name some character traits that you and your closest friends share.

Making Friends

Life would be much simpler if there were a recipe for making friends. It might begin, "Combine loyalty and caring. Stir in respect." Of course, no such recipe exists. There are, however, suggestions that you can follow to make new friends.

One of the most important things to remember is to be yourself. Do not pretend to be someone you are not. If you do, you will eventually get tired of having to hide your true self. Besides, good friendships are rooted in honesty, and people tend to appreciate others who are genuine and sincere.

One thing you can do to make new friends is make an effort to meet new people. The people around you play an important part in your personal health and well-being. The positive influence of good friendships can impact your physical, mental/emotional, and social health. Think about joining a club or other group, either at school or in your community. What are your interests, talents, and hobbies? There are bound to be others with whom you share common interests.

Another way to make new friends is to join a worthwhile effort or cause. You could volunteer for a community project, such as a park cleanup, or become a tutor at your local elementary school. You could find out if a classmate needs a study partner. Another benefit of participating in these kinds of activities is the sense of accomplishment you will experience. You will feel better about yourself because you will be making a positive contribution to your community.

Reading Check **Give Examples** What are some things you could do to meet new people?

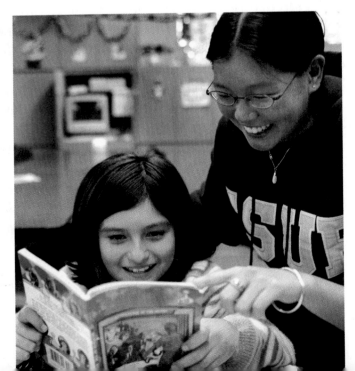

▶ Volunteering for a project or other activity is an opportunity to make a difference. **What character trait does this show?**

Health Skills Activity

"Breaking the Ice"

Outgoing people often have an easier time making friends than those who are shy. For some people, meeting and getting to know others can be difficult. If this sounds like you, here are some strategies to try:

- Friendships start with a simple conversation. This can be as simple as asking a classmate a question. You can always talk about school. Gradually try to talk about other topics, such as movies or sports. Ask about your classmate's interests.
- Are there others in your class who tend to keep quiet and seem a bit shy? They may also find it hard to meet people. Make an effort to start a conversation with one of them.

On Your Own

Try using one of the above strategies to meet a new person.

Cliques

People tend to feel comfortable around others like themselves. This sometimes leads to the formation of cliques during adolescence. A **clique** is *a group of friends who hang out together and act in similar ways.* Cliques can be a close-knit group of people with a strong common interest or bond. Cliques can satisfy a teen's need to belong and feel accepted. They can also be harmful, especially when members feel negative peer pressure from other members.

Peer pressure is *the influence to go along with the beliefs and actions of other people your age.* Peer pressure is negative when it involves behavior that can damage your health or hurt others. It is positive, however, when peers encourage and support healthy behaviors.

Some cliques are exclusive groups that limit membership to a chosen few. Cliques like this are sometimes hurtful to outsiders. Members may go out of their way to make nonmembers feel bad by teasing or laughing at them. A more positive approach would be to show respect and kindness to others, even those with whom you have nothing in common.

Reading Check

Compare In what ways can cliques benefit teens? In what ways can they be harmful?

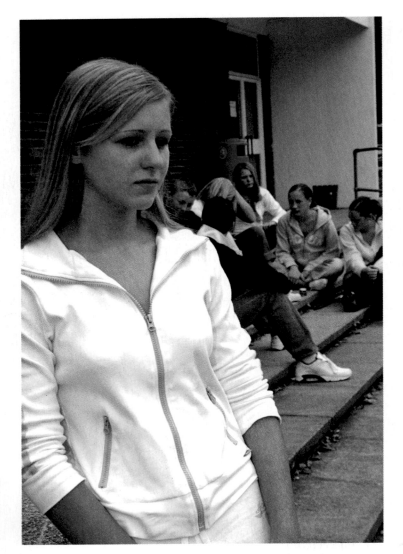

▲ Cliques can help
satisfy the emotional
need to belong.
**What are some ways
that cliques can be
harmful?**

Dating

During your teen years, you may begin feeling attracted to others. These feelings may take the form of strong emotions. Yesterday, the girl who lives across the street was "just another kid on the block." Today, you find it hard to stop staring at her when she is around. Yesterday, your older brother's best friend was a pest or a bore. Today, you find yourself worrying about your appearance when you know he is coming to your house. These new feelings cause some teens to begin—or at least begin thinking about—dating. Dating is a way to get to know other people better.

There is no specific time when you are supposed to start dating. Some people feel ready to date in their teens, while others do not feel ready until much later. Some teens choose to put off dating because they want to focus on other activities or interests.

Spending Time With a Group

An alternative to individual dating is to spend time in a group setting. A mixed group of teens might get together to watch a movie or play a game. Other fun group activities include dancing, skating, and playing volleyball. An added health benefit of these activities is that they keep you physically active.

There are other advantages to going out with a group as well. One advantage is that it takes the pressure off you to keep the conversation flowing. When there are several teens present, as opposed to only two, you do not have to talk as much. Having to come up with conversation topics on a date can add stress to a situation that might already have you feeling nervous.

 Reading Check **Explain** What are some reasons why people begin dating at different times?

Individual Dating

At some point, you might feel ready to go out on a date with just one other person. Perhaps your parents will let you know that they feel you are ready for individual dating. Dating is a big step

Health Online

Visit **health.glencoe.com** and complete the Interactive Study Guide for Lesson 1.

that should be taken for the right reasons. Some reasons might include having an interest in what another person has to say, and wanting to know that person better. Reacting to peer pressure is not a good reason to begin dating someone.

Think of dating as a special form of friendship. It should involve two people who enjoy each other's company, and who share common interests and values. Like any other friendship, a dating relationship should be based on caring and respect.

▲ Doing group activities is an alternative to individual dating. **What are some advantages of spending time with other teens in a group setting?**

Lesson 1 Review

 After You Read

Review this lesson for new terms, major headings, and Reading Checks.

What I Learned

1. *Vocabulary* Define *peer pressure*. Use it in an original sentence.

2. *Identify* Name two qualities of a good friend.

3. *Recall* Name two advantages of going out with a group as opposed to individual dating.

Thinking Critically

4. *Evaluate* Art and Jake have been friends since kindergarten. Recently, they have begun to drift apart. Jake feels rejected and is wondering if Art is mad at him for some reason. What advice would you give Jake?

5. *Apply* Janine, who is new at school, has become part of a clique. Today at lunch, members of the group talked about skipping school to go to the beach. What do you think Janine should do? How could Janine influence her friends to make healthful choices?

Applying Health Skills

6. *Communication Skills* With a group, develop a "Friends' Bill of Rights." This document should spell out the things that friends have a right to expect of each other. The bill should contain examples.

Practicing Communication Skills

● **Building Vocabulary**
Make a word diagram that shows the relationship among the terms below. Decide which term is the most general and the one all the others relate to.

- communication (p. 108)
- body language (p. 108)
- mixed message (p. 109)
- "I" message (p. 110)
- active listening (p. 110)

● **Focusing on the Main Ideas**
In this lesson, you will learn to

- **describe** types of nonverbal communication.
- **explain** how to be a more effective speaker.
- **identify** ways of being a good listener.
- **communicate** effectively with the use of "I" messages.

● **Reading Strategy**
Finding the Main Idea For each major heading in this lesson, write one sentence that states the main idea.

Quick Write

Make a list of different ways people communicate, such as speaking, writing letters, instant messaging, and so on. Identify similarities and differences among these methods.

What Is Communication?

An essential skill in building healthy relationships is communication. **Communication** is *the exchange of thoughts, feelings, and beliefs between two or more people.* Good communication is not only about getting a message across successfully. It is also about being able to listen to messages you hear. This means paying attention to and hearing what the other person is saying.

In this lesson, you will take a look at the factors that make up good communication skills. You will learn ways to keep the lines of communication open.

Nonverbal Communication

You have probably noticed that when two people carry on a conversation, they often move their hands around as they talk. Also, the looks on their faces may reveal clues about what they are saying. Gestures and facial expressions are features of *nonverbal communication*—communication without words.

There are two main types of nonverbal communication. One is **body language,** *the use of visual cues to communicate information or feelings.* In addition to gestures and facial expressions, body language includes posture.

The second type of nonverbal communication is *intonation,* or tone of voice. When you speak, the sound of your voice alone can send a message. You may sound angry or unhappy without even realizing it. How you say something can be just as important as what you say.

Mixed Messages

Body language and intonation often occur naturally without any effort. Some people, for example, use hand gestures when speaking. Sometimes, however, verbal and nonverbal messages can send two different messges. For that reason, you should try to become aware of the nonverbal messages you send. Otherwise, you run the risk of sending mixed messages. A **mixed message** occurs *when your words say one thing but your body language and/or intonation say another.* Saying you are sorry while grinning is an example of a mixed message. It tells the person you are apologizing, but that you do not really mean it. Can you think of other examples of mixed messages?

Reading Check **Define** What is *intonation?*

▲ Notice that you do not have to hear this teen's words to get a sense of what she is saying or feeling. **What body language tells you that the teen on the right is listening to what the other teen is saying?**

Effective Verbal Communication

Communication is a two-way street. In order for it to be effective, two different sets of skills need to be present. The first set is speaking skills. These skills determine how a message is delivered. The second is listening skills, which determine how a message is received. Listening skills are the part of the communication process that is most often overlooked.

Speaking Skills

One rule of effective speaking is to make your message as clear as possible. Consider this message: "You can't do anything right!" These words were spoken by a teen named Josh to his younger brother Chris. The two had planned to work together on a project. Chris, however, decided to get a head start before Josh got home from school. When Josh came home, he saw that Chris had glued a few parts together incorrectly.

Josh is clearly angry, but his message is not an example of effective speaking. It does nothing more than place blame. Most importantly, it leaves little room for a positive response. Chris will probably feel hurt and may answer back in anger.

Health Online

Topic: Body Language Basics

Visit **health.glencoe.com** for Student Web Activities to learn about how people use body language to communicate.

Activity: Using the information provided at the link above, create a body language game that teaches players how to communicate with their partners using only nonverbal clues.

Compare that message with this one: "I'm mad because I wanted to work on the project together. I wanted you to wait for me." This is an example of an **"I" message.** This is *a statement that presents a situation from the speaker's personal viewpoint.* "I" messages do not accuse or scold the way "you" messages do. "I" messages tell how the speaker feels. This makes them very powerful communication tools.

"I" messages are a key speaking skill. Here are some other skills for good communication:

- **Stay calm.** Remember, the louder you speak, the less likely you are to be heard. Few arguments are ever settled by screaming or slamming a door.

- **Stick to the point.** Think your ideas through before you begin to speak. Be specific.

- **Choose the right time and place.** Find a time when the other person is not in a hurry or busy with something else. Find a quiet place where there is little chance of interruption.

- **Be aware of your body language and intonation.** Do not send mixed messages. Be sure to maintain eye contact with the other person. Eye contact is a way of showing that you are sincere.

Reading Check **Identify** What are two advantages of "I" messages over "you" messages?

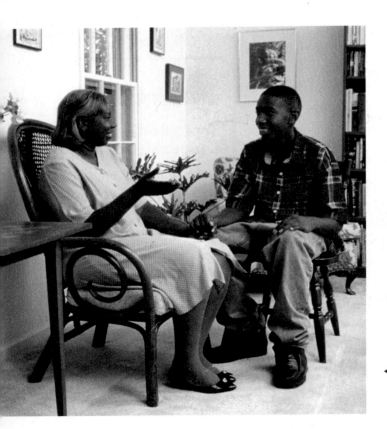
◀ An important factor of active listening is appropriate body language. **What are some other skills of active listening?**

Listening Skills

Have you ever spoken to someone whose attention was on something else—the TV, maybe? It can be a frustrating experience. Good listening skills are just as important to interpersonal communication as speaking skills. A speaker's message has meaning only if the listener receives it.

A good listener is an active listener. **Active listening** is *hearing, thinking about, and responding to the other person's message.* The following suggestions can help you become a more active listener.

- **Pay careful attention to all that the speaker has to say.** Do not begin forming your answer while the other person is still speaking. If the two of you are working through a problem, keep an open mind. There are at least two sides to every disagreement. You may end up seeing things in a different way. Also, if you carefully listen to people, others will appreciate this. They will be more likely to carefully listen to you when you speak.

- **Use body language that shows you are listening.** Make eye contact with the speaker. Nod your head from time to time to show that you are paying attention. Back up your body language with comments such as "Really?" or "What happened next?" You can also use body language to show emotion.

- **Think for a moment before speaking.** Take time to collect your thoughts. Decide exactly how you want to respond. Once you do respond, "mirror" the speaker's thoughts and feelings. Repeat what the person said as a way of confirming what you heard.

- **Ask questions.** After the person has finished talking, ask questions or add your own comments or opinions. If you do not understand something, say so.

Health Online

Visit **health.glencoe.com** and complete the Interactive Study Guide for Lesson 2.

Lesson 2 Review

After You Read

Review this lesson for new terms, major headings, and Reading Checks.

What I Learned

1. *Vocabulary* What is a *mixed message*?

2. *List* What are the two main types of nonverbal communication?

3. *Identify* Besides active listening, what are some tips for effective listening?

Thinking Critically

4. *Synthesize* Respond to the statement "Actions speak louder than words." Explain the relevance of this expression to the skill of communication.

5. *Apply* Kelly is really upset. A jacket she loaned to a friend came back with a tear in it. How can Kelly express her feelings using an "I" message?

Applying Health Skills

6. *Communication Skills* With a group, develop a booklet on the importance of good communication skills. The booklet should describe and demonstrate techniques such as using "I" messages and active listening.

Peer Pressure and Refusal Skills

Guide to Reading

Building Vocabulary
As you read this lesson, write each new highlighted term and its definition in your notebook.

- refusal skills (p. 115)
- aggressive (p. 116)
- passive (p. 116)
- assertive (p. 116)

Focusing on the Main Ideas
In this lesson, you will learn to
- **explain** the differences between positive and negative peer pressure.
- **identify** risks of negative peer pressure.
- **develop** refusal skills to resist negative peer pressure.

Reading Strategy
Comparing and Contrasting Create a graphic that shows the difference between positive and negative peer pressure. Be sure to include examples of each.

Quick Write

Describe a time when you were inspired to do something good because of positive peer pressure.

Peer Pressure

Lately, Stephanie has been spending lunchtime with a new group of girls. She shares some common interests with them, but she does not like the way they gossip and treat some of the girls outside their group. "What is she wearing? That's horrible!" Stacy said, pointing to a girl across from them.

As the girls laughed and pointed, Stephanie stood there feeling bad, wishing they would stop talking about the other girl. "Doesn't she look ridiculous?" Stacy said to Stephanie. Stephanie was not sure what to say. She felt pressured to join in, but she did not want to. "No. She doesn't look ridiculous. She just dresses a little different than us," Stephanie said.

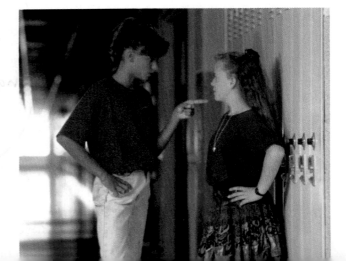

▶ Peer pressure can influence your decisions positively or negatively. **What is peer pressure?**

Peer Pressure and Decisions

Peer pressure can be a powerful force during the teen years. Teens look to members of their peer group for acceptance, sometimes without knowing it. Pressure to fit in can have an impact, good or bad, on a person's decisions. Peer pressure can influence healthful choices.

Some peer pressure is direct—it takes the form of words or actions directed toward you. Indirect peer pressure is more subtle than direct peer pressure. For example, you may notice many people at school wearing the latest shoe style. Maybe you want to go out and buy those shoes too, because you think you will fit in with everyone else if you wear them. It is important to be aware of indirect peer pressure.

Reading Check **Explain** What is the difference between direct and indirect peer pressure?

Positive Peer Pressure

In addition to being direct or indirect, peer pressure may also be positive or negative. Positive peer pressure can inspire you to be the best person you can be. When Sally saw a news story about victims of a deadly flood, she decided to take action. The story showed pictures of a teen her age who had lost her home. The image affected Sally in a way that made her want to help. The next day, she started collecting money in her neighborhood. Her goal was to send the money to a national organization in charge of the relief effort.

Sally asked her friends and other teens she knew to help raise money, too. Her efforts became a source of direct peer pressure on these teens. Within several days, the teens had raised hundreds of dollars.

Positive peer pressure can benefit your own life, too. You can be positively influenced to do something that improves your own well-being and health. Don was encouraged by a friend to try out for his school's choir. The experience opened Don up to music he might otherwise have never heard. Don really liked the music. He now listens to choral music to relax when he is feeling stressed.

▼ Positive peer pressure can encourage healthy habits. **What is an example of positive peer pressure that you have experienced?**

Negative Peer Pressure

Negative peer pressure is pressure to do something that could hurt you or others. It often goes against your own wants, needs, or values. For example, the pressure that Stephanie felt to laugh at another girl was negative peer pressure. If Stephanie had gone along with her friends, she would have felt bad about herself.

Some teens endanger their health when they let themselves be influenced by negative peer pressure. For example, they might use alcohol, tobacco, or other drugs. Giving into these pressures can negatively affect your performance at school, your health, and your future. That is a good reason to choose friends who share your values.

Negative peer pressure takes many forms. Teens who put negative pressure on you may try to manipulate your emotions or find your weaknesses. The pressure may come as a dare or threat. It may come in the form of a bribe, teasing, or name-calling. Recognizing negative peer pressure in all its forms is important. This is a first step toward standing your ground and protecting your beliefs. **Figure 5.1** lists questions you can ask yourself to help you decide if peer pressure is negative.

Reading Check **List** Name some forms that negative peer pressure can take.

▼ **FIGURE 5.1**

RECOGNIZING NEGATIVE PEER PRESSURE

When you feel you are being pressured, analyze the possible outcomes and health consequences. **What are two questions to ask yourself when you are feeling peer pressure?**

Possible Outcomes	Health Consequences
• Is this activity dangerous?	• How will this activity affect my physical health?
• Does it break the law?	• Am I being asked to do something that could bring me physical harm?
• Can it lead to punishment, such as suspension from school, or arrest?	• Is the activity something that can lead to an addiction?
• Will it lead to disapproval or disappointment from parents or guardians?	• What effect will it have on my emotional health?
• Will property be destroyed or damaged?	• Will I feel guilty if I do this activity?
	• Will I disappoint myself?
	• Is it something I simply do not feel ready for?
	• How will this decision affect the health of others?
	• Could someone else be hurt?

Refusal Skills

Negative peer pressure can be very strong. When anyone challenges your beliefs or values, you need to be strong, too. This strength will help you resist negative peer pressure. While negative pressure is often easy to recognize, it can be difficult to resist. One way to resist negative pressure is by using refusal skills. **Refusal skills** are *communication strategies that help you say no effectively.* They help you avoid doing things you do not want to do without feeling uncomfortable about your decision. By using refusal skills, you stand up for your values, which builds self-respect. You also show others that you have strength and character. These qualities will win their respect as well.

A Strategy for Refusing

Like other skills, refusal skills take practice. Many teens find the S.T.O.P. strategy an effective way to use refusal skills. The letters in S.T.O.P. represent the four steps in the strategy. You can use one or all of the following steps:

- **Say no in a firm voice.** State your feelings firmly but politely. Just say, "No, I don't want to." Make your "no" sound like you really mean it. Use body language to support your words. Make eye contact with the person.

- **Tell why not.** If the other person keeps up the pressure, explain why you feel the way you do. You do not need to use phony excuses or make up reasons. Simply say, "No thanks, I care about my health." Do not apologize. You have done nothing wrong.

- **Offer other ideas.** If the person pressuring you to do something is a friend, you can choose to suggest alternatives. Recommend an activity that is safe and fun.

- **Promptly leave.** If all else fails, just walk away. Make your actions match your words. If you are someplace where you need a ride, phone a parent to come and pick you up.

Reading Check **Identify** Tell what the letters in the S.T.O.P. strategy stand for.

Styles of Communication

When you use refusal skills, your goal is to say no. You are not trying to start an argument. However, the other person does need to hear you and understand your position. How your words are received is largely a matter of your communication *style*. There are three basic styles of communication: aggressive, passive, and assertive.

▶ Your communication style can affect how well you communicate. **What style of communication do you think the teen on the left is using?**

Aggressive communication means *speaking in a way that is overly forceful, pushy, hostile, or otherwise attacking in approach.* The speaker may talk in a loud voice, leaning in toward the other person. This approach is not an effective way to communicate and get a message across. People are not likely to listen to what you are saying if they feel like you are being pushy. Aggressive communication can stir up anger in the listener, and can even lead to violence.

The **passive** style of communication includes *a tendency to give up, give in, or back down without standing up for your rights and needs.* A passive communicator might speak in a very quiet voice and avoid looking directly at the listener. This style of communication suggests that the person might be uncertain and easy to persuade. Speaking in a firm voice and making eye contact are important strategies for refusal.

One effective style of communication is an assertive style. Being **assertive** means *behaving with confidence and clearly stating your intentions.* Speak in a firm but positive voice. Your body language and attitude should back up your words. Hold your head high and make eye contact. When you are assertive you stand up for your own rights while respecting the rights of others.

Health *Online*

Visit **health.glencoe.com** and complete the **Interactive Study Guide for Lesson 3.**

Reading Check **Recall** What is an assertive communication style?

Health Skills Activity

Refusal Skills

Responding to "Lines"

Teens who use negative peer pressure can often be persuasive. They may flatter you or even beg you to do something. They may also use common phrases, or "lines," such as "Everyone's doing it." It is a good idea to have a response planned for common lines. Here are some possibilities:

"LINE"	POSSIBLE RESPONSES
• Everyone's doing it.	• You're wrong. I'm not doing it.
• A real friend would do it.	• A real friend wouldn't ask.
• Are you afraid?	• No, just smart.

With a Group

Practice these lines. Add some responses of your own. Which responses do you think are most effective, and why?

Lesson 3 Review

After You Read

Review this lesson for new terms, major headings, and Reading Checks.

What I Learned

1. **Vocabulary** What are *refusal skills*?

2. **Give Examples** Give one example of positive peer pressure and one of negative peer pressure.

3. **Identify** Name the three communication styles. Tell which one is the most effective in helping you say no to negative peer pressure.

Thinking Critically

4. **Analyze** Ralph has told Peter twice that he does not want to sneak into the movies. He has even offered to pay for Peter's ticket to the show. Peter insists on sneaking in. What should Ralph do next?

5. **Apply** Zoey is pressuring Alicia to let her copy Alicia's homework assignment. Alicia knows this is wrong. How can she express her feelings to Zoey in an assertive way?

Applying Health Skills

6. **Communication Skills** Act out body language that reflects one of the three communication styles. Challenge classmates to guess which style you are demonstrating.

Limits and Abstinence

Guide to Reading

Building Vocabulary
As you read this lesson, write each new highlighted term and its definition in your notebook.

- limits (p. 118)
- consequences (p. 119)
- abstinence (p. 119)
- affection (p. 120)

Focusing on the Main Ideas
In this lesson, you will learn to

- **explain** why it is important to set limits.
- **identify** reasons why teens should choose abstinence.
- **demonstrate** care and respect for someone in a healthy way.

Reading Strategy
Predicting Look over the lesson, including the headings and pictures. Then write a sentence predicting what information you think the lesson will provide.

Quick Write

Identify some limits that are set by the law. Write a sentence explaining why these limits are set.

Limits: Invisible Boundaries

Can you imagine playing a sport or game that had no rules? The activity would seem pointless, and would likely be dangerous. Rules bring a sense of order and purpose to games. They serve a similar purpose in daily life, where they sometimes take the form of limits. **Limits** are *invisible boundaries that protect you*. The laws used by a society are an example of limits.

As a teen, you probably have limits set by your parents or guardians. Your limits may include what TV shows you can watch, what Web sites you can visit, and how late you can stay up at night. Like laws, these limits are meant to keep you safe and protect your health. Internet browsing rules, for example, may keep you away from dangerous chat rooms or inappropriate Web sites.

◀ A STOP sign is a limit set by law. **What is the purpose of this limit? What are the possible consequences facing people who choose not to obey this limit?**

Also, having a fixed bedtime ensures that you will get the sleep you need as a growing teen. These are some of the ways to promote good health and prevent illness.

Recognizing Your Own Limits

As you grow older, you will probably spend more and more time outside your home. Sometimes adults will not be present to enforce limits. Knowing your own limits will become increasingly important for you because where you go and who you spend time with can directly affect your personal safety. You will need to be able to evaluate situations and avoid people who might be bad influences.

Consider the decision made by a teen named Steve. On Sunday night, Steve spent the night at his friend Tom's house. Though Tom's parents thought they were sleeping, Tom and Steve stayed up all night watching television, playing video games, and eating pizza. Monday morning, both boys could hardly find the energy to get out of bed for school. Throughout their classes they could hardly keep their eyes open, let alone take a test. These were the negative consequences of their actions. **Consequences** are *outcomes or effects that may occur as a result of a decision or an action.*

One way to establish limits in your own life is to write down goals you wish to achieve. Once you understand what you would like to achieve, you will have a better idea of boundaries you need to set that will help you reach your goal. Chapter two describes the goal-setting process in detail.

Reading Check **Give Examples** What are two typical limits for teens?

Choosing Abstinence

One of the most important limits you can set for yourself during adolescence is choosing abstinence. **Abstinence** is *the conscious, active choice not to participate in high-risk behaviors.* When you begin dating, choosing abstinence from sexual activity is the responsible choice. It is a choice more and more teens are making. The Centers for Disease Control and Prevention does a yearly report on high-risk behaviors among teens. One recent report shows that over the past ten years, the percentage of teens choosing abstinence has steadily increased.

▼ Choosing abstinence allows you to focus on positive activities that will maintain your health. **What are some positive activities you can do with your friends?**

The Cost of Raising a Family

Raising a child is a huge responsibility, both emotionally and financially. To get a sense of this responsibility, find out about the costs of diapers and baby food. These are just two of the many expenses related to parenting.

Multiply the price of these items to determine their cost in weeks, months, and years. Share your findings with classmates.

Reasons for Choosing Abstinence

Practicing sexual abstinence shows respect for yourself. It also shows respect for the physical and emotional well-being of others.

The choice to be sexually abstinent has other benefits as well. You promote good health and avoid the risks that many sexually active people face. One of these is the risk of being infected with a sexually transmitted disease (STD). Many STDs show no visible symptoms, which means only a doctor can tell whether someone is infected. STDs can damage the reproductive system, preventing the person from ever having children. Some STDs remain in the body for life—even after they are discovered. Still others—especially HIV/AIDS—can lead to death.

Another risk of sexual activity is unplanned pregnancy, which can change the entire course of a person's life. It can be particularly difficult for teens, who typically do not have the emotional or financial resources to be parents. As a teen, you are beginning an exciting and challenging period of self-discovery. Over the next few years you will begin to realize what you want out of life. Parenthood at this time will complicate an already complex time in your life. When people wait until adulthood to become parents, they are better able to achieve long-term goals, such as attending college.

Reading Check **List** Give reasons why abstinence is an important choice for teens.

Healthy Ways of Displaying Affection

Finding someone special—someone to care about deeply—is a goal most people share. It is one of the great gifts and joys of life. Showing **affection,** or *feelings of love for another person,* can take many different forms. One of these is sexual intimacy. This expression of caring is best postponed until adulthood and marriage. Becoming sexually active during the teen years, as you have read, carries risks. It also involves an emotional commitment that most teens are not prepared to make.

◀ Showing affection lets someone know that you care. **Why do you think it is important to show someone that you care?**

There are plenty of healthy ways for teens to show their affection. One way is to do something thoughtful for the other person. For example, you might give him or her a card or a small gift. Show the other person that you are a good friend. Make it clear you are willing to listen to his or her thoughts and ideas. Actions such as these deepen the bonds of affection. They also display good character, a sure sign that you are maturing. Holding hands and hugging are physical ways to show affection.

Reading Check **Define** What is *affection*?

Dealing with Sexual Feelings

Sexual feelings are normal and healthy. You cannot prevent them, but you do have control over how you deal with them. There are ways of managing these feelings during the teen years. Think about talking through your feelings with a trusted adult. A parent, coach, counselor or teacher will be able to offer useful suggestions. They will be able to answer questions you might have about sexual feelings.

Health Online

Visit health.glencoe.com and complete the Interactive Study Guide for Lesson 4.

Lesson 4 Review

After You Read

Review this lesson for new terms, major headings, and Reading Checks.

What I Learned

1. *Vocabulary* What are *limits*?

2. *Recall* What are some negative consequences of sexual activity during adolescence?

3. *List* Name two healthy ways for teens to show affection.

Thinking Critically

4. *Apply* Connie is at a party. One of the teens suggests turning out the lights and playing a kissing game. What action can Connie take that shows she understands the importance of limits?

5. *Analyze* Gayle and Eddie have been dating for a while. Eddie recently suggested that he and Gayle explore their affection physically. What would you advise Gayle to tell him?

Applying Health Skills

6. *Goal Setting* Make a contract with yourself in which you set the goal of choosing abstinence. The contract should establish limits that you set for yourself. Sign your contract and keep it in a safe place.

Health Online For more review questions for Lesson 4, go to health.glencoe.com.

Lesson 4: Limits and Abstinence **121**

Setting Limits

DIRECTIONS

Goal Setting involves setting positive goals and taking steps to achieve them. This activity will give you the opportunity to develop and master this important health skill. Here's a guide to the different parts of this activity:

❶ In the **Model** section, you will read about a teen who performs the health skill successfully. This "model" scenario will show you how the skill is done.

❷ The **Practice** section will help guide you in practicing the skill.

❸ In the **Apply** section, you will have a chance to perform the skill on your own. You can use the Self-Check to check your work.

To complete this activity, first read the scenario presented in the Model. Then move on to the Practice. Finally, go ahead and try the Apply.

❶ Model

Ron's family had just moved to a new city at the beginning of the school year. Knowing that he might be faced with negative peer pressure, Ron wanted to be prepared. He wrote out the following steps to help him achieve his goal.

1. *Identify a specific goal.* "I want to avoid negative peer pressure."

2. *List the steps you will take.* "I will set limits for myself to help me avoid pressure that may come up. I will not go anywhere where tobacco, alcohol, or other drugs are present."

3. *Get help and support from others.* "My neighbor John, a student at the same school, feels the same way I do. He can introduce me to his friends."

4. *Set up checkpoints.* "Anytime someone mentions using drugs, I will state my limits. I will not be friends with anyone who does not agree to respect my limits."

5. *Reward yourself.* "I will feel good about myself because I am sticking to my goal."

② Practice

Shortly after Ron started school, he became friends with Reggie. The two began spending a lot of time together. When the first big social studies test of the semester came up, the boys studied together. As they were studying, Reggie commented that Ron looked tense. He then said, "I have something you can smoke that can help you calm down." What response could Ron give that would help him stick to his goal? Use the following questions to help you decide.

1. Which step of Ron's action plan best addresses this situation?

2. Where could Ron get help and support from others?

3. In your opinion, which goal-setting step is most important? Tell why.

Skill Summary
GOAL SETTING

The strategy of goal setting includes the following:

- Identify a specific goal.
- List the steps you will take.
- Get help and support from others.
- Set up checkpoints.
- Reward yourself.

③ Apply

Think about long-term goals of your own. Then think about how yielding to negative peer pressure might interfere with achieving those goals. Develop an action plan for achieving one of your goals. At each step, identify actions you could take to resist negative peer pressure.

Self-Check

- Did I identify a long-term goal I hope to achieve?
- Does my action plan show ways of resisting negative peer pressure at each step?
- Did I explain how negative peer pressure might interfere with my goal?

How to Deal With
TRICKY SITUATIONS

What do you do when friends get pushy or just plain mean?

Friends can make life a blast—but they can also present a problem or two. Here's some *friendly* advice on what to do when things get tricky.

THE SITUATION

You have been snubbed by the popular crowd!

THE FIX

First, feel empowered—you can handle this. Now, try talking one-on-one with individual kids in the group—away from the others. It can be easier to connect with one person rather than many. This will help you determine if the crowd is really for you anyway.

THE SITUATION

Your friends are pushing you to drink or smoke.

THE FIX

Be prepared with smart reasons to just say no. For example, find out how many people die from lung cancer each year and drop that data on the friends urging you to smoke.

THE SITUATION

Your best friend has a new friend, and now they're totally ignoring you.

THE FIX

Have a heart-to-heart with your friend and explain how this hurts your feelings. He or she might start to include you. But sometimes friends drift apart. If you're still feeling left out, it might be time to start forming new friendships.

THE SITUATION

You're clueless about making new friends.

THE FIX

Rehearse icebreakers on safe topics like the big game or cafeteria food. Once someone responds, chat him or her up, but resist the urge to spill your whole life story right away.

SIX SIGNS THAT SOMEONE MIGHT MAKE A GOOD FRIEND

He or she is...

1. reading your favorite book.
2. making comments that are very similar to what you'd say.
3. called a "good guy" or "very nice" by his or her friends.
4. speaking passionately in class about an issue you care about, too.
5. playing on the same team or is in the same club as you.
6. giving you a friendly wave or smile.

Reading Review

Foldables™ and Other Study Aids Take out the Foldable™ that you created for Lesson 1 and any graphic organizers that you created for Lessons 1–4. Find a partner and quiz each other using these study aids.

Lesson 1 Friendships During Adolescence

Key Ideas

- During adolescence, friendships take on a greater importance than ever before.
- Good friends are trustworthy, sympathetic, caring, and respectful.

Vocabulary

- relationships (p. 102)
- sympathetic (p. 103)
- clique (p. 105)
- peer pressure (p. 105)

Lesson 2 Practicing Communication Skills

Key Ideas

- Nonverbal messages are important to communication because they give a more reliable reading of a person's feelings than words.
- You can be a more effective speaker by using "I" messages, staying calm, sticking to the point, choosing the right time and place, and being aware of your body language and intonation.

Vocabulary

- communication (p. 108)
- body language (p. 108)
- mixed message (p. 109)
- "I" message (p. 110)
- active listening (p. 110)

Lesson 3 Peer Pressure and Refusal Skills

Key Ideas

- Positive peer pressure and negative peer pressure both influence your behavior.
- An effective strategy for refusing is the S.T.O.P. formula.

Vocabulary

- refusal skills (p. 115)
- aggressive (p. 116)
- passive (p. 116)
- assertive (p. 116)

Lesson 4 Limits and Abstinence

Key Ideas

- Setting limits is important because it keeps you safe and protects your health.
- Teens who choose abstinence avoid serious health consequences, such as an unplanned pregnancy and infection with an STD.

Vocabulary

- limits (p. 118)
- consequences (p. 119)
- abstinence (p. 119)
- affection (p. 120)

HEALTH QUIZ

Now that you have read the chapter, look back at your answers to the Health Quiz on the chapter opener. Would you change any of them? What would your answers be now?

Reviewing Vocabulary and Main Ideas

On a sheet of paper, write the numbers 1–6. After each number, write the term from the list that best completes each sentence.

- active listening
- body language
- clique
- "I" message
- mixed message
- peer pressure
- relationships
- sympathetic

Lesson 1 Friendships During Adolescence

1. Connections you have with other people and groups in your life are known as _____.

2. Good friends are _____, meaning they are aware of how you may be feeling at a given moment.

3. A(n) _____ is a group of friends who hang out together and act in similar ways.

Lesson 2 Practicing Communication Skills

4. A(n) _____ occurs when your words say one thing but your body language and/or intonation say another.

5. A statement that presents a situation from the speaker's personal viewpoint is known as a(n) _____.

6. _____ is hearing, thinking about, and responding to the other person's message.

*On a sheet of paper, write the numbers 7–12. Write **True** or **False** for each statement below. If the statement is false, change the underlined word or phrase to make it true.*

Lesson 3 Peer Pressure and Refusal Skills

7. <u>Peer pressure</u> may be direct or indirect, positive or negative.

8. One way to resist negative peer pressure is by using <u>refusal skills</u>.

9. When you use a <u>passive</u> style of communication, you show confidence and clearly state your intentions.

Lesson 4 Limits and Abstinence

10. Like laws or rules, <u>consequences</u> are meant to keep you safe and protect your health.

11. When you choose to be sexually <u>abstinent</u>, you avoid the risk of STDs.

12. Showing <u>sympathy</u> toward another person is showing feelings of love for that person.

Thinking Critically

Using complete sentences, answer the following questions on a sheet of paper.

13. Analyze Della was invited to a get-together at the home of a friend's friend. Della found out the girl's parents would not be home and that there would be drinking and smoking. What would be an assertive way for Della to let her friend know she is no longer interested in going?

Write About It

14. Analyzing Influences Take a stand on whether or not you think cliques are a positive or negative influence. Write a paragraph supporting your position.

Career Corner

School Counselor Many teens will go to a school counselor for help in handling emotions or resolving conflicts. School counselors help students with school, family, or personal problems. They also work with students to help plan their futures. This profession requires a four-year degree and two years of graduate training in counseling. If you think you might like to help young people solve problems, visit the *Career Corner* at **health.glencoe.com** to find out more about this career.

15. Refusal Skills Write a short story about a teen who uses effective refusal skills when confronted with negative peer pressure.

Standardized Test Practice

Math

Teens who are sexually active run the risk of getting STDs. The most serious of those is HIV/AIDS. Below are some statistics of HIV/AIDS from the Centers for Diseases Control and Prevention (CDC). Use the information to answer the questions that follow.

- In a recent year, an estimated 38,490 teens in the United States were found to have AIDS.

- These individuals accounted for 4 percent of all people found to have AIDS in this country.

- Of these teens, an estimated 10,041 died the same year.

- This number accounted for 2 percent of all deaths from AIDS in the United States.

TEST-TAKING TIP

Make sure you understand the relationships between number statements.

1. Based on the statistics shown, which of the following CANNOT be inferred?
   - **A.** Of the teens found to have AIDS, 28,449 did not die that year.
   - **B.** Some of these teens became infected by sharing needles.
   - **C.** 96 percent of the people found to have AIDS that year were not teens.
   - **D.** AIDS is a deadly disease.

2. Based on the statistics, the total estimated deaths for the year noted was
   - **A.** Under 20,000.
   - **B.** Between 21,000 and 100,000.
   - **C.** Between 100,000 and 300,000.
   - **D.** Over half a million.

Chapter Preview

▲ *Working With the Photo*

Your social health is a measure of how well you get along with others. **Your friendships are one set of relationships that define your social health. What are some others?**

Start-Up Activities

Before You Read

Look at the Instant Message below. What would you say to "topothekey"? Keep a record of your answer.

IM *Express*

gregtheman: how's it going?

topothekey: ever since my mom got married again, I sort of feel like she doesn't know I'm there.

FOLDABLES™ Study Organizer

As You Read

Make this Foldable™ to help you organize what you learn in Lesson 1 about building healthy relationships. Begin with a plain sheet of 11" × 17" paper.

1 Fold a sheet of paper in half along the long axis, then fold in half again. This makes four rows.

3 Label the chart with the health skills shown.

Trust	
Respect	
Patience	
Tolerance	

2 Open and fold the short side on the left to make a 3" column.

Take notes on the character traits that help build healthy relationships.

Health Online Visit health.glencoe.com and complete the Health Inventory for Chapter 6.

You and Your Relationships

Guide to Reading

● Building Vocabulary

As you read this lesson, write each new highlighted term and its definition in your notebook.

■ social health (p. 131)
■ role (p. 131)
■ tolerance (p. 132)

● Focusing on the Main Ideas

In this lesson, you will learn to

■ **explain** differences among relationships.
■ **identify** needs that relationships satisfy.
■ **develop** skills to build strong, healthy relationships.

● Reading Strategy

Classifying Make a chart of the kinds of relationships described. Identify people in your life that fit each type of relationship.

FOLDABLES Study Organizer Use the Foldable™ on p. 129 as you read this lesson.

Quick Write

Write a short paragraph describing a successful relationship you have. Tell what makes the relationship work.

Relationships: The Foundation of Social Health

Josh balanced his school work and other responsibilities with the activities he enjoyed doing with his family and friends. He enjoyed talking with his friends at soccer practice and meeting new people at his school. He was also looking forward to the family reunion that was coming up. Every summer his extended family gathered for a picnic in the park. It was a time to laugh, share new experiences, and play games together. This year Josh decided to invite a friend from school to the family picnic. What are some activities you enjoy doing with your family and friends?

◀ An important factor of your social health is how you relate to others. **Who are some of the people you interact with every day?**

Social health is *your ability to get along with the people around you.* The relationships you form with other people are the foundation of your social health. Relationships are the connections you have with groups and people in your life. In your teen years, your relationships are mainly with family, friends, peers, and teachers. These relationships are part of your environment, and they can impact your health. Healthy relationships are important to good social health.

Differences Among Relationships

Not all relationships are the same. Some relationships are close and familiar, and others are more formal.

Different relationships also meet different needs. Some relationships, such as those with family and friends, meet emotional needs. They satisfy your need to feel that you are loved and that you belong. Other relationships meet more practical needs. Your relationships with teachers, for example, are based on your need to learn.

Another factor that makes different relationships unique is the role you play. A **role** is *a part you play when you interact with another person.* Everyone plays many different roles. **Figure 6.1** shows some typical teen roles. Each role you play carries responsibilities and expectations. The responsibilities that come with a role may change over time. You will also take on new roles and responsibilities as you get older.

Reading Check **Compare** How are relationships different?

DEVELOPING Good Character

Respect

Every relationship benefits from respect. One way to show respect for another person is through simple courtesies—for example, holding the door for the person behind you. Using good manners when you are in someone else's home is another sign of respect.

What other ways can you think of to show respect for people in your life?

▼ **FIGURE 6.1**

SOME TEEN ROLES

Roles like these carry responsibilities. **Which of these roles describe you? What responsibilities do they carry?**

- Daughter/Son
- Sister/Brother
- Friend
- Granddaughter/Grandson
- Niece/Nephew
- Babysitter
- Student
- Peer tutor
- Teammate
- Club member
- Volunteer

▲ Tolerance is important to healthy relationships. **How can you benefit from having relationships with people from different backgrounds?**

Building Healthy Relationships

Relationships can grow just like other living things. When a plant is neglected, its leaves droop and turn brown. As a living thing, it needs to be watered and cared for. In the same way, relationships need attention if they are to grow and thrive. One way to care for a relationship is to practice traits of good character. These traits include:

- **Trust.** If you are honest in what you say and do, others will be more willing to trust you. They will be able to rely on you because they know that when you say something, you mean it. For example, when Janet's mom said she was going to pick her up after school, Janet did not wonder if she would actually show up or not. She trusted her mom to be there.

- **Respect.** Showing respect in a relationship means being polite and considerate. It also means knowing and accepting a relationship's "social boundaries"—the appropriate ways of behaving in a relationship. For example, whenever Enrique meets an adult, he addresses the person by the title, "Mr." or "Ms." Another way to show respect is to listen to people before you respond.

- **Patience.** No one is perfect. Everyone has behaviors that can annoy others. Being patient with people is an important trait to develop. Waiting in line requires patience and so does helping a younger brother or sister who may be learning something new that you are already familiar with.

- **Tolerance.** Accepting people who are different than you is an example of tolerance. **Tolerance** is *the ability to value other people as they are.* This includes people of different races, cultures, and religions, as well as those who have disabilities or impairments. Building relationships with people from other backgrounds can be enriching. For example, Sergio invited Steve to his house for a Cinco de Mayo dinner. Steve enjoyed the time he spent with Sergio's family because it allowed him to experience some of the Latino customs practiced by Sergio's family.

Health Online

Visit **health.glencoe.com** and complete the Interactive Study Guide for Lesson 1.

Reading Check **Define** What is *tolerance?*

Health Skills Activity

Advocacy

Relating to Your Community

Building a healthy relationship with the community includes the following skills:

- **Respect.** Show your respect for your community by taking pride in it. Help keep it clean. Avoid littering or defacing property.

- **Tolerance.** Demonstrate tolerance by getting to know people in your community who are different than you. When you demonstrate tolerance, you encourage others around you to do the same.

With a Group

Create several posters encouraging teens to show respect for their community and to demonstrate tolerance of others.

Lesson 1 Review

After You Read

Review this lesson for new terms, major headings, and Reading Checks.

What I Learned

1. *Vocabulary* What is a *role*?

2. *Recall* What are some needs that relationships meet?

3. *Identify* Which character traits are found in strong, healthy relationships?

Thinking Critically

4. *Analyze* Denise was elected to her school's student council, but realized that soccer practice would conflict with most student council meetings. In what way is Denise failing to meet the responsibilities of her role as a student-council representative? What should she do?

5. *Apply* Suzy often disagrees with her history teacher. Sometimes she interrupts him when he is speaking, and raises her voice when addressing him. How can Suzy disagree with her teacher in a way that shows respect?

Applying Health Skills

6. *Communication Skills* With a group, discuss the role of communication in building strong, healthy relationships. Role-play a situation in which you use communication skills to show respect for a friend.

Getting Along with Your Family

Guide to Reading

Building Vocabulary
Define each term as best as you can. Then check your definitions as you read the lesson.

- family (p. 134)
- extended family (p. 135)
- single-parent family (p. 135)
- blended family (p. 137)

Focusing on the Main Ideas
In this lesson, you will learn to

- **identify** the different types of families.
- **describe** responsibilities within the family.
- **explain** changes that affect families.
- **develop** healthy ways to deal with family changes.

Reading Strategy
Comparing and Contrasting Read about the different family types described in the lesson. Find the similarities and differences among them.

Quick Write

Write a short essay titled "My Family is _____." Fill in the blank with a word that best describes your family.

The Family Unit

When you look closely at the words *relationship* and *relative*, you discover that they share a common root: *relate*. Your earliest and most important relationships are with family—your relatives. The **family** is *the basic unit of society, and includes two or more people brought together by blood, marriage, adoption, or a desire for mutual support.*

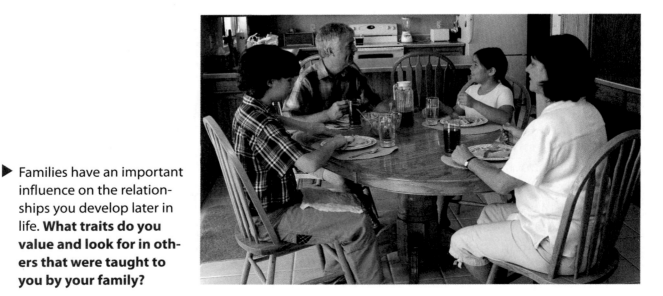

► Families have an important influence on the relationships you develop later in life. **What traits do you value and look for in others that were taught to you by your family?**

The way you relate with your family prepares you for all future relationships. It is within your family that you begin developing social skills. Through your family, you form a sense of who you are, and you learn to care for and share with others. Developing a positive relationship with your family helps you keep all three sides of the health triangle in balance.

Types of Families

Shari's family consists of her younger brother, her mother, and herself. Her neighbor, Latesha, lives with her mother, her father, and her grandfather. These family units are just two of the many types of families that exist.

Latesha lives in an **extended family,** *a family in which one or more parents and children live with other relatives such as grandparents, aunts, uncles, and cousins.* Shari, by contrast, lives in a **single-parent family,** *a family made up of one parent plus a child or children.* **Figure 6.2** shows some other types of family units. Which type describes your family?

Reading Check **Give Examples** List two different types of families, and identify the members that might belong to each family.

Television Families

Many television programs focus on the daily challenges of family life. These programs often show a variety of different family types. Some have couples with no children and some have nuclear families with a mom, dad, and children. Some programs show more than one type of family in the same program.

Think of several different television "families." What types of families are they? Are the challenges they face similar or are they different? Explain.

▼ **FIGURE 6.2**

FAMILY TYPES

There are many different types of families. **Do you know families who are examples of some of the family types shown?**

Family Type	Composition
Nuclear Family	Two parents and one or more children
Couple	Married people with no children
Adoptive family	A couple plus one or more adoptive children
Foster family	Adults caring for a child or children born to different parents
Joint-custody family	Two parents living apart, sharing custody of their children
Single-custody family	Two parents living apart, and a child or children living with only one parent
Single-parent family	One parent and child or children

Families Meet Needs

As you learned in Lesson 1, relationships satisfy needs. This includes family relationships. The most important function that a family performs is meeting the physical, mental/emotional, and social needs of its members.

- **Physical needs.** Families provide physical necessities, such as food, clothing, safety, and shelter. They care for family members when they are sick. They protect members from accidents and other threats. Finally, they teach members how to achieve and maintain good health.

- **Mental/emotional needs.** Families teach members love and acceptance and help them feel emotionally secure. Having your emotional needs met promotes a positive self-image and high self-esteem. Family members can turn to each other when they feel hurt or discouraged.

- **Social needs.** Families guide members in developing social skills, such as effective communication and good manners. Families also teach children values. The family can share cultural traditions with its members and encourage them to be proud of their heritage.

Responsibilities Within the Family

Different family members have different roles and responsibilities. **What are your responsibilities within your family?**

As with any other group, family members have individual roles, which have their own responsibilities and expectations. Parents or guardians have the most responsibility. They are responsible for financially supporting other family members. Parents also are the emotional anchor of the family. It is their job to establish a loving environment in which children can grow. Parents or guardians are often the first to teach their children values—the difference between right and wrong.

Children may play many roles in a family. For example, you may be responsible for helping prepare meals or other chores. Maybe you look after a younger sibling while adults are at work.

Some teens volunteer for responsibilities in the home that go beyond what their

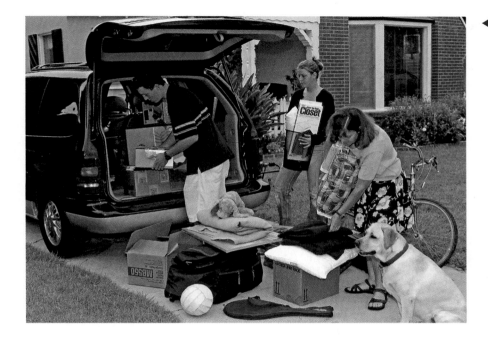

Families experience many changes. **What change might the family in this picture be going through?**

parents or guardians expect from them. Taking responsibility is one way of showing maturity within the family.

Reading Check **Identify** What kinds of responsibilities might children in a household be expected to take on?

Changes in the Family

Families sometimes face changes. When Teresa's older brother graduated from high school and joined the Navy, she became the oldest child living at home. She is now expected to do the chores that her brother used to do. She also receives some of the privileges of being the oldest child at home.

Some changes that occur in a family are unexpected or beyond the family's control. These changes include the end of a marriage or death of a family member. These kinds of changes can create stress for all members of the family.

Changes in Family Structure

The last fifty years have brought about big changes in the structure of the American family. Couples today are having fewer children. More marriages end in divorce. In 1960, nine percent of children under the age of 18 lived with only one parent. Since then, that percentage has more than tripled.

Many adults who get divorced eventually remarry. This trend has led to an increase in the number of blended families. A **blended family** is *a family that consists of a parent, a stepparent, and the children of one or both parents.* For children, becoming part of a blended family often involves making hard adjustments. These changes can sometimes be hard to deal with both emotionally and socially. It is important to talk with parents or other trusted adults about these difficulties.

Changes in Family Circumstances

Changes in the family's circumstances can also result in added stress. For example, families sometimes have to move to a new city or town. For children, moving means not only saying goodbye to old friends, but also having to make new ones.

Financial problems or the loss of a parent's job can also put an emotional strain on a family. Teens in the family may be asked to help out in various ways, such as earning their own spending money.

The serious illness of a family member can also disrupt daily life. Adult family members may be unavailable or unable to perform normal duties and responsibilities. Again, the teens in the family may be called upon to help out.

Reading Check **Describe** What are some changes that can be stressful for families?

Coping with Family Changes

Most families are able to work through problems caused by change. One skill that can be especially useful during difficult times is good communication. Talk with a parent or guardian. Explain how you feel. Being scared or uncertain about what lies ahead is a normal reaction. Your parents or guardians may have similar feelings.

In some situations, parents may feel overwhelmed and may even be the source of the problem. If this is the case, talk to a trusted adult outside the family. Your teachers and school counselors are trained to help. Religious leaders may also be able to help.

Some family problems are too big to solve by family members alone. Families who need guidance can find it through counseling or other community resources. Check your local phone directory for numbers you can call.

Health Online

Visit **health.glencoe.com** and complete the Interactive Study Guide for Lesson 2.

Abuse

One family problem that always requires outside help is abuse. Abuse can take several different forms, including neglect, physical and sexual abuse, and substance abuse. Neglect occurs when parents do not provide food, clothing, housing, medical care, and emotional support to their children. Children and infants who are neglected may suffer what is called *failure to thrive,* meaning that they don't develop physically, emotionally, and socially. Children who are emotionally neglected may suffer from low self-esteem.

Physical abuse involves the use of physical force. It can cause injuries such as bruises, cuts, or broken bones. Every year, about 1,500 children die as a result of physical abuse. Another 140,000 are injured. Sexual abuse involves any mistreatment of a child or adult involving sexual activity. Substance abuse involves addiction to alcohol or drugs. Even if only one family member has a substance abuse problem, it affects every family member.

Any teen who is a victim of abuse needs to seek help. Speak with a teacher, school counselor, or other adult you trust. You will learn more about getting help for abuse in Chapter 8.

> **Reading Check** **Identify** What are two types of abuse?

Health Online

Topic: Coping with Abuse

Visit health.glencoe.com for Student Web Activities to learn about the different kinds of abuse and what can be done about them.

Activity: Using the information provided at the link above, create a brochure that lists the kinds of abuse, what a teen can do to stop abuse, and the names and numbers of local resources that can help.

Lesson 2 Review

> **After You Read**

Review this lesson for new terms, major headings, and Reading Checks.

What I Learned

1. *Vocabulary* What is a *blended family*?

2. *Give Examples* Name two physical needs that a family provides.

3. *Identify* What can a teen do to cope with family changes?

Thinking Critically

4. *Evaluate* Which family change described in the lesson do you think would be the hardest to deal with?

5. *Apply* Carla's mother and stepfather recently had a new baby. How might this change affect Carla? What effect might it have on her responsibilities within the family?

Applying Health Skills

6. *Accessing Information* Use the phone book to find names of organizations that provide support to family members of substance abusers. Create a card showing how to contact these places.

Marriage and Parenthood

Guide to Reading

● Building Vocabulary
Write what you think each term below means. As you read, make corrections as needed.

- commitment (p. 140)
- divorce (p. 142)
- unconditional love (p. 143)

● Focusing on the Main Ideas
In this lesson, you will learn to

- **identify** the factors that affect the success of a marriage.
- **describe** the responsibilities involved in being a parent.
- **identify** the consequences of teen parenthood.

● Reading Strategy
Drawing Conclusions Based on this lesson, what assumptions can you make about teen marriage and parenthood?

Quick Write

Write a paragraph describing what you think is one of the challenges of being a parent.

Marriage

The tradition of marriage—a union between two people—is very old. Some people view marriage as something that should happen automatically when you become an adult. Others wait until they are truly ready for a long-term commitment. A **commitment** is *a pledge or promise.*

When two people get married, they make a legal and social commitment to each other. They pledge to live together and care for each other for the rest of their lives. They agree to respect each other's needs and desires. They agree to work at all times to make their relationship as strong as possible. The decision to marry is one of the biggest decisions a person can make.

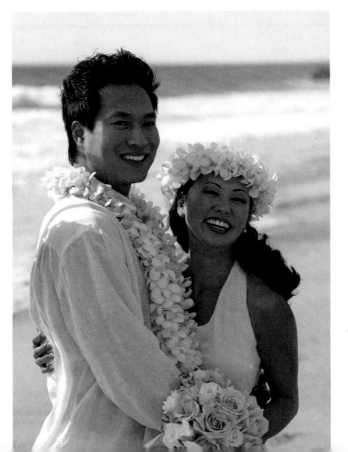

◀ Couples who are ready for marriage need a strong commitment to each other. **What does this mean? Why is a commitment so important?**

Factors Affecting Marriage

A successful marriage depends on many factors. Marriage requires emotional and physical maturity. Being emotionally mature means knowing yourself and accepting your strengths and weaknesses. It means knowing what you value. People who are emotionally mature also have life goals and a plan for reaching them. They are able to understand and respect someone else's feelings and needs.

Besides emotional maturity, other factors that lead to a successful marriage are the same as those that build good friendships. These factors include common interests and shared values. In fact, many married couples see each other as best friends. **Figure 6.3** shows some other factors that affect the success of a marriage.

Reading Check **Identify** What are some commitments that married couples make to each other?

▼ **FIGURE 6.3**

FACTORS THAT AFFECT THE SUCCESS OF A MARRIAGE

These are some of the factors that can help a marriage last. Why do you think communication is important to a healthy marriage?

Factors that Affect the Health and Strength of a Marriage

 Effective communication between partners. This includes the ability to share feelings, needs, and concerns as they arise.

 Similar values, goals, outlooks, and spiritual beliefs. When couples share the things that are most important to them, they move forward in their lives together.

 Ability to solve problems through compromise and conflict resolution. This requires both partners in a marriage to respect, trust, and care for each other.

 Emotional maturity. This involves understanding a partner's needs and wants. Each partner is able to consider what is best for the relationship, not just for him or herself.

Marital Problems

Even the best marriages sometimes have problems. Couples may disagree or argue over money, children, or other issues. When the marriage is based on a foundation of trust, respect, and communication, these disagreements can usually be resolved.

Sometimes, however, married people cannot overcome their differences or solve the problems they face as a couple. In such cases, one or both spouses may seek a **divorce,** *a legal end to a marriage contract.*

Teen Marriage

According to a recent government survey, four out of every ten adult marriages end in divorce. For teens, the divorce rate is closer to six out of ten. Why do teen marriages fail so often? One reason is that most people are not ready for marriage during adolescence. Most teens are just beginning to learn about themselves and what they want out of life. They have not had enough experience with relationships to make a long-term commitment to another person.

Most teens are also not ready to be parents. This is another factor that contributes to the high divorce rate among teens. Many teens get married because of an unplanned pregnancy. Taking care of a baby is often a bigger responsibility than many teen couples can handle.

A lack of money is another factor that can cause marital problems. Teens lack the work experience and education needed to get most high-paying jobs. This can make it difficult to support a family. These responsibilities and pressures can put strain on a teen marriage.

Reading Check **List** What are some reasons teen marriages fail?

▶ Marriage is one of the biggest decisions a person can make. **What are some factors to consider before getting married?**

◄ Parenthood can be very rewarding, but it also involves many challenges. **What are some of the challenges of being a responsible parent?**

Parenthood

Parenthood involves making a life-long commitment to another person. It involves meeting the physical, mental/emotional, and social needs of a child. Parenthood can be a wonderful experience, but it is important to wait until you are ready for the responsibilities that come with parenthood.

The Responsibilities of Becoming a Parent

Parenthood can be very challenging. It requires a person to juggle many responsibilities and fill many roles. Parents are responsible for the health and safety of their children. Additional responsibilities include the following:

- **Setting fair limits.** Small children need to know their limits—what they can and cannot do. It is up to parents to set fair rules and then enforce them.

- **Teaching values.** Parents are their children's first teachers. Children learn social skills and values by watching or listening to their parents. Parents need to be good role models for their children and demonstrate fairness, trust, caring, and respect.

- **Providing patience and love.** Raising children can be a difficult and sometimes exhausting job. When it comes to their children, parents must be slow to anger and quick to forgive. They must show their children **unconditional love.** This is *love without limitation or qualification.* Devoted parents support their children through good times and bad.

▶ It is a parent's job to establish a loving environment in which a child can grow. **What are some ways a parent can establish a loving environment?**

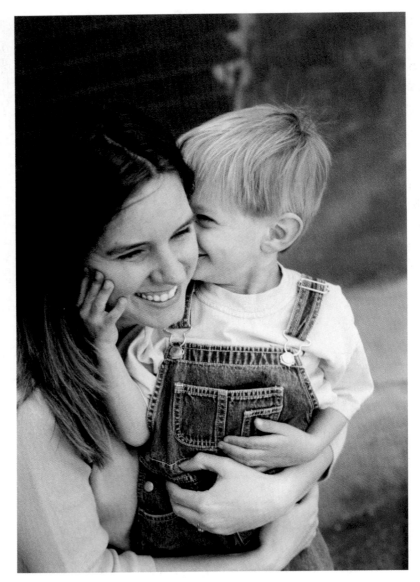

Risks of Teen Parenthood

The decision to become a parent is one that requires serious thought and planning. Most teens do not have the emotional maturity to plan for parenthood.

Teen pregnancy can also create health risks for both mother and baby. A female teen's body is still developing and may not be ready to support and nourish an unborn child. Babies born to teen mothers are at an increased risk of being born prematurely, or before they are ready to be born. They are more likely to have low birth weights which can lead to serious health problems. A pregnant teen may not be aware of the things she can do to protect the health of her developing baby. She may not be able to afford proper prenatal care.

Reading Check **Describe** What are some of the risks associated with teen pregnancy?

Health Online

Visit **health.glencoe.com** and complete the Interactive Study Guide for Lesson 3.

Consequences of Teen Parenthood

Teen parents who are committed to raising their child face many challenges. One of these challenges is meeting the expenses of raising a child. This includes the cost of baby food, diapers, clothes, medical care, and more.

Between school, work, and raising a child, many teen parents find themselves physically and emotionally exhausted. They may begin to envy their peers who are not raising children. Some teen parents may have to put education plans on hold, limiting their career choices. All of these difficulties can put a great deal of stress on a teen parent.

▶ Teen parenthood can be difficult both emotionally and financially. **What are some challenges this teen might face?**

Lesson 3 Review

After You Read

Review this lesson for new terms, major headings, and Reading Checks.

What I Learned

1. *Vocabulary* What is *unconditional love*?

2. *Recall* What are two factors that contribute to the success of a marriage?

3. *Identify* What are some of the responsibilities of parenthood?

Thinking Critically

4. *Evaluate* How might a person's emotional maturity affect his or her marriage?

5. *Synthesize* What have you learned from this lesson that helps you better understand or appreciate your own parent or guardian?

6. *Analyze* Roseanne discovered that her older teen sister was planning to elope with her boyfriend. Roseanne shared with her sister what she learned about teen marriage. Her sister responded, "Maybe that's all true, but Robert and I really love each other." How could Roseanne help her sister make a healthful choice?

Applying Health Skills

7. *Goal Setting* Identify a goal you hope to accomplish in the next five years. Explain how becoming a parent would affect your success in reaching that goal. Be prepared to share your ideas in a class discussion.

Building Health Skills

Sending the Right Message

DIRECTIONS

Communication Skills involve learning how to efficiently express yourself and understand others. This activity will give you the opportunity to develop and master this important health skill. Here's a guide to the different parts of this activity.

❶ In the **Model** section, you will read about a teen who performs the health skill successfully. This "model" scenario will show you how the skill is done.

❷ The **Practice** section will help guide you in practicing the skill.

❸ In the **Apply** section, you will have a chance to perform the skill on your own. You can use the Self-Check to check your work.

To complete this activity, first read the scenario presented in the Model. Then move on to the Practice. Finally, go ahead and try the Apply.

❶ Model

An important ingredient in any healthy relationship is communication. Gil was planning to practice fielding with his teammate Chris. Gil's mother, however, reminded him that he had promised to help clean out the garage. Read how Gil and his mother used communication skills to solve this problem.

Gil made eye contact with his mother and said, "Mom, I know I made a promise to you, but I forgot we had a big game coming up. Can I clean out the garage next weekend?"

Gil's mother responded, "I wish I could say yes, but I can't. A local charity is picking up old clothes on Tuesday, and we have some that I want to give them."

Gil's mother saw the look of disappointment on his face. "I'll tell you what," she said. "I'll ask your brother if he's willing to swap chores with you. If he agrees to clean the garage, will you do some of his chores in exchange?"

Gil smiled. "That sounds like a deal, Mom," he said.

② Practice

Notice that Gil and his mother used effective communication skills when speaking and listening. When Gil first spoke, he made eye contact with his mother. He used an "I" statement: "*I know I made a promise.*" As he spoke, his mother nodded her head to show she was listening. When she spoke, she also used "I" statements.

1. What is an example of an "I" statement that Gil's mother used?
2. Can you find evidence of body language in the conversation between Gil and his mother?
3. Did their conversation have a positive outcome? How does it affect their relationship?

Skill Summary
COMMUNICATION SKILLS

Speaking Skills:
- "I" messages
- Clear, simple statements
- Honest thoughts and feelings
- Appropriate body language

Listening Skills:
- Appropriate body language
- Conversation encouragers
- Mirror thoughts and feelings
- Ask questions

③ Apply

With a partner, develop a skit that is a fictional relationship between a parent and child or two friends. Your dialogue should reflect at least two speaking skills and two listening skills. Perform your skit for classmates. See if they are able to identify the communication skills used.

Self-Check

- Did we use two speaking skills in our conversation?
- Did we use two listening skills?

A Taste of Parenthood

Many teens do not understand how demanding parenthood can be. This brief experiment will give you a glimpse of the responsibilities.

What You Will Need

- Help of a parent, guardian, brother, or sister
- Clock or watch with an alarm feature
- Paper
- Pencil or pen

What You Will Do

1 Select an evening or weekend when you have a light workload. Arrange with a family member to help you out with your experiment.

2 Go about your normal activities. These might include watching a favorite TV program or speaking to a friend on the phone.

3 Without warning, your partner is to set off the alarm. He or she should be close enough to where you are so that you can hear the alarm.

Stop what you are doing and go to the alarm and turn it off. The alarm interruption represents the attention a baby requires.

4 On your paper, note the time when you heard the alarm, and what you were doing when the alarm went off.

5 Return to your normal activities. Your partner is to set the alarm off a minimum of five times.

Wrapping It Up

Write about this experience and what it has taught you. As you write your thoughts, imagine what it would be like to respond to the alarm every day. How might this be like caring for a child? Share your report with classmates, comparing your experience with theirs.

Reading Review

FOLDABLES Study Organizer

Foldables™ and Other Study Aids Take out the Foldable™ that you created for Lesson 1 and any graphic organizers that you created for Lessons 1–3. Find a partner and quiz each other using these study aids.

Lesson 1 You and Your Relationships

Key Ideas

- Relationships vary in terms of the degree of closeness, the needs they satisfy, and the roles involved.
- Relationships satisfy emotional needs, such as the need to feel loved and to belong.
- Features found in strong, healthy relationships include trust, respect, patience, tolerance, and caring.

Vocabulary

- social health (p. 131)
- role (p. 131)
- tolerance (p. 132)

Lesson 2 Getting Along with Your Family

Key Ideas

- Families meet the physical, mental/emotional, and social needs of their members.
- Parents or guardians must provide financial support, create a loving environment, and teach values. A child's responsibilities may include helping with chores and being respectful.

- Changes in a family's structure include divorce and remarriage. Changes to a family's circumstances can include moving to a new city, financial problems, job loss, and illness.

Vocabulary

- family (p. 134)
- extended family (p. 135)
- single-parent family (p. 135)
- blended family (p. 137)

Lesson 3 Marriage and Parenthood

Key Ideas

- Factors that affect the success of a marriage include good communication skills, sharing similar goals and values, emotional maturity, and the ability to compromise.
- Responsible parents set fair limits and provide safety, support, encouragement, patience, and love.
- Consequences of being a teen parent include financial problems, physical and emotional exhaustion, changed relationships with peers, and stress.

Vocabulary

- commitment (p. 140)
- divorce (p. 142)
- unconditional love (p. 143)

After You Read

IM Express

Now that you have read the chapter, review your answer to the I.M. Express on the chapter opener. Have your ideas changed? What would your answer be now?

Reviewing Vocabulary and Main Ideas

On a sheet of paper, write the numbers 1–6. After each number, write the term from the list that best completes each sentence.

- blended families
- family
- role
- single-parent family
- social health
- tolerance

Lesson 1 You and Your Relationships

1. Your ability to get along with the people around you is your _____.

2. A(n) _____ is a part you play when you interact with another person.

3. The ability to accept other people as they are is known as _____.

Lesson 2 Getting Along with Your Family

4. A(n) _____ is the basic unit of society, and includes two or more people.

5. A family made up of one parent plus a child or children is known as a(n) _____.

6. Remarriage among divorced adults has led to an increase in the number of _____.

Lesson 3 Marriage and Parenthood

On a sheet of paper, write the numbers 7–10. After each number, write the letter of the answer that best completes each statement.

7. Being emotionally mature includes all of the following *except*:
   a. accepting your strengths and weaknesses.
   b. knowing what is important to you.
   c. putting another person's needs ahead of your own.
   d. marrying a person because you reached a certain age.

8. Which is *not* a commitment of marriage or parenthood?
   a. Pledging to care for each other.
   b. Making sure that a child does not become a financial burden.
   c. Setting and enforcing fair rules for a child.

9. Giving birth to a child prematurely is an example of:
   a. A risk facing teen females who become pregnant.
   b. A consequence faced by parents who fail to set limits.
   c. Prenatal care.

10. The statement about teen parents that is true is:
    a. They may face serious money problems.
    b. They may find themselves physically and emotionally exhausted.
    c. They may feel added stress.
    d. All of the above.

Health Online Visit health.glencoe.com and take the Online Quiz for Chapter 6.

Thinking Critically

Using complete sentences, answer the following questions on a sheet of paper.

11. Analyze How do your relationships affect your mental/emotional health?

12. Apply Create a list of topics you think a couple should discuss before getting married.

Write About It

13. Stress Management Write a short story about a family that is coping with problems brought on by a change in circumstances.

14. Decision Making Write an article that could be published in a school newspaper that explains the consequences of teen pregnancy.

Career Corner

Social Worker Would you like to help children and families in need? A career as a social worker might be for you. Social workers help with problems related to poverty, sickness, and family crises. To become a social worker, you need a college education and a master's degree in social work. To find out more about this and other health careers, visit the *Career Corner* at **health.glencoe.com**.

Standardized Test Practice

Reading

Read the passage and then answer the questions.

In Japan, the ancient practice of *arranged marriage* is still common. In this custom, the bride and groom see each other for the first time at an arranged meeting.

When a woman in Japan whose family practices this tradition turns 25, she and her parents assemble an "information kit." The kit contains photos and descriptions of her background, education, hobbies, and interests. The parents then pass out copies of the information kit to friends and neighbors. These people ask around to see if anyone knows of an eligible bachelor. Once an interested male is located, he will prepare an information kit of his own. This is then sent to the woman and her family.

If the two parties are willing, a meeting is arranged. Members of both families go to the meeting, which takes place in a fancy restaurant. Upon meeting, the couple decides if they are interested in dating. A woman might have as many as ten such meetings before she finds a marriage partner.

1. The main idea of this passage is best summed up by which statement?

   A. Arranged marriages are the best kind.

   B. Every married couple should have an information kit.

   C. Marriage customs are different in different places.

   D. In an arranged marriage, the couple sees each other only once.

2. The following are steps in the modern Japanese version of an arranged marriage. Which step is in the wrong order?

   A. The woman reaches the age of 25.

   B. A meeting at a fancy restaurant is arranged between the willing parties.

   C. The women and her parents assemble an "information kit."

   D. Upon meeting, the couple decides if they are interested in dating.

CHAPTER

7 Conflict Resolution

Peer Medi

Chapter Preview

▲ *Working With the Photo*

Conflict resolution involves peacefully finding a solution to a problem. **How are the teens in this picture resolving their conflict peacefully?**

Start-Up Activities

Before You Read Do you know how to deal with conflict positively and effectively? Take the short health inventory on this page. Keep a record of your answers.

HEALTH INVENTORY

1. When I am involved in a conflict, I try to listen to what the other person has to say.
   (a) always   (b) sometimes   (c) never

2. I walk away from conflicts that are not worth my time and energy.
   (a) always   (b) sometimes   (c) never

3. I seek help when I cannot resolve a conflict on my own.
   (a) always   (b) sometimes   (c) never

FOLDABLES™ Study Organizer

As You Read Make this Foldable™ to help you organize what you learn in Lesson 1 about the nature of conflict. Begin with a plain sheet of 8½″ × 11″ paper or notebook paper.

1 Fold the sheet of paper from top to bottom, leaving a 2″ tab at the bottom.

3 Unfold the paper once. Cut along the center fold line of the top layer only. This makes two tabs.

2 Fold in half from side to side.

4 Label the tabs as shown.

Under the appropriate tab, record information on some common causes of conflict at home and outside of the home.

Health Online Visit **health.glencoe.com** and use the e-flashcards to preview Chapter 7 vocabulary terms.

The Nature of Conflict

Guide to Reading

Building Vocabulary

Choose the term from the list below that is central to the lesson's main idea. Explain the relationship this term has with each of the other terms.

- conflict (p. 154)
- bully (p. 157)
- labeling (p. 158)
- prejudice (p. 158)

Focusing on the Main Ideas

In this lesson, you will learn to

- **explain** some reasons why conflicts occur.
- **describe** different kinds of conflict.
- **develop** healthy and effective ways to deal with bullying.

Reading Strategy

Comparing and Contrasting As you read the lesson, list similarities and differences between conflicts at home and those outside the home.

FOLDABLES Study Organizer Use the Foldable™ on p. 153 as you read this lesson.

Quick Write

List any disagreements you've had in the last month, what they were about, and with whom you disagreed.

▼ Conflicts can start for a variety of reasons. **What kinds of conflicts can occur at school?**

What Is Conflict?

It began as an innocent episode. Tyler was waiting patiently in the cafeteria line when someone accidentally bumped into him from behind. He fell against Frank, a classmate standing in line in front of him. "What's your problem?" Frank asked, shoving Tyler back. Tyler got angry and shoved Frank back. A campus supervisor spotted the boys and took them both to the vice-principal's office. Tyler felt that he had been wrongly accused, but he was as much to blame as Frank was for contributing to the conflict. A **conflict** is *a disagreement between people with opposing viewpoints, ideas, or goals.*

Conflicts can be caused by a difference of opinion over just about anything. They can occur over relationships, space, or property. They can also be about power, rewards, or privileges.

Reading Check

Define What is *conflict*?

Kinds of Conflict

Conflicts can take many different forms depending on what and who is involved. Some conflicts involve only a simple exchange of words. These conflicts are fairly minor. Others, such as gang confrontations, can be ongoing and severe. When conflicts involve weapons that can lead to injury or death, they are extremely serious.

Many conflicts are interpersonal—between two or more people. Others are internal—they take place inside your own mind. Imagine being asked to judge a talent contest in which your best friend is a contestant. You might be torn between loyalty to a friend and responsibility for choosing the best act.

People have different needs and wants, and conflicts are often unavoidable. Maybe you want to watch a certain TV show, but your sister wants to watch a different one. Maybe two girls have a crush on the same boy. Conflicts are not necessarily negative. They are a part of everyday life. In fact, they can be a good force in people's lives. Resolving conflicts can help people settle their differences, get along peacefully, and move on to positive action.

Reading Check List What are two types of conflict?

Conflicts at Home

The more time you spend with people, the more chances there are for disagreements to arise. If you spend a large part of your day with family, conflicts with family members may be common. It is important to maintain a positive relationship with your family members because these relationships can affect your overall health.

Conflicts with parents or guardians usually occur over limits, responsibilities, or expectations. You may feel that a rule set by a parent is unfair. Maybe, in your opinion, you should be able to stay up—or out—later. Perhaps you feel that you have been asked to do more chores than other family members. As a maturing teen, you may feel that you have proven yourself ready for more independence. Your parent or guardian, however, may feel differently. When conflicts like these come up, try to remember

Health Online

Topic: Handling Conflict at Home

Visit health.glencoe.com for Student Web Activities to learn about the different kinds of conflict and what you can do to resolve conflict when it happens at home.

Activity: Using the information provided at the link above, create a "Conflict Tip Sheet" that will remind you of things you can do to resolve conflicts that occur at home.

▼ Conflicts with parents or guardians can be over restrictions, responsibilities, or expectations. **What do you need to remember when you have a conflict with an adult in charge at your home?**

Health Skills Activity

Decision Making

You Be the Judge

Mike and his friends were having a party and needed a CD player. Mike borrowed his brother's without asking. As Mike was riding his bike over to his friend's house, he dropped the CD player on the road, breaking it. When Mike told his brother what happened, his brother was angry. "How could you take my things without asking? I thought I could trust you," his brother said and then walked away.

Mike did not know what to do next. How could he mend his relationship with his brother?

What Would You Do?

Apply the six steps of decision making to Mike's problem. With a partner, role-play a scene in which Mike thinks through his decision, and then acts on it.

1. State the situation.
2. List the options.
3. Weigh the possible outcomes.
4. Consider your values.
5. Make a decision and act.
6. Evaluate your decision.

that parents set limits to ensure their children's well-being. As parents, they are responsible for keeping you safe and healthy. You, in turn, have a responsibility to respect their authority and to try to keep a positive relationship with them.

Conflicts between siblings—sisters or brothers—often involve property or space. Older siblings may be upset by younger siblings who get in their way or who use their possessions without asking first. This often happens when siblings share a room. Also, conflict between siblings often involves competition. One sibling may feel that another is getting more attention from parents or guardians. A younger sibling may resent an older sibling because they have more privileges. Although conflicts are a normal part of family life, it is important to behave positively toward family members in order to build strong family relationships.

Reading Check

Identify: What are conflicts between siblings often about?

Conflicts Outside the Home

At this point in your life, you spend much of your day in school. As a result, many of the conflicts you have outside the home relate to school, friends, and peers.

Conflicts at school may be with teachers or other authority figures. More often, however, they happen between peers or friends. These conflicts can involve an incident, like Tyler experienced in the chapter-opening paragraph. Other times differences in personality, beliefs, or opinions are involved.

Sometimes conflicts are one-sided and unprovoked. One person may not take the time to understand another. Sometimes a person seeks power and attention by putting others down. This type of conflict is a form of bullying. The person who is the target of these behaviors usually feels upset and possibly helpless.

Bullying

A **bully** is *someone who picks on individuals who are smaller or weaker.* Bullies can be males or females of any age. Bullies may limit their behavior to teasing and name-calling, or they may become physical. Some bullies try to show how tough they are by taking away the property of others. The best way to deal with bullies is to walk away and share the matter with a trusted adult. Bullies expect victims to react with fear or anger. When you walk away, you take away the bully's power. Bullying can be serious. If you know someone who is a bully or if you are targeted by a bully in your school, talk with a person in authority. Bullying should not be allowed under any circumstances. You can use the resources available to you to improve the safety of your environment inside and outside the home.

Teasing is a form of bullying. Everyone has been teased at one time or another. The person doing the teasing may think it is harmless, though it might not be. When Joel started wearing braces on his teeth, an older student, Max, started teasing him. Max and his friends found the teasing hilarious. Joel found it irritating. At first he tried ignoring it and avoiding Max whenever he could. When that did not work, Joel made his own joke about his braces. That did the trick. If Joel was in on the joke, there was nothing for Max to make

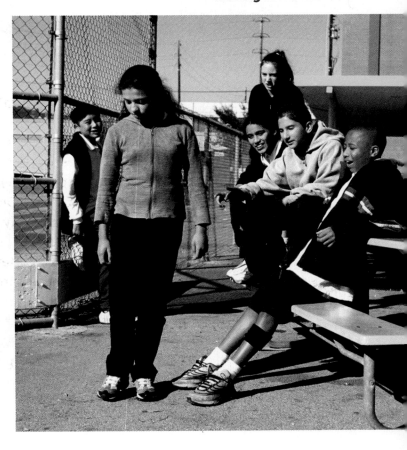

▼ Teasing can seem harmless but can be hurtful. **If you are teased, what is your best course of action? What is your second best option if the teasing continues?**

fun of. Joel was glad the teasing was over, but if his approach had not worked, he still had the option of confronting Max. He could have explained to Max how the teasing made him feel so that Max would hopefully understand and decide to stop.

Labeling, or *name-calling,* is another form of bullying. Name-calling is hurtful, especially when it is based on **prejudice**—*a negative and unjustly formed opinion, usually against people of a different racial, religious, or cultural group.* A student who is a target of this kind of labeling should attempt to resolve the matter by talking with a school counselor, parent, or other trusted adult. This is a very serious problem that needs action right away.

Being teased, labeled or bullied can be an emotionally painful experience. It is difficult not to feel hurt by what others say. Remember that words should be used to build others up, not to tear them down.

Health Online

Visit health.glencoe.com and complete the Interactive Study Guide for Lesson 1.

Reading Check

Recall What should a person do if he or she is being bullied?

Lesson 1 Review

After You Read

Review this lesson for new terms, major headings, and Reading Checks.

What I Learned

1. *Vocabulary* What is *prejudice?* Use the term in a sentence.

2. *Give Examples* Give an example of an interpersonal and internal conflict.

3. *Recall* What kinds of conflicts often occur in the home?

4. *Explain* What are some forms of bullying?

Thinking Critically

5. *Analyze* Alisa and her mother had an argument over the amount of time she spends watching TV. Alisa is feeling angry with her mother. What do you think Alisa could do to maintain a positive relationship with her mother?

6. *Apply* Ever since Dave got his hair cut in a new style, he has been feeling self-conscious about it. To make matters worse, Ted makes fun of Dave every time he sees him. What type of hurtful behavior is Ted using to target Dave? What should Dave do?

Applying Health Skills

7. *Analyzing Influences* Sometimes negative song lyrics or other media messages encourage negative behaviors. Evaluate song lyrics that promote positive behavior. Write a review of these lyrics to share with classmates.

Health Online For more review questions for Lesson 1, go to **health.glencoe.com.**

Preventing Conflicts

Guide to Reading

● Building Vocabulary
As you read this lesson, write the three new highlighted terms in your notebook. Next to each, write its definition.

- escalate (p. 159)
- revenge (p. 161)
- mob mentality (p. 162)

● Focusing on the Main Ideas
In this lesson, you will learn to

- **identify** factors that build conflicts.
- **prevent** conflicts from becoming serious.
- **develop** stress management techniques to release anger.

● Reading Strategy
Classifying Using the diagram to the right as a guide, create a concept map that shows why conflicts build.

Why Conflicts Build

Many conflicts do not go beyond an exchange of words. Others **escalate,** or *become more serious.* Fortunately, this can be avoided. You can take steps to prevent conflicts from becoming violent. One step is recognizing signs that a conflict is building. Some well-known signs appear in **Figure 7.1.** Another step toward prevention is identifying the emotions and other factors that fuel conflict. These include anger, jealousy, group pressure, and the use of alcohol and other drugs.

Quick Write

Write a paragraph describing what you typically do when you get angry.

The Warning Signs of Building Conflict	
Physical Signs	*Emotional Signs*
• A knot in the stomach	• Feeling concerned
• Faster heart rate	• Getting defensive
• A lump in the throat	• Wanting to cry
• Balled-up fists	• Not feeling valued
• Cold or sweaty palms	• Wanting to lash out
• A sudden surge of energy	• Wanting to escape

◀ **FIGURE 7.1**

Some warning signs that a conflict is building are physical. Others are emotional. **Can you think of other signs of building conflict?**

Citizenship

When a fight is developing, you can show good citizenship by encouraging those involved to find a positive way to resolve the conflict. However, if the fight turns violent, do not get involved. Instead, get help from a trusted adult right away.

Who would be an appropriate person at your school to report a fight to?

Anger

Nearly everyone gets angry at some point. Imagine that you and a friend have plans to meet outside a movie theater. Your friend arrives after the film has started, and does not give a reason for why he is late. Or imagine that you arrive at school after being out sick for several days. You discover that your sister failed to tell you about an important test even though you asked her to keep you informed about what you were missing. Anger would be a natural response to these situations. When you get angry, it is important to express your anger in a healthy way. In fact, keeping anger inside can harm you emotionally and physically.

Dealing with anger in an appropriate way can be challenging. Yelling at another person never accomplishes anything positive. This will only hurt or annoy the other person, creating a larger conflict. The best strategy when emotions are running high is to step away from the situation. Be quiet for a few moments and allow yourself to cool down. Share your feelings with a friend or trusted adult who is not directly involved in the situation. Focus your attention on something other than your anger and its source. When you are ready to speak calmly, let the other person know what is bothering you. Be sure to concentrate on the problem, not the person.

Reading Check **Recall** What should you do when you are angry?

Jealousy

"Why does *she* always get special treatment? It's not fair! I can't believe you got picked and I didn't!"

Have you ever heard statements like these? They are expressions of jealousy, a gateway to other emotions. It leads to feelings of anger and resentment. Jealousy has been known to ruin friendships, especially when the jealous person feels wronged. It is normal to feel jealous sometimes, especially when someone

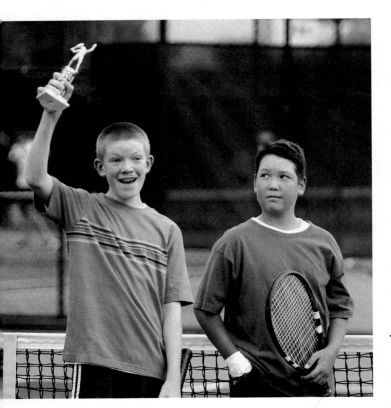

◀ Talking about feelings of jealousy with a trusted adult is a better idea than seeking revenge. **What are some situations that might cause teens to feel jealous of someone else?**

Health Skills Activity

Stress Management

Letting Off Steam

It is not always easy to know how or when to deal with anger. Sometimes you may think it is best to say nothing only to later realize that you are still angry. When you allow anger to build, the emotion becomes like water heating up in a kettle. At such times, you need to let off steam. Here are some suggestions that can help you release built-up anger or frustration:

- Close your eyes and focus on relaxing and breathing.
- Find a way to turn your negative energy into positive energy. Write in your journal or work on a hobby. Look for an opportunity to laugh.
- Do some physical activity. Go for a run, bike ride, or walk.
- Talk to a friend, parent, or trusted adult.

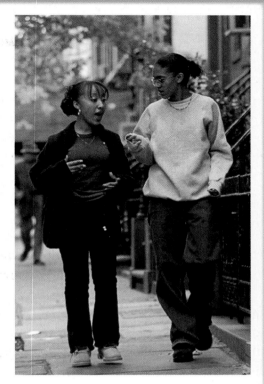

With a Group

Make a list of some of the different techniques each member in your group has used to redirect negative energy. Share your list with other groups in the class.

---

does better than you or gets more attention than you. Just be sure to deal with these feelings in a healthy way. Talk to a friend or trusted adult. You can also write down your feelings in a private journal.

When you are jealous of someone, seeking revenge is not a healthy way to deal with your feelings. **Revenge** is *punishment, injury, or insult to the person seen as the cause of the strong emotion.* Revenge is often seen as "payback" or an opportunity to "even the score." Seeking revenge, however, never helps a jealous person get what he or she really wants. It also has a way of turning a minor conflict into a major one. You could end up hurting someone or getting hurt yourself. Instead, manage your feelings of jealousy by talking about them with someone you trust or writing them down in a private journal.

Group Pressure

Sometimes when people have a disagreement in public, a crowd forms. Usually this begins with one or two curious people who stop to watch. Eventually, others join in as a result of **mob mentality.** This is *acting or behaving in a certain and often negative manner because others are doing it.* The onlookers may "egg on" the people involved in the conflict.

When this type of situation arises, the people in the middle of the conflict can get swept up in the mob mentality themselves. This can cause them to put aside their own thoughts of right and wrong and give in to the crowd. These situations usually have bad outcomes. If you find yourself in such a crowd, you should go get help from an adult right away.

Reading Check **Explain** How can pressure from a group of peers cause a conflict to escalate?

Alcohol and Other Drugs

Alcohol and conflicts do not mix well. Typically, alcohol only makes matters worse—in some instances, causing the situation to become violent.

Using alcohol affects a person's emotional state and understanding of a problem. The same is true of many other drugs. Teens who use alcohol or other drugs may lose self-control. They may lash out at others in violent ways. In fact, violent crimes committed under the influence of alcohol are a leading cause of teen deaths. The use of alcohol and other drugs can make it difficult to resolve conflicts in a peaceful way. To protect themselves from violence and other harmful effects, teens should avoid using alcohol and other drugs.

▼ Reaching an agreement that puts an end to a conflict is gratifying. **What are some other ways to prevent conflicts from building?**

Preventing Conflicts from Building

Conflicts are a normal part of life. You can usually prevent a conflict from building by dealing with the problem in appropriate ways. The following strategies can help:

• **Learn to understand your feelings.** It is especially important to recognize why you are angry. It is also helpful to understand that some emotions are impulsive, they last for a moment. Other emotions are more steady.

- **Keep your conflicts private.** Find a quiet, out-of-the-way spot to share your differences with another person. Trying to resolve a conflict in public may draw a crowd. This invites mob mentality, which can lessen the chances of resolving the conflict peacefully.

- **Avoid using alcohol or other drugs.** Using alcohol and drugs can affect a person's emotions, judgment and decision-making ability, making it difficult to resolve conflicts peacefully.

- **Show respect for yourself and for others.** This will help you build healthy relationships, which in turn will help you resolve conflicts when they arise.

- **Learn to accept others.** Enjoying people who have different views and customs than you can enrich your life.

- **Try putting yourself in the other person's situation.** If you understand the other person's point of view, you may be more sympathetic, understanding, and willing to resolve the conflict in a positive way.

Health Online

Visit **health.glencoe.com** and complete the Interactive Study Guide for Lesson 2.

Reading Check

Explain Why is it important to keep conflicts private?

Lesson 2 Review

After You Read

Review this lesson for new terms, major headings, and Reading Checks.

What I Learned

1. **Vocabulary** What is *mob mentality*?

2. **Recall** Name two factors that fuel conflicts.

3. **List** Name two ways to prevent conflicts from building.

Thinking Critically

4. **Evaluate** Andy and his best friend Jake tried out for the concert band. Jake made it, but Andy did not. Now Andy cannot bring himself to congratulate Jake, but he is not sure why. Tell what Andy may be feeling and what he can do about it.

5. **Synthesize** Jill and Connie were discussing a problem. Connie began to raise her voice out of anger. What strategies should Jill take to resolve the conflict in a positive way? Why are these strategies important?

Applying Health Skills

6. **Practicing Healthful Behaviors** On a sheet of paper, describe your strengths and weaknesses when preventing conflicts from growing. List ways to change your weaknesses to strengths that will help you improve your ability to deal with conflict.

Resolving Conflicts

Guide to Reading

● Building Vocabulary
Write what you think each term means. As you come across the word in the lesson, make changes as needed.

- conflict resolution (p. 164)
- win-win solution (p. 165)
- mediation (p. 165)
- compromise (p. 166)

● Focusing on the Main Ideas
In this lesson, you will learn to
- **demonstrate** effective skills for resolving conflicts.
- **recall** the steps of the mediation process.
- **identify** traits of a good mediator.

● Reading Strategy
Sequencing Explain the order in which the steps in the T.A.L.K. strategy should be carried out.

Quick Write
Write two ways of communicating that could lead to conflict. Next to each, write how the same idea could be expressed in a more positive way.

Finding Constructive Solutions

Sometimes it is easy to find a solution to a conflict. When this task is more difficult, however, you might be tempted to ignore the conflict or set it aside. Yet, conflicts or other differences that remain unsettled or unresolved can damage relationships. Avoiding a conflict is likely to make it worse. Fortunately, there is a constructive approach to dealing with any conflict—an approach in which the parties involved work together toward a positive, healthy outcome. This approach uses the skill of **conflict resolution,** which involves *solving a disagreement in a way that satisfies both sides.*

◀ There are constructive ways of dealing with conflict. **Can you name the steps in the T.A.L.K. strategy?**

Conflict Resolution

The skill of conflict resolution starts with the word *TALK*. Each letter represents one step in the T.A.L.K. strategy. This strategy can effectively end conflicts and improve and maintain your personal and family health. The meaning of the letters is as follows:

- **Take a time-out.** Wait at least 30 minutes before you discuss the situation with the other person. This will give both of you a chance to calm down and think more clearly.

- **Allow each person to tell his or her side.** Each person should have the chance to explain his or her feelings without interruption.

- **Let each person ask questions.** Each person should have the chance to question the other. Stay calm and respectful.

- **Keep brainstorming.** Be open to trying different solutions that will satisfy both of you. Do not let your emotions prevent you from trying different solutions.

Conflict-resolution skills tie in with other health skills—especially communication skills.

Conflict Resolution: Win-Win Outcomes

People have a natural tendency to think of conflicts in terms of winners and losers. This is not always accurate, however. If one person gets his or her way when a conflict is settled, does that mean that the other person automatically ends up losing? Not necessarily. When the T.A.L.K. strategy is used, a **win-win solution** is possible. This is *an agreement or outcome that gives each party something it wants*. Win-win solutions are more desirable than win-lose solutions. That is because both parties come away with something.

> **Reading Check**   **Define** What is a *win-win solution*?

A Need for Mediation

In some instances, you and another person might reach a win-win solution on your own. This will give both of you the satisfaction of knowing that you worked together to achieve a constructive solution.

Suppose that you and the other person are unable to come to an agreement. When this happens, your best bet is to seek outside help. One form of help is **mediation.** This is *a process in which a third person, a mediator, helps those in conflict find a solution*. A mediator can be an adult or a student. With the help of a mediator, most people discover creative ways to solve problems. **Figure 7.2** details the steps in the mediation process.

Connect To... Language Arts

Word Parts

The words *constructive* and *destructive* are opposites. Yet both words share the common root *struct-,* meaning "build." The difference between the two lies in the prefixes *con-* and *de-*. The first word part, con-, means "with or together." The second part, de-, means "away from."

Looking at the root and these prefixes, which word is considered positive and which word is negative? How are these words used to describe criticism? Which type of criticism achieves the best outcome?

A key element to successful mediation is cooperation. Each party must be willing to work with the other and the mediator. **How does a mediator help people in conflict find a solution?**

Steps in the Mediation Process

1. The parties involved in the conflict agree to seek an independent mediator's help.

2. The mediator hears both sides of the dispute.

3. The mediator and the parties work to clarify the wants and needs of each party.

4. The parties and mediator brainstorm possible solutions.

5. The parties and mediator evaluate each possible outcome.

6. The parties choose a solution that works for each of them.

The Mediation Process

The mediation process begins in a private location. The only people present are the mediator and the two parties with the problem. Each party presents his or her side. The mediator, who is neutral, listens carefully. The mediator may ask questions to make sure each side understands the other's point of view. Finally, the mediator will steer both sides toward a **compromise.** This is *an arrangement in which each side gives up something to reach a satisfactory solution.*

Effective mediators must be good communicators. They must have good listening skills, enabling them to hear each side of an argument. They must also be fair and neutral judges. Finally, good mediators need to be effective problem solvers. They need to be able to get to the root of the conflict.

Peer Mediation

Do you think you have what it takes to be a good mediator? If you do, you may want to find out if your school has a peer-mediation program. Many schools today do. Teens are often good mediators because they can put problems into words that other students understand. **Figure 7.3** shows some other traits of an effective peer mediator. Which of these traits do you have?

Students who want to be peer mediators need to go through a training program. This is done on the students' own time and is voluntary. Ask your teacher or school counselor if your school has a peer-mediation program.

Health Online

Visit health.glencoe.com and complete the Interactive Study Guide for Lesson 3.

Reading Check **Identify** What are two skills shared by effective mediators?

TRAITS OF AN EFFECTIVE PEER MEDIATOR

One trait of an effective peer mediator is good listening skills. Why do you think it is important for a peer mediator to have many of these traits?

Problem Solver
Easy to Talk to
Enthusiastic
Responsible

Mature
Effective Listener
Decisive
Interested
Alert
Trustworthy
Open-minded
Reliable

Lesson 3 Review

After You Read

Review this lesson for new terms, major headings, and Reading Checks.

What I Learned

1. **Vocabulary** What is *compromise*? How is it used in conflict resolution?

2. **Recall** What are the four steps in the T.A.L.K. strategy?

3. **Identify** Name a skill or value that an effective mediator has.

Thinking Critically

4. **Apply** Think about an actual conflict you experienced. Then explain how the skill of conflict resolution helped or could have helped you reach a solution.

5. **Evaluate** Can learning peer-mediation skills be useful to teens even if they are not interested in becoming peer mediators? Why or why not?

Applying Health Skills

6. **Communication Skills** Imagine a situation in which younger students are involved in a conflict. With several classmates, role-play how peer mediators might interact with the students involved.

Building Health Skills

TALKing Out a Problem

DIRECTIONS

Conflict Resolution involves finding a peaceful solution to a disagreement or preventing it from becoming a larger conflict. This activity will give you the opportunity to develop and master this important health skill. Here's a guide to the different parts of this activity:

❶ In the **Model** section, you will read about a teen who performs the health skill successfully. This "model" scenario will show you how the skill is done.

❷ The **Practice** section will help guide you in practicing the skill.

❸ In the **Apply** section, you will have a chance to perform the skill on your own. You can use the Self-Check to check your work.

To complete this activity, first read the scenario presented in the Model. Then move on to the Practice. Finally, go ahead and try the Apply.

❶ Model

Mary and Ally were having trouble working together on a class project. The girls decided to use the T.A.L.K. strategy to help find a solution.

Mary: Let's take a break for a minute and then try to work out a plan.

> *T—Take a time-out.*

Ally: I feel like you want to decide who does what part without considering my thoughts.

> *A—Allow each person to tell his or her side uninterrupted.*

Mary: I'm sorry. What part of the project would you like to do?

> *L—Let each person ask questions.*

Ally: Since it is hard for me to get to the library, how about if you do the library research and I do research on the Internet at home.

> *K—Keep brainstorming to find a good solution.*

Mary: That sounds good! Then we can both write parts of the paper and combine our work into a finished project.

❷ Practice

Mary used the T.A.L.K. strategy a week later at home. Mary and her brother are having a disagreement over whose turn it is to wash after-dinner dishes. Mary had taken her brother's turn the week before so that he could make soccer practice. Now it is her brother's turn to do the dishes but he claims not to recall this agreement.

Write a conversation between Mary and her brother in which they use the T.A.L.K. strategy. Label each step with a T., A., L., or K. Write an end to the conversation where Mary and her brother find an agreeable solution.

Skill Summary
CONFLICT RESOLUTION

The T.A.L.K. strategy for resolving conflicts has several steps:

- *Take a time-out.*
- *Allow each person to tell his or her side.*
- *Let each person ask questions.*
- *Keep brainstorming.*

❸ Apply

Imagine that you are dealing with one of the conflicts in the box below. Write out the steps in the T.A.L.K. strategy as you would use them to resolve this conflict. Identify the specific steps you would take to do your part to find a win-win solution. Share your strategy with classmates.

- You and a friend each want to see a different movie. Neither one of you is willing to compromise.
- Your backpack is missing from your locker. Several days later you see a student wearing an identical backpack.

Self-Check

- Did I use each step in the T.A.L.K. strategy?
- Did I show what I would do to reach a win-win solution?

Bad behavior is increasing at sporting events—and both fans and players are crying "foul."

UNNECESSARY ROUGHNESS

Nine fans were injured in a fight between National Basketball Association (NBA) players and fans in Auburn Hills, Michigan. In Philadelphia, crowds frustrated by the team's awful play booed Santa Claus during a half-time show. Behavior at some Philadelphia Eagles' football games got so bad that officials set up a court in the stadium—with a jail—to handle the worst offenders.

WHO'S TO BLAME?

How did fan behavior become so horrible? University of Pennsylvania professor Ken Shropshire thinks the change in the way fans relate to their teams is fueled by everything from close-up TV coverage to video games. "With the realistic, violent sports video games and the pervasiveness of sports on television, fans feel they're actually part of things now," he says. "All the major sports convey that fans are right in the middle. So they feel they should be part of the game."

Games aren't mere athletic contests. They are in-your-face productions. Laser-light-show introductions and scoreboard messages calling for more noise contribute to an atmosphere of confrontation.

"There is no question that the anger in the voice of a small percentage of fans has escalated," says Tom Gamboa, first-base coach for Kansas City Royals. "I have no idea when this started, but there are some people now, when they pay for a sports event, instead of watching it, they feel like they're entitled to take part in it."

REMEMBER: IT'S JUST A GAME

The bad behavior isn't limited to pro sports either. Many colleges take pride in their lack of hospitality for visiting teams. Players shooting free throws at basketball games used to be given respectful silence. Now fans attempt to distract them by jeering and waving towels.

At Duke University, a group called the Cameron Crazies specializes in personal

taunts that often cross the line. They once dangled chicken nuggets near an overweight visiting player. Many argue that the Crazies are just having fun.

That visiting player might have a different opinion.

© Grant Halverson/AP

Reading Review

Lesson 1 The Nature of Conflict

Key Ideas

- Conflicts can be minor or major, interpersonal or internal.

- Conflicts with parents or guardians can be over limits, responsibilities, or expectations. Conflicts between siblings can involve property or space, or can take the form of competition or rivalry.

- Conflicts at school can be over an incident or differences in personality, beliefs, or opinions.

Vocabulary

- conflict (p. 154)
- bully (p. 157)
- labeling (p. 158)
- prejudice (p. 158)

Lesson 2 Preventing Conflicts

Key Ideas

- Factors that cause conflicts to build include anger, jealousy, group pressure, and the use of alcohol and other drugs.

- Ways to prevent conflicts from building include learning to understand your feelings; keeping your conflicts private; avoiding alcohol or other drugs; showing respect for yourself and for others; accepting people who are different from you; and trying to put yourself in another person's situation.

Vocabulary

- escalate (p. 159)
- revenge (p. 161)
- mob mentality (p. 162)

Lesson 3 Resolving Conflicts

Key Ideas

- Effective skills for resolving conflicts include the T.A.L.K. strategy. The letters stand for _T_ime-out, _A_llow each person to tell his or her side, _L_et each person ask questions, and _K_eep brainstorming.

- Compromise is important in conflict resolution because it helps achieve a win-win solution.

- Traits of a good mediator include conflict-resolution skills, good communication skills, fairness, and an ability to help solve problems.

Vocabulary

- conflict resolution (p. 164)
- win-win solution (p. 165)
- mediation (p. 165)
- compromise (p. 166)

After You Read

HEALTH INVENTORY

Now that you have read the chapter, look back at your answers to the Health Inventory in the chapter opener. Is there anything that you should do differently?

Reviewing Vocabulary and Main Ideas

On a sheet of paper, write the numbers 1–6. After each number, write the term from the list that best completes each sentence.

- bully
- conflict
- conflict resolution
- escalate
- labeling
- mob mentality
- prejudice
- revenge

Lesson 1 The Nature of Conflict

1. A(n) _____ is a disagreement between people with opposing viewpoints, ideas, or goals.

2. _____ is a negative and unjustly formed opinion, usually against people of a different racial, religious, or cultural group.

3. A(n) _____ is someone who picks on individuals who are smaller or weaker.

Lesson 2 Preventing Conflict

4. A conflict that becomes more serious is said to _____ .

5. _____ is punishment, injury, or insult to the person seen as the cause of the strong emotion.

6. People who act or behave in a certain and often negative manner because others are doing it have a _____ .

Lesson 3 Resolving Conflict

*On a sheet of paper, write the numbers 7–10. Write **True** or **False** for each statement below. If the statement is false, change the underlined word or phrase to make it true.*

7. The *T* in the T.A.L.K. strategy stands for <u>Tell the other person to cooperate.</u>

8. When a conflict is resolved to the satisfaction of both parties, a <u>win-lose</u> solution has been achieved.

9. <u>Mediation</u> can help two people unable to reach a compromise on their own.

10. An arrangement in which each side gives up something to reach a satisfactory solution is known as <u>resolution.</u>

Thinking Critically

Using complete sentences, answer the following questions on a sheet of paper.

11. **Synthesize** Zoey recently moved from a different part of the country. She speaks with an accent that is different than the students in her new school. Kathy, a girl in class, imitates Zoey's accent, teasing her whenever she speaks. Kathy's teasing really bothers Zoey. What should she do?

Health Online Visit **health.glencoe.com** and take the Online Quiz for Chapter 7.

12. **Evaluate** Which step in the peer mediation process do you think would be the most challenging? Explain your answer.

Write About It

13. **Decision Making** Think about a difficult decision you have had to make that involved an internal conflict. Explain how you resolved this conflict.

14. **Conflict Resolution** Write a story about an imaginary conflict between two people. Tell how conflict-resolution skills were used to bring about a win-win solution.

Career Corner

Professional Mediator Are you a good listener and able to see both sides of a disagreement? If so, then you may have what it takes to be a professional mediator. These professionals work in corporations, government agencies, and schools, helping people solve problems peacefully. To enter this career, you will need a four-year college degree and training in mediation. If you think this career might match your skills, read more about it in *Career Corner* at **health.glencoe.com**.

Standardized Test Practice

Reading

The following are observations made by famous people about conflict. Read the quotes, and then answer the questions.

A. Conflict is inevitable, but combat is optional.
—Max Lucado

B. Whenever you're in conflict with someone, there is one factor that can make the difference between damaging your relationship and deepening it. That factor is attitude.
—William James

C. A good manager doesn't try to eliminate conflict; he tries to keep it from wasting the energies of his people.
—Robert Townsend

D. You can't shake hands with a clenched fist.
—Indira Gandhi

E. Don't be afraid of conflict. Remember, a kite rises against, not with, the wind.
—Hamilton Mabie

TEST-TAKING TIP

When reading, make sure you understand all words and phrases. If you are not sure of a meaning, look the word up in a good dictionary.

1. The two quotes that suggest conflict is a fact of life are
   A. A and B.
   B. B and C.
   C. A and C.
   D. D and E.

2. Which two quotes carry the message that "violence never solves a problem"?
   A. The quotes by Max Lucado and Robert Townsend
   B. The quotes by William James and Hamilton Mabie
   C. The quotes by Robert Townsend and Indira Gandhi
   D. The quotes by Max Lucado and Indira Gandhi

Stop
Violence
in Our
Community!

Chapter Preview

▲ **Working With the Photo**

Preventing violence improves the quality of life for everyone in a community. **Does your school protect members of the school community?**

Violenc

Start-Up Activities

Before You Read

What do you know about violence and abuse? Take the short quiz on this page. Keep a record of your answers.

HEALTH QUIZ Answer *true* or *false* for each of the following statements:

1. Violent gangs are found only in large cities.
2. Victims of violence can suffer emotional and physical injuries.
3. There are no effective ways to deal with bullies.
4. The term *abuse* refers only to physical violence.
5. When abuse occurs in a family, all members may be affected.

ANSWERS: 1. False; 2. True; 3. False; 4. False; 5. True

FOLDABLES™ Study Organizer

As You Read

Make this Foldable™ to record what you learn about violence prevention at home and away from home. Begin with a sheet of 11″ × 17″ paper.

1 Fold the short sides of the sheet of paper inward so they meet at the middle.

2 Label the Foldable™ with the title "Violence Prevention" in bold letters along the upper edge. On one of the front sides of the Foldable™, write "Home." On the other front side, write "Away from Home."

3 Under the appropriate tabs, list ways you can reduce your risk of becoming a victim of violence both at home and away from home.

Health Online Visit **health.glencoe.com** and play the Chapter 8 crossword puzzle game.

Avoiding and Preventing Violence

Guide to Reading

Quick Write

Write about what you think is most responsible for school violence and why.

The Many Faces of Violence

On most days, the front page of any major newspaper will carry at least one story involving violence. **Violence** is *any behavior that causes physical or psychological harm to a person or damage to property.* Violence can take the form of words as well as actions. Threatening another person with physical harm is considered violence. So is defacing or destroying public or private property. Homicide is violence at its worst. **Homicide** is *the killing of one human being by another.*

Violence involving teens is on the rise. According to the National Center for Juvenile Justice, the number of 10- to 17-year-olds arrested for violent crimes more than doubled in the last decade. The number of teen homicides more than tripled. The study also found that teens are more likely to encounter violence than any other age group.

◀ Cleaning up graffiti is an ongoing challenge in many cities. **What do you think could be done about this problem?**

Factors in Teen Violence

Why are more and more young people becoming involved in violence? One factor that appears to have a strong influence on this trend is the media. Statistics show that by age 18, a child will have witnessed as many as 200,000 acts of violence on television. Movies and popular music often portray violence as acceptable. Many researchers see a connection between these messages and the rise in teen crime. Other factors in teen violence include the influence of gangs, and the availability of weapons and drugs in the person's environment.

Gangs, Weapons, and Drugs: A Vicious Cycle

At one time the word *gang* referred to a group of loyal friends. Today, a **gang** is *a group whose members often use violence or take part in criminal activity.* While gangs are most often found in cities, they also form elsewhere.

Gangs contribute to violence on the streets and in schools. Their violence frequently leads to the injury and death of innocent people. Gang members may carry weapons and sell drugs. In fact, gang members are 50 percent more likely to carry guns than any other youth group. Most gangs that have guns buy them illegally, often with money made through **drug trafficking**—*the buying or selling of drugs.* Drug trafficking is a serious crime.

Weapons

Gang members are not the only ones carrying weapons. In a nationwide survey, 17 percent of students reported carrying a gun, knife, or other weapon on one or more days the previous month before the survey. In 2001, 5,486 young people were murdered. Seventy-nine percent of these deaths occurred as a result of gunshot wounds. If you carry a gun, you are twice as likely to be injured by gun violence. You also increase your risk of hurting or killing an innocent person.

Drugs

Teens who engage in violent behavior are more likely to use drugs. One national survey found that 85 percent of violent teens reported using marijuana. Some 55 percent reported using several illegal drugs. Drugs affect a person's ability to think clearly, show good judgment, and make wise decisions. A person under the influence of a drug is more likely to be involved in violent crime. He or she may commit an act of violence in order to get money to buy drugs.

Reading Check **Explain** What is the relationship between gangs, weapons, and drugs?

School Violence

Most schools are safe places. Every year, however, three million young people in the United States become victims of crime at school. Two-thirds of these incidents are violent. Many schools have responded to this problem by adopting a **zero tolerance policy.** This is *a policy that makes no exceptions for anybody for any reason.* In schools with zero tolerance policies, any student who brings a weapon to school is expelled. Students who take part in any violent act are also expelled.

Many schools have taken other measures to improve safety and reduce violence. These actions include limiting entry to a single door, and keeping all others locked. Many schools have also begun performing random searches of lockers and backpacks. Still others have added metal detectors at entrances to prevent students from bringing weapons into their schools.

Protecting Yourself from Violence

You can reduce your risk of becoming a victim of violence by avoiding unsafe situations. Be alert to what is going on around you and trust your instincts. If a situation feels unsafe, it probably is. **Figure 8.1** lists some additional precautions you can take to protect yourself at home and away from home.

▶ **FIGURE 8.1**

PROTECTING YOURSELF FROM VIOLENCE

These strategies can help you reduce the risk of becoming a victim of violence. **What other strategies could you use to avoid violence, gangs, and weapons?**

At Home
- Lock doors and windows when you are home alone.
- Open the door only to people you know well.
- Do not give personal information over the telephone or computer.
- Never tell a stranger that you are home alone. Say your parents are busy and can't come to the phone.
- Never agree to meet with a person you met online.
- When you come home, have your key ready before you reach the door.
- Never shoot a gun or pick it up, even if it is unloaded.
- If someone comes to the door or window and you feel you are in danger, call 911.

Away from Home
- Walk in pairs or in a group. Stay in familiar neighborhoods.
- Tell your family where you are going and what time you will be home.
- If you think someone is following you, go into a store or other public place.
- Never hitchhike or accept a ride from strangers.
- If a stranger stops his or her car to ask you for help or directions, walk or run the other direction. Do not get close to the car.
- Don't look like an easy target. Stand tall and walk confidently.
- Never carry your wallet, purse, or backpack in a way that is easy for others to grab.
- If someone wants your money or possessions, give them up.
- If someone tries to grab you, scream and run away.

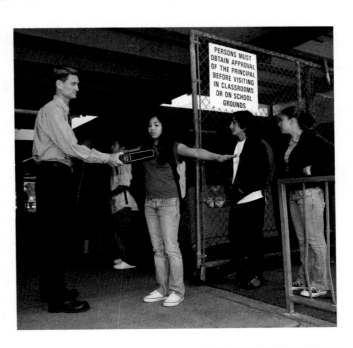

▶ Many schools today are stepping up measures to prevent acts of violence. **What steps have officials in your school taken to make you feel safer?**

Preventing Violence

You can do your part to help stop the spread of violence. Develop your own personal zero tolerance policy regarding violence. Make a pact with yourself never to fight with or threaten others. Encourage others to resolve conflicts peacefully. Be a role model for nonviolence. Encourage your family to become a member of your Neighborhood Watch program. If you see or hear anything that may lead to violence, talk to a trusted adult right away.

Reading Check

Recall What can you do to help stop the spread of violence?

Health *Online*

Visit **health.glencoe.com** and complete the Interactive Study Guide for Lesson 1.

Lesson 1 Review

After You Read

Review this lesson for new terms, major headings, and Reading Checks.

What I Learned

1. *Vocabulary* What is *violence*? Use the word in an original sentence.

2. *List* Name three factors that contribute to teen violence.

3. *Recall* What steps are schools taking to help prevent the spread of violence?

Thinking Critically

4. *Evaluate* Greg has been studying at a friend's house until after dark. He is uncomfortable walking home alone after dark. What could Greg do?

5. *Analyze* Some people feel that school searches violate a person's right to privacy. How might you respond to this argument?

Applying Health Skills

6. *Conflict Resolution* Some violent acts happen because conflicts are allowed to escalate. With a partner, develop a story about two teens in conflict. Show how the teens use the T.A.L.K. strategy of conflict resolution to peacefully resolve their differences.

Dealing with Violence

Guide to Reading

Building Vocabulary

As you read this lesson, write each new highlighted term and its definition in your notebook.

- victim (p. 180)
- assault (p. 181)
- battery (p. 181)
- rape (p. 181)

Focusing on the Main Ideas

In this lesson, you will learn to

- **identify** several types of violent crimes.
- **describe** actions that victims of violence need to take.
- **advocate** for the prevention of violence in America.

Reading Strategy

Predicting Look at the main headings, figures, and captions before you read this lesson. Predict the kinds of information you think you might learn.

*Q*uick Write

Find and write a summary of a news story about someone victimized by crime or violence.

Effects of Violence on Victims

Did you know teens are twice as likely as adults to be victims of violent crime? A **victim** is *any individual who suffers injury, loss, or death due to violence.* Victims who survive violent attacks are affected in different ways. In addition to the physical injuries that can result from violence, a victim's emotional injuries can be even more painful and long-lasting. Victims of any kind of violence should seek help to deal with the effects. Talking with a trusted adult or a mental health professional can lessen some of the pain. With help, victims of violence can recover.

► A school counselor can be one source of help for victims of violence. **What are some other sources of help for victims?**

Assault and Battery

Two violent crimes that often go hand in hand are assault and battery. **Assault** is *an unlawful threat or attempt to do bodily injury to another person.* Assault can be with a weapon or with bare hands. **Battery** is *the unlawful beating, hitting, or kicking of another person.* Often people who threaten to assault go on to batter, or beat, their victims. Assault and battery can occur anywhere, and anyone can be victimized.

One category of battery victims is people injured by domestic abuse. This crime involves beating or doing other physical harm to a family member. Women and children are the most common targets of domestic abuse. Anyone who is a victim of domestic abuse needs to get outside help right away.

Reading Check **Compare** What is the difference between assault and battery?

Rape

Rape is *any kind of sexual intercourse with a person against her or his will.* Most rape victims are female; however, males can also be victims.

In most rape cases involving teens, the attacker and victim know each other. Sometimes the person who commits the rape is a peer whom the victim has dated or is dating. No matter what the circumstances are, rape is always a crime and is *never* the victim's fault.

The best way to avoid becoming a rape victim is to avoid situations that might lead to attack. Stay with a group of peers when you go places. Avoid walking alone, especially at night. Avoid going anywhere with a date where there are no other people around. Instead, go on group dates with other couples and stay in public places. Do not let anyone touch you in a way that makes you feel uncomfortable. Remember, it is your right to say no and to have control over your own body. No one should be forced to engage in sexual activity against his or her will.

Reading Check **Recall** Who can become a victim of rape?

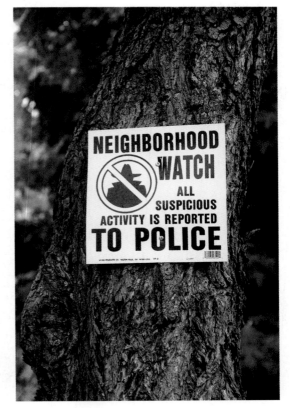

▶ Many communities work together with law enforcement to make their neighborhoods safer. **What is being done in your community?**

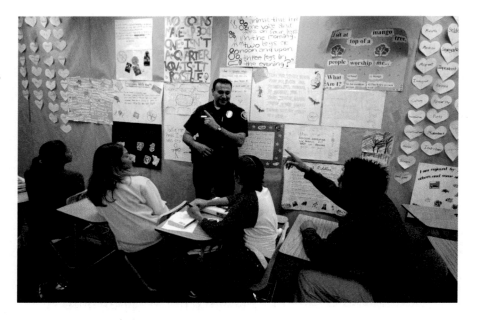

One way to help defeat violence is through education. **What can you do to advocate for an end to violence?**

Getting Help

One of the worst things a victim can do after an attack is nothing. Unfortunately, that is exactly what most people do, especially victims of rape. A report by the National Institute of Justice estimates that 95 percent of all rapes go unreported. Perhaps the biggest reason why this number is so high is that many rape victims feel ashamed or embarrassed. They somehow feel that they are partly or totally to blame for the attack.

If you are a victim of violent crime, you need to take three important actions. The first is to get medical attention. Sometimes victims of crime have been injured and are not even aware of it. Many are in a state of shock, which can temporarily block out pain.

The second action you need to take is to report the incident to the police. This is especially important in the event of rape. Making a report can be difficult, but it is a necessary step. Revealing the incident to the police can help them bring the person responsible to justice. It can also be a step toward preventing that person from harming others.

Third, seek out treatment for the emotional effects of what you have been through. Being a victim of violence is a traumatic experience for most people. It has long-term emotional effects that can interfere with normal life. Victims may have flashbacks and nightmares. They may also have trouble forming relationships. Counseling can help most victims recover from the experience and move on with their lives.

Reading Check **Recall** What is the first action that a victim of violence needs to take?

Helping Defeat Violence

Violence has lasting effects on both the victims and their families. Violent crime affects society as well, costing American taxpayers $675 billion each year.

Both the government and private organizations work to help reduce and prevent youth violence. You can also help stamp out the epidemic of violence. Here are some ways:

- Anytime you witness an act of violence, report what you have seen. Talk to a trusted adult first. He or she will take the necessary steps to involve law enforcement.

- Become an advocate for safety and victims' rights. One is the Youth Outreach for Victim Assistance (YOVA) program. Sponsored by the National Center for Victims of Crime, this youth-adult partnership educates teens about what victims go through. It also tells young people where they can go for help if they are victimized.

Health Online

Visit **health.glencoe.com** and complete the Interactive Study Guide for Lesson 2.

Reading Check **Identify** Who does violence affect?

Lesson 2 Review

After You Read

Review this lesson for new terms, major headings, and Reading Checks.

What I Learned

1. **Vocabulary** Define the term *assault*.

2. **List** Name two ways a person can avoid becoming a victim of rape.

3. **Identify** What are three actions a victim of violence should take?

4. **Recall** How can you personally help stamp out violence?

Thinking Critically

5. **Explain** Why is it important to tell someone if you are a victim of violence?

6. **Apply** Jacob and Tom are walking home from a movie when some older teens grab and shove them. After the incident has ended, Tom says he wants to forget about it and just go home. As Tom speaks, his voice is shaking. What might you say to your friend if you were in Jacob's place?

Applying Health Skills

7. **Advocacy** Find out about programs in your community that work to prevent violence. How can students get involved? Report your findings in the form of a chart.

Bullying and Harassment

Guide to Reading

● Building Vocabulary
Each of the terms below is an act of wrong-doing. Define each as best you can. Be prepared to change or correct your definitions as you read the lesson.

- intimidation (p. 185)
- harassment (p. 186)
- gender discrimination (p. 186)

● Focusing on the Main Ideas
In this lesson, you will learn to

- **describe** ways of dealing with bullies.
- **identify** different forms of harassment.
- **develop** effective communication skills to deal with harassment.

● Reading Strategy
Finding the Main Idea For each of the main headings in this lesson, write one sentence that states the main idea.

Q *uick Write*

Write a poem or short story involving a bully. Give your poem or story a positive ending.

Bullying

Vic was waiting patiently in line at school. It was a hot day and he wished the line would move faster. Just then he felt someone push him, almost causing him to fall over. Vic turned and saw Tony and three of his buddies. "Out of the way, loser," Tony said as the four cut in front of Vic. Tony glared at Vic and then grinned at his friends. They all started laughing. Vic felt an immediate urge to push back, but he noticed that a teacher was walking toward him. He was glad that the teacher intervened.

▶ Most students have been bullied at one time or another. **What actions can you take if you are confronted by a bully?**

Dealing with a Bully

Have you ever been bullied? If so, you are not alone. Three out of every four students have been bullied at one time or another. Bullying is reported to be the most severe in grades 7 through 9. Dealing with bullies can be a source of frustration and fear.

Bullies often taunt people who are shy or stand out in some way. Bullies can be male or female. Male bullies often use threats of physical violence. Female bullies often use verbal put-downs that hurt other people's feelings. Sometimes bullying takes the form of **intimidation.** This is *purposely frightening another person through threatening words, looks, or body language.*

People who are victims of bullying can feel helpless. They may believe there is nothing they can do to change the situation. Their self-esteem may suffer as a result of repeated put-downs. Although the victim is seldom aware of it, bullies have low self-esteem, too. Many bullies have been bullied by peers themselves. They usually pick on others to make themselves feel better. Also, bullies almost always have an audience that supports his or her actions.

If you are being bullied, try to ignore the person and, if possible, just walk away. If the bully refuses to be ignored, walk away anyway. If the bully blocks you, try to remain calm. Be forceful without being physical. Stand up for yourself. Whatever happens, it is important to report the incident to a person in authority. At school, let a teacher, counselor, or other trusted adult know what is going on. No one should have to put up with bullying. All students have a right to learn in a safe environment.

Health *Online*

Topic: Stopping the Bullies

Visit **health.glencoe.com** for Student Web Activities to learn about bullying and what can be done to stop it.

Activity: Using the information provided at the link above, create a "Bully Bookmark" with tips for what to do if you are bullied on one side, and tips for what to do if you see someone else bullied on the other.

Reading Check **Define** What is *intimidation*? How should a person react if he or she feels intimidated?

◀ Making fun of others is a form of bullying. **How might this behavior affect a person's self-esteem?**

Health Skills Activity

Communication Skills

Using "I" Messages

Sometimes the person making ethnic jokes or inappropriate remarks may be a friend of yours. He or she may not realize that you find this conduct offensive. When a friend behaves in a way that offends you, you need to let her or him know that you are offended by these actions. At the same time, you may not want to jeopardize the friendship or create a conflict. You can express your feelings in a positive way by using "I" statements instead of "you" statements. Here are a few examples of "you" statements that can be substituted with "I" statements.

Instead of "You" Statements...	...Use "I" Statements
✗ You're being offensive.	✔ I am offended by what you are saying.
✗ You're embarrassing me.	✔ I feel embarrassed.
✗ You aren't being funny.	✔ I don't think that is funny.

With a Partner

Both you and your partner should each write three "you" statements. Trade papers and change the "you" statements to "I" statements.

Harassment

Joking can be fun, not to mention a sign of good mental health. However, a joke is neither funny nor healthy when it disrespects another person. When this kind of disrespectful behavior happens repeatedly, it is considered **harassment** (huh·RAS·muhnt). This is *ongoing conduct that offends another person by criticizing his or her race, color, religion, physical disability, or gender.* Harassment can take many forms. It can be a spoken or written comment, gesture, or unwanted physical contact.

Harassment that involves obscene behavior or remarks of a sexual nature is labeled *sexual harassment.* Sexual harassment includes unwelcome touching and inappropriate or offensive sexual remarks, or jokes. Sending obscene or inappropriate e-mail, text-messaging, or voice mail can also be a form of sexual harassment. Lesson 4 contains additional information on sexual harassment.

A type of conduct related to sexual harassment is **gender discrimination**—*singling out or excluding a person based on gender.* Gender discrimination can be directed at a male or a female. Either way, gender discrimination is wrong. You should never judge or presume something about a person based on his or her gender.

Dealing with Harassment

"What's the matter—can't you take a joke? You're just too sensitive." Comments like these are often directed at people who are targets of harassment. These remarks can make the victim feel as though he or she deserves the harassment.

No one, however, has to put up with harassment. If you are a target of harassment, here are some strategies for dealing with the problem:

- Tell the person to stop what he or she is doing. Make it clear that this pattern of behavior is hurtful and unacceptable. Explain that if it continues, you will report the harassment.

- Use an assertive communication style. Speak in a firm but positive voice with your head and shoulders up.

- Look the person in the eye as you speak.

- Let your family know what is happening and seek their advice. Get help if you need it and do not allow the behavior to continue.

- If the harassment continues, tell a trusted adult. Charges can then be filed against the peer. If the harassment takes place at school, tell a teacher or a school administrator.

Health Online

Visit **health.glencoe.com** and complete the Interactive Study Guide for Lesson 3.

Lesson 3 Review

After You Read

Review this lesson for new terms, major headings, and Reading Checks.

What I Learned

1. **Vocabulary** What is *gender discrimination*?

2. **List** Name two ways of dealing with bullies.

3. **Recall** What are some forms harassment can take?

Thinking Critically

4. **Analyze** Shelby is being teased repeatedly by Matt. His sexual remarks bother her. She doesn't know what to do. What advice would you have for Shelby?

5. **Apply** Your cousin writes to tell you about a "really funny kid" who just came to his school. He explains that this new person gets a laugh by knocking other students' books out of their hands. How would you explain to your cousin that the action is inappropriate behavior?

Applying Health Skills

6. **Accessing Information** Harassment is considered a hate crime in 46 of the 50 states. Find out what the laws are in your community regarding harassment. Make a poster explaining the penalties for this behavior.

Abuse

Guide to Reading

Building Vocabulary
As you read this lesson, write each new highlighted term and its definition in your notebook.

- abuse (p. 188)
- domestic violence (p. 189)
- neglect (p. 190)
- sexual abuse (p. 190)
- sexual harassment (p. 191)

Focusing on the Main Ideas
In this lesson, you will learn to

- **explain** different forms of abuse.
- **describe** the effects of abuse on its victims.

Reading Strategy
Classifying Make a chart identifying the four types of abuse. For each type, identify what action a victim of abuse can take.

Quick Write

Write a paragraph describing problems that might affect a relationship. Identify healthy ways of dealing with such problems.

What Is Abuse?

Every close relationship has its ups and downs, its good days and bad days. When the relationship is healthy, the people involved care for and respect each other.

When a relationship is unhealthy or unbalanced, difficulties that arise can become worse. In some cases, abuse may occur. **Abuse** is *the physical, emotional, or mental mistreatment of one person by another.*

Abuse is a problem that affects people of all ages, skin colors, and economic groups. Any type of abuse is a crime. It is damaging to everyone involved and is never the victim's fault.

Reading Check **Define** What is *abuse*?

◄ Abuse can affect the physical, social, and mental/emotional health of the victim. **What are some types of abuse?**

Kinds of Abuse

Abuse takes place mostly in close relationships, often between people who are related by blood or marriage. Parents or guardians may abuse their children or each other. Abuse may also occur between siblings or other family members. Many abusers try to make their victims feel as if they deserve to be treated harshly. Abuse is not an acceptable form of discipline. No one ever deserves to be abused.

Physical Abuse

The most common type of abuse is **domestic violence,** *physical abuse that occurs within a family.* The term *domestic* refers to the home or family setting, which is where most abuse occurs. Domestic violence is about power and control. The abuser seeks to establish and maintain authority over the family or a family member. Half of all reported abuse cases involve domestic violence.

Physical abuse ranges from pushing and slapping to punching and choking. Sometimes a household item may be used as a weapon. When the victim is a small child, the abuser often makes up excuses for the child's injuries. For example, the abuser may claim that the child fell down. Adults who are physically abused sometimes make excuses for their own injuries. Victims may also make excuses for the abuser. This type of behavior, which is called *enabling,* establishes a pattern of abuse.

Emotional Abuse

While physical abuse can leave visible signs, emotional abuse is harder to spot. The effects, however, can be just as severe and last longer than bruises. Emotional abuse uses words or gestures to mistreat another person. It may include yelling, bullying, teasing, or threats of violence. All share the same intent, which is to make the victim feel stupid, worthless, or helpless.

Neglect

People need basic necessities such as food, clothing, a place to live, and medical care. In addition, they have emotional needs, such as the need for love and nurturing. Children rely on their parents and guardians to meet those needs.

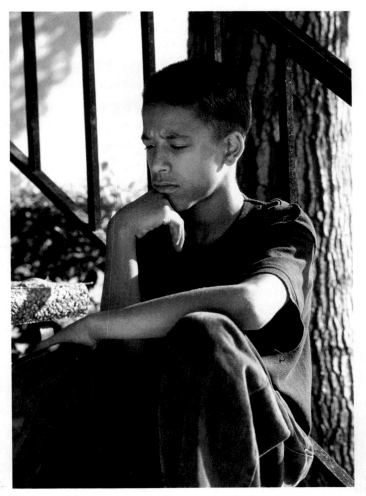

▼ Emotional abuse can make a person feel isolated or unwanted. **How could you reach out to a person who needs help?**

When parents or guardians do not meet their children's basic needs, they are guilty of the crime of neglect. **Neglect** is *the failure to meet a person's basic physical and emotional needs.* Children are the most common targets of neglect, but elderly people and people with disabilities may also suffer neglect. More than two million cases of child abuse and neglect are reported every year in the United States. Abuse and neglect can have long-lasting effects on a child. **Figure 8.2** lists some of the physical, mental/emotional, and social effects.

Reading Check **Identify** Who are typical targets of neglect?

Sexual Abuse

Sexual abuse occurs when *a person forces another person to participate in a sexual act against his or her will.* According to one estimate, 150,000 to 200,000 new cases of sexual abuse occur each year. Often the targets of sexual abuse are children, and the abuser is an adult in the household or a relative or friend of the family. People who commit the crime of sexual abuse do not always use physical force. They may use bribes, trickery, or other means to persuade a child to perform sexual acts. All sexual abuse is illegal and damaging.

▶ **FIGURE 8.2**

CHILD ABUSE AND NEGLECT

The effects of child abuse and neglect can appear on all three sides of the health triangle. **What are some mental/ emotional effects?**

Long-Term Consequences of Child Abuse and Neglect

Physical Health Consequences
- Impaired brain development
- Impaired physical, mental, and emotional development
- A "hyper-arousal" response by certain areas of the brain, which may result in hyperactivity, and sleep disturbances
- Poor physical health, including various illnesses

Mental/Emotional Health Consequences
- Increased risk for emotional problems such as depression, panic disorder, and post-traumatic stress disorder
- Alcohol and drug abuse
- Difficulty with language development and academic achievement
- Suicide

Social Health Consequences
- Difficulty forming secure relationships
- Difficulties during adolescence
- Criminal and/or violent behavior
- Abusive behavior

A kind of sexual abuse that may happen at school is **sexual harassment** which is *uninvited and unwelcome sexual conduct directed at another person.* As mentioned in the previous lesson, sexual harassment includes words, touching, jokes, looks, notes, or gestures with a sexual manner or meaning. This kind of unwelcome and uninvited behavior is illegal and must be reported to school personnel.

Reading Check **Define** What is *sexual abuse?*

Effects of Abuse

Abuse can leave emotional scars that remain long after physical signs have gone away. Victims often blame themselves for what happened. They may be too afraid or ashamed to get the help they need. Children who suffer abuse often have a number of emotional problems, including low self-esteem. These problems may show up in the form of self-destructive behaviors, including attempts at suicide, alcohol and drug abuse, and eating disorders. Some victims of abuse turn to criminal or violent behavior. Many go on to become abusers themselves.

Help exists for victims of abuse. You will learn about available resources in the next lesson.

Health Online

Visit health.glencoe.com and complete the Interactive Study Guide for Lesson 4.

Lesson 4 Review

After You Read

Review this lesson for new terms, major headings, and Reading Checks.

What I Learned

1. **Vocabulary** What is *domestic violence?*

2. **List** Name several forms of abuse.

3. **Identify** What are some ways in which abuse can affect its victims?

Thinking Critically

4. **Evaluate** Respond to the statement "All forms of abuse negatively affect the victim's physical health." Tell whether you agree or disagree, and why.

5. **Analyze** Why do you think it is important for victims of abuse to get help?

Applying Health Skills

6. **Advocacy** With classmates, develop a handbook for identifying and dealing with different types of abuse. In your handbook, define the different types of abuse, and steps to take when dealing with abuse. Also, list trustworthy organizations that can help victims of abuse. Make a copy available to everyone in the class.

Health Online For more review questions for Lesson 4, go to health.glencoe.com.

Lesson 4: Abuse **191**

Preventing and Coping With Abuse

Building Vocabulary
As you read this lesson, be on the lookout for the terms below. Write each term and its definition in your notebook.

- cycle of abuse (p. 193)
- crisis hot line (p. 193)

Focusing on the Main Ideas
In this lesson, you will learn to

- **describe** the cycle of abuse.
- **develop** a plan to stop the cycle of abuse.
- **identify** where to get help if you are abused.

Reading Strategy
Identifying Cause and Effect Explain why a victim of abuse may be unwilling to say anything.

Quick Write

Identify a phenomenon that might be described as a *vicious cycle*. Write a brief description of this phenomenon.

Those Affected by Abuse

Whenever abuse is present in a family, all family members are affected. The effects of abuse are serious and long-lasting. For this reason, all members of the family need help.

Abused spouses are sometimes enablers in domestic violence. By concealing the true cause of their injuries, they help maintain the cycle of violence. They prevent themselves and their abusers from getting the help they need. In this lesson you will learn about where victims of abuse can get help.

▶ Help is available in any community for abuse victims and their families. **Who can students in your school turn to if they need to report an abuse problem?**

The Cycle of Abuse

The cycle of violence in abusive relationships goes beyond domestic partners. In fact, mental-health experts have found that patterns of abuse often go back many generations. Many children who were abused or who witnessed abuse see this behavior as an acceptable model for how to treat people. As adults, they often go on to become abusers themselves. This *pattern of repeating abuse from one generation to the next* is known as the **cycle of abuse.** Breaking this cycle of abuse can be difficult and often requires outside help.

Breaking the Cycle of Abuse

Each of us has the power to break the cycle of abuse. If you suspect that a friend is being abused, it is important to ask your friend about it. If you are still concerned, tell a trusted adult. The first step a victim of abuse should take is to confide in a trusted adult. This can be a parent, another family member, a teacher, a school nurse or counselor, or a doctor. Victims can also call a **crisis hot line,** *a toll-free telephone service where abuse victims can get help and information.* **Figure 8.3** lists some organizations that provide toll-free crisis hot lines for victims of abuse, parents, and other concerned individuals. The people who staff these phone lines have received special training in dealing with abuse problems and helping victims of abuse. The person who calls is not asked to give his or her name. Conversations are kept strictly confidential.

Organization	Whom They Help
Childhelp USA	Child abuse victims, parents, concerned individuals
Youth Crisis Hotline	Individuals reporting child abuse, youth ages 12 to 18
Stop it Now!	Child sexual abuse victims, parents, offenders, concerned individuals
National Domestic Violence Hotline	Children, parents, friends, offenders
Girls and Boys Town	Abused, abandoned, and neglected girls and boys, parents, and family members

NAIC, U.S. Department of Health and Human Services.

◀ **FIGURE 8.3**

CRISIS HOT LINES FOR VICTIMS OF ABUSE

These organizations help victims of abuse by providing hot lines, where victims can talk about the abuse and get advice. Who else do these organizations help?

Ending abuse is not easy. Abused people—especially children—may feel ashamed, especially if the abuse was sexual. They may have fears over what will happen if they tell. They may fear that talking about the abuse will lead to the break-up of their family. They may also have concerns about getting someone in trouble with the law, particularly if the abuser is a family member. Even though these concerns are understandable, the cycle of abuse will not end until someone reports the problem.

Sometimes victims are reluctant to say anything because they promised the abuser to keep the abuse secret. Sometimes abusers threaten their victims to keep them quiet. If you are the victim of abuse or you know someone who is, you need to be aware that keeping it a secret is never a good idea. The only way an abuser will ever stop is by getting help. It is important for you to know that you are not alone. Others have experienced the same thing, and there are people who are willing to help you.

 Reading Check **Identify** Who can victims of abuse turn to for help?

▲ Some families who are living in abusive homes might go to shelters, where they can be safe and get emotional support. **How can you help another teen in need of emotional support?**

Help with Abuse Problems

Most people need professional help to overcome the emotional trauma of abuse. For many, help means counseling—talking through their problems with someone trained to listen. Teens who have been abused sometimes find comfort in group counseling sessions. These sessions give teens an opportunity to discuss their situation with others who have experienced similar problems.

In extreme situations or ones where abuse is ongoing, abused family members may be sent to shelters—community-run residences where victims of abuse can feel safe. They can stay at the shelter while getting help putting their lives back together.

If you suspect that a friend is a victim of abuse, share what you have learned. Strongly urge the person to seek help.

Reading Check **List** Name some sources of help for abuse problems.

Health Online

Visit **health.glencoe.com** and complete the Interactive Study Guide for Lesson 5.

Lesson 5 Review

After You Read

Review this lesson for new terms, major headings, and Reading Checks.

What I Learned

1. **Vocabulary** What is the *cycle of abuse*?

2. **Identify** What is the first step any abuse victim can take to end the cycle of abuse?

3. **List** What are some crisis hot lines for victims of abuse?

Thinking Critically

4. **Apply** Debbie, a victim of family abuse, says she really wants to report the problem but doesn't know who to turn to. What might you tell Debbie that would encourage her to make a healthful choice to call for help?

5. **Analyze** Why might some victims of abuse be reluctant to report the abuse?

6. **Explain** Why do children who are abused sometimes become abusers themselves?

Applying Health Skills

7. **Accessing Information** With a group, learn about specific resources in your community for abused families. Identify what types of resources they are, such as shelters, counseling, or hot lines. Share your findings with other groups.

Building Health Skills

Standing Up to Harassment

DIRECTIONS

Decision Making involves taking steps to make healthy and responsible choices. This activity will give you the opportunity to develop and master this important health skill. Here is a guide to the different parts of this activity.

❶ In the **Model** section, you will read about a teen who performs the health skill successfully. This "model" scenario will show you how the skill is done.

❷ The **Practice** section will help guide you in practicing the skill.

❸ In the **Apply** section, you will have a chance to perform the skill on your own. You can use the Self-Check to check your work.

To complete this activity, first read the scenario presented in the Model. Then move on to the Practice. Finally, go ahead and try the Apply.

❶ Model

Marcus had worked hard to make the football team. Gil, one of his teammates, was continually making fun of him, which really brothered Marcus.

Marcus used the decision-making process to help him decide what to do. Here is how he mapped out his choices:

Step 1: State the Situation: I am being harassed by a member of my team, and I would like it to end.

Step 2: List the Options: I could talk to the coach or directly to Gil. I could also quit the team.

Step 3: Weigh the Possible Outcomes: Talking to the coach would probably help. If I talk to Gil he may get angry. It might also lead to even more teasing.

Step 4: Consider Your Values: I am not a quitter. I worked hard to make the team.

Step 5: Make a Decision and Act: I will tell the coach what the problem is. I know he will be able to help.

Step 6: Evaluate the Decision: The coach talked to both Gil and me and helped us work out the problem.

② Practice

Marcus' friend Carl is being teased by classmates about his clothes. Marcus wants to help Carl put an end to the harassment. Imagine that you are Marcus. Use the decision-making steps to guide you in helping Carl make a good decision.

1. What is Carl's situation?
2. What are some of Carl's options?
3. What are the possible outcomes?
4. Consider what Carl's values might be.
5. What decision does Carl make?

Skill Summary
DECISION MAKING

- State the situation.
- List the options.
- Weigh the possible outcomes.
- Consider your values.
- Make a decision and act.
- Evaluate the decision.

③ Apply

With a small group, brainstorm some other situations a teen might face that involve harassment. Then write a story about the teen and explain the type of harassment he or she is experiencing. Show how decision making is used to end the harassment.

Self-Check

- Did we use each step in the decision-making process?
- Did we include an explanation of the harassment the teen was experiencing?

A Nonviolent Response to a Threatening Situation

When faced with a threatening situation, a common reaction is to want to lash out in anger. When people are pushed, either physically or emotionally, they want to push back. This chapter presents a number of different situations that are threatening, which include harassment, intimidation, abuse, and bullying. When you are faced with a threatening situation, be prepared to respond in a nonviolent way. This activity can help you learn some nonviolent responses.

What You Will Need

- Poster board
- Markers or crayons

What You Will Do

1. Your teacher will divide the class into six small groups and assign each group one of the following threatening behaviors: harassment, intimidation, emotional abuse, and bullying.

2. In your group, brainstorm nonviolent ways of responding to your threatening situation. First, imagine an instance in which the threatening behavior takes place. For example, if your group was assigned the behavior of bullying, think of a situation in which someone your age might be bullied. Discuss how this young person might respond in a nonviolent way.

3. Now, create a colorful poster. On one side of the poster write "The Situation" at the top. Below that, describe the situation your group has come up with. On the other side of the poster write "A Nonviolent Response." Below that write a nonviolent way of responding to the situation.

Wrapping It Up

After all the groups have presented their posters, discuss these questions as a class: How can teens help other teens respond to threatening situations in a nonviolent way? Also, discuss the benefits of responding in a nonviolent way.

Display your posters where your classmates can see them. This will help students learn a variety of nonviolent responses.

Reading Review

Lesson 1 Avoiding and Preventing Violence

Key Idea

- Factors that contribute to teen violence include media influence, gangs, weapons, and drugs.

Vocabulary

- violence (p. 176)
- homicide (p. 176)
- gang (p. 177)
- drug trafficking (p. 177)
- zero tolerance policy (p. 178)

Lesson 2 Dealing with Violence

Key Ideas

- Ways to avoid becoming a victim of rape include going out with a group of peers, avoiding going anywhere with a date where you are alone, and refusing to allow someone to touch you in a way that makes you feel uncomfortable.
- Victims need to get help to recover from the effects of violence.

Vocabulary

- victim (p. 180)
- assault (p. 181)
- battery (p. 181)
- rape (p. 181)

Lesson 3 Bullying and Harassment

Key Idea

- Forms of harassment include bullying, intimidation, teasing, and sexual harassment.

Vocabulary

- intimidation (p. 185)
- harassment (p. 186)
- gender discrimination (p. 186)

Lesson 4 Abuse

Key Idea

- Abuse can take several forms, including physical abuse, emotional abuse, neglect, and sexual abuse.

Vocabulary

- abuse (p. 188)
- domestic violence (p. 189)
- neglect (p. 190)
- sexual abuse (p. 190)
- sexual harassment (p. 191)

Lesson 5 Preventing and Coping with Abuse

Key Ideas

- Victims and abusers need help in order to end the cycle of abuse.
- Ways for abuse victims to get help include talking to a trusted adult, calling a crisis hot line, counseling, and staying in community shelters.

Vocabulary

- cycle of abuse (p. 193)
- crisis hot line (p. 193)

HEALTH QUIZ

Now that you have read the chapter, look back at your answers to the Health Quiz on the chapter opener. Would you change any of them? What would your answers be now?

Reviewing Vocabulary and Main Ideas

On a sheet of paper, write the numbers 1–6. After each number, write the term from the list that best completes each sentence.

- assault
- battery
- gang
- homicide
- rape
- victim
- violence
- zero tolerance policy

Lesson 1 Avoiding and Preventing Violence

1. _____ is any behavior that causes physical or psychological harm to a person or damage to property.

2. The killing of one human being by another is known as _____.

3. _____ is a policy that makes no exceptions for anybody for any reason.

Lesson 2 Dealing with Violence

4. A(n) _____ is any individual who suffers injury, loss, or death due to violence.

5. An unlawful threat or attempt to do bodily injury to another person is known as _____.

6. _____ is any kind of sexual intercourse against a person's will.

On a sheet of paper, write the numbers 7–13. Write **True** *or* **False** *for each statement below. If the statement is false, change the underlined word or phrase to make it true.*

Lesson 3 Bullying and Harassment

7. <u>Intimidation</u> is purposely frightening another person through threatening words, looks, or body language.

8. A repeating pattern of behavior that includes making fun of someone is called <u>violence</u>.

9. When harassment involves obscene behavior or remarks of a sexual nature it is called <u>sexual harassment</u>.

Lesson 4 Abuse

10. The most common type of abuse is <u>zero tolerance</u>.

11. Children, <u>older adults</u>, and people with disabilities all may be targets of neglect.

Lesson 5 Preventing and Coping with Abuse

12. The <u>cycle of abuse</u> is a pattern in which children of abuse go on to become abusers.

13. If abuse is ongoing or violent, family members may go to community-run residences known as <u>crisis hot lines</u>.

Thinking Critically

Using complete sentences, answer the following questions on a sheet of paper.

14. Analyze A teen named Tom lives in a community that has gangs. Tom does not want to join a gang, but he feels that doing so is the only sure way of surviving. What information does Tom need to have that might help him make a healthier decision?

Write About It

15. Analyzing Influences Write a paragraph describing how the media might influence violent behavior.

16. Practicing Healthful Behaviors Create a list of positive health behaviors you will practice to reduce your risk of being a victim of violence.

Standardized Test Practice

Math

The table below contains data about victims of violence for a 10-year period. Use the data to answer the questions that follow.

Violent Victimization Rates by Age, 1994–2003*

Year	12–15	16–19	20–24
1994	118.6	123.9	100.4
1995	113.1	106.6	85.8
1996	95.0	102.8	74.5
1997	87.9	96.3	68.0
1998	82.5	91.3	67.5
1999	74.4	77.5	68.7
2000	60.1	64.4	49.5
2001	55.1	55.9	44.9
2002	44.4	58.3	47.6
2003	51.6	53.1	43.5

*Violent crime per 1,000 persons in age group

TEST-TAKING TIP

When dealing with tables or charts, read the title and examine the information. Make sure you understand what type of data the table or chart contains.

1. The only year in which 20- to 24-year-olds experienced a higher rate of crime than 12- to 15-year-olds was

A. 2002

B. 1996

C. 1998

D. 2003

2. For the years 2000 to 2003, the mean victim rate for 12- to 15-year-olds was

A. 51.6

B. 55.1

C. 56.4

D. 52.8

Physical Activity and Fitness

Chapter Preview

▲ Working With the Photo

Physical activity is one way to build the physical side of your health triangle. **What are some other habits that promote good physical health?**

Start-Up Activities

Before You Read

Look at the Instant Message below. How would you respond to kregmar's answer? Keep a record of your answer.

IM Express

4keeblin: Gotta run. I'm meeting some of the guys over at the park for softball. You interested?

kregmar: Nah, softball isn't really my thing. I have a TV show to watch. I'll catch up with you at school tomorrow.

FOLDABLES™ Study Organizer

As You Read

Make this Foldable™ to help you organize the information on physical activity, exercise, and physical fitness presented in Lesson 1. Begin with a plain sheet of 11" × 17" paper.

1 Fold the sheet of paper in half along the short axis, then fold in half again. This forms four columns.

2 Open the paper and refold it in half along the long axis, then fold in half again. This forms four rows.

3 Unfold and draw lines along the folds.

4 Label the chart as shown.

Chapter 9	Definition	Examples	Impact on my life
Physical Activity			
Exercise			
Physical Fitness			

In the appropriate section of the chart, write down definitions and examples of physical activity, exercise, and physical fitness, as well as the impact each has on your daily life.

Health Online Visit health.glencoe.com and complete the Health Inventory for Chapter 9.

The Benefits of Physical Activity

Guide to Reading

● Building Vocabulary
Write each term below in your notebook and add a definition in pencil. As you read the lesson, be prepared to make corrections to your definitions.

- physical activity (p. 204)
- coordination (p. 205)
- balance (p. 205)
- calories (p. 205)
- physical fitness (p. 206)
- exercise (p. 207)
- aerobic exercise (p. 207)
- anaerobic exercise (p. 208)

● Focusing on the Main Ideas
In this lesson, you will learn to

- **identify** the benefits of physical activity.
- **develop** habits to improve your physical health.
- **describe** various types of physical activities.
- **explain** the importance of exercise to overall fitness.

● Reading Strategy
Predicting Examine the headings, figures, and captions before you read this lesson. Predict what kinds of information you think you will learn.

FOLDABLES Study Organizer Use the Foldable™ on p. 203 as you read this lesson.

ⓠuick Write
Write a short paragraph about the kinds of physical activity you do in a typical day.

Choosing an Active Lifestyle

Connor and Marcus are identical twins. Although they look alike, their interests and health habits are different. When they have a choice between playing basketball or a video game, Connor chooses basketball and Marcus chooses the video game. When there is a choice between taking the stairs or an elevator, Connor walks up. Can you guess which choice Marcus makes?

Which brother are you more like? If you are like Connor, you follow an active lifestyle that includes plenty of physical activity. **Physical activity** is *any form of bodily movement that uses up energy*. Health experts advise teens to get 60 minutes of physical activity on most days. This can be done all at once or divided into 10- or 15-minute bursts of activity.

Reading Check **Identify** How much physical activity is recommended for teens?

Why Is Physical Activity Important?

Like a machine, your body is made up of many moving parts. Staying physically active helps keep those parts in good working order. Physical activity benefits each side of the health triangle:

- **Physical Health:** When you choose to make regular physical activity a part of your life, you create more energy for completing your activities. Physical activity helps your heart and lungs work more efficiently and strengthens your bones. It improves **coordination,** *the smooth and effective working together of your muscles and bones.* It also improves your **balance,** *the feeling of stability and control over your body.* Physical activity during the day helps you sleep better and more soundly at night. It also helps you maintain a healthy weight by burning **calories.** These are *units of heat that measure the energy available in foods.* Physical activity helps "use up" calories that could lead to unwanted extra pounds. **Figure 9.1** shows the calories burned doing various activities for one hour.

- **Mental/Emotional Health:** Physically active people are better able to handle the stress and challenges of everyday life. They also tend to have a higher self-esteem. Being physically active will help you think more clearly and concentrate better in school.

◀ Some forms of physical activity are done in a group. **What are some social benefits of these kinds of activities? How do they benefit your health triangle?**

CALORIES BURNED IN ONE HOUR FOR VARIOUS PHYSICAL ACTIVITIES

Activities that burn the most calories are shown in green. Those that burn the least amount are shown in red. **How does burning calories affect your physical health?**

ACTIVITY	If You Weigh 130 Lbs	If You Weigh 155 Lbs
Backpacking	413	493
Basketball (game)	472	563
Basketball (shooting baskets)	266	317
Bicycling (average effort)	472	563
Bowling	177	211
Canoeing (moderate effort)	413	493
Dancing (general)	266	317
Football, touch	472	563
Frisbee playing (general)	177	211
Frisbee playing (ultimate)	207	246
Golf (general)	236	281
Horseback riding (general)	236	281
House cleaning (general)	207	246
Mowing lawn	325	387
Stair climbing	472	563
Swimming (general)	590	704
Water volleyball	177	211
Weight lifting (moderate)	177	211

- **Social Health:** Whether you are on a team or working out with a partner, physical activity can benefit your social health. Physical activity can help you meet new people with similar interests. It also improves your ability to resolve conflicts effectively and work with others as a team.

Reading Check **Recall** What are two physical and two social benefits of being physically active?

Physical Activity and Fitness

Physical activity is also a key to **physical fitness,** *the ability to handle the physical demands of everyday life without becoming overly tired.* People who are physically fit have enough energy to do the

Health Skills Activity

Practicing Healthful Behaviors

Activity + Eating + Sleeping = Good Physical Health

In a way, physical health can be viewed as a health triangle within a health triangle. The three sides to physical health—physical activity, good eating habits, and adequate rest—are interrelated. Teens who are active during the day tend to get more restful sleep during the night. When you eat the right foods, you give your body the fuel it needs for physical activity. It is important for you to assume responsibility for taking care of your physical health.

On Your Own

Describe your own physical health triangle. If the sides are not balanced, identify which areas need work. Tell what habits you can adopt that will improve your overall physical health. Develop a plan to practice these habits regularly.

things they want to do. They also have a reserve of energy for times when their bodies need it.

People who are physically fit tend to live longer and healthier lives. Later in this chapter, you will learn how to set fitness goals that will help you improve your fitness level.

The Importance of Exercise

Look again at Figure 9.1 on page 206. Several of the activities shown, including weight lifting and stair climbing, are exercises. **Exercise** is *planned physical activity done regularly to build or maintain one's fitness.* Exercise is an important ingredient in an overall fitness plan. The reason is simple: while every physical activity works various muscles, exercise targets specific muscles.

Exercises fall into two basic categories—aerobic and anaerobic—though many exercises have elements of both. Each of these categories serves an important role in physical fitness. **Aerobic exercise** is *rhythmic, nonstop, moderate to vigorous activity that requires large amounts of oxygen.* Aerobic exercise works a very important muscle in your body—your heart. It also benefits the lungs. Stair climbing, swimming, running, biking, and many forms of dancing are examples of aerobic exercise.

▶ Swimming can be a leisure activity, a sport, or an exercise. **Which kind of exercise is swimming?**

Health Online

Visit health.glencoe.com and complete the Interactive Study Guide for Lesson 1.

Anaerobic exercise is *intense physical activity that requires little oxygen but uses short bursts of energy.* Lifting weights, gymnastics, and football are examples of anaerobic exercises. In the next lesson you will learn more about the benefits of aerobic and anaerobic exercise.

Reading Check   **Define** What is *exercise*?

Lesson 1 Review

After You Read

Review this lesson for new terms, major headings, and Reading Checks.

What I Learned

1. *Vocabulary* What is *physical activity*?

2. *Recall* What are some health benefits of becoming and staying physically active?

3. *Identify* What are the two types of exercise? Describe each of them.

Thinking Critically

4. *Evaluate* Evaluate your current physical activity level by noting how many minutes you are active in a typical day. Tell what steps, if any, you need to take to boost your current activity level.

5. *Analyze* Alex would like to become more physically active but only if he can avoid exercising. What advice would you give Alex?

Applying Health Skills

6. *Advocacy* Develop a poster campaign that emphasizes the importance of physical activity. Include ideas for different types of physical activity that would appeal to teens. Get permission to post these in school hallways.

Endurance, Strength, and Flexibility

Guide to Reading

Building Vocabulary
List each term below in your notebook. As you come across it in your reading, write the definition.

- heart and lung endurance (p. 210)
- muscle strength (p. 211)
- muscle endurance (p. 211)
- flexibility (p. 212)
- body composition (p. 213)
- heredity (p. 214)

Focusing on the Main Ideas
In this lesson, you will learn to

- **identify** the four measures of physical fitness.
- **describe** exercises that improve different areas of physical fitness.
- **develop** behaviors that will improve your body composition.

Reading Strategy
Organizing Information
Copy the graphic organizer below onto a sheet of paper. Complete the organizer with information from the lesson.

Measures of Fitness

Quick Write

Write a paragraph describing why you think flexibility is important. What activities do you think can help improve flexibility?

Measures of Fitness

When you feel sick, your parent or guardian may take your temperature. When you go for a medical checkup, the doctor takes your blood pressure. It is also possible to measure a person's level of physical fitness. There are four separate measurements of physical fitness. These are heart and lung endurance, muscle strength and endurance, flexibility, and body composition.

▶ Types of physical activity that can improve heart and lung endurance include running, walking, and cycling. **Why are activities that involve endurance important to the health of your heart and lungs?**

Heart and Lung Endurance

Blood pressure is a measure of how well your heart pumps blood through your body. It is an indicator of heart health. In a way, the same thing can be said about **heart and lung endurance.** This endurance is *a measure of how efficiently your heart and lungs work when you exercise and how quickly they return to normal when you stop.* The word *endure* means "to last." When you have high heart and lung endurance, you can work or play for long periods without running out of "steam." **Figure 9.2** shows a test that measures heart and lung endurance.

If your score is low, do not be discouraged. Heart and lung endurance can be improved. Try doing nonstop moderate to vigorous exercise for at least 20 minutes, three to five times a week. You will notice an improvement after a few weeks.

Activities that build heart and lung endurance include swimming and cycling. Swimming carries the added advantage of providing a total body workout.

Other related exercises that can improve heart and lung endurance are walking, jogging, and running. If you walk, your goal should be 30 minutes at a brisk pace. If you jog or run, aim for at least 20 minutes. If that is difficult, try alternating walking and jogging and slowly work up to 20 minutes of jogging.

Reading Check **Describe** What are some ways of improving heart and lung endurance?

▼ FIGURE 9.2

MEASURING HEART AND LUNG ENDURANCE

This test will help you determine if you need to improve your heart and lung endurance. **Why is heart and lung endurance important?**

1. Work with a partner, taking turns. Using a sturdy bench about 8 inches high, step up in 2 seconds and down in 2 seconds for 3 minutes.

2. Fully extend each leg as you step. Step up with your right foot, then your left. Step down with your right foot first. Stepping should be continuous.

3. Step at the rate of 24 steps per minute for 3 minutes.

4. Find your pulse on the side of your neck. Count the number of pulses you feel for 1 minute.

5. To rate your heart and lung endurance, find your recovery heart rate on the chart. This term refers to how quickly your heart rate returns to normal right after exercise is stopped.

Scoring (number of heartbeats)	Rating
70-100	Acceptable heart and lung endurance
101 or more	Low heart and lung endurance

Muscle Strength and Endurance

The ability of your muscles to exert a force is called strength. **Muscle strength** is *a measure of the most weight you can lift or the most force you can exert at one time*. **Muscle endurance** is *a measure of a muscle's ability to repeatedly exert a force over a prolonged period of time*. Both measures are important to overall fitness.

Figures 9.3 and **9.4** provide two different tests of muscle strength and endurance. Figure 9.3 tests the strength and endurance of the muscles in your mid-section. These muscles make up what fitness experts refer to as your *core*. Core muscles are important to safe lifting as well as balance. Developing a strong, durable core will lessen the risk of injury to your back.

Figure 9.4 tests strength and endurance of the muscles in your upper body. These muscles, which include those of the arms, shoulders, and chest, provide power. Players in contact sports, such as basketball, baseball and football, all work their upper bodies.

Like heart and lung endurance, muscle strength and endurance can be improved. The tests in Figures 9.3 and 9.4 are great strengthening exercises. Others include step-ups, which you practiced in Figure 9.2, and push-ups. Push-ups strengthen muscles in your arms and chest. **Figure 9.5** illustrates a technique for doing push-ups.

▼ FIGURE 9.3

MEASURING ABDOMINAL STRENGTH AND ENDURANCE

Abdominal strength helps reduce the risk of injury to your back. What are some ways to build abdominal strength?

1. Work with a partner, taking turns. Lie on your back with your knees slightly bent. Your partner should hold your feet.
2. With your arms crossed on your chest, curl your upper body forward. Return to the starting position. Your head should never touch the floor.
3. Continue to do curl-ups at the rate of about 20 per minute, stopping when you can no longer continue, or have completed 60 curl-ups.
4. To rate your abdominal strength and endurance, find your score on the chart. The range shown is acceptable for your age and gender. If you do not score with this range, continue working at this exercise until you do.

Age	Female	Male
12	18–32	18–36
13	18–32	21–40
14	18–32	24–45
15	18–35	24–47

▼ FIGURE 9.4

MEASURING UPPER-BODY STRENGTH AND ENDURANCE

You can measure your upper-body strength and endurance by measuring the time you can hang from a bar with your chin above the bar. **What do you think are the benefits of building upper-body strength?**

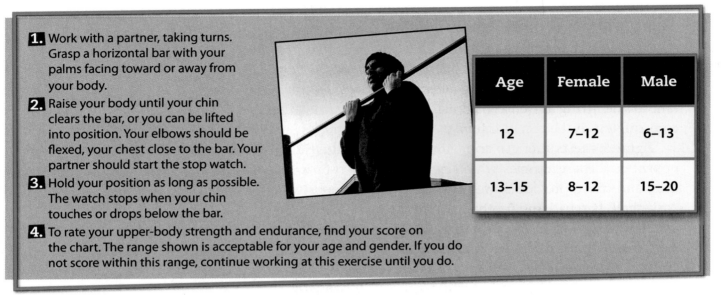

1. Work with a partner, taking turns. Grasp a horizontal bar with your palms facing toward or away from your body.

2. Raise your body until your chin clears the bar, or you can be lifted into position. Your elbows should be flexed, your chest close to the bar. Your partner should start the stop watch.

3. Hold your position as long as possible. The watch stops when your chin touches or drops below the bar.

4. To rate your upper-body strength and endurance, find your score on the chart. The range shown is acceptable for your age and gender. If you do not score within this range, continue working at this exercise until you do.

Age	Female	Male
12	7–12	6–13
13–15	8–12	15–20

Another approach to building muscle strength is weight lifting. Also known as *resistance training,* weight lifting can be used to strengthen every muscle group. Just make sure that a fitness instructor or other expert supervises your workout.

Reading Check **Compare** What is the difference between muscle strength and muscle endurance?

▼ FIGURE 9.5

DOING A PUSH-UP

1. **Lie facedown on the floor. Bend your arms and place your palms flat on the floor beneath your shoulders.**

2. **Straighten your arms, pushing your entire body upward. Then lower your body to the floor. Repeat.**

Flexibility

Are you able to bend and touch your toes? If you can, you probably have good flexibility. **Flexibility** is *the ability of your body's joints to move easily through a full range of motion.* Flexibility permits bending, turning, and stretching. It helps you reduce your risk of muscle injury. Gymnasts and dancers need a high level of flexibility.

You can improve your flexibility through regular stretching, bending, and twisting exercises. Move slowly and gently, holding each stretch. This will gradually improve the flexibility of your muscle groups.

Body Composition

The last measure of physical fitness is body composition. It is different from the other measures you have learned about. **Body composition** is *the ratio of body fat to lean body tissue, such as bone, muscle, and fluid.* There is no exercise used to measure body composition, and the improvements you make in this area have as much to do with diet as with exercise.

The main method for measuring body composition is the skinfold test, which involves pinching a fold of skin on the back of your upper arm and on the inside of your lower leg. Each fold is measured with an instrument called a skinfold caliper. The two numbers are then added together. Ask your fitness instructor about the skinfold test.

One of the keys to improving body composition is to eat healthy foods and increase your physical activity. Teens with too much body fat generally have a weight problem. Taking in fewer calories and burning more calories through exercise will help shed some of the excess weight. Physical activities and exercise build muscle mass while reducing the percentage of body fat. By decreasing the amount of calories you consume and increasing your physical activity, you are choosing positive health behaviors that can protect your health.

Reading Check **Explain** How do you measure body composition?

▶ Eating nutritious foods and exercising regularly can improve your body composition. **What is body composition?**

Fitness and a Healthy Attitude

How a person performs on fitness tests depends on a variety of factors. An important one is **heredity,** *the passing of traits from parents to their children.* Speed, for example, is a trait that is often inherited, or passed down, from parents. People who can run fast have more of one type of muscle fiber than another.

Differences likes these don't make one person better—or worse—than another. If you want to improve your level of physical fitness, you will need to set goals for yourself. It is perhaps even more important to keep a positive outlook about what you *can* do. Remember that improvement is possible in every area of fitness and that each improvement you make gives a boost to your physical health. Also remember, however, that everyone has limits. You can make only so much progress in a short period of time. In the next lesson, you will learn how to set up a fitness plan.

Health *Online*

Visit **health.glencoe.com** and complete the Interactive Study Guide for Lesson 2.

Reading Check   **Explain** How does attitude affect your fitness level?

Lesson 2 Review

After You Read

Review this lesson for new terms, major headings, and Reading Checks.

What I Learned

1. *Vocabulary* What is *heart and lung endurance*?

2. *List* Name the four measures of fitness.

3. *Identify* What are some exercises that will improve muscle strength and endurance? What are some that will improve flexibility?

4. *Describe* What are some ways to improve body composition?

Thinking Critically

5. *Evaluate* Natalie wants to become a ballet dancer. What area of fitness should she concentrate on improving? How should she go about doing this?

6. *Synthesize* When Don scored low on the test for muscle strength and endurance, he decided that fitness is simply "not for him." What is wrong with Don's attitude? What advice could you give him?

Applying Health Skills

7. *Accessing Information* Research different activities and exercises that can help you improve your physical fitness levels. With classmates, make a list of your findings. Include reliable sources that teens could go to find more information on the exercises or activities that interest them.

Health *Online*   For more review questions for Lesson 2, go to **health.glencoe.com**.

Setting Fitness Goals

Guide to Reading

Building Vocabulary
As you read this lesson, write each new highlighted term and its definition in your notebook.

- cross-training (p. 216)
- FITT principle (p. 218)
- resting heart rate (p. 219)
- target heart rate (p. 219)
- warm-up (p. 219)
- cool-down (p. 220)

Focusing on the Main Ideas
In this lesson, you will learn to

- **identify** factors to consider when choosing activities and exercises.
- **explain** the parts of the FITT principle.
- **develop** warm-up and cool-down techniques for preventing injuries.

Reading Strategy
Sequencing Describe the sequence that should be followed in a workout, along with a short summary of what occurs at each stage.

Identifying Your Fitness Goals

You wouldn't start a long road trip without first mapping out a route. In the same way, reaching a fitness goal requires a plan. A first step in developing such a plan is deciding what your goals are. What do you personally hope to accomplish? Maybe you want to compete in a certain sport or event. If so, your goal will probably focus on a specific fitness measure. Your goals should include strategies that will help you improve and maintain all three sides of your health triangle.

Choosing Activities and Exercises

Once you have identified your goal, you need to select activities and exercises that will help you meet it. **Figure 9.6** on page 216 lists some activities and rates each in terms of its fitness benefits. Your coach or physical education teacher can give you guidance on other activities and exercises. Other factors to consider when selecting activities and exercises include the following:

- **Personal tastes.** Make sure you choose activities that you will enjoy doing. You are more likely to stick with such activities. Another way to keep your interest level high is to vary your routine. *Switching between different activities and exercises on different days* is known as **cross-training.**

Quick Write
Write a brief description of the type of terrain and weather in your area. Tell what kinds of physical activities would make the most sense in these surroundings.

SELECTED ACTIVITIES AND THEIR FITNESS BENEFITS

The ratings in this chart show the benefits of activities done for 30 minutes or more. **Which activities have a high rating for heart and lung endurance?**

Activity or Exercise	Low	Midway	High
Handball			
Swimming			
Jogging			
Bicycling			
Tennis			
Brisk walking			
Softball			
Weight Training			

■ Heart and Lung Endurance
■ Muscle Strength and Endurance
■ Flexibility

Working on improving many areas should be a goal of every fitness plan. Your plan, for example, should include at least 20 to 30 minutes of aerobic exercise 3 to 5 times a week.

- **Requirements.** Some activities will require special equipment, such as racquets, balls, gloves, and so on. Many require protective gear, such as helmets or knee pads. Before you start an activity, find out what kind of equipment you will need. Also decide if you will need lessons or special instruction before you start.

Reading Check

Identify What kinds of questions do you need to ask yourself when choosing activities?

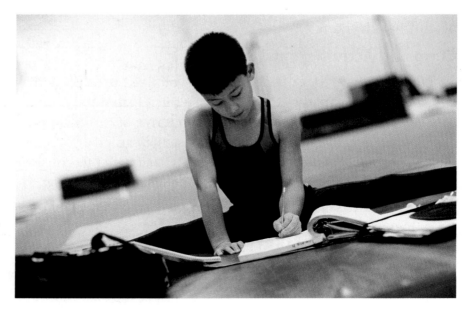

▶ Keeping a fitness log or journal is a good way to identify your fitness goals as well as track your progress. **What are some fitness goals that you might set for yourself?**

Creating a Schedule

Think about the time of day when you will do a particular activity or exercise. Be practical and realistic. If you have a 7:30 ride to school, it will probably be difficult to fit in an activity before you leave. Another aspect of scheduling has to do with season and climate. Do you live in a region that gets snow? If so, and if one of your exercises is running, you will need an indoor track or a treadmill during the winter months. Most communities have centers that are open to the public, and which offer pools and other exercise facilities.

Be sure to put your plan in writing. A written plan will help you stay on track and stick with your goal. Start by listing all physical activities that are currently part of your routine. For example, most teens have gym class on certain school days. If you are a member of a sports team, include practice sessions and game days. Be sure to count any outside activities that involve physical movement, such as dance lessons. **Figure 9.7** shows one teen's weekly fitness plan.

Reading Check **Recall** What type of information should go into a fitness plan?

▼ **FIGURE 9.7**

SAMPLE WEEKLY FITNESS PLAN

A written plan will help you stick with your goals. **Which activities has this teen added to his or her existing schedule? How many hours per day on average is this teen active?**

| Calendar | Edit | Settings |
| Monthly | Weekly | Daily |

Sun	Mon	Tues	Wed	Thurs	Fri	Sat
1 Ride bike (1 hr)	2 Gym class (30 min)	3 Basketball after school (40 min)	4 Gym class (30 min)	5 Ride bike after school (40 min)	6 Gym class (30 min)	7 Soccer game (50 min)
8	9 Soccer practice (1 hr)	10 Karate class (1 hr)	11 Soccer practice (1 hr)	12 Karate class (1 hr)	13 Walk home briskly from soccer practice (20 min)	14 Karate class (1 hr)
15	16 Walk home briskly from soccer practice (20 min)	17	18	19	20	21
22	23	24	25	26	27	28

Health Skills Activity

Accessing Information

Measuring Your Heart Rate

There are several reliable methods for determining your heart rate, or pulse. One of the easiest is to place two fingers at the base of your neck. Do not use your thumb, which has a pulse of its own. Feel for a throbbing sensation. This sensation is your heart pumping blood through an artery in your neck. Using a clock with a second hand, count the number of throbs in ten seconds. Multiply this number by six to get your heart rate.

On Your Own

Take your current resting heart rate using this method. Investigate other reliable methods for taking this measurement. Share your findings.

Connect To... Math

Target Heart Rate

The best way to become used to calculating your target heart rate is to practice. Try it right now. If you are 13 years old, for example, your target heart rate will be within this range:

$(220 - 13) \times 0.6 = 124$ low end

$(220 - 13) \times 0.8 = 166$ high end

Compute the range for a 14-year-old.

Building Fitness Levels

Whatever activity you choose to do, remember to start small. If you have never swum laps, you are probably not ready to compete on the school swimming team. Take each activity one day at a time and build up gradually. As you progress, adjust each activity using the **FITT principle,** *a method for safely increasing aspects of your workout without injuring yourself.* The letters in the name stand for Frequency, Intensity, Time, and Type.

Frequency is how often you work different muscle groups. Gradually increase the number of times per week you work a muscle group. You might start by working out two or three times per week. Eventually, you can work out every day.

Intensity refers to how hard you work different muscle groups. If you are lifting weights, you increase intensity by adding more weight. If you are running laps, you increase intensity by increasing your speed.

Time, or *duration*, is a measure of how long you spend per session. Teens should get a total of 60 minutes of activity on most days. If you are just beginning an activity or exercise, you will need to start by doing less than that. You can eventually build up your endurance to a point where you can do the full hour.

Type refers to the type of activity you choose to do. A complete workout package should feature both aerobic and anaerobic exercises. For some fitness goals, you will want to do more of one type of exercise than another.

It is important that any changes to your workouts be made gradually. Adjust only one FITT element at a time. Trying to do too much, too soon, can result in injury.

Reading Check **Explain** What do the letters in the *FITT principle* stand for?

Monitoring Your Heart Rate

How can you tell when you are ready to step up an element of your workout? One way is to check your heart rate. The Health Skills Activity on page 218 gives you instructions on how to measure your heart rate.

During exercise, there are two measures to take. They are resting heart rate and target heart rate. **Resting heart rate** is *the number of times your heart beats per minute when you are relaxing.* Take this measurement at the very beginning of a workout session, before you start any exercise. **Target heart rate** is *the range of numbers between which your heart and lungs receive the most benefit from a workout.* Finding your target heart rate is simple. You start by subtracting your age from 220. Then you multiply the resulting number by 0.6 and again by 0.8. The range of numbers between the two products represents your target heart rate.

Reading Check **Define** What is *target heart rate*?

Warming Up and Cooling Down

Every exercise or activity session should begin with a warm-up and end with a cool-down. A **warm-up** is *a period of low to moderate exercise to prepare your body for more vigorous activity.* Warming up helps prevent injuries to muscles, joints, and connective tissue. Warm-ups should last around ten minutes and should include light aerobic exercise to get your blood flowing. Walking or jogging in place is an excellent choice. Warming up can also include practicing skills related to the activity you will be doing. Complete your warm-up with simple stretches such as those shown in **Figure 9.8.** Your goal should be to get your muscles, tendons, ligaments, and joints primed for action. Stretch only the muscles that have been warmed up. Stretching cold muscles could lead to injury.

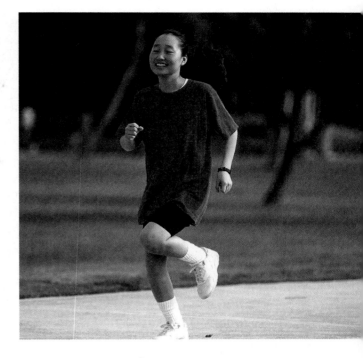

▲ When choosing activities and exercises, be aware of your environment. **What types of activities would be suitable for the environment in this picture?**

Health *Online*

Topic: Stretching for Fitness

Visit **health.glencoe.com** for Student Web Activities to learn about why stretching is so important, and how you can make stretching part of your overall health plan.

Activity: Using the information provided at the link above, create a personal stretching routine that you can use before and after strenuous exercise.

A **cool-down** is *a period of low to moderate exercise to prepare your body to end a workout session.* Cooling down helps return blood circulation and body temperature to normal. A cool-down should last around ten minutes and include gentle stretching exercises. You might repeat the same stretches you did during your warm-up.

▼ FIGURE 9.8

BASIC STRETCHES

Learning good stretching techniques can help prevent injury. Try the two techniques illustrated and tell where you feel the "pull."

Health *Online*

Visit **health.glencoe.com** and complete the Interactive Study Guide for Lesson 3.

Lesson 3 Review

After You Read

Review this lesson for new terms, major headings, and Reading Checks.

What I Learned

1. *Vocabulary* What is the *FITT principle*?

2. *Recall* Name two factors that need to be considered when choosing activities or exercises.

3. *Explain* Why are warm-ups and cool-downs important parts of any fitness routine?

Thinking Critically

4. *Synthesize* Rich has made more progress than he expected in the first three weeks of weight lifting. He now plans to increase his load and the length of his sessions. Do you think Rich has made a good decision? What positive health behavior should Rich do to prevent health problems?

5. *Evaluate* Anne has planned out a schedule that includes four hours of activity and exercise each day. Previously she has been sedentary. What do you think are her chances of success with her fitness program?

Applying Health Skills

6. *Goal Setting* Create a schedule that includes any current physical activity you get. Add at least one new exercise and show where it fits into your schedule. Write the date by which you hope to improve in one or more specific fitness areas. Identify steps you will take to achieve your goals.

Health *Online* For more review questions for Lesson 3, go to **health.glencoe.com**.

Sports Conditioning and Avoiding Injury

Guide to Reading

● **Building Vocabulary**
As you read this lesson, write each new highlighted term and its definition in your notebook.

■ conditioning (p. 222)
■ PRICE formula (p. 224)
■ dehydration (p. 225)
■ heat exhaustion (p. 225)

● **Focusing on the Main Ideas**
In this lesson, you will learn to

■ **describe** the benefits of conditioning.
■ **develop** nutrition habits for athletes.
■ **identify** ways of minimizing injury risks during sports or activities.
■ **show** how to treat sports-related injuries.

● **Reading Strategy**
Identifying Problems and Solutions As you read the lesson, identify injuries described and ways of dealing with each.

Quick Write

Describe an injury you had while playing a physical game or sport. Tell how this injury was treated.

Sports Conditioning

Standing behind the center, Evan barked signals. Everyone in the stands sat silently, breathlessly watching. There was one second left on the clock, time for one last play. North High was down by four points. The game—and season—was on the line.

"Hut! Hut! *Hut!*" Evan called. He took the snap from the center and moved back in the pocket. Out of the corner of his eye he saw a large linebacker barreling toward him from the right. Evan scrambled left and threw the ball as he skillfully dodged the tackler. Time seemed to stand still as the ball floated downfield. It fell gracefully into the hands of Evan's target. "Touchdown!" the official shouted. The North High fans went wild. "Evan!" they cheered. "Evan! Evan! Evan!"

▶ Proper conditioning will strengthen your muscles so you can play your best when you compete. **What type of conditioning exercises do you think the tennis player in this picture practices?**

▲ Drinking water before and during a game is a good sports nutrition habit. **What is another?**

Playing a sport can seem glamorous, especially when you are a star quarterback. It is also a fun way to make physical activity part of your life. Playing a sport involves much more than showing up for games, however. Athletes devote many hours off the field to physical **conditioning,** *a regular activity and exercise that prepares a person for a sport.* Some conditioning takes place right before a game. Baseball players, for example, practice batting and fielding. Basketball players do passing drills and take practice shots from different spots on the court. Conditioning may also include weight training and other exercises. Additionally, maintaining a healthy diet and getting enough rest are important aspects of conditioning.

Reading Check

Identify Besides practice and exercise, what are two conditioning practices every athlete should follow?

Sports Nutrition

Everyone needs proper nutrition. The term *nutrition* refers to a person's eating habits. For athletes, good nutrition includes following specific guidelines on and off the field.

One common guideline is to eat carbohydrates before a game or event. Whole-grain products, fruits, and vegetables are good energy sources. Avoid foods high in simple sugars, such as candy bars. These will provide a burst of energy, but one that lasts only briefly.

Before and during a game, you should drink plenty of water. Your body loses water through perspiration, even outdoors in winter. Health authorities advise drinking at least eight ounces of water before a game. Then take sips periodically during the game to replenish your fluids. Drinking water is important for any strenuous workout.

Reading Check

Give Examples Name specific foods that athletes might eat before a game for added energy.

Minimizing Risk

Whether your fitness program includes sports or some other activity, safety should be your first concern. You have already learned some guidelines for minimizing the risk of an activity-related injury. These guidelines include progressing gradually, warming up, and cooling down. Other guidelines include using the right equipment and knowing your limits.

Proper Gear

In sports, proper gear starts with equipment used in your game. For some team sports, you wear cleats. These are shoes with spikes on the bottom that grip the ground and provide traction. Whatever shoes you wear should be suitable to your activity or game. Shoes should also fit properly, feel comfortable, and provide adequate support.

For games played in bright sunlight, a good pair of sunglasses is more than a fashion statement. It is a necessity. Choose shatterproof glasses with lenses that offer UV protection. UV protection will shield your eyes from the same harsh rays that cause sunburns on unprotected skin.

Other protective gear includes athletic supporters, knee pads, elbow pads, and helmets. Specific needs and equipment will depend on your activity or sport. You want to be sure to choose the appropriate gear in order to reduce your risk of injury.

For non-sports activities, wear clothing that is loose-fitting or stretchable. This type of clothing will give you freedom of movement and help you stay cool in warm weather. In cool weather, dress in layers to trap warm air against your body.

Know Your Limits

As Rod stood in his outfield position, his shoulder hurt from where a ball had struck it earlier. The game was important, however, so Rod decided to play through the pain. When Rod learned later that he had separated his shoulder, he felt bad in more than one way. He would be on the bench for the rest of the baseball season.

Do not make the same mistake Rod did. Learn to listen to your body whether you play a sport or exercise. If someone tells you "No pain, no gain," do not believe them. Pain is your body's way of telling you to slow down or stop, if you have been injured. If you experience pain, you should take the appropriate health care measure to protect yourself from further injury.

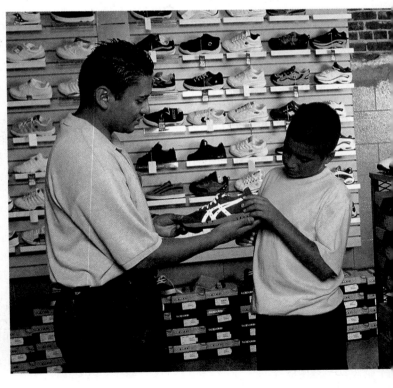

▼ You should remember to use appropriate athletic gear. **What are some features to consider when buying shoes for a sport or physical activity?**

Treating Injuries

Sometimes even when you are cautious, injuries can occur, especially when you are playing *contact sports*. This term is used for any sport where physical contact between players is normal. Football, hockey, and boxing are examples of contact sports.

Even if you are not injured through contact, you might experience muscle soreness. When a muscle stiffens or aches, the **PRICE formula** will provide some relief. The letters stand for *Protect, Rest, Ice, Compress, and Elevate.* Apply the following treatment as soon as possible after the game, event, or activity:

- **Protect** the injured part from further injury by keeping it still. Try not to move it too much. Moving it may make the pain worse.

- **Rest** the injured part.

- **Ice** the part using an ice pack.

- **Compress**, or put pressure on, the part using an elastic bandage. This will keep the injury from swelling. It will also help keep that part of your body motionless. Just be careful not to wrap the bandage too tightly. This could cut off the flow of blood.

- **Elevate** the injured part above the level of the heart.

Reading Check

Explain What do the letters in the PRICE formula stand for?

Weather-Related Injuries

Some sports and activities, such as ice hockey, skiing, and ice skating, are done in cold weather. Other activities tend to be played

▶ Treat an injury such as muscle soreness as soon as possible after it occurs. **Which steps in the PRICE formula is this teen demonstrating?**

in hot weather. Temperatures at both extremes pose a health risk to the body. You should follow practices that will reduce your risk of injury.

When the temperature rises in the summer, so does your body's. You perspire more, which is your body's way of cooling you down. If you are not careful to replace this lost water, you risk **dehydration.** This *condition caused by excessive water loss* can lead to other, more serious health problems. One of these is **heat exhaustion**—*an overheating of the body that can result from dehydration.* People with heat exhaustion often feel dizzy and have a headache. Their skin feels clammy when touched. Anyone who shows the symptoms of heat exhaustion needs to be taken to a cool, shady spot. The person should receive plenty of fluids. If the symptoms do not go away, call for help immediately.

Cold weather can bring its own share of problems, including frostbite and hypothermia. Chapter 20 will discuss weather-related risks in further detail.

Health Online

Visit **health.glencoe.com** and complete the Interactive Study Guide for Lesson 4.

Reading Check **Define** What is *dehydration*?

Lesson 4 Review

After You Read

Review this lesson for new terms, major headings, and Reading Checks.

What I Learned

1. *Vocabulary* What is *conditioning*? What are some specific practices that are part of conditioning for most sports?

2. *Identify* Name two ways to minimize the risk of injury during sports or activities.

3. *Recall* What type of treatment is used for an exercise-related or sport-related injury such as muscle soreness?

Thinking Critically

4. *Analyze* Mel has tried on several pairs of cleats. The only pair he thinks look good on him are a size too small. He plans to buy the shoes anyway. How could you help Mel make a healthful decision if you were the salesperson?

5. *Apply* Angela has one more lap to run around the track to finish her routine for the day. She is feeling light-headed and dizzy. What steps would you take to help Angela if you were there at the track?

Applying Health Skills

6. *Communication Skills* Working with a small group, develop a public service announcement for teens. Your announcement should communicate ways to avoid injury and minimize other risks while being physically active.

Building Health Skills

Playing It Safe

DIRECTIONS

Practicing Healthful Behaviors involves taking specific actions to stay healthy and avoid risky behaviors. This activity will help you develop and master this important health skill. Here's a guide to the different parts of this activity:

❶ In the **Model** section, you will read about a teen who performs the health skill successfully. This "model" scenario will show you how the skill is done.

❷ The **Practice** section will help guide you in practicing the skill.

❸ In the **Apply** section, you will have a chance to perform the skill on your own. You can use the Self-Check to check your work.

To complete this activity, first read the scenario presented in the Model. Then move on to the Practice. Finally, go ahead and try the Apply.

❶ Model

Sometimes exercise-related problems can be prevented by being aware of weather-related risks.

"All set," Connie said. She and Rebecca had decided that they would jog together.

"Wait," Rebecca said. "I just heard that the temperature right now is in the low 90s."

"So?" Connie said. "No pain, no gain!"

"Exercising in the heat can cause heat exhaustion," Rebecca said. "I think we need to wait until it cools down. We should also drink plenty of water before we go."

The girls waited a few hours. In the late afternoon when the temperature had dropped, Connie went to Rebecca's room. "Now can we go?" she asked.

"Not like that, Sis," Rebecca replied. "The clothes you're wearing are dark."

"Now that it's starting to get dark out, we need to wear light-colored clothing. That will help drivers see us. Here, put this on, too." She handed her sister a reflective armband. "This will also make us easier to see."

② Practice

Connie's friend Lisa invited her to go for a bike ride on a trail that was a few miles outside of town. The countryside surrounding the trail was scenic and peaceful. Connie was looking forward to the bike ride. As Connie was getting ready to join Lisa, she remembered that temperatures sometimes drop quickly during this time of the year.

1. What advice should Connie give Lisa about her clothing?

2. What other safety tips should Connie share with Lisa before going on the bike ride?

Skill Summary
PRACTICING HEALTHFUL BEHAVIORS

When working out or playing a sport:
- Avoid extreme temperatures.
- Drink water before and during exercise.
- Wear appropriate clothing and protective gear.

③ Apply

Working with a partner, develop a pamphlet that would be useful to teens exercising in your community. What weather-related factors or other safety risks exist in your community? How can these dangers be avoided? With your teacher's permission, display your pamphlet in the classroom or school library.

Self-Check

- Did we mention specific safety risks or weather-related factors in our community?
- Did we show how these dangers can be avoided?

Looking for an inexpensive activity that will make you feel good?

RUN FOR IT!

Experts agree. Running relaxes you—and doing something physical helps your self-esteem. Follow these basic steps, and you'll be running a 5K (or 3.1 mile) race in no time.

1 GET IN GEAR

Head to your local sporting-goods store and ask the salesperson for a pair of running shoes with good support and cushioning. Mention that you're just starting out, so he or she can recommend the right type of shoe for your needs. When the weather turns cooler, be sure to have warm running gear for the rest of your body.

2 MAKE A GOAL

Check out the Road Runners Club of America's local race schedules. Register for a 5K race for teens that is a few weeks or months away. Then get motivated by imagining yourself crossing the finish line.

3 FUEL UP

Drink at least eight ounces of water up to five minutes before your run, and then again during and after your run. (Avoid caffeinated beverages, which dehydrate you.) You should have a carbohydrate snack about two to three hours before you run. Carbohydrates give you the energy you need to keep going. Perfect pre-run foods include oatmeal or bananas.

4 GET MOVING

After you've warmed up your muscles by stretching, start with a slow-paced jog. If you feel tired, it's okay to walk for a bit and pick up the pace again when you're ready. Once you've finished, you should stretch.

5 TAKE IT UP A NOTCH

Run three to five times a week for eight weeks before a race. Go a little farther each week while gradually picking up your pace. By your third week, you should be up to about 20 minutes (or roughly two miles at an easy 10-minute-per-mile pace). At that rate, you'll be hitting that 5K finish line in about 31 minutes. Then, get ready for your victory lap!

Reading Review

FOLDABLES Study Organizer

Foldables™ and Other Study Aids Take out the Foldable™ that you created for Lesson 1 and any graphic organizers that you created for Lessons 1–4. Find a partner and quiz each other using these study aids.

Lesson 1 The Benefits of Physical Activity

Key Idea
- Physical activity benefits your physical, mental/emotional, and social health.

Vocabulary
- physical activity (p. 204)
- coordination (p. 205)
- balance (p. 205)
- calories (p. 205)
- physical fitness (p. 206)
- exercise (p. 207)
- aerobic exercise (p. 207)
- anaerobic exercise (p. 208)

Lesson 2 Endurance, Strength, and Flexibility

Key Ideas
- The four measures of physical fitness are heart and lung endurance, muscle strength and endurance, flexibility, and body composition.
- Different exercises improve different areas of physical fitness.

Vocabulary
- heart and lung endurance (p. 210)
- muscle strength (p. 211)
- muscle endurance (p. 211)
- flexibility (p. 212)
- body composition (p. 213)
- heredity (p. 214)

Lesson 3 Setting Fitness Goals

Key Ideas
- The parts of the FITT principle are Frequency, Intensity, Time, and Type.
- Warming up is important because it prevents injuries to muscles, joints, and connective tissue. Cooling down is important because it helps return blood circulation and body temperature to normal.

Vocabulary
- cross-training (p. 215)
- FITT principle (p. 218)
- resting heart rate (p. 219)
- target heart rate (p. 219)
- warm-up (p. 219)
- cool-down (p. 220)

Lesson 4 Sports Conditioning and Avoiding Injury

Key Idea
- The main treatment for sports-related injuries is the PRICE formula—short for Protect, Rest, Ice, Compress, and Elevate.

Vocabulary
- conditioning (p. 222)
- PRICE formula (p. 224)
- dehydration (p. 225)
- heat exhaustion (p. 225)

Reviewing Vocabulary and Main Ideas

On a sheet of paper, write the numbers 1–6. After each number, write the term from the list that best completes each sentence.

- balance
- coordination
- flexibility
- heart and lung endurance
- physical activity
- muscle strength

Lesson 1 The Benefits of Physical Activity

1. Any form of bodily movement that uses up energy is known as _____.
2. _____ is the smooth and effective working together of your muscles and bones.
3. _____ is the feeling of stability and control over your body.

Lesson 2 Endurance, Strength, and Flexibility

4. _____ is a measure of how efficiently your heart and lungs work when you exercise and how quickly they return to normal when you stop.
5. The ability of your body's joints to move easily through a full range of motion is known as _____.
6. _____ is a measure of the most weight you can lift or the most force you can exert at one time.

*On a sheet of paper, write the numbers 7–12. Write **True** or **False** for each statement below. If the statement is false, change the underlined word or phrase to make it true.*

Lesson 3 Setting Fitness Goals

7. Switching between different activities and exercises on different days is known as <u>cross-training</u>.
8. Your <u>resting heart rate</u> is the range of numbers between which your heart and lungs receive the most benefit from a workout.
9. Warm-ups should consist of low to <u>vigorous</u> activity to prepare you for your workout.

Lesson 4 Sports Conditioning and Avoiding Injury

10. Regular activity and exercise that prepare a person for a sport are known as <u>nutrition</u>.
11. Before a game or event, you should eat foods high in <u>protein</u>.
12. The <u>PRICE formula</u> can provide relief from muscle stiffness or soreness.

230 Chapter 9: Physical Activity and Fitness

Health Online Visit health.glencoe.com and take the Online Quiz for Chapter 9.

Thinking Critically

Using complete sentences, answer the following questions on a sheet of paper.

13. Synthesize Janice understands that physical fitness is important. She says that she plans to start becoming physically active as an adult. How would you encourage Janice to become physically active now as a teen?

Write About It

14. Advocacy Write an article for your school paper on the importance of becoming and staying physically active.

Career Corner

Athletic Trainer Athletes often meet with athletic trainers to get advice on fitness programs. These professionals help athletes maintain their physical fitness. They also treat sports injuries. Athletic trainers need at least a four-year degree and successful completion of a certification test. Find out more about this and other health careers by clicking on *Career Corner* at **health.glencoe.com.**

15. Goal Setting Write an extended journal entry about an activity or exercise you would like to try. Set a goal to try this activity and develop a plan to achieve your goal.

Standardized Test Practice

Reading

Read the passage and then answer the questions.

Many teens dream of competing in the Olympic Games. The Olympic spirit of universality, excellence, peace, and friendship is represented in many symbols that date back to early modern Games.

The Olympic motto is one symbol of the Olympic spirit. The Olympic motto is *Citius—Altius—Fortius,* which is Latin for "faster, higher, stronger." The intended meaning is that each athlete should focus on improving his or her own ability, rather than on coming in first.

Another Olympic symbol is the five rings. Each ring is a different color and together they represent the five major continents. (The Americas are treated as one continent.) The rings are interlaced to represent the universality of the Olympics, bringing together athletes from around the world.

The flame is another Olympic symbol, linking the ancient Games to the modern Games. The Olympic flame is lit in Greece and carried by a relay of runners to the site of the Games. There, it is used to light the cauldron that burns until the Closing Ceremony.

TEST-TAKING TIP

Read the passage carefully once to find out what information it contains. After you read each question, look back at the passage to find the answer.

1. The five rings represent
   A. the number of athletes in the first modern Games.
   B. the Olympic motto.
   C. the five major continents in the world.
   D. the five major countries in the world.

2. Which statement best represents the main idea of the passage?
   A. Many teens want to compete in the Olympics.
   B. Athletes from all over the world compete in the Olympics.
   C. There are many Olympic symbols.
   D. Symbols are used to represent the spirit of the Olympics.

Chapter Preview

▲ *Working With the Photo*

Many factors affect your food choices. **What are some of your favorite foods?**

Start-Up Activities

Before You Read Do you make healthy choices when selecting the foods you eat? Take the short health inventory on this page. Keep a record of your answers.

HEALTH INVENTORY

1. I try to eat plenty of fruits and vegetables.
   (a) always   (b) sometimes   (c) never

2. I try to eat foods that are rich in fiber.
   (a) always   (b) sometimes   (c) never

3. I use the MyPyramid food guidance system as a guide when choosing foods.
   (a) always   (b) sometimes   (c) never

4. I choose healthful, low-fat snacks.
   (a) always   (b) sometimes   (c) never

FOLDABLES™ Study Organizer

As You Read Make this Foldable™ to record what you learn about the body's need for nutrients in Lesson 1. Begin with two plain sheets of 8½" × 11" paper.

1 Collect two sheets of paper and place them 1 inch apart.

3 Crease the paper to hold the tabs in place. Staple along the fold.

2 Fold up the bottom edges, stopping them 1 inch from the top edges. This makes all tabs the same size.

4 Turn and label the tabs as shown.

The Importance of Nutrition
Why You Need Nutritious Foods
Influences on Your Food Choices
Getting the Nutrients You Need

Under the appropriate tab of your Foldable™, define terms and record information on nutrients and influences on food choices.

Health Online Visit **health.glencoe.com** and use the e-flashcards to preview Chapter 10 vocabulary terms.

The Importance of Nutrition

Guide to Reading

Building Vocabulary
Write the terms you think you know in your notebook. Add a definition in pencil. As you read the lesson, be prepared to correct your definitions.

- nutrients (p. 235)
- nutrition (p. 235)
- appetite (p. 236)
- hunger (p. 236)

Focusing on the Main Ideas
In this lesson, you will learn to

- **explain** why the body needs nutrients.
- **identify** factors that influence which foods you choose.
- **describe** how emotions can affect your food choices.

Reading Strategy
Making Inferences Look briefly at the headings, figures, and captions in the lesson. Based on the words and images you see, what do you think you will learn in this lesson?

FOLDABLES Study Organizer Use the Foldable™ on p. 233 as you read this lesson.

Quick Write

Create a menu that contains your favorite foods. Next to each food, write what nutrients you think it provides.

The Role of Food

Food, like water and air, is one of life's necessities. Your relationship to food affects all three sides of your health triangle. For example, if you do not eat breakfast before going to school, you might have a hard time focusing in class. Have you ever had days when you could not seem to concentrate because you were hungry? That was your body's way of telling you that it was running low on fuel. Your body needs food to function properly. Choosing healthy foods is a positive behavior that can help you prevent certain health problems.

◀ Food affects all sides of your health triangle, including your ability to concentrate in school. **Describe other effects food has on your health triangle.**

Food, Nutrients, and Nutrition

Your body depends on nutrients in food to function properly throughout the day. **Nutrients** are *substances in food that your body needs*. They help the body build new tissue, repair damaged cells, and produce energy. The energy from food is measured in units called calories. Each calorie is equal to a certain amount of energy. Chocolate, for example, is high in calories but provides few nutrients. Fruit, on the other hand, has few calories but has more nutrients the body needs. Calories are further discussed in Lesson 3.

There are two main kinds of nutrients: those that provide energy and those that help your body run smoothly. Proteins, carbohydrates, and fats are examples of nutrients that provide energy. Vitamins, minerals, and water are examples of nutrients that help the body run well.

Which nutrients does your body need the most? The best way to answer that question is to learn about **nutrition**—*the study of nutrients and how the body uses them*. Someone who eats well-balanced meals with plenty of fresh fruits and vegetables has good nutrition. Eating well-balanced meals is a good way to promote good health and prevent diseases.

Reading Check **Define** What are *nutrients*?

What Influences Your Food Choices?

Now you know why it is important to eat—but have you ever thought about how people decide *what* to eat?

Yoshi, who grew up in Japan, prefers miso soup and rice for breakfast, while his American friend Carl likes cereal and milk. Both Yoshi's and Carl's tastes in food are influenced by their families' cultural backgrounds.

Another factor that influences the foods many people choose to eat is availability. Melissa's family enjoys fresh fruits and vegetables. The meals they prepare depend on which foods are in season. **Figure 10.1** shows several other factors that influence which foods we choose to eat.

▼ **FIGURE 10.1**

INFLUENCES ON FOOD CHOICES

Your family and culture is one influence on the foods you eat. **Which factors in this figure play the biggest role in your personal food choices?**

Peer Pressure · Availability · Convenience · Knowledge of Nutrition · Advertising · Family and Culture

Appetite and Hunger

Another factor that influences what you choose to eat is **appetite,** or *the psychological desire for food.* The aroma of fresh-baked bread, for example, might make you crave a piece of toast, even if you are not hungry. Psychological desires for food are often connected to memories and feelings. If the smell of fresh-baked bread reminds you of happy times with your family, you might feel like eating some even if your body does not really need fuel at the moment.

People sometimes confuse hunger with appetite. **Hunger** is *the body's physical need for food.* It is important to learn to tell the difference so that you will know why you eat. This will help you make healthy choices when it comes time to satisfy your body's physical need for food. You will learn more about how to make healthy choices later in this chapter.

Food and Emotions

In addition to appetite and hunger, emotions also influence your food choices. Foods bring up feelings connected to past experiences. For example, certain foods may remind you of loved ones or of fun times. If a food is associated with a pleasant or comforting memory people often crave it even when they are not hungry. The craving can be especially strong when people feel sad, lonely, or discouraged. What they are really craving, however, is not the food, but the pleasant emotions associated with the food. Using food in this way is not a good idea because it can lead to unhealthy eating habits and weight problems. Healthier ways to cope with negative feelings include writing in a journal, listening to music, and talking to a friend.

Reading Check

Recall List four factors that influence what a person chooses to eat.

Meeting Nutrient Needs

All bodies need the same nutrients, but the amount a body needs depends upon the person's age, gender, general health, and level of activity. When you do not get enough of a particular nutrient, you could have a *nutrient deficiency,* a shortage of a nutrient.

As a growing teen on the go, your energy demands are greater than those of an older person who is less active. You also need calcium to build strong bones and teeth. A calcium deficiency could affect the strength of your bones as you get older. You also need iron to help your body make enough red blood cells as you grow. A shortage of iron can lead to a blood disease called anemia.

In general, teens need more of most nutrients to support growth and satisfy energy needs.

Most people in the United States get plenty of food, yet many still do not get the nutrients they need. This is partly because of lifestyles that include too much fast food and foods that are high in fat and sugar. Eating low-nutrient, high-fat foods, along with overeating, can lead to long-term health problems such as obesity, diabetes, heart disease, and cancer. Developing healthy eating habits, which includes limiting high-fat and high-calorie foods, is your best defense against poor nutrition.

▲ Food labels can tell you which nutrients are in a product, as well as how much fat and calories. **Why is it important to provide your body with enough nutrients?**

Lesson 1 Review

After You Read

Review this lesson for new terms, major headings, and Reading Checks.

What I Learned

1. *Vocabulary* Define *appetite*, and explain how it can affect which foods you choose to eat.

2. *Recall* What do nutrients do for your body?

3. *Describe* What role do emotions play in your food choices?

Thinking Critically

4. *Apply* Which factors do you think influence a teen's food choices the most? Explain your answer.

5. *Analyze* How is it possible to have plenty of food and yet be poorly nourished?

Applying Health Skills

6. *Accessing Information* Using online or print resources, locate a country that has famine problems. Research the causes of the famine and what steps are being taken to solve the problem. Share your findings with your classmates.

Health Online For more review questions for Lesson 1, go to health.glencoe.com.

Lesson 1: The Importance of Nutrition **237**

Nutrients for Wellness

● Building Vocabulary

Write the terms below in your notebook. As you come across each one in your reading, write a definition beside it.

- carbohydrates (p. 238)
- fiber (p. 239)
- proteins (p. 240)
- saturated fat (p. 240)
- unsaturated fat (p. 240)
- vitamins (p. 240)
- minerals (p. 240)

● Focusing on the Main Ideas

In this lesson, you will learn to

- **identify** the six major classes of nutrients.
- **explain** specific ways your body uses nutrients.

● Reading Strategy

Organizing Information Make a diagram similar to the one below. Include a box for each nutrient and foods that are sources of that nutrient.

Carbohydrate	Protein
↓	↓

Food Sources ⟶

Quick Write

Make a list of foods that you think are high in nutrients. After reading the lesson, check to see if you were right.

Nutrients and Nutrition

Scientists who study the nutrients in food have found more than forty different kinds. These nutrients are divided into six groups: carbohydrates, proteins, fats, vitamins, minerals, and water. Choosing a variety of healthy foods can help you get enough nutrients from each of these important groups.

Carbohydrates

What does a steaming plate of spaghetti have in common with a ripe peach? Both foods contain carbohydrates, your body's main energy source. **Carbohydrates** are *sugars and starches that occur naturally in foods, mainly in plants.* There are two kinds of carbohydrates: simple and complex.

◀ An apple is a great source of carbohydrates. **What are some other sources of carbohydrates?**

Nutrition from Nature

When carbohydrate-rich foods are processed they can lose some of their nutrients. The process that turns wheat into white flour is a good example of how nutrients can be lost. In this process the inner and outer parts of the wheat grain are separated, and only the inner portion is used to make the flour. All the nutrients in the grain's outer covering are lost. Heating, freezing, dehydrating, and canning are other processes that remove nutrients from food.

When shopping for carbohydrate-rich foods, try to choose whole grains—like barley, millet, and brown rice—or foods that contain them such as whole wheat bread, popcorn, and oatmeal. Likewise try to snack on fresh fruits and vegetables. They are naturally rich in nutrients and haven't been processed.

On Your Own

Make a list of carbohydrate-rich foods that you enjoy eating. Which of these foods contain whole grains? Develop a plan for including more whole grains in your food choices.

All carbohydrates are made of sugar molecules. When these molecules remain separate, they are called *simple carbohydrates*. Foods that contain simple carbohydrates include fruits, many vegetables, milk, and milk products.

Sugar molecules that join together to form long chains are called *starches*, or *complex carbohydrates*. Foods that contain complex carbohydrates include grains such as rice and pasta, dried beans, and starchy vegetables such as potatoes. Nutritionists say that about half to two-thirds of your daily energy should come from carbohydrates.

▼ A great way to include fiber in your diet is by eating whole-grain cereals. **Why is it important to get enough fiber?**

Reading Check **Identify** What are complex carbohydrates? Name some foods that contain this nutrient.

Fiber

Fiber is *the parts of fruit, vegetables, grains, and beans that your body cannot digest.* It is a special type of complex carbohydrate, found in raw fruits, vegetables, and whole grains. As it passes through the digestive system, fiber pushes other food particles along. Choosing to eat high-fiber foods can help reduce your risk of certain types of cancer and heart disease.

MediaWatch

Sports Drinks

Staying hydrated—making sure your body has enough water—is especially important during strenuous exercise. Sports drinks can help your body stay hydrated and give you an energy boost. Do a little research on the various kinds of sports drinks, comparing their ingredients and price.

Which drinks do you think are best? Why?

Proteins

Proteins are *nutrients your body uses to build, repair, and maintain cells and tissues.* They are made up of chemical building blocks called *amino acids.* Anyone who has had a stiff muscle get better after a few days of rest has experienced proteins at work. Proteins also play an important role in fighting disease since parts of your immune system are made of proteins.

Foods that contain protein include beef, pork, veal, fish, poultry, eggs, and most dairy products. Notice that all these foods are animal products or byproducts. These foods are called *complete proteins* because they contain all nine of the essential amino acids. Most plant proteins—available from nuts, peas, and dried beans—lack one or more essential amino acids.

Reading Check **Define** What are *proteins*?

Fats

Fats are an important part of good nutrition. They promote healthy skin and normal cell growth, and they carry vitamins A, D, E, and K to wherever they are needed in your body.

However, eating a large amount of **saturated fats,** *fats that are solid at room temperature*, is not good for your health. Foods like butter, cheese, and fatty meats are high in saturated fats. Eating too much of these foods can increase your risk of heart disease.

Most of the fats in your diet should be **unsaturated fats.** These are *fats that remain liquid at room temperature*. They come mainly from plant foods such as olive oil, nuts, and avocados.

Cholesterol

Cholesterol is a fatty substance found in the blood. There are two kinds of cholesterol. The "bad" cholesterol is LDL (low-density lipoprotein), which collects on the walls of arteries and forms a thick, hard substance called plaque. If too much plaque builds up it can block the arteries and cause heart attacks and strokes. The "good" cholesterol is called HDL (high-density lipoprotein). This type of cholesterol helps remove LDL from the arteries so it can be disposed of in the liver. Eating too much saturated fat can increase your body's level of cholesterol.

Vitamins and Minerals

Two other kinds of nutrients that the body needs are vitamins and minerals. Though only small quantities of each are needed, they are essential to your body's health. **Vitamins** are *substances that help your body fight infections and use other nutrients, among other jobs*. **Minerals** are *elements that help form healthy bones and teeth, and regulate certain body processes*.

There are two kinds of vitamins: water-soluble and fat-soluble. Water-soluble vitamins, which include vitamins C and B, dissolve in water. Your body cannot store them, so you need to consume them regularly. Fat-soluble vitamins, including vitamins A, D, E, and K, are stored in the body's fat until they are needed. **Figure 10.2** lists the functions and food sources of some vitamins and minerals. Most teens do not get enough vitamin E, calcium, or iron. The best way to get vitamins and minerals is to choose nutritious foods.

Health Online

Visit **health.glencoe.com** and complete the Interactive Study Guide for Lesson 2.

▼ FIGURE 10.2

VITAMINS AND SELECTED MINERALS: FUNCTIONS AND SOURCES

Vitamins and minerals are essential to your body's health. **What foods do you eat that provide your body with vitamins?**

	Functions	Food Sources
Vitamins	**Vitamin A** Promotes healthy skin and normal vision	Dark-green leafy vegetables (such as spinach); dairy products (such as milk); deep yellow-orange fruits and vegetables (such as carrots, winter squash, apricots); eggs; liver
	B Vitamins Needed for a healthy nervous system; help in energy production	Poultry; eggs; meat; fish; whole-grain breads and cereals
	Vitamin C Needed for healthy teeth, gums, and bones; helps heal wounds and fight infection	Citrus fruits (such as oranges and grapefruit); cantaloupe; strawberries; mangoes; tomatoes; cabbage and broccoli; potatoes
	Vitamin D Promotes strong bones and teeth and the absorption of calcium	Fortified milk; fatty fish (such as salmon and mackerel); egg yolks; liver
	Vitamin K Helps blood clot	Dark-green leafy vegetables (such as spinach); egg yolks; liver; some cereals
Minerals	**Calcium** Needed to build and maintain strong bones and teeth	Dairy products (such as milk, yogurt, cheese); dark-green leafy vegetables (such as spinach); canned fish with edible bones (such as sardines)
	Fluoride Promotes strong bones and teeth; prevents tooth decay	Fluoridated water; fish with edible bones
	Iron Needed for hemoglobin in red blood cells	Red meat; poultry; dry beans (legumes); fortified breakfast cereal; nuts; eggs; dried fruits; dark-green leafy vegetables
	Potassium Helps regulate fluid balance in tissues; promotes proper nerve function	Fruits (such as bananas and oranges); dry beans and peas; dried fruits, tomato juice
	Zinc Helps heal wounds; needed for cell reproduction	Meat; poultry; eggs; dry beans and peas; whole-grain breads and cereals

▲ Water is all around us. The water that we drink comes from natural sources like the one in this picture. **What functions does water perform as a nutrient?**

Water

Water plays a role in many of the body's functions. It helps you digest and absorb food, it regulates body temperature and blood circulation, and it carries nutrients and oxygen to cells. It also removes toxins and other wastes, cushions joints, and protects tissues and organs from shock and damage.

Dehydration, or lack of water in the body, can cause problems like fatigue, confusion, and inability to focus. You need to replace the water your body loses by drinking at least eight 8-ounce cups of fluid a day. Even more water is needed during vigorous activity or hot weather. Choose water or milk most of the time and limit your intake of juice or soda.

Reading Check **Explain** Why does the body need plenty of water?

Lesson 2 Review

After You Read

Review this lesson for new terms, major headings, and Reading Checks.

What I Learned

1. *Vocabulary* What is *fiber*? What function does it have in the body?

2. *List* Name the six major classes of nutrients.

3. *Identify* Name some sources of complete proteins.

Thinking Critically

4. *Apply* Make a list of the foods you have eaten today. Identify which nutrients can be found in each food. Are there any nutrient groups that you have left out?

5. *Hypothesize* How can the food you choose to eat today affect your health in the future?

Applying Health Skills

6. *Analyzing Influences* As you learned earlier in this chapter, the media play a role in people's food choices. Find an ad for a food or food product. What methods does the ad use to encourage you to buy the food? Share your findings with those of your classmates.

Health Online For more review questions for Lesson 2, go to **health.glencoe.com**.

Following Nutrition Guidelines

Guidelines for Healthy Eating

Choosing foods that provide the right nutrients can be a challenge. To help you meet this challenge, the United States Department of Agriculture (USDA) has created a program called the **MyPyramid food guidance system.** This is *a system designed to help Americans make healthful food choices.*

A Closer Look at MyPyramid

MyPyramid includes an illustration (see **Figure 10.3**) that shows a pyramid with six colored sections, each representing a different food group. A well-balanced eating plan should contain a variety of foods from the five main food groups. These are grains, vegetables, fruits, milk, and meat and beans. The sixth group, oils and other fats, should only be eaten in very small amounts. MyPyramid can help you develop a personalized eating plan based on your age, gender, and activity level.

Look at Figure 10.3. Notice the figure walking up the steps of the pyramid. The figure is there to remind you to make physical activity a part of your daily routine.

Reading Check

Identify What do the colored bands in MyPyramid represent?

Quick Write

Describe your current eating habits in a short paragraph. Include a list of the foods you eat the most and the kinds of snacks you enjoy.

MyPyramid

The goal of MyPyramid is to help you develop a healthy lifestyle. What does the figure in the illustration remind you to do?

Other Guidelines for Good Health

MyPyramid reflects science-based advice from the *2005 Dietary Guidelines for Americans*. These guidelines were released by the U.S. Department of Agriculture (USDA) and the U.S. Department of Health and Human Services (HHS). The guidelines encourage people who are two years of age and older to develop healthful eating habits and increase their level of activity. Doing both improves health and reduces the risk of certain diseases.

Eat a Variety of Foods

Have you ever heard the expression, "Variety is the spice of life?" That means life is better when things are not always the same. Healthy eating includes choosing a variety of foods so that your body gets all the nutrients it needs. Ask a parent or guardian to help you create some meals and snacks that include a variety of healthy foods.

Eat More Fruits, Vegetables, and Whole Grains

When it comes to eating enough fruits, vegetables, and whole grains, many teens fall short. The guidelines recommend making half the grains you eat each day whole grains. Including leafy greens and colorful vegetables and fruits in your meals will make your food more attractive as well as more nutritious.

Balance the Calories You Consume with Physical Activity

Consume only as many calories as your body needs. A **calorie** is *a unit of heat that measures the energy available in food.* It also measures how much energy your body uses. Most teens need around 2,000 calories a day. If you are involved in regular, strenuous exercise such as running on your school's track team, you may need more. If you eat more calories than your body needs you could gain more weight than is healthy for your body.

Staying physically active will help you burn some of the calories you take in from food. **Figure 10.4** shows the relationship between calories consumed and calories burned.

Teens should be physically active for at least 60 minutes on most days. In addition to helping you maintain a healthy weight, physical activity builds strength, gives you energy, and helps you feel good about yourself.

Reading Check **Explain** Why is physical activity important?

Limit Fats, Sugar, and Salt

Look at the MyPyramid illustration in Figure 10.3 again. Can you see the narrow yellow band? This category represents fats. A healthy choice for good nutrition is to limit your intake of oils, butter, salad dressing, and other high-fat foods. Many processed and prepared foods contain hidden fats. To find out how much fat a single serving of packaged food contains, read the Nutrition Facts

Health Online

Topic: MyPyramid

Visit **health.glencoe.com** for Student Web Activities that will help you develop a personal eating plan using MyPyramid.

Activity: Using the information from the link above, create a personal eating plan based on your age, gender, and activity level.

▼ FIGURE 10.4

THE ENERGY "EQUATION"

You can burn off some of the calories you eat with physical activity. **What activities are you involved in that help your body burn calories?**

Food	Calories In		Calories Out	Activity
3-Ounce Lean Cooked Hamburger Patty	245	=	227	Playing Frisbee
English Muffin with Egg, Cheese, and Ham	360		356	Mowing the Lawn
Corn Muffin	510		522	Riding Your Bike
Grilled Chicken Sandwich, Plain Baked Potato, and Bottled Water	640		647	Swimming

panel. A typical Nutrition Facts panel appears in **Figure 10.5.** Notice that this product contains a total of 12 grams (g) of fat. How much of this fat is saturated fat?

The *Dietary Guidelines* recommend that you limit added sugars and salt. One way to cut back on added sugars is to limit foods such as cookies, cake, candy, and regular soft drinks. Enjoy these sweet treats occasionally, rather than every day. Be aware that added sugars may be present in unexpected foods, such as salad dressings and many breakfast cereals.

Salt contains **sodium,** *a nutrient that helps control the amount of fluid in your body.* Too much sodium can lead to high blood pressure in some people. Once again, you can find out how much sodium a food has by checking the Nutrition Facts panel.

Reading Check **Define** What is *sodium?*

▶ **FIGURE 10.5**

NUTRITION FACTS PANEL

Food labels provide important nutritional information that can help you make sensible food choices. **How many servings does this product contain?**

Nutrition Facts
Serving Size 1 cup (226 g)
Servings Per Container 2

Amount Per Serving	
Calories 250	Calories from Fat 110

	% Daily Value*
Total Fat 12g	18%
Saturated Fat 3g	15%
Trans Fat 3g	
Cholesterol 30g	10%
Sodium 470mg	20%
Potassium 700mg	20%
Total Carbohydrate 31g	10%
Dietary Fiber 0g	0%
Sugar 10g	
Protein 5g	
Vitamin A	4%
Vitamin C	2%
Calcium	20%
Iron	4%

*Percent Daily Values are based on a 2,000 calorie diet. Your Daily Values may be higer or lower depending on your calorie needs.

	Calories	2,000	2,500
Total Fat	Less than	65g	80g
Saturated Fat	Less than	20g	25g
Cholesterol	Less than	300mg	300mg
Sodium	Less than	2,400mg	2,400mg
Total Carbohydrate		300g	375g
Dietary Fiber		25g	30g

Keep Foods Safe to Eat

Foods must be handled and prepared properly in order to be safe to eat. If foods are improperly handled, they can become contaminated with bacteria that can cause illness. Also known as food poisoning, a **foodborne illness** is *a sickness resulting from eating food that is not safe to eat.* To maintain your health, it is important that you take steps to make sure your food is free from contamination.

The most important thing you can do to protect yourself against foodborne illness is to wash your hands with hot soapy water before handling food. Another way to keep foods safe to eat is by storing and preparing them at the right temperatures. In addition, use a separate cutting board and knife when cutting raw meat to avoid contaminating other foods.

▲ When food shopping, buy perishable foods last. Get them home and into the refrigerator promptly. **What are some other ways to prevent foodborne illness?**

Lesson 3 Review

After You Read

Review this lesson for new terms, major headings, and Reading Checks.

What I Learned

1. *Explain* Who created the MyPyramid food guidance system and what is its purpose?

2. *List* Name the five main food groups in the MyPyramid food guidance system. What does the sixth group represent?

3. *Identify* What are two things you can do to keep your foods safe from harmful bacteria?

Thinking Critically

4. *Synthesize* Explain how the MyPyramid food guidance system graphic is designed to help you know what foods to eat.

5. *Apply* Tom had a peanut butter sandwich and a glass of milk for lunch. Which food groups do these foods represent from the MyPyramid food guidance system? What else could Tom eat to add more food groups to his lunch?

Applying Health Skills

6. *Accessing Information* Check the Nutrition Facts panel of several snack foods you enjoy eating. Compare the nutrients in a single serving of each food and decide which one provides the most nutrients.

Planning Meals and Snacks

Guide to Reading

Building Vocabulary

As you read this lesson, write the two new highlighted terms and their definitions in your notebook.

- empty-calorie foods (p. 249)
- nutrient density (p. 250)

Focusing on the Main Ideas

In this lesson, you will learn to

- **explain** why breakfast is important.
- **describe** meal-planning tips.
- **identify** healthy ways to snack.

Reading Strategy

Finding the Main Idea For each of the main sections in this lesson, write one sentence that states the main idea in the section.

Quick Write

Write a short description of your favorite snack and when you tend to eat it.

▼ A healthful breakfast gives you energy that lasts throughout the morning. **Why is this important for teens in particular?**

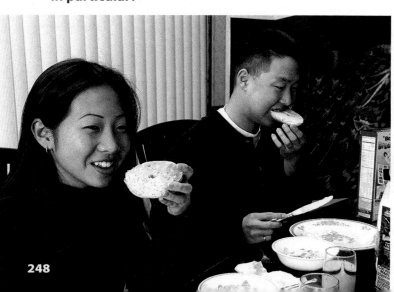

Planning Healthy Meals

The advice in the MyPyramid food guidance system can be summed up by the three words *variety, moderation*, and *balance*. Variety, as you have seen, can make your meals and snacks more nutritious and interesting. Moderation, which includes eating reasonable portions and limiting fats, sugars, and salt, can lower your risk of developing certain diseases. Balance, which means being careful not to eat more calories than your body can burn, can help you maintain a healthy weight.

In this lesson you will see how these ideas can be applied to planning healthful meals and snacks. You will learn ways to eat well, both at home and on the go.

Breakfast: Start the Day Out Right

Breakfast has been called the most important meal of the day, and for good reason. After a night of sleep, in which your body rests and repairs itself, you need breakfast to turn your body's fuel-producing mechanism back on. Breakfast gets the body going and provides the fuel you will need later in the morning. This fuel helps you to stay alert so you can concentrate in school. Research suggests that students who make time for breakfast are less likely to be absent or late for school. They also tend to do better academically than teens who do not eat breakfast.

When planning breakfast or any meal, remember that any food that supplies calories and nutrients can be part of a healthful breakfast. Round out your meal with a cup of fruit and a glass of low-fat milk. Trail mixes and packaged breakfast bars can also be good as long as the sugar content is not too high. The Nutrition Facts label on the wrapper of a breakfast bar will tell you how much sugar the bar contains.

Reading Check **Give Examples** What are some ways you can make breakfast more interesting?

Lunch and Dinner

For most Americans, lunch is a relatively small meal and dinner is large. In other cultures, the opposite is true: the largest meal is consumed at lunchtime. Instead of eating large meals, try eating four or five small meals spread out over the whole day. This will help keep your body burning calories throughout the day. Aim for variety, moderation, and balance in your food choices. By doing so, you will be planning for good health and taking measures to help prevent disease. Here are some suggestions:

- **Vary your proteins.** As a growing teen you need about five 1-ounce servings of meat and beans daily. If you are bored with regular sandwich fillings, try a fish like salmon or a nut butter made from something other than peanuts.

- **Use limited amounts of fats, sugars, and salt.** If you are someone who really likes dessert, try substituting fresh fruit or yogurt for empty-calorie foods like cake and cookies. **Empty-calorie foods** are *foods that offer few, if any, nutrients but do supply calories.*

- **Balance your eating plan.** Use a food log to write down what and how much you eat. This will help you identify which food groups you are eating too little of or too much of. Keeping track of what you eat will also give you a good idea of how many calories you are taking in.

▼ Eating well-balanced meals will give your body the nutrients it needs and keep you feeling healthy. **How can you plan a meal that includes a variety of food items?**

Health Online

Visit **health.glencoe.com** and complete the Interactive Study Guide for Lesson 4.

If you are eating more calories than your body can burn during your daily activities, you may want to cut back on calories or increase your exercise. Your eating habits may show you ways you can balance your eating plan and prevent disease and health problems.

Snacking Smart

During adolescence, your body is growing rapidly. Snacking can help you meet your nutritional needs during this period of change, especially if you choose healthy snacks.

When you snack, pay attention to what you are eating. Eating absent-mindedly can lead to overeating. Also, avoid snacking just before mealtime so that you will be able to eat your regular meal.

As for *what* to eat, remember to choose healthy foods. Healthy snacks will provide your body with important nutrients. Foods that have more nutrients than calories are considered nutrient-dense. **Nutrient density** is *the amount of nutrients relative to the number of calories they provide.* The more nutrients a food has in relation to calories, the more nutrient-dense it is. **Figure 10.6** provides some specific ideas for nutrient-dense snacks. You can probably add some snack ideas of your own.

Reading Check **Define** What is *nutrient density*?

Eating Out, Eating Right

Choosing nutritious foods and controlling your portion sizes are important strategies for maintaining your health and preventing future health problems. This can often be challenging when eating out. Portions of food tend to be larger at restaurants. Another challenge is not knowing what is in a dish.

▶ **FIGURE 10.6**

SOME SMART SNACKS

Snacking can help you meet your nutritional needs during the teen years. **What other foods do you enjoy eating that would make healthful snacks?**

Food	Calories from Fat	Food Group Equivalent
Air-popped popcorn, plain, 1 cup	0	1 cup Grains
Applesauce, ½ cup	0	½ cup Fruit
Gelatin with ½ cup sliced banana	0	½ cup Fruit
Graham crackers, 2	2	1 ounce Grains
1½ ounces of low-fat cheese and 4 saltines	52	1 ounce Grains, 1 cup Milk

When it comes to portion control, try ordering an appetizer as your meal. These are usually smaller servings. Just make sure you choose a dish that is nutrient-dense. If you do decide to order a main course, eat only half and take the other half home for a later meal. Make sure to refrigerate your leftovers as soon as you get home so they do not spoil.

Here are some other tips to help you eat healthy in restaurants:

- Check the menu for heart-healthy selections. Many restaurant menus feature dishes approved by the American Heart Association. These items appear with a small red heart next to them.

- Select foods that are grilled, broiled, or roasted, instead of fried. These foods usually contain less fat.

- Ask for salad dressing on the side. Use just enough to flavor the greens without smothering them. Do the same with sauces, gravies, and other toppings.

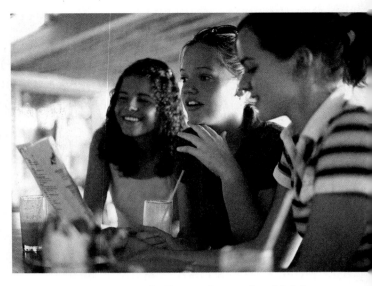

▲ Try to choose healthful foods when eating out. **What descriptions on a menu can tell you whether a food item is healthful?**

Lesson 4 Review

After You Read

Review this lesson for new terms, major headings, and Reading Checks.

What I Learned

1. *Vocabulary* What makes a food an *empty-calorie food*?

2. *Recall* Why is breakfast important?

3. *Identify* Give three meal-planning tips that can add variety, moderation, and balance to your eating plan.

Thinking Critically

4. *Explain* How can you avoid overeating when you eat at a restaurant?

5. *Apply* You are hungry, but dinner is still an hour away. Can you think of a snack that would help you feel less hungry but still leave you ready to eat dinner? How much of the snack food do you think you should eat?

Applying Health Skills

6. *Practice Healthful Behaviors* Keep a food log for two days. Record every food you eat and the nutrients that each food contains. Identify ways to improve your eating habits.

Building Health Skills

Eating for Your Health

DIRECTIONS

Goal Setting involves setting positive goals and taking steps to achieve them. This activity will give you the opportunity to develop and master this important health skill. Here's a guide to the different parts of this activity:

❶ In the **Model** section, you will read about a teen who performs the health skill successfully. This "model" scenario will show you how the skill is done.

❷ The **Practice** section will help guide you in practicing the skill.

❸ In the **Apply** section, you will have a chance to perform the skill on your own. You can use the Self-Check to check your work.

To complete this activity, first read the scenario presented in the Model. Then move on to the Practice. Finally, go ahead and try the Apply.

❶ Model

Don wanted to change his eating habits to include more healthy foods. He used the goal-setting process to develop an action plan for himself.

- **Identify a specific goal.** Don's goal was to improve his eating habits.

- **List the steps to reach your goal.** Don wrote down the following ideas:
  - Choose more fruits and vegetables.
  - Eat smaller portions of food.
  - Limit how much fast food and other high-fat foods I eat.

- **Get help from others.** Don told his parents about his plan.

- **Evaluate your progress.** Don kept a food log to help him keep track of his food choices.

- **Reward yourself.** After two weeks, Don rewarded himself by going to a movie with a friend.

❷ Practice

Don decided he also wants to change his habit of skipping breakfast. He usually gets up late every morning and does not have time to eat before he leaves for school. Don knows that eating breakfast is an important part of a healthy eating plan. Use the goal-setting process to help Don develop a plan to eat breakfast on a regular basis. Show how Don can use each step in the goal-setting process to help him reach his goal.

Skill Summary
GOAL SETTING

- Identify a specific goal.
- List the steps to reach your goal.
- Get help from others.
- Evaluate your progress.
- Reward yourself.

❸ Apply

Think about a food habit you would like to change. For example, maybe you tend to snack in front of the TV or maybe you like to eat two helpings of dessert. In a notebook, tell how accomplishing this goal will improve your health. Then, set a goal to change your habit and create an action plan to help you reach your goal. List the steps you will take to reach your goal. Decide whom you can turn to for help and support in reaching your goal. Keep track of your progress in a daily log. Bring your results to class.

Self-Check

- Did my action plan contain each step in the goal-setting process?
- Did I tell how this goal will improve my health?
- Did I keep track of my progress?

Jars of Sugar

According to some estimates, the average American eats 100 pounds of sugar each year. Some of the sources of this sugar are obvious. For example, it is clear that regular soft drinks contain a lot of sugar. However, some sources of sugar can be hidden. Sugar can also appear in foods under a variety of names. These include *corn sweetener, corn syrup, fructose, sucrose,* and others.

What You Will Need

- Seven empty baby food jars
- A container of sugar
- A set of measuring spoons

What You Will Do

1. The table shown here lists the amount of sugar, in grams, found in several popular foods. Note that 5 grams of sugar is equivalent to 1 level teaspoon of sugar. 1 gram is just under $1/4$ teaspoon and 2 grams is a little under $1/2$ teaspoon.

2. Calculate how many teaspoons of sugar each product in the list contains.

3. Using the spoons, measure out the amount of sugar in each product and place it in a jar. Label the jar with the name of the product it corresponds to.

Wrapping It Up

Evaluate your findings. Which foods contain the most sugar? Which foods contain other nutrients? What are some ways to reduce your sugar intake?

Food	Grams of Sugar
Cola (12 oz.)	42
Fat-free fruit yogurt (8 oz.)	35
Light popcorn (1 c.)	0
Fruit punch drink (8 oz.)	27
Sweetened breakfast cereal (¾ c.)	15
Three reduced-fat chocolate sandwich cookies	14
Chocolate candy bar (1.55 oz.)	40

Reading Review

FOLDABLES™ Study Organizer

Foldables™ and Other Study Aids Take out the Foldable™ that you created for Lesson 1 and any graphic organizers that you created for Lessons 1–4. Find a partner and quiz each other using these study aids.

Lesson 1 The Importance of Nutrition

Key Ideas

- Nutrients in the body do many jobs.
- Emotions can cause you to like or dislike foods because of associations with past experiences.
- You can get the nutrients your body needs by eating a variety of healthful foods.

Vocabulary

- nutrients (p. 235)
- nutrition (p. 235)
- appetite (p. 236)
- hunger (p. 236)

Lesson 2 Nutrients for Wellness

Key Ideas

- The six major kinds of nutrients are carbohydrates, proteins, fats, vitamins, minerals, and water.
- Your body uses nutrients for energy, for building and repairing tissue, and for aiding in body processes such as digestion.

Vocabulary

- carbohydrates (p. 238)
- fiber (p. 239)
- proteins (p. 240)
- saturated fats (p. 240)
- unsaturated fats (p. 240)
- vitamins (p. 240)
- minerals (p. 240)

Lesson 3 Following Nutrition Guidelines

Key Ideas

- The MyPyramid system is designed to make it easy for you to choose healthful foods, and to encourage you to be physically active.
- The five main food groups in MyPyramid are grains, vegetables, fruits, milk, and meat and beans.
- Balancing the calories you take in with the calories you burn off can help you maintain a healthy weight.

Vocabulary

- MyPyramid food guidance system (p. 243)
- calorie (p. 245)
- sodium (p. 246)
- foodborne illness (p. 247)

Lesson 4 Planning Meals and Snacks

Key Ideas

- Effective meal planning can add variety, moderation, and balance to your eating plan.
- Breakfast is one of the most important meals of the day.
- Healthy snacking involves being aware of your snack habits and choosing to snack on mostly nutrient-dense foods.

Vocabulary

- empty-calorie foods (p. 249)
- nutrient density (p. 250)

Reviewing Vocabulary and Main Ideas

On a sheet of paper, write the numbers 1–6. After each number, write the term from the list that best completes each sentence.

- nutrition
- appetite
- unsaturated **fat**
- carbohydrates
- fiber
- proteins
- nutrients
- saturated **fat**

Lesson 1 The Importance of Nutrition

1. Substances in food your body needs are called _____.
2. The study of nutrients and how the body uses them is known as _____.
3. _____ is the psychological desire for food.

Lesson 2 Nutrients for Wellness

4. _____ are sugars and starches that naturally occur, mainly in plant sources of food.
5. Nutrients your body uses to build, repair, and maintain cells and tissues are called _____.
6. Eating too much _____ can increase a person's risk of heart disease.

*On a sheet of paper, write the numbers 7–12. Write **True** or **False** for each statement below. If the statement is false, change the underlined word or phrase to make it true.*

Lesson 3 Following Nutrition Guidelines

7. The MyPyramid food guidance system reflects advice from <u>The Dietary Guidelines for Americans</u>.
8. The <u>yellow</u> wedge in MyPyramid represents grains.
9. Teens should be physically active at least <u>30</u> minutes per day.

Lesson 4 Planning Meals and Snacks

10. Many health experts think <u>dinner</u> is the most important meal of the day.
11. One way to limit fats, sugars, and salt in your eating plan is to substitute <u>nutrient-dense</u> foods for empty-calorie foods.
12. One way to <u>control portions</u> when you eat out is to eat half of your meal and take the rest home.

Thinking Critically

Using complete sentences, answer the following questions on a sheet of paper.

13. **Explain** Why should calcium-rich foods be an important part of a teen's eating plan?
14. **Evaluate** Explain how the media influences food choices.

Health Online Visit health.glencoe.com and take the Online Quiz for Chapter 10.

Write About It

15. Practicing Healthful Behaviors Write an essay that explains clearly how teens can use MyPyramid to guide their food choices.

16. Goal Setting Set a goal to change one of your eating habits. Develop a plan to reach this goal.

Standardized Test Practice

Math

Use the Nutrition Facts label to answer the questions.

Nutrition Facts	
Serving Size 3 pieces (314g)	
Servings Per Container 14	
Amount Per Serving	
Calories 359	**Calories from Fat** 219
	% Daily Value*
Total Fat 24g	36%
Saturated Fat 12g	60%
Trans Fat 4g	
Cholesterol 60g	20%
Sodium 235mg	10%
Potassium 0mg	0%
Total Carbohydrate 31g	10%
Dietary Fiber 0g	0%
Sugars 10g	
Protein 5g	
Vitamin A	2%
Vitamin C	0%
Calcium	0%
Iron	2%

* Percent Daily Values are based on a 2,000 calorie diet. Your Daily Values may be higher or lower depending on your calorie needs.

	Calories	2,000	2,500
Total Fat	Less than	65g	80g
Saturated Fat	Less than	20g	25g
Cholesterol	Less than	300mg	300mg
Sodium	Less than	2,400mg	2,400mg
Total Carbohydrate		300g	375g
Dietary Fiber		25g	30g

TEST-TAKING TIP

Make sure you understand the problem you have been asked to solve. Always check your math, if there is time, by reversing the operation. Use subtraction to check addition, for example.

1. The total calories in two servings is
  A. 36
  B. 359
  C. 718
  D. None of the above

2. Charlie ate three servings of this product in one day. How much of the Daily Value for sodium did he receive from just this one food?
  A. 10 percent
  B. 30 percent
  C. 100 percent
  D. 235 percent

Chapter Preview

▲ *Working With the Photo*

Managing your weight in healthful ways can help you feel good about your body. **How are these teens taking care of their bodies in a healthful way?**

Start-Up Activities

Before You Read How much do you know about body image? Take the short quiz on this page. Keep a record of your answers.

HEALTH QUIZ Choose the best answer for each of the following questions:

1. Which of the following statements is true?
   - **a.** It does not matter how much you weigh, as long as you like yourself.
   - **b.** Being realistic about your body is important.
   - **c.** The thinner you are, the better.
   - **d.** Being overweight does not affect your overall health.

2. The best weight for a teen is:
   - **a.** the lowest number of pounds possible.
   - **b.** whatever weight makes the teen happiest.
   - **c.** the weight that fits the teen's height, gender, and age.
   - **d.** None of the above.

ANSWERS: 1: b; 2: c

FOLDABLES™ Study Organizer

As You Read Make this Foldable™ to help you record what you learn about body weight in Lesson 1. Begin with a plain sheet of 8½" × 11" paper.

1 Fold the sheet of paper in half along the long axis.

4 Turn the paper vertically and label the tabs as shown.

2 Turn the paper and fold it into thirds.

3 Unfold and cut the top layer along both fold lines. This makes three tabs.

Under the appropriate tab of your Foldable™, record definitions and take notes on each term relating to body weight.

Health Online Visit **health.glencoe.com** and complete the Chapter 11 crossword puzzle.

Maintaining a Healthy Weight

Guide to Reading

● **Building Vocabulary**
Try to define the terms below in your own words. As you read, check and revise your definitions.

- body image (p. 260)
- appropriate weight (p. 261)
- body mass index (BMI) (p. 262)
- overweight (p. 262)
- underweight (p. 262)

● **Focusing on the Main Ideas**
In this lesson, you will learn to

- **identify** the importance of a healthy body image.
- **explain** how eating and physical activity affect weight.
- **describe** ways to maintain a healthy weight.

● **Reading Strategy**
Identifying Cause and Effect As you read, identify factors that can have an effect on your body image.

FOLDABLES Study Organizer Use the Foldable™ on p. 259 as you read this lesson.

Quick Write

Write a paragraph describing what actions you currently take to try and maintain a healthy body weight.

Body Image

A group of teens were sitting in a circle eating lunch at school talking about their weight. Crystal, who studies ballet and is tall and slender, said she wished she could lose ten pounds.

Craig had never been very athletic and was a little thin. "Personally, I'd like to look like a bodybuilder," he said with a laugh.

Have you ever wished you could change something about your body or compared yourself to a celebrity or professional athlete? If so, you are not alone. As a teen, your body is going through big changes. As your body changes in your teen years, so do your thoughts and feelings about how you look. *The way you see and feel about your body* is called your **body image.**

◀ Sometimes the media seem to suggest that there is one perfect body type. **How can this cause teens to develop a distorted body image?**

Body Image and Self-Esteem

How you feel about your body can affect your self-esteem. Self-esteem refers to what you value about yourself, both inside and out. If you feel uncomfortable about how your body looks, your self-esteem can be negatively affected.

It is important to understand that the changes your body is going through are normal. It is also important to remember that every person is unique. Though the media tend to portray females as thin and males as muscular, the real world is very different. People come in all shapes and sizes. It is more important for you to be healthy than to try to look like someone else.

The key to positive body image and high self-esteem is having an optimistic attitude and a healthy lifestyle. Know what makes you happy, set realistic goals, and spend time with people who appreciate you. Eat well, get plenty of rest and exercise, and work on developing a personal style that is all your own. Avoid comparing yourself to people in the media or to those around you. All these things will help you feel good about yourself and your body. A healthy body image will also have a positive effect on the way you interact with others.

Reading Check **List** What are some of the keys to a positive body image and high self-esteem?

Your Appropriate Weight

Many people who have an unhealthy body image complain about their weight. They think they are too fat or too thin. Is there a "right" weight for every person, and if so, how do you find it?

Everyone has an **appropriate weight.** This is *the weight that is best for your body,* and is given as a range. For example, the appropriate weight of a 5-foot, 5-inch female is between 117 and 155 pounds. A range is given because height is not the only factor that affects how much a person should weigh. To determine your appropriate weight, you need to consider your gender, age, height, and body build or frame. People are said to have small, medium, or large frames. Your frame is the size of your bone structure. Teens must also consider their growth pattern. During adolescence people grow at different rates.

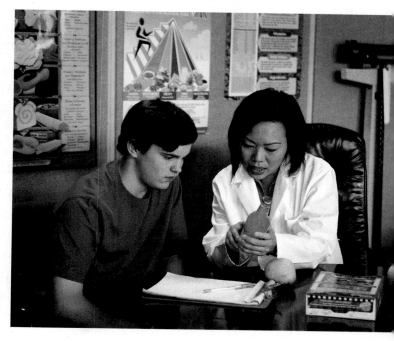

▼ A nutritionist can help you manage your weight in a healthful way. **What kind of advice do you think a nutritionist might give you?**

Health Skills Activity

Accessing Information

Finding Your BMI

To determine your BMI, follow these steps:

1. Multiply your weight by 703. If, for example, you weigh 125 pounds, you would get a result of 87,875. Write the result you get on a sheet of paper.
2. Next multiply your height in inches times itself. Write this result down as well.
3. Finally, divide your answer from Step 1 by your answer from Step 2. If you divide 87,875 by 4,225, you get 20.8. This number is your BMI.
4. Find your BMI on the grid for your gender. Remember, however, that this is only an estimate.

On Your Own

Complete the steps above to find your own BMI. Is your weight in the appropriate range for someone your age?

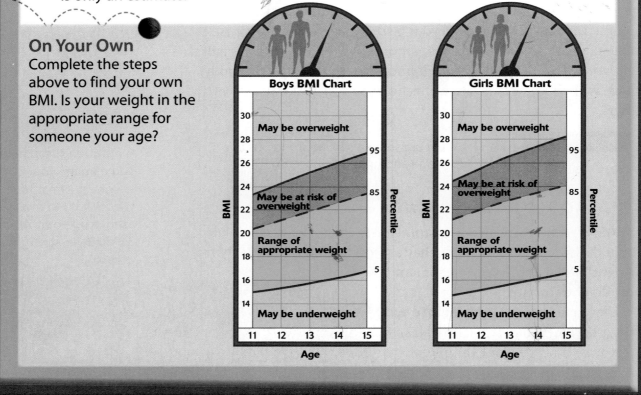

Body Mass Index

You can determine if your weight is in an appropriate range for your age by calculating your **body mass index (BMI).** This is *a measurement that allows you to assess your body size, taking your height and weight into account.* The Health Skills Activity above shows how to figure out your BMI. Your BMI is based on your weight, gender, height, and age.

Reading Check **Define** What is the *body mass index*?

Weight Problems

Many teens who compute their BMI will find that they fall within the range of appropriate weight. Some teens will find that their BMI falls above the appropriate range. This means they may be overweight or at risk of being overweight. **Overweight** means *weighing more than what is appropriate for your gender, height, age, body frame, and growth pattern.* Other teens may find that their BMI falls below the appropriate range, meaning they may be underweight. **Underweight** is *weighing less than is appropriate for your gender, height, age, body frame, and growth pattern.*

Overweight Teens

The number of overweight children and teens in the United States is at an all-time high. Over the past 40 years, the number of overweight teens has risen by 300 percent. The increase among children 6 to 11 years old is 400 percent.

This trend can be traced to lifestyle factors. These include overeating or eating too many empty-calorie foods, and getting too little physical activity. The extra pounds mean added stress on the heart and lungs. They also mean an increased risk of lifestyle-related illnesses. One such illness, type 2 diabetes, has spread rapidly among young people. At one time type 2 diabetes showed up almost exclusively in adults. As recently as 20 years ago, only 2 percent of new cases involved children and teens. Today, the number of new childhood and teen cases is almost 20 percent. Those who are overweight are also at risk of developing heart disease, cancer, and stroke.

Underweight Teens

With all the concern about overweight teens, it is easy to overlook the problem of teens who are underweight. Teens who are too thin lack body fat, which is an important source of energy. Underweight teens may also be undernourished. This means their bodies are not getting enough of the nutrients they need to grow and function normally. The absence of some nutrients, especially proteins, makes it hard for the body to fight infection. Underweight teens are also at risk of developing anemia. This is a blood condition caused by a lack of iron in the diet. Anemia can make you feel tired and rundown.

Reading Check

Explain What are two factors that have caused a rise in the number of overweight teens?

▲ Spending too much time in front of a computer can contribute to weight problems. **What are some activities you can participate in to maintain a healthy and balanced lifestyle?**

Health Online

Topic: The Lowdown on Diets

Visit **health.glencoe.com** for Student Web Activities to learn about the wide variety of diets on the market and how to tell the difference between the healthy ones and the dangerous ones.

Activity: Using the information provided at the link above, make a flyer entitled "Dieting Do's and Don'ts" that includes important facts all teens should know about dieting.

Reaching an Appropriate Weight

The secret to reaching or maintaining a healthful weight is to adjust your "energy equation." This is the balance between "calories in" (from food) and "calories out" (from physical activity). A pound of weight equals about 3,500 calories. If you are underweight, you need to take in more calories from food than your body burns off. If you are overweight, the opposite is true: you need to burn more calories than you take in. Exercise or other physical activities can help you burn some of the calories you take in from food.

The MyPyramid food guidance system recommends that teens get approximately 60 minutes of physical activity per day on most days. Calorie needs vary by age, gender, and activity level. Females between the ages of 14 and 18 need approximately 1,800 to 2,400 calories each day depending on how active they are. Males in the same age group need approximately 2,200 to 3,200 depending on activity level.

Beyond the Energy Equation

It is important to recognize that healthy weight management is more than just counting calories. You need to pay attention to the source of the calories you eat. For example, the average chocolate bar provides 250 calories. A turkey breast sandwich on whole-wheat bread has the same number of calories. However, the chocolate bar contains empty calories—there are very few nutrients. The turkey sandwich, by contrast, provides nutrients from two different food groups. The point is to make sure that most of the calories you take in provide nutrients your body needs.

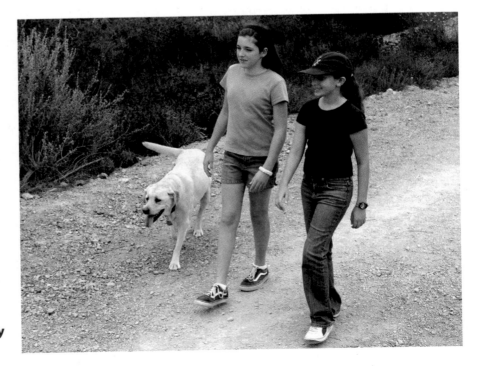

▶ Physical activity can help burn some of the calories you take in from food. **Why is it important to balance the calories you take in with the calories your body burns off?**

The MyPyramid food guidance system, discussed in Chapter 10, can help you develop a personalized eating plan based on the number of calories your body needs.

 Reading Check **Recall** How much physical activity is recommended for teens?

Managing Weight in a Healthy Way

Some people who need to lose weight look for shortcuts. Instead of eating right and getting reasonable exercise, they turn to fad diets, diet pills, and extreme workout programs that promise fast results. Though the products claim to help people shed pounds quickly, some of these products may be ineffective and also unsafe. A person who needs to lose weight should do so gradually by slowly increasing physical activity and eating only as many calories as his or her body needs.

People needing to gain weight also should carefully analyze how they can gradually add calories and nutrients. If you need to adjust your weight, talk to your health care provider. He or she can recommend a safe, healthy approach that will help you reach your goal in a reasonable amount of time.

Health Online

Visit **health.glencoe.com** and complete the Interactive Study Guide for Lesson 1.

Lesson 1 Review

After You Read

Review this lesson for new terms, major headings, and Reading Checks.

What I Learned

1. *Vocabulary* What is the meaning of *appropriate weight*?

2. *Recall* Why is a healthy body image important?

3. *Explain* What factors is your BMI based on? What does your BMI tell you?

4. *Identify* What are some healthful ways to reach an appropriate weight?

Thinking Critically

5. *Describe* How can eating and physical activity habits affect weight? What can you do to assure your habits are healthy?

6. *Apply* Imagine that a teen takes in 2,000 calories each day and burns 2,300 calories. Over time, what will happen to the teen's weight? Explain your answer.

Applying Health Skills

7. *Practicing Healthful Behaviors* With a small group, brainstorm good health habits that could affect the energy equation. Make a list of these habits and their impact. Be prepared to share your list with other groups.

Eating Disorders

Guide to Reading

● **Building Vocabulary**

As you read this lesson, write each new highlighted term and its definition in your notebook.

- eating disorder (p. 266)
- binge eating disorder (p. 267)
- obese (p. 267)
- anorexia nervosa (p. 267)
- bulimia nervosa (p. 268)

● **Focusing on the Main Ideas**

In this lesson, you will learn to

- **describe** the symptoms of various eating disorders.
- **explain** the health risks associated with an eating disorder.
- **identify** sources of help that are available for a person with an eating disorder.

● **Reading Strategy**

Comparing and Contrasting Create a chart that shows the similarities and differences between the eating disorders discussed in the lesson.

Quick Write

Write a paragraph explaining why you think some teens develop an eating disorder.

What Are Eating Disorders?

Patricia's parents were worried about her. She had been eating almost nothing at mealtime for several weeks and had lost a lot of weight. When her mother tried to talk to her about how little she was eating, Patricia got angry. "Why do you keep bugging me about eating?" she shouted. "Can't you see how fat I am?" Her mother looked at Patricia in disbelief. The last word anyone would use to describe Patricia was *fat*. If anything, she seemed too thin.

By thinking she was fat and not wanting to eat, Patricia was showing signs of an **eating disorder**—*an extreme and damaging eating behavior that can lead to sickness and even death.* She is one of an estimated 36 million people in this country who have an eating disorder. Many of these people suffer from unrealistic and unhealthy body images.

Eating disorders have little to do with physical hunger. Often, these disorders are brought on by mental/emotional problems, such as depression or low self-esteem. Having an eating disorder places a person at risk for developing severe medical problems. The risk is especially great for teens whose bodies are already undergoing dramatic physical changes.

Reading Check **Define** What is an *eating disorder*?

Binge Eating Disorder

A **binge eating disorder,** which is *compulsive overeating,* is the most common eating disorder. A compulsion is something you feel you cannot control. Binge eaters cannot control their desire to eat, so they compulsively overeat. About 25 million Americans suffer from this disorder.

People with this disorder eat even when they are not hungry. They also eat food in amounts large enough to make them physically uncomfortable. They often eat alone so that others do not see the amount of food they eat. They may also hide food for the same reason. Because of the excessive amounts of food they eat, most compulsive eaters have serious weight problems, and many are obese. **Obese** means *weighing more than 20 percent higher than what is appropriate for their height, age, and body frame.*

The guilt and depression that compulsive eaters feel about their problem can contribute to a low self-esteem and poor body image.

Reading Check **Explain** What can a binge eating disorder lead to?

Anorexia Nervosa

Patricia's symptoms described in the lesson opener are typical of **anorexia nervosa.** This is *an eating disorder characterized by self-starvation leading to extreme weight loss.* Anorexia means "without appetite," and nervosa means "of nervous origin."

Anorexia is most common among female teens between the ages of 14 and 18, though the disorder can occur in males as well. People with anorexia often do well in school, but have low self-esteem and a poor body image. In an effort to gain control over their lives and bodies, they begin to change their diet. This usually means eating less and less food in an effort to lose weight. Even when a person with anorexia is dangerously thin, she may still see herself as being overweight.

When the body is deprived of adequate food, a number of serious problems can develop. The person may become significantly underweight. Without proper nutrients, the body cannot grow and repair itself

▼ An unhealthy body image can lead to an eating disorder. **What are some ways to build a healthy body image?**

Caring

An eating disorder is a cry for help. If you believe that a friend has an eating disorder, talk with a trusted adult such as a school counselor or nurse. Consulting an adult is not an act of betrayal. It is the best way to show you care about your friend. Who are some other trusted adults you could turn to if you suspect a friend has an eating disorder?

▼ People with bulimia often binge on foods high in calories and fat. **How does this type of eating pattern damage the body?**

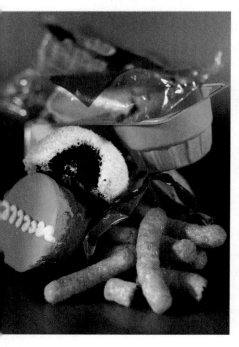

in normal ways. For example, bones become thin and brittle from lack of calcium, and body temperature and blood pressure drop.

If left untreated, a person with anorexia could die from starvation, heart failure, kidney failure, or other medical complications. The depression that often comes with anorexia can sometimes lead to thoughts of suicide.

Reading Check **Identify** Name two symptoms of anorexia nervosa.

Bulimia Nervosa

Bulimia nervosa is another eating disorder that primarily affects female teens. However, one in ten people with bulimia is male. **Bulimia nervosa** is *a condition in which a person eats large amounts of food and then secretly purges.* Purging means to get rid of or remove something. People with bulimia purge the food they have eaten by vomiting or taking laxatives. They may also exercise too much in an effort to work off the calories they have eaten.

Like with anorexia, people with bulimia are very concerned with losing weight and maintaining strict control of their bodies. They do not usually become extremely thin, however. For this reason it can be hard to tell if a person is suffering from bulimia and needs help. The signs of bulimia are subtle. For example, the person might go into a bathroom immediately after eating a large meal and vomit. He or she may run water to cover the sound of vomiting. Another sign is swollen cheeks caused by vomiting.

Although people with bulimia are not usually at risk of starving to death, the disorder can seriously damage their health in other ways. Stomach acids from frequent vomiting eat away at tooth enamel and injure the mouth and throat. Frequent vomiting can also cause a hormone imbalance, dehydration, damage to the kidneys and liver, and loss of important minerals.

Reading Check **Describe** What are some health risks of bulimia nervosa?

Help for People with Eating Disorders

A person with an eating disorder needs help. Treatment can involve working with a counselor, primary care doctor, and nutritionist. These health care providers can help the person rebuild his or her physical and mental/emotional health. When an eating disorder involves serious medical problems or severe depression, a hospital or special treatment facility may be recommended.

◀ Getting help is the first step toward recovery. **What are some treatments for people with eating disorders?**

Health Online

Visit **health.glencoe.com** and complete the Interactive Study Guide for Lesson 2.

Lesson 2 Review

 After You Read

Review this lesson for new terms, major headings, and Reading Checks.

What I Learned

1. *Vocabulary* What is another name for *binge eating disorder*?

2. *List* What are two health risks associated with anorexia nervosa?

3. *Identify* What are two signs of bulimia nervosa?

4. *Describe* What kinds of help are available to a person with an eating disorder?

Thinking Critically

5. *Evaluate* In what ways are the symptoms of anorexia and bulimia similar? In what ways are the two disorders different?

6. *Apply* Shauna suspects that her friend Jenna has an eating disorder. Lately, Jenna hardly eats anything and is getting thin. What could Shauna do to help? Explain your answer.

Applying Health Skills

7. *Advocacy* With a group, create a documentary titled "The Truth Behind Eating Disorders." Reveal facts and statistics you think the average teen may not be aware of. If you have access to a video camera, record your documentary. Otherwise, arrange to perform your documentary live for other classes.

Building Health Skills

Changing Your Weight Safely

DIRECTIONS

Accessing Information involves finding reliable information to make healthy choices. This activity will give you the opportunity to develop and master this important health skill. Here's a guide to the different parts of this activity:

❶ In the **Model** section, you will read about a teen who performs the health skill successfully. This "model" scenario will show you how the skill is done.

❷ The **Practice** section will help guide you in practicing the skill.

❸ In the **Apply** section, you will have a chance to perform the skill on your own. You can use the Self-Check to check your work.

To complete this activity, first read the scenario presented in the Model. Then move on to the Practice. Finally, go ahead and try the Apply.

❶ Model

Before you make changes to your weight, be sure to get reliable information that will help you come up with a sensible plan.

When Allyson went for her yearly medical checkup, she learned she was underweight. The doctor recommended that she take a nutrient supplement.

Allyson and her mother went to the grocery store. They found a dozen different nutrient supplements on the shelves. Allyson took the following steps to find out which product would be the most effective.

- *Read product labels.* Allyson turned her attention to the information panel that listed the ingredients.

- *Consult Internet Sources.* Allyson used Web sites ending in .gov, .org, and .edu to look up information on the different products.

- *Follow up by consulting an independent, reliable authority.* Allyson later spoke to a pharmacist who said that the extra fat and sugar in some products were not a good idea.

② Practice

Allyson's experience soon came in handy. Her sister was home from college and wanted to lose some weight. Allyson was able to help her make an informed decision. She recommended using reliable, independent sources to check out claims about each diet. Government health agency Web sites, she said, were good options. Finally, she told her sister that she should speak to their family doctor before starting any diet.

1. What source of information did Allyson suggest?

2. Why did Allyson advise her sister to use .gov sources?

Skill Summary
ACCESSING INFORMATION

- Read product labels.
- Consult Internet sources (.gov, .org, or .edu).
- Get advice from a reliable authority.

③ Apply

With a small group, find an ad for a popular weight-loss or weight-gain product. Make a poster showing the front and back label of the product. Circle any claims or information that you believe is questionable. Below the labels, list an online or print resource you found that could provide reliable information about the product. Share and compare your poster with the other groups.

Self-Check

- Did we show the front and back labels of our product?
- Did we circle any claim or piece of information that was questionable?
- Did we find an independent source of reliable information about this product?

The heat is on young celebrities to look thinner than ever. Unfortunately, some fans will do almost anything to be just like them.

Pressure to be PERFECT

Surrounded by images of young celebrities who are painfully thin, teens can feel lots of pressure to meet the same standard. Trying hard to look like their idols, some can starve themselves and literally make themselves sick.

"Glamorous teen celebrities seem to have it made," says Dr. Susan Sabin, an expert on body image problems. "It appears that their lives are trouble-free, happy, and constantly entertaining— and the way to get all that is a perfect, skinny body."

STARS IN THEIR EYES

Even young celebrities themselves are not immune from the pressure. "I've been there, trust me," says one young pop star who has appeared in a few movies. "When I was younger, I tried to be skinny. There is so much pressure in today's society to look like the girl on the cover of the magazine. But those photos are airbrushed and have special lighting. The model has gone through two hours of hair and makeup. That just sets expectations really high for girls."

For teens, aspiring to unrealistic standards can lead to self-doubt, depression, extreme dieting—and in some cases, eating disorders. Dr. Sabin notes that many of her patients idolize one young TV star who is extremely thin. Nobody has said the star has an eating disorder, but Dr. Sabin believes that her very thin image is glamorized and admired.

A GROWING PROBLEM

Because many cases go unreported, the statistics vary, but 5 million or more girls and women in America are estimated to suffer from anorexia and other eating disorders. While anorexia is relatively rare—affecting up to 3.7 percent of the female population at some point in their lifetime—it is the most deadly of all mental diseases. About 5 to 10 percent of anorexics die from it or its complications.

LOOK SMART

Here are few ways to keep you—and your friends—on track when it comes to body image.

- Avoid idealizing celebrities whose bodies appear thinner than normal.
- Remember there is no perfect body shape.
- Don't worry about clothing sizes. Just find clothes that fit you best.
- If you're worried that a friend might have an eating disorder, talk to an adult.

Reading Review

Lesson 1 Maintaining a Healthy Weight

Key Ideas
- Teens with a healthy body image are more likely to have positive self-esteem. This in turn affects the way they interact with others.
- To build a healthy body image, teens should keep a positive attitude, eat healthy, exercise, get plenty of rest, set realistic goals, and spend time with people who appreciate them.
- To maintain a healthy weight, you need to adjust your "energy equation." This means balancing "calories in" from food with "calories out" from physical activity.

Vocabulary
- body image (p. 260)
- appropriate weight (p. 261)
- body mass index (BMI) (p. 262)
- overweight (p. 263)
- underweight (p. 263)

Lesson 2 Eating Disorders

Key Ideas
- Symptoms of anorexia nervosa include extreme weight loss and depression. Health risks include starvation, heart and kidney failure, and other medical complications.
- Signs of bulimia nervosa include vomiting after meals and swollen cheeks, caused by vomiting. Health risks include loss of tooth enamel and injury to the mouth and throat from stomach acids, dehydration, loss of important minerals, hormone imbalances, and damage to the kidneys and liver from laxative abuse.
- Symptoms of binge eating disorder include eating when not hungry, eating beyond the point of feeling comfortably full, and depression. Health risks from binge eating disorder include obesity.
- Help for a person with an eating disorder includes treatment by a team of health care providers. If the symptoms are extreme, the patient may be sent to a hospital or a treatment facility.

Vocabulary
- eating disorder (p. 266)
- binge eating disorder (p. 267)
- obese (p. 267)
- anorexia nervosa (p. 267)
- bulimia nervosa (p. 268)

After You Read

HEALTH QUIZ

Now that you have read the chapter, look back at your answers to the Health Quiz on the chapter opener. Would you change any of them? What would your answers be now?

Reviewing Vocabulary and Main Ideas

On a sheet of paper, write the numbers 1–5. After each number, write the term from the list that best completes each sentence.

- anorexia nervosa
- appropriate weight
- body image
- body mass index (BMI)
- bulimia nervosa
- obese
- overweight
- underweight

Lesson 1 Maintaining a Healthy Weight

1. The way you see and feel about your body is your _____.

2. _____ is the weight range that is best for your body.

3. A formula you can use to determine if your weight is appropriate for you is called _____.

4. _____ means weighing more than what is appropriate for gender, height, age, body frame, and growth pattern.

5. _____ is weighing less than what is appropriate for gender, height, age, body frame, and growth pattern.

Lesson 2 Eating Disorders

On a sheet of paper, write the numbers 6–10. After each number, write the letter of the answer that best completes each statement.

6. In this country, anorexia nervosa affects mostly
- **a.** female teens.
- **b.** male teens.
- **c.** male adults.
- **d.** female adults.

7. Losing weight to the point of becoming dangerously thin is a sign of
- **a.** all eating disorders.
- **b.** anorexia nervosa.
- **c.** bulimia nervosa.
- **d.** binge eating disorder.

8. The condition in which a person secretly eats large amounts of food and then tries to purge is called
- **a.** obesity.
- **b.** anorexia nervosa.
- **c.** bulimia nervosa.
- **d.** compulsive eating.

9. Obesity is a health risk of which of the following conditions?
- **a.** anorexia
- **b.** bulimia
- **c.** compulsive eating
- **d.** None of the above

10. Which of the following health care providers usually treats people with eating disorders?
- **a.** counselor
- **b.** primary care doctor
- **c.** nutritionist
- **d.** All of the above

Health Online Visit **health.glencoe.com** and take the Online Quiz for Chapter 11.

Thinking Critically

Using complete sentences, answer the following questions on a sheet of paper.

11. **Apply** A number of teens are invited to a swim party. Kim, one of the teens, says she does not want to be seen in a bathing suit. Imagine you are Kim's best friend. What might you tell her?

12. **Explain** Why is it often difficult to tell if a person has an eating disorder?

Write About It

13. **Accessing Information** Using online or print resources, research alternate formulas for computing BMI. Then develop your findings into an article.

14. **Practicing Healthful Behaviors** Write a journal entry in which you identify three positive health behaviors that can help a teen develop a healthy body image. Explain why a healthy body image is important.

Career Corner

Psychologist Are you fascinated by how the mind works? Perhaps you should consider a career as a psychologist. Psychologists study human behavior. In practice, they help people understand and improve their behaviors. A doctoral degree in psychology is required to enter this profession. Find out more about this and other health careers by visiting the *Career Corner* at **health.glencoe.com**.

Standardized Test Practice

Reading

Read the passage and then answer the questions.

Dieting is a very popular pastime in America. Everywhere you look you can find advertisements for diets that claim they will help you "Lose Pounds Fast!" Most diets that make this claim focus on helping dieters lose weight by getting rid of excess water rather than fat. Although water is easy to lose, it is also easy to gain. This often leads to what health experts call "seesaw dieting," "weight cycling," or "yo-yo dieting" in which a person gains and loses weight rapidly.

Since part of the weight that many people regain is fat, yo-yo dieting can be unhealthier than being overweight. Any teen who needs to lose weight should do so in a healthy way. This means losing the weight gradually by eating smaller portions and exercising under the supervision of a doctor or other health professional.

TEST-TAKING TIP

Make sure you grasp the main idea of the reading passage as a whole. Make sure that you also understand the main point of each paragraph.

1. Which of the following is *not* a name for "rapid ups and downs in weight"?
   A. seesaw dieting
   B. weight cycling
   C. yo-yo dieting
   D. burning calories

2. Which sentence *best* captures the main point of the second paragraph?
   A. Water is replaced by more body fat.
   B. Yo-yo dieting may be less healthy than being slightly overweight.
   C. Body fat is hard to lose.
   D. Losing weight gets harder the more you diet.

CHAPTER

12 Alcohol

Chapter Preview

▲ **Working With the Photo**

Alcohol is a powerful drug. It affects individuals differently. **Do you know some of alcohol's effects on the body?**

Start-Up Activities

Before You Read

Read the Instant Message below. Suppose you were geobot171. How would you respond to your friend's comment? Keep a record of your answer.

IM Express

geobot171: You hear about Jimmy? He got caught with a beer at the dance. They suspended him.

zzzgetfish: That was dumb. I told him he'd get caught. If he's gonna drink, he should never do it in public!

FOLDABLES™ Study Organizer

As You Read

Make this Foldable™ to organize the information in Lessons 2 and 3 on alcohol and its effects on the body. Begin with a plain sheet of 11" × 17" paper.

1 Fold the sheet of paper into thirds along the short axis. This forms three columns.

2 Open the paper and refold into thirds along the long axis, then fold in half lengthwise. This forms six rows.

3 Unfold and draw lines along the folds.

4 Label the chart as shown.

Effects	Short-Term	Long-Term
Mouth and Esophagus		
Heart and Blood Vessels		
Brain and Nervous System		
Liver		
Stomach and Pancreas		

In the appropriate section of the chart, take notes on the short- and long-term effects of drinking alcohol.

Health Online Visit **health.glencoe.com** and complete the Health Inventory for Chapter 12.

Why Alcohol Is Harmful

Guide to Reading

Building Vocabulary
Read the terms in the list below. Then, write what you think the definitions are in your notebook. Make any corrections that are needed as you read the text.

- alcohol (p. 278)
- depressants (p. 278)
- alternatives (p. 281)

Focusing on the Main Ideas
In this lesson, you will learn to

- **explain** why some teens drink alcohol.
- **state** reasons not to drink alcohol.
- **identify** alternatives to drinking alcohol.

Reading Strategy
Organizing Information Make a diagram titled *What Teens Should Know About Alcohol*. Draw spokes from the heading. Under each, note one of the facts from the lesson.

*Q*uick Write

Find a news story about a traffic accident involving alcohol. Write a short summary of the story.

What Is Alcohol?

Alcohol is *a drug that is produced by a chemical reaction in fruits, vegetables, and grains.* There are, however, several kinds of alcohol. Some are used to kill germs. Others can be found in medicines, cleaners, and fuels. The kind of alcohol we are talking about in this chapter is a beverage. It is called *ethanol* alcohol. Ethanol alcohol is produced by a chemical reaction called *fermentation.*

Alcohol is a drug. That means that it affects the brain and central nervous system, causing changes in behavior. Alcohol belongs to a group of drugs known as depressants. **Depressants** are *drugs that slow down the body's functions and reactions.* Even small amounts of alcohol can affect how a person feels and behaves. For example, many people have mood changes when they drink alcohol. Some become

◀ Many teens are making the decision to stay alcohol free and are finding many healthier social activities to engage in. **How can abstaining from alcohol improve your health triangle?**

relaxed and friendly. Others become depressed and angry. Having alcohol in the body makes it hard to think clearly and make good decisions. That is why many people say and do things they regret after they drink.

Reading Check **Define** What are *depressants*?

Alcohol Use and Teens

A teen's body and mind are still growing and developing. Research has shown that alcohol use can interfere with long- and short-term growth. Alcohol can harm the brain's ability to learn, and make it hard to remember. Teens who drink are more likely to fall behind in school. Alcohol also increases the risk of social problems, depression, suicidal thoughts, and violence.

Teens who drink alcohol risk getting into trouble with the law. It is illegal for anyone under the age of 21 to use alcohol. If you are caught buying or drinking alcohol, you could be arrested, fined, or sent to a youth detention center.

Finally, alcohol is the cause of hundreds of traffic accidents every year. One third of all teen traffic deaths are related to alcohol.

▲ Alcohol is a depressant that can cause changes in mood. **What other negative effects does alcohol have on your health?**

Why Some Teens Drink Alcohol

Teens who drink risk damaging their health. Why, then, do some young people drink alcohol? Here are some reasons teens give.

What Teens May Say	What Teens Should Know
• "Drinking will help me forget about my problems."	• The problems will still be there when the effects of alcohol wear off.
• "I'll look more grown-up with a drink in my hand."	• You won't look mature getting in trouble for illegal underage drinking.
• "Movies make drinking look cool."	• Filmmakers want you to spend money to see their movie.
• "My friends keep pressuring me to try alcohol."	• Real friends won't pressure you to do something that you don't want to do.
• "I'm stressed out about school. A drink will help me relax."	• Alcohol interferes with sleep and performance in school or other activities, creating more stress.

Reading Check **Identify** What are some reasons teens give for trying alcohol?

Health Skills Activity

Refusal Skills

Life of the Party

Kim has been invited to a party at her friend Terry's house. When she arrives, she finds that Terry's parents are not at home and many teens are drinking beer. Terry tells her that her older brother brought the beer. She urges Kim to try some. Kim knows that it is illegal for teens to drink and has learned about the risks of using alcohol. What do you think Kim should do when her friend laughs at her concerns and continues to offer her a drink?

On Your Own

Apply the S.T.O.P. strategy described below to help Kim say no to using alcohol.
1. **S**ay no in a firm voice.
2. **T**ell why not.
3. **O**ffer other ideas.
4. **P**romptly leave.

Health Online

Visit **health.glencoe.com** and complete the Interactive Study Guide for Lesson 1.

Reasons Not to Drink

Does the phrase "just say no" sound familiar? Choosing not to use alcohol is a healthy choice. It shows you understand how risky drinking can be and are choosing to stay alcohol free. Some teens may believe that drinking alcohol will help them fit in with their peers.

In reality, the Centers for Disease Control and Prevention's most recent report reveals that the majority of teens do *not* drink. Many teens realize the negative effects alcohol can have on their health and are saying no to alcohol use.

► Alcohol is one of the biggest factors in teen traffic deaths. **Can you think of a better reason to stay alcohol free?**

There are important reasons why you should join this majority. First, you are risking your health when you drink. Second, using alcohol is against the law for teens. Finally, you want to make decisions that will help you become a strong person. Teens who stay alcohol free are better able to handle the challenges of everyday life.

Reading Check **Explain** Why is drinking a bad idea for teens?

Alternatives to Drinking Alcohol

Teens who avoid alcohol may want to seek positive alternatives to drinking. But what **alternatives** or *other ways of thinking or acting* are available to teens who choose not to drink? One positive alternative is sports. Learning new skills, discovering a new talent, challenging your body, and being part of a team are all alternatives to drinking alcohol.

Other alternatives include pursuing interests in theater or the arts, volunteering in your community, and advocacy. Becoming an advocate gives you a chance to make a difference in the lives of others. There are many advocacy groups that try to help teens like yourself make smart choices. Some of these include Students Against Destructive Decisions (SADD), Teens Against Tobacco Use (T.A.T.U.), and Youth for Environmental Sanity.

▲ There are much more fun ways to spend time with friends than drinking alcohol. **What activities do you enjoy?**

Lesson 1 Review

After You Read

Review this lesson for new terms, major headings, and Reading Checks.

What I Learned

1. *Vocabulary* Define *alcohol,* and use it in a sentence.

2. *State* What are three reasons not to drink alcohol?

3. *Explain* What are two reasons teens give for using alcohol?

Thinking Critically

4. *Evaluate* How can positive alternatives help a teen avoid using alcohol?

5. *Apply* You are at an amusement park with several friends. When it is time to leave, a friend's brother offers to give you a ride. You believe you smell alcohol on his breath. What should you do, and why?

Applying Health Skills

6. *Advocacy* Create a TV ad that encourages teens *not* to drink. Use images and reasons you think will appeal to teens your age. Share your ad with your classmates.

Short-Term Effects of Alcohol Use

Guide to Reading

● **Building Vocabulary**
As you read this lesson, write each new highlighted term and its definition in your notebook.

■ reaction time (p. 282)
■ intoxication (p. 283)
■ blood alcohol content (BAC) (p. 283)
■ alcohol poisoning (p. 283)
■ malnutrition (p. 285)

● **Focusing on the Main Ideas**
In this lesson, you will learn to

■ **describe** how alcohol travels through the body.
■ **explain** the short-term effects alcohol has on a person.
■ **identify** factors that account for different reactions to alcohol among different people.

● **Reading Strategy**
Sequencing Using Figure 12.1, trace the course alcohol takes after it enters the body. Name the various organs it reaches.

FOLDABLES Study Organizer Use the Foldable™ on p. 277 as you read this lesson.

Quick Write

Write a paragraph describing how you think alcohol affects the body.

◀ Alcohol consumption can cause delays in reaction time. **How can this make the activity in this picture very dangerous?**

Alcohol and the Body

Alcohol is a very fasting-acting drug. It begins to affect the body the moment it enters the mouth, so it can be felt almost immediately. If there is no food in the stomach, alcohol can reach the brain in under a minute and slow reaction time. **Reaction time** is *the ability of the body to respond quickly and appropriately to situations.* This is what makes drinking and driving so deadly. People with slowed reaction time cannot respond quickly enough to dangers on the road.

Reading Check **Define** What is *reaction time?*

Intoxication

As you can see from the diagram in **Figure 12.1**, the liver's job is to break down alcohol once it enters the bloodstream. This process takes time. The liver can only process about half an ounce of alcohol per hour. Anything

▼ FIGURE 12.1

ALCOHOL'S JOURNEY THROUGH THE BODY

Alcohol travels through the body, where it is filtered by the liver. What effects can alcohol have on the liver?

Brain and Nervous System
In the brain, alcohol affects memory, speech, judgment, vision, and hearing.

Mouth and Esophagus
Alcohol enters the body through the mouth. It travels down the esophagus to the stomach.

Liver
In the liver, alcohol is broken down. It is changed into water and carbon dioxide gas. Ninety percent leaves the body. Much of the remainder is eliminated as liquid waste or escapes through the pores or breath.

Heart and Blood Vessels
The heart pumps the alcohol throughout the body.

Stomach and Pancreas
Some people become sick to the stomach, especially first-time drinkers. Many vomit. Most of the alcohol passes into the small intestine. Some, however, is absorbed into the bloodstream. From there some of it passes into the liver.

more stays in the blood and travels through the body causing intoxication. **Intoxication** means *a person's mental and physical abilities have been impaired by alcohol.*

If a person continues to drink, his or her blood alcohol content will continue to rise. **Blood alcohol content** or **BAC** is *a measure of the amount of alcohol present in a person's blood.* BAC is expressed as a percentage of the total amount of blood in the body. A BAC of 0.02% is enough to make most people feel lightheaded. A BAC of 0.08% is enough to make it dangerous for a person to drive a car. If a person has a BAC of 0.08% he or she is considered legally intoxicated.

People who are heavily intoxicated are at risk of alcohol poisoning. **Alcohol poisoning** is *a dangerous condition that results when a person drinks excessive amounts of alcohol over a short time period.* And as with any drug overdose, alcohol poisoning can kill you.

Reading Check **Identify** What is the BAC of a legally drunk driver?

Connect To... Language Arts

Intoxication

The word *intoxicate* contains the prefix *in-*, meaning "having or toward," and the suffix *–ate*, meaning "the action of." That leaves the root word, *toxic*. Look this root up in the dictionary.

Tell how this root's meaning relates to the terms intoxication *and* alcohol poisoning.

How Alcohol Affects the Individual

One of the greatest dangers of alcohol is that there is no way to tell how a person will act when alcohol is in his or her body. Several things determine the effect alcohol may have:

- **Gender and body size:** Females and smaller people are affected more quickly than males and larger people.

- **Other drugs:** Alcohol mixed with other drugs or medicines can be deadly. Each drug can make the effects of the others stronger.

- **Food:** Food in the stomach slows down alcohol absorption.

- **General health:** How healthy and well-rested a person is, affects how the body responds to alcohol. Someone who is over tired or sick will be affected more quickly.

- **How fast you drink:** The faster a person drinks, the more he or she will be affected by alcohol.

- **How much you drink:** The amount a person drinks affects how his or her body reacts. Different alcoholic beverages contain different amounts of alcohol. **Figure 12.2** shows a comparison of alcohol content in a variety of beverages. Drinking a lot or very quickly overworks the liver and causes intoxication.

Reading Check **Explain** What role does a drinker's weight and gender play in how he or she is affected?

▼ FIGURE 12.2

ALCOHOL CONTENT OF DIFFERENT DRINKS

Alcoholic drinks are only partly alcohol. The rest is water, flavoring, and minerals. Each of the drinks shown contains the same amount of alcohol—0.6 oz. of pure alcohol. **How much beer would a person need to drink to consume the same amount of alcohol in two 5 oz. glasses of wine?**

Beer 12 oz.   **Wine** 5 oz.   **Liquor** 1.5 oz.

Alcohol Use and Violence

Those who drink are more likely to fight or behave violently. This is because alcohol makes many people aggressive. Alcohol use causes a great deal of violence both in and outside the home. Two-thirds of all domestic violence cases are related to alcohol abuse. Violence also increases at sporting events where alcohol is served.

Alcohol and Nutrition

Alcohol affects the body's ability to use nutrients. Long-term use of alcohol can lead to **malnutrition,** *a condition in which the body doesn't get the nutrients it needs to grow and function properly.* Because alcohol comes from the breakdown of sugar, it has calories. These calories have almost no nutritional value. When a person drinks alcohol for a long period of time and is not eating enough healthy food, he or she may not be getting enough nutrients. The calories in alcohol can also cause unwanted weight gain, especially when combined with other high-calorie beverages like soda and fruit juice.

Health Online

Visit health.glencoe.com and complete the Interactive Study Guide for Lesson 2.

Lesson 2 Review

After You Read

Review this lesson for new terms, major headings, and Reading Checks.

What I Learned

1. *Vocabulary* What is *blood alcohol content?*

2. *Recall* How long does it take alcohol to reach the brain of a person who has not eaten recently?

3. *Give Examples* List three factors that can influence the effect alcohol has on a person.

Thinking Critically

4. *Apply* Review alcohol's journey through the body in Figure 12.1. Explain why people who have been drinking might smell like alcohol.

5. *Analyze* Allie is at a party at a friend's house. She has had trouble sleeping lately because of worries over a big exam. Someone at the party suggests everyone have a beer. What are at least two good reasons Allie should say no?

Applying Health Skills

6. *Accessing Information* Some teens may believe myths about alcohol. With classmates, research several of these myths. Use your findings to create a poster showing the truths about these concepts.

Long-Term Effects of Alcohol Use

Guide to Reading

● **Building Vocabulary**
Look at the terms below. Can you see how they might be related? Write down any relationships you see.
- fatty liver (p. 287)
- cirrhosis (p. 287)
- binge drinking (p. 289)
- inhibition (p. 289)
- fetal alcohol syndrome (FAS) (p. 290)

● **Focusing on the Main Ideas**
In this lesson, you will learn to
- **identify** body organs and systems negatively affected by long-term alcohol use.
- **describe** the long-term effects of alcohol use.
- **explain** the risks to a fetus if its mother drinks alcohol.

● **Reading Strategy**
Identifying Cause-and-Effect List the long-term effects caused by alcohol as described in the lesson.

Quick Write

Write a short paragraph explaining what you know about the dangers of using alcohol.

Long-Term Physical Effects of Alcohol Use

It is important to remember that alcohol is a drug. Its effects impact all areas of a person's life. Drinking alcohol regularly can lead to a number of serious health problems. These include damage to major organs like the stomach, liver, pancreas, and heart. It can also make existing health problems worse. A special concern is alcohol's effect on the teenaged brain. Research has shown that drinking alcohol as a teen can lead to long-lasting learning and memory problems.

Since alcohol is a depressant, it affects a person's emotional health. The more a person drinks, the more problems he or she is likely to have at home, work, with friends, and even strangers. Many people have mood changes when they drink. Those who are depressed often feel worse with alcohol in their bodies.

For some, alcohol can become addictive. This means that the person needs the drug both physically and emotionally.

Alcohol and the Mouth

Alcohol is not digested like other foods. It is absorbed by tissues lining the mouth and stomach, and goes directly into the blood. Studies show that people who drink large amounts of alcohol are six times more likely to develop mouth or throat cancer.

Alcohol and the Stomach

Alcohol irritates the stomach lining and increases the amount of acid there. Extra acid makes the lining red and swollen, and can produce ulcerations. Ulcerations are sores that cause bleeding.

Drinking alcohol also weakens the valve that separates the stomach from the esophagus. This valve is like a door that prevents stomach acid from entering the esophagus. When the valve is weak, acid flows back into the esophagus and causes heartburn. Many people who drink regularly have ongoing heartburn.

◀ The picture on the left shows a normal liver. The one on the right shows one damaged by alcohol. **What can happen if your liver stops functioning?**

Alcohol and the Liver

One of the most serious effects of alcohol is damage to the liver. If alcohol is frequently in the blood, liver cells die. When this happens, **fatty liver** can develop. This is *a condition in which fats build up in the liver and cannot be broken down.* The increased amount of fat prevents the liver from working normally and from repairing itself.

A life-threatening problem also associated with heavy alcohol use is **cirrhosis.** This is *a disease characterized by scarring and eventual destruction of the liver.* The scarring from cirrhosis reduces blood flow in the liver. The damaged liver is unable to carry out one of its key functions—removing poisons from the blood. These poisons can eventually reach and damage the brain.

Alcohol and the Brain

Even mild-to-moderate drinking can have a negative effect on how the brain works. For example, alcohol disrupts the parts of the brain responsible for memory and problem solving. The brain can also shrink in size. This damage can be serious enough to interfere with everyday functions.

Alcohol can also block messages that are sent to the brain. This can cause problems with movement, vision, and hearing.

▼ Even simple acts can be difficult when intoxicated. **How might intoxication affect a person's daily activities?**

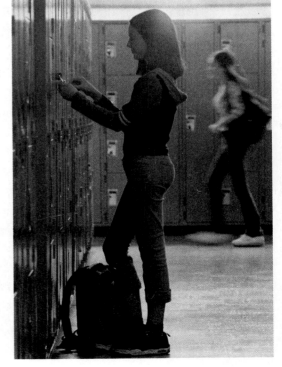

Alcohol and the Heart

Heavy drinking damages the heart muscle, causing the heart to become enlarged, and leads to high blood pressure. It also increases the number of fat cells in the blood, and puts a strain on the blood vessels. All these conditions put a person who drinks at risk of heart failure or stroke.

Reading Check **List** Name two problems of the stomach related to long-term alcohol use.

Driving While Intoxicated

As stated earlier, *a person with a BAC of 0.08% is considered* legally intoxicated or drunk. If the person is also driving a car, he or she is said to be driving while intoxicated or DWI.

A devastating long-term consequence of driving while intoxicated is causing your own death or the death of another. On average, someone is killed in a crash involving alcohol every 31 minutes. In 2004, over 16,000 people were killed in alcohol-related crashes. That accounts for 39 percent of all traffic deaths that year. Remember, the driver is not the only person at risk. Passengers, pedestrians, and other drivers are all potential victims of a person who is DWI.

People who are DWI are eleven times more likely to die in a crash than sober drivers. **Figure 12.3** shows a numerical link between the amount of alcohol in a driver's blood and the likelihood of a deadly accident occurring.

▼**FIGURE 12.3**

TRAFFIC DEATHS AND BAC

Drivers with a BAC of 0.10% are *48 times* as likely to be involved in a fatal crash. **How can you reduce your risk of being involved in an alcohol-related crash?**

Likelihood of Fatal Crash

Source: U.S. Dept. of Transportation, 2000.

◀ Binge drinking can prevent teens from reaching their long-term goals. **What are some other effects of binge drinking?**

Binge Drinking

Teens who experiment with alcohol also risk becoming binge drinkers. **Binge drinking** is *the consumption of a large quantity of alcohol in a very short period of time*. Although binge drinking is dangerous at any age, it is a special problem for teens.

Binge drinking is harmful because of the potential long-term consequences. Since teens frequently combine high-risk activities with binge drinking, their potential for death or serious injury is very high. Some of the dangers include:

- Death due to falls, drowning, or drunk driving
- Pregnancy or contraction of sexually transmitted diseases due to sexual activity
- Being a victim of violent behavior
- Death from alcohol poisoning

Reading Check   **Define** What is *binge drinking*?

Alcohol Use and Teen Pregnancy

Unplanned pregnancies are sometimes a long-term consequence of alcohol use. Using alcohol can lower a person's inhibitions and affects the ability to make healthy decisions. An **inhibition** is *a conscious or unconscious restraint of a person's own behaviors or actions*. Many inhibitions are normal and healthy because they prevent people from taking dangerous risks.

When using alcohol, people are much more likely to say and do things they normally would not. Misunderstandings and hurt feelings are a common result of lowered inhibitions. Teen pregnancy is a very serious and long-lasting result of lowered inhibitions.

Visit **health.glencoe.com** and complete the Interactive Study Guide for Lesson 3.

GOVERNMENT WARNING: (1) ACCORDING TO THE SURGEON GENERAL, WOMEN SHOULD NOT DRINK ALCOHOLIC BEVERAGES DURING PREGNANCY BECAUSE OF THE RISK OF BIRTH DEFECTS. (2) CONSUMPTION OF ALCOHOLIC BEVERAGES IMPAIRS YOUR ABILITY TO DRIVE A CAR OR OPERATE MACHINERY, AND MAY CAUSE HEALTH PROBLEMS.

1.5L CONTAINS SULFITES

▲ Signs like this appear in some restaurants and other locations where alcohol is available. **Why do you think it is important to post these types of warning labels?**

Pregnancy among teens is usually unplanned. One study of female teens with unplanned pregnancies found that one-third had been using alcohol.

An unplanned pregnancy complicates a teen's life. It can disrupt long-term plans and goals, such as going to college. Most teens are not prepared emotionally or financially to be parents. For this reason, pregnancy can be very difficult for teens.

Fetal Alcohol Syndrome

When a female is pregnant, everything she eats and drinks affects her unborn baby. This includes alcohol, which is passed into the baby's blood. A baby's liver is not developed enough to break down alcohol. Therefore, when an unborn baby is exposed to alcohol, it can develop **fetal alcohol syndrome (FAS).** FAS is *a group of alcohol-related birth defects that include both physical and mental problems.* Babies with FAS have smaller body sizes, lower birth weight, and other problems. Babies with FAS frequently develop problems with their hearts and kidneys as well. Because alcohol limits the supply of oxygen to the baby's brain, learning disabilities and mental retardation can also occur.

Reading Check

List What are some health problems that occur in babies with FAS?

Lesson 3 Review

After You Read

Review this lesson for new terms, major headings, and Reading Checks.

What I Learned

1. *Vocabulary* What is *cirrhosis*? What are the long-term risks associated with this health problem?

2. *Explain* How are three body organs or systems negatively affected by long-term alcohol use?

3. *Recall* What are the risks to the fetus of a pregnant female who uses alcohol?

Thinking Critically

4. *Hypothesize* What are some ways in which experimenting with alcohol can interfere with a teen's future?

5. *Apply* At a party, Cindy sees a pregnant female reach for a beer. What could Cindy say to help the woman understand the health risks of drinking during pregnancy?

Applying Health Skills

6. *Practicing Healthy Behaviors* Some people say that alcohol helps them relax and sleep better. Make a list of things you could do that would help your body relax and sleep better without using alcohol.

Health Online For more review questions for Lesson 3, go to **health.glencoe.com**.

Alcoholism and Alcohol Abuse

Guide to Reading

● Building Vocabulary
Read the terms below and try to define them. Write your definitions in pencil and make any changes that are needed as you read this lesson.

- addiction (p. 291)
- alcoholism (p. 291)
- tolerance (p. 292)
- physical dependence (p. 292)
- enablers (p. 294)
- alcohol abuse (p. 295)

● Focusing on the Main Ideas
In this lesson, you will learn to

- **identify** symptoms of alcoholism and alcohol abuse.
- **describe** the stages of alcoholism.
- **explain** how alcoholism affects families and society.

● Reading Strategy
Sequencing As you read the lesson, be aware of the progression of alcoholism. Make notes about what occurs at each stage of the problem.

*Q*uick Write
Make a list of all the reasons you can think of to avoid alcohol use.

Alcohol's Addictive Power

One of the biggest problems with alcohol is that it is habit-forming. Like other drugs, using alcohol repeatedly can lead to **addiction.** This is *a physical or psychological need for a drug.* Teens 15 and younger are four times more likely to become addicted than older individuals.

An addiction to any drug can change a person's life. It takes the focus off of healthy goals and damages relationships with family and friends. In the following lessons, you will learn more about the dangers of alcohol addiction, and about where people can turn for help.

The Disease of Alcoholism

People who are addicted to alcohol suffer from alcoholism. **Alcoholism** is *a progressive, chronic disease involving a mental and physical need for alcohol.* People with alcoholism are called *alcoholics.* The disease affects all parts of an alcoholic's life—physical, mental, emotional, and social. Currently, an estimated 14 million Americans are alcoholics or have an alcohol abuse problem.

Millions more take part in risky drinking that could lead to mental, emotional, and health problems.

People with this disease typically have five major symptoms:

- **Denial.** The person has a hard time believing they have a problem. They are usually the last to admit they need help.

- **Craving.** The person has a strong need, or compulsion, to drink.

- **Loss of control.** The person is unable to limit her or his drinking on any given occasion.

- **Tolerance.** A person who drinks regularly can develop a tolerance. **Tolerance** is *a process in which your body needs more and more of a drug to get the same effect.* For alcoholics, tolerance means needing to drink more and more in order to feel the effects of intoxication.

- **Physical dependence. Physical dependence** is *a type of addiction in which the body itself feels a direct need for a drug.* If the person stops drinking abruptly, his or her body may experience symptoms, such as sweating, shakiness, and anxiety.

Figure 12.4 lists some other symptoms associated with alcoholism. If you know someone who displays some of these symptoms, encourage them to get help.

Reading Check **Define** What is *physical dependence*?

▼ **FIGURE 12.4**

COMMON SYMPTOMS OF ALCOHOLISM

As shown, alcohol affects all areas of life and leads to negative consequences to your physical, mental/emotional, and social health. **What should you do if you think that someone you are close to has an alcohol related problem?**

- Drinking alone

- Making excuses to drink

- Need for daily or frequent use of alcohol in order to function

- Lack of control over drinking, with inability to stop or reduce the amount of alcohol being consumed

- Episodes of violence associated with drinking

- Secretive behavior to hide alcohol-related behavior

- Hostility when confronted about drinking

- Neglecting to eat regularly

- Neglecting to take care of physical appearance

- Nausea and vomiting

- Shaking in the morning

- Abdominal pain

- Numbness and tingling

- Confusion

Source: National Institutes of Health

Stages of Alcoholism

There are four stages of alcoholism. They develop over a period of time. Each stage can be long or short, depending on the individual and the age at which he or she begins drinking.

Stage One

Most people in the first stage are surprised by how much they can drink. Other symptoms of this first stage include:

- Drinking to relax or get relief from stress and mental fatigue
- Looking for opportunities to drink
- A gradual increase in tolerance

Stage Two

In the second stage, the person has short-term memory loss and blackouts. These are periods of time the alcoholic cannot remember. Other symptoms include:

- Saying or doing hurtful things
- Sneaking extra drinks and feeling guilty
- Making excuses for drinking

Stage Three

In stage three the alcoholic loses control. He or she cannot predict what will happen. For example, though the alcoholic intends to have only one drink, he or she cannot stop after just one. The alcoholic's body depends on the drug. Other symptoms include:

- Aggressive or resentful behavior
- Making and failing to keep promises
- Losing interest in anything but alcohol
- Avoiding family and friends
- Trouble with money, work, and the law
- Tremors and the start of severe physical problems

Stage Four

The fourth and final stage is chronic, or ongoing. Up until now, the alcoholic may have been able to keep a job. Now, however, he or she lives to drink, and drinking can go on all day. Symptoms include:

- Long periods of being intoxicated all the time
- Strange or unreasonable fears
- Faulty thinking or hallucinations
- Malnutrition caused by not eating properly

Reading Check

Explain What problems and behaviors occur during stage two of the disease of alcoholism?

▲ Alcoholism is a disease that can shatter a person's entire life and disrupt the lives of those around them. **How widespread is this disease in the United States?**

Health Online

Topic: Speaking Out About Alcohol

Visit **health.glencoe.com** for Student Web Activities to learn about the effects of alcohol and what teens around the country are doing to encourage their peers not to drink.

Activity: Using the information provided at the link above, write a letter to the editor of your local newspaper suggesting ways that underage drinking can be prevented in your community.

Costs to the Family

Alcoholism affects others apart from the alcoholic. Denial—the biggest symptom of this disease—is a problem for family and friends as well. Often they don't believe the drinker has a problem. They think he or she just needs to stop drinking or cut down. Family members often neglect their own needs to focus on helping the alcoholic. This can have a very negative effect on self-esteem, especially if the alcoholic is abusive.

In some families, members who try to help the alcoholic make the problem worse by becoming enablers. **Enablers** are *persons who create an atmosphere in which the alcoholic can comfortably continue his or her unacceptable behavior.* Enabling includes making excuses for or lying on behalf of the alcoholic. Enablers believe that these actions help, but they do not. An unhealthy cycle of dependency develops between the alcoholic and the enabler. This cycle allows the alcoholic to avoid getting treatment for his or her disease.

Reading Check **Define** What is *enabling*?

Costs to Society

The nation spends about $148 billion on alcohol abuse every year. More than half of this is paid by the American taxpayer. Alcohol's cost to the national economy is also very high. As noted earlier, alcohol abusers are likely to miss or skip work. This costs business an estimated $80.9 billion in lost productivity. Productivity is how much work a person produces when he or she is on the job.

► Speaking honestly to a family member about an alcohol problem is better than trying to hide the problem. **How can enabling be harmful to both an alcoholic and family members?**

Alcohol Abuse

Although the terms *alcoholism* and *alcohol abuse* are sometimes used interchangeably, there is a difference. People who abuse alcohol are not physically dependent on the drug. Rather, **alcohol abuse** is *a pattern of drinking that results in one or more well-defined behaviors within a twelve-month period.* The four symptoms are:

- Failure to fulfill major work, school, or home responsibilities.
- Drinking in situations that are physically dangerous. For example, driving while intoxicated, or riding in a car driven by someone who is drinking alcohol.
- Having ongoing alcohol-related legal problems. These may include arrests for DWI or physically hurting someone while drunk.
- Continuing to drink even when relationships have been negatively affected by the person's use of alcohol.

Visit health.glencoe.com and complete the Interactive Study Guide for Lesson 4.

Reading Check **Identify** Name a behavior associated with alcohol abuse.

Lesson 4 Review

 After You Read

Review this lesson for new terms, major headings, and Reading Checks.

What I Learned

1. *Vocabulary* Define *alcoholism*.

2. *Explain* What is the difference between alcohol abuse and alcoholism?

3. *Describe* Briefly describe the four stages of alcoholism.

Thinking Critically

4. *Analyze* Over the past year, Andrew has secretly been drinking alcohol. He has missed a lot of school and has been in trouble with the law. Would you say Andrew is an alcoholic? Explain your answer.

5. *Synthesize* You are at a friend's house. You overhear your friend's father say,

"I do *not* have a drinking problem." Your friend looks uncomfortable, then says, "He really doesn't have a problem you know." What kind of behavior is your friend demonstrating?

Applying Health Skills

6. *Stress Management* Some people use alcohol to relieve stress. Make a list of healthy activities a person can do to manage stress without the use of alcohol. As a class, compile the best ideas into a brochure on stress management techniques. Share copies of your brochure with family and friends.

Getting Help for Alcohol Abuse

Guide to Reading

● Building Vocabulary
As you read this lesson, write each new highlighted term and its definition in your notebook.

- intervention (p. 296)
- relapse (p. 296)
- recovery (p. 297)
- withdrawal (p. 297)
- detoxification (p. 297)

● Focusing on the Main Ideas
In this lesson, you will learn to

- **explain** what a person experiences during withdrawal from alcohol.
- **describe** the steps in the process of recovery.
- **identify** community resources that can help alcoholics, alcohol abusers, and their families.

● Reading Strategy
Predicting Based on the headings and photos in this lesson, describe what you think you will learn from reading it.

*Q*uick Write

Name a person you turn to when you need help with a problem. Write a brief description of qualities this person has, such as good listening skills.

Help for People with Alcohol Problems

People who are struggling with alcohol use need help. However, many of them may be in denial. Being in denial means refusing to admit a problem with alcohol. To overcome this obstacle, family and friends can hold an intervention. An **intervention** is *a gathering in which family and friends get the problem drinker to agree to seek help.* The drinker is confronted with the facts of his or her problem and strongly urged to stop drinking.

Starting Down the Road to Recovery

Treatment for alcoholism begins with the alcoholic's understanding that he or she has an addiction and must never drink again. If an alcoholic takes even one drink there is the chance that he or she will have a relapse. A **relapse** is *a return to the use of a drug after attempting to stop.*

◀ Counseling can help a person recover from alcohol abuse. **What are some organizations that provide this type of counseling?**

Recovery starts only after the alcoholic makes the commitment never to drink again. **Recovery** is *the process of learning to live an alcohol-free life,* and is usually long and difficult. The alcoholic must cope with the symptoms of withdrawal that occur when he or she stops drinking. **Withdrawal** is *the physical and psychological reactions that occur when someone stops using an addictive substance.* These can be mild to very severe and include headaches, tiredness, strong mood swings, and nausea.

Steps Along the Road

The road to recovery consists of a number of steps. Every person who wants to get better must take all the steps. There are no shortcuts. These are as follows:

- **Admission.** At the start of recovery, the person must admit that he or she has an addiction and ask for help.

- **Counseling.** Alcoholics need outside help from counselors and support groups to recover. Many people find the group Alcoholics Anonymous (AA) helpful. AA is an organization that is made up entirely of recovering alcoholics. They all know from firsthand experience how difficult it can be to break an addiction.

- **Detoxification.** This is *the physical process of freeing the body of an addictive substance.*

- **Resolution.** Once recovery has begun, the alcoholic resolves or makes the decision to accept responsibility for his or her actions. It is time to move forward, and the person is now referred to as a *recovering alcoholic*. A recovering alcoholic is someone who has an addiction to alcohol but chooses to live without it.

Reading Check **Explain** What makes recovery from alcoholism so difficult?

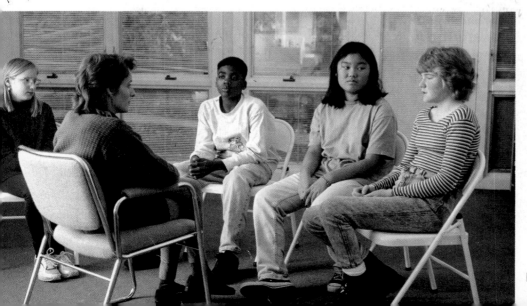

◀ Support groups are available to teens with an alcoholic in their family. **What are the benefits of joining such a group?**

Health Skills Activity

Communication Skills

When Communication Counts Most

If a friend or family member has a problem with alcohol, you may be able to help. Here's how.

- **Have an honest talk with the drinker.** Choose a time when the person is sober. Make eye contact and talk honestly about your concerns. Tell him or her about the serious effects alcohol can have on a person's physical, mental, and emotional health.
- **Encourage the person to seek help.** After expressing your concerns, explain why support is needed. Ask the person to get help.
- **Offer Information.** Finally, provide useful information about where the person can go for help. Facts and details are important at this stage. Make sure that the person understands what kind of help is available and how to get it.

With a Group

Role-play a conversation in which you use the skills outlined above. Think about specific words that would express your concern and encourage the person to get help.

Health Online

Visit **health.glencoe.com** and complete the Interactive Study Guide for Lesson 5.

Help for the Family

The families of alcoholics need to recover from the effects of living with alcoholism as well. This is especially true when members of the family have been enablers. There are several organizations that offer help. One well-known example is Al-Anon. This non-profit group teaches family and friends about alcoholism and helps them understand how they have been affected. It also teaches them skills for coping with the many problems alcoholism creates. Another group that exists within Al-Anon is Alateen. It is specially designed to help teens deal with alcoholic parents. Both groups do community outreach work as well. They educate the public and direct families to counselors, support groups, and mental health facilities.

Ways to Stay Alcohol Free

You have learned that alcohol use can damage a teen's physical, mental/emotional, and social health. The best way to avoid these risks is to choose to be alcohol free. Avoid situations where

Staying alcohol free involves knowing how to say no to high-risk situations like the teen in this picture. **What refusal skills do you use to abstain from high-risk situations?**

alcohol may be present. Choose friends who are alcohol free. They will support your decision not to use alcohol.

If you find yourself in a situation in which you feel pressured to try alcohol, use refusal skills. Practice the S.T.O.P. strategy discussed in Chapter 2. State your decision clearly and assertively. When you speak assertively, you are letting people know you are serious. If the pressure continues, walk away. If needed, get help from a parent or other adult.

Reading Check **Identify** What are some ways to stay alcohol free?

Lesson 5 Review

After You Read

Review this lesson for new terms, major headings, and Reading Checks.

What I Learned

1. *Vocabulary* Define *withdrawal*.

2. *List* Name the steps in the recovery process.

3. *Identify* What community organizations are available to help alcoholics and their families?

Thinking Critically

4. *Evaluate* What is the one fact about alcohol addiction you think a problem drinker needs most?

5. *Apply* Imagine that a friend admits to having a drinking problem. The way he plans to handle the problem is to gradually cut down on his drinking. Is this a wise plan? Why or why not?

Applying Health Skills

6. *Goal Setting* Think about personal goals you have. Write one or two of these down on a sheet of paper, leaving space under each one. In the spaces, explain how using alcohol could interfere with your goals.

Helping Someone Get Help

DIRECTIONS

Decision Making involves taking steps to make healthy and responsible choices. This activity will give you the opportunity to develop and master this important health skill. Here's a guide to the different parts of this activity:

❶ In the **Model** section, you will read about a teen who performs the health skill successfully. This "model" scenario will show you how the skill is done.

❷ The **Practice** section will help guide you in practicing the skill.

❸ In the **Apply** section, you will have a chance to perform the skill on your own. You can use the Self-Check to check your work.

To complete this activity, first read the scenario presented in the Model. Then move on to the Practice. Finally, go ahead and try the Apply.

❶ Model

Darcy recently realized that her close friend, Ellie, has a drinking problem. Darcy used the decision-making process to help her decide what to do.

1. **State the situation:** I'm afraid my friend might have a drinking problem and needs help.

2. **List the options:** I could just do nothing. I could talk to the guidance counselor at school. I could try talking to Ellie.

3. **Weigh the possible outcomes:** If I do nothing, Ellie's problem could get worse. If I talk to her about it, she might get mad.

4. **Consider values:** Ellie is my friend. I care about what happens to her.

5. **Make a decision and act:** I will try to talk to Ellie about her problem.

6. **Evaluate your decision:** I spoke to Ellie today after school. She said she knows she has a problem. She asked me go to the school guidance counselor with her to get help.

❷ Practice

Darcy's cousin, Stacy, told her a secret, after making Darcy promise not to say anything. "There's this club I want to join," she said. "Before I can be a member, I have to pass a test. I have to steal beer from a convenience store." When Darcy told Stacy this was a bad idea, Stacy frowned. "I thought you'd understand how important this is to me," she said.

1. What decision is Darcy faced with this time?
2. What do you think Darcy's options are?
3. What are the possible outcomes of these options?
4. What would you do if you were Darcy?

Skill Summary
DECISION MAKING

1. State the situation.
2. List the options.
3. Weigh the possible outcomes.
4. Consider values.
5. Make a decision and act.
6. Evaluate your decision.

❸ Apply

In a small group, think of a situation where a decision needs to be made involving teens and alcohol use. Write your situation down, then trade situations with another group. Each group should write an original story using the situation they have been given. The story should show how the six steps of decision making can be used to make a choice. Make your story realistic. Share your story with the class.

Self-Check

- Did our story illustrate the six steps of decision making?
- Did our story show how decision making can be used to make choices involving alcohol?
- Was our story realistic?

Refusing to Get in a Car with a Driver Who Has Been Drinking

You have learned that you should not drink and drive. You should also avoid getting into a car with someone who has been drinking. If someone who has been drinking alcohol invites you to ride in a car with them, you should know how to refuse that invitation. The following are some suggestions that can help you avoid an unsafe situation.

- Make a decision to never ride with someone who has been drinking and stick to it.
- Do not make arrangements to go places with a driver who you know will likely drink at an event you are going to.
- Find other ways to get a ride home if you are with a driver who has been drinking.
- Use direct statements: "I am not riding with you. You have been drinking. Don't drive. I'll find us another ride."

What You Will Need

- 1 index card per student
- Colored pencils or markers

What You Will Do

1 Working with a small group, brainstorm a list of refusal statements a teen can use to avoid riding in a car with a driver who has been drinking.

2 Write a skit that has dialogue showing successful use of refusal skills. Be sure that every group member has a part.

3 Act out your skit for the class.

Wrapping It Up

As a class, discuss the dialogue used in each of the skits. Decide which skit presented the most effective refusal statements. Then, on your own, take your index card and write "Don't Ride With a Drunk Driver" on the card. Then, write at least two statements you can use to refuse such a ride. Use markers or colored pencils to make the card creative and colorful. The most creative cards can be displayed in the classroom.

12 Reading Review

FOLDABLES™ Study Organizer

Foldables™ and Other Study Aids Take out the Foldable™ that you created for Lessons 2 and 3 and any graphic organizers that you created for Lessons 1–5. Find a partner and quiz each other using these study aids.

Lesson 1 Why Alcohol Is Harmful

Key Ideas
- Alcohol is a drug that can damage a person's physical, mental/emotional, and social health.
- Some of the reasons teens use alcohol include media messages, stress relief, peer pressure, and to look more mature.

Vocabulary
- alcohol (p. 278)
- alternatives (p. 281)
- depressants (p. 278)

Lesson 2 Short-Term Effects of Alcohol Use

Key Ideas
- Alcohol enters the bloodstream quickly. It slows down a person's reaction time. This creates serious safety risks for the drinker and others.
- Factors that influence the effects of alcohol include weight, gender, rate of consumption, amount consumed, amount eaten, other drugs in the system, state of health, and how well-rested the person is.

Vocabulary
- reaction time (p. 282)
- intoxication (p. 283)
- blood alcohol content (BAC) (p. 283)
- alcohol poisoning (p. 283)
- malnutrition (p. 285)

Lesson 3 Long-Term Effects of Alcohol Use

Key Ideas
- Body organs affected by long-term alcohol use include the mouth, stomach, liver, brain, and heart.
- Babies born to mothers who use alcohol are more likely to have health problems, learning disabilities, or even mental retardation.

Vocabulary
- fatty liver (p. 287)
- inhibition (p. 289)
- cirrhosis (p. 287)

Lesson 4 Alcoholism and Alcohol Abuse

Key Idea
- Symptoms of alcoholism include denial, craving, loss of control, tolerance, and physical dependence.

Vocabulary
- addiction (p. 291)
- enablers (p. 294)
- alcoholism (p. 291)
- alcohol abuse (p. 295)
- tolerance (p. 292)
- physical dependence (p. 292)

Lesson 5 Getting Help for Alcohol Abuse

Key Idea
- The process of recovery includes admission, detoxification, counseling, and resolution.

Vocabulary
- intervention (p. 296)
- relapse (p. 296)
- withdrawal (p. 297)
- recovery (p. 297)
- detoxification (p. 297)

After You Read

I.M. *Express*

Now that you have read the chapter, review your answer to the I.M. Express on the chapter opener. Have your ideas changed? What would your answer be now?

Reviewing Vocabulary and Main Ideas

On a sheet of paper, write the numbers 1–6. After each number, write the term from the list that best completes each sentence.

- alcohol
- alcohol poisoning
- alternatives
- drug
- depressant
- intoxication
- malnutrition
- reaction time

Lesson 1 Why Alcohol Is Harmful

1. A _____ is a substance that changes the structure or function of the body or mind.

2. A(n) _____ is a drug that slows down the body's functions and reactions.

3. _____ to drinking include finding a hidden skill and volunteering.

Lesson 2 Short-Term Effects of Alcohol Use

4. _____ can occur when the body does not receive enough nutrients to function properly.

5. The ability of the body to respond quickly and appropriately to any situation is called _____.

6. _____ means a person is physically and mentally impaired by the use of alcohol.

*On a sheet of paper, write the numbers 7–13. Write **True** or **False** for each statement below. If the statement is false, change the underlined word or phrase to make it true.*

Lesson 3 Long-Term Effects of Alcohol Use

7. A disease characterized by scarring and eventual destruction of the liver is called <u>fatty liver</u>.

8. The consumption of a large quantity of alcohol in a very short period of time is known as <u>inhibition</u>.

Lesson 4 Alcoholism and Alcohol Abuse

9. A person with a blood alcohol content (BAC) of <u>0.80%</u> is legally considered to be DWI, short for driving while intoxicated.

10. An <u>addiction</u> is a physical or psychological need for a drug.

Lesson 5 Getting Help for Alcohol Abuse

11. Loss of control is one symptom of <u>alcoholism</u>.

12. <u>Alcohol abuse</u> is a pattern of drinking that results in one or more well-defined behaviors within a twelve-month period.

13. <u>Resolution</u> is a process in which the alcoholic's body adjusts to functioning without the drug.

Health Online Visit health.glencoe.com and take the Online Quiz for Chapter 12.

Thinking Critically

Using complete sentences, answer the following questions.

14. Evaluate How can alcohol use as a teen cause health problems later in life?

15. Analyze Why is an alcoholic always said to be recovering rather than cured?

16. Apply Imagine you are planning a birthday party for a friend. What are some fun activities you could choose that do not include the use of alcohol?

Write About It

17. Refusal Skills What reasons might teens use to persuade others to use alcohol? What are some refusal responses to these statements?

18. Decision Making Write a short story or play about a teen faced with a decision involving alcohol. Show how the teen made a healthy decision.

Standardized Test Practice

Reading

Read the passage and then answer the questions.

A SADD Story

In 1981, a group of students from Wayland, Massachusetts, wanted to make a statement. Having watched peers die in accidents involving drunk driving, the group formed SADD. Back then, the letters in the name stood for "Students Against Driving Drunk." The students' goal was to spread the word that drunk driving kills.

Today, SADD has thousands of chapters in middle schools, high schools, and colleges. In 1997, the letters in SADD were changed to stand for "Students Against Destructive Decisions." The group is now dedicated to preventing all high-risk behaviors among teens. These include underage drinking, substance abuse, violence, and suicide.

1. Which best describes the way in which SADD changed since it was founded?

   A. The founders moved the organization's headquarters to a city out west.

   B. The founders sold the organization to its adult backers.

   C. SADD grew to have thousands of chapters.

   D. The group is no longer dedicated to preventing drunk driving.

2. Sixteen years after SADD was founded, the organization's name was changed to

   A. Students Against Drunk Driving.

   B. Students Against Doing Drugs.

   C. Students Against Dealing Drugs.

   D. Students Against Destructive Decisions.

Chapter Preview

▲ **Working With the Photo**

The healthy habits you develop in your teen years will benefit you now and for the rest of your life. **How does staying tobacco free benefit your health now and in the future?**

Start-Up Activities

📘 **Before You Read** Do you take action to stay tobacco free? Take the health inventory on this page. Keep a record of your answers.

HEALTH INVENTORY

1. I stay away from tobacco products.
   (a) always   (b) sometimes   (c) never

2. I stay up-to-date on the health risks related to tobacco use.
   (a) always   (b) sometimes   (c) never

3. I encourage others to stay tobacco free.
   (a) always   (b) sometimes   (c) never

FOLDABLES™ Study Organizer

📘 **As You Read** Make this Foldable™ to record what you learn in Lesson 1 about tobacco's harmful effects. Begin with a plain sheet of 8½" × 11" paper.

1 Fold a sheet of paper in half along the short axis.

2 Open and fold the bottom edge up to form a pocket. Glue the edges.

3 Label the front of the booklet as shown. Label the pockets "Tobacco Products" and "Harmful Effects." Place an index card or quarter sheet of notebook paper into each pocket.

How Tobacco Affects the Body

On index cards or quarter sheets of notebook paper, take notes on the different types of tobacco products and how they harm the body. Store these cards in the appropriate pocket of your Foldable.

🖱️ **Health Online** Visit **health.glencoe.com** and use the e-flashcards to preview vocabulary terms for Chapter 13.

Facts About Tobacco

Guide to Reading

● Building Vocabulary

As you read this lesson, write each new highlighted term and its definition in your notebook.

- nicotine (p. 308)
- addictive (p. 309)
- tar (p. 309)
- bronchi (p. 309)
- carbon monoxide (p. 309)
- smokeless tobacco (p. 310)

● Focusing on the Main Ideas

In this lesson, you will learn to

- **recognize** the various forms of tobacco.
- **identify** some of the harmful substances in all forms of tobacco.
- **describe** the negative effects tobacco use can have on appearance.

● Reading Strategy

Making Inferences Look briefly at the headings, figures, and captions in this lesson. Discuss what kinds of information you think this lesson will provide.

FOLDABLES Study Organizer Use the Foldable™ on p. 307 as you read this lesson.

Quick Write

Make a list of as many tobacco products as you can think of prior to reading. Briefly describe each product.

What Is Tobacco?

Tobacco is a woody, shrub-like plant with large leaves. It is estimated that there are more than 4,000 chemicals in tobacco, many of which have been proven to cause cancer. One of these is **nicotine**—*an addictive drug found in tobacco leaves and in all tobacco products.*

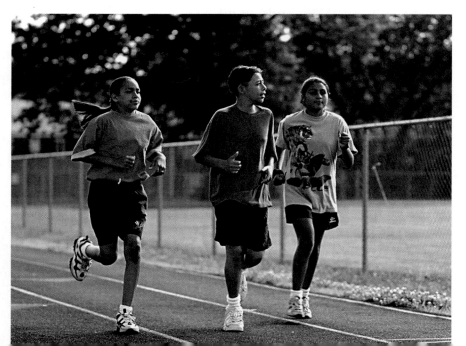

▶ Smoking can make it difficult to breathe during physical activity. **What physical activities do you enjoy that would become much more difficult if you smoked?**

Nicotine is an **addictive** drug, meaning it is *capable of causing a user to develop intense cravings.* Once the drug has been in the body regularly for some time, a person begins to depend on it.

Another dangerous ingredient in tobacco is **tar,** *a thick, oily, dark liquid that forms when tobacco burns.* When smokers inhale, tar deposits form on the **bronchi** (BRONG·ky), which are *passages through which air enters and spreads through the lungs.* If tar builds up, serious diseases such as emphysema and lung cancer can develop. These diseases make it very difficult for a person to breathe.

Carbon monoxide is a third harmful substance that is released when tobacco is burned. **Carbon monoxide** is *a poisonous, colorless, odorless gas.* The carbon monoxide in smoke passes through the lungs and into the bloodstream. There it reduces the amount of oxygen the blood vessels can carry. This weakens muscles and blood vessels, which can lead to heart attack and stroke.

Reading Check **Define** What is *carbon monoxide?*

Different Tobacco Products

There are many different tobacco products on the market today. These include cigarettes, cigars, pipes, specialty cigarettes, and smokeless tobacco.

Cigarettes

Of the many different products that contain tobacco, the most commonly used is cigarettes. Cigarettes put smokers at risk for emphysema and other lung and heart diseases, cancer, infertility, and stroke. Cigarettes and other forms of tobacco can cause bad breath, stain teeth and fingers, and cause the skin to wrinkle prematurely. More than 400,000 cigarette smokers die from smoking-related illnesses every year.

Cigars and Pipes

Cigars contain larger quantities of the same harmful substances as cigarettes. One large cigar can contain as much tobacco as a pack of cigarettes. Cigar smokers have a higher risk of developing cancer of the mouth, larynx, and throat. They are also at greater risk of dying from heart disease.

▼ Cigarette smoke releases carbon monoxide. **What does this gas do inside the smoker's lungs?**

Some people smoke pipes using loose tobacco. Pipe smokers usually inhale less than cigarette smokers. However, they are still at risk of developing cancer of the lip, mouth, and throat.

Specialty Cigarettes

Two other tobacco products are bidis and kreteks. Bidis (BEE·deez) are flavored, unfiltered cigarettes imported from India and other countries in Southeast Asia. Kreteks (KREE·teks), also called clove cigarettes, are imported from Indonesia. Kreteks typically contain a mixture of tobacco, cloves, and other additives. Both can have higher concentrations of nicotine, tar, and carbon monoxide than regular cigarettes.

Smokeless Tobacco

Smokeless tobacco is *ground tobacco that is chewed or inhaled through the nose.* Smokeless tobacco contains 15 times more nicotine than cigarettes. It can lead to cancers of the mouth, esophagus, larynx, stomach, and pancreas. Chewing tobacco also stains the teeth and causes bad breath, tooth decay, and gum disease.

Health Online

Visit health.glencoe.com and complete the Interactive Study Guide for Lesson 1.

Lesson 1 Review

After You Read

Review this lesson for new terms, major headings, and Reading Checks.

What I Learned

1. *Vocabulary* What is *nicotine?*

2. *List* Identify and describe the risks associated with three harmful substances found in all forms of tobacco.

3. *Recall* What is the most common form in which tobacco is used? Name three other tobacco products.

Thinking Critically

4. *Analyze* Julia is at a party where another girl lights a cigarette. When Julia points out that smoking is bad for her health, the other girl shrugs. "I'm a strong person," she says. "I can quit anytime I want." How might Julia reply?

5. *Evaluate* Pete chews smokeless tobacco. He uses it when no one else is around so others do not have to watch him spitting tobacco juice. "It's a win-win situation," says Pete. Do you agree with Pete's point of view? Explain your answer.

Applying Health Skills

6. *Analyzing Influences* Some teens start smoking because they see their peers smoking. With a group, brainstorm other reasons teens might start to use tobacco. Make a list of the reasons and compare it with those from other groups.

310 Chapter 13: Tobacco

Health Online For more review questions for Lesson 1, go to **health.glencoe.com**.

Health Risks of Tobacco Use

📖 Guide to Reading

● Building Vocabulary

Write the terms below in your notebook. Add a definition for each term as you read this lesson.

- chronic obstructive pulmonary disease (COPD) (p. 313)
- cardiovascular disease (p. 313)

● Focusing on the Main Ideas

In this lesson, you will learn to

- **describe** how tobacco use effects the body systems.
- **practice** decision making to protect your health against tobacco smoke.

● Reading Strategy

Drawing Conclusions Based on this lesson, list the effects of tobacco use on the body systems.

Tobacco Use Is Hazardous to Your Health

The message that smoking is bad for the health is not new. In 1965, Congress passed a law requiring tobacco manufacturers to print health warnings on cigarette packages. Similar labeling laws have since been passed for other tobacco products.

❓uick Write

List two future goals. Then write a short paragraph telling how a tobacco-related illness could affect each of these goals.

SURGEON GENERAL'S WARNING: Smoking Causes Lung Cancer, Heart Disease, Emphysema, And May Complicate Pregnancy.

SURGEON GENERAL'S WARNING: Quitting Smoking Now Greatly Reduces Serious Risks to Your Health.

SURGEON GENERAL'S WARNING: Smoking By Pregnant Women May Result in Fetal Injury, Premature Birth, And Low Birth Weight.

SURGEON GENERAL'S WARNING: Cigarette Smoke Contains Carbon Monoxide.

SURGEON GENERAL'S WARNING: Smoking By Pregnant Women May Result in Fetal Injury,

◀ Federal law requires that cigarette packages have one of four different warning labels. **Which of these health warnings do you think is most important for teens?**

How Tobacco Use Affects the Body

The chemicals in tobacco and tobacco smoke can cause damage to most of the body's systems. Tobacco use is particularly damaging to teens because their bodies are still growing and developing. Some of the effects of tobacco use are evident almost immediately. Others become apparent over time. **Figure 13.1** shows both the short-term and the long-term harmful effects of tobacco use on body systems.

▼ **FIGURE 13.1**

IMPACT OF SMOKING ON THE BODY SYSTEMS

The negative health effects of smoking begin immediately and grow progressively worse the longer you smoke. **What are the short-term and long-term effects on the nervous system?**

A Nervous System
Short-term effects:
Changes take place in brain chemistry. Withdrawal symptoms (nervousness, shakes, headaches) may occur as soon as 30 minutes after the last cigarette. The heart rate and blood pressure increase.
Long-term effects: There is an increased risk of stroke due to decreased flow of oxygen to the brain.

B Circulatory System
Short-term effects:
Heart rate is increased. Energy is reduced because less oxygen gets to body tissues.
Long-term effects: Blood vessels are weakened and narrowed. Cholesterol levels increase. Blood vessels are clogged due to fatty buildup. Oxygen flow to heart is reduced. Risk of heart disease and stroke is greater.

C Respiratory System
Short-term effects:
User has shortness of breath, reduced energy, coughing, and more phlegm (mucus). Colds and flus are more frequent. Allergies, asthma, bronchitis, and other serious respiratory illnesses increase.
Long-term effects:
Risk of lung cancer, emphysema, and other lung diseases increases.

D Digestive System
Short-term effects: User has upset stomach, dulled taste buds, and tooth decay.
Long-term effects: Risk of cancer of the mouth and throat, gum and tooth disease, stomach ulcers, and bladder cancer increases.

One long-term physical effect of smoking is a dry, hacking cough. This indicates that the tobacco has done permanent damage to the smoker's body. A dry cough is often a symptom of **chronic obstructive pulmonary disease (COPD),** *a condition in which passages in the lungs become swollen and irritated, eventually losing their elasticity.* This condition includes chronic bronchitis, asthma, and emphysema. In the United States, COPD causes over 100,000 deaths per year. Ninety percent of these deaths are linked to smoking.

Smokers are also at an increased risk of developing lung cancer. **Figure 13.2** gives some important facts about the link between smoking and lung cancer.

Smoking is also a leading cause of **cardiovascular disease,** *a disease of the heart and blood vessels.* Long-term smoking increases cholesterol levels and contributes to arteriosclerosis, a hardening of the arteries. Both conditions reduce oxygen flow to the heart, dramatically increasing a smoker's risk of stroke and heart attack. Other long-term effects of smoking include cancers of the brain, throat, breast, and bladder.

Reading Check   **Define** What do the letters *COPD* stand for?

Health Online

Visit **health.glencoe.com** and complete the Interactive Study Guide for Lesson 2.

▼**FIGURE 13.2**

THE FACTS ABOUT LUNG CANCER

Smoking can cause serious damage to the lungs. **What can you do to decrease your chances of getting lung cancer?**

Compare the healthy lung with the cancerous lung. Now think about the following facts:

1. Smoking is the number one cause of lung cancer, causing 87 percent of lung cancer cases.

2. Cigarette smoke contains more than 4,000 different chemicals, many of which are cancer-causing substances.

3. Lung cancer is the leading cancer killer in the United States, causing more deaths than the next three most common cancers combined.

4. Secondhand smoke is also an important cause of lung cancer.

Healthy Lung   **Cancerous Lung**

Health Skills Activity

Decision Making

Fresh-Air Friend

Mike gets a ride to school with a girl in his class named Ashley. Mike is concerned about his health because Ashley's mom smokes in the car. Mike hasn't mentioned his concern because he doesn't want to sound rude or ungrateful. He's tried opening a window, but Ashley says it makes her cold. Mike doesn't know what to do or say. Use the decision-making process to help him make a decision.

- State the situation
- List the options
- Weigh the possible outcomes
- Consider your values
- Make a decision and act
- Evaluate the decision

What Would You Do?

Apply the six steps of the decision-making process to Mike's problem. What are Mike's options? Show how Mike makes a healthful decision.

Lesson 2 Review

After You Read

Review this lesson for new terms, major headings, and Reading Checks.

What I Learned

1. **Vocabulary** What is *cardiovascular disease?* How is this caused by smoking?

2. **List** What are some ways that tobacco use damages the circulatory system?

3. **Describe** What is the relationship between smoking and lung cancer?

Thinking Critically

4. **Analyze** Of the health risks associated with tobacco use, which one do you consider the most serious? Explain your answer.

5. **Explain** Why do you think it is important to put warning labels on cigarette packages?

Applying Health Skills

6. **Advocacy** Make a poster encouraging teens not to smoke. One part of your poster should clearly state the health risks associated with various tobacco products. The other part should try to persuade teens not to use tobacco.

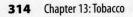 **Health Online** For more review questions for Lesson 2, go to **health.glencoe.com**.

Tobacco Addiction

Guide to Reading

● Building Vocabulary
As you read this lesson, write each new highlighted term and its definition in your notebook.

- tolerance (p. 316)
- physical dependence (p. 316)
- psychological dependence (p. 316)
- withdrawal (p. 317)
- nicotine replacement therapies (NRT) (p. 317)
- relapse (p. 318)

● Focusing on the Main Ideas
In this lesson, you will learn to

- **explain** how a person becomes addicted to tobacco.
- **identify** the different types of dependence that occur as a result of tobacco use.
- **describe** the symptoms of withdrawal.

● Reading Strategy
Sequencing Make a flow diagram that outlines the steps in the addiction process.

Tobacco's Web of Addiction

Nicotine is an extremely powerful and addictive drug. It is just as addictive as heroin or cocaine. When nicotine enters the body, it interacts with receptors in the brain. The brain sends a message to the body to speed up heart and breathing rates. As these feelings go away, they leave the user wanting more. Tobacco use soon becomes a habit, and the user can quickly become addicted. Once addicted, it becomes very difficult to quit smoking.

Quick Write

Make a list of habits you know are hard to break. Choose one you find interesting and write a paragraph describing what you think it would be like to change that habit.

▶ The best way to prevent tobacco addiction is to never start using tobacco. **Why is it difficult to stop smoking once a person has started?**

Tolerance and Dependence

As the body gets used to nicotine, it develops a tolerance to the drug. **Tolerance** is *a process in which the body needs more and more of a drug to get the same effect.*

Any time the nicotine level drops or is absent, the body experiences a craving. This is a sign that the body has a physical dependence on nicotine. **Physical dependence** is *a type of addiction in which the body itself feels a direct need for a drug.* The cravings that result from a physical dependence can only be satisfied by more nicotine.

Addiction to a drug affects the mind as well as the body. Some people begin to believe they need tobacco to perk up or relax. What these people are experiencing is a psychological dependence on nicotine. A **psychological dependence** is *an addiction in which the mind sends the body a message that it needs more of a drug.* Certain events, situations, and habits trigger a desire to use tobacco. For example, some people feel the need to smoke at parties or night clubs.

Studies have reported that a staggering 90 percent of the people who start smoking become addicted. Teens are more likely to develop a severe level of addiction than people who begin smoking at a later age. Teens who use tobacco are also much more likely to use drugs such as marijuana, cocaine, and alcohol. **Figure 13.3** provides greater detail on nicotine addiction among teens.

Reading Check **Identify** What percentage of people who start smoking become addicted?

▼ FIGURE 13.3

THE PATH TO SMOKING ADDICTION

The nicotine in tobacco is very addictive. **Based on the facts below, how would you react if a friend said to you, "No way, I won't get addicted"?**

The Path to Smoking Addiction
1. More than 80 percent of all adult smokers first become regular smokers before the age of 18.
2. More than a third of all teens who ever try one cigarette become regular, daily smokers before leaving high school.
3. Teens can feel symptoms of nicotine addiction only days or weeks after they first start smoking on an occasional basis. Addiction symptoms are felt well before teens begin to smoke daily.
4. The earlier in life smoking is first tried, the higher the chances are of becoming a regular smoker and the lower the chances are of ever being able to quit.

◀ Although quitting smoking is hard, it can be done. **How might friends, family members, and health professionals help in accomplishing this goal?**

Breaking the Tobacco Habit

Though some of the damage done by smoking cannot be reversed, it is amazing how much the body can help. For that reason, it is never too late to quit using tobacco. Here are some steps to do just that.

- **Prepare to stop.** Set a specific date for quitting.
- **Get support and encouragement.** Let family and friends know you are quitting and ask for help and support.
- **Find out about health services.** Doctors, support groups, and certain organizations can help users quit.
- **Change your daily routine.** It helps to avoid smokers and routines that were part of the smoking life.
- **Follow a healthy lifestyle.** Eat well, manage stress, and get plenty of physical activity to help you feel good without the use of tobacco.

Withdrawal

Some people choose to quit smoking *cold turkey,* meaning they stop all use of tobacco immediately. When a person stops using tobacco, he or she may experience symptoms of **withdrawal.** These are *physical and psychological reactions that occur when someone stops using an addictive substance.* The physical symptoms of withdrawal include headaches, tiredness, increased hunger, and a jittery, restless feeling. **Nicotine replacement therapies (NRT)** are *products that assist a person in breaking a tobacco habit.* These products reduce the amount of nicotine in the body slowly, reducing the symptoms of withdrawal.

The psychological symptoms of withdrawal can include irritability, sudden cravings for tobacco in certain situations or at certain times, and difficulty concentrating or sleeping. Counseling or support groups can help a user overcome a psychological dependence on tobacco.

Reading Check   **Define** What are *nicotine replacement therapies*?

Dealing with Relapse

The body undergoes physical changes when a person no longer uses tobacco. Learning to live without tobacco takes time and a lot of willpower.

Many people who decide to quit tobacco suffer a relapse within the first three months of quitting. A **relapse** is *a return to the use of a drug after attempting to stop.* Resuming the habit after working hard to quit can be discouraging. Self-esteem often drops and people may feel frustrated and angry.

Most people attempt to quit several times before they succeed. Reviewing what caused a relapse and taking steps to prevent it from happening again can help. For example, if a person is in the habit of smoking after a meal, planning another activity can take the person's mind off smoking.

Health Online

Visit **health.glencoe.com** and complete the Interactive Study Guide for Lesson 3.

Lesson 3 Review

After You Read

Review this lesson for new terms, major headings, and Reading Checks.

What I Learned

1. *Vocabulary* Define *tolerance*. How does a tolerance to nicotine form?

2. *Recall* Explain the difference between physical dependence and psychological dependence.

3. *Give Examples* What are the symptoms of nicotine withdrawal?

Thinking Critically

4. *Analyze* What specific dangers does trying tobacco pose for teens?

5. *Synthesize* How do nicotine replacement therapies help a person stop smoking?

6. *Apply* Madison's mother has been trying to quit smoking, but has had several relapses. What can Madison do to help her mother quit smoking?

Applying Health Skills

7. *Refusal Skills* Some teens try tobacco for the first time because of peer pressure. With a small group, brainstorm effective ways to say no when peers offer or suggest that you use tobacco. Make a list of the best ideas and share them with your classmates in a roundtable discussion.

Tobacco's Costs to Society

Guide to Reading

● **Building Vocabulary**
Explain how the terms below are related. Then find each in the lesson and write a definition for each term.

- secondhand smoke (p. 320)
- sidestream smoke (p. 320)
- mainstream smoke (p. 320)
- passive smoker (p. 320)

● **Focusing on the Main Ideas**
In this lesson, you will learn to

- **identify** ways in which tobacco harms nonsmokers.
- **describe** the costs tobacco use has on society.

● **Reading Strategy**
Identifying Problems and Solutions After reading this lesson, state why secondhand smoke is a problem. Offer your suggestions for dealing with this problem.

Tobacco's Many Costs

For every dollar spent to spread the word about the dangers of tobacco, tobacco companies spend $23 on marketing. Marketing is a method used by businesses to make the public aware of their product. Each year tobacco companies spend $12.7 billion on advertising alone. It is only a fraction, however, of the $157 billion the U.S. spends on health care costs related to tobacco use. That averages $632 per American per year. There are many more costs associated with tobacco use. This lesson takes a look at some of them.

Cost to the Individual

A study on smoking habits was conducted several years ago. Researchers discovered that the average smoker smokes a pack and a half a day. The average price per pack in most states is up to $5. This means the typical smoker spends $7.50 per day on tobacco. Over the course of a month, that works out to $225. In 10 years' time, the smoker will have spent $27,000 on tobacco.

Quick Write

Make a list of the costs associated with tobacco use. As you read, add costs to your list.

▶ The average smoker spends $225 a month on cigarettes. **How would you put this money to better use?**

Buying tobacco products is not the only cost of smoking. Smokers pay higher health insurance rates than nonsmokers. They can also expect to live shorter lives and have more health problems than nonsmokers. This is especially true for females, whose lives are shortened by an average of five years from smoking.

Smoking is costly in two other ways as well. Burning tobacco is a leading cause of forest fires and fires in the home.

 Reading Check **Recall** How much does the U.S. spend each year on health care costs related to tobacco use?

Costs to the Nonsmoker

Smokers are not the only individuals who pay a price for their habit. The health of those who don't smoke is also affected. Whenever a smoker lights up, smoke is released into the air that everyone breathes. This is referred to as **secondhand smoke,** or *environmental tobacco smoke (ETS)*. ETS is a mixture of two forms of smoke from burning tobacco products. The first is **sidestream smoke,** or *smoke that comes directly from a burning cigarette, pipe, or cigar*. The second type is **mainstream smoke,** or *smoke that is exhaled by a smoker*. Sidestream smoke contains twice as much tar and nicotine as mainstream smoke.

A *nonsmoker who breathes in secondhand smoke* is said to be a **passive smoker.** Passive smokers develop many of the same health problems as people who actually light and smoke tobacco products. An estimated 40,000 nonsmokers die each year from heart disease. About 3,000 additional nonsmokers die of lung cancer.

Secondhand smoke is particularly hard on children younger than 18 months and people with asthma. Each year, between 150,000 and 300,000 infants and toddlers develop pneumonia or bronchitis from secondhand smoke. Of these, some 15,000 need to be hospitalized. Secondhand smoke is also estimated to cause between 200,000 to 1 million asthma attacks each year.

▼ Secondhand smoke can create health problems such as asthma for the nonsmoker. **What are some actions that you can take to eliminate secondhand smoke in certain places?**

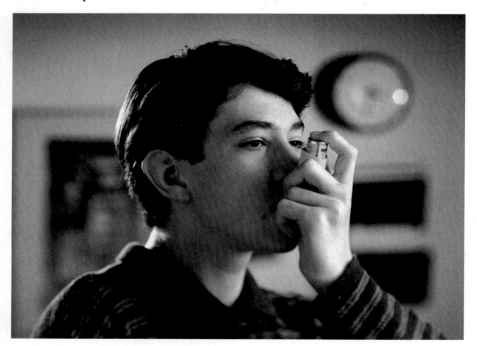

Costs to the Unborn Child

Health experts have long recognized that pregnancy and tobacco do not mix. Smoking during pregnancy increases the risk that the baby will be born too soon and have developmental problems. Babies born to smoking mothers also have lower birth weights than those born to nonsmoking mothers. One reason for the lower birth weight is that the developing baby gets too little oxygen. The lack of oxygen is caused by the presence of carbon monoxide gas in the mother's blood.

Reading Check **Identify** If a pregnant female smokes, how is her baby affected?

Costs of Lost Productivity

Productivity is a measure of how much a person is able to produce based on how much time he or she works. If you finish most of your homework in study hall, you might say study hall is "productive." People who use tobacco have lower productivity levels on the job. They are sick more often than nonsmokers and, therefore, get less done. This reduced or lost productivity is costly to businesses. It is also costly to the nation as a whole. It is estimated that smoking costs the U.S. economy $80 billion per year in lost productivity.

Countering the Costs of Tobacco

America's tobacco habit costs the nation nearly $240 billion a year. Some public action groups and Congress have been investigating ways to lower that cost. Some have proposed a ban on the manufacture and sale of tobacco products. Many smokers, however, claim that would interfere with their constitutional rights. Others claim that banning tobacco products would go against the nation's commitment to having a free economy.

Another proposal is to increase the amount of excise tax on cigarettes. This would make it more costly to purchase tobacco products and give the government more money to educate people about the dangers of tobacco use. The graph in **Figure 13.4** on page 322 shows the portion of the retail price of cigarettes that goes to excise tax in selected states. Which solution do you think would work best to reduce the costs of tobacco use on society?

Reading Check **Explain** What are two possible solutions to offsetting the costs of tobacco on society?

Connect To... Math

Cigarette Taxes

Research has shown that higher cigarette taxes have been one of the most effective ways to reduce smoking. State and federal taxes can really increase the cost of a pack of cigarettes. For example, in New Jersey the average price of a pack is $6.06. This price includes the following taxes:

$2.40 state excise cigarette tax
.39 federal tax
.34 sales tax

Compute the total tax included in the price of a pack of cigarettes in New Jersey. What percent of the price is tax? What effect would increasing the state cigarette tax have on the average price?

Health Online

Visit **health.glencoe.com** and complete the Interactive Study Guide for Lesson 4.

STATE EXCISE TAX RATES ON CIGARETTES

Since January 1, 2002, 41 states have increased their cigarette tax in an effort to reduce smoking. **What is the tax rate for a pack of cigarettes in Florida? In New York?**

State	Tax Rate (¢ per pack)	State	Tax Rate (¢ per pack)
Alaska	160	New York	150
Arizona	118	North Carolina	5
Connecticut	151	Rhode Island	246
Florida	33.9	South Carolina	7
Georgia	37	Vermont	119
Michigan	200	Washington	142.5
Montana	170	Wisconsin	77
New Jersey	240	District of Columbia	100

Source: Compiled by FTA various sources, 2005.

Lesson 4 Review

After You Read

Review this lesson for new terms, major headings, and Reading Checks.

What I Learned

1. *Vocabulary* What is *secondhand smoke?* How does it affect the nonsmoker?

2. *Identify* How much money do tobacco companies spend each year on advertising?

3. *Vocabulary* What is smoking's cost to the U.S. in terms of business productivity?

Thinking Critically

4. *Evaluate* Why are pregnant women advised not to smoke?

5. *Analyze* Erin was waiting in line for the movies. When the man in front of Erin lit a cigarette, the woman standing beside the man said it was rude. "Why?" the man asked. "I'm not hurting anyone else, am I?" How would you respond to this question?

Applying Health Skills

6. *Advocacy* With a group, brainstorm ways to lessen the cost of tobacco to the nation and/or individual. Once you come up with a plan, share it with those in other groups. Take the best ideas from all plans. Share these with a local government representative in the form of a class letter or email.

Choosing to Be Tobacco Free

📘 Guide to Reading

● Building Vocabulary
Write the terms that follow in your notebook. Next to each write the definition that is highlighted in the lesson.

- negative peer pressure (p. 323)
- point-of-sale promotions (p. 324)

● Focusing on the Main Ideas
In this lesson, you will learn to

- **identify** ways teens are influenced to try tobacco.
- **explain** how to avoid pressure to use tobacco.
- **describe** the rights of nonsmokers.

● Reading Strategy
Predicting Glance at the headings and pictures in this lesson. Predict what this lesson will teach you.

Why Some Teens Start Using Tobacco

With everything you have read in this chapter, you may wonder why any teen would use tobacco. Here, you will find some answers and learn about ways to stay tobacco free.

Pressure from Peers

At some point, most teens will be offered tobacco. Some will not only have it offered to them, but be strongly encouraged to use it as well. This *pressure you feel to go along with harmful behaviors or beliefs of others your age* is called **negative peer pressure.**

🅠 uick Write

Write a short dialogue between yourself and a peer who wants you to try tobacco. Show how you can politely but firmly refuse.

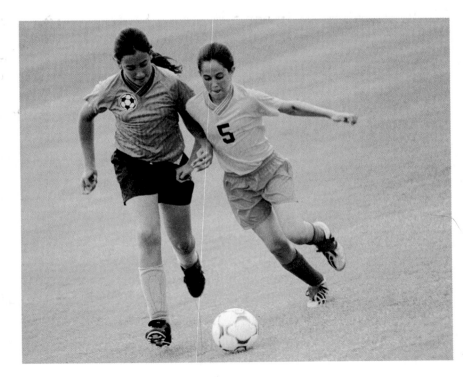

▶ Choosing to be tobacco free is a commitment to yourself to live a longer and healthier life. **What are some benefits of a tobacco-free lifestyle?**

Other Pressures

Some of the pressures to smoke can come from indirect sources, such as the following:

- **Family members.** Teens who live in homes where tobacco is used are more likely to use tobacco themselves.

- **Advertising.** Tobacco companies use strategies such as **point-of-sale promotions,** which are *advertising campaigns in which a product is promoted at a store's checkout counter.* They effectively capture the attention of shoppers as they are waiting to pay.

- **Media.** TV shows and movies often show characters having fun while smoking.

The good news is that fewer and fewer teens are using tobacco every year. **Figure 13.5** shows what teens really think about tobacco.

Reading Check

Describe What are some ways in which teens are pressured to smoke?

▼ FIGURE 13.5

TEEN OPINIONS ON SMOKING

Here is what teens across the United States said in response to statements about tobacco use. **How would you respond to these statements?**

All numbers are percentages	Agree	Disagree	No Opinion or Do Not Know
Seeing someone smoke turns me off.	67	22	10
I would only date people who don't smoke.	86	8	6
It is safe to smoke for only a year or two.	7	92	1
Smoking can help you when you're bored.	7	92	1
Smoking helps reduce stress.	21	78	3
Smoking helps keep your weight down.	18	80	2
Chewing tobacco and snuff cause cancer.	95	2	3
I strongly dislike being around smokers.	65	22	13

Source: Centers for Disease Control and Prevention, 2005.

Staying Tobacco Free

You can protect your health now and in the future by making a commitment to stay tobacco free. Nearly 85 percent of adult smokers report having started smoking before age 18. If you avoid using tobacco now, as a teen, there is a strong possibility that you won't start smoking as an adult.

There is no question that resisting negative peer pressure can be difficult, but you can do it. Start by choosing friends who do not use tobacco. Also, avoid situations where tobacco is likely to be used. Finally, if you do feel pressure to try tobacco, remember to use the S.T.O.P. strategy to help you say no. The S.T.O.P. strategy is explained in Chapter 5.

Nonsmokers' Rights

You have the right to breathe air that is free of tobacco smoke. Laws have been passed in recent years to protect the rights of non-smokers. Many local laws forbid smoking in designated areas such as businesses, schools, and public transportation vehicles.

Reading Check **Identify** What action has been taken to protect nonsmokers' rights?

Health Online

Visit **health.glencoe.com** and complete the Interactive Study Guide for Lesson 5.

Lesson 5 Review

After You Read

Review this lesson for new terms, major headings, and Reading Checks.

What I Learned

1. *Vocabulary* What is *negative peer pressure?*

2. *Describe* Name ways of avoiding pressure to try tobacco.

3. *Recall* What right is shared by all nonsmokers?

Thinking Critically

4. *Evaluate* Which of the influences you read about to try tobacco do you find the most persuasive, and why?

5. *Analyze* You are sitting in a nonsmoking area of a restaurant. A person at the next table lights up. When you point to the nonsmoking sign, the person extinguishes the cigarette. She then says, "You know, smokers have rights, too." How do you respond?

Applying Health Skills

6. *Communication* With a classmate, practice polite ways of asking another person to put out a cigarette. Pay attention to body language and tone of voice. Demonstrate your technique for the class.

Building Health Skills

Saying No to Tobacco

DIRECTIONS

Goal Setting involves setting positive goals and taking steps to achieve them. This activity will give you the opportunity to develop and master this important health skill. Here's a guide to the different parts of this activity:

1 In the **Model** section, you will read about a teen who performs the health skill successfully. This "model" scenario will show you how the skill is done.

2 The **Practice** section will help guide you in practicing the skill.

3 In the **Apply** section, you will have a chance to perform the skill on your own. You can use the Self-Check to check your work.

To complete this activity, first read the scenario presented in the Model. Then move on to the Practice. Finally, go ahead and try the Apply.

1 Model

Carrie is going to be a bridesmaid in her cousin Rebecca's wedding. The wedding reception is being held at the home of another relative named Dan.

As Carrie and Rebecca were discussing plans for decorating Dan's house, Carrie remembered that Dan and many of his friends smoke. "What are we going to do?" Carrie asked Rebecca.

Carrie and Rebecca came up with a plan and talked it over with Dan. Fortunately, Dan is very understanding and willing to follow their plan.

1. ***Identify a specific goal***. Rebecca wants to have a smoke-free reception.

2. ***List the steps you will take***. All the guests who smoke will be asked ahead of time not to smoke in the house.

3. ***Get help and support from others***. Rebecca and her fiancé will ask their parents and other non-smoking relatives to help them notify the smokers about the decision.

4. ***Reward yourself***. Rebecca's reward will be a smoke-free reception.

② Practice

Carrie is on her way to a birthday party with relatives. Her aunt Emily, who smokes, is going to be there. Though Carrie is looking forward to seeing her aunt, she wants to protect her health by avoiding environmental tobacco smoke.

1. What is Carrie's specific goal?
2. What are some steps she could take?
3. How could she get help and support from others?
4. What is Carrie's reward?

Skill Summary
GOAL SETTING

The strategy of goal setting includes the following:

- Identify a specific goal.
- List the steps you will take.
- Get help and support from others.
- Reward yourself.

③ Apply

Imagine that you are planning to take a vacation with your relatives. Some of your relatives smoke. You know issues will come up about when and where smoking will be allowed. For example, the smokers in the group will want to sit in the smoking section at restaurants. Use your goal-setting skills to help you stay tobacco free.

Self-Check

- Did I make a plan for achieving my goal of remaining tobacco free?
- Did I get help and support from my relatives?

UP IN SMOKE

Secondhand smoke might be even more dangerous than experts first thought.

Recently, many people were surprised to hear that the Centers for Disease Control and Prevention (CDC) issued a warning about secondhand smoke. It advised anyone at risk of heart disease to avoid any indoor public spaces where smoking is allowed. According to the CDC, exposure to secondhand smoke for as little as 30 minutes can significantly increase a person's risk of heart attack.

DETECTING A HIDDEN DANGER

The health risks posed by secondhand smoke are well documented, but what triggered the warning was a small study out of Helena, Montana. When the city passed a law banning indoor smoking, Helena's only heart hospital recorded a 40 percent drop in the number of heart attacks. They went from an average of 40 per six months to just 24.

What's more, when a court order lifted the ban half a year later, the heart-attack rate bounced right back. Dr. Robert Shepard, who wrote the Helena study, offers this explanation: "There is laboratory evidence that secondhand smoke makes platelets in the blood stickier.

This causes clots and sends arteries into spasm—both of which can lead to heart attacks." The chemical reaction and the resulting damage occur quickly.

WHAT DOES IT MEAN FOR EVERYONE ELSE?

The study's findings could be very important. The CDC estimates that in the United States, secondhand smoke causes 35,000 deaths a year from heart disease. This figure, some experts believe, will have to be revised upward. Why? Because 60 percent of Americans—both smokers and nonsmokers—show biological effects of tobacco-smoke exposure.

Shepard did offer some reassurance for people who cannot avoid groups of smokers when they walk outside. Exposure for a few seconds probably doesn't do much harm, he says, because the toxins in cigarette smoke are diluted in outside air.

CHAPTER 13 Reading Review

Lesson 1 Facts About Tobacco

Key Idea

- Harmful substances in tobacco include nicotine, tar, and carbon monoxide.

Vocabulary

- nicotine (p. 308)
- addictive (p. 309)
- tar (p. 309)
- bronchi (p. 309)
- carbon monoxide (p. 309)
- smokeless tobacco (p. 310)

Lesson 2 Health Risks of Tobacco Use

Key Idea

- The long-term effects of tobacco include chronic obstructive pulmonary disease, cardiovascular disease, stomach ulcers, infertility, and cancer.

Vocabulary

- chronic obstructive pulmonary disease (COPD) (p. 313)
- cardiovascular disease (p. 313)

Lesson 3 Tobacco Addiction

Key Ideas

- A tolerance to nicotine forms as the body adjusts to the effects of the drug.
- Breaking the tobacco habit is hard because nicotine is a powerfully addictive drug.

Vocabulary

- tolerance (p. 316)
- physical dependence (p. 316)
- psychological dependence (p. 316)
- withdrawal (p. 317)
- nicotine replacement therapies (NRT) (p. 317)
- relapse (p. 318)

Lesson 4 Tobacco's Costs to Society

Key Idea

- Tobacco's costs to society are to the individual, the nonsmoker, and to unborn children of mothers who smoke. Costs include property damage through fire and lost productivity.

Vocabulary

- secondhand smoke (p. 320)
- sidestream smoke (p. 320)
- mainstream smoke (p. 320)
- passive smoker (p. 320)

Lesson 5 Choosing to Be Tobacco Free

Key Ideas

- Pressure to use tobacco can come from peers, family members, advertising, and the media.
- Ways to avoid using tobacco include choosing friends who do not use tobacco, avoiding situations where tobacco is likely to be used, and using refusal skills.

Vocabulary

- negative peer pressure (p. 323)
- point-of-sale promotions (p. 324)

Assessment

Reviewing Vocabulary and Main Ideas

On a sheet of paper, write the numbers 1–5. After each number, write the term from the list that best completes each sentence.

- addictive
- bronchi
- carbon monoxide
- cardiovascular **disease**
- chronic obstructive pulmonary disease (COPD)
- nicotine
- smokeless tobacco
- tar

Lesson 1 Facts About Tobacco

1. _____ is an addictive drug found in tobacco leaves and in all tobacco products.

2. A poisonous, odorless gas found in tobacco is _____.

3. _____ is ground tobacco that is chewed or inhaled through the nose.

Lesson 2 Health Risks of Tobacco Use

4. A condition in which passages in the lungs become swollen and irritated, eventually losing their elasticity, is known as _____.

5. _____ is a disease of the heart and blood vessels.

*On a sheet of paper, write the numbers 6–11. Write **True** or **False** for each statement below. If the statement is false, change the underlined word or phrase to make it true.*

Lesson 3 Tobacco Addiction

6. A process in which your body needs more and more of a drug to get the same effect is called <u>withdrawal</u>.

7. A form of addiction in which the mind sends the body a message that it needs more of a drug is called <u>physical addiction</u>.

Lesson 4 Tobacco's Costs to Society

8. <u>Sidestream smoke</u> is smoke from a lighted cigarette, pipe, or cigar.

9. When people miss work because of a tobacco-related illness, the result is <u>lost productivity</u>.

Lesson 5 Choosing to Be Tobacco Free

10. An advertisement that catches your attention at a checkout is an example of <u>negative peer pressure</u>.

11. Teens who avoid smoking are <u>more likely</u> to start smoking as adults.

Health Online Visit health.glencoe.com and take the Online Quiz for Chapter 13.

Thinking Critically

Using complete sentences, answer the following questions on a sheet of paper.

12. Apply Nadine smells tobacco on her sister Shari's hair and clothes one afternoon. How could Nadine talk to her sister about the tobacco smell without accusing her of smoking?

13. Synthesize Explain how a person becomes addicted to tobacco.

Write About It

14. Decision Making Write a story about a teen faced with a difficult decision. The decision is whether to join a club in which the members smoke. Use the decision-making process to show how the teen makes a healthy choice.

15. Advocacy Create a "how-to" pamphlet explaining how to avoid tobacco. Include some of the dangers of tobacco use.

Career Corner

Respiratory Therapist Smokers who seriously damage their lungs may need the help of a respiratory therapist. These professionals evaluate, treat, and care for patients with breathing disorders such as chronic obstructive pulmonary disease. Respiratory therapists can become registered after attending a two-year program at a community college or vocational school. Learn more about this and other health careers by clicking on *Career Corner* at **health.glencoe.com**.

Standardized Test Practice

Math

The pie graph shows the causes of smoking-related deaths by percentage. Use the graph to answer the questions that follow.

Pie graph:
- Other 17%
- Lung cancer 30.7%
- Stroke 4.3%
- Cardiovascular disease 20.2%
- COPD 20.2%
- Other causes 7.6%

TEST-TAKING TIP

When problems include graphs, make sure you understand the kind of graph and what type of data it shows.

1. The wedges in the chart for cardiovascular disease and COPD reveal

   A. that fewer people die of lung cancer than of either one of these illnesses.

   B. that more people die of COPD than of cardiovascular disease.

   C. that the two causes of smoking-related deaths claim roughly the same number of lives.

   D. None of the above.

2. Based on pie wedge for "Other causes," you can assume all of the following *except*

   A. that combined these illnesses account for some 17% of the total deaths.

   B. that a greater percentage of smoking-related deaths are caused by lung cancer.

   C. that combined these illnesses account for more deaths than stroke.

   D. that these illnesses are unimportant.

CHAPTER
14 Drugs

Chapter Preview

▲ Working With the Photo

By learning about the risks associated with drug use, you can take a stand and help others stay drug free too. **What are some ways that you can advocate for a drug-free environment?**

332

Start-Up Activities

FOLDABLES Study Organizer

As You Read Make this Foldable™ to help you organize the information on medicines and drugs in Lesson 1. Begin with a sheet of notebook paper.

1 Fold a sheet of paper along the long axis, leaving a ½" tab along the side.

3 Cut the top layer along both folds. Then cut each tab in half to make six tabs.

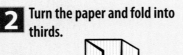

2 Turn the paper and fold into thirds.

4 Turn the paper vertically and label the tabs as shown.

1. Drugs
2. Medicines
3. Prescription Medicines
4. OTC Medicines
5. Side Effects
6. Tolerance

Under the appropriate tab, write notes and define terms related to medicine and drugs.

Drug Misuse and Abuse

Guide to Reading

Building Vocabulary
List each new highlighted term and its definition in your notebook.

- drug (p. 334)
- prescription medicines (p. 335)
- over-the-counter medicines (OTC) (p. 335)
- drug misuse (p. 335)
- side effect (p. 335)
- tolerance (p. 335)
- drug abuse (p. 336)

Focusing on the Main Ideas
In this lesson, you will learn to

- **explain** the difference between drug misuse and drug abuse.
- **identify** the risks of drug abuse.
- **develop** strategies for making healthful choices about taking medicines.

Reading Strategy
Drawing Conclusions Based on this lesson, list three different ways drug abuse can affect your health.

FOLDABLES Study Organizer Use the Foldable™ on p.333 as you read this lesson.

Quick Write

Write a sentence explaining why it is important to read the label directions on medicines before taking them.

Drug Use

People often define the word "drug" differently. A **drug** is *a substance other than food that changes the structure or function of the body or mind.* A "medicine" is a drug used to prevent or treat illnesses and disease.

▶ Medicines help treat many kinds of illnesses and diseases. **Why is it important to use medicines only as directed?**

All medicines are drugs, but not all drugs are medicines. All drugs, including medicines, can be misused and abused.

Types of Medicines

Medicines can be categorized into two general types. The first type, **prescription medicines,** are *medicines that can be sold only with a written order from a physician.* With this type of medicine, a doctor or pharmacist gives specific directions on its use—how much to take, how often, and for how long.

Have you ever taken aspirin for a headache, or used cough syrup for a cold? If so, you have used another type of medicine. **Over-the-counter medicines (OTC)** are *medicines that are safe enough to be taken without a written order from a physician.* They are sold in pharmacies and other stores.

▲ Prescription drugs are available only with a written order from a doctor. **What type of directions are provided with prescription drugs?**

Reading Check **Compare** What is the difference between prescription and over-the-counter medicines?

Drug Misuse

Both prescription medicines and over-the-counter medicines can be misused. **Drug misuse** is *taking or using medicine in a way that is not intended.* A person who does any of the following is misusing drugs:

- Using the drug without following the instructions on the label
- Using a drug not prescribed for you
- Allowing someone else to use a drug prescribed for you
- Taking more of the drug than the doctor prescribed
- Using the drug longer than advised by the doctor

Even when taken correctly, some medicines will cause a side effect. A **side effect** is *any effect of a medicine other than the one intended.* Common side effects include stomach upset, drowsiness, sleeplessness, and headache. Side effects should be discussed with your doctor if they occur.

When a physician prescribes a medicine that must be taken for a long period of time, a drug tolerance may develop. **Tolerance** is *a condition in which a person's body becomes used to the effect of a medicine and needs greater and greater amounts of it in order for it to be effective.*

Medicine Ads

Find several magazine ads for medicines. Look for common information in the ads.

Use critical thinking skills to interpret the ads' messages. What conclusions can you draw about the legal requirements for medicine ads?

Health Skills Activity

Practicing Healthful Behaviors

Handling Medicine Safely in Your Home

What do you know about medicine safety in the home? Follow these guidelines to store, use, and dispose of medicine safely.

- Know what medicines are in your home and what they are used to treat.
- Store medicines in a cool, dry place.
- Keep medicines safely sealed in childproof containers, and keep them out of the reach of children.
- Never share prescription medicines. They could cause serious harm to someone else.
- Do not use OTC medicines for more than ten days at a time unless you check with your doctor.
- Before taking two or more medicines at the same time, get your doctor's approval. Combining medicines can cause harmful side effects.
- Do not use medicines that have passed their expiration date.
- To safely dispose of outdated or unused liquid or pills, flush them down the toilet.

On Your Own

Create a "Medicine Safety Checklist" suitable for home use. Review the completed checklist with your family. Post the list in an appropriate place in your home.

Health Online

Visit **health.glencoe.com** and complete the Interactive Study Guide for Lesson 1.

Drug Abuse

When you hear the term *drug abuse,* what do you think of? **Drug abuse** is *intentionally using drugs in a way that is unhealthy or illegal.* Certainly the person using illegal drugs is abusing drugs. However, using illegal drugs is only one form of drug abuse. Using *legal* drugs for non-medical reasons or using a medication for something other than its intended use is also drug abuse.

Drug abuse can affect all three sides of your health triangle. The physical effects range from sleeplessness and irritability to heart failure and stroke. Drug abuse interferes with brain function, affecting your mental/emotional health. Some drugs make it difficult to think or concentrate. Other drugs cause depression or anxiety. Your social health is also affected. Teens who abuse drugs may withdraw from family and friends. They may lose interest in school or other activities.

Addiction

People who abuse drugs are at risk of developing an addiction. An addiction is a physical or psychological need for a drug. When a person uses a drug regularly, he or she will develop a tolerance to the drug. The user needs more and more of the drug to get the same effect. Eventually, the user becomes addicted. There is no telling how many times a person can use a drug before becoming addicted. Once addicted, the user can no longer function without the drug. It becomes the focus of his or her daily life.

Drug addition, like alcoholism, is a disease. Once a person becomes addicted, it is very difficult to quit using the drug. Treatment options exist that can help drug users overcome their addiction. You will learn more about the different treatment options available to drug users in Lesson 5.

▲ Drug abuse takes you away from your friends and other people in your life who you love. **Can you imagine what your life would be like without those who are closest to you?**

Reading Check **Recall** Name two different forms of drug abuse.

Lesson 1 Review

After You Read

Review this lesson for new terms, major headings, and Reading Checks.

What I Learned

1. *Vocabulary* Define *drug*. Use the word in an original sentence.

2. *Identify* Name two side effects that can occur when taking medicine.

3. *Compare* What is the difference between drug misuse and drug abuse?

Thinking Critically

4. *Explain* How does drug addiction occur?

5. *Hypothesize* What might you say to persuade a friend not to take a medicine that has not been prescribed to him or her?

Applying Health Skills

6. *Accessing Information* Use library resources and the Internet to research drug misuse and abuse in the United States. Create a pamphlet to educate others about the dangers.

Marijuana and Other Illegal Drugs

Guide to Reading

● **Building Vocabulary**

In your notebook, use each of the new vocabulary terms in an original sentence that illustrates its meaning.

- marijuana (p. 338)
- THC (p. 338)
- amnesia (p. 341)
- anabolic steroids (p. 343)

● **Focusing on the Main Ideas**

In this lesson, you will learn to

- **describe** the effects and risks of marijuana use.
- **identify** the most commonly used club drugs.
- **explain** the reasons that teens abuse anabolic steroids.
- **list** the physical effects of anabolic steroid abuse.

● **Reading Strategy**

Finding the Main Idea For each major heading in this lesson, write one sentence that states the main idea.

*Q*uick Write

List one physical, mental/emotional, and social risk of using marijuana.

What Is Marijuana?

You may have heard the different names people use when referring to marijuana. **Marijuana** is *dried leaves and flowers of the hemp plant, called cannabis sativa.* It is also commonly called *pot* or *weed*. Marijuana is an illegal drug that is usually smoked.

What Are Marijuana's Effects?

Marijuana affects the brain of the person using the drug. *The main active chemical in marijuana is* **THC.** THC alters the way the brain processes sensory information.

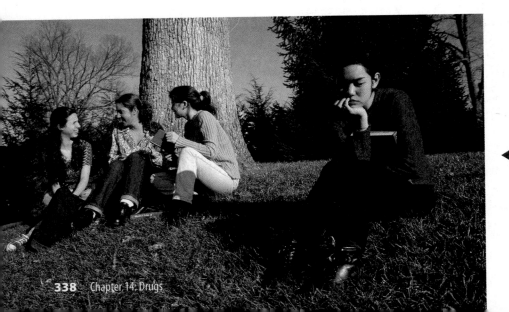

◀ Marijuana use can cause a lack of interest in the things you once enjoyed. **What are some other reasons to avoid marijuana?**

Marijuana can cause a variety of reactions. Some people experience a pleasant sensation for a short while. Others may experience unpleasant reactions to the drug. It is also impossible to know what other harmful substances may be mixed in with marijuana.

Short-Term Effects

Marijuana use has many negative effects. It reduces reaction time and coordination, and impairs judgment. It also increases heart rate and appetite. High doses of marijuana can cause anxiety and panic attacks. **Figure 14.1** lists some additional effects of marijuana use.

Long-Term Effects

Long-term effects of marijuana use are serious. Since the drug contains many of the same chemicals found in tobacco smoke, users are at risk for the same lung diseases that tobacco users confront, including cancer.

There are over 400 chemicals in the marijuana plant. Research has found that people who abuse marijuana for a long period of time experience changes to the region of the brain that processes information. It has been associated with depression, anxiety, and personality disturbances. Users may fall behind in school or at work.

Marijuana use can also affect a person's social health. The loss of motivation that comes with continued marijuana use can lead to problems with friends or family members.

Reading Check **Explain** How does marijuana affect the user?

▼ **FIGURE 14.1**

EFFECTS OF MARIJUANA USE

Marijuana affects your ability to think clearly, concentrate on goals, and relate to people in healthful ways. **What are some other effects of marijuana use?**

Health Effects of Marijuana Use	
Brief Description	The most commonly used illegal drug in the U.S. The main active chemical is THC.
Street Names	Pot, ganja, weed, grass, and many others.
Effects	Short-term effects include memory and learning problems, distorted perception, and difficulty thinking and solving problems.

Safety Risks

Using marijuana puts teens at risk in a number of ways. Since it is an illegal substance, users are at risk of getting arrested. Users may also say or do things that could get them into trouble or hurt them. Impaired reaction time and coordination can make driving a car dangerous while under the influence of marijuana.

Since marijuana can affect judgment, its use can lead to participation in other risky behaviors. These can include using alcohol or other drugs, or engaging in sexual activity. This can increase the risk of sexually transmitted diseases and unplanned pregnancy.

Marijuana and Addiction

Perhaps you have heard someone say, "Marijuana? What's the big deal? It's not like you can get hooked or anything." Not true. Frequent users of marijuana can develop a tolerance to the drug. Developing a tolerance often leads to physical dependency and addiction. Each year more than 120,000 people seek treatment for addiction to marijuana.

Reading Check **Recall** What are some of the safety risks involved in using marijuana?

▲ Driving under the influence of marijuana can be dangerous. **What are some effects of marijuana use that could impair a person's ability to drive safely?**

Health Skills Activity

Accessing Information

Marijuana Myths

Marijuana is the most commonly used illegal drug. Because its effects are not as dramatic as some other illegal drugs, it is often mistakenly believed to be a harmless drug. Here are some common myths about marijuana use:

Myth: "Marijuana is not addictive—users can stop whenever they want."

Myth: "Smoking marijuana is safer than using other drugs."

Myth: "Everyone smokes marijuana."

On Your Own

Using this lesson and other reliable print or online resources, find information that shows how these myths may not be true. Develop a fact sheet listing each myth and the truths behind each myth.

What Are Club Drugs?

Club drugs take their names from dance clubs or raves where they are often used. Some people may falsely believe that club drugs are safe to use. However, research shows that these drugs may produce harmful effects.

Hallucinations, paranoia, and amnesia are among the harmful effects of club drugs. **Amnesia** is *partial or total loss of memory.* When club drugs are mixed with alcohol, which they often are, the effects of both substances are increased. These effects are also unpredictable. People react differently to club drugs. No one can tell ahead of time what their reaction will be. Two forms of club drugs are ecstasy and date rape drugs.

Ecstasy

Ecstasy is a club drug that affects the user in similar ways to hallucinogens and stimulants. It speeds up the central nervous system, making a person feel very alert or "hyper." The scientific name for ecstasy is MDMA. Unlike marijuana, which comes from a plant, MDMA is a synthetic chemical, created in illegal laboratories. Makers of the drug often add other substances to ecstasy, such as caffeine or amphetamines. As a result, an ecstasy user may not even know what drug is being ingested.

Ecstasy is usually taken as a pill, tablet, or capsule. When combined with alcohol, the effects can be even more dangerous.

It is hard to predict how ecstasy will affect a user. Some users might feel energized, happy, and relaxed, while others become nervous and agitated. Initial effects can last for three to six hours. However, after-effects such as sadness, depression, and memory problems can last for several days or longer. Researchers are currently studying how long-term use of ecstasy may affect the brain.

The wide-ranging effects of taking ecstasy start within 30 minutes of taking the drug. They can include:

- increased heart rate
- nausea
- anxiety
- elevated blood pressure
- dizziness
- chills
- sweating
- increased sense of confidence
- feelings of well-being
- loss of appetite

Date Rape Drugs

Rohypnol, commonly called roofie, is a club drug that appeared in the United States in the 1990s. It works by suppressing the central nervous system. Rohypnol has no odor, color, or taste. In pill form, it can easily be slipped into someone's drink. When a person unknowingly takes Rohypnol, he or she is unaware of what is happening and is unable to resist an attack or unwanted sexual advances. The drug also produces amnesia, so the person who has taken it often has no memory of what has occurred.

GHB is another depressant of the central nervous system. Until 1992, GHB was available as an over-the-counter drug used by bodybuilders to increase muscle mass and decrease fat. GHB usually comes in liquid form. Like Royhpnol, it has been linked to sexual assault.

Ketamine, sometimes called Special K, is an anesthetic used in medical procedures for humans and animals. When abused as a club drug, ketamine is usually snorted, or sprinkled over marijuana or tobacco and smoked. Ketamine is so powerful that only a small amount may cause serious health effects, such as hallucinations, memory loss, and severe breathing problems—even respiratory failure.

▼ Drug use has many harmful consequences. **What are some short-term and long-term health effects of club drugs?**

Anabolic Steroids

Anabolic steroids are *synthetic substances related to the male sex hormones.* Physicians sometimes prescribe these drugs to treat growth problems, lung diseases, and skin conditions. Anabolic steroids are similar to the male hormone testosterone. They help build muscle mass and enhance the development of male characteristics.

Steroids are most often abused by people who want to enhance their athletic abilities by adding muscle mass and increasing their strength and endurance. Abuse of these drugs has become a serious concern in professional sports in the United States. **Figure 14.2** lists some of the harmful effects of using anabolic steriods.

▲ The best way to improve your athletic performance is to practice. **How could using drugs stand in the way of reaching your goals?**

Reading Check **Define** What are *anabolic steroids*?

▼ **FIGURE 14.2**

HEALTH EFFECTS OF ANABOLIC STEROIDS

A person caught using steroids can face social consequences, such as being kicked off a team or expelled from school. **Can you think of some consequences of steroid use related to mental/emotional health?**

Health Effects of Anabolic Steroids	
Brief Description	Human-made substances related to male sex hormones. Some athletes abuse anabolic steroids to enhance performance. Abuse of anabolic steroids can lead to serious health problems, some of which are irreversible.
Effects	Major side effects can include liver tumors and cancer, jaundice, high blood pressure, kidney tumors, severe acne, and trembling.
	In males, side effects may include shrinking of the testicles and breast development.
	In females, side effects may include growth of facial hair, menstrual changes, and deepened voice.
Statistics and Trends	In NIDA's 2004 *Monitoring the Future* study, 3.4% of high school seniors reported using steroids at least once.

Source: NIDA Infofacts: High School and Youth Trends.

Health Online

Visit **health.glencoe.com** **and complete the Interactive Study Guide for Lesson 2.**

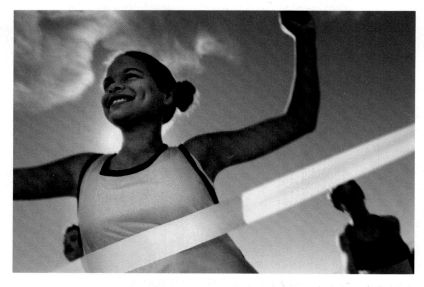

Teens and Steroid Use

Most teens avoid using steroids. Those that do risk damaging their health. They also risk negatively affecting their appearance. Steroids can put acne on your face, make your hair fall out, and stunt your growth. They can also cause a person to become angry or violent, which can result in personal injury or injury to others.

Steroid use can also cause a hormonal imbalance. Hormones are important during the teen years. They are responsible for the physical, mental/emotional, and social changes that all teens go through on their way to adulthood. When hormone levels are not balanced, problems with the development of female and male characteristics can occur. Boys can grow breasts and girls can develop mustaches or beards.

▲ Playing well after hard work and practice can give you a deep sense of pride and accomplishment. **Have you ever felt this way after achieving something that you worked hard for?**

Reading Check **Explain** How might anabolic steroids affect a teen's health?

Lesson 2 Review

After You Read

Review this lesson for new terms, major headings, and Reading Checks.

What I Learned

1. *Vocabulary* What is *THC*?

2. *Recall* What are some negative consequences of using anabolic steroids?

3. *Explain* What are two long-term effects of marijuana use?

Thinking Critically

4. *Analyze* Why do you think steroid abuse is a concern in competitive sports?

5. *Hypothesize* What might happen to a person who unknowingly ingests Rohypnol while at a club?

Applying Health Skills

6. *Advocacy* Write a script for a public service announcement for radio or television, explaining the short- and long-term effects of marijuana use.

Health Online For more review questions for Lesson 2, go to health.glencoe.com.

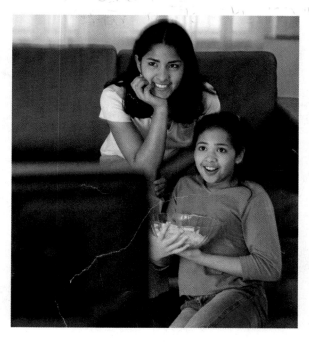

Narcotics, Stimulants, and Depressants

Guide to Reading

Building Vocabulary
As you read this lesson, write each new highlighted term and its definition in your notebook.

- narcotics (p. 345)
- opium (p. 345)
- euphoria (p. 346)
- withdrawal symptoms (p. 346)
- stimulants (p. 348)
- amphetamine (p. 348)
- binge (p. 348)
- CNS depressants (p. 350)

Focusing on the Main Ideas
In this lesson, you will learn to

- **name** the most commonly abused narcotics.
- **describe** the effects that narcotics can have on a user's health.
- **identify** specific stimulants and CNS depressants.
- **name** the health risks linked to stimulant and CNS depressant abuse.

Reading Strategy
Identifying Cause-and-Effect Make a two-column chart. In the first column, write the names of drugs presented in this lesson. In the second, list the effects of these drugs.

Quick Write
Make a list of reasons why you should avoid using drugs.

What Are Narcotics?

Narcotics are *specific drugs that are obtainable only by prescription and are used to relieve pain.* Historically, narcotics were made from **opium,** which is *a liquid from the poppy plant containing substances that numb the body.* When used under a doctor's supervision, narcotics are effective in the treatment of extreme pain. However, they are also highly addictive. As a result, their sale and use is controlled by law.

▶ Spending time with your family can help you avoid pressure to use drugs. **What are some healthful activities you can do with your family?**

Narcotics and Addiction

Narcotics affect the body by attaching themselves to certain receptors in the brain to block any painful messages that are being sent. These drugs can also produce **euphoria,** or *a feeling of well-being or elation* because they affect the areas of the brain that perceive pleasure.

When narcotics are abused, the threat of serious health risk increases drastically. Abusing these drugs can result in tolerance, physical and psychological dependence, and addiction. The body becomes accustomed to having the drug and when it is taken away, the user experiences **withdrawal symptoms.** These are *symptoms that occur after chronic use of a drug is reduced or stopped.* Withdrawal symptoms can be unbearable. They can include pain in the muscles and bones, sleeplessness, diarrhea, agitation, and vomiting. **Figure 14.3** on the next page shows some of the effects of narcotic drug abuse.

Heroin

Heroin is an illegal narcotic. It is made from morphine, another narcotic. Heroin is most often inhaled or injected intravenously, although sometimes users smoke the drug.

Heroin users can become easily addicted. Users can develop a psychological dependence, craving the feelings the drug brings. Regular users build up a tolerance to the drug and then need it in ever-increasing doses. Over time, the user becomes physically addicted and quitting becomes very difficult. If the user tries to quit, he or she may experience painful withdrawal symptoms.

◀ When prescribed by a doctor, narcotics are used to treat extreme pain, such as the pain endured by cancer patients. **Why are patients strictly supervised by doctors when using narcotics?**

EFFECTS OF NARCOTIC DRUG ABUSE

When narcotics are abused, there is a high risk of addiction and other health consequences. **What are some of these consequences?**

Health Effects of Narcotic Drug Abuse

- Can cause drowsiness, constipation, and depress breathing.
- Taking a large single dose could cause severe respiratory depression or death.
- Can cause death if taken with certain medications or alcohol.
- Can lead to physical dependence and tolerance. The body becomes used to the substance and higher doses are needed to feel the same initial effect.
- Narcotics are highly addictive, often causing uncontrollable drug use in spite of negative consequences.
- Withdrawal symptoms occur if use is reduced abruptly. Symptoms can include restlessness, muscle and bone pain, insomnia, diarrhea, vomiting, cold flashes with goose bumps, and involuntary leg movements.
- Withdrawal from narcotics usually requires detoxification in a hospital. People who suffer from long-term addictions may never be able to withdraw completely, because withdrawal is so severe it can leave lasting harmful effects on the body.

OxyContin

OxyContin is a legal narcotic, available through a doctor's prescription. When used in the approved manner, it can control severe pain in patients with cancer, back pain, or arthritis.

However, OxyContin is also abused by users. The long-term effect of OxyContin use is an increased tolerance to the drug, which leads to physical addiction. Withdrawal symptoms when the drug is stopped are similar to those of other narcotics.

Reading Check

Recall What are some of the effects of narcotic drug abuse?

► The effects of drug abuse include the loss of ability to concentrate. **How would this affect your performance at school?**

What Are Stimulants?

Stimulants are *drugs that speed up activity in the human brain and spinal cord.* They cause the heart to beat faster and blood pressure and metabolism to rise. A person using this type of drug will often move and speak more quickly than usual. The user may feel exhilarated, or excited. Others may become anxious.

Some stimulants are so mild that people may not realize they are ingesting a drug. Caffeine, found in coffee, tea, many soft drinks, and chocolate, is a stimulant. Some stimulants are prescribed by doctors for patients with certain physical or emotional problems. Stimulant abuse, however, can be dangerous. **Figure 14.4** on the next page shows several types of stimulants and their harmful effects.

Reading Check **Define** What are *stimulants*?

Amphetamines

An **amphetamine,** also known as speed, is *a drug that stimulates the central nervous system.* Amphetamines are highly addictive. Using large amounts of amphetamines can result in aggressive behavior that is difficult to predict. Other effects include extreme weight loss and loss of physical strength.

Cocaine

Cocaine is an illegal stimulant derived from the coca plant. Usually sold as a fine white powder, cocaine is often mixed with water and injected into the body *intravenously,* or administered into a vein. Cocaine can also be smoked or taken in through the nose, which is known as *snorting.* Cocaine is one of the most addictive drugs on the street today.

Cocaine affects the user almost immediately. The effects can last up to a few hours. Taking large amounts of the drug increases these effects, but can also lead to violent and unpredictable behavior. As cocaine use continues, the user develops a tolerance for the drug. Larger and more frequent doses of cocaine are needed. During a cocaine **binge,** *when a drug is taken repeatedly and at increasingly high doses,* the possible consequences are very dangerous.

Reading Check **Identify** What is a cocaine binge?

EFFECTS OF STIMULANTS

The biggest risk associated with stimulant abuse is damage to your heart, sometimes causing heart attacks or death. **What are some other harmful effects of stimulant abuse?**

Substance	Other Names	Forms	Methods of Use	Harmful Effects
Amphetamine	Crystal, ice, glass, crank, speed, uppers	Pills, powder, chunky crystals	Swallowed, snorted up the nose, smoked, injected	Uneven heartbeat, rise in blood pressure, physical collapse, stroke, heart attack, and death
Methamphetamine	Meth, crank, speed, ice	Pills, powder, crystals	Swallowed, snorted up the nose, smoked, injected	Memory loss, damage to heart and nervous system, seizures, and death
Cocaine	Coke, dust, snow, flake, blow, girl	White powder	Snorted up the nose, injected	Damage to nose lining and liver; heart attack, seizures, stroke, and death
Crack	Crack, freebase rocks, rock	Off-white rocks or chunks	Smoked, injected	Damage to lungs if smoked, seizures, heart attack, and death

Crack

When cocaine is heated and processed with baking soda and water, it forms a substance that is smoked. The drug that is created is called *crack*. It gets its name from the cracking sound that occurs when the mixture is smoked. Crack is an extremely addictive and dangerous drug.

Methamphetamine

Methamphetamine is a highly addictive stimulant drug that strongly affects the central nervous system. It is becoming an epidemic in the United States. This drug is produced in illegal laboratories that exist in every state, in small towns and cities, and are popping up in disturbing numbers.

Methamphetamine, or "meth" as it is commonly known, is taken into the body in a variety of ways. Its effects are similar to those of cocaine.

▲ When you abstain from using drugs you can concentrate on activities that you enjoy. **Do you have any interests that you would like to spend more time pursuing?**

Health *Online*

Visit **health.glencoe.com** and complete the Interactive Study Guide for Lesson 3.

The Effects of Methamphetamine

Initially, methamphetamine can make users feel confident and full of energy. Because of these feelings, users often binge, sometimes for days without food or sleep. The user's behavior is often unpredictable.

When a methamphetamine user becomes addicted to the drug, it often becomes difficult, if not impossible, to feel any sense of pleasure without the drug. Methamphetamine abuse is so rampant that in 2004, the Drug Enforcement Administration (DEA), the federal government agency responsible for enforcing laws and regulations governing narcotics and controlled substances, set aside $151.4 million just for its methamphetamine budget.

What Are Central Nervous System (CNS) Depressants?

CNS depressants are *substances that slow down normal brain function.* They are sometimes called sedatives or tranquilizers. Physicians can prescribe some CNS depressants for relief of sleeplessness, anxiety, or tension. However, these drugs are sometimes abused. When used for extended periods of time, they can result in drug tolerance and addiction.

CNS depressants produce a feeling of calm or drowsiness in the person taking the drug. Two CNS depressants that are commonly prescribed are:

- **barbiturates** (bar·BI·chur·ruhts), which are prescribed for the treatment of anxiety or tension, or for people with sleep disorders.

- **benzodiazepines,** to treat patients with more serious anxiety and panic attacks.

Like all prescription medicines, CNS depressants should only be taken as prescribed, and under a doctor's supervision. Long-term users can develop a tolerance in which larger doses are needed to achieve the desired effect. **Figure 14.5** shows some of the effects of depressants.

Reading Check **Explain** How do CNS depressants affect the body?

EFFECTS OF DEPRESSANTS

Depressants are sometimes prescribed to treat certain conditions, but when abused, they are dangerous. **What are some harmful effects of depressants?**

Substance	Other Names	Forms	Methods of Use	Harmful Effects
Tranquilizer	Valium, Librium, Xanax	Pills or capsules	Swallowed	Anxiety; reduced coordination and attention span. Withdrawal can cause tremors and lead to coma or death.
Barbiturate	Downers, barbs, yellow jackets, reds	Pills or capsules	Swallowed	Causes mood changes and excessive sleep. Can lead to coma.
Hypnotic	Quaaludes, Ludes, Sopor	Pills or capsules	Swallowed	Impaired coordination and judgment. High doses may cause internal bleeding, coma, or death.

Lesson 3 Review

After You Read

Review this lesson for new terms, major headings, and Reading Checks.

What I Learned

1. **Vocabulary** Define *narcotics*.

2. **List** Name two commonly abused narcotics.

3. **Give Examples** Give three examples of harmful effects that can result from abusing stimulants.

Thinking Critically

4. **Evaluate** Explain the physical and psychological effects that can cause a person to become addicted to heroin.

5. **Analyze** Think of a high-risk behavior that could result from the abuse of narcotics.

Applying Health Skills

6. **Goal Setting** Make a contract with yourself in which you set the goal of remaining drug free. Develop a plan to help you reach this goal. Sign your contract and keep it visible to help you remember your goal.

Hallucinogens and Inhalants

Guide to Reading

● **Building Vocabulary**
In your notebook, write a sentence that describes the meaning of each new term in your own words.

■ hallucinogens (p. 352)

■ inhalant (p. 354)

● **Focusing on the Main Ideas**
In this lesson, you will learn to

■ **define** hallucinogens.

■ **explain** how hallucinogens affect the user.

■ **identify** the health risks to a person who uses inhalants or hallucinogens.

● **Reading Strategy**
Make an Outline Using the main heads in this lesson, make an outline of the lesson. As you read, fill in your outline with details.

*Q**uick Write***

Write down three facts you know about inhalants.

▼ Many activities can be very difficult while under the influence of hallucinogens. **What are some other effects of hallucinogens?**

Hallucinogens

Hallucinogens are *drugs that distort moods, thoughts, and senses.* Some of these drugs are made from natural substances in plants, such as cactus and mushrooms. Hallucinogens can also be manufactured.

How Do Hallucinogens Affect the User?

Hallucinogens get their name from the word *hallucinate,* which means to have visions. Hallucinogens affect how a user perceives the passage of time, sees colors, senses motion, or hears sound. These drugs can interfere with a person's thought process and ability to communicate. The user can no longer distinguish between what is real and what is not. This can lead to strange or risky behavior. LSD and PCP are examples of hallucinogens. **Figure 14.6** on the next page shows some additional effects of hallucinogens.

▼ FIGURE 14.6

EFFECTS OF HALLUCINOGENS

Hallucinogens can cause many harmful effects, including death. **What are two examples of hallucinogens?**

Substance	Other Names	Forms	Methods of Use	Harmful Effects
PCP	Angel dust, supergrass, killer weed, rocket fuel	White powder, liquid	Applied to leafy materials and smoked	Loss of coordination; increased heart rate, blood pressure, and body temperature; convulsions; heart and lung failure; broken blood vessels; bizarre or violent behavior; temporary psychosis; false feeling of having super powers
LSD	Acid, blotter, microdot, white lightning	Tablets; squares soaked on paper	Eaten or licked	Increased blood pressure, heart rate, and body temperature; chills, nausea, tremors, and sleeplessness; unpredictable behavior; flashbacks; false feeling of having super powers

LSD

LSD, a drug made from lysergic acid, is one of the strongest and most widely abused hallucinogens. It is sold as tablets, capsules, liquid, or on absorbent paper. A tiny amount produces a powerful effect. The psychological effects of LSD are often very difficult to predict. Users may experience hallucinations. They may not know where they are—or even who they are.

Hallucinogens such as LSD can also produce flashbacks. Weeks or even months after taking the drug, a user may relive terrifying thoughts or feelings.

PCP

PCP (phencyclidine) is not a true hallucinogen in its chemical makeup. It is grouped with this category of drugs because its effects are similar to those of LSD. PCP can become addictive, and cause violent and unpredictable behavior. For this reason, PCP users are a threat to others and themselves.

Reading Check **Identify** What are some of the harmful effects of hallucinogens?

Inhalants

An **inhalant** is *any substance whose fumes are sniffed and inhaled to produce mind-altering sensations.* They can be found in any kitchen, garage, or bathroom—household products that are readily available.

Toxic, or poisonous, inhalants include paint, vegetable cooking sprays, air freshener, lighter fluid, markers and pens, correction fluid, and hair sprays. Using a product for something other than its intended use is drug abuse.

Toxic inhalants are not meant to be put into the human body. They can cause serious health effects and even death. **Figure 14.7** lists some of the health effects that can result from abusing inhalants. Hundreds of teens die each year from sniffing or huffing inhalants. However, most teens do not abuse inhalants.

What Damage Do Inhalants Cause?

Abusing inhalants can damage the protective coating that surrounds brain cells, called *myelin.* If myelin is damaged, nerve cells may not be able to send messages to other parts of the body. These results can be permanent and severe. They can affect a person's ability to walk, talk, or think. Inhalant abuse can also kill the user instantly. Even a person experimenting with inhalants for the first time can die from choking, suffocation, or a heart attack.

▼ **FIGURE 14.7**

HEALTH EFFECTS OF INHALANTS

The greatest risk of inhalant use is death, which can occur with a person's first use of the drug. **What are some other health effects of inhalant use?**

Health Effects of Inhalants	
Brief Description	Breathable chemical vapors that users intentionally inhale because of the chemicals' mind-altering effects. The substances inhaled are often common household products that contain harmful solvents or aerosols.
Street Names	Whippets, poppers, snappers.
Effects	Most inhalants produce a rapid high that resembles alcohol intoxication. If sufficient amounts are inhaled, nearly all solvents and gases produce anesthesia, a loss of sensation, and even unconsciousness. They can also cause suffocation, choking, seizures, and death.

◀ One symptom of inhalant abuse is red or runny eyes. **What other parts of the body can inhalant abuse damage?**

Warning Signs of Inhalant Abuse

Here are some symptoms that may indicate a person is abusing inhalants. If you notice these symptoms in someone you know, speak to a teacher or trusted adult about your concerns.

- Eyes that are red or runny.
- Sores or spots near the mouth.
- Breath that smells strange or like chemicals.
- Holding a marker or pen near the nose.

Reading Check **Give Examples** What are two symptoms of inhalant abuse?

Health Online

Visit **health.glencoe.com** and complete the Interactive Study Guide for Lesson 4.

Lesson 4 Review

After You Read

Review this lesson for new terms, major headings, and Reading Checks.

What I Learned

1. *Vocabulary* What are *hallucinogens*?

2. *Recall* What are two possible consequences of using hallucinogens?

3. *Identify* List the health risks to a person who uses inhalants.

Thinking Critically

4. *Hypothesize* What might you say to someone you know who is thinking of abusing an inhalant for the first time?

5. *Analyze* Why do you think inhalant abuse might be a serious problem among 12- to 14-year-olds?

Applying Health Skills

6. *Advocacy* Using pictures from magazines, create a poster showing household substances that are abused as inhalants. Add a caption or slogan to let other students know about the dangers of inhalant abuse.

Getting Help

Guide to Reading

● **Building Vocabulary**
As you read this lesson, write the new highlighted term in a sentence that illustrates its meaning.

■ detoxification (p. 359)

● **Focusing on the Main Ideas**
In this lesson, you will learn to

■ **explain** why it is important to get help for drug use.
■ **identify** the symptoms of drug abuse.
■ **describe** different treatment options for drug abuse.

● **Reading Strategy**
Predicting Look over the lesson, including the headings and pictures. Then write a sentence predicting what information you think the lesson will provide.

Quick Write

List three sources of help for drug use.

▼ Getting help is an important step in kicking a drug habit. **Who would you feel comfortable talking to if you needed help?**

Getting Help

The first step in getting help for drug abuse is for the user to recognize that he or she has a problem. This can be very difficult for users. It can also be difficult for family members or health care professionals to see that a problem exists. Users may try to hide the problem or deny that one exists.

If you have a drug problem, you need to get help. Talk to a trusted adult. If it is too uncomfortable talking with someone you know, you can turn to organizations that offer counseling and treatment. These sources of help include support groups, alcohol or drug treatment centers, and toll-free hot lines staffed by drug counselors.

Although some effects of drug abuse are permanent, drug addiction is treatable. In this lesson, you will learn about some of the different treatment options available.

Reading Check **Recall** What is the first step in getting help for drug abuse?

Recognizing When Someone Needs Help

There are different signs that show that someone may be dealing with a drug abuse problem. Users may lose interest in activities or family and friends. They may also frequently lie to cover up their addiction. **Figure 14.8** lists some of the symptoms of drug abuse. Recognizing these symptoms can help you identify if someone you know has a drug problem.

What should you do if someone you care about has a drug problem? If you think a friend needs help, try talking to him or her about your concerns. If you do not want to talk to the person directly, ask for help from a trusted adult. Encourage him or her to get help.

Reading Check **Give Examples** What are some signs that a person may have a drug problem?

▼ FIGURE 14.8

SYMPTOMS OF DRUG ABUSE

Recognizing the symptoms of drug abuse can help you identify if someone needs help. **What should you do if you recognize these signs in someone you know?**

Tolerance	A person will need increasingly larger amounts of drugs to get high.
Craving	A person will feel a strong need, desire, or urge to use drugs, will use a drug despite negative consequences, and will feel anxious and irritable if he or she can't use them. Craving is a primary symptom of addiction.
Loss of control	A person often will take more drugs than he or she meant to, or may use drugs at a time or place he or she had not planned. A person also may try to reduce or stop using drugs many times, but may fail.
Physical dependence or withdrawal symptoms	In some cases when drug use is stopped, a person may experience withdrawal symptoms from a physical need for the substance. Withdrawal symptoms differ depending on the drug, but they may include nausea, sweating, shakiness, and extreme anxiety.

Drug Treatment Options

Once a person has recognized that he or she has a drug problem, the recovery process can begin. Recovery begins when the person stops using the drug so the body can rid itself of the drug and its effects. If the person is physically and psychologically addicted to the drug, he or she may experience withdrawal. Withdrawal symptoms vary depending on the drug used, but may include headaches, vomiting, chills, and hallucinations.

Drug users need help to recover from a drug addiction. Many communities offer treatment programs, counseling, and support groups to help people recover from drug abuse.

Treatment Programs

Treatment programs include both inpatient and outpatient programs. **Figure 14.9** lists some of the different treatment programs that are available depending on the level of addiction, the type of drug, and the patient. Some hospitals and treatment

▼ **FIGURE 14.9**

TREATMENT PROGRAMS FOR SUBSTANCE ABUSE

There are many options available for those who need help recovering from a drug addiction. **Why do you think different treatment programs work better for some than others?**

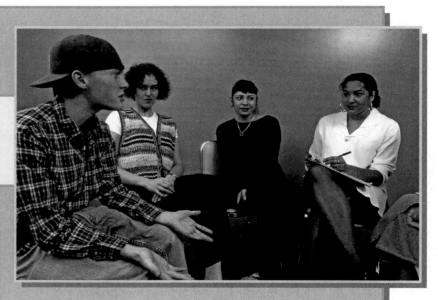

- **Inpatient treatment** is provided in special units of hospitals or medical clinics, and offers both detoxification and rehabilitation services.

- **Residential programs** provide a living environment with treatment services. Treatment in these programs lasts from a month to a year or more.

- **Partial hospitalization or day treatment** programs may be provided in hospitals or free-standing clinics. In these programs, the person attends treatment for 4 to 8 hours per day but lives at home.

- **Outpatient programs** provide treatment at a program site. Many meet in the evenings and on weekends so participants can go to school or work. Some programs meet daily while others meet less frequently.

- **Intensive outpatient treatment** programs require a person to attend 9 to 20 hours of treatment activities per week. These programs last from about 2 months to 1 year.

centers have detoxification units for people going through withdrawal. **Detoxification** is *the physical process of freeing the body of an addictive substance.* Once the physical dependency is overcome, the person can focus on changing his or her thinking and habits that led to the drug use.

Counseling

Some people find the support and help they need to stay drug free through counseling. Counseling provides an opportunity to openly share thoughts and feelings with a trained expert. It can help addicts deal with their psychological dependency on drugs. Counseling may involve only the addict, or it may involve the entire family.

Support Groups

A support group is a group of people who work together to help one another stay drug free. Often, recovering addicts find strength in being surrounded by people who are working toward the same goal. Common support groups for addiction include Narcotics Anonymous and Cocaine Anonymous. Nar-Anon provides help for those who have been affected by someone else's drug use.

Reading Check **Recall** What are some drug treatment options?

Health Online

Visit **health.glencoe.com** and complete the Interactive Study Guide for Lesson 5.

Lesson 5 Review

After You Read

Review this lesson for new terms, major headings, and Reading Checks.

What I Learned

1. *Vocabulary* Define *detoxification*.

2. *Describe* What are some of the ways support groups help people become drug free? Why are they effective?

3. *List* Name three symptoms of drug abuse.

Thinking Critically

4. *Analyze* Why do you think there are so many different drug treatment options available?

5. *Apply* Imagine your friend comes to you and tells you that he has been abusing inhalants and feels that he cannot stop. He begs you not to tell anyone. What would you do?

Applying Health Skills

6. *Decision Making* Imagine that you suspect a friend has a drug problem. Use the decision-making process to help you decide whether to speak to your friend about your concerns or speak to a trusted adult.

Staying Drug Free

● **Building Vocabulary**
As you read this lesson, write the new highlighted term and its definition in your notebook.

■ drug free (p. 361)

● **Focusing on the Main Ideas**
In this lesson, you will learn to

■ **explain** the health benefits of staying drug free.

■ **demonstrate** alternative behaviors to drug use.

● **Reading Strategy**
Organizing Information Create a chart that lists the ways staying drug free will benefit each side of your health triangle.

Quick Write

Describe how the different sides of your health triangle benefit if you avoid using drugs.

Choosing to Be Drug Free

The choice to refuse drugs is not always an easy one. Negative peer pressure can be a powerful force during the teen years. Yet, however challenging it may be to resist negative peer pressure to experiment with drugs, stopping drug abuse once it has started is much harder. It is also important to be true to yourself and make decisions that will promote a healthy body and mind.

▶ Staying drug free helps you maintain healthy relationships with your family and friends. **What are some other benefits of staying drug free?**

◀ Staying drug free can help you build a positive self-image. **What are some ways to say no to drug use?**

Choosing to be drug free is one of the most important decisions you can make. **Drug free** is *a characteristic of a person not taking illegal drugs or of a place where no illegal drugs are used.*

Refusing Drugs

Developing skills for refusing drugs is very important. Refusal skills can help you say no to unhealthy behaviors. These skills can help you resist negative peer pressure without feeling guilty or uncomfortable. Saying no in a clear and confident way lets others know you respect yourself and your health. If you feel pressure to experiment with drugs, remember the S.T.O.P. strategy.

- **S**ay no in a firm voice.
- **T**ell why not.
- **O**ffer alternative ideas or activities.
- **P**romptly leave.

Using this strategy is useful when you are approached by someone pressuring you to use drugs. However, you can take steps now that will help you to avoid such a situation. Choose friends who are also drug free. Avoid going to places where you know drugs will be present. Finally, always look for healthful ways to deal with problems you are facing. If you feel lonely or depressed, or if you need help solving personal problems, talk to an adult you trust. The people you are with, the places you happen to be, and how you are feeling, all play a role in your ability to be drug free. Your awareness of positive alternatives to drug use and the benefits of staying drug free also play a role.

Reading Check **Explain** What is a strategy to resist negative peer pressure?

▼ FIGURE 14.10

REASONS TO BE DRUG FREE

Avoiding drugs will benefit all three sides of your health triangle. **What are your own personal reasons for staying drug free?**

- You will not be breaking the law.
- You will have more natural energy.
- You will have better concentration and memory.
- You will be able to focus on improving your talents and enjoying your interests.
- You will look better because your appearance will not be affected by drugs.
- You will have better control over your feelings and actions.
- You will not regret foolish actions caused by drug-impaired judgment.
- You will not waste money on drugs.
- You will have better relationships with friends and family members.
- You will respect yourself for taking care of your body and mind.

The Benefits of Staying Drug Free

Making wise decisions about drugs will have a positive effect on your physical, mental/emotional, and social health. You protect your body against the harmful effects of drugs. You are able to concentrate better and will do better in school. You are able to enjoy other interests with family and friends. **Figure 14.10** above lists some additional benefits of being drug free.

 Reading Check **Explain** Name three benefits of being drug free.

Positive Alternatives to Drug Use

Positive alternatives to drug use are everywhere if you look for them. Positive alternatives allow you to have fun and spend time with family and friends in more healthful ways. Here are some strategies for staying drug free. Can you think of any others?

- Begin a regular physical activity routine.
- Volunteer to help someone in your school or community.
- Join a school club or organize a new one.
- Take part in a drug-free event. Bring a friend.
- Write down your thoughts, or express yourself through art.
- Balance enough physical activity with enough rest.
- Form friendships with people who are drug free.

Reading Check **Recall** Name three healthy alternatives to drug use.

▶ Staying away from drugs enables you to pursue and achieve your goals. **What steps are you taking to achieve your goals?**

Health Online

Visit **health.glencoe.com** and complete the Interactive Study Guide for Lesson 6.

Lesson 6 Review

After You Read

Review this lesson for new terms, major headings, and Reading Checks.

What I Learned

1. *Vocabulary* Define the term *drug free*.

2. *Recall* What are different strategies for choosing to be drug free?

3. *List* Give five reasons for being drug free.

Thinking Critically

4. *Apply* Imagine talking with a friend who is thinking about experimenting with drugs. What might you say to encourage him or her to stay drug free?

5. *Analyze* Every time someone offers you drugs, you say no. What else can you do to help you stay drug free?

Applying Health Skills

6. *Practicing Healthful Behaviors* Create a poster listing activities that you consider positive alternatives to illegal drug use. With permission from school administrators, hang your poster in a school hallway.

Building Health Skills

Saying No to Drugs

DIRECTIONS

Refusal Skills involve saying no to behavior that is unhealthy or unsafe. This activity will give you the opportunity to develop and master this important health skill. Here's a guide to the different parts of this activity:

❶ In the **Model** section, you will read about a teen who performs the health skill successfully. This "model" scenario will show you how the skill is done.

❷ The **Practice** section will help guide you in practicing the skill.

❸ In the **Apply** section, you will have a chance to perform the skill on your own. You can use the Self-Check to check your work.

To complete this activity, first read the scenario presented in the Model. Then move on to the Practice. Finally, go ahead and try the Apply.

❶ Model

Jeff and Mark have been friends since grade school, and have always enjoyed the same activities. This year, however, Jeff has noticed some changes in Mark. When Mark's older brother began smoking marijuana, Mark experimented with it, too. On a hike one day, Mark stopped at a clearing and took a joint out of his pocket and looked at Jeff saying, "Want some?"

Jeff uses the S.T.O.P. strategy to help him say no effectively.

Say no in a firm voice. "No thanks. I'm not interested."

Tell why not. "The hike is already good. I don't need drugs to make it better."

Offer another idea. "Let's get back to the road and get some lunch. I'm starving."

Promptly leave. "If that's what you want to do, I'm out of here."

② Practice

It is not always easy to turn away from negative peer pressure. Having a plan in place can help.

On another occasion, Jeff and Mark are studying for a test that will decide if they qualify for a science camp next summer. They know the exam will be hard. After a few hours of intense studying, Mark comes out of his parents' bathroom, holding a prescription bottle. "I bet these pills will help us study," Mark tells Jeff.

In small groups, discuss the ways in which Jeff could refuse the drugs. Use the S.T.O.P. strategy to develop your refusals.

Skill Summary
REFUSAL SKILLS

S.T.O.P. is effective and easy to remember in a tough situation.

Say no in a firm voice.
Tell why not.
Offer another idea.
Promptly leave

③ Apply

Jeff sees one of the soccer players from his team hanging out with older boys. Jeff goes up to say hello and discovers that the guys are talking about using drugs to improve their athletic skills.

Imagine you are Jeff. Use what you've learned about the S.T.O.P. strategy to complete the following dialogue. Include a reason why drug use is an unhealthy choice.

Older Boy:	"Hey, Jeff. How about a little something to boost your game?"
Jeff:	_____
Older Boy:	"Give me a break! You haven't even tried it."
Jeff:	_____
Older Boy:	"Lots of people get help this way. It's nothing new."
Jeff:	_____
Older Boy:	"You may be passing up a chance to be great!"
Jeff:	_____

Self-Check

■ Do your responses follow the S.T.O.P. strategy?

■ Did you include a reason why drug use is unhealthy?

Memory Obstacles

Many drugs make it difficult to process information. In this activity, loud music and disruptive talk mimics the effects of some drugs. How will these distractions interfere with your ability to recall information?

What You Will Need

- Paper for each member of the group
- Pencil for each member of the group
- 2 posters with 25 pictures of everyday items on each
- A source of loud music

What You Will Do

1. Using pictures from magazines, one person in the group will make 2 posters with 25 everyday items on each one.

2. The leader will hold up the first poster and give the group 30 seconds to look at it. Each student should try to remember as many items as possible.

3. The leader then puts the poster down, and the students write down as many of the items as they can recall.

4. Now loud music is turned on. The leader also asks two people on opposite sides of the room to have a loud conversation with each other.

5. Then the leader holds up the second poster and repeats step 3.

Wrapping It Up

How many people in the group had more trouble remembering items on the second poster than on the first? Why?

Compare what just happened to what can happen to your brain when under the influence of a drug.

Reading Review

Lesson 1 Drug Misuse and Abuse

Key Idea

- All drugs, including over-the-counter drugs, can be misused or abused.

Vocabulary

- drug (p. 334)
- prescription medicines (p. 335)
- over-the-counter medicines (p. 335)
- drug misuse (p. 335)
- side effect (p. 335)
- tolerance (p. 335)
- drug abuse (p. 336)

Lesson 2 Marijuana and Other Illegal Drugs

Key Idea

- Marijuana and anabolic steroids affect all three sides of the health triangle.

Vocabulary

- marijuana (p. 338)
- THC (p. 338)
- amnesia (p. 341)
- anabolic steroids (p. 343)

Lesson 3 Narcotics, Stimulants, and Depressants

Key Idea

- Stimulants and depressants have opposite effects on the body.

Vocabulary

- narcotics (p. 345)
- opium (p. 345)
- euphoria (p. 346)
- withdrawal symptoms (p. 346)
- stimulants (p. 348)
- amphetamine (p. 348)
- binge (p. 348)
- CNS depressants (p. 350)

Lesson 4 Hallucinogens and Inhalants

Key Idea

- Hallucinogens and inhalants interfere with a user's thought process.

Vocabulary

- hallucinogens (p. 352)
- inhalant (p. 354)

Lesson 5 Getting Help

Key Idea

- Treatment for drug abuse includes treatment programs, counseling, and support groups.

Vocabulary

- detoxification (p. 359)

Lesson 6 Staying Drug Free

Key Ideas

- There are many physical, mental/emotional, and social benefits of staying drug free.
- Refusal skills can help you say no to drugs.

Vocabulary

- drug free (p. 361)

14 Assessment

HEALTH QUIZ

Now that you have read the chapter, look back at your answers to the Health Quiz on the chapter opener. Would you answer any of the questions differently?

Reviewing Vocabulary and Main Ideas

On a sheet of paper, write the numbers 1–6. After each number, write the term from the list that best completes each sentence.

- information
- nervous
- chemical
- depressants
- side effect
- prescription medicines

Lesson 1 Drug Misuse and Abuse

1. _____ are medicines that can be sold only with a written order from a physician.

2. Any effect of a medicine other than the one intended is known as a _____.

Lesson 2 Marijuana and Other Illegal Drugs

3. THC is a powerful _____ that is the main ingredient of marijuana.

4. Long-term marijuana use affects the region of the brain that processes _____.

Lesson 3 Narcotics, Stimulants, and Depressants

5. Methamphetamine affects the user's central _____ system.

6. Stimulants and _____ have opposite effects on the body

*On a sheet of paper, write the numbers 7–12. Write **True** or **False** for each statement below. If the statement is false, change the underlined word or phrase to make it true.*

Lesson 4 Hallucinogens and Inhalants

7. <u>Hallucinogens</u> are drugs that can distort moods, thoughts, and senses of the users.

8. <u>Depressants</u> are any substance whose fumes are sniffed and inhaled to produce mind-altering sensations.

9. <u>LSD</u>, a drug made from lysergic acid, is one of the strongest and most widely abused hallucinogens.

Lesson 5 Getting Help

10. The physical signs of drug abuse are the <u>same</u> in people who abuse drugs.

11. <u>Inpatient</u> treatment programs are places where people get treatment for a few hours and then go home.

Lesson 6 Staying Drug Free

12. Staying drug free is one of the <u>least</u> important decisions you can make to be the healthiest person you can be.

Health *Online* Visit health.glencoe.com and take the Online Quiz for Chapter 14.

Thinking Critically

Using complete sentences, answer the following questions on a sheet of paper.

13. Hypothesize What are three reasons someone might begin experimenting with drugs?

14. Explain How can taking club drugs put a person's physical health at risk?

Write About It

15. Analyzing Influences Write a journal entry that states your own reasons for making a commitment to be drug free.

16. Refusal Skills Write a short story about a teen who is pressured to use a drug and uses refusal skills to say no.

Career Corner

Social Worker A social worker is a professional who often works with families in crisis. Drug abuse is one of the common problems that causes great stress for the family of the abuser. Family members may be at risk themselves, or be unsure how to best help their loved one. A social worker can counsel the drug user as well as the family. This health care professional can also help families work through federal, state, and local paperwork or court proceedings that are often part of the user getting help for the addiction. Find out more about this and other health careers by clicking on *Career Corner* at **health.glencoe.com**.

Standardized Test Practice

Math

The National Institute on Drug Abuse recently conducted its **Monitoring the Future Survey.** The survey found that drug use among eighth graders decreased or stayed steady from 2003 to 2004. In 2004, however, there was a significant increase in inhalant abuse among eighth graders. Use the information below from the survey to answer the questions that follow.

- Lifetime use of inhalants increased significantly among eighth graders, from 15.8 percent in 2003 to 17.3 percent in 2004.

- 30-day use of marijuana was down significantly among eighth graders, from 7.5 percent in 2003 to 6.4 percent in 2004.

- Use of anabolic steroids decreased significantly among eighth graders from 2.5 percent in 2003 to 1.9 percent in 2004 for annual use.

- Use of methamphetamine decreased significantly among eighth graders, from 3.9 percent in 2003 to 2.5 percent in 2004.

1. Based on the statistics shown, which of the following *cannot* be inferred?
  - **A.** In 2003 approximately 92.5 percent of all eighth graders did not abuse marijuana.
  - **B.** Fewer eighth graders abused marijuana in 2003 than those eighth graders who abused methamphetamine in 2004.
  - **C.** Approximately 82.7 percent of eighth graders did not abuse inhalants in 2004.
  - **D.** The rate of methamphetamine use among eighth graders decreased from 2003 to 2004.

2. Based on the statistics, the greatest decrease in one year occurred with which drug?
  - **A.** marijuana
  - **B.** methamphetamine
  - **C.** inhalants
  - **D.** anabolic steroids

CHAPTER

15 Personal Care and Consumer Choices

Chapter Preview

▲ **Working With the Photo**

Good health habits are easy to develop if you build them into your daily routine. **Can you think of two healthy habits you could add to your day?**

Start-Up Activities

Before You Read Look at the Instant Message below. What could you tell jelyrole94 about protecting her skin from the sun? Keep a record of your answer.

IM Express

nuffsed: U want to meet us? We'll be at the beach around lunchtime.

jelyrole94: I don't think I can. My skin burns really fast.

FOLDABLES™ Study Organizer

As You Read Make this Foldable™ to help you organize what you learn about personal care. Begin with a plain sheet of 8½" × 11" paper.

1 Fold the sheet of paper along the long axis, leaving a 2" tab along the side.

3 Label the tabs as shown.

Personal Care

| Skin | Eyes | Ears |

2 Unfold and cut the top layer along both fold lines. This makes three tabs.

Under the appropriate tab, write down what you learn about caring for your skin, eyes, and ears.

Health Online Visit **health.glencoe.com** and complete the Health Inventory for Chapter 15.

Personal Health Care

Guide to Reading

● Building Vocabulary
As you read this lesson, write each new highlighted term and its definition in your notebook.

- epidermis (p. 373)
- dermis (p. 373)
- dandruff (p. 374)
- plaque (p. 375)
- tartar (p. 375)
- decibel (p. 377)

● Focusing on the Main Ideas
In this lesson, you will learn to

- **identify** common skin and hair problems.
- **explain** functions of the mouth and teeth.
- **describe** how to protect your eyes and ears.

● Reading Strategy
Classifying Make a chart with four columns, one each for skin, mouth, eyes, and ears. Identify a way of caring for each of these.

FOLDABLES Study Organizer Use the Foldable™ on p. 371 as you read this lesson.

Quick Write

Write a short description of your daily hygiene routines. Hygiene is practices of cleanliness that help maintain health.

Functions of Skin

The skin is your body's largest organ. Like other organs of the body, it has several important functions. It is a watertight barrier when you swim or take a bath. It also helps control your body temperature. It releases perspiration when you are hot and tells your brain to slow blood circulation when you are cold.

The skin also allows you to feel textures, such as rough and smooth, and alerts you when something is hot, cold, or painful. Your skin also protects you from germs.

▶ Your skin enables you to experience the sense of touch: the roughness of tree bark, the smooth, silky feel of satin, or the softness of a rabbit. **What are some other functions of the skin?**

Parts of the Skin

The skin is composed of three main layers. The *outermost layer of the skin* is the **epidermis** (e·puh·DER·mis). The *thick inner layer of skin* underneath it is the **dermis.** This is where nerve endings, blood vessels, and oil and sweat glands are found. The innermost layer of skin, the *subcutaneous* (sub·kyoo·TAY·nee·uhs) *layer,* connects your skin to muscle and bone.

Reading Check **List** Name the three main layers of the skin.

Skin Problems

Oil glands help the skin stay soft. During the teen years, too much oil can cause clogged pores which leads to acne. Acne sores include whiteheads, blackheads, and pimples.

Minor acne can be treated with over-the-counter products and good hygiene. More serious cases may require visits to a dermatologist (DER·muh·TAHL·uh·jist), a physician who specializes in skin problems.

Other skin problems are caused by sun exposure. Exposure to the sun's ultraviolet (UV) rays increases the risk of developing skin cancer. Sun exposure also damages the skin, causing wrinkles and premature aging.

Viruses can also affect the skin. Cold sores and warts are both caused by viruses. Both can be treated, but are contagious. Contagious means the virus can be spread to others. Anyone with a wart or cold sore should avoid skin contact with others, and should wash his or her hands often.

Skin Care

Having clean, healthy skin is part of your overall appearance. During the teen years, you may notice an odor in areas where you sweat heavily. The odor is caused by bacteria. Bathing or showering regularly and using anti-perspirants and deodorants can eliminate body odor.

If you have acne, gently wash the infected area with mild soap and warm water. Repeat this twice a day. Never scrub or irritate the skin, though. This can cause even more acne.

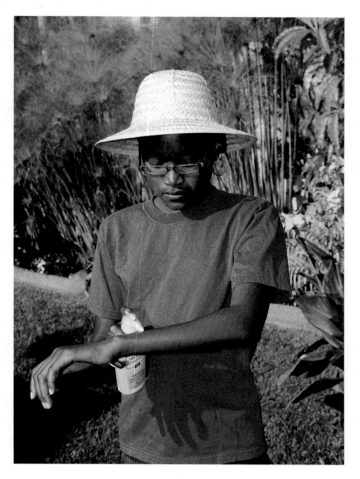

▲ It is healthy to be involved in outdoor activities, but measures must be taken to protect yourself from the sun's harmful rays. **What are some of these protective measures?**

Wear sunscreen and protective clothing when you're in the sun. Avoid sunlight or use extra sunscreen protection between 10:00 A.M. and 4:00 P.M. Avoid body piercings and tattoos. Even under sterile conditions, the skin is exposed to germs.

Reading Check **Identify** Name two ways of caring for your skin.

Your Hair and Nails

Your hair and nails are composed of a tough substance called keratin. Both grow out of living tissue located in the dermis. Each nail is surrounded by a fold of epidermis called a *cuticle* (KYOO·ti·kuhl).

Hair and Nail Problems

The same oil glands that cause acne can also affect hair, making it look and feel greasy. Another common hair problem is **dandruff,** *a flaking of the outer layer of dead skin cells.* Try using shampoos made for oily hair or flaking scalp.

Head lice is another common hair problem. These are tiny insects that live in hair and spread easily. To prevent the spread of lice, avoid sharing combs, brushes, and hats. If you get lice, you can treat it with a medicated shampoo. You will also need to wash all bedding, towels, combs, brushes, and clothing. Your family will also need to do this.

There are some nail problems, too. A hangnail is a split in the cuticle near the fingernail's edge. Carefully trim the skin. The cuticle should heal in a few days. An ingrown toenail occurs when the toenail pushes too far into the skin along the side of the toe. This can result from trimming the nail on a curve rather than straight across or wearing shoes that are too tight. See a doctor if your toe becomes inflamed and sore as it may be infected.

Reading Check **Identify** What substance makes up your hair and nails?

◀ Brushing or combing your hair regularly can keep it looking healthy. **What are some other things you can do to take care of your hair?**

Your Teeth

Like your skin, your teeth are vital to your appearance and health. They chew and grind food, making it easier to digest. They are also necessary for proper speech.

Tooth and Gum Problems

Taking care of your teeth and gums can prevent tooth decay. **Figure 15.1** shows the stages of tooth decay.

The gums serve as anchors for your teeth. Like the teeth, they can also develop problems. One problem is gingivitis (jin·juh·VY·tis). This is a condition in which the gums become inflamed and bleed easily. If left untreated, gingivitis can cause tooth loss.

Tooth and Gum Care

Caring for the teeth and gums is essential. Make it a habit to floss and gently brush the teeth and gums for at least two to three minutes, twice a day. Brushing and flossing clean the teeth and remove plaque.

▼ FIGURE 15.1

THE PROCESS OF TOOTH DECAY

When teeth are not cared for properly, tooth decay results. **What regular habits can help you prevent tooth decay?**

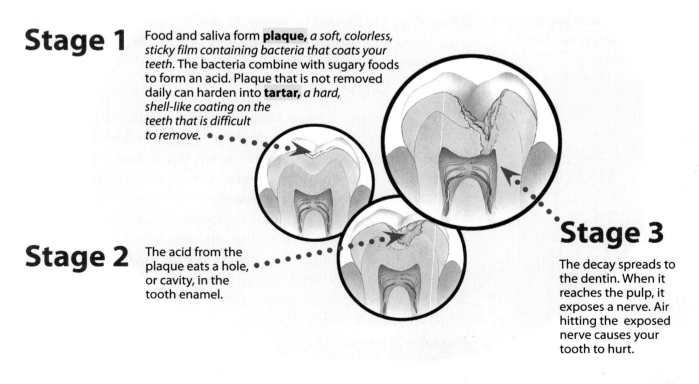

Stage 1 Food and saliva form **plaque,** *a soft, colorless, sticky film containing bacteria that coats your teeth.* The bacteria combine with sugary foods to form an acid. Plaque that is not removed daily can harden into **tartar,** *a hard, shell-like coating on the teeth that is difficult to remove.*

Stage 2 The acid from the plaque eats a hole, or cavity, in the tooth enamel.

Stage 3 The decay spreads to the dentin. When it reaches the pulp, it exposes a nerve. Air hitting the exposed nerve causes your tooth to hurt.

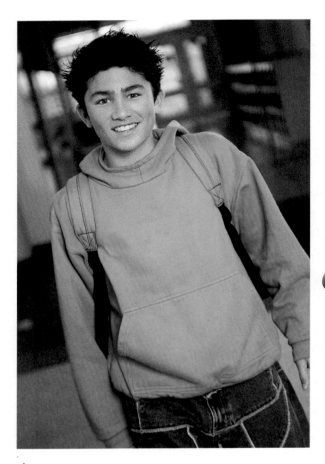

▲ Your smile is an important part of your appearance. **What steps can you take to keep your smile bright and your teeth healthy?**

Good eating habits also help keep your teeth healthy. Dairy products and other foods high in calcium will help keep teeth strong. You should also limit the number of sugary foods you eat.

You should see a dentist twice a year. The dentist or a dental hygienist will clean and remove hard-to-reach plaque and tartar. The dentist can also treat any cavities and gum problems. If your teeth are growing in crooked, your dentist may recommend that you see an orthodontist. An orthodontist may put braces on your teeth to straighten them.

Reading Check **Describe** Tell how tooth decay occurs.

Your Eyes

Your eyes are your organ of sight. The main parts of the eye are shown in **Figure 15.2** on the next page.

Vision Problems

There are several common vision problems. Nearsightedness is when a person can see nearby objects clearly, but distant objects are blurred. With farsightedness, the reverse is true. With astigmatism (ah·STIG·muh·tizm), images appear blurred or distorted due to an irregularly shaped lens or cornea. Most vision problems can be corrected by using eyeglasses or contact lenses.

Eye Care and Protection

It is important to protect your eyes from injury, dust, and overexposure to sunlight. Wear sunglasses that have lenses with UV protection. Wear protective gear when doing any activity that could injure your eyes. Watch television or use a computer in a well-lit room. Avoid rubbing your eyes. This can irritate them and spread bacteria. If you wear contact lenses, always wash your hands before putting in or taking out your lenses. Change your lenses regularly according to your eye doctor's instructions.

Regular vision screenings and eye exams are also important. See an eye doctor for an exam every two years if you don't wear corrective lenses, yearly if you do.

Reading Check **Explain** What is an astigmatism?

PARTS OF THE EYE

Each part of the eye has a specific function. **What is the function of the optic nerve?**

A The **cornea** is a clear protective structure that lets in light.

B The **aqueous** (AY·kwee·uhs) **humor** is the watery fluid in between the cornea and lens. It helps maintain pressure in the eye.

C The **iris** is the colored part of the eye. It controls the size of the pupil.

D The **pupil** is a dark opening in the center of the iris. The pupil controls the amount of light that enters the eye.

E The **lens** is a clear flexible structure that focuses light on the retina.

F The **retina** (RE·tin·uh) is a thin layer of nerve cells that absorb light. It covers the interior back of the eye.

G The **optic nerve** is a cord of nerve fibers that carries messages from the retina to the brain.

H The **sclera** (SKLEHR·uh) is the white of the eye. It protects the eyeball and gives it its shape.

Your Ears

Your ears provide information in the form of sound. Your ears also enable you to control your balance. Fluid and tiny hair cells inside your ears send messages to your brain when you move or shift positions. The brain interprets the messages and tells your body what adjustments it needs to make. **Figure 15.3** on the next page shows the different parts of the ear.

Hearing Problems

The most common ear problem is hearing loss. Middle ear infections and punctured eardrums can cause hearing loss. Loud noises can also cause hearing loss. Any noise above 85 decibels can be harmful. A **decibel** is *a measure of the loudness of sound.*

Prolonged exposure to loud noise can also lead to *tinnitus* (TIN·uh·tuhs). This is a constant ringing in the ears.

Ear Care and Protection

To protect your ears, never insert anything into the ear. Avoid loud noises. Cover the ears in cold weather to avoid frostbite. See a doctor for an earache or to treat ringing in the ears.

Health Online

Visit **health.glencoe.com** and complete the Interactive Study Guide for Lesson 1.

► **FIGURE 15.3**

PARTS OF THE EAR

The ear has three main parts: the outer ear, the middle ear, and the inner ear. **What are the functions of the ear?**

Oval Window

Stirrup

Anvil

Semicircular Canals

Hammer

Auditory Nerve

Eardrum

Cochlea

External Auditory Canal

Eustachian Tube

Outer Ear   **Middle Ear**   **Inner Ear**

Lesson 1 Review

After You Read

Review this lesson for new terms, major headings, and Reading Checks.

What I Learned

1. *Identify* What are the three layers of the skin called?

2. *Vocabulary* What is *plaque*? Why should plaque be removed?

3. *Recall* Name two ways of caring for and protecting the ears.

Thinking Critically

4. *Apply* A friend of yours is planning to get a pierced lip. What potential risks does this plan involve?

5. *Analyze* Tim likes playing handball. However, he doesn't like the way the protective goggles look. What decision does Tim need to make?

Applying Health Skills

6. *Accessing Information* Choose one of the body areas discussed in this chapter. Using reliable sources, find out four new facts about the care of this part of the body. Share your findings with classmates.

Health Online For more review questions for Lesson 1, go to **health.glencoe.com**.

Being a Smart Health Consumer

Becoming an Informed Consumer

Each day American consumers spend millions of dollars for goods or services. A **consumer** is *anyone who uses products or services.*

As a teen you are making more consumer decisions on your own. As you grow older, you will be responsible for more consumer choices. Learning **consumer skills,** *techniques that enable you to make wise, informed purchases,* will help you become a smart shopper. Smart shoppers know how to compare products in terms of quality, effectiveness, safety, and cost. They also know how to resolve problems with purchases.

Reading Check **Define** What is a *consumer*?

Quick Write

Write a letter to the maker of a product you bought that doesn't work. Explain the problems you had.

▶ Consumer skills help you to make wise, informed purchases. **What are some examples of consumer skills?**

Health Skills Activity

Analyzing Influences

Reading Between the Lines

As a consumer you can use ads to your advantage. This means cutting through what the advertiser wants you to hear or see and getting to the information you need. Here are some ways for doing that:

- **Consider the Source.** Where is the information in the ad from? When possible, trace a health claim back to its source. Claims like "nine out of ten doctors recommend" are meaningless. Also, beware of infomercials, ads meant to look like impartial TV programs.

- **Consider the Approach.** What techniques are being used to attract your attention or appeal to you? Some advertisers use celebrities to promote their products. Admiring a person's talents or looks is not a good reason for choosing a product. Another technique advertisers use is hidden messages. These are often pictures showing seemingly happy, attractive people. The message implies that the product will make you happier and healthier. One last advertising approach is the "testimonial." Ordinary-looking people claim to have gotten great results, but they may be paid actors. Learning to identify these techniques will help you avoid being swayed by them.

On Your Own

Analyze an ad for a health product or service. What technique did the advertiser use? Are the health claims in the ad from a reliable source?

Influences on Your Buying Decisions

Informed consumers are aware of the many factors that play a role in their buying decisions. One factor is personal taste. Many of the products people buy are items they have tried and liked. Another factor is personal need.

A number of external factors also impact your buying decisions. One of the most important outside influences is media messages. Each day you receive hundreds of messages from TV, radio, the Internet, newspapers, and magazines. One of the strongest influences is advertising. According to one industry source, around 3,000 ads a day are seen by the average American. Informed consumers know how to analyze information in ads. The Health Skills Activity above gives some useful tips for evaluating ads.

Comparison Shopping

"Compare and save!" You've probably seen lines like this in ads or on store displays. This advice relates to the consumer skill of **comparison shopping,** or *a method of judging the relative benefits of competing products or services based on quality, effectiveness, safety, and cost.* Suppose you want to purchase a sunscreen that offers maximum protection against the sun's UV rays. You might compare different brands. Read the ingredients and the application instructions. Look for one that has a *sun protection factor (SPF)* of at least 15. This will help protect you against the sun's harmful rays.

How about cost? Some brands may have identical volume and ingredients but vary in cost.

Another factor that may affect your purchase is whether an item carries a **warranty.** This is *a promise to refund your money if the product doesn't work as claimed.* A warranty shows that a company stands behind its product.

Reading Check **List** What factors are evaluated in comparison shopping?

Connect To...

Math

Unit Price

One important piece of information to understand when it comes to comparing costs is *unit price.* This is cost per unit of weight or volume. To figure out unit price, first find the weight or volume given on each product container. (Make sure that both products are measured in the same type of units.) Next divide the price of the product by its weight or volume. The amount you end up with is the unit price.

An 8 fl. oz. bottle of lotion costs $3.89. What is its unit price?

Managing Consumer Problems

Products usually work as advertised. Unfortunately, some people and businesses sell products or services that don't work. When this is done purposefully to deceive the buyer, the seller has committed *fraud.* This is a crime punishable by law.

One of the most serious kinds of fraud is **health fraud.** This is *the selling of products or services to prevent diseases or cure health problems which have not been scientifically proven safe or effective for such purposes.* Making inaccurate claims about a health product can give false hope to people who are seriously ill. Some products may even pose a risk to your health. If you believe you have been a victim of health fraud, contact the Food and Drug Administration. You will learn more about this agency in the next lesson.

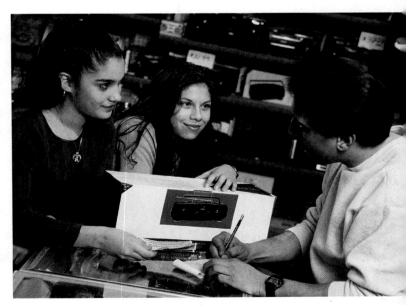

▶ The teen in this picture is returning an item that does not work properly. **What should you do before you buy a product to ensure that your money will be refunded if the product does not work as it should?**

Problems with Products

In spite of a manufacturer's best efforts, a particular product may be defective. Sometimes, the store where you bought the item will be willing to take it back. For example, you may have bought a bottle of aspirin and opened it to find they were all stuck together. With your receipt, a reputable store will have no problem returning your money. A good consumer habit is to keep your sales receipts until you are certain you are satisfied with the product. You should also ask about the store's return policy before purchasing from a store. In some cases, your only remedy will be to send the product back to its manufacturer.

Online Shopping

Buying over the Internet can be fun, easy, and convenient. However, just like buying in a store, consumers need to be aware and take precautions to prevent problems.

When buying online, know who you are dealing with. Anyone can set up a shop online. Confirm the seller's physical address and phone number in case you need to get in touch with them.

Check different Web sites and compare prices of the same item including shipping costs. Find out what their return policies are and whether or not you will have to pay shipping costs to return the item. Always pay by credit card, never send cash. Print and save records or receipts of your online purchases.

Health Online

Visit **health.glencoe.com** and complete the Interactive Study Guide for Lesson 2.

Lesson 2 Review

After You Read

Review this lesson for new terms, major headings, and Reading Checks.

What I Learned

1. *Vocabulary* What are *consumer skills*?

2. *Recall* Name two factors a comparison shopper evaluates.

3. *Describe* What should you do if a product you purchased is defective?

Thinking Critically

4. *Evaluate* Which factor(s) most influence your shopping decisions—price, quality, effectiveness, or safety? Explain.

5. *Analyze* Why are consumer skills important? Explain your answer.

Applying Health Skills

6. *Analyzing Influences* Another influence on teen buying habits is peer pressure. Think about brands of clothing or footwear popular among your peers. Identify which of these items teens might be influenced to buy. Share your thoughts in class.

Using Medicines Wisely

Guide to Reading

● **Building Vocabulary**
Organize the terms into a word web. Decide which term is central to all other terms.
- medicines (p. 383)
- prescription medicines (p. 383)
- over-the-counter (OTC) medicines (p. 384)
- vaccine (p. 384)
- antibiotics (p. 385)
- side effect (p. 386)

● **Focusing on the Main Ideas**
In this lesson, you will learn to
- **identify** types of medicines.
- **explain** ways medicines are taken into the body.
- **describe** factors that determine how medicines affect the body.

● **Reading Strategy**
Classifying Make a chart of the kinds of medicines mentioned in the lesson.

Medicines

When sickness or injury occurs, medicines can often help a person feel and/or get better. **Medicines** are *drugs that are used to treat or prevent diseases and other conditions.* Medicines in the United States are carefully controlled. The Food and Drug Administration (FDA), sets standards for medicine safety and effectiveness. Before a medicine can be manufactured and sold, it must be tested and approved by the FDA.

Prescription and Nonprescription Medicines

One of the FDA's roles is to determine how a new medicine should be released to the public. The FDA releases drugs in two forms:

- **Prescription medicines** are *medicines that can be sold only with a written order from a physician or nurse practitioner.* The FDA requires standard information to appear on the label of any prescription medicine. This information includes instructions on how much medication to take, how often, and how long to continue taking the medicine. A sample label appears in **Figure 15.4.** As a smart health consumer, you should always read these labels carefully before taking any medicine.

Quick Write

Describe a time when you took a medicine. State what the medicine was meant to treat and how you took it.

PRESCRIPTION MEDICINE LABEL

Medicine labels provide important information. How many times can this prescription be refilled?

Lowe's Pharmacy
672 Miller Road
Oakville, TX
(214) 555-6666
Pharmacist: T. NEWHOUSE
Rx 7578034   Dr. FISCHER
06/30/07
MARIA CORA   Refills 0
ONE TEASPOON THREE TIMES DAILY.
PEDIAPRED LIQUID 5MG/5ML
USE THIS MEDICATION EXACTLY
AS DIRECTED: DO NOT SKIP
DOSES OR DISCONTINUE WITHOUT
INSTRUCTIONS FROM YOUR
PHYSICIAN.   TAKE WITH MEALS

- **Nonprescription medicines.** Some medicines are less risky than others. They are sold as nonprescription, or **over-the-counter (OTC) medicines.** These are *medicines that are safe enough to be taken without a written order from a physician.* Even OTC medicines can be harmful if used incorrectly. You should read OTC labels as carefully as you would prescription labels.

▼ There are different medicines for many types of illnesses and conditions. **What type of medicine is used to treat strep throat?**

Reading Check   **Identify** What is another name for over-the-counter medicines?

Types of Medicines

Relieving symptoms of a chronic condition is one function of medications. Others include preventing disease, fighting infection, and easing pain.

Medicines to Prevent Diseases

A **vaccine** is *a medicine that prevents a disease from developing.* Vaccines are made from dead or weakened germs that cause the immune system to produce antibodies. *Antibodies* are proteins that attack and kill or disable specific germs that cause disease. Some vaccines provide protection over a number of years. Others, such as the flu vaccine, are given once a year. The chart in **Figure 15.5** shows some common vaccines given today.

TYPES OF MEDICINES

Different types of medicines treat or prevent different illnesses. Which of these medicines have you been given?

Type of Medicine	Some Examples	Disease or Problem
Vaccines	MMR vaccine, Varicella vaccine, Havrix, Vaqta	Diphtheria, whooping cough, measles, mumps, rubella, chicken pox, pneumonia, hepatitis A and B
Antibiotics	• Penicillin • Cephalosporin • Tetracycline • Macrolides	• Strep throat, pneumonia, STDs • Meningitis, skin rash • Urinary tract infections, Rocky Mountain spotted fever • Given to patients allergic to penicillin
Pain Reliever	Aspirin, acetaminophen, ibuprofen, codeine	General pain relief

Medicines to Fight Infection

When a person develops a bacterial infection, his or her doctor may prescribe an antibiotic to treat the infection. **Antibiotics** are *medicines that reduce or kill harmful bacteria in the body.* Several common classes of antibiotics appear in Figure 15.5. Each type of antibiotic fights specific strains of bacteria.

Medicines to Relieve Pain

Have you ever had a sore back, toothache, or headache? If you took medicine to feel better, it was most likely a pain reliever. Some common pain relievers are shown in Figure 15.5. Pain relievers block or lessen pain signals sent through the nervous system. Many pain relievers are available over-the-counter. Some are used to treat more serious pain and are available only with a prescription.

Reading Check **List** Name three different types of medicine.

How Medicines Enter the Body

There are several common ways medicines enter the body. Swallowing, or ingestion, is the most common way medicines are taken. Pills, tablets, capsules, and liquids are taken this way. The medicine moves through the stomach and small intestine. From there it passes into the bloodstream and circulates throughout the body. Cold medicines and pain relievers are often delivered this way.

Injection, or shot, is another way in which medicines are given. Injected medicines enter the bloodstream and begin to work more quickly.

Medicine can also be inhaled as a mist or fine powder. Inhalation is a relatively new delivery system. People with asthma often use an inhaler. Cold or sinus medication can be breathed in through the nostrils.

Medicines are also given topically, or applied to the skin. Creams and ointments are often applied this way. Skin patches that release medicine over time are a fairly new delivery method.

Reading Check **Describe** What types of medicines are swallowed?

Medicine in the Body

How medicines affect the body depends on the type and amount of medicine taken. The individual's chemical makeup, age, gender, and body size also matter. An allergic reaction to a medicine is an unwanted effect that can be deadly.

In general, *any effect of a medicine other than the one intended* is considered a **side effect.** Typical side effects include headache, upset stomach, and drowsiness. Commonly reported side effects of a medicine are listed on or inside the product's packaging. Any reaction that is unexpected or unwanted should be reported to the doctor or pharmacist.

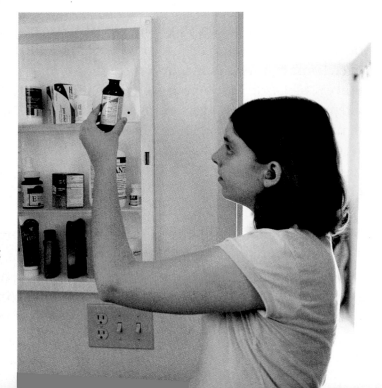

▶ When using medicines, it is important to keep them out of reach of young children. **Why is it important to be responsible when using medicines?**

Risks of Medicines

When a person uses a particular medication for a long period of time, he or she develops a tolerance. This is a process in which your body needs more and more of a medicine to get the same effect. In some cases, the medicine loses its effectiveness altogether and the doctor will need to prescribe a different medication.

Overuse is another problem. The more an antibiotic is used, the less effective it becomes. Why? Bacteria build up a resistance to antibotics with frequent exposure. They adapt to—or overcome—the antibotic. Bacteria can also develop a resistance when antibiotics are not taken as prescribed. For example, if the prescription label says to take the medicine for 14 days and you stop after 7 days, the bacteria may still be present and could make you feel sick again. Medicines should always be used wisely and only as directed.

Finally, taking two or more medicines at once can be dangerous. Always let your doctor and pharmacist know what other medicines you are taking before starting a new medicine.

> **Reading Check** **Identify** Name two risks of medicines.

Health Online

Visit **health.glencoe.com** and complete the Interactive Study Guide for Lesson 3.

Lesson 3 Review

> **As You Read**

Review this lesson for new terms, major headings, and Reading Checks.

What I Learned

1. *Vocabulary* What type of medicine prevents a disease from developing?

2. *List* Name two ways medicines are taken into the body.

3. *Describe* What factors determine a medicine's effect on the body?

Thinking Critically

4. *Analyze* A friend of yours on the football team wants an energy burst before a game. He wants to take a handful of vitamins. When you express concern, he says, "They're over-the-counter vitamins." Respond to this comment.

5. *Hypothesize* Laura's doctor has prescribed a medicine to treat a case of poison ivy. She also regularly takes medicine because she has trouble concentrating. Should Laura tell her doctor what medicine she is already taking? Why or why not?

Applying Health Skills

6. *Accessing Information* The Internet makes it easier than ever to get information about medications. As part of a group, visit a Web site that offers information about medicines. Identify two pieces of information not covered in the lesson. Share your findings with other groups.

Choosing Health Services

Quick Write

Write a brief description of your health care team. Name all the doctors and other people who provide health care services to you.

The Role of Health Care

When Rick fell and hurt his leg, his dad took him to the hospital emergency room. There, a nurse wrote down information about Rick's health and medicines he was taking. Rick was taken to another room, where a technician took X rays. A doctor looked at the X ray, examined his leg, and told him it was broken.

The people Rick saw at the hospital are part of our **health care system.** This term refers to *the medical services available to a nation's people and manner in which these services are paid for.* Different countries have different kinds of health care systems. Originally, health care in America served people who were sick or injured. Today the system also provides preventive care. **Preventive care** is *the steps taken to keep disease or injury from happening or getting worse.*

◄ Health care includes diagnosing illnesses and treating injuries. **When was the last time you were treated by a health care professional?**

Health Care Providers

Rick was treated by a team of health professionals. Your health care is probably also a "team" effort. The leader of your personal health care team is your primary care physician. This is the medical professional who provides physical checkups and general care.

Sometimes a problem will be beyond your primary care physician's specific training or experience. When this happens, she or he will refer you to a **specialist.** This is *a doctor trained to handle particular kinds of patients or medical conditions.* An allergist is one type of specialist. A dermatologist, or skin doctor, is another. **Figure 15.6** lists different kinds of specialists and the conditions they treat.

Still other medical professionals you routinely see may include a dental hygienist. If you wear glasses or contacts, you may have your eyes checked by an ophthalmic (oph·THAL·mik) technician. Professionals like these are known as **allied health professionals.** They are *medical professionals who perform duties which would otherwise have to be performed by doctors or nurses.*

Types of Health Care

Rick's treatment at the hospital was as an *outpatient.* In outpatient care, the person receives treatment and then returns home. *Inpatient* care involves staying at a hospital or other health care facility. Many surgeries are done on an inpatient basis, though more often, minor surgeries are being done at outpatient surgical

Specialist	Conditions They Treat
Cardiologist	Treats diseases and conditions of the heart.
Psychiatrist	Treats and prescribes medication for patients who have mental, behavioral, or emotional problems.
Osteopath	Treats disorders of the human body, with special emphasis on bones, muscles, and nerves.
Oncologist	Treats patients with all types of cancer.
Dietitian	Treats nutrition-related diseases, works with patients to develop nutritious eating habits.
Neurologist	Treats diseases of the brain and nervous system.

◀ FIGURE 15.6

HEALTH CARE SPECIALISTS

Health care specialists treat specific conditions to provide patients with the best care. **What conditions do oncologists treat?**

centers. In these facilities, the person is operated on, and released the same day. An example of a surgery done at an outpatient center is the repair of a hernia.

Reading Check **Identify** Name two types of health care professionals.

Changes in Health Care Settings

Health care used to be delivered mainly in doctor's offices or hospitals. Over the years, additional types of health care delivery settings have been created.

- **Surgery centers** are facilities that offer outpatient surgical care. For general outpatient care, many people go to clinics. Clinics often have primary care physicians and specialists on staff.

- **Hospice care** provides a place where terminally ill patients can live out the remainder of their lives. Hospice workers are experts at pain management. They are also skilled at giving emotional support to the patient and family. Terminally ill patients can also receive hospice care in their own homes.

- **Assisted living communities** offer older people an alternative to traditional nursing homes. In assisted living communities, older adults are permitted to select the services they need. For example, they may only need help with transportation, remembering to take their medicines, or making meals. As long as they are able, residents live in their own private living quarters. A medical staff is available if and when residents need help.

▶ This teen is visiting a grandparent at an assisted living center. **How do these communities differ from traditional nursing homes?**

Covering the Costs of Health Care

Another area of health care that is changing is the way in which costs are covered. Many people have health insurance to help cover costs. **Health insurance** is *a plan in which private companies or government programs pay for part of a person's medical costs.* Traditional health insurance plans may pay up to 80 percent of the cost of outpatient care. They pay an even greater percentage of inpatient care. Many businesses pay a portion of their employees' and their families' health insurance costs.

With recent increases in the cost of health insurance, the insurance industry and care providers have worked to develop lower cost alternatives, such as **managed care.** This is *a plan that saves money by limiting the choice of doctors to patients who are members.* People pay a monthly fee called a *premium* to the insurance company for health insurance. They are able to save money by seeing doctors and other health care providers who participate in the managed care plan.

Other health insurance alternatives available to some Americans are two government insurance programs, Medicaid and Medicare. The first is designed to assist people with limited income. The second is for adults over the age of 65, and for those with certain disabilities.

Reading Check **Compare** Tell how traditional health insurance differs from managed care.

Health Online

Visit **health.glencoe.com** and complete the Interactive Study Guide for Lesson 4.

Lesson 4 Review

After You Read

Review this lesson for new terms, major headings, and Reading Checks.

What I Learned

1. *Recall* Name two types of health care providers.

2. *Give Examples* Name two types of health care settings.

3. *List* What are some ways in which people pay for health care?

Thinking Critically

4. *Evaluate* How does managed care help reduce health care costs?

5. *Synthesize* How might an assisted living community affect the health of a senior citizen?

Applying Health Skills

6. *Practicing Healthful Behaviors* One way of reducing health care costs in America is developing positive health behaviors. What are some behaviors that you could do to stay healthy? Make a list of these.

Public Health

Building Vocabulary
As you read this lesson, write each new highlighted term and its definition in your notebook.
- public health (p. 392)
- recall (p. 393)
- famine (p. 395)

Focusing on the Main Ideas
In this lesson, you will learn to
- **explain** the role of government agencies in public health.
- **identify** the health related jobs done by nongovernment agencies.

Reading Strategy
Organizing Information Using headings from this lesson, create a graphic that shows different ways in which public health is protected.

Quick Write

State what you think the term *public health* means. Then add a short explanation of why public health is important.

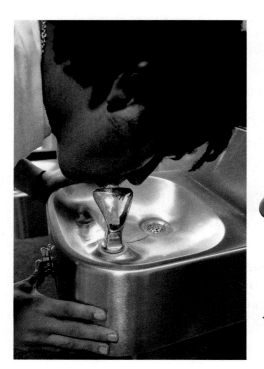

◀ Each community maintains its own safe water supply. **Do you know where the water that comes through your tap originates?**

What Is Public Health?

Tim had been running non-stop for a half hour. He stopped at a water fountain in the park and took a drink. By drinking the water in the public fountain, Tim assumed that the water was safe to drink. Who is responsible for the safety of your drinking water? How about the food you eat or medicines you take?

You can be confident your food, medicine, and water are safe because Americans have systems for public health. **Public health** *involves efforts to monitor and promote the welfare of the population.*

Public health occurs on many levels. Every county in every state has its own public health department. The nation as a whole has agencies to protect the well-being of the American people. The world also has organizations that monitor the health of the "global community."

Reading Check **Define** What is *public health*?

Federal Health Agencies

At the federal level, public health is overseen by the Department of Health and Human Services (HHS). HHS includes more than 300 programs in a variety of health areas. Among these programs are research, disease prevention, and food and drug safety. HHS is also responsible for the Medicare and Medicaid systems, as well as abuse prevention. **Figure 15.7** shows a list of the main agencies of HHS.

The Consumer Product Safety Commission (CPSC), works to reduce risks from unsafe products. If a product is found to cause health problems, or injury, the CPSC will issue a **recall**—*an announcement that informs the public that a product has been determined unsafe.* This is done through media announcements and by direct mail. The recall will list specific model numbers and the addresses where the defective goods should be returned.

▼ FIGURE 15.7

MAIN AGENCIES OF THE DEPARTMENT OF HEALTH AND HUMAN SERVICES

There are several government agencies that work to protect public health. **What is the function of the Centers for Disease Control and Prevention?**

National Institutes of Health (NIH)	World's premier medical research organization. Supports over 38,000 research projects nationwide in diseases.
Food and Drug Administration (FDA)	Assures the safety of foods, cosmetics, medicines, and medical devices.
Centers for Disease Control and Prevention (CDC)	Provides a system of health monitoring to prevent disease outbreaks and maintain national health statistics.
Indian Health Service (HIS)	Provides health services to American Indians and Alaska Natives of federally recognized tribes.
Health Resources and Services Administration (HRSA)	Provides access to essential health care services for people who are low-income, uninsured, or live in areas where health care is scarce.
Substance Abuse and Mental Health Services Administration (SAMHSA)	Works to improve the quality and availability of substance abuse prevention, addiction treatment, and mental health services.
Agency for Healthcare Research and Quality (AHRQ)	Supports research on health care systems, health care quality and cost issues, access to health care, and effectiveness of medical treatments.

Health Skills Activity

Accessing Information

International Red Cross

The Red Cross is an international agency that helps people worldwide during times of war or disaster. The Red Cross was started in Switzerland during the 1800s. Its goal then was to care for wounded soldiers. Today, the Red Cross has chapters in nearly 200 nations.

In times of need, the International Red Cross provides medical treatment, food, clothing, and shelter. It also sponsors classes in first-aid and cardiopulmonary resuscitation (CPR). You may also know the American Red Cross for its blood donation work in the United States. Like the International Red Cross, the agency collects blood from volunteers. After processing, this blood is used for blood transfusions where needed.

On Your Own

Find out what services your local chapter of the American Red Cross provides. Share your findings with the class.

Health *Online*

Topic: Knowing Community Resources

Visit health.glencoe.com for Student Web Activities to learn about different kinds of public health information and services available.

Activity: Using the information provided at the link above, make a list of public health resources that are available in your community.

Nongovernmental Health Organizations

Federal agencies are paid for by tax dollars. Other health organizations exist purely through donations of money and/or time. The American Heart Association and American Cancer Society are two such organizations. Staffed by employees and volunteers, these organizations provide important health information. They help the public to keep informed about research and new developments to treat these diseases. They also help fund research efforts for ways to prevent and cure diseases and respond to sudden illness and injury. Finally, non-governmental organizations provide programs that teach prevention of disease and respond to health emergencies and disasters.

Reading Check

Explain How are organizations like the American Heart Association funded differently than government organizations?

Public Health at the International Level

Americans have a vast network of health agencies to rely on. The same is not true for people throughout the world and especially those in developing nations. A lot of diseases that no longer pose a health threat to Americans are still problems in developing countries. In many places throughout the globe, populations are faced with **famine,** *a widespread shortage of food.* Famine leads to starvation and death.

Fortunately, the international community has made world health a priority. International organizations that head this effort include the World Health Organization (WHO). WHO is an agency of the United Nations with members in 200 countries and territories. Another organization, Doctors Without Borders, is a group of physicians, allied health professionals, and other volunteers. Doctors Without Borders provides care to people in 70 countries who are affected by disasters, medical emergencies, or wars. These groups provide information and aid to struggling communities and nations. Like the nongovernmental agencies mentioned earlier, they rely on donations to continue their efforts.

Health Online

Visit **health.glencoe.com** and complete the Interactive Study Guide for Lesson 5.

Reading Check

List Name an international organization that does public health work in developing countries.

Lesson 5 Review

 After You Read

Review this lesson for new terms, major headings, and Reading Checks.

What I Learned

1. **Describe** What are some agencies of the Department of Health and Human Services? What kinds of efforts do these groups make in support of public health?

2. **Vocabulary** What is a *recall*? What information is included in a recall?

3. **Recall** Name two nongovernmental health organizations. Tell what types of help these organizations offer.

Thinking Critically

4. **Analyze** Look again at Figure 15.7. Tell which of these agencies look after the well-being of less fortunate Americans. Briefly explain your answer.

5. **Synthesize** Imagine that a river floods halfway around the world, destroying farms and homes. Which public health organizations would be most likely to spring into action? What steps might they take to help the people of this region?

Applying Health Skills

6. **Advocacy** Some Americans may not be aware of the role public health agencies play in protecting our health. Working in a group, develop a public service announcement (PSA) that highlights the work of two public health agencies. Share your PSA with other groups.

Building Health Skills

Finding Reliable Online Information

DIRECTIONS

Accessing Information involves finding reliable information to make healthful choices. This activity will give you the opportunity to develop and master this important health skill. Here's a guide to the different parts of this activity:

❶ In the **Model** section, you will read about a teen who performs the health skill successfully. This "model" scenario will show you how the skill is done.

❷ The **Practice** section will help guide you in practicing the skill.

❸ In the **Apply** section, you will have a chance to perform the skill on your own. You can use the Self-Check to check your work.

To complete this activity, first read the scenario presented in the Model. Then move on to the Practice. Finally, go ahead and try the Apply.

❶ Model

Judy needed to do a report for health class on recent research on vaccines. She knew the Internet would be a good source for finding the latest information.

Judy remembered that government agencies, non-profit organizations, and universities provide the most reliable sources of information. She did a search for vaccines and scanned the pages for links that ended in .gov, .org, and .edu. Judy clicked on the link which took her to the home page of the Centers for Disease Control and Prevention (CDC). At the CDC Web site, Judy found a listing of current links that gave her everything she needed for her report.

② Practice

For her next health report on "bone health," Judy tried the CDC Web site again. This time the site directed her to information that was too technical to understand. What Judy needed was a site designed for teens. She tried typing the word "teen" into the CDC internal search engine. She discovered a whole page with the heading "Health Topic: Adolescents and Teens." She clicked the link to *bone health* and scrolled down to the bottom of the page. Once again Judy was in business!

1. Identify the things Judy did that helped her get reliable information.

2. What problem did Judy encounter? How did she solve the problem?

3. If the CDC site did not provide the information Judy needed, what else could she do?

Skill Summary
ACCESSING INFORMATION

Accessing reliable information online involves:

- Using a government, non-profit organization, or university Web site.
- Looking for the *.gov, .org,* or *.edu.*
- Finding the most recent links.

③ Apply

Work with a small group to prepare a short report on insect repellants. Use your textbook to find some basic information about the connection between insects, ticks, and disease. Then visit a reliable Internet site to find four interesting facts about this topic. List the facts you discover and the Web address of the Internet site you visited. Record the date your sources were reviewed. Share your report with the class.

Self-Check

- Did we provide basic information?
- Did we include four facts?
- Did we use a reliable source?
- Was our source current?

DANGER
In The Locker Room

A strain of antibiotic-resistant bacteria is striking athletes at an increased rate.

Twelve-year-old Nicolas Johnson scraped his shoulder during football practice. Infection from the wound spread to his lungs, and Nicolas spent five weeks recovering in a Texas hospital.

What turned this simple scrape into a dangerous illness? The culprit was the bacterium called *methicillin-resistant staphylococcus aureus*— or MRSA for short. It is a highly contagious bug that is resistant to most commonly used antibiotics.

STUDENT OR PRO ATHLETES— THIS BUG DOESN'T CARE

MRSA is infecting the world of sports, from high school wrestling mats and neighborhood health clubs to the locker rooms of colleges and professional teams.

"We're seeing it more and more," says Ron Courson, head athletic trainer at the University of Georgia. "You would be hard-pressed to find a football team at any level that hasn't had to deal with it one way or another."

In some people, the bacteria causes a minor infection. In others, it can lead to more severe illness. When a staphylococcus infection does develop, it's usually treatable with powerful antibiotics.

KEEP IT CLEAN

The Centers for Disease Control and Prevention estimates that roughly 130,000 people are hospitalized with MRSA each year. Why is MRSA difficult to control? Its early symptoms are so tame that people with the infection often don't seek medical attention until it has begun to spread. Plus, MRSA can be passed easily from one person to another.

For example, scrapes on the skin from artificial turf can provide the entry point into an athlete's body. Then the germ can be passed around in any number of ways—by sharing towels, for instance, or using locker room facilities that aren't completely disinfected.

PREVENTING INFECTION

Some simple steps to keep MRSA from spreading:

- ▶ Wash hands regularly. Soap and water can effectively remove the bacteria before it causes trouble.
- ▶ Cover all wounds, even small ones. This closes off the potential entry points for MRSA.
- ▶ See a doctor at the first sign that a boil or welt seems to be worsening.
- ▶ Don't share towels or other gear, and wipe down heavily used equipment such as weight machines before and after use.

Reading Review

Lesson 1 Personal Health Care

Key Ideas

- Skin problems include acne, sunburn, cold sores, and warts. Hair problems include oily hair, dandruff, and head lice.
- Protecting your eyes includes wearing sunglasses, never rubbing your eyes, and getting regular eye exams.
- Protecting your ears involves avoiding loud noises and using earplugs.

Vocabulary

- epidermis (p. 373)
- dermis (p. 373)
- dandruff (p. 374)
- plaque (p. 375)
- tartar (p. 375)
- decibel (p. 377)

Lesson 2 Being a Smart Health Consumer

Key Ideas

- Consumer skills include knowing how to comparison shop and resolve problems with purchases.
- Smart shoppers compare products for quality, effectiveness, safety, and cost.

Vocabulary

- consumer (p. 379)
- consumer skills (p. 379)
- comparison shopping (p. 381)
- warranty (p. 381)
- health fraud (p. 381)

Lesson 3 Using Medicines Wisely

Key Idea

- Factors that determine how medicines affect the body include type and amount of medicine taken and the individual's chemical makeup, age, gender, and body size.

Vocabulary

- medicines (p. 383)
- prescription medicines (p. 383)
- over-the-counter (OTC) medicines (p. 384)
- vaccine (p. 384)
- antibiotics (p. 385)
- side effect (p. 386)

Lesson 4 Choosing Health Services

Key Idea

- Health care providers include primary care physicians, specialists, and allied health professionals.

Vocabulary

- health care system (p. 388)
- preventive care (p. 388)
- specialist (p. 389)
- allied health professionals (p. 389)
- health insurance (p. 391)
- managed care (p. 391)

Lesson 5 Public Health

Key Idea

- Both government and nongovernment agencies work to protect the health and safety of the public.

Vocabulary

- public health (p. 392)
- recall (p. 393)
- famine (p. 395)

Reviewing Vocabulary and Main Ideas

On a sheet of paper, write the numbers 1–6. After each number, write the term from the list that best completes each sentence.

- consumer skills
- decibel
- dermis
- epidermis
- health fraud
- lens
- plaque
- warranty

Lesson 1 Personal Health Care

1. The outermost layer of the skin is the _____.

2. _____ is a soft, colorless, sticky film containing bacteria that grow on your teeth.

3. A(n) _____ is a measure of the loudness of sound.

Lesson 2 Being a Smart Health Consumer

4. A(n) _____ is a promise to refund your money if the product doesn't work as claimed.

5. The selling of products or services that claim to prevent diseases or cure health problems which have not been scientifically proven safe or effective for such purposes is known as _____.

6. _____ are techniques that enable you to make wise, informed purchases.

*On a sheet of paper, write the numbers 7–15. Write **True** or **False** for each statement below. If the statement is false, change the underlined word or phrase to make it true.*

Lesson 3 Using Medicines Wisely

7. <u>Over-the-counter (OTC) medicines</u> are medicines that can be sold only with a written order from a physician.

8. A medicine that prevents a disease from developing is called an <u>antibiotic</u>.

9. Medicines applied to the skin are said to be taken <u>topically</u>.

Lesson 4 Choosing Health Services

10. <u>Preventive care</u> is medical care that keeps disease or injury from happening or getting worse.

11. <u>Outpatient</u> care involves a stay at a hospital or some other health care facility.

12. In managed care, the health consumer pays a small fee known as a <u>co-pay</u>.

Lesson 5 Public Health

13. A recall will generally be issued by the <u>HHS</u>.

14. A <u>famine</u> is a widespread shortage of food.

15. The <u>World Health Organization</u> is one international organization that has made world health a priority.

Health Online Visit **health.glencoe.com** and take the Online Quiz for Chapter 15.

Thinking Critically

Using complete sentences, answer the following questions on a sheet of paper.

16. Synthesize One skill emphasized in the chapter was learning to analyze advertising claims for health care products. How can this skill benefit you when you are making purchases?

17. Analyze How can taking care of your teeth, hair, and nails affect your total health?

Write About It

18. Communication Skills Imagine you are teaching a younger sibling about personal care. Write a dialogue between you and your sibling in which you explain how to care for the eyes, ears, and skin.

19. Analyzing Influences Write a paragraph describing some of the factors that can influence a teen's buying decisions.

Career Corner

Speech Therapist Students interested in how people communicate might want to consider a career as a speech therapist. These professionals work with people who have hearing and speech impairments to find possible causes and treatments. They also help patients improve their speaking skills. Speech therapists need a master's degree in audiology or speech therapy. Read more about this and other health careers by clicking on *Career Corner* at **health.glencoe.com**.

Standardized Test Practice

Math

Read the following statistics on hearing loss. Then answer the questions that follow.

- A survey by the National Center for Health Statistic reveals 23.3 million Americans have hearing loss.

- About 1.3 million of these people are 18 years old or younger.

- The National Institutes of Health reports that one-third of all hearing loss results from loud noises. Sources of these noises include power lawn mowers, jet engines, city traffic, loud appliances, rock music, and digital music earpieces.

TEST-TAKING TIP

Make sure you understand the relationship between integers and percentages in number statements.

1. What percentage of hearing loss cases reported by the National Center for Health Statistic involves teens?
   A. 1.3 percent
   B. 5.6 percent
   C. 23.3 percent
   D. None of the above

2. What approximate percentage of all hearing loss results from loud noises?
   A. 33.3 percent
   B. 25.5 percent
   C. 55 percent
   D. 80.5 percent

16 Your Body Systems

Chapter Preview

▲ **Working With the Photo**

Every movement you make or action you take involves one or more body systems. **Can you name any of these systems?**

Start-Up Activities

Do you have lifestyle habits that protect your body systems? Take the short health inventory below. Keep a record of your answers.

HEALTH INVENTORY

1. I sit, stand, and walk with straight posture.
   (a) always   (b) sometimes   (c) never

2. I participate in regular physical activity.
   (a) always   (b) sometimes   (c) never

3. I avoid using tobacco, alcohol, and other drugs.
   (a) always   (b) sometimes   (c) never

4. I wear a safety helmet when riding my bike.
   (a) always   (b) sometimes   (c) never

FOLDABLES™ Study Organizer

As You Read Make this Foldable™ to organize what you learn about the skeletal system in Lesson 1. Begin with two plain sheets of 8 ½" × 11" paper.

1 Collect two sheets of paper, and place them 1" apart.

2 Fold up the bottom edges of the paper, stopping them 1" from the top edges. This makes all tabs the same size.

3 Crease the paper to hold the tabs in place. Staple along the fold.

4 Turn and label the tabs as shown.

Skeletal System

Parts
Problems
Care

Under the appropriate tab, record main ideas and supporting facts about the parts, problems, and care of the skeletal system.

Health Online Visit **health.glencoe.com** and use the e-flashcards to preview vocabulary terms for Chapter 16.

Your Skeletal System

Guide to Reading

● **Building Vocabulary**
Make a word web using these terms. Decide which term should be the central term.

- skeletal system (p. 404)
- marrow (p. 405)
- joint (p. 406)
- cartilage (p. 406)
- tendons (p. 406)
- ligaments (p. 406)

● **Focusing on the Main Ideas**
In this lesson, you will learn to

- **explain** the functions of the skeletal system.
- **identify** four types of joints.
- **list** some problems of the skeletal system.
- **practice** healthful behaviors to keep your skeletal system healthy.

● **Reading Strategy**
Analyzing a Graphic Using Figure 16.1 on page 405, find examples of each kind of joint discussed in the lesson.

FOLDABLES | Study Organizer | Use the Foldable™ on p. 403 as you read this lesson.

Quick Write

Describe a sport or physical activity you enjoy doing. Tell what role you think your skeletal system plays in this activity.

Your Body's Framework

When a tall building is constructed, the steel beams go up first. Without this framework, the building could not stand. The same is true of your **skeletal system**—*a body system made up of bones, joints, and connective tissue.* **Figure 16.1** shows the parts of the skeletal system. The skeletal system does a lot more than help you stand up. Along with your muscles, it allows you to walk, run, jump, bend, lift, and carry.

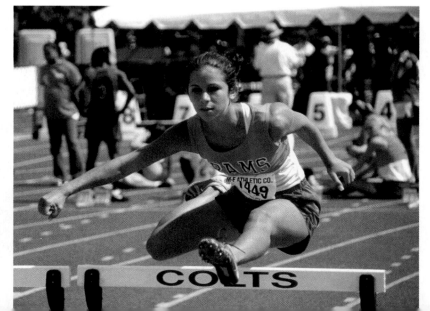

▶ Your skeletal system helps you run and jump. **What are some other functions of the skeletal system?**

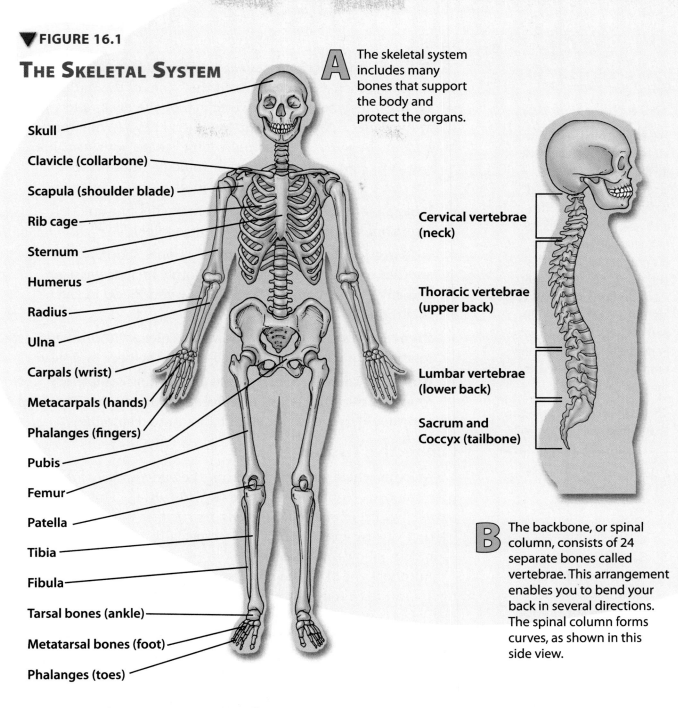

▼ FIGURE 16.1

THE SKELETAL SYSTEM

A The skeletal system includes many bones that support the body and protect the organs.

Skull

Clavicle (collarbone)

Scapula (shoulder blade)

Rib cage

Sternum

Humerus

Radius

Ulna

Carpals (wrist)

Metacarpals (hands)

Phalanges (fingers)

Pubis

Femur

Patella

Tibia

Fibula

Tarsal bones (ankle)

Metatarsal bones (foot)

Phalanges (toes)

Cervical vertebrae (neck)

Thoracic vertebrae (upper back)

Lumbar vertebrae (lower back)

Sacrum and Coccyx (tailbone)

B The backbone, or spinal column, consists of 24 separate bones called vertebrae. This arrangement enables you to bend your back in several directions. The spinal column forms curves, as shown in this side view.

Functions of Your Skeletal System

The skeletal system has a number of important functions. It provides a strong, stable framework capable of movement. It also supports and protects your delicate internal organs.

The 206 bones that make up your skeleton are living structures that function as storage centers for minerals, such as calcium and phosphorus. They also produce the body's blood cells. Red bone marrow makes millions of blood cells each day. **Marrow** is *a soft tissue in the center of some bones.*

Reading Check **Explain** What is the function of bone marrow?

▼ Getting enough calcium is important for strong bones. **What are some good sources of calcium?**

Joints

The point at which two bones meet is called a **joint.** Some joints do not move, such as those between the bones of the skull. Other joints, like those between the vertebrae of the back, allow only slight movement. Mobile joints, however, allow a wide range of movement. Imagine not having a joint where your arm bones meet at your elbow. Many activities would be impossible.

There are several types of mobile joints:

- **Hinge joints.** These joints allow movement in one direction. Knees and elbows are hinge joints.
- **Gliding joints.** Gliding joints help bones slide over one another without twisting. Gliding joints include wrists and ankles, and connect bones below your neck, in the collarbone.
- **Pivot joints.** These joints allow movement with limited rotation. A pivot joint is found between the neck and head.
- **Ball-and-socket joints.** These joints allow complete rotations, allowing bones to move in all directions. Your hips and shoulders are examples of ball-and-socket joints.

Connective Tissues

At joints where movement occurs, the bone surfaces are coated with smooth, slippery **cartilage** (KAHR·tuhl·ij). This is *a strong flexible, gel-like tissue that cushions your joints.* Cartilage reduces friction during movement and is especially important in your shoulders, elbows, and knees.

Another type of connective tissue is **tendons**—*tough bands of tissue that attach your muscles to bones.* A large tendon that you can easily feel is your Achilles tendon. It is located on the back of your leg just above your heel. Finally, **ligaments** are *cord-like tissues that connect the bones in each joint.* They help hold bones in place.

> **Reading Check** **Define** What is *cartilage?*

Problems of the Skeletal System

Bones, joints, and connective tissues are strong and durable. Yet, like most structures made of living cells, they can develop problems. Injuries, infections, poor posture, and a lack of nutritious foods can cause some of the following problems of the skeletal system.

Health Skills Activity

Practicing Healthful Behaviors

Got Calcium?

Calcium builds healthy bones and teeth. It also keeps your heartbeat steady and your nerves and muscles in good condition. If your blood levels of calcium are too low, your body draws it from your bones. Removing calcium from your bones without replacing it can lead to osteoporosis, a condition where bones become weak and can break easily. To keep your bones strong, exercise and eat plenty of calcium-rich foods. These include low-fat or fat-free dairy products, broccoli, spinach, and calcium-fortified orange juice.

On Your Own

Think of ways to incorporate calcium-rich foods into meals and snacks. For example, throw some spinach leaves into a salad or melt some reduced-fat cheese on top of cooked broccoli. Create a list of your ideas and share them with the class.

- **A fracture** is a break in a bone caused by an injury. It results in swelling and sometimes extreme pain.

- **A dislocation** occurs when a bone is pushed out of its joint, usually stretching or tearing a ligament. This type of injury can also cause extreme pain.

- **A sprain** is a stretching or twisting of ligaments in a joint, causing swelling. It can be treated using the P.R.I.C.E. formula discussed in Chapter 9.

- **Overuse injuries** happen over time and make up about half of the sports injuries that occur in teens. A shin splint, common among runners and aggressive walkers, is an example of an overuse injury.

- **Scoliosis** is a disorder in which the spine curves to one side of the body. It appears to have a slight S- or C-shaped curve. It is usually painless, but it can cause back pain and difficulty with breathing. In most cases, the cause is not known.

- **Osteoporosis** is a condition characterized by brittle and porous bones. It develops because of long-term deficiencies of calcium and certain hormones, insufficient vitamin D, and lack of exercise.

Health Online

Visit **health.glencoe.com** and complete the Interactive Study Guide for Lesson 1.

◀ Wearing protective gear during sports can help prevent injuries to the skeletal system. **Do you play any sports that require protective gear?**

Caring for Your Skeletal System

You can add bone mass only while you are still growing, so now is the time to focus on building healthy bones. Start with good nutrition. Low-fat and fat-free dairy products contain calcium and other nutrients important to good bone health. These include phosphorus, magnesium, and added vitamin D in milk. Regular physical activity increases bone mass, especially weight-bearing exercises such as walking and jogging. Remember to use good posture when you sit, stand, or walk. Good posture keeps your spine healthy.

Sports injuries in the United States are on the rise for teens. If you are injured, take the time to heal completely before you go back to your sport. Use protective gear when playing sports, riding your bike, or in-line skating.

Reading Check **Explain** What behaviors help keep the skeletal system healthy?

Lesson 1 Review

After You Read

Review this lesson for new terms, major headings, and Reading Checks.

What I Learned

1. *Vocabulary* What are *joints*? Name four types.

2. *List* Name three functions of the skeletal system.

3. *Identify* What are two problems of the skeletal system?

Thinking Critically

4. *Apply* You and another teen on the gymnastics team are practicing. You see your teammate doing an exercise that the coach said not to do. What risk is your teammate taking?

5. *Synthesize* Jan understands the importance of eating foods rich in calcium. She is allergic to milk, however. What suggestions can you make that might help Jan?

Applying Health Skills

6. *Practicing Healthful Behaviors* During most sports and other physical activities, your body parts are in motion. Name some ways to protect the bones from injury when playing a specific sport.

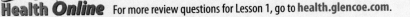

Health Online For more review questions for Lesson 1, go to **health.glencoe.com**.

Your Muscular System

Guide to Reading

● Building Vocabulary
As you read this lesson, write each new highlighted term and its definition in your notebook.

- muscular system (p. 409)
- skeletal muscles (p. 410)
- smooth muscles (p. 410)
- cardiac muscles (p. 410)

● Focusing on the Main Ideas
In this lesson, you will learn to

- **explain** the functions of the muscular system.
- **identify** how muscle types differ.
- **describe** ways to keep your muscular system healthy.

● Reading Strategy
Comparing and Contrasting Explain similarities and differences among the different muscle types in the lesson.

Q uick Write
Write a short journal entry about a time you had a muscle ache or pain. Tell what you did to relieve the symptoms.

Your Muscles

Your muscles make it possible for your body to move. They also pump blood throughout your body and move food through your digestive system. Muscles also control the movement of air in and out of your lungs.

Your **muscular system** is *the group of structures that give your body parts the power to move.* **Figure 16.2** shows some of the different muscles that make up the muscular system. It also tells which tasks each muscle performs.

◀ Muscles have a number of important functions. **What is one function of the muscular system?**

▼ **FIGURE 16.2**

THE MUSCULAR SYSTEM

This figure shows the major skeletal muscles of your body. **What does your trapezius muscle do?**

Extensors straighten your hand at the wrist.

Sternomastoid turns your head.

Trapezius raises your head and shoulders.

Flexors bend your hand at the wrist.

Biceps bend your arm at the elbow.

Pectoralis major moves your arm across your chest.

Abdominal rectus flexes your torso.

External obliques assist in breathing.

Quadriceps straighten and raise your leg.

Sartorius muscle bends your leg at the knee.

Triceps straighten your arm at the elbow.

Deltoids raise your upper arm.

Latissimus dorsi muscles lower your upper arm.

Gluteus maximus extends your thigh and raises your torso from a stooping position.

Abductors move your legs apart.

Gastrocnemius extends or lowers your foot when you walk or tiptoe.

Hamstrings bend your leg at the knee.

Abductors move your legs together.

Achilles tendon attaches your calf muscles to your heel bone.

Anterior tibial muscle flexes your ankle and your foot.

Types of Muscles

Different muscle types carry out different tasks. *The muscles attached to bones that enable you to move* are called **skeletal muscles.** Skeletal muscles are the largest part of the body's muscular system. There are more than 600 skeletal muscles. These muscles are voluntary. You have the power to control their movement.

Smooth muscles are *the muscles found in organs, blood vessels, and glands.* The mouth, stomach, and lungs are all composed largely of smooth muscles. Smooth muscles are *involuntary* because they operate without your awareness. **Cardiac muscles** are *muscles found only in the walls of your heart.* They are involuntary muscles, working continuously even when you are asleep.

Reading Check **List** Name the three types of muscles.

How Muscles Work

Muscle movement is triggered by messages or impulses. These impulses are sent to muscle fiber— narrow strands of tissue within the muscle. There are two basic and opposite actions that account for all muscle movement. The first is contraction, the shortening of muscle fibers. The second is extension, the lengthening of muscle fibers. **Figure 16.3** shows these actions at work in two muscles of the arm.

Problems of the Muscular System

Have your muscles ever ached after strenuous exercise or a tough competition? Sore muscles are a temporary condition. Other muscle problems, however, may have a lasting effect on your body. One such problem is muscle strain, which is caused by small tears to a muscle or tendon. Strains usually occur in large muscles that have been overworked. If you feel pain when you exercise, stop what you are doing.

A serious problem that sometimes occurs in teens is muscular dystrophy. This disorder is usually inherited and causes the skeletal muscle tissue to gradually waste away. Eventually, the person can no longer stand or walk.

Reading Check

Explain What should you do if you develop sore muscles from exercising?

Connect To... Science

Fast-Twitch, Slow-Twitch

Every muscle is made of two different types of fiber. Fast-twitch fibers provide quick bursts of intense energy. Slow-twitch fibers use little energy, but have more energy to burn over time. Most people are born with about half of each fiber type. Some people, however, inherit more fast-twitch muscles and this helps them naturally excel in sports.

Do you think you have more of one type of fiber than the other? If so, which one?

▼ FIGURE 16.3

HOW MUSCLES WORK

Many of your skeletal muscles work in pairs. **When you bend your arm, which muscle contracts and which muscle extends?**

1 When you bend your arm, your biceps contract and pull on a bone of your lower arm. At the same time, the triceps extend.

biceps

triceps

2 When you straighten your arm, your triceps contract and pull on the other bone in your lower arm. At the same time, the biceps extend.

biceps

triceps

Care of the Muscular System

You may know the expression "Use it or lose it." This saying is certainly true about muscles. Using muscles helps maintain the natural tension in the fibers. This natural tension is called *muscle tone.* The best way to keep your muscles toned is to stay active and eat well. Remember that the heart is also a muscle, and that regular exercise makes it stronger. A healthy heart pumps more blood and has more time to rest between beats.

Be sure to warm up before exercising or playing sports and to cool down afterwards. This will help prevent muscle strain. Using exercise or sports equipment properly can also help prevent muscle injury.

Another way to keep your muscles healthy is to lift properly. Never bend over to lift a heavy object. This puts a lot of strain on your back muscles and can cause injury. Instead, bend your knees, keeping your back straight. Then stand up to lift the load, letting your leg muscles do the work.

> **Health Online**
>
> Visit **health.glencoe.com** and complete the Interactive Study Guide for Lesson 2.

Reading Check **Recall** What is the proper way to lift a heavy object?

Lesson 2 Review

After You Read

Review this lesson for new terms, major headings, and Reading Checks.

What I Learned

1. *Vocabulary* What are *skeletal muscles*? What other term is used to describe these muscles?

2. *Describe* What are the functions of the muscular system?

3. *List* Give two suggestions for keeping the muscular system healthy.

Thinking Critically

4. *Apply* A teen is doing bench presses in the school's weight room. During each repetition, he groans loudly. When you ask if he is in pain, he replies, "Yes—but it's *good* pain." How might you respond?

5. *Evaluate* A teen has been asked to carry some boxes of books to a classroom. He stoops over and pulls a box upward toward his chest. Should he continue lifting this way?

Applying Health Skills

6. *Advocacy* Review the recommendations in the lesson for taking care of your muscular system. Choose one that you think many teens are likely to ignore or be unaware of. Develop a guest editorial for the school paper regarding this habit.

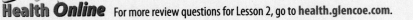

Your Circulatory System

Guide to Reading

● Building Vocabulary
As you read this lesson, write each new highlighted term and its definition in your notebook.

- circulatory system (p. 413)
- cell respiration (p. 414)
- arteries (p. 415)
- veins (p. 415)
- capillaries (p. 415)

● Focusing on the Main Ideas
In this lesson, you will learn to

- **explain** the process of circulation.
- **identify** the parts of the circulatory system.
- **describe** ways to keep your circulatory system healthy.

● Reading Strategy
Sequencing Using Figure 16.4 as a guide, trace the path of blood flowing to and from the heart.

Quick Write

Tell in a sentence or two what you know about your own blood. Mention blood type and blood pressure.

The Body's Transport System

Even when you are sound asleep, parts of your body are awake. Some of your muscles, for example, never stop working. One of those muscles is your heart. Your heart's job is to pump blood to all parts of your body.

The heart is the main organ of the **circulatory** (SUR·kyuh·luh·tohr·ee) **system.** This system is *a group of organs and tissues that move essential supplies to body cells and remove their waste product*s. This system is also sometimes called the cardiovascular (KAR·dee·oh· VAS·kyoo·lur) system.

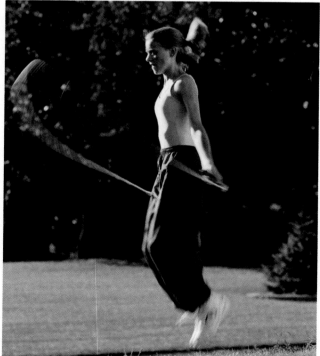

▶ Exercise can help keep your heart healthy. **What are some other ways to care for your heart?**

Circulation and the Body's Cells

Your circulatory system, shown in **Figure 16.4,** is made up of your heart, blood vessels, and blood. Pumped by your heart, blood travels through the blood vessels carrying nutrients and oxygen throughout the body. *The process in which the body's cells are nourished and energized* is called **cell respiration.** As blood

▼FIGURE 16.4

THE CIRCULATORY SYSTEM

In this figure, red represents oxygen-rich blood and blue represents blood containing carbon dioxide. **What do the pulmonary veins carry?**

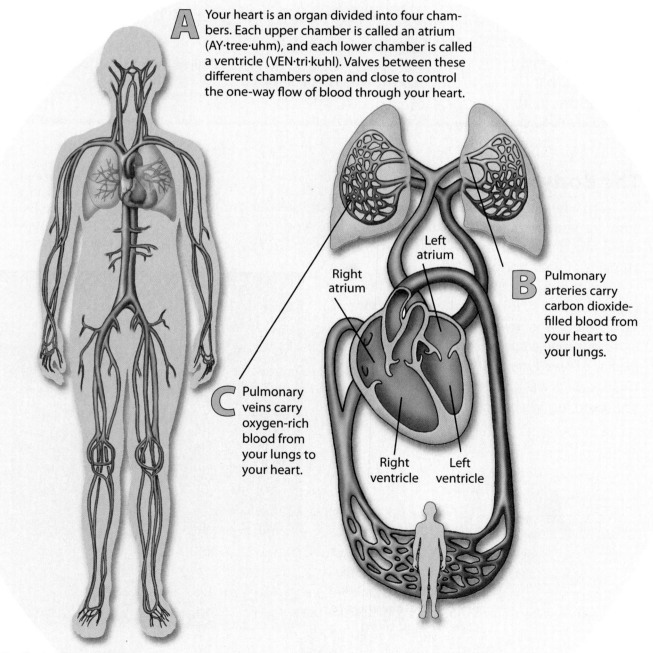

A Your heart is an organ divided into four chambers. Each upper chamber is called an atrium (AY·tree·uhm), and each lower chamber is called a ventricle (VEN·tri·kuhl). Valves between these different chambers open and close to control the one-way flow of blood through your heart.

Left atrium

Right atrium

B Pulmonary arteries carry carbon dioxide-filled blood from your heart to your lungs.

C Pulmonary veins carry oxygen-rich blood from your lungs to your heart.

Right ventricle

Left ventricle

flows, it picks up nutrients from the digestive system and oxygen from the lungs, which it delivers to the body's cells. The cells use these materials to produce energy for the body. This process creates waste products, which include carbon dioxide gas. The blood picks up these wastes and delivers them to the liver, kidneys, and lungs for removal from the body.

Reading Check **Define** What is *cell respiration*?

Blood

Like the heart, blood plays an important role in circulation. It may surprise you to learn that blood is made up in nearly equal parts of solids and liquids. The liquid part of blood, *plasma* (PLAZ·muh), is about 92 percent water. The solids in blood consist mainly of blood cells and cell parts called *platelets*. There are two kinds of blood cells. Red blood cells carry oxygen to cells and carry carbon dioxide away from them. White blood cells carry germ fighters from the immune system to areas of the body that need them. Platelets help blood clot at the site of a wound. Clotting seals the wound and prevents excessive blood loss.

Blood Vessels

Look again at Figure 16.4. The thick red lines are **arteries.** These are *blood vessels that carry blood away from the heart to other parts of the body.* The thick blue lines are **veins.** These are *blood vessels that carry blood from the body back to the heart.* The thin red and blue lines branching off from the main ones are **capillaries.** These are *tiny blood vessels that connect the veins and arteries to the body's cells.*

Giving and Receiving Blood

Even though platelets work to stop bleeding, the circulatory system is not designed to handle major wounds. When a serious injury occurs, the body can lose a lot of blood. If too much blood is lost, the person will die if the blood is not replaced. Blood can be replaced by means of a *transfusion.*

Before transfusions can be done, however, the doctors need to make sure that the blood type of the injured person matches the blood type of the donated blood. There are four main blood types: A, B, AB, and O. Everyone is born with one of these types. If a person receives blood of the wrong type, their body will reject it. Their immune system will treat the blood as a threat and serious health complications can result, even death.

Blood safety is a concern since viruses such as HIV can be passed through infected blood. In the United States, the Food and

Connect To... Science

Anemia and Teens

Anemia is a condition in which the body is not producing enough red blood cells needed to carry oxygen to other cells. Iron-deficiency anemia is the most common type of anemia in teens. You can increase the iron levels in your diet by eating lean meat, eggs, spinach, raisins, dried beans, and iron-fortified cereal.

Research the symptoms of anemia. Find out what the health risks are if left untreated.

▶ Having your blood pressure checked is part of a physical exam. **Why is maintaining a normal blood pressure important?**

Drug Administration (FDA) is responsible for regulating organizations that collect and distribute donated blood. FDA regulations make it very safe to give and receive blood. All donated blood is tested for HIV and other diseases. Blood that fails any test is discarded.

Reading Check **Identify** Why is it important to know your blood type?

Problems of the Circulatory System

Some of the problems of the circulatory system affect the heart and blood vessels. Others affect the blood itself.

- **Hypertension** is also called high blood pressure. It can lead to kidney failure, heart attack, or stroke.
- **Heart attack** is the blockage of blood flow to the heart.
- **Stroke** usually results from blood clots that block vessels in the brain, or from the rupture of a blood vessel.
- **Arteriosclerosis** is a condition in which arteries harden, reducing the amount of blood that can flow through them.
- **Anemia** is an abnormally low level of hemoglobin, a protein that binds to oxygen in red blood cells.
- **Leukemia** is a type of cancer in which large amounts of abnormal white blood cells are produced that interferes with the production of other blood cells.

Care of the Circulatory System

One way of keeping your heart healthy is to be physically active. Teens should get 60 minutes of physical activity on most days. Regular activity strengthens your heart muscle and allows it to pump more blood with each beat.

Limit the amount of fat in your eating plan. Fats, especially the saturated kind, can cause fat deposits to form on artery walls. These deposits increase blood pressure. As you lower your fat intake, increase your intake of dietary fiber. Whole grains and raw vegetables are a great source of fiber. They also make a filling and satisfying snack.

Another way to keep your heart healthy is to avoid tobacco. Tobacco use can cause lung cancer, emphysema, and other lung diseases. It can also lead to heart disease. Finally, learn to manage the stress in your life. Stress can cause high blood pressure, which puts a strain on the entire cardiovascular system.

Reading Check

List Name two habits that help keep your circulatory system healthy.

Health Online

Visit **health.glencoe.com** and complete the Interactive Study Guide for Lesson 3.

Lesson 3 Review

After You Read

Review this lesson for new terms, major headings, and Reading Checks.

What I Learned

1. *Vocabulary* Define *circulatory system*.

2. *Explain* Tell what happens during cell respiration.

3. *Recall* What are two problems of the circulatory system?

4. *Identify* What are three types of blood vessels? Explain the function of each.

Thinking Critically

5. *Analyze* When a person donates blood, why is it necessary to find out his or her blood type?

6. *Apply* Devin's father recently had a mild heart attack. Devin is concerned about his own heart health. What advice can you give Devin about ways to keep his heart healthy?

Applying Health Skills

7. *Analyzing Influences* In addition to lifestyle, heredity also influences circulatory health. With a group, investigate the role that heredity plays in hypertension and other problems of the circulatory system.

Your Respiratory System

Guide to Reading

● Building Vocabulary
Read each of the words below. If the word is familiar, write down what you think its meaning is. If it's not, guess at its meaning.

- respiratory system (p. 418)
- respiration (p. 418)
- bronchi (p. 420)
- alveoli (p. 420)
- diaphragm (p. 420)
- asthma (p. 420)
- Air Quality Index (AQI) (p. 421)

● Focusing on the Main Ideas
In this lesson, you will learn to

- **explain** how your body uses the air you breathe.
- **identify** the parts and functions of the respiratory system.
- **describe** ways to maintain the health of your respiratory system.
- **analyze** the role of posture on respiratory health.

● Reading Strategy
Organizing Information Create an outline using the major and minor headings in the lesson. As you read, take notes under each heading on your outline.

Quick Write

Write about a time when you felt out of breath. Tell what caused this and what, if anything, you did to get your breath back.

Breathing

While reading this paragraph you will breathe in and out four or five times. This will happen without you even thinking about it. Breathing is a function of your body's **respiratory system**— *a system that consists of organs that supply the body with constant oxygen and rid the body of carbon dioxide.* Your body needs oxygen to survive. In fact, a person can live only a few minutes without oxygen.

Functions of the Respiratory System

The respiratory system's main job, as its name suggests, is **respiration.** This is *the exchange of gases between your body and the air.* There are two major types of respiration: external and internal.

- **External respiration.** This is the exchange of oxygen and carbon dioxide between the blood and the air in the lungs. As you inhale, you breathe oxygen-rich air into your lungs. The oxygen exchanges with carbon dioxide inside your lungs. When you exhale, you release carbon dioxide into the air.

- **Internal respiration.** This is the exchange of gases between the blood and the cells of the body. Oxygen moves from your lungs to your blood where it is carried to all the cells of the body. In the cells, oxygen combines with nutrients to provide energy. This process produces carbon dioxide—a waste gas. Blood carries the carbon dioxide to the lungs where it is released outside the body. Another name for this process, which you already read about in Lesson 3, is *cell respiration*.

Reading Check   **Identify** What is the main function of the respiratory system?

Main Parts of the Respiratory System

The main structures of the respiratory system are shown in **Figure 16.5.** Find the lungs in this diagram. These are the system's main organ. Every day, your lungs take in enough air to fill a large room.

▼ **FIGURE 16.5**

THE RESPIRATORY SYSTEM

The respiratory system allows the body to take in oxygen and remove carbon dioxide. **Where in the respiratory system does oxygen exchange with carbon dioxide?**

A Air enters through the **nose** and **mouth,** both of which are lined with mucous (MYOO·kuhs) membranes. Fine hairs called cilia (SIL·ee·uh) trap dirt that you breathe in.

B The **throat** has two passageways—one for air and one for food.

C The **epiglottis** (e·puh·GLAH·tis) is a flap of tissue that closes over the trachea when you swallow.

D The **larynx** (LA·ringks) is the upper part of the respiratory system, which contains the vocal cords.

E The **trachea** (TRAY·kee·uh) is a windpipe that directs air to the lungs.

F The **bronchi** (BRAHN·ky) are passages through which air enters the lungs.

G In the **lungs,** oxygen is transferred to the blood, and carbon dioxide is removed from the blood.

H The **diaphragm** (DY·uh·fram) is a dome-shaped muscle that separates the lungs from the abdomen.

Each lung is divided into sections called *lobes*. Notice that there are three lobes in the right lung and two in the left. The *main openings through which air enters the lungs* are the **bronchi** (BRAHNG·ky). From the bronchi, air moves into smaller tubes called bronchioles. These passages branch into even smaller spaces called **alveoli** (al·VEE·uh·ly). The alveoli are *tiny air sacs in the lungs where carbon dioxide is exchanged with oxygen.*

The Role of the Diaphragm

Have you have heard of a blacksmith? Blacksmiths use fire to shape metal into tools and other goods. They use devices called bellows to fan the flames of the fire. Human lungs have a lot in common with bellows. Both are responsible for introducing oxygen and both rely on muscle power to accomplish this task. However, while bellows are powered by arm muscles, lungs get their power from the diaphragm. The **diaphragm** is *a dome-shaped muscle that separates the chest from the abdomen.* When you inhale, the diaphragm contracts and flattens. Its downward motion permits the lungs to fill with air. When you exhale, the opposite happens. The diaphragm moves upward, squeezing the lungs and forcing the air out.

Reading Check

Explain What happens in the lungs when the diaphragm contracts?

Problems of the Respiratory System

One of the most common respiratory diseases suffered by young people is **asthma,** *a serious chronic condition that causes tiny air passages in the respiratory system to become narrow or blocked.* Its symptoms are wheezing, shortness of breath, and coughing. About 4 million Americans under age 18 have asthma. Asthma attacks are often triggered by an allergic reaction to substances in the environment.

Other respiratory problems include bronchitis, pneumonia, tuberculosis (TB), and influenza ("flu"). Symptoms include coughing, wheezing, and difficulty breathing. Fever may be present as well. Tuberculosis and pneumonia are serious problems and may require hospitalization.

◀ One common respiratory illness is the flu. **What are some more serious respiratory illnesses?**

Chronic obstructive pulmonary disease (COPD) is a condition in which the lungs lose their elasticity. It can be caused by asthma that is not controlled properly, as well as tobacco smoke. Emphysema is a form of COPD in which the alveoli are damaged or destroyed and breathing becomes difficult. Lung cancer is a disease in which tissues of the lung are destroyed by the growth of a tumor.

Care of the Respiratory System

Taking care of your respiratory system includes staying physically active, which makes your lungs stronger. It also includes avoiding tobacco smoke and polluted air. Many communities, especially in or near big cities, report local air quality on the news or in the newspaper. An **Air Quality Index (AQI)** is *a measure of ozone, sulfur dioxide, carbon monoxide, and fine particles close to the ground.* On days when the air quality is poor, avoid doing activity outdoors. Knowing your area's AQI can help you maintain your respiratory health.

In addition to exercising regularly, it is important to protect yourself from respiratory infections. When someone in your home is sick with the flu or a cold, wash your hands often with soap and water and avoid touching your nose and mouth.

Health Online

Visit **health.glencoe.com** and complete the Interactive Study Guide for Lesson 4.

Lesson 4 Review

After You Read

Review this lesson for new terms, major headings, and Reading Checks.

What I Learned

1. **Vocabulary** What is *asthma*?

2. **Explain** Explain external and internal respiration.

3. **List** Name the main parts of the respiratory system.

Thinking Critically

4. **Apply** A friend calls to ask if you want to ride bikes. Your local news is reporting poor air quality. What choice do you make? What advice do you give your friend?

5. **Evaluate** Marie arrives home from school feeling feverish and coughing. Based on what you have learned, which respiratory illness might Marie possibly have? Are there any illnesses that you can rule out?

Applying Health Skills

6. **Analyzing Influences** Investigate the role of posture on the health of the respiratory system. Share your findings with the class. Use this example to discuss how the health of one body system can affect another body system.

Your Nervous System

Guide to Reading

Building Vocabulary
As you read, write each term and its definition in your notebook.

- nervous system (p. 422)
- central nervous system (CNS) (p. 423)
- peripheral nervous system (PNS) (p. 423)
- neurons (p. 423)
- somatic system (p. 424)
- autonomic system (p. 424)
- traumatic brain injury (TBI) (p. 425)

Focusing on the Main Ideas
In this lesson, you will learn to

- **explain** the functions of your nervous system.
- **identify** the different parts of the nervous system.
- **describe** ways of protecting your nervous system from injury.

Reading Strategy
Predicting Before you read, glance at the main headings, figures, and captions. Predict the kinds of tasks carried out by your nervous system.

Quick Write
Write a detailed step-by-step procedure of a very simple action. An example might be washing your face.

Your Body's Command Center

Computers are amazing machines, capable of doing billions of calculations in a second. Yet, even the fastest computer cannot compose music or write a play. Only the human brain is able to do such work.

Your brain is just one part of your **nervous system.** This is *your body's message and control center.* Your nervous system controls all your body's actions and jobs.

▶ Your nervous system warns you when food is too hot to eat. **What are some other ways that your nervous system helps you to prevent injury?**

Parts of the Nervous System

The nervous system has two main divisions:

- The **central nervous system (CNS)** includes *the brain and spinal cord.*

- The **peripheral nervous system (PNS)** includes *the nerves that connect the central nervous system to all parts of the body.*

The PNS sends the information it gathers to the CNS. The CNS examines the information, and then sends directions back to the PNS on how to respond. These messages are carried by means of electrical charges called *impulses.* They travel along body pathways at speeds up to 248 miles per hour. The senders and receivers of these transmissions are called neurons. **Neurons** are *specialized nerve cells.*

Reading Check **List** Name two parts of the nervous system.

Central Nervous System

The central nervous system (CNS) has two parts: the brain and the spinal cord. The brain is the largest, most complex part of your entire nervous system. This remarkable structure, which weighs about 3 pounds, contains at least 100 billion neurons. Messages from your brain take the form of thoughts, memories, and commands to carry out actions. Your brain allows you to reason and to direct your muscle movement. It is involved in your emotions and everything you sense. Your brain also controls involuntary processes, such as heartbeat and respiration. **Figure 16.6** on the next page shows the different parts of the brain and their functions.

The spinal cord is a column of nerve tissue about 18 inches long and about as thick as your index finger. This precious cord is protected by *vertebrae,* bones that make up the spine. It is further protected by fluid that surrounds it, acting like a shock absorber. Your spinal cord relays messages to and from the brain and body.

▼ Whether you play a sport or do other activities, protect yourself. **What risks can you avoid by wearing protective gear like the teen in this picture?**

PARTS OF THE BRAIN

Like a computer, the brain is made up of many distinct parts, each with a different function. **What is the function of the brain stem?**

A The **cerebrum** is the largest portion of the brain. It controls the senses, movement of muscles, thinking, and speech.

B The **cerebellum** controls balance, posture, and coordination.

C The **brain stem** controls some important automatic body functions such as heartbeat, breathing, blood pressure, and digestion.

D The **meninges** are membranes that cover the brain and the spinal cord.

Skull

Midbrain

Pons

Medulla

Spinal Cord

Vertebrae

Health Online

Visit **health.glencoe.com** and complete the Interactive Study Guide for Lesson 5.

Peripheral Nervous System

The word *peripheral* means "located away from the center." The peripheral nervous system (PNS) is made up of nerves that fan out from the CNS. These nerves connect to the muscles, skin, organs, and glands. The PNS carries messages between the CNS and the rest of the body.

Like the CNS and nervous system as a whole, the PNS has two parts. The **somatic** (soh·MA·tik) **system** is *the part of the nervous system that deals with actions that you control.* For example, the nerves to and from your arm muscles are part of the somatic system. The **autonomic** (aw·tuh·NAH·mik) **system** is *a system dealing with actions you do not control.*

Reading Check **Identify** What two body parts make up the central nervous system?

Problems of the Nervous System

For teens, the most common cause of nervous-system problems is a blow to the head. Head injuries during sports or other activities can cause **traumatic brain injury (TBI)**—*a condition caused by the brain being jarred and striking the inside of the skull.* Traumatic brain injury is the number one cause of death and disability in children and young adults. It can also cause memory loss, loss of one or more senses, and psychological problems.

Spinal-cord injuries from accidents can also lead to serious problems. This includes paralysis, an inability to move body parts. Other problems include nerve inflammation, or "pinched nerve." This condition is very painful. Besides pain medication, the only way to treat nerve inflammation is to rest the affected area.

Not all nervous system problems are caused by injury. Diseases can also affect the nervous system, including the following:

- **Meningitis.** This is a potentially life-threatening infection of the *meninges,* connective membranes in the spine.

- **Brain tumor.** This is an abnormal growth of tissue that kills normal neurons around it. It is also called brain cancer.

- **Epilepsy.** This is an illness in which a small area of the brain is damaged. The result is *seizures,* episodes of uncontrollable muscle activity.

- **Multiple Sclerosis (MS).** With this disease, the protective outer coating of the nerves is damaged. They no longer work properly. Multiple Sclerosis is a *degenerative* disease, meaning it becomes worse over time.

Connect To... Science

Technology and the Brain

Using magnetic resonance imaging (MRI) technology, researchers have learned that the brain develops in stages, generally from back to front. The first part to develop controls the sensory functions such as vision, hearing, and touch. The last part, reaching full development around age 25, controls judgment and decision making.

Research other ways MRI technology is being used in science or health care.

Care of the Nervous System

Always wear protective head gear during sports or physical activities such as skateboarding and bicycling. Always use your safety belt when riding in a car. In addition, get plenty of rest and avoid alcohol and other drugs. These chemicals can destroy brain cells and interfere with thoughts, emotions, and judgment.

Reading Check **Identify** What are some ways to care for your nervous system?

▶ Helmets can prevent traumatic brain injury. **What are some activities that require a helmet?**

Health Skills Activity

Practicing Healthful Behaviors

Avoiding Repetitive Motion Injuries

Many people use a computer for long periods at a time, either at work or at home. Some of these people may develop a nervous system problem called *repetitive motion injury*. This injury is an inflammation of the nerves in the wrists caused by prolonged, repeated movements. The following strategies can help you prevent this type of injury when using a computer.

1. Keep wrists relaxed and straight. Use only finger movements to strike the keys.
2. Press keys with the least pressure that is necessary.
3. Move your entire hand to press hard-to-reach keys.
4. Take frequent breaks, which is also good for your eyes.

On Your Own
Practice these strategies each time you use a computer.

Lesson 5 Review

After You Read

Review this lesson for new terms, major headings, and Reading Checks.

What I Learned

1. *Vocabulary* What is the *somatic system*?

2. *Explain* What jobs are done by your brain?

3. *List* Name the two main parts of the nervous system.

Thinking Critically

4. *Apply* You are sitting at home when the telephone rings. Explain the steps that your nervous system takes between the time that the phone rings and the time that you answer it.

5. *Evaluate* Many states now have laws requiring people to wear safety belts in motor vehicles. Tell whether you think this type of law is a good idea. Explain your answer.

Applying Health Skills

6. *Accessing Information* With a group, research current efforts to treat spinal-cord injuries. Determine what makes it so difficult to heal a damaged spinal cord so it works properly again. Share your findings in a brief oral report.

Health Online For more review questions for Lesson 5, go to **health.glencoe.com**.

Your Digestive and Excretory Systems

Quick Write

Water is important to healthy digestion. Make a list of ways you could increase your water intake.

The Digestive System

Like a car, train, or airplane, your body cannot operate without fuel. The fuel your body uses is food. *The body system that converts this fuel into usable energy* is your **digestive system.** This system also helps control the elimination of used-up fuel in the form of wastes. **Figure 16.7** shows the parts of the digestive system.

◄ The digestive system converts the food you eat into active energy. **What are some processes involved in digestion?**

427

The process of changing food into material the body can use is called **digestion** (dy·JES·chuhn). Digestion involves both mechanical and chemical processes. Mechanical processes include chewing and mashing food into smaller pieces. The chemical process involves breaking food down into particles with digestive enzymes. **Enzymes** are *proteins that affect the many body processes.* Digestive enzymes speed up the breakdown of food. Many enzymes are produced in the body.

The Mouth and Teeth

The digestive process starts in the mouth. The teeth tear and grind food into small pieces. When the taste buds on your tongue sense flavor, your mouth produces saliva (suh·LY·vuh). **Saliva** is *a fluid made by the salivary glands* that moistens and softens food, making it easier to swallow. Saliva also contains enzymes that begin breaking down the food.

Reading Check **Define** What is *saliva*?

▼ FIGURE 16.7

THE DIGESTIVE SYSTEM

The digestive process begins in the mouth. **Where does partially digested food go when it leaves the mouth?**

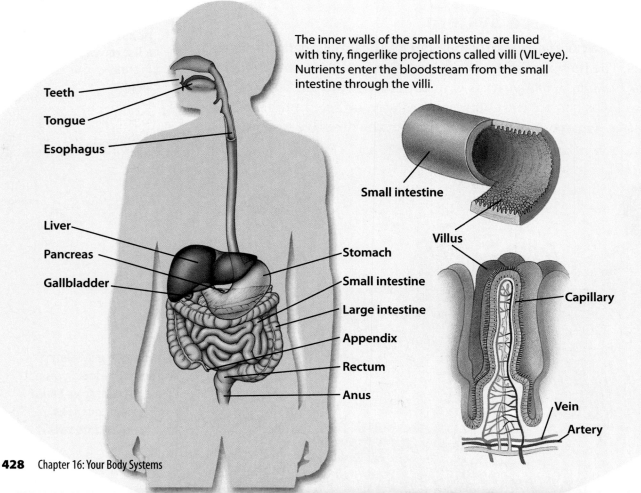

The inner walls of the small intestine are lined with tiny, fingerlike projections called villi (VIL·eye). Nutrients enter the bloodstream from the small intestine through the villi.

Teeth
Tongue
Esophagus
Liver
Pancreas
Gallbladder
Stomach
Small intestine
Large intestine
Appendix
Rectum
Anus
Small intestine
Villus
Capillary
Vein
Artery

The Stomach and the Small Intestine

As food continues its journey through the digestive system, it passes from the mouth to the esophagus. This is a muscular tube that pushes food down into the stomach in a process called *peristalsis* (pehr·uh·STAHL·sis). Peristalsis is a series of involuntary waves that carry food particles along.

Once it has reached the stomach, food continues to be broken down. Glands in the stomach wall release gastric juices, a blend of hydrochloric acid and enzymes. Hydrochloric acid is strong enough to dissolve metal. A protective stomach lining prevents this powerful acid from digesting the stomach itself. Besides breaking down food, the acid kills most of the bacteria contained in the food.

The stomach also serves as a temporary storage area for food that is not ready for further digestion. Some food remains in your stomach for as long as four hours. The rate at which your stomach empties depends on what you ate.

Most of digestion takes place at the next stage, in the small intestine. The **small intestine** is *a coiled, tubelike organ that is about 20 feet long.* It is here that nutrients are separated from the bulk of the food. The nutrients then enter the bloodstream and travel to body cells where they are used for growth, energy, and repair.

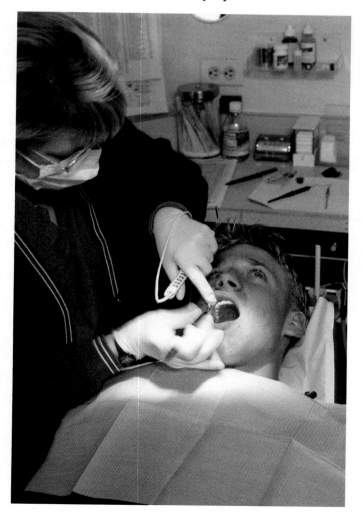

▼ Regular dental checkups will help keep your teeth healthy. **What role in the digestive process do your teeth play?**

Organs That Aid Digestion

The digestive system is assisted in its work by three important organs through which food does not pass. These are the liver, gallbladder, and pancreas. The liver is the second-largest organ in your body. With more than 500 functions, it is also one of your body's busiest organs. To aid digestion, the liver produces *bile,* a substance that helps break down fats.

The gallbladder stores the bile and releases it into the small intestine as needed. The pancreas makes additional digestive enzymes which are released directly into the small intestine.

Reading Check

Explain Explain the role of the liver and pancreas in digestion.

Health Skills Activity

Practicing Healthful Behaviors

Adding Sources of Fiber

Eating high-fiber foods and drinking plenty of water helps move food through the digestive process and protects you against colon cancer, constipation, and diabetes. Fiber also reduces the risk of heart disease. High-fiber foods are also filling, therefore discouraging overeating. To get more fiber from the foods you eat:

- **Start the day with a good breakfast.** If you do not eat breakfast regularly, now is the time to start. Breakfast cereals made with oats or bran are excellent sources of soluble fiber. So are whole-grain muffins.
- **Eat meatless meals several times a week.** Try a bean burrito with cheese at lunch or dinner. The beans will give you a fiber boost.
- **Eat high-fiber snacks.** Popcorn is a great source of fiber, and so are nuts and fruit.

On Your Own

Research additional foods with a high fiber content. Make a list of ways to incorporate these foods into an eating plan.

The Excretory System

Once all the nutrients are extracted from food, all that remains is liquid and solid waste. Body wastes consist of food materials that cannot be digested. Natural plant fiber is one such material. The job of removing this matter from the body falls to the **excretory system**—*your body's waste removal system. The process of removing wastes from the body* is known as **excretion** (ek·SKREE·shuhn).

The Process of Excretion

Food particles that cannot be digested move from the small intestine to *the large intestine,* or **colon** (KOH·luhn). The lining of the colon absorbs much of the liquid contained in this material. Some liquid waste leaves the body through pores in the skin, as perspiration. Other liquid wastes are sent to the **kidneys.** These are *organs that filter water and dissolved wastes from the blood and help maintain proper levels of water and salts in the body.* The waste materials filtered out by the kidneys leave the body as urine. The solid waste products that remain are called *feces* (FEE·seez) and leave the body through the anus (AY·nuhs).

Problems of the Digestive and Excretory Systems

Have you ever overeaten or eaten too fast? The discomfort you may have felt afterward was a warning from your digestive system. Indigestion is your body's way of telling you to eat slowly and to control the amount you eat. If you have diarrhea, or watery feces, your food might have been contaminated with bacteria. Diarrhea can also be a symptom of a more serious colon disease.

Heartburn is a common name for a burning sensation in the center of the chest or throat. Despite its name, it has nothing to do with your heart. Heartburn is a result, rather, of stomach acids flowing backward into the esophagus. This problem is sometimes related to diet but can have other causes as well. If you have heartburn that will not go away, tell your doctor.

Ulcers are sores in the stomach or small intestine. They are painful and may cause internal bleeding. Ulcers are usually caused by bacterial infection. Alcohol use, however, can also be a factor. Alcohol use has also been linked to liver disease and colon cancer.

Other problems that can affect the structure of the digestive and excretory systems include the following:

- **Gallstones and kidney stones.** These are both painful blockages, caused by mineral crystals. Gallstones affect the gallbladder, while kidney stones affect the kidneys.

- **Appendicitis.** This is the inflammation of the appendix. Appendicitis is a serious condition that requires emergency surgery.

- **Hemorrhoids.** These are masses of swollen veins at the opening of the anus. They may be painful and can bleed.

▲ Your body needs plenty of fluids to keep your excretory system working properly. **What are some other ways to keep your excretory system healthy?**

Reading Check

List Identify two problems of the digestive or excretory system.

Care of the Digestive and Excretory Systems

The following suggestions will help you maintain the health of your digestive and excretory systems.

- Eat a variety of healthful foods. Choose low-fat and high-fiber foods from all food groups. Include plenty of fruits and vegetables.

- Do not rush your meals. Taking your time to eat will help prevent you from overloading your digestive system. It will also help you avoid overeating.

- Chew your food thoroughly. Do not try to wash large pieces of food down with a beverage.

- Drink plenty of water. Your digestive system needs water to work properly. Drink six to eight 8-ounce glasses each day.

- Wash your hands regularly. Before preparing or eating food, always wash your hands with soap and water. This will help prevent the spread of bacteria that could upset your digestive system.

Health Online

Visit **health.glencoe.com** and complete the Interactive Study Guide for Lesson 6.

Reading Check **Explain** Why is it important to eat slowly?

Lesson 6 Review

After You Read

Review this lesson for new terms, major headings, and Reading Checks.

What I Learned

1. *Vocabulary* What is *excretion*?

2. *List* Name three organs of the digestive system.

3. *Explain* How does the liver aid digestion?

4. *Identify* Name two habits that will help prevent problems of the digestive and excretory systems.

Thinking Critically

5. *Apply* Explain what happens to an apple from the time you begin eating it to the time that it reaches your colon.

6. *Synthesize* What role does fiber play in the health of the digestive system?

Applying Health Skills

7. *Goal Setting* Identify a behavior that promotes digestive health but which you are not currently practicing. Use the skill of goal setting to help you make this behavior a habit. Share the steps in your action plan with classmates.

Health Online For more review questions for Lesson 6, go to **health.glencoe.com**.

Your Endocrine System

Guide to Reading

● **Building Vocabulary**
As you read this lesson, write each new highlighted term and its definition in your notebook.

- endocrine system (p. 433)
- gland (p. 434)
- pituitary gland (p. 434)

● **Focusing on the Main Ideas**
In this lesson, you will learn to

- **describe** the main function of the endocrine system.
- **explain** the jobs done by different hormones.
- **identify** disorders of the endocrine system.

● **Reading Strategy**
Identifying Cause-and-Effect List several effects caused by glands of the endocrine system.

The Endocrine System and Growth

When you started school this year, were you surprised by how much some classmates had grown? Maybe you underwent a growth spurt yourself that surprised others. Fast growth is common during the teen years. The body system responsible for this and other changes is the **endocrine** (EN·duh·krin) **system.** This is *a chemical communication system that controls many body functions.*

Quick Write

Write what you already know about hormones and the role they play during adolescence.

◀ Hormones secreted by the glands of the endocrine system are responsible for growth. **What other changes are brought about by these glands?**

Parts of the Endocrine System

The endocrine system is made up of glands located throughout your body. A **gland** is *a group of cells or an organ that secretes a substance.* The major glands of the endocrine system include the pituitary, thyroid, parathyroids, adrenals, pineal body, and the reproductive glands. The pancreas is also part of the endocrine system because it releases insulin, a hormone that regulates the level of glucose in the blood. The pancreas also produces enzymes that aid in the digestive process.

The endocrine glands work by responding to signals from the brain or from the **pituitary** (pih·TOO·ih·tehr·ee) **gland.** This is *a gland that signals other endocrine glands to produce hormones when needed.* This pea-sized gland is located at the midpoint of the skull, behind the eyes.

Hormones

The chemicals secreted by the endocrine glands are called *hormones.* Hormones travel in the bloodstream to the cells that need them. Some hormones are produced continuously, while others are produced only at certain times. Each hormone has a specific job. **Figure 16.8** lists some of the hormones released by the endocrine system and their function.

Reading Check **List** Name three glands of the endocrine system.

▼ **FIGURE 16.8**

SELECTED GLANDS AND HORMONES THEY PRODUCE

Glands and hormones are the foundations of the endocrine system. **What is the function of the thyroid gland?**

Gland	Hormone	Function
adrenals	corticosteroids	Regulates salt and water balance, metabolism, the immune system, and the body's response to stress
	adrenaline	Increases heart rate and blood pressure when the body experiences stress
parathyroids	parathyroid	Regulates the level of calcium in the blood
pineal body	melatonin	Regulates the wake-sleep cycle
pituitary	growth	Stimulates the growth of bone and other body tissues
	thyrotropin	Stimulates the thyroid gland to produce thyroid hormones
	corticotropin	Stimulates the adrenal glands to produce certain hormones
thyroid	thyroxine	Regulates the rate at which cells burn fuel from food to produce energy

The Body's Response to Stress

Can you remember the last time you felt restless or nervous? You may have had trouble sitting still or sweaty palms. When your brain recognizes a stressful situation, your adrenal glands release the hormone adrenaline. This hormone allows your body to respond to stress.

Heart rate and blood flow to the brain increase during a stress response. Blood sugar levels and blood pressure rise. Sweat production increases and air passages expand. Digestion and other bodily processes may slow down to conserve energy in other parts of the body. After the stressful stimulus has passed, the body returns to its normal state.

Problems of the Endocrine System

The most common problem of the endocrine system is diabetes. Type 1 diabetes occurs when the pancreas cannot produce enough insulin. Type 2 diabetes occurs when the body cannot use the insulin it produces properly. This usually occurs in people who are overweight and who do not get enough physical activity. Recently, there has been an increase in the number of teens and children with type 2 diabetes. Maintaining a healthy weight and staying physically active can help prevent type 2 diabetes.

Another common endocrine problem is an overactive or underactive thyroid gland. Symptoms of an overactive thyroid gland include swelling in the front of the neck, nervousness, increased sweating, and weight loss. Symptoms of an underactive thyroid gland include tiredness, depression, weight gain, hair loss, and muscle and joint pain.

Connect To... Language Arts

Chemical Messengers

Hormones are chemical messengers secreted by glands in your body. They travel to other parts of the body, helping cells and organs do their work. The word *hormone* comes from the Greek word *horman,* which can mean to "stir up, activate, or set in motion."

Choose one of the glands shown in Figure 16.8. Use a dictionary to find what language its name came from and how the gland's name evolved.

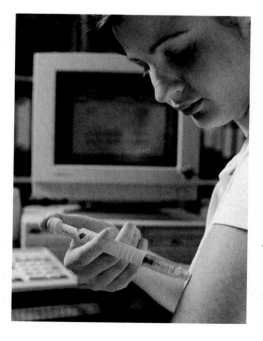

◀ The teen in this picture has diabetes and needs daily shots of insulin. **What can you do to lower your risk of developing diabetes?**

Endocrine problems can also occur in the pituitary gland. When the pituitary gland releases too much growth hormone, it can result in a very tall person. Too little growth hormone can result in a very small person. Many of these and other problems of the endocrine system can be treated with medicine under a doctor's care.

Reading Check **Give Examples** Name two problems of the endocrine system.

Care of the Endocrine System

The best thing you can do to care for the endocrine system is practice good health habits. Regular physical activity, good nutrition, and adequate rest all contribute to endocrine health. Learn to manage stress in healthful ways. Stress can be harmful if it goes on for too long or occurs too often. Regular medical check-ups are also important. Some hormonal disorders have symptoms that are unusual or hard to notice. Your health professional can perform tests to make sure your hormones are working the way they should.

Reading Check **Identify** What are two habits that are good for the endocrine system?

Health Online

Visit health.glencoe.com and complete the Interactive Study Guide for Lesson 7.

Lesson 7 Review

After You Read

Review this lesson for new terms, major headings, and Reading Checks.

What I Learned

1. *Vocabulary* What is a *gland*?

2. *Describe* Name the main function of the endocrine system.

3. *Identify* What hormone is released during a stressful situation?

4. *Recall* What are some common problems of the endocrine system?

Thinking Critically

5. *Analyze* Which gland of the endocrine system do you think is most important? Explain your answer.

6. *Synthesize* In what way is the pancreas part of both the endocrine and the digestive systems?

Applying Health Skills

7. *Advocacy* Type 2 diabetes in children and teens is on the rise. With a group, research this trend. Find out what strategies are available to help reduce the risk of developing type 2 diabetes. Use your findings to create a poster or brochure to inform other teens in your school.

Health Online For more review questions for Lesson 7, go to health.glencoe.com.

Your Reproductive System

Guide to Reading

● **Building Vocabulary**
As you read this lesson, write each new highlighted term and its definition in your notebook.

- reproductive system (p. 437)
- sperm (p. 437)
- hernia (p. 439)
- fertilization (p. 439)
- ovulation (p. 439)
- menstruation (p. 439)
- menstrual cycle (p. 439)

● **Focusing on the Main Ideas**
In this lesson, you will learn to

- **identify** the parts of the male and female reproductive systems.
- **explain** the three functions of the female reproductive system.
- **identify** problems of the male and female reproductive systems.
- **describe** ways to keep your reproductive system healthy.

● **Reading Strategy**
Comparing and Contrasting Make a list of similarities and differences between the male and female reproductive systems.

Quick Write

Write what you think is the single most important thing teens can do to care for their reproductive system.

The Reproductive System

The body systems you have read about so far are the same for both genders. In this lesson, you will learn about the one body system that is different for males and females: the **reproductive system.** This is *the body system containing the organs that make possible the production of offspring.*

The Male Reproductive System

During puberty the testes, the male reproductive glands, produce testosterone, a male hormone. The testes also produce **sperm,** *the male sex cell.* The testes, along with other parts of the male reproductive system, are shown in **Figure 16.9.**

Sperm are stored in the epididymis, a network of tubes located behind the testes. When sperm leave the epididymis, they pass through the vas deferens (vas·DEF·uh·ruhnz). There they mix with secretions from the seminal vesicles, the prostate gland, and the Cowper's glands. This mixture of fluids and sperm is called *semen* (SEE·muhn). Semen exits the penis through *ejaculation* (ih·ja·kyuh·LAY·shuhn), a series of forceful muscular contractions.

MALE REPRODUCTIVE SYSTEM

A Seminal vesicles

B Prostate gland

C Cowper's glands

D The **urethra** (yoo·REE·thruh) is a tube that carries urine and sperm to the outside of the body.

E The **penis** is the external sexual organ.

F The **testes** (TES·teez), or testicles, are two small glands that produce sperm and hormones.

G The **scrotum** (SKROH·tuhm) is a muscular sac that contains the testes.

H The **vas deferens** (vas DEF·uh·ruhnz) are tubes that extend from each epididymis to the urethra.

I Behind each testicle is the **epididymis** (ep·uh·DID·uh·muhs), a network of tubes in which the sperm mature and are stored temporarily.

Problems of the Male Reproductive System

For teen males, a common reproductive-system problem is injury to the testes. Wearing appropriate protective gear during sports is one way to avoid this type of injury. A far more serious problem is cancer of the testes, which is one of the most common cancers for males ages 14 to 34. Testicular cancer can spread to other parts of the body. If it is detected and treated early, however, the person has an excellent chance of recovering.

A **hernia** *occurs when an internal organ pushes against or through a surrounding cavity wall.* The most common type of hernia, inguinal hernia, occurs when the intestine pushes into the scrotum. Eighty percent of all hernias are inguinal. Hernias are mainly caused by incorrect heavy lifting, though other health problems can also be a factor. A hernia appears as a lump or swelling in the groin or lower abdomen. It can be corrected with surgery.

The health of the male reproductive system can also be affected by sexually transmitted diseases (STDs), which are spread through sexual contact. Some STDs if left untreated can cause sterility. Sterility means the person cannot produce offspring.

Reading Check **List** Name two reproductive system problems among teen males.

▲ The woman in this picture just gave birth to a baby. **What part of the female reproductive system nourishes the baby during pregnancy?**

The Female Reproductive System

The female reproductive system shown in **Figure 16.10** has three key functions. The first is to store egg cells. The second function is to create offspring, or babies. New life is formed through the process of fertilization. **Fertilization** (fur·tuhl·lih·ZAY·shuhn) occurs *when a male's sperm cell joins with a female's egg cell.*

Once an egg is fertilized it travels from the fallopian tube to the uterus where it attaches to the wall of the uterus and begins to grow. During the first eight weeks, it is called an embryo. After eight weeks, the embryo becomes a fetus. In approximately nine months, the fetus is mature and is ready to be born. The third function of the female reproductive system is to give birth to the baby.

The Menstrual Cycle

During puberty, egg cells mature and are released by the ovaries in a process called ovulation. **Ovulation** is *the release of one mature egg cell each month.* Just before one of the ovaries releases an egg cell, the uterus lining thickens. The uterus is getting ready to receive and nourish a fertilized egg. If an egg is not fertilized, the lining breaks down and is shed by the body through menstruation (men·stroo·AY·shuhn). **Menstruation** is *when the lining material, the unfertilized egg, and some blood flow out of the body.* Menstruation, also called a period, usually lasts from 5 to 7 days and happens about every 28 days. This cycle is called the menstrual cycle. The **menstrual** (MEN·stroo·uhl) **cycle** results from *hormonal changes that occur in females from the beginning of one menstruation to the next.*

FIGURE 16.10

FEMALE REPRODUCTIVE SYSTEM

A The **ovaries** contain ova, or eggs, and produce hormones.

B The **fallopian** (fuh·LOH·pee·uhn) **tubes** carry eggs from the ovaries to the uterus.

C The **uterus** shelters and nourishes the fetus.

D The **endometrium** is the lining of the uterus.

E The **cervix** (SER·viks) is the opening of the uterus.

F The **vagina** (vuh·JY·nuh) is a muscular passageway from the uterus to outside the body.

For most girls, menstruation begins anywhere from age 9 to age 16. During the first few years of menstruation, the menstrual cycle may be irregular. It is also normal for females to have cramps before or during their period.

Reading Check **Explain** What happens during menstruation?

Problems of the Female Reproductive System

Among the most serious female reproductive problems is cancer. Cancer can occur in the breasts, ovaries, uterus, or cervix. Breast cancer is the second-leading cause of death in women. Other reproductive problems include:

- **Infertility.** This is the inability to get pregnant. It may be due to blocked fallopian tubes or a failure to produce eggs.
- **Ovarian cysts.** These are growths on the ovary. Symptoms of ovarian cysts include a feeling of heaviness in the abdomen and abdominal pain, swelling, and bloating.
- **Sexually transmitted diseases (STDs).** As mentioned earlier, these diseases are spread through sexual contact.

Care of the Reproductive System

Both males and females can maintain the health of their reproductive system by practicing good hygiene. Bathe or shower regularly. Abstain from sexual activity, which will protect you against STDs and unplanned pregnancy.

Males should also avoid wearing tight clothing and check their testes monthly for lumps, swelling, or soreness. Your doctor or other health care professional can show you how to perform a testicular self-exam.

Females should perform a breast self-exam once a month. If you feel any unusual lumps or thickening, see your doctor right away. Females also need to have regular physical exams, beginning at about age 18. Keep a record of your menstrual cycle. Your doctor may need to know how regularly your periods occur and how long they last. During your period, change your tampons or sanitary pads about every four hours. See your doctor if you have severe cramps or unusually heavy bleeding.

Reading Check **Explain** How does abstinence benefit a teen's reproductive health?

Health Online

Visit **health.glencoe.com** and complete the Interactive Study Guide for Lesson 8.

Lesson 8 Review

After You Read

Review this lesson for new terms, major headings, and Reading Checks.

What I Learned

1. *Vocabulary* What is *fertilization*?

2. *List* What are three functions of the female reproductive system?

3. *Describe* Describe two ways to keep your reproductive system healthy.

4. *Identify* What are the male reproductive cells called?

5. *Recall* Name two female reproductive system problems.

Thinking Critically

6. *Analyze* How are the female and male reproductive systems similar? How are they different?

7. *Apply* Mario will be the catcher this year on his baseball team. What special precautions does Mario need to take to prevent injury to his reproductive system?

Applying Health Skills

8. *Accessing Information* Using print or online resources, research how a testicular or breast self-exam is done. When should these exams be performed? Why are they important?

Getting the Facts About Your Body

DIRECTIONS

Accessing Information involves finding reliable information to make healthy choices. This activity will give you the opportunity to develop and master this important health skill. Here's a guide to the different parts of this activity:

❶ In the **Model** section, you will read about a teen who performs the health skill successfully. This "model" scenario will show you how the skill is done.

❷ The **Practice** section will help guide you in practicing the skill.

❸ In the **Apply** section, you will have a chance to perform the skill on your own. You can use the Self-Check to check your work.

To complete this activity, first read the scenario presented in the Model. Then move on to the Practice. Finally, go ahead and try the Apply.

❶ Model

Terry needed a new helmet to wear while riding his bike or skateboarding. Terry used the following steps to find reliable information about helmets.

1. He went to a Web site his health teacher recommended. It was a government-run site for teens about preventing sports injuries.

2. Terry clicked on a link at the Web site. It took him to another site specializing in information about skateboarding safety. The site provided information on selecting a helmet as well as other tips on skateboard safety.

3. Terry's final stop was the sporting goods store. He brought his older brother, Chuck, with him. Terry knew Chuck might think of questions to ask that wouldn't occur to him.

② Practice

Terry recently began playing basketball regularly. Terry remembers from health class that he should warm up before participating in sports, but he needs details—how should he warm up? How long should he spend warming up?

1. Where can Terry go to find this information?
2. How can Terry tell which sources are accurate?
3. Are there places in the community where Terry can get help?

Skill Summary
ACCESSING INFORMATION

Using the skill of accessing information involves:

- Seeking information from reliable sources.
- Asking parents, teachers or others for help.

③ Apply

Choose a body system that you want to learn more about. Use reliable sources of information from school, the Internet, and home to learn at least three new facts about this system. Develop a fact sheet about your body system that includes a diagram of the system, three new facts, and two sources of reliable information. Explain why your sources of information are reliable.

Self-Check

- Did I include a diagram of the body system?
- Did I provide three new facts?
- Did I include two reliable sources?

How Muscles and Bones Work Together

The muscles, bones, and joints in the body work like living levers. They use the same principles used in lifting and moving machines such as cranes. The small movement of one arm of a lever causes a larger movement in the other arm. This activity will show you how to make a model arm. Your finished arm will demonstrate how muscles and bones work together in a system of joints and levers.

What You Will Need

- 2 strips of stiff poster board 10" × 2"
- Hole punch
- Metal fastener
- 2 long balloons
- String

What You Will Do

1. Round off one end of each strip. Punch holes about 1 inch from both ends of one strip. This strip will represent the upper arm. In the other strip, punch one hole about 1 inch from the rounded end. Punch another hole 4 inches from that same end. This strip will be the forearm.

2. With a fastener, loosely join the rounded ends of the two strips. This represents the elbow joint.

3. Slightly inflate the balloons. Tie knots in both ends of each balloon.

4. Tie the end of one balloon to each end of the upper arm. This balloon represents the triceps muscle on the back of the arm. Tie the second balloon between the top of the upper arm and the second hole in the forearm. This represents the biceps muscle.

5. Experiment with moving the upper arm while the elbow joint rests on a surface. Observe what happens to the balloons and to the forearm.

Wrapping It Up

What happens to the biceps when the forearm is extended? What happens when it is closed? How do the triceps and biceps work together? Observe how far the forearm moves when the upper arm is moved a short distance. Compare these distances.

Reading Review

FOLDABLES Study Organizer

Foldables™ and Other Study Aids Take out the Foldable™ that you created for Lesson 1 and any graphic organizers that you created for Lessons 1–8. Find a partner and quiz each other using these study aids.

Lesson 1 Your Skeletal System

Key Ideas

- Functions of the skeletal system include providing a framework capable of movement, supporting and protecting the internal organs, storing minerals, and making blood cells.

Lesson 2 Your Muscular System

Key Ideas

- Functions of the muscular system include allowing movement, pumping blood, moving food through your digestive system, and controlling the movement of air in and out of the lungs.

Lesson 3 Your Circulatory System

Key Ideas

- The circulatory system transports oxygen and nutrients to the body's cells and removes the cells' waste products.

Lesson 4 Your Respiratory System

Key Ideas

- Your respiratory system supplies your body with oxygen and removes carbon dioxide.
- The lungs are the main organ of the respiratory system.

Lesson 5 Your Nervous System

Key Ideas

- The nervous system controls all of your body's actions.
- The nervous system has two parts: the central nervous system and the peripheral nervous system.

Lesson 6 Your Digestive and Excretory Systems

Key Ideas

- Digestion is the process of converting food into energy.
- Excretion is the process of removing wastes from the body.

Lesson 7 Your Endocrine System

Key Ideas

- The main function of the endocrine system is to secrete chemicals, called hormones, that regulate many body functions.

Lesson 8 Your Reproductive System

Key Ideas

- The reproductive system makes it possible to produce offspring, or babies.
- Fertilization occurs when a male's sperm cell joins with a female's egg cell.

After You Read

HEALTH INVENTORY

Now that you have read the chapter, look back at your answers to the Health Inventory on the chapter opener. Is there anything you should do differently?

Reviewing Vocabulary and Main Ideas

On a sheet of paper, write the numbers 1–5. After each number, write the term from the list that best completes each sentence.

- cardiac muscles
- cartilage
- hemoglobin
- joint
- ligaments
- marrow
- skeletal muscles
- smooth muscles

Lesson 1 Your Skeletal System

1. _____ is a soft tissue in the center of some bones.

2. The point at which two bones meet is called a _____.

Lesson 2 Your Muscular System

3. The muscles attached to bones that enable you to move your body are called _____.

4. _____ are found only in the walls of your heart.

Lesson 3 Your Circulatory System

5. Blood gets its red color from a protein called _____.

*On a sheet of paper, write the numbers 6–14. Write **True** or **False** for each statement below. If the statement is false, change the underlined word or phrase to make it true.*

Lesson 4 Your Respiratory System

6. <u>Respiration</u> is the exchange of gases between your body and your environment.

7. The <u>bronchi</u> is a muscle that separates the chest from the abdomen.

Lesson 5 Your Nervous System

8. The <u>peripheral nervous system (PNS)</u> includes the brain and spinal cord.

9. The <u>autonomic</u> system deals with actions that you control.

Lesson 6 Your Digestive and Excretory Systems

10. Enzymes are <u>proteins</u> that affect the rate of many body processes.

11. Another name for the colon is <u>small intestine</u>.

Lesson 7 Your Endocrine System

12. The chemicals secreted by the endocrine glands are called <u>hormones</u>.

Lesson 8 Your Reproductive System

13. <u>Sperm</u> is a mixture of fluids including secretions from the seminal vesicles, prostate gland, and Cowper's glands.

14. The release of one egg cell each month is called <u>fertilization</u>.

Thinking Critically

Using complete sentences, answer the following questions on a sheet of paper.

15. Analyze Which body systems do you think benefit most from positive eating habits? Explain your answer.

16. Explain What happens to an egg cell after it is fertilized?

Write About It

17. Advocacy Choose one of the body systems discussed in the chapter. Write an article for teens on ways they can protect this body system. Include information on the function of this body system and how it can affect other body systems.

Standardized Test Practice

Reading

Read the passage and then answer the questions.

Have you ever heard that cracking your knuckles is harmful? Some people believe this habit can cause skeletal-system problems such as arthritis. It can't. That is just a myth. The popping noise you hear when you flex your knuckles is gas bubbles escaping inside the joint.

Another urban legend about the skeletal system is that people who can bend their fingers far back are double-jointed. There is actually no such thing as being double-jointed. People who can bend their fingers back have the same number of joints that everyone else does. The real difference is that the ligaments surrounding their joints stretch more than normal.

1. The phrase urban legend in the second paragraph seems to mean
   A. city dweller.
   B. knuckle.
   C. joint.
   D. myth.

2. Which statement best captures the main idea of the passage?
   A. Cracking your knuckles is not really harmful.
   B. People who can bend their fingers far back are not really double-jointed.
   C. A number of myths exist about the skeletal system.
   D. Hitting your elbow hurts even if there is no funny bone.

Chapter Preview

▲ *Working With the Photo*

Your teen years are just one of several life stages you will go through. **Can you think of three other stages of life?**

Start-Up Activities

Before You Read What do you already know about growth and development? Take the short Health Quiz on this page. Keep a record of your answers.

HEALTH QUIZ Answer *true* or *false* to each of the following statements:

1. All human life begins as a single cell.
2. Your eye color is inherited from your parents.
3. Physical changes are not common in adolescence.
4. Late adulthood is the time most people start families.

ANSWERS: 1. true; 2. true; 3. false; 4. false

FOLDABLES™ Study Organizer

As You Read Make this Foldable™ to help you organize what you learn in Lesson 1 about the beginnings of life. Begin with a plain sheet of 8½" × 11" paper.

1 Fold the sheet of paper along the long axis, leaving a half-inch tab along the side.

2 Turn the paper, fold it in half, and then fold it in half again.

3 Unfold and cut the top layer along the three fold lines. This makes four tabs.

4 Turn the paper vertically and label the tabs as shown.

Cells
Tissues
Organs
Body Systems

Under the appropriate tab, write down major concepts related to cells, tissues, organs, and body systems.

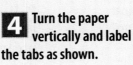 **Health Online** Visit **health.glencoe.com** and use the e-flashcards to preview Chapter 17 vocabulary terms.

The Beginning of Life

Guide to Reading

● Building Vocabulary
Write the terms below in your notebook. As you read the lesson, write down their definitions.

- fertilization (p. 450)
- egg cell (p. 450)
- sperm cell (p. 450)
- uterus (p. 452)
- embryo (p. 452)
- fetus (p. 452)
- placenta (p. 453)
- umbilical cord (p. 453)
- cervix (p. 454)

● Focusing on the Main Ideas
In this lesson you will learn to

- **identify** the building blocks of life.
- **explain** how a single cell develops into a baby.
- **describe** the stages of birth.
- **access** information on the physical and emotional changes a pregnant female experiences.

● Reading Strategy
Analyzing a Graphic Using Figure 17.2 on page 452, summarize the process that a fetus goes through during the months before its birth.

FOLDABLES Study Organizer Use the Foldable™ on p. 449 as you read this lesson.

Quick Write

Write a short paragraph explaining why you think some twins are identical and others are not.

Building Blocks of Life

The cell is the basic unit of life. The human body is composed of trillions of cells, each with its own job to do. Cells that do similar jobs come together to form tissues. Tissues combine to form organs, and organs group together to form body systems. **Figure 17.1** illustrates how cells organize themselves into body systems.

Fertilization

Your body started as a single fertilized cell. **Fertilization** is *the joining together of a male sperm cell and a female egg cell,* to form one cell. *The reproductive cell from the female that joins with a sperm cell to make a new life* is called an **egg cell.** *The cell from the male that enters the egg cell during fertilization* is called a **sperm cell.**

Fertilization takes place in the mother's reproductive system. The egg cell is fertilized in one of her two fallopian tubes. As soon as a sperm cell meets the egg cell, a film is produced around the egg. This prevents any additional sperm cells from entering the egg cell. Once fertilization takes place, a new life begins to grow.

FROM CELL TO SYSTEM

Cells work together in the body to create tissues, organs, and systems. Can you name some of the body's organs?

1. Cells

Cells are the basic building blocks of life. There are many different kinds of cells. Some cells come from the stomach where they play a role in digestion. Other kinds of cells in the body include heart, skin, and nerve cells.

2. Tissues

When cells get together to do similar jobs, tissues are created. There are many kinds of tissues in the body, including muscle tissue and brain tissue.

3. Organ

When tissues combine to form a structure designed to do a particular job, an organ is created. Examples of organs in your body include the heart, kidneys, lungs, and brain.

4. Body System

When organs work together to do a particular job, they form a body system. For example, the digestive system shown here is made up of the mouth, esophagus, stomach, liver, and intestines. These organs work together to help your body digest food. Other systems in the body, such as the circulatory system, have their own jobs. Systems cooperate with one another to keep your body balanced and running smoothly.

Growth During Pregnancy

Once an egg cell is fertilized it travels from the fallopian tube to the uterus. The **uterus** (YOO·tuh·ruhs) is *a pear-shaped organ inside a female's body where the embryo is protected and nourished.* The egg cell begins to divide into a group of cells called a *cluster of cells.* This cluster of cells is an **embryo**—*the developing organism from fertilization to about the eighth week of its development.* The embryo attaches itself to the inside wall of the mother's uterus. Once the embryo is attached to the uterus, the cells continue to divide into cells that do specific jobs.

Over time, cells combine to form tissues. Tissues that do similar jobs combine to form organs, and organs combine to form body systems. By the end of the eighth week, the embryo's organs have started to develop. The embryo is now called a **fetus**—*the developing organism from the end of the eighth week until birth.* The fetus will continue to grow and develop for about nine months. **Figure 17.2** shows how the embryo and fetus develop during those months.

▼ **FIGURE 17.2**

NINE MONTHS OF DEVELOPMENT

In just nine months, a single cell develops into a full-grown baby. **How big is the fetus at the end of the fifth month?**

End of First Month
The heart, brain and lungs of the embryo are forming. It is about one-third of an inch long.

End of Second Month
The heart of the fetus begins to beat, and all other organs are developing. It is about 1 inch long.

End of Third Month
The fetus begins to move around. It weighs about 1 ounce and is about 3 inches long.

End of Fourth Month
The facial features of the fetus are well developed and its mother can feel it move. It weighs about 6 ounces and is about 5 inches long.

End of Fifth Month
The eyelashes and nails of the fetus appear and its heartbeat can be heard. It weighs about 1 pound and is just under 10 inches long.

Growth Inside the Uterus

In order for a fetus to develop, it must get food from its mother. The fetus receives nourishment through the placenta. The **placenta** (plu·SEN·tuh) is *a thick, rich tissue that lines the walls of the uterus during pregnancy and that nourishes the fetus.* The fetus gets food and oxygen through a blood vessel in the **umbilical** (uhm·BIL·i·kuhl) **cord,** *a tube that connects the mother's placenta to the fetus.* The umbilical cord also carries away the wastes produced by the growing fetus.

Substances such as tobacco, alcohol, and other drugs can do harm to a fetus. For that reason, females should avoid using harmful substances when they are pregnant.

Reading Check

Compare What is the difference between an embryo and a fetus?

Health Online

Visit **health.glencoe.com** and complete the Interactive Study Guide for Lesson 1.

End of Sixth Month
The fetus can hear, kick, swallow, and open and close its mouth. It weighs about 1.5 pounds and is about 12.5 inches long.

End of Seventh Month
The fetus can open its eyes and move its arms and legs freely. It weighs about 2 to 2.5 pounds and is about 14.5 inches long.

End of Eighth Month
The fetus's hair is getting longer and its skin becomes smoother. The fetus weighs about 4 pounds and is almost 18 inches long.

End of Ninth Month
The baby's organs are all ready to work on their own. It weighs 7 to 9 pounds and is 18 to 20 inches long.

Stages of Birth

After growing and developing for about nine months inside its mother's body, a fetus is ready to be born. Birth occurs in three stages:

- **Stage One.** The muscles in the uterus begin to squeeze and release gently. These muscle movements, called contractions, mean that birth is starting. At this point, *the entry to the uterus,* called the **cervix,** begins to *dilate,* or open.

▲ Nine months after becoming pregnant, a woman gives birth to her baby. **In which stage of birth are contractions the strongest?**

- **Stage Two.** The cervix continues to dilate, preparing for the baby to pass through. Contractions become very strong, helping to push the baby through the cervix, down the birth canal, and out of the mother's body.

- **Stage Three.** Once the baby is born, the placenta is no longer needed. The muscles of the uterus keep contracting until the placenta is pushed out of the mother's body.

Reading Check

Recall What happens during stage two of birth?

Lesson 1 Review

 After You Read

Review this lesson for new terms, major headings, and Reading Checks.

What I Learned

1. *Vocabulary* Define *fertilization.*

2. *Identify* What structure carries food and oxygen from the mother's body to her developing fetus?

3. *Recall* How is an organ different from a body system?

Thinking Critically

4. *Analyze* How does a woman know that her baby is ready to be born?

5. *Apply* Janice is thinking about having a baby, but she likes to smoke cigarettes. Based on what you learned in this lesson, what advice would you give her?

Applying Health Skills

6. *Accessing Information* A pregnant woman experiences many physical and emotional changes. Use reliable sources to learn more about these changes. Make a list of some of the physical and emotional changes that occur during pregnancy.

Health *Online* For more review questions for Lesson 1, go to **health.glencoe.com.**

Heredity and Environment

Guide to Reading

● Building Vocabulary
Review the terms below. See if you can determine which terms are related to heredity and which terms are related to environment.

- heredity (p. 455)
- chromosomes (p. 456)
- genes (p. 456)
- genetic disorder (p. 456)
- environment (p. 456)
- prenatal care (p. 457)
- birth defects (p. 458)

● Focusing on the Main Ideas
In this lesson you will be able to

- **explain** how characteristics are passed from parent to child.
- **identify** factors that could cause birth defects.
- **explain** the importance of prenatal care.
- **access** information on your family's health history.

● Reading Strategy
Finding the Main Idea Read the main headings in this lesson. For each heading, write one sentence that describes the main idea.

Quick Write

What steps should a pregnant woman take to care for herself and her developing baby?

The One and Only You

Each and every person is a one-of-a-kind individual. This means that no two people share exactly the same looks, personality, or abilities. Many factors influence the way a person develops. Some factors are related to heredity, and others are environmental factors.

Heredity

Heredity is *the passing of traits from parents to their children.* Traits include characteristics such as eye color, hair color, and body shape. Inherited traits can also include talents and abilities. Children can also inherit a tendency to develop certain diseases and other health problems.

▶ The genetic information passed from parent to child can mean that they look a lot alike. **What are some of the physical traits that this parent and child share?**

▲ A fetus needs nourishment to grow. **How does a fetus receive the food and oxygen it needs?**

Traits are passed on through chromosomes and genes. **Chromosomes** are *threadlike structures found within the nucleus of a cell that carry the codes for inherited traits.* All but two kinds of cells in the human body have 46 chromosomes positioned in pairs. Sperm and egg cells contain only 23 chromosomes. When a sperm and egg cell combine, the newly formed cell will have 46 chromosomes—23 from the sperm cell and 23 from the egg cell.

The tiny bits of information carried in chromosomes are called **genes**—*the basic units of heredity.* Genes carry codes for traits such as eye color and height. Each child inherits different combinations of chromosomes and genes from his or her parent. This means that even children with the same parents do not look exactly the same, or have the same personality.

Genetic Disorders

When the genes from one or both parents are abnormal or changed in some way a baby can be born with a **genetic** (juh·NE·tik) **disorder.** This is *a disorder caused partly or completely by a defect in genes.* A defect is a flaw or the absence of something needed.

Genetic disorders can occur when a fertilized egg has more or fewer than 46 chromosomes. For example, people with Down syndrome have an extra chromosome that causes them to have certain facial features and learning disabilities.

Other genetic disorders are caused by abnormal or defective genes. Sickle-cell anemia is a blood disorder caused by an abnormal gene. People with this disorder have abnormally shaped red blood cells that can block blood vessels and cause pain in the bones and joints.

Reading Check   **Explain** What role do genes play in heredity.

Environment

As a fetus develops, its health is affected by its environment. **Environment** is *the sum total of a person's surroundings.* A fetus's environment is its mother's uterus. If the mother is unhealthy or engages in harmful activities, the fetus can be affected. A healthy mother is more likely to have a healthy baby.

Accessing Information

Your Family's Health History

Researching your family's health history will let you know if you are at risk for developing certain diseases. It will also help you make healthy decisions that can prevent or lower your risk of disease. One way to learn about the health histories of family members is to create a questionnaire and ask them to fill it out. You will want to know what diseases or other health problems your family members have now or have had in the past.

On Your Own

Brainstorm a list of questions to include on a health history questionnaire. Create the questionnaire and give it to your parents, their siblings, and—if possible—your grandparents. Also ask your grandparents about diseases or other health problems their parents may have had.

Prenatal Care

When a female learns that she is pregnant, it is important that she begin prenatal care right away. **Prenatal** (pree·NAY·tuhl) **care** includes *steps taken to provide for the health of a pregnant female and her baby.* Prenatal care includes regular visits to an obstetrician (ahb·stuh·TRI·shuhn). This is a doctor whose specialty is the care of a pregnant female and her unborn child. During a regular visit, the obstetrician may look at the baby using ultrasound. This technology uses sound waves to form a picture of the fetus in its mother's uterus. Doctors use these pictures to check the growth of the fetus and to detect any problems that might exist. A good prenatal program also includes the following positive health behaviors:

- Eating healthful foods
- Participating in moderate exercise
- Getting plenty of rest
- Avoiding alcohol, tobacco, and other drugs
- Talking to a doctor or other health care provider before taking any medicines

Reading Check

List Name two health behaviors that are part of a good prenatal program.

Treatment of a Premature Infant

When a baby is born premature, he or she may be taken to the neonatal intensive care unit of the hospital. Here, sick and extremely premature infants will receive additional treatment, depending on the nature of their medical condition. Babies who need help breathing are given a ventilator or oxygen tube. Some require medication, and sometimes even surgery.

▼ Using alcohol during pregnancy can result in premature birth and low birth weight. **What factors help determine whether or not a baby will be born healthy?**

Birth Defects

Birth defects are *abnormalities present at birth that cause physical or mental disability or death*. Good prenatal care can help prevent birth defects. Some birth defects, however, are caused by genetic disorders or problems with the fetus's environment. For example, certain infections during pregnancy can cause birth defects.

The following are six kinds of environmental factors that can contribute to a birth defect:

Poor Nutrition

One way a mother can make sure she has a healthy baby is to eat well while she is pregnant. While in the uterus, the fetus relies on its mother for all of its needs. If a mother has an unhealthy diet, her baby could be born prematurely, or too soon. The baby may also have a low birth weight and is at risk of developing physical and mental problems.

Alcohol Use

Everything a pregnant woman drinks is carried in her blood to the fetus. Alcohol makes it difficult for the baby to get the oxygen and nourishment it needs for cell development. If a woman drinks during pregnancy, her baby may develop fetal alcohol syndrome (FAS). Children born with FAS may have physical problems and learning disabilities. Women who are pregnant, or want to become pregnant, should avoid using alcohol.

Medicine and Other Drugs

Medicines and other drugs affect both the mother and her baby. Pregnant women should take only medicines that are approved by a doctor or other health care provider. If a pregnant woman takes certain illegal drugs or prescription drugs, her baby may be born with a drug addiction.

Infections

When a pregnant woman develops an infection, it can sometimes cause serious harm to the fetus. For example, if a woman develops Rubella (German measles) during pregnancy, her baby might be born deaf or suffer from other health problems. To avoid serious problems, women should be vaccinated against certain diseases before they become pregnant.

▶ Smoking during pregnancy can negatively affect a fetus's health. **What other behaviors during pregnancy affect the health of the unborn child?**

SURGEON GENERAL'S WARNING: Smoking By Pregnant Women May Result in Fetal Injury, Premature Birth, And Low Birth Weight.

Tobacco

When a pregnant woman smokes or spends time around smokers, she risks damaging the health of her unborn child. Tobacco can have a negative effect on a fetus's growth and cause it to be born prematurely. Babies whose mothers smoke while pregnant are also at risk of having a low birth weight.

STDs

Certain sexually transmitted diseases (STDs) can be passed from a mother to her fetus causing serious health problems. Herpes and syphilis are two examples. A mother infected with herpes or syphilis may not even know it because there may be no visible symptoms. STDs can cause brain damage, blindness, and even death. A pregnant woman who thinks she might have an STD should talk to her doctor immediately.

Health Online

Visit **health.glencoe.com** and complete the Interactive Study Guide for Lesson 2.

Lesson 2 Review

After You Read

Review this lesson for new terms, major headings, and Reading Checks.

What I Learned

1. *Vocabulary* Define *prenatal care.*

2. *Identify* What are the structures in the nucleus of every cell that carry genetic information?

3. *Give Examples* List two substances that could harm a fetus if its mother takes them into her body while she is pregnant.

Thinking Critically

4. *Analyze* Why should a pregnant female be concerned if she gets sick before she has her baby?

5. *Apply* Cynthia's aunt just learned that she is pregnant. Cynthia knows that her aunt wants to do everything she can to have a healthy baby. What could Cynthia do to help her aunt stay healthy?

Applying Health Skills

6. *Advocacy* Create a brochure that will encourage pregnant women to practice positive health behaviors during their pregnancies. Include actions they can take to stay healthy as well as behaviors they should avoid.

From Childhood to Adolescence

Guide to Reading

Building Vocabulary
In your own words, write the definition of each of the following terms. Check to see if you are correct as you read the lesson.

- developmental tasks (p. 460)
- infancy (p. 462)
- toddlers (p. 462)
- preschoolers (p. 462)
- puberty (p. 463)

Focusing on the Main Ideas
In this lesson, you will learn to

- **explain** Erikson's stages of life.
- **identify** some developmental tasks facing adolescents.
- **describe** the stages of childhood.
- **practice** stress management to help you cope with mood swings.

Reading Strategy
Predicting Look over the headings in this lesson. Write a question that you think the lesson will answer. When you are finished reading the lesson, see if your question has been answered.

Quick Write

Make a list of all the ways you think adolescence is different from childhood.

Stages of Development

From the day a baby is born, he or she begins to develop in all three areas of the health triangle. The process of developing from a baby to an adult is often explained in stages or steps. According to psychologist Erik Erikson, there are eight stages in the human life cycle. Each stage has its own **developmental tasks.** These are *events that need to happen in order for you to grow toward becoming a healthy, mature adult.* The eight stages of life and their developmental tasks are illustrated in **Figure 17.3.**

When people master the developmental tasks in one stage and move on to the next stage, they improve their emotional and social health. They build confidence and are better able to relate to others.

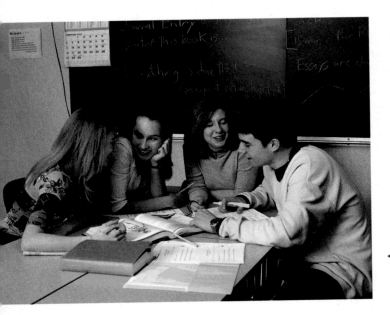

◄ One developmental task of adolescence is to find and express your unique self. **What makes you unique?**

▼ FIGURE 17.3

ERIKSON'S STAGES OF LIFE

In each stage, there is a developmental task that involves relating to other people. **What is the developmental task for late childhood?**

❶ Infancy
Birth to 1 year
Characteristic of stage: child must depend on others to meet every need
Developmental task: learn to trust

❷ Early Childhood
1 to 3 years
Characteristic of stage: child is learning to do things on his or her own
Developmental task: to develop the ability to do things for oneself

❸ Middle Childhood
3 to 5 years
Characteristic of stage: child begins to make decisions and to think of and carry out tasks
Developmental task: to develop initiative — ability to create one's own play

❹ Late Childhood
6 to 11 years
Characteristic of stage: child explores surroundings and masters more difficult skills
Developmental task: to develop interest in performing activities

❺ Adolescence
12 to 18 years
Characteristic of stage: adolescent searches for his or her own identity
Developmental task: to develop a sense of who one is

❻ Young Adulthood
19 to 30 years
Characteristic of stage: young adult tries to establish close personal relationships
Developmental task: to develop intimacy — a strong relationship with another person

❼ Middle Adulthood
31 to 60 years
Characteristic of stage: adult focuses on accomplishment in workplace and is concerned with the well-being of others
Developmental task: to develop the sense of having contributed to society

❽ Maturity and Old Age
61 years to death
Characteristic of stage: person reflects on and tries to understand meaning of own life
Developmental task: to develop a sense of satisfaction with one's life

Stages of Childhood

The physical and mental/emotional growth that occurs during childhood can be grouped into four stages. These stages are called infancy, early childhood, middle childhood, and late childhood.

Infancy

The first year of life is called **infancy.** During infancy, a child doubles in height and triples in weight. A child begins to move around and to explore the world during the first year of life. When an infant's needs are met in a loving and consistent way, he or she learns to trust people and feel safe.

Early Childhood

Toddlers are *children between the ages of one and three who are learning to walk and talk.* This is an exciting time for children. They are learning to do things on their own. They are also running into stumbling blocks along the way. As children explore and test their abilities, they learn a lot from their failures as well as their successes.

Middle Childhood

Children between the ages of three and five are often called **preschoolers.** This age is a time of curiosity when children ask a lot of questions and use their imaginations. They often enjoy pretending to be adults, so how adults behave around them is important. Preschoolers need lots of encouragement and praise for trying new things. This praise helps them feel good about themselves and builds positive self-esteem. An adult or older sibling who is critical or impatient can lower a child's self-esteem.

As preschoolers grow, they develop better physical coordination. They like to use their bodies in active play, such as drawing pictures and jumping rope.

Late Childhood

Between the ages of six and eleven, school becomes an important part of most children's lives. At school they practice social skills, make friends, and discover a whole world outside their families. At this stage, children's physical growth is a little slower and steadier. This is a creative time, and many children put a lot of energy into artistic projects such as drawing and building.

Adolescence

Adolescence is a time when you are no longer a young child, but are not yet an adult. During adolescence, you will experience many physical, mental/emotional, and social changes. These changes will help prepare you for adulthood.

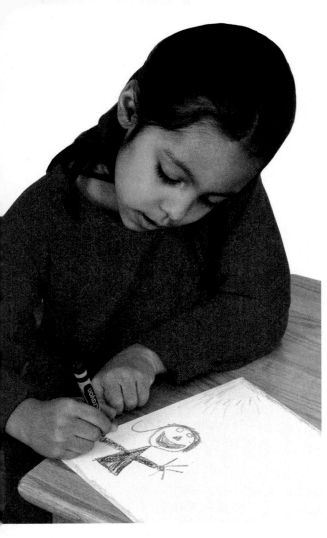

▲ Creativity plays an important role in a child's development. **Why do you think it is so important for young children to be proud of their creative projects?**

Physical Development

After infancy, the second-fastest period of physical growth is adolescence. These physical changes are the result of puberty. **Puberty** is *the time when you start developing physical characteristics of adults of your gender.* Puberty usually starts between the ages of 8 and 14. Most girls typically begin puberty earlier than boys do, but this is not always the case. Each individual grows and develops at his or her own rate. Many of the physical changes that males and females go through during puberty are listed in **Figure 17.4.** These changes are the result of hormones produced by the body's endocrine system.

▼ FIGURE 17.4

PHYSICAL CHANGES DURING PUBERTY

Males and females go through a variety of changes. How are they similar and how are they different?

Female	Both	Male
• Female hormone production increases. • Breasts develop. • Hips get wider. • Uterus and ovaries enlarge. • Ovulation occurs. • Menstruation begins. • Body fat increases.	• Growth spurt occurs. • Acne may appear. • Perspiration increases. • Pubic hair appears. • Underarm hair appears. • External genitals enlarge. • Most permanent teeth have come in.	• Male hormone production increases. • Facial hair appears. • The larynx enlarges and the voice gets deeper. • Shoulders broaden. • Muscles develop. • Sperm production begins. • Breasts can become tender and enlarged temporarily.

Health Skills Activity

Stress Management

Coping with Mood Swings

The mood swings you experience during your teen years can feel like you are on an emotional roller coaster. Below are some tips for dealing with mood swings in healthful ways.

- **Do something nice for yourself.** For example, listen to your favorite music or get together with a friend.
- **Be creative.** Write about what you are feeling or express your emotions through painting or another form of artwork.
- **Get moving.** Physical activities help the body stay in balance. They will also help take your mind off whatever is bothering you.
- **Get some help.** When you are sad or angry it is easy to feel alone. Talk to friends, family, or other trusted adults about what you are feeling.
- **Get some rest.** With all the changes going on in your body, extra rest can really help. Try taking a nap or just relaxing with a book or magazine.
- **Eat well.** Help your body through its many changes by eating nutritious foods.

On Your Own

Create a poster for teens listing healthful ways to cope with mood swings. Include the tips described above and other suggestions you can think of. With permission, hang your posters where other students can see them.

Emotional Development

Emotional changes are a normal part of adolescence. The hormones that control your physical growth and development can also affect your thoughts and feelings. You begin to think and act more independently. You are aware of how your opinions and actions affect others. You might have mood swings, where you are happy one minute and sad the next. Mood swings can be confusing and unpleasant, but they are a normal part of adolescence.

You cannot control your hormones or the emotional changes they cause. You can, however, control your response to these changes. Express your emotions in healthy ways. Talk about your feelings with others. Do activities that help you relax. Listen to music, play sports, take a walk, or spend time with family and friends. Managing your emotions in a healthy way will help you build strong emotional health.

Social Development

As you make the transition from child to adult, you face developmental tasks. These tasks help you develop your self-concept, or the view you have of yourself. They also help you grow socially, by helping you relate to others in a positive way. As you master these developmental tasks, you are preparing for a successful transition to adulthood. Here are some of those tasks:

- Establish independence from your parents and other adults.
- Spend time alone and learn more about yourself.
- Consider what is important to you in life.
- Approach life like an adult, using your intelligence and reason to solve problems.
- Accept your body and its characteristics.
- Form mature relationships with people of both genders.
- Become interested in your community and show that you care about it.

Health Online

Visit **health.glencoe.com** and complete the Interactive Study Guide for Lesson 3.

Reading Check **Identify** What are two developmental tasks associated with adolescence?

Lesson 3 Review

After You Read

Review this lesson for new terms, major headings, and Reading Checks.

What I Learned

1. **Vocabulary** Define *puberty*.

2. **Identify** What are the four main stages of childhood?

3. **Give Examples** List three physical changes that females experience during puberty, and three that males experience.

Thinking Critically

4. **Analyze** Why is it important for adults to support and encourage children?

5. **Apply** Kottiya seems to be on an emotional roller coaster every day. She was cheerful and talkative this morning, but she felt sad and grumpy at lunchtime. All of these emotions leave her feeling confused and worried. What advice would you give Kottiya to help her understand and cope with her mood swings?

Applying Health Skills

6. **Analyzing Influences** Look at several teen magazines. In what ways do the articles, advertisements, and photos try to influence teens? Give an example of a positive influence and an example of a negative influence.

Adulthood and Aging

Guide to Reading

Building Vocabulary
Chrono is the Greek word for "time." Choose the term from the list below that you think describes a person's age by the number of years lived. Write down what you think the definitions are for the other two terms. Check your definitions as you read.

- chronological age (p. 468)
- biological age (p. 468)
- social age (p. 468)

Focusing on the Main Ideas
In this lesson, you will learn to

- **identify** the three stages of adulthood.
- **explain** the difference between chronological, biological, and social age.
- **describe** how to keep your health triangle in balance during your later years.

Reading Strategy
Organizing Information Create a chart that is divided into three parts. Describe one of the stages of adulthood in each of the three parts.

Quick Write

Pretend that you are an older person. Write a letter to the person you are now. What kinds of stories or advice would the older you want to share with the younger you?

Stages of Adulthood

Like childhood, adulthood can be divided into stages. These stages are early, middle, and late adulthood. Each stage is marked by certain milestones such as starting a career, raising children, retiring, and so on. While many people go through these stages in a predictable way, some do not. For example, some adults choose to marry later in life or not at all. Some adults retire early, while others continue working as long as they can.

▶ For many people, establishing a career is an important part of early adulthood. **What do you think your goals will be when you reach early adulthood?**

Early Adulthood

In early adulthood, many people are busy pursuing an education or training for a job or career. They may try several different jobs before they find something they enjoy doing. People form new interests and friendships during this stage. This is also the time when many people choose to get married and start a family. Some people, however, wait until middle adulthood to marry or have children.

Middle Adulthood

At the beginning of this stage, many people are focused on advancing in their jobs. This could mean developing new skills or taking on more responsibility at work. This stage is also a time when many people are raising children. People in middle adulthood are often interested in contributing to their communities. They may volunteer to help young people or raise money for their favorite charity. As people move through middle adulthood, they may begin planning for retirement. Some people may even choose to retire early during this stage.

Late Adulthood

This stage begins around age 60 when many people look forward to retiring from their jobs. When people retire, they often pursue interests they did not have time for while they were working or raising children. Some people continue to work during late adulthood and some pursue new careers. People at this stage may also choose to stay active by doing volunteer work or spending time with their grandchildren. Maintaining good health will help you stay active during late adulthood. Develop good eating and exercise habits now during your teen years. People who develop good habits early are more likely to stick with them later in life.

Reading Check **Compare** What is the difference between early and middle adulthood?

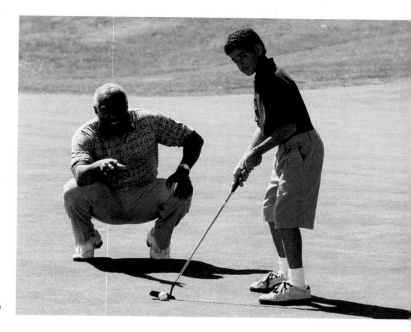

▶ Staying active and being involved with people of all ages is fun for everyone. **Can you think of other sports or activities that older and younger people can enjoy together?**

▼ When you stay active, biological age may be younger than chronological age. **How can actions as a teen affect your biological age as you reach late adulthood?**

Measuring Age

Many older people will tell you they feel much younger than their years. As you get older, good health and a positive attitude can help you feel younger than you are. Age can be measured in three different ways:

- **Chronological** (krah·nuh·LAH·ji·kuhl) **age.** You learned earlier that *chrono* is the Greek word for "time." Therefore, your **chronological age** is your *age measured in years*. It is the amount of time you have been living since you were born. You have no control over this number.

- **Biological age.** *Age determined by how well various body parts are working* is your **biological age.** It is affected by diet, exercise, and heredity, among other factors. If you make healthy choices throughout your life, your body will stay healthier longer. However, physical changes will occur naturally as your body ages—no matter how healthy you are.

- **Social age.** *Age measured by your lifestyle and the connections you have with others* is your **social age.** Social age has to do with the activities that society expects you to participate in at certain stages of life. For example, as a young child you were expected to grow, learn, and play. As an adult, you will be expected to work and perhaps contribute to your community. Some adults choose to delay entering the workforce or accepting other responsibilities. These people may have a younger social age than other adults of similar age.

Reading Check   **Recall** Name the three different ways to measure age.

Aging: A Positive Experience

Good health is an important part of the aging process. That is why older people need to pay attention to the health triangle, just as teens do. When adults are careful to keep all sides of their triangle in balance, they help to make their later years rewarding and productive. Here are some tips for keeping your health triangle balanced during late adulthood:

- **Physical health.** Older adults who take care of their physical health usually have a biological age that is younger than their chronological age. They may face fewer illnesses and disabilities that could prevent them from enjoying themselves.

▶ This adult is volunteering to help children become skilled readers. **How do they both benefit from this relationship?**

- **Mental and emotional health.** Staying mentally active is just as important as being physically active. Older adults who read, take classes, work, or volunteer are more likely to maintain good mental/emotional health.

- **Social health.** Being involved with other people is important to good social health. When older people stay in contact with family and friends, they are better able to cope with the challenges of aging.

Reading Check

Identify Why is it important for older adults to keep their health triangles balanced?

Health *Online*

Visit **health.glencoe.com** and complete the Interactive Study Guide for Lesson 4.

Lesson 4 Review

After You Read

Review this lesson for new terms, major headings, and Reading Checks.

What I Learned

1. *Vocabulary* Define *social age*.

2. *Compare and Contrast* How is chronological age different from biological age?

3. *Give Examples* List three things that adults are usually focused on during early adulthood.

Thinking Critically

4. *Analyze* How can developing good health habits as a teen affect your adult years?

5. *Apply* Stan thought he would spend all his time working in his garden when he retired. After only a few months, however, he began to feel that gardening was not enough. He missed his friends at work, and he felt lonely. What would you suggest that Stan do to bring his health triangle into balance?

Applying Health Skills

6. *Setting Goals* Choose a goal you would like to accomplish during your adulthood. Using the goal-setting process, develop a plan to achieve your goal. List the steps you can take now as a teen to help you reach this goal.

Building Health Skills

PRACTICING HEALTHFUL BEHAVIORS

Coping With the Highs and Lows of Puberty

DIRECTIONS

Practing Healthful Behaviors involves taking specific actions to stay healthy and avoid risky behaviors. This activity will give you the opportunity to develop and master this important health skill. Here's a guide to the different parts of this activity:

❶ In the **Model** section, you will read about a teen who performs the health skill successfully. This "model" scenario will show you how the skill is done.

❷ The **Practice** section will help guide you in practicing the skill.

❸ In the **Apply** section, you will have a chance to perform the skill on your own. You can use the Self-Check to check your work.

To complete this activity, first read the scenario presented in the Model. Then move on to the Practice. Finally, go ahead and try the Apply.

❶ Model

Theresa has been experiencing a lot of highs and lows lately. One morning she woke up in a great mood. At school she felt tired and irritable and did not want to talk to her friends at lunch. By early afternoon, she was feeling happy again and really enjoyed softball practice. Her good mood lasted until after dinner, when her mother asked her to take out the trash.

The next day, Theresa talked to the counselor at school. She gave Theresa the following practical tips for coping with her changing emotions.

1. Ask yourself what you are feeling and why.

2. Express what you are feeling. Try talking to someone, writing in a journal, painting, or dancing.

3. Find a way to relax. Try exercising, listening to music, or doing some deep breathing exercises.

4. Ask for help if you need it.

② Practice

Theresa was having another roller-coaster day. She was feeling pretty good until she got to school and discovered that she had gotten a low grade on her English paper. This made her so upset that she ran to the bathroom and cried. She felt like her whole life was a mess.

1. What was Theresa feeling, and why?
2. What steps can Theresa take to cope with her changing emotions?
3. What are some healthful ways that Theresa could express her feelings?

③ Apply

Think of a day when your emotions seemed to change all the time. Make a chart of how your emotions changed throughout the day. Divide a piece of paper into six parts. Label the parts: morning, mid-morning, lunch, afternoon, early evening, and night.

1. Write the emotions you felt under each part.
2. Tell how you could express each feeling in a positive way.
3. On the back of your paper, list one way that would help you relax.
4. Finally, write the name of someone you can ask for help when you need it.

Self-Check

■ Did I identify what I was feeling and why?
■ Did I tell how to express my emotions in a positive way?
■ Did I list one way to relax?
■ Did I name someone who can help?

Secrets of a
LONG LIFE

Why do some people live long? One woman may have had the answer.

What do you eat? Are you a non-smoker? Are you physically active? Do you have a healthy attitude? Do you keep stress under control? How about your genes—have your relatives lived long lives?

Scientists say responses to these questions can indicate how long a person will live. Here is the story of one woman who may have had all the right answers.

Verona Johnston

A Sharp Mind

Verona Johnston was 114 when she died in December 2004. Until her death, she was the oldest documented person in the United States. TIME spoke with her a few months before she died about her secret of longevity.

"I can remember names pretty well," said Johnston. She lived on her own until age 98 but then moved in with her daughter, Julie Johnston, 81. In fact, Verona Johnston's mind was so sharp until her death, that she solved word jumbles in her head and remembered joke punch lines.

At 114, her vision was nearly gone, and she relied on a cane to take steps, but Johnston could still hear fairly well. Did she dwell on what age had taken away from her? "No. She was never a complainer," says daughter Julie. That attitude may have had

much to do with Verona's long life. Not to mention good genes and a whopping dose of good luck.

Small Portions Mean Big Paybacks

Verona had always been big on moderation. At 114, her daily snack consisted of orange juice and exactly one cracker, one cinnamon-drop candy, and one cashew. "That's enough," she insisted.

Johnston never smoked. As for exercise, it was always part of her active lifestyle. Well into her 90s, she climbed up and down seven flights of stairs to her old apartment.

Verona knew how to roll with changes. "Electricity was the most important thing that happened to us," she reflected. The computer was intimidating, but she gave it a whirl. For Verona, every day brought exciting surprises. That curiosity may have been just one more reason for her long and healthy life.

Reading Review

Lesson 1 The Beginning of Life

Key Ideas

- The cell is the basic building block of life.
- Cells combine to form tissues, tissues combine to form organs, and organs work together to form body systems.
- Two sex cells, one female and one male, combine to create a fertilized cell that will develop into a baby.
- It takes about nine months for a fetus to develop into a full-grown baby inside the mother's uterus.

Vocabulary

- fertilization (p. 450)
- egg cell (p. 450)
- sperm cell (p. 450)
- uterus (p. 452)
- embryo (p. 452)
- fetus (p. 452)
- placenta (p. 453)
- umbilical cord (p. 453)
- cervix (p. 454)

Lesson 2 Heredity and Environment

Key Ideas

- Chromosomes and genes carry the information that parents pass on to their children.
- Genetic disorders are problems caused when the genetic material is damaged or changed in some way.
- A pregnant female needs to take good care of her body to help prevent birth defects.

Vocabulary

- heredity (p. 455)
- chromosomes (p. 456)
- genes (p. 456)
- genetic disorder (p. 456)
- environment (p. 456)
- prenatal care (p. 457)
- birth defects (p. 458)

Lesson 3 From Childhood to Adolescence

Key Ideas

- All human beings go through stages as they develop from infants to adults.
- The stages of development involve physical, mental/emotional, and social changes.
- Adolescence is a time of transition from child to adult.
- Puberty is the time during adolescence when your body changes to take on the physical characteristics of your gender.

Vocabulary

- developmental tasks (p. 460)
- infancy (p. 462)
- toddlers (p. 462)
- preschoolers (p. 462)
- puberty (p. 463)

Lesson 4 Adulthood and Aging

Key Ideas

- Adulthood can be divided into three stages: early, middle, and late.
- All adults do not age at the same rate or in the same way.
- There are three ways to measure age: chronological, biological, and social.
- Older adults need to focus on all three sides of their health triangle in order to stay healthy and active.

Vocabulary

- chronological age (p. 468)
- biological age (p. 468)
- social age (p. 468)

📖 **After You Read**

HEALTH QUIZ

Now that you have read the chapter, look back at your answers to the Health Quiz on the chapter opener. Would you change any of them? What would your answers be now?

Reviewing Vocabulary and Concepts

On a sheet of paper, write the numbers 1–5. After each number, write the term from the list that best completes each statement.

- fetus
- sperm cell
- prenatal care
- uterus
- chromosomes
- obstetrician
- placenta
- umbilical cord
- cervix

Lesson 1) The Beginning of Life

1. The _____ must unite with the egg cell in order for fertilization to occur.

2. In order for a baby to be born, the mother's _____ has to widen so the baby can pass through.

3. A baby develops in its mother's _____.

Lesson 2) Heredity and Environment

4. When a woman becomes pregnant, she needs to see an _____ for regular check-ups.

5. Each parent contributes 23 _____ to create an embryo.

Lesson 3) From Childhood to Adolescence

On a sheet of paper, write the numbers 6–7. After each number, write the letter of the answer that best completes each statement.

6. The time when a child doubles in height and triples in weight is _____.

    a. early childhood   **c.** infancy

    b. adolescence   **d.** late childhood

7. There are _____ stages of life according to scientist Erik Erikson.

    a. eight   **c.** three

    b. six   **d.** ten

Lesson 4) Adulthood and Aging

On a sheet of paper, write the numbers 8–11. Write **True** *or* **False** *for each statement below. If the statement is false, change the underlined word or phrase to make it true.*

8. All adults age at the <u>same</u> time and in the <u>same</u> way.

9. <u>Middle</u> adulthood is when most people retire from their jobs.

10. The age determined by how well your body parts are working is your <u>chronological</u> age.

11. Volunteering is one way for older adults to build good <u>mental/emotional</u> health.

Thinking Critically

Using complete sentences, answer the following questions on a sheet of paper.

12. **Interpret** How might the environment inside a mother's uterus affect her baby's health?

13. **Analyze** What are some ways an older adult can keep his or her health triangle balanced?

Write About It

14. **Accessing Information** Find out what organizations in your community pair teens and older adults. Then, write a short letter to the editor of your school paper describing these projects.

Career Corner

Genetic Counselor Genetic counselors help people who have family members with birth defects or a history of health problems caused by a genetic disorder. They work as members of a complete medical team, and they help identify people who might be at risk for genetic problems. They also offer counseling and support to families, and can help them get assistance from community or state services. To become a genetic counselor, you need a master's degree in genetic counseling, and you need to pass a certification test. Read more about this and other health careers by clicking on *Career Corner* at **health.glencoe.com**.

Standardized Test Practice

Reading

Read the passage and then answer the questions.

In addition to physical changes, puberty brings with it many emotional changes. During puberty, young people develop intense friendships, especially with members of the same sex. They care a lot about what other people think, and they want to be liked and accepted by their friends. Sometimes they may want to spend more time with friends and less time with family. This can be a difficult time of adjustment for parents and guardians, who are used to being the center of their child's life.

Many pre-teens feel anxious or self-conscious about the physical changes of puberty. This is especially true when they compare themselves with others. Young people need to be aware that while their friends may grow at different rates, they will eventually catch up with one another. During puberty, many parents also notice their child's moods change quickly and often. Although it can be frustrating, parents need to remember that these mood swings are normal and are probably related to changes in hormone levels in the body.

1. When young people go through puberty, they experience the following emotional changes *except*
   A. They have intense friendships with members of the same sex.
   B. They care deeply about what other people think.
   C. They do not care if they are liked or not.
   D. Sometimes they may want to spend more time with friends and less time with family.

2. During puberty, many parents may notice that their child's moods can
   A. remain steady.
   B. always be positive.
   C. always be negative.
   D. can change quickly and often.

18 Communicable Diseases

Chapter Preview

▲ *Working With the Photo*

You can protect yourself against some communicable diseases by wearing appropriate clothing during certain outdoor activities. **Do you know some other ways to prevent the spread of disease?**

Start-Up Activities

Before You Read Look at the Instant Message below. What would you tell AlinaGLUV? Keep a record of your answer.

IM *Express*

> **Corndog54:** I feel lousy. I think I'm getting the flu.☹
>
> **AlinaGLUV:** Maybe you should stay home...but we have that big test tomorrow in health.

FOLDABLES™ Study Organizer

As You Read Make this Foldable™ to help you record main ideas about the causes of communicable diseases. Begin with a plain sheet of 11″ × 17″ paper.

1 Hold the paper like a placemat. Fold the short sides inward so they meet in the middle.

2 Fold the top to the bottom.

3 Open and cut along the inside fold lines. This makes four tabs.

4 Label the tabs as shown.

| Pathogens and Disease | Types of Pathogens |
| How Pathogens Are Spread | Preventing the Spread of Disease |

Under the appropriate tab, summarize what you learn about pathogens and how to prevent communicable diseases from spreading.

Health Online Visit **health.glencoe.com** and complete the Health Inventory for Chapter 18.

Preventing the Spread of Disease

Guide to Reading

Building Vocabulary
Fold a sheet of paper in half, lengthwise. As you read this lesson, write each new term on the left side of the fold and its definition on the other side.

- disease (p. 478)
- communicable disease (p. 478)
- pathogens (p. 478)
- infection (p. 478)
- viruses (p. 479)
- bacteria (p. 479)
- fungi (p. 479)
- protozoa (p. 479)
- vector (p. 480)
- hygiene (p. 480)

Focusing on the Main Ideas
In this lesson you will be able to

- **name** some causes of communicable diseases.
- **explain** how germs are spread.
- **describe** how to protect yourself against pathogens.

Reading Strategy
Organizing Information Create a table like the one shown below. As you read, describe how pathogens spread in the first column. In the second column, describe ways you can prevent spreading pathogens.

Pathogens	
How Pathogens Spread	Preventing the Spread of Pathogens

FOLDABLES Study Organizer Use the Foldable™ on p. 477 as you read this lesson.

Quick Write

How do you think people catch colds? Explain your answer.

Common Diseases

You wake up with a runny nose and your eyes itch. Your throat is sore, you sneeze and cough, and your head aches. You have a cold. A cold is one kind of disease. A **disease** is *any condition that interferes with the proper functioning of the body or mind.*

A cold is a **communicable disease,** *a disease that can be passed to a person from another person, animal, or object.* The agents that cause communicable diseases are called pathogens. **Pathogens** are *disease-causing organisms that are so small they can only be seen through a microscope.* Pathogens are also known as germs. When germs enter your body, you can develop an infection. An **infection** is *a condition that occurs when pathogens enter the body, multiply, and cause harm.* **Figure 18.1** shows several kinds of pathogens and the diseases they cause.

COMMON PATHOGENS AND DISEASES THEY CAUSE

All communicable diseases are caused by pathogens. What type of pathogen causes chicken pox?

Pathogens	Diseases
Bacteria	Pink eye, pertussis (whooping cough), strep throat, tuberculosis, Lyme disease, most foodborne illnesses, diphtheria, bacterial pneumonia, cholera
Viruses	Colds, influenza, hepatitis, chicken pox, measles, mumps, mononucleosis, herpes, HIV/AIDS, fever, polio, rabies, viral pneumonia
Fungi	Athlete's foot, ringworm
Protozoa	Dysentery, malaria

Types of Pathogens

Not all pathogens are alike, yet they can all cause diseases. As shown in Figure 18.1, there are four common pathogens:

- **Viruses** (VY·ruh·suhz) are *the smallest pathogens.* Viruses cause common diseases, such as colds and the flu. Most viral infections *cannot* be treated and cured with antibiotics.

- **Bacteria** are *tiny one-celled organisms.* Certain bacteria can be helpful. Bacteria that live in your digestive tract help you digest food. Other bacteria are harmful. They can cause diseases, such as strep throat and pneumonia. Most bacterial infections *can* be treated and cured by antibiotics.

- **Fungi** (FUHN·jy) are *organisms that are more complex than bacteria, but cannot make their own food.* They are primitive life-forms that feed on organic materials. They thrive in warm, moist environments. Fungi cause ringworm and athlete's foot.

- **Protozoa** (proh·tuh·ZOH·uh) are *one-celled organisms that are more complex than bacteria.* Malaria is a disease caused by a protozoa that can live in mosquitoes. If an infected mosquito bites a person, the protozoa transfers into the body through the skin.

Reading Check **Compare** How are bacterial infections different from viral infections?

▼ One way in which communicable diseases can be spread is through touch. **What is another way in which communicable diseases are spread from person to person?**

How Do Pathogens Spread?

Disease can occur when pathogens enter the body. Here are common ways pathogens are spread:

- **Direct contact with others.** Pathogens can spread directly from one person to another. For example, you can pick up a virus or bacteria by shaking hands with or kissing an infected person. Some pathogens are spread through sexual contact.

- **Indirect contact with others.** Pathogens can enter your body by sharing drinking glasses or eating utensils with an infected person. Pathogens can also be spread by contaminated needles used for tattoos, body piercings, and drug injection.

- **Contact with contaminated food and water.** Some pathogens infect people through contaminated food or water. Food that is improperly stored or undercooked provide an environment where pathogens can multiply. Illnesses people get from pathogens in food are called *food borne illnesses.*

- **Contact with animals or insects.** Animals and insects can spread pathogens. *An organism, such as an insect, that transmits pathogens* is called a **vector.** For example, the bite of a tick can spread the virus that causes Lyme disease. Mosquitoes infected with the West Nile virus can spread that virus to birds, horses, and humans through their saliva.

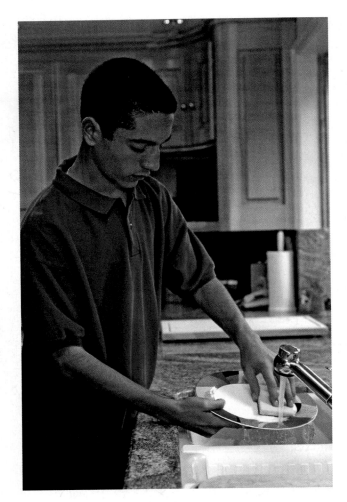

▲ When you immediately wash glasses, plates, or other utensils after using them, you keep bacteria from growing. **Is it important to use warm soapy water when you wash dishes? Why or why not?**

Reading Check **Recall** What are four ways that pathogens are spread?

How to Keep Pathogens from Spreading

There is no way to completely avoid pathogens. However, you can help protect yourself from them by practicing good personal **hygiene,** or *cleanliness.* Here are some other actions you can take to help prevent the spread of pathogens:

- Eat nutritious foods. Get enough physical activity and rest.

- Avoid close contact with people infected with a communicable disease, especially if they are still contagious.

Health Skills Activity

Practicing Healthful Behaviors

Keep Your Hands Clean!

One of the best ways of stopping pathogens from entering your body or spreading to others is to wash your hands frequently. Practice washing your hands thoroughly using the following steps:

1. Use warm water to wet your hands, and then apply soap.
2. Vigorously rub your hands together, scrubbing your whole hand for 30 seconds or more.
3. Rinse your hands thoroughly. Use a paper towel to turn off the water in public restrooms.
4. Use a clean towel or paper towel to dry your hands. In a public restroom, use a paper towel to open the door when you leave.

With a Group

Create a poster encouraging students to wash their hands regularly. Include the hand-washing steps listed above. With permission from school administrators, hang your poster in a school restroom or hallway.

- Never share eating or drinking utensils.

- Do not share toothbrushes or other personal hygiene items.

- Wash your hands thoroughly in warm, soapy water, especially before eating and after using the bathroom, playing with pets or handling garbage.

- Avoid touching your mouth, nose, and eyes. Do not bite your nails.

- Handle and prepare food safely, especially poultry and fish. Wash vegetables and cook meat thoroughly.

- Wipe counters thoroughly with a clean sponge or cloth. Wash or replace the sponge or cloth frequently. If these items are dirty or overused, they can actually spread more germs than they remove.

- Keep your environment clean. Empty trash frequently. Keep trash cans clean.

Reading Check **Identify** What five habits can you practice to keep yourself safe from pathogens?

Helping Others Stay Healthy

You may be carrying pathogens and not even know it. When you come in contact with others, these pathogens can easily spread. You can help protect the people around you from the spread of pathogens. Here are some healthful behaviors to practice:

- If you are ill, stay home from school and other public places. Avoid close contact with others.

- When you sneeze, cover your mouth and nose, and turn your head away from others. Wash your hands immediately.

- Do not share eating utensils, drinking glasses, toothbrushes, or other personal items.

- If a health care professional prescribes medicine for you, follow the directions exactly. Take all medicine that is prescribed.

- Again, prepare and store food safely. Wash vegetables and cook meat thoroughly. Always wash your hands before handling food.

Health Online

Visit health.glencoe.com and complete the Interactive Study Guide for Lesson 1.

Reading Check

Explain Give three suggestions for protecting others from the pathogens you could spread.

Lesson 1 Review

After You Read

Review this lesson for new terms, major headings, and Reading Checks.

What I Learned

1. **Vocabulary** Define *infection.* Use it in a sentence.

2. **Identify** What is a communicable disease?

3. **Give Examples** What are four types of pathogens? Give an example of a disease caused by each kind.

4. **Describe** What are some ways that pathogens can be spread by indirect contact?

Thinking Critically

5. **Analyze** Why do you think it is important for teens to practice good personal hygiene?

6. **Apply** Brendan is coughing and sneezing at school. What should Brendan do to help prevent the spread of pathogens? Explain your answer.

Applying Health Skills

7. **Practicing Healthful Behaviors** Think of four behaviors that you can practice to help stop the spread of pathogens. Create a plan to practice two of these behaviors during the next week. Follow the plan and write a paragraph describing the results.

 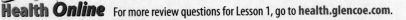 **Health Online** For more review questions for Lesson 1, go to **health.glencoe.com.**

The Body's Defenses Against Infection

Guide to Reading

● Building Vocabulary
As you read this lesson, write each new term and its definition in a list. Then draw three or four circles. Within each circle, group related terms together.

- immune system (p. 483)
- immunity (p. 483)
- inflammation (p. 484)
- lymphatic system (p. 485)
- lymphocytes (p. 485)
- antigen (p. 486)
- antibodies (p. 486)
- vaccine (p. 486)

● Focusing on the Main Ideas
In this lesson you will be able to

- **name** the body's first line of defense against pathogens.
- **describe** how the immune system functions.
- **explain** how antibodies protect the body.
- **practice** behaviors that keep your immune system healthy.

● Reading Strategy
Sequencing Draw a concept map that shows different ways your body works to defend itself from pathogens entering your body. Use Figure 18.2 as a guide.

Body's Defenses

Your Body Defends Itself

Pathogens are everywhere. They are in the air you breathe, the water you drink, and on objects you touch. Most bacteria, viruses, and other pathogens never get the chance to make you sick. Your body has natural barriers between you and pathogens. Your body's five major barriers to pathogens are shown in **Figure 18.2.**

These barriers are your body's first line of defense. If a pathogen gets past them, your body's immune system responds. Your **immune** (i·MYOON) **system** is *a combination of body defenses made up of the cells, tissues, and organs that fight off pathogens and disease.* Your immune system has two main responses—the nonspecific response and the specific response. Together these responses provide **immunity**—*your body's ability to resist the germs that cause a particular disease.*

Reading Check **Explain** What is the function of the immune system?

Quick Write

Think about a time you were ill and had a fever. How does a fever help your body fight an infection?

THE FIVE MAJOR BARRIERS

Barriers help keep pathogens out of your body. Which barrier protects you from pathogens that might enter your body through your mouth?

•Tears

cover and protect the eye from dust and pathogens. As they flow, tears carry foreign material away from the eye. Tears contain chemicals that kill pathogens.

•Mucous Membranes

are the soft skin that lines the nose, mouth, eyes, and other body openings. They are coated in a sticky material called mucus (MYOO•kuhs) that traps pathogens. When you cough, sneeze, or clear your throat, the pathogens trapped in the mucus are expelled.

•Saliva

washes germs away from your teeth. It contains chemicals that kill pathogens trying to enter through your mouth.

•Skin

provides a tough, outer protective surface that keeps pathogens from entering your blood. If you get a cut, burn, or scrape, pathogens can get past this barrier.

•Stomach Acid

is a gastric juice produced by the lining of your stomach. It kills many of the pathogens that make it past the saliva and mucus membranes of your mouth.

Nonspecific Immune Response

When pathogens enter your body, the immune system reacts with a nonspecific immune response. This response begins with inflammation. **Inflammation** is *the body's response to injury or disease, resulting in a condition of swelling, pain, heat, and redness.* The brain sends signals telling white blood cells to rush to the affected area and destroy the pathogens. Circulation to the area slows down.

With inflammation, the body starts producing a protein called interferon (in·ter·FIR·ahn) to stimulate the body's immune system. If pathogens multiply and spread, your body temperature may rise and cause a fever. A higher body temperature makes it harder for pathogens to reproduce. A fever also signals the body to produce more white blood cells to destroy the pathogens.

Reading Check

Explain How does the body first respond to invading pathogens?

Health Skills Activity

Practicing Healthful Behaviors

Keeping a Healthy Immune System

Good health habits can keep your immune system healthy. A healthy immune system means your body is better able to fight off infection. Commit to these habits to keep your immune system in top condition!

- Follow a healthful eating plan. Eat plenty of vitamin-rich fruits, vegetables, and whole grains.
- Participate in regular physical activity.
- Learn to manage stress in healthy ways.
- Get plenty of sleep. Rest strengthens your body's defenses.
- Avoid tobacco, alcohol, and other drugs.
- Drink plenty of water.
- Bathe and shower regularly.
- Get regular check-ups from a health care professional.

On Your Own

Using print or online resources, research other good health habits that can help you look and feel your best.

Specific Immune Response

Some pathogens can survive the body's nonspecific response. When this happens, the body sets in motion a specific immune response. Each specific response is customized to attack a particular pathogen and its toxins. Our immune system can "recognize" pathogens it has already battled. Once our immune system creates a specific response, cells from that response are ready to attack when the pathogen reappears. As a result, the second response is much quicker than the first.

The Lymphatic System

The **lymphatic** (lim·FA·tik) **system** is *a secondary circulatory system that helps the body fight pathogens and maintains its fluid balance.* The fluid circulating in the lymphatic system is called lymph (LIMF). *The white blood cells in the lymphatic system* are called **lymphocytes** (LIM·fuh·sytes). There are two main kinds of lymphocytes: B cells and T cells. B cells form in the bone marrow. T cells develop in the thymus gland.

▲ Vaccinations protect the body against certain communicable diseases. **How do vaccines help fight pathogens?**

Macrophages (MA·kruh·fay·juhz) are also found in the lymph. Their purpose is to attach themselves to invading pathogens and destroy them. Macrophages surround foreign substances and destroy them. Macrophages help the lymphocytes recognize the invader and prepare for future attacks.

Antibodies and Antigens

Lymphocytes react to *antigens*. An **antigen** is *any substance released by invading pathogens.* The immune system responds to these antigens by producing antibodies. **Antibodies** are *proteins that attach to antigens, keeping them from harming the body.* B cells produce a specific antibody for each specific antigen. If the same type of pathogen invades the body again, these antibodies are ready to attack.

T cells either stimulate the production of B cells or attack pathogens directly. There are two main types of T cells: helper cells and killer cells. Helper cells activate the production of B cells. Killer cells attach to invading pathogens and destroy them.

Immunity

Everyone is born with a natural immunity. Even before a baby is born, the mother's antibodies pass from her body to her developing fetus. After a baby is born, antibodies are passed on to the baby through the mother's milk. However, these immunities last for only a few months. Then the baby's immune system becomes active, and produces antibodies on its own to fight pathogens.

Immunity also develops when a vaccine is used. A **vaccine** (vak·SEEN) is *a preparation of dead or weakened pathogens that causes the immune system to produce antibodies.* They help the immune system make antibodies for certain diseases. This process is called immunization.

Vaccines have been developed for many diseases, such as polio, measles, and chicken pox. Some vaccinations, such as those for hepatitis B, must be given in a series over a span of a few months. Others, such as the tetanus shot, must be given repeatedly during your lifetime. To keep your body healthy, it is important to keep vaccinations current. **Figure 18.3** provides the vaccination schedule for many common vaccines. Remember that vaccinations protect not only you but also those around you!

Visit health.glencoe.com and complete the Interactive Study Guide for Lesson 2.

Reading Check   **Explain** How does your immune system react to a vaccination?

▼ **FIGURE 18.3**

VACCINATION SCHEDULE

This table lists common vaccines and the ages at which each vaccine is given. At what ages is the vaccine for polio given?

Vaccine	Recommended Ages for Vaccine
Hepatitis B	Birth, 2 months, 15–18 months
DTaP, Diphtheria, tetanus, pertussis (whooping cough)	2, 4, 6, and 15–18 months; 4–6 years; Td (tetanus and diptheria toxiod) boosters at 11–12 years and every 10 years thereafter
HIB (*H. influenzae* type b)	2, 4, and 6–18 months
IBV: Polio	2, 4, and 12–15 months, 4–6 years
MMR: measles, mumps, rubella	12–15 months; 4–6 years
Varicella: chicken pox	5 months; can be given any time after 12 months
Hepatitis A	2 doses a least 6 months apart, anytime between 2 and 18 years; used only in high-risk areas or for high-risk groups

Source: American Academy of Pediatrics, 2000.

Lesson 2 Review

📖 **After You Read**

Review this lesson for new terms, major headings, and Reading Checks.

What I Learned

1. *Vocabulary* Define the term *antigen*. Name two types of white blood cells your immune system produces to fight antigens.

2. *Recall* What is the lymphatic system? How does it protect your body against disease?

3. *Explain* What is the body's first line of defense against pathogens?

Thinking Critically

4. *Analyze* How does fever help fight an infection?

5. *Evaluate* How do vaccines help protect the health of the community?

Applying Health Skills

6. *Decision Making* A teen wakes up with a cold yet wants to go to school to take final exams. Use the decision-making process to help the teen make a healthy decision.

Common Communicable Diseases

Guide to Reading

● **Building Vocabulary**
As you read, write each term on one side of an index card and its definition on the other. Use the cards to quiz yourself on the definitions.

- contagious period (p. 489)
- mononucleosis (p. 489)
- hepatitis (p. 490)
- tuberculosis (p. 491)
- pneumonia (p. 491)
- strep throat (p. 491)

● **Focusing on the Main Ideas**
In this lesson you will learn to

- **explain** what causes colds and how they can be treated.
- **identify** some common communicable diseases.
- **describe** the symptoms of some common communicable diseases.

● **Reading Strategy**
Predicting Look at the main headings, figures, and captions in the lesson. Predict what kind of information you think you might learn.

Quick Write

List your symptoms if you had a cold or the flu. What actions could you take to prevent others from catching your disease?

Colds

The common cold occurs more frequently than any other communicable disease. Colds are caused by hundreds of different viruses, and can be spread by direct or indirect contact.

You can help treat a cold by getting plenty of rest and drinking lots of fluids. Some over-the-counter (OTC) medicines can help relieve your symptoms. You should stay at home for at least 24 hours after your cold symptoms appear. This is when your cold is most contagious, meaning it is easily spread to others. Anyone who comes in contact with cold viruses can become infected. That is why it is so important to take an active role in preventing the common cold.

Reading Check **Recall** Why is it important to stay home at least the first 24 hours after becoming infected with a cold virus?

◀ Cold germs spread quickly and easily. **How can you help stop the spread of cold viruses to others?**

The Flu

Influenza, or "the flu," is another common communicable disease. Flu symptoms include fever, chills, fatigue, headache, muscle aches, and respiratory problems. Like the cold, the flu can be spread through both direct and indirect contact.

The flu is caused by one of three main types of influenza viruses, each with several different strains. Every year, certain strains of the flu virus spread more quickly than others. Scientists try to anticipate which strains will spread fastest and create enough flu vaccines for the following year. Most strains of the flu are relatively harmless, but some can be serious.

▲ Eating healthy foods can help your body fight off communicable diseases such as the flu. **What other choices can you make that will help keep you healthy?**

Reading Check **Compare** How are the flu and the common cold similar? How are they different?

Other Common Communicable Diseases

Every communicable disease has a contagious period. The **contagious period** is *the length of time that a particular disease can be spread from person to person.* Quite often, the contagious period includes a length of time before the infected person starts to show symptoms. Chicken pox, measles, and mumps all have specific contagious periods. Several communicable diseases and their contagious periods are listed in **Figure 18.4.** Other common communicable diseases are described below.

Mononucleosis

Mononucleosis (MAH·noh·nook·klee·OH·sis), or "mono," is *a viral disease characterized by a severe sore throat and swelling of the lymph glands in the neck and around the throat area.* Mono most commonly infects teens and young adults. Known as "the kissing disease," it is spread through contact with the saliva of an infected person. Mono is also spread through sharing contaminated eating utensils and drinking glasses.

Reading Check **Define** What is a *contagious period*?

Connect To...
Social Studies

Fighting Disease

Diseases have shaped the lives of many famous athletes and historical leaders throughout the world. For example, United States President Franklin D. Roosevelt continued to lead our nation after contracting polio.

Research the life of a famous person, either from the past or currently living, who had to fight disease. Write a brief report. Tell about the disease and how this person prevailed.

COMMON COMMUNICABLE DISEASES

This figure shows the symptoms and contagious periods of several communicable diseases. **Which diseases have similar symptoms? What are those symptoms?**

Disease	Symptoms	Contagious Period	Vaccine
Chicken pox	Itchy rash, fever, muscle aches	One to five days before symptoms appear to when spots crust over	Yes
Pneumonia	High fever, chest pain, cough	Varies	For some types
Rubella	Swollen lymph nodes, rash, fever	Seven days before rash starts to five days after	Yes
Measles	Fever, runny nose, cough, rash	Three to four days before rash starts to four days after	Yes
Mumps	Fever, headache, swollen areas in neck and under jaw	Seven days before symptoms to nine days after	Yes
Whooping cough	Fever, runny nose, dry cough (with a whooping sound)	From inflammation of mucous membranes to four weeks after	Yes
Tuberculosis	Fever, fatigue, weight loss, coughing blood	Varies	Yes

Hepatitis

Hepatitis (hep·uh·TY·tis) is *a viral disease of the liver characterized by yellowing of the skin and the whites of the eyes.* Other symptoms might include loss of appetite, weakness, lack of energy, fever, headaches, and a sore throat. Hepatitis A, B, and C are three different virus types.

Hepatitis A is common in areas with poor sanitation. It is spread through food or water that has been contaminated by human waste. People can also become infected if the virus enters the body through an open wound.

Hepatitis B and C are most commonly spread through contact with contaminated blood or other body fluids. Vaccines can protect people from contracting hepatitis A and B. Medications can help treat people infected with hepatitis C.

Tuberculosis

Tuberculosis (too·ber·kyuh·LOH·sis), or TB, is *a bacterial disease that usually affects the lungs.* Since TB can spread easily through the air, people are tested periodically to see if they have the disease. Sometimes people who test positive for TB show no symptoms. Even without symptoms, they can still spread the disease to others.

Pneumonia

Pneumonia is *a serious inflammation of the lungs.* Symptoms include fever, chills, and difficulty breathing. People infected with other diseases are especially vulnerable to pneumonia. This infection can be spread though direct or indirect contact. A virus or bacteria can cause pneumonia. Pneumonia caused by a bacteria can be treated with antibiotics.

Strep Throat

Strep throat is *a sore throat caused by streptococcal bacteria.* Strep throat produces a red and painful throat, fever, and swollen lymph nodes in the neck. It might also cause headaches, nausea, and vomiting. It is spread through direct or indirect contact with an infected person. Left untreated, strep throat can lead to serious complications, such as heart or kidney damage. Fortunately, strep throat is caused by a bacteria and can be treated with antibiotics.

▲ Getting a blood test will determine if a person has mononucleosis. **What are the symptoms of mono?**

Visit **health.glencoe.com** and complete the Interactive Study Guide for Lesson 3.

Lesson 3 Review

After You Read

Review this lesson for new terms, major headings, and Reading Checks.

What I Learned

1. *Vocabulary* Define *mononucleosis.*

2. *Give Examples* What are two examples of how someone might become infected with hepatitis A?

3. *List* Name two symptoms of strep throat.

Thinking Critically

4. *Analyze* Why are hospital patients often at risk for developing pneumonia?

5. *Evaluate* If someone has symptoms such as a fever and fatigue, how will that person know when to seek help from a health care professional?

Applying Health Skills

6. *Practicing Healthful Behaviors* Write a short article describing healthful behaviors teens can use to control the spread of disease. Include a list of some common communicable diseases and how they are spread.

Sexually Transmitted Diseases

Guide to Reading

● Building Vocabulary
As you read this lesson, write the term below and its definition in your notebook.

■ sexually transmitted diseases (STDs) (p. 492)

● Focusing on the Main Ideas
In this lesson you will be able to

■ **identify** common STDs and the problems they cause.
■ **state** how to protect yourself from STDs.
■ **explain** why abstinence is the best way to avoid getting an STD.

● Reading Strategy
Organizing Information Create a chart listing each STD described in this lesson, its symptoms, and treatment.

Quick Write

Write a paragraph about why it is important for teens to avoid sexual activity.

What Are STDs?

Sexually transmitted diseases (STDs) are *infections that are spread from person to person through sexual contact.* They are sometimes called sexually transmitted infections (STIs). In the United States, STDs are a major health problem for teens. Each year, one-quarter of all new cases of STDs appear among 15- to 19-year olds. One in four sexually active teens has an STD, although many do not even know it. However, STDS are completely preventable. This lesson will help you learn more about STDs, their causes, and how to avoid them. **Figure 18.5** lists some important facts about STDs.

Common STDs

STDs can cause serious health problems if left untreated. Anyone who suspects he or she may have an STD should see a doctor right away. Some common STDs are described below:

- **Chlamydia** (kluh·MI·dee·uh) is a bacterial STD that may affect the reproductive organs, urethra, and anus. Chlamydia can be treated with antibiotics. It is a "silent" disease because in many cases there are no symptoms. Symptoms can include genital discharge and pain when urinating. If left untreated, chlamydia can seriously damage the reproductive organs in both males and females, leading to infertility.

WHAT YOU SHOULD KNOW ABOUT STDS

Learning the facts about STDs can help you avoid them. What is the best way for teens to avoid getting STDs?

- Most STDs are spread only through sexual contact.

- You cannot tell if someone has an STD by his or her appearance.

- Most STDs have either very mild or no symptoms.

- Many STDs can be treated and cured, but early diagnosis is important.

- Because treatments for STDs vary, they must be accurately identified.

- STDs can recur because the body does not build up an immunity to them.

- STDs are serious diseases that can cause sterility, blindness, deafness, insanity, and death.

- STDs can cause birth defects.

- **Genital herpes** (HER·peez) is a viral STD that produces painful blisters on the genital area. This STD is transmitted by skin-to-skin contact that can occur without having sexual intercourse. It results in periodic outbreaks of painful blisters or sores on the genitals. Herpes can be passed on to another person even when the blisters are not present. Although there is no cure, medicines are available to lessen the outbreaks.

- **Genital warts** are growths or bumps in the genital area caused by certain types of the human papillomavirus (HPV). This STD is also transmitted by skin-to-skin contact. Genital warts can be treated, but there is no cure for HPV infection. These infections are the most common type of STD in the United States. Like genital herpes and chlamydia, HPV is often a silent disease. Some strains of HPV are linked to the cause of cervical and skin cancers.

- **Trichomoniasis** (TREE·koh·moh·NI·ah·sis) is an STD caused by the protozoan Trichomonas vaginalis. Trichomoniasis can be treated and cured with medications. The disease may be silent, but symptoms can include discomfort during urination, genital discharge, and irritation or itching in the genital area.

- **Gonorrhea** (gah·nuh·REE·uh) is a bacterial STD that affects the mucous membranes of the body, particularly in the genital area. Symptoms include a thick yellowish discharge from the genitals and a burning sensation when urinating. The infection can be treated with antibiotics. Untreated, it can infect other parts of the body, such as the heart, and cause fertility problems for both women and men.

- **Syphilis** (SIH·fuh·luhs) is a bacterial STD that can affect many parts of the body. It can damage body organs, such as the brain. During the advanced stage, the disease can cause mental disorders, blindness, heart problems, paralysis, and even death. If diagnosed early, syphilis can be treated and cured with antibiotics.

- **Pelvic inflammatory disease (PID)** is a general infection of the female reproductive organs. Most females become infected with PID as a result of contracting another STD, such as chlamydia or gonorrhea. When PID is untreated, the infection may worsen over time and cause sterility.

- **HIV/AIDS** is a serious STD covered in the next lesson.

Reading Check **Give Examples** Name three STDs that are caused by bacteria.

Practicing Abstinence

The best way to avoid getting an STD is to abstain from sexual activity. As a teen, deciding to say no to sexual activity is one of the most important health choices that you can make.

▼ Group activities can help you avoid situations where you may feel pressure to engage in sexual activity. **What activities do you and your friends like to do together?**

Make a commitment to practice abstinence and demonstrate your commitment through words and actions. Choose friends who share your values and support your decisions.

Avoid being alone on a date. By participating in group activities, you can avoid the pressures of sexual activity. If you do go on a one-on-one date, communicate your limits to your date before you go out. Practice how to respond to a date who tries to pressure you into sexual activity. For example, if your date says, "If you really care for me, you would have sex with me," you can say, "If you really care for me, you would respect my decision."

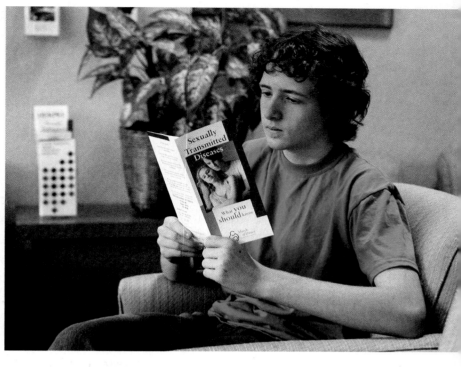

▲ Learning the facts about STDs can help teens make a commitment to practice abstinence. **What can you do to help spread awareness of STDs?**

Reading Check   **Describe** What are some ways to avoid being pressured to engage in sexual activity?

Lesson 4 Review

After You Read

Review this lesson for new terms, major headings, and Reading Checks.

What I Learned

1. **Vocabulary** Define *sexually transmitted disease*.

2. **Give Examples** What are three examples of STDs that are considered "silent diseases"?

3. **List** Name three consequences of untreated chlamydia.

Thinking Critically

4. **Apply** Why is abstinence the best choice for teens?

5. **Evaluate** Why is it important to immediately seek help from a health care professional if you suspect you have an STD?

Applying Health Skills

6. **Advocacy** Create a booklet that tells teens about the dangers of STDs. It should highlight the most common STDs and their symptoms. Also include how teens can avoid getting STDs.

HIV/AIDS

Guide to Reading

● **Building Vocabulary**
Write each term and what you think it means. As you find the terms in this lesson, make any necessary corrections.

- HIV (human immunodeficiency virus) (p. 496)
- AIDS (acquired immunodeficiency syndrome) (p. 496)
- opportunistic infection (p. 496)
- carrier (p. 496)

● **Focusing on the Main Ideas**
In this lesson you will be able to

- **define** HIV and AIDS.
- **explain** how people become infected with HIV and develop AIDS.
- **describe** how to avoid getting HIV and AIDS.

● **Reading Strategy**
Identify Problems and Solutions After reading this lesson, identify ways that HIV is transmitted. Then, identify ways to prevent the spread of HIV.

Quick Write

List what you have heard about HIV or AIDS. Are they myths or facts?

What Is HIV? What Is AIDS?

HIV (human immunodeficiency virus) is *the virus that causes AIDS.* **AIDS (acquired immunodeficiency syndrome)** is *a deadly disease that interferes with the body's natural ability to fight infection.* HIV attacks the body's T cells. As mentioned in Lesson 2, T cells are a type of lymphocyte that help the body fight off pathogens. When the HIV virus attacks a T cell, it replaces the cell's genetic information with its own and then multiplies. As more T cells are taken over, the immune system becomes weaker.

Eventually, the body can no longer fight the pathogens that a healthy immune system would destroy. When this happens, AIDS develops. One symptom that signals the onset of AIDS is the presence of opportunistic infections. An **opportunistic infection** is *an infection that rarely occurs in a healthy person.* For example, many AIDS patients develop a type of pneumonia that can cause death.

A person can be a carrier of HIV, without having AIDS. A **carrier** is *a person who appears healthy but is infected with HIV and can pass it to others.* A person may be infected with HIV for ten years or more before starting to show symptoms of AIDS. A blood test is the only way of knowing if a person is infected with the HIV virus. AIDS can affect men, women, and children of all ages. **Figure 18.6** shows the number of new AIDS cases diagnosed by age group in 2003. The table also shows how many total AIDS cases have been diagnosed by age group through the end of 2003. How do you think this information is used to help reduce the spread of HIV?

How Does HIV Spread?

HIV is spread from person to person through contact with specific body fluids. These fluids are sperm, fluid from the vagina, blood, and breast milk.

One of the ways HIV spreads is through sexual contact with an infected person. Just one incident of sexual activity with an infected person can spread the virus. People who have more than one sex partner are at greatest risk.

Another way HIV is spread is through sharing needles. Many injection drug users have contracted HIV. Tattoos and body piercings can also spread HIV if performed with contaminated needles.

HIV can also be spread from mother to child. This can occur either before or after delivery, or through breast-feeding. In recent years, new drug therapies have reduced the rate of transmission of HIV to the fetus during pregnancy.

Health Online

Topic: Staying Alive

Visit health.glencoe.com for Student Web Activities to learn more about HIV/AIDS, and what teens are doing to help stop the spread of HIV.

Activity: Using the information provided at the link above, create a FAQ sheet about HIV and AIDS that can be made available to teens throughout your community.

▼ FIGURE 18.6

U.S. AIDS CASES AT AGE OF DIAGNOSIS, 2003

AIDS develops months or even years after infection with HIV. Why would this long span of time make the spread of the disease harder to control?

Age	Estimated # of AIDS Cases in 2003	Cumulative Estimated # of AIDS Cases, Through 2003
Under 13:	59	9,419
Ages 13 to 14:	59	891
Ages 15 to 24:	1,991	37,599
Ages 25 to 34:	9,605	311,137
Ages 35 to 44:	17,633	365,432
Ages 45 to 54:	10,051	148,347
Ages 55 to 64:	2,888	43,451
Ages 65 to older:	886	13,711

Source: Centers for Disease Control and Prevention—Division of HIV/AIDS Prevention

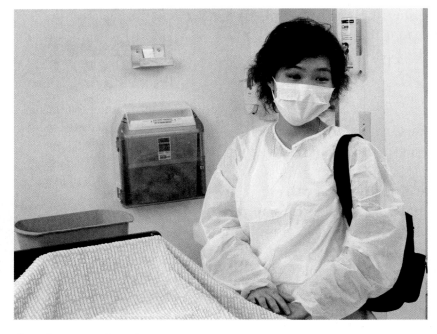

▲ When people visit an AIDS patient in the hospital, they need to take precautions to protect the patient from infection. **Why is it necessary for these actions to be taken?**

At one time, HIV was spread through donated blood. Since 1985, all donated blood in the United States is tested for HIV. As a result, the risk of getting HIV from a blood transfusion is extremely low.

How HIV Is NOT Spread

False ideas and myths about how HIV is spread have circulated for many years. They have even made people reluctant to donate blood. It is important to be aware of these myths and to learn the facts. HIV is spread only through contact with specific body fluids. It is not spread through casual touching or any of the following ways:

- Breathing the air
- Being bitten by a mosquito
- Swimming in a pool
- Sharing utensils
- Donating blood
- Hugging or shaking hands
- Using the same shower, bathtub, or toilet as an infected person

Reading Check **Recall** What are four ways that HIV is not spread?

Fighting AIDS

Scientists continue to work on improved medical treatments for people with HIV and AIDS. Currently, there is no cure for HIV or AIDS. However, drugs are available that slow down the progress of HIV infection. Unfortunately, many of these drugs are costly and can have serious side effects. Scientists are also working on a vaccine for HIV, but this will probably take many more years. The best weapons in the fight against HIV and AIDS are knowledge and abstinence.

Reading Check **Identify** What treatment is available for people with HIV infection?

► Practicing abstinence allows you to enjoy healthful activities with your friends. **How can friends help you practice abstinence?**

Preventing HIV/AIDS

HIV infection and AIDS can be prevented. There are three main ways to avoid these diseases:

- **Practice abstinence.** Abstinence is the conscious, active choice not to participate in high-risk behaviors. This includes avoiding sexual activity.

- **Avoid drugs and alcohol.** Using drugs and alcohol can impair your ability to make healthful decisions. This can lead to participation in other risky behaviors, such as sexual activity.

- **Avoid sharing needles.** Needles can carry HIV into your bloodstream. This includes needles that are used for tattoos or body piercings.

Health Online

Visit **health.glencoe.com** and complete the Interactive Study Guide for Lesson 5.

Lesson 5 Review

After You Read

Review this lesson for new terms, major headings, and Reading Checks.

What I Learned

1. *Vocabulary* Define *HIV* and *carrier.*

2. *Give Examples* What are two ways teens can get infected with HIV?

3. *Recall* How does HIV weaken the body's immune system?

Thinking Critically

4. *Analyze* Why is HIV an extremely dangerous virus?

5. *Apply* Jasmine doesn't want to share tennis rackets with Mei, who has HIV.

Jasmine is afraid of getting infected with HIV. What could you tell Jasmine?

Applying Health Skills

6. *Goal Setting* Think of how you want to avoid exposure to HIV infection, AIDS, or other STDs. Set a goal to protect yourself from these diseases. Develop a plan to help you reach your goal. Be clear and specific about the steps you will take to reach your goal.

Health Online For more review questions for Lesson 5, go to **health.glencoe.com**.

Lesson 5: HIV/AIDS **499**

Protect Yourself From Pathogens

DIRECTIONS

Goal Setting involves setting positive goals and taking steps to achieve them. This activity will give you the opportunity to develop and master this important health skill. Here's a guide to the different parts of this activity:

1 In the **Model** section, you will read about a teen who performs the health skill successfully. This "model" scenario will show you how the skill is done.

2 The **Practice** section will help guide you in practicing the skill.

3 In the **Apply** section, you will have a chance to perform the skill on your own. You can use the Self-Check to check your work.

To complete this activity, first read the scenario presented in the Model. Then move on to the Practice. Finally, go ahead and try the Apply.

1 Model

Jennifer noticed that she was sick a lot during the school year. She admitted that she never cleaned her room. Jennifer set a goal to keep her room clean to help reduce the number of pathogens that could be making her sick. Here is the plan she developed to meet her goal:

1. **Identify a specific goal and write it down.**

   Keep my room clean for one month.

2. **List the steps you will take to reach your goal.**

   Put dirty clothes in a hamper.

   Put clean clothes and shoes away.

   Throw trash in the wastebasket.

   Empty wastebasket when it is full.

   Vacuum the carpet and dust the furniture weekly.

   Clean up drink and food spills right away.

3. **Get help and support from others.**

   Ask my mother's advice on the best way to clean.

4. **Set up checkpoints to evaluate your progress.**

   After two weeks, evaluate my overall health and cleanliness of my room.

5. **Give yourself a reward once you have achieved your goal.**

   If I keep my room clean for one month, I will buy myself a new CD.

② Practice

Jennifer likes having a clean, uncluttered room. She also likes how achieving a goal builds her self-confidence. Now Jennifer wants to reduce the number of colds she gets every school year. She believes that she could achieve this if she washed her hands more frequently.

1. What is Jennifer's goal?
2. What steps can help Jennifer reach her goal?
3. Who can Jennifer get to help her?
4. How can Jennifer evaluate her progress?
5. How can she reward herself for following her plan?

Skill Summary
GOAL SETTING

1. Identify a specific goal and write it down.
2. List the steps you will take to reach your goal.
3. Get help and support from others.
4. Evaluate your progress.
5. Reward yourself.

③ Apply

Think of how you can better protect yourself from disease. How would you accomplish this goal? Take a piece of paper and make a reminder to post in your room. On your reminder include: 1) your goal; 2) steps to reach your goal; 3) names of people who can help you; 4) how you'll check your progress; and 5) a reward. Use art to illustrate how achieving your goal will improve your physical, mental/emotional or social health.

Self-Check

- Did I set a specific goal?
- Does my reminder contain the steps for achieving my goal?
- Did I show how my goal will improve my health?

Healthy Habits

How healthy are your habits? This activity will help you find out.

What You Will Need

- pencil and paper

What You Will Do

Write *yes* or *no* for each statement.

1 I avoid sharing eating utensils or drinking glasses with others.

2 I avoid drinking water from streams and lakes.

3 I cover my nose and mouth when I cough or sneeze.

4 I make sure leftover food is properly stored.

5 I wash my hands after using the bathroom and before preparing or serving food.

6 When I am sick, I get medical care.

7 When I am sick, I avoid others during the contagious period.

8 I avoid sharing combs, brushes, and towels with others.

9 I avoid contact with people who have a cold or other communicable diseases.

10 I have received all the recommended vaccinations.

Wrapping It Up

Give yourself 1 point for each yes. A score of 8–10 is very good. A score of 6–7 is good. A score of 4–5 is fair. If you score below 4, you need to work on improving your health behaviors.

Reading Review

Lesson 1 Preventing the Spread of Disease

Key Idea

- Communicable diseases can be spread by direct and indirect contact, animals and insects, and contaminated food and water.

Vocabulary

- disease (p. 478)
- communicable disease (p. 478)
- pathogens (p. 478)
- infection (p. 478)
- viruses (p. 479)
- bacteria (p. 479)
- fungi (p. 479)
- protozoa (p. 479)
- vector (p. 480)
- hygiene (p. 480)

Lesson 2 The Body's Defenses Against Infection

Key Idea

- The immune systems reacts to pathogens with nonspecific and specific responses.

Vocabulary

- immune system (p. 483)
- immunity (p. 483)
- inflammation (p. 484)
- lymphatic system (p. 485)
- lymphocytes (p. 485)
- antigens (p. 486)
- antibodies (p. 486)
- vaccine (p. 486)

Lesson 3 Common Communicable Diseases

Key Idea

- Common communicable diseases include colds, the flu, mononucleosis, hepatitis, tuberculosis, pneumonia, and strep throat.

Vocabulary

- contagious period (p. 489)
- mononucleosis (p. 489)
- hepatitis (p. 490)
- tuberculosis (p. 491)
- pneumonia (p. 491)
- strep throat (p. 491)

Lesson 4 Sexually Transmitted Diseases

Key Idea

- Chlamydia, genital warts, genital herpes, trichomoniasis, gonorrhea, syphilis, and hepatitis B are common STDs.

Vocabulary

- sexually transmitted diseases (STDs) (p. 492)

Lesson 5 HIV/AIDS

Key Ideas

- HIV is spread through contact with sperm, vaginal fluid, blood, or breast milk.
- Abstinence is the only sure way to protect yourself against HIV infection, AIDS, and other STDs.

Vocabulary

- HIV (human immunodeficiency virus) (p. 496)
- AIDS (acquired immunodeficiency syndrome) (p. 496)
- opportunistic infection (p. 496)
- carrier (p. 496)

Assessment

Reviewing Vocabulary and Main Ideas

On a sheet of paper, write the numbers 1–9. After each number, write the term from the list that best completes each statement.

- disease
- immune system
- infection
- viruses
- antibodies
- vaccine
- influenza
- contagious period
- tuberculosis
- inflammation

Lesson 1 — Preventing the Spread of Disease

1. A(n) _____ is any condition that interferes with the proper functioning of the body or mind.

2. A(n) _____ is a condition that occurs when pathogens enter the body, multiply, and cause harm.

3. _____ are the smallest kinds of pathogens.

Lesson 2 — The Body's Defenses Against Infection

4. _____ is the body's response to injury or disease, resulting in a condition of swelling, pain, heat and redness.

5. The _____ is a combination of body defenses made up of the cells, tissues, and organs that fight pathogens in the body.

6. _____ are proteins made by B cells that bind to specific antigens.

Lesson 3 — Common Communicable Diseases

7. _____ is a communicable disease characterized by fever, chills, fatigue, headache, muscle aches, and respiratory symptoms.

8. The _____ is the length of time that a particular disease can be spread from person to person.

9. _____ is a bacterial disease that usually affects the lungs.

*On a sheet of paper, write the numbers 10–15. Write **True** or **False** for each statement below. If the statement is false, change the underlined word or phrase to make it true.*

Lesson 4 — Sexually Transmitted Diseases

10. Sexually transmitted diseases are infections that spread from person to person through <u>casual</u> contact.

11. Syphilis is a bacterial STD that can affect <u>many parts of the body</u>.

12. Genital herpes <u>can</u> be transmitted when symptoms are not present.

Lesson 5 — HIV/AIDS

13. HIV is the virus that causes <u>AIDS</u>.

14. You <u>can</u> become infected with HIV by shaking hands with an infected person.

Health Online Visit health.glencoe.com and take the Online Quiz for Chapter 18.

15. Scientists have developed powerful new drugs to <u>cure</u> HIV infections.

Thinking Critically

Using complete sentences, answer the following questions on a sheet of paper.

16. Explain Why do people who have AIDS actually die from other diseases?

17. Interpret Sometimes after you get a vaccination, years later you have to get more of the same vaccine. Why do you think you might need this "booster shot"?

Write About It

18. Analyzing Influences Write a journal entry describing what factors can influence a teen's attitude toward sexual activity. Are these influences positive or negative?

19. Accessing Information Write a paragraph that explains why some people may not realize that they are infected with an STD.

Standardized Test Practice

Reading

Read the passage and then answer the questions.

During the Middle Ages, hundreds of people were killed by the bubonic plague in a very short time. The pathogen for the bubonic plague is a bacterium called *Yersinia pestis*. It lived inside fleas, which lived on rats. The rats became infected when the fleas bit them. Even uninfected fleas that bit infected rats could become infected. When the fleas jumped from rat to rat, the plague spread quickly. As the disease moved through the cities' rat populations, the rats died off. As the number of rats decreased, more and more infected fleas started living on and biting humans. People became hosts for the bacterium. During 1347 to 1350, the bubonic plague killed one-third of Europe's population.

TEST-TAKING TIP

When a question asks for the main point of the passage, reread the first and last sentences. This is where the authors often place the most important information.

1. The main point of this passage is to explain how

  A. fleas can live on rats and humans.

  B. the plague killed so many people so quickly.

  C. to prevent the plague from killing humans.

  D. Europe's population became so low.

2. Read this sentence from the passage. The pathogen for the bubonic plague is a bacterium called *Yersinia pestis*. What does *pathogen* mean?

  A. path

  B. antigen

  C. name

  D. germ

Chapter Preview

▲ *Working With the Photo*

Some noncommunicable diseases are present at birth. **What are two other causes of noncommunicable diseases?**

Start-Up Activities

Before You Read Do you practice healthy lifestyle behaviors that help to prevent noncommunicable diseases? Take the Health Inventory below. Keep a record of your answers.

HEALTH INVENTORY

1. I limit foods that are high in salt and fat.
   (a) always   (b) sometimes   (c) never

2. I am physically active each day.
   (a) always   (b) sometimes   (c) never

3. I manage stress in healthful ways.
   (a) always   (b) sometimes   (c) never

4. I apply sunscreen before I go outside.
   (a) always   (b) sometimes   (c) never

FOLDABLES™ Study Organizer

As You Read Make this Foldable™ to record and collect information on the causes of noncommunicable diseases presented in Lesson 1. Begin with a plain sheet of 11″ × 17″ paper.

1 Fold the sheet of paper into thirds along the short axis.

2 Open and fold the bottom edge up to form a pocket. Glue the edges.

3 Label each pocket as shown.

Diseases Present at Birth | Lifestyle Choices | Environmental Factors

Summarize key points on index cards on the different causes of noncommunicable diseases. Store these cards in the appropriate pocket of your Foldable™.

Health Online Visit **health.glencoe.com** and use the e-flashcards to preview Chapter 19 vocabulary terms.

Causes of Noncommunicable Diseases

Guide to Reading

● **Building Vocabulary**
As you read the lesson, write each term and its definition in your notebook.

- noncommunicable diseases (p. 508)
- chronic diseases (p. 508)
- degenerative disease (p. 508)
- congenital disorder (p. 508)
- heredity (p. 509)

● **Focusing on the Main Ideas**
In this lesson you will learn to

- **identify** various types of noncommunicable diseases.
- **explain** what causes noncommunicable diseases.
- **describe** some health lifestyle behaviors that can prevent diseases.

● **Reading Strategy**
Skimming Glance at the headings of this lesson. By looking over the major and minor headings, you will have an idea of what the lesson is about. Write three main ideas of the lesson you learn from skimming.

FOLDABLES Study Organizer Use the Foldable™ on p. 507 as you read this lesson.

Quick Write

Make a list of as many factors as you can think of that can cause noncommunicable diseases.

What Is a Noncommunicable Disease?

As you learned in Chapter 18, you can get communicable diseases from other people. Some diseases, however, are noncommunicable. **Noncommunicable diseases** are *diseases that cannot be spread from person to person.* For example, you cannot catch diabetes from someone who has this disease. Some noncommunicable diseases are chronic. **Chronic diseases** are *present either continuously or on and off over a long period of time.* Asthma is a chronic disease.

Other noncommunicable diseases are considered degenerative. A **degenerative disease** is *a disease that causes breakdown in the body cells, tissues, and organs as it progresses.* Multiple sclerosis is an example of a degenerative disease.

Diseases Present at Birth

Some babies are born with physical or mental disabilities caused by birth defects or genetic disorders. The causes of many birth defects are unknown. *All disorders that are present when the baby is born* are called **congenital disorders.** Examples of congenital disorders include cystic fibrosis and sickle-cell anemia. These two diseases are caused by hereditary factors.

Heredity is *the passing of traits from parents to their children.* Some birth defects are caused by the mother's choice of lifestyle. For example, a pregnant woman who drinks alcohol may give birth to a child with fetal alcohol syndrome (FAS).

Reading Check **Recall** List three types of noncommunicable diseases.

Lifestyle Choices and Disease

While it is hard to determine who will develop a particular disease, researchers have found that certain risk factors increase a person's chance of developing a disease. Heredity, age, gender, and ethnic group are factors over which people have no control.

People can, however, control one major group of risk factors—their lifestyle choices. When people make unhealthy choices, they increase their risk of disease. Drinking too much alcohol, for example, can cause cirrhosis of the liver. Smoking tobacco can cause lung cancer and other respiratory diseases. Heart disease can result from eating too many foods that are high in saturated fat, and from a lack of physical activity. To decrease your risk of disease, practice the following healthy lifestyle behaviors:

▲ Multiple sclerosis (MS) is a degenerative disorder of the brain and spinal cord that causes problems with the use of limbs. **How might discovering the cause of MS help scientists find a cure or treatment?**

- **Eat healthful foods.** Eat plenty of whole grains, fruits, and vegetables. Go easy on foods high in fat, sugar, or salt.

- **Stay physically active.** Teens should be physically active at least 60 minutes on most days. Regular physical activity strengthens the heart and lungs, and helps the body systems work better.

- **Maintain a healthy weight.** Keep your weight within the recommended range for your gender, age, height, and body frame.

- **Get enough sleep.** Teens need at least nine hours of sleep a night.

- **Manage stress.** Use time management and other healthful strategies to reduce stress.

- **Avoid tobacco, alcohol, and other drugs.** These substances harm many parts of the body.

◀ Smog is one environmental factor that can cause respiratory diseases. **What are other environmental factors that can cause disease?**

Environmental Factors and Disease

Your environment affects your personal health. Many substances in the environment can cause serious health problems. When houses are built near landfills, for example, they can become contaminated by fumes from the chemical waste buried in the landfills. Illness can result years after initial exposure.

Carbon monoxide—a colorless, odorless gas—is another harmful environmental substance. Fumes from car exhaust and some furnaces and fireplaces emit carbon monoxide when used. High levels of carbon monoxide gas can be dangerous and cause serious illness or even death.

Smog is another environmental factor that can cause disease. Smog is a yellow-brown haze that forms when sunlight reacts with air pollution. Breathing smog can cause respiratory diseases in some people. When smog is especially heavy, people with respiratory diseases may need to limit their outdoor activities.

Health Online

Visit **health.glencoe.com** and complete the Interactive Study Guide for Lesson 1.

Lesson 1 Review

After You Read

Review this lesson for new terms, major headings, and reading checks.

What I Learned

1. *Vocabulary* Define *chronic diseases*. Give an example of one.

2. *Identify* What are three risk factors that can cause noncommunicable diseases?

3. *Describe* What are two environmental factors that can cause disease?

Thinking Critically

4. *Synthesize* How can lifestyle choices affect a person's health?

5. *Evaluate* How can communities lower the risk of diseases caused by the environment?

Applying Health Skills

6. *Accessing Information* Using print or online resources, research some common noncommunicable diseases. Choose one and create a fact sheet describing what causes the disease and how it affects the body. Include information on how this disease is treated or managed. Share your findings with the class.

Health Online For more review questions for Lesson 1, go to **health.glencoe.com**.

Cancer

Guide to Reading

● **Building Vocabulary**
Write each term below and its definition on separate index cards. Mix up the cards and try to match each term to its definition.

- cancer (p. 511)
- tumor (p. 511)
- benign (p. 512)
- malignant (p. 512)
- risk factors (p. 513)
- carcinogens (p. 513)
- biopsy (p. 513)
- radiation therapy (p. 514)
- chemotherapy (p. 514)
- remission (p. 515)
- recurrence (p. 515)

● **Focusing on the Main Ideas**
In this lesson you will learn to

- **identify** common types of cancer.
- **recognize** some causes of cancer.
- **explain** ways that cancer can be treated.
- **describe** how to reduce the risk of developing cancer.

● **Reading Strategy**
Organizing Information Create a chart that shows the different types and treatments of cancers.

Quick Write

Write a couple of sentences that explain why people need to wear sunscreen when they go outdoors.

What Is Cancer?

Cancer is *a disease characterized by the rapid and uncontrolled growth of abnormal cells.* It can affect people of any age. Although many cancers can be treated, cancer is the second-leading cause of death in the United States.

How does cancer develop? More than 50 trillion cells make up the adult human body. Most of the cells are normal, but some are abnormal cells. Usually, your body's immune system destroys abnormal cells. When these cells survive, however, they begin to divide. As they divide, some of them grow into tumors. A **tumor** is *a mass of abnormal cells.*

▶ Before you go outdoors, apply sunscreen with an SPF of 15 or higher. **What other precautions can you take to protect your skin from the sun's ultraviolet rays?**

Tumors can be either benign or malignant. **Benign** tumors are *not cancerous* and do not spread to other parts of the body. **Malignant** tumors are *cancerous*. They can spread to other parts of the body.

Types of Cancer

Cancer can develop in many parts of the body. Some types of cancer are more common than others. See **Figure 19.1** for some common types of cancer. Skin cancer is the most common type. Fortunately, if skin cancer is discovered early enough, it can be successfully treated.

Lung cancer is the leading cause of cancer deaths. In 2005, almost one out of every three people who died from cancer had lung cancer. There is good news, however. In recent years, the number of lung-cancer deaths has fallen because fewer people are smoking. Smoking is the leading cause of lung cancer.

▼ **FIGURE 19.1**

COMMON TYPES OF CANCER

This chart lists some common types of cancer. **What is the leading cause of skin cancer?**

Type of Cancer	Important Facts
Skin cancer	is the most common kind of cancer. Excessive exposure to direct sunlight is the major cause of skin cancer.
Breast cancer	most often occurs in women over 50. It can occur in younger women and occasionally in men.
Reproductive organ cancer	can occur in the testicles and prostate gland in men. It can occur in the ovaries, cervix, and uterus in women.
Lung cancer	is the leading cause of cancer deaths in the United States. Smoking is the biggest risk factor for both males and females.
Colon and rectal cancer	develop in the digestive tract. Early detection and better screening have greatly reduced the number of cases of colon and rectal cancers.
Leukemia	is a cancer of the white blood cells that starts in the bone marrow. An increase in cancerous white blood cells interferes with the healthy white blood cells' immune response.
Lymphoma	is a cancer that starts in the lymphatic system. It weakens the immune system and increases the risk of developing infections.

Risk Factors and Causes of Cancer

Although the causes of some types of cancers are unknown, scientists have identified certain risk factors. **Risk factors** are *characteristics or behaviors that increase the likelihood of developing a medical disorder or disease.* Heredity, age, lifestyle choices, and environmental factors are some of the risk factors that can increase a person's risk of cancer. For example, someone whose diet is high in saturated fats and low in fiber is at an increased risk for colon and rectal cancers.

Some types of cancer are caused by exposure to carcinogens (kar·SI·nuh·juhnz). **Carcinogens** are *substances that cause cancer.* For example, asbestos is a carcinogen. This material was used in construction and manufacturing until it was discovered to contain cancerous substances. Other common carcinogens are the chemicals in tobacco, which are linked to lung and mouth cancers. Not all carcinogens are chemicals. For instance, ultraviolet light from the sun can cause skin cancer. Radiation, including X-rays, can also cause cancer in large doses.

Reading Check

Recall Name two carcinogens and the types of cancers they cause.

Diagnosing Cancer

Health care professionals have many ways to begin checking for cancer. They can identify a group of abnormal cells when looking at the skin. They might feel a lump where the tissue should be soft. X-rays and other scanning equipment can also locate abnormal cell formations. If a suspicious lump or formation is discovered, a biopsy is usually done on the tissue. A **biopsy** is *the removal of a sample of tissue from a person for examination.* To diagnose cancer, the physician will examine tissue samples under a microscope to see if the cells are cancerous. If the cells are found to be cancerous, the patient will begin treatment. In order to diagnose cancer early, it is important to watch for warning signs. **Figure 19.2** on page 514 shows some of the warning signs of cancer. A person who shows a warning sign of cancer should be examined by a physician as soon as possible.

▲ Most cells in your body divide at a controlled rate. Cancer cells divide at an uncontrolled rate. **How are the normal cells in the top picture different from the cancer cells in the bottom picture?**

The Warning Signs of Cancer

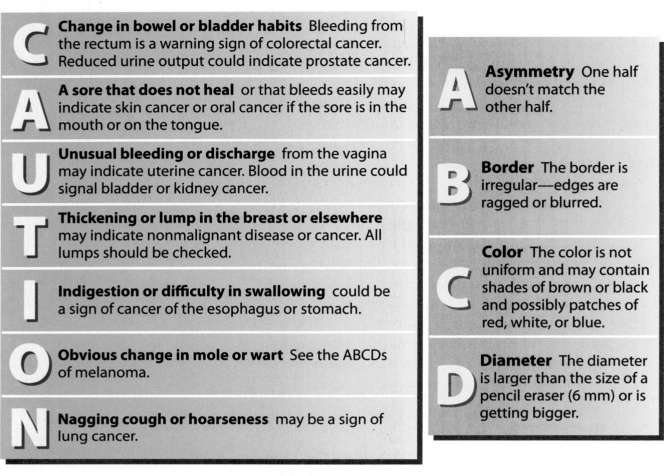

C — **Change in bowel or bladder habits** Bleeding from the rectum is a warning sign of colorectal cancer. Reduced urine output could indicate prostate cancer.

A — **A sore that does not heal** or that bleeds easily may indicate skin cancer or oral cancer if the sore is in the mouth or on the tongue.

U — **Unusual bleeding or discharge** from the vagina may indicate uterine cancer. Blood in the urine could signal bladder or kidney cancer.

T — **Thickening or lump in the breast or elsewhere** may indicate nonmalignant disease or cancer. All lumps should be checked.

I — **Indigestion or difficulty in swallowing** could be a sign of cancer of the esophagus or stomach.

O — **Obvious change in mole or wart** See the ABCDs of melanoma.

N — **Nagging cough or hoarseness** may be a sign of lung cancer.

A — **Asymmetry** One half doesn't match the other half.

B — **Border** The border is irregular—edges are ragged or blurred.

C — **Color** The color is not uniform and may contain shades of brown or black and possibly patches of red, white, or blue.

D — **Diameter** The diameter is larger than the size of a pencil eraser (6 mm) or is getting bigger.

Treating Cancer

The best way to treat cancer depends on many factors. These include the type of cancer, the stage of the disease, and the age and general health of the patient. The following are the most common cancer treatments:

- **Surgery** removes cancer cells from the body. It is used for treating breast, skin, lung, and colon cancer, among others.

- **Radiation therapy** is *a treatment that uses X-rays or other forms of radiation to kill cancer cells.* The high-energy rays from radioactive substances destroy or shrink the cancer cells.

- **Chemotherapy** is *the use of powerful medicines to destroy cancer cells.* It is often used to fight cancers that have spread throughout the body, such as leukemia.

All treatments have side effects. For example, the side effects of radiation therapy and chemotherapy include nausea, fatigue, and temporary hair loss. When cancer treatment is successful, the

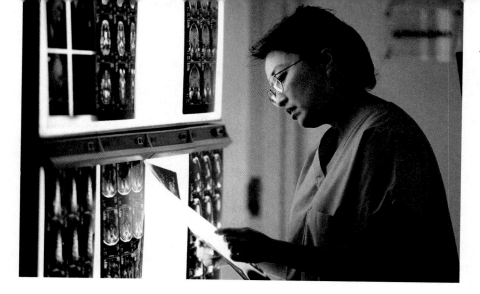

◄ Health care professionals can often detect signs of cancer in several ways. **Why is early detection of some types of cancer so important?**

cancer is in remission. **Remission** is *when cancer signs and symptoms disappear.* Cancer that is in remission can sometimes return. *The return of cancer after a remission* is called a **recurrence.**

Reading Check **Recall** What are two treatments commonly used for a cancer?

Reducing the Risk of Cancer

You can take an active role in promoting good health and reducing cancer risks. Here are some tips:

- **Avoid tobacco and alcohol.** Cigarette smoking is the single major cause of cancer deaths in the United States. Excessive alcohol use increases the risk of several types of cancer.

- **Limit sun exposure.** One way to protect yourself from UV rays is to limit your time in the sun. You should also apply a sunscreen with an SPF of at least 15 before you go outdoors. Wearing a hat that shades your neck, your face, and the tops of your ears is also a way to limit sun exposure.

- **Be physically active.** Be at least moderately active for 60 minutes or more on most days.

- **Perform self-examinations.** Females should perform monthly self-exams of their breasts. Males should perform a testicular self-exam once a month. Ask your health care provider for information on how to conduct both of these exams. In addition, check your skin regularly for moles and other skin growths. If you notice any changes in them, see a health care provider right away.

Reading Check **Explain** What is meant by the ABCDs of checking moles?

Visit **health.glencoe.com** and complete the Interactive Study Guide for Lesson 2.

Health Skills Activity

Advocacy

Reducing the Risk of Cancer

You can make healthy choices that will reduce your risk of getting certain cancers. Create a resource for your school. Collect information on some preventable cancers. Create a booklet on what teens can do to reduce their risk of getting some types of cancer. Start with this information:

- Lung and mouth cancer: avoid chewing and smoking tobacco.
- Skin cancer: limit exposure to the sun, and wear sunscreen with an SPF of at least 15 when outdoors.
- Liver cancer: avoid excessive use of alcohol.

In a Group

Design a booklet or computer presentation on healthy behaviors to prevent cancer. Think of a memorable title for your booklet. Include a slogan and logo. Give your presentation or present your booklet to the class.

Lesson 2 Review

After You Read

Review this lesson for new terms, major headings, and Reading Checks.

What I Learned

1. **Vocabulary** Define *cancer*.

2. **Identify** What are four common types of cancer?

3. **Describe** Describe ways that cancer can be treated.

4. **Give Examples** What are three ways to reduce the risk of cancer?

Thinking Critically

5. **Synthesize** Why is it important to diagnose cancer as early as possible?

6. **Apply** Why do people with outdoor jobs have a higher risk of skin cancer than people who work indoors?

Applying Health Skills

7. **Accessing Information** Living with cancer can be very difficult for both cancer patients and their families. Research the type of support groups available in your community for people dealing with cancer.

Heart and Circulatory Problems

Guide to Reading

● Building Vocabulary
To help you learn each vocabulary term, divide it into syllables. The smaller parts make the longer terms easier to pronounce and understand.

- arteriosclerosis (p. 518)
- atherosclerosis (p. 518)
- hypertension (p. 519)
- stroke (p. 519)
- heart attack (p. 519)
- angioplasty (p. 519)
- Body Mass Index (BMI) (p. 521)

● Focus on the Main Ideas
In this lesson you will be able to

- **identify** and describe different types of heart disease.
- **describe** how to treat heart disease.
- **explain** ways to reduce the risk of heart disease.

● Reading Strategy
Identifying Cause-and-Effect List three lifestyle behaviors that can cause heart disease.

What Is Heart Disease?

The term *heart disease* describes any condition that weakens the heart and blood vessels and makes them less functional. More adults in the United States die from heart disease than from any other cause. In fact, about 13 million people in the United States have heart disease, and about 1 million people die from this condition every year. The risk of heart disease depends partly on age and heredity. However, most heart disease is the result of lifestyle behaviors, such as smoking, eating too many foods high in

Quick Write

What are three ways to keep your heart healthy?

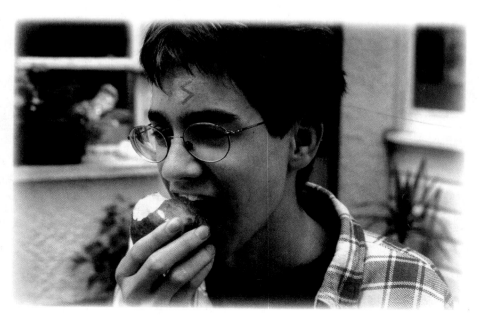

► Eating nutritious foods can help you maintain a healthy heart. **What other factors contribute to the health of your heart?**

saturated fat, and not getting enough regular physical activity. Teens who make healthy lifestyle choices are less likely to develop heart disease as adults.

Types of Heart Disease

Body cells must have a constant supply of fresh oxygen to survive. The body's tissues and organs depend on the flow of blood through the arteries to deliver oxygen to the cells. When the arteries are clear and healthy, the blood flows through them freely. When the arteries are damaged or blocked, the blood does not flow as well.

Two disorders can result from problems with the blood flow through the arteries. **Arteriosclerosis** is *a group of disorders in which arteries harden and become more rigid.* When the arteries become rigid, less blood is able to flow through them. **Atherosclerosis** *occurs when fatty substances in the blood build up on the walls of the arteries.* This buildup shrinks the space through which blood can travel. **Figure 19.3** shows how arteries can become blocked. If the space in the coronary arteries narrows, the heart may not get enough oxygen.

▼ **FIGURE 19.3**

How Arteries Become Blocked

The heart's muscle tissue gets blood from the coronary arteries. When arteries become blocked, the heart is prevented from getting the blood it needs. **What do you think might happen when the heart does not get enough blood?**

Partially Blocked Artery
A buildup of plaque slows the flow of blood.

Plaque

Healthy Artery
Blood is able to flow freely.

Blood Flow

Blood Flow

Other Cardiovascular Problems

As your heart beats, it pushes blood through your body's blood vessels, creating pressure on the blood vessels' walls. This force is called blood pressure. When a person's blood pressure is higher than normal, he or she has high blood pressure, or hypertension. **Hypertension** is *a condition in which the pressure of the blood on the walls of the blood vessels stays at a level that is higher than normal.* High blood pressure can lead to a heart attack or a stroke. A **stroke** is *a serious condition that occurs when an artery of the brain breaks or becomes blocked.* Brain cells die from lack of oxygen, affecting the part of the body controlled by those cells.

Have your blood pressure checked regularly by a health care professional. Most hypertension can be treated with a healthful eating plan, physical activity, stress management, and medication.

Heart Attack

A **heart attack** is *a condition in which blood flow to a part of the heart is greatly reduced or blocked.* If the blood is cut off for more than a few minutes, the heart muscle cells are damaged and die. Heart attacks usually cause pain, tightness, or pressure in the chest, or pain spreading in the arms, jaw, back, or abdomen. Other symptoms may include cold skin, shortness of breath, sweating, fainting, nausea, and lightheadedness.

> **Reading Check**
>
> **Compare** What do heart attacks and strokes have in common?

Health Online

Topic: Taking Positive Action

Visit health.glencoe.com for Student Web Activities to learn more about how young people are taking action to help find cures for noncommunicable diseases like cancer, diabetes, and heart disease.

Activity: Using the information provided at the link above, create your own plan to help find a cure for one of the diseases mentioned in this lesson.

Treating Heart Disease

To help people with heart disease, health care professionals use some of the following treatments:

- **Angioplasty** (AN·je·uh·plas·tee) is *a surgical procedure in which an instrument with a tiny balloon, drill bit, or laser attached is inserted into a blocked artery to clear a blockage.* These devices either flatten, cut, or burn away the blockage.

- **Medications** can dissolve blood clots that block arteries. Sometimes aspirin is prescribed to prevent platelets from clumping together to form blood clots.

▼ Medication is one way to treat heart disease. **What are some other ways?**

Analyzing Influences

Heart-Healthy Ads

Teens are surrounded by food ads in magazines, television, radio, newspapers, billboards, and other media. With heart disease receiving so much attention in the media, food makers have begun advertising many foods as "heart-healthy." Find two advertisements in print, on the radio, or on television that advertise heart-healthy foods. Study the ads. How do the ads promote the foods? What language do they use? How do you think the ad writers want you to feel about eating the food? Do the ads contain any facts? Are these facts reliable? How can you tell?

In a Group

Create an advertisement for a delicious, heart-healthy meal. Include creative lettering, clipped magazine or newspaper pictures, and information about the food. Make your ad inviting, so teens are persuaded to try your heart-healthy meal.

- **Pacemakers** are electronic devices implanted into the chest to help the heart beat regularly. The pacemaker creates electrical signals that control the heartbeat.

- **Bypass surgery** creates new pathways for blood to flow around blockages. Surgeons can take a healthy blood vessel from another part of the body, such as the leg, and make a detour around the blocked part of the coronary artery.

- **Heart valve surgery** is when a faulty valve can be replaced with an artifical one made of metal or plastic.

- **Heart transplants** completely replace a person's damaged heart with the healthy heart of someone who recently died. Heart transplants are extremely complicated, so they are done only when the heart is severely damaged and no other treatment will work.

How to Prevent Heart Disease

Although symptoms of heart disease usually do not appear until adulthood, heart disease can begin developing in child-hood. Making healthy choices today can decrease your risk of developing heart disease when you are older. Here are some strategies for keeping your heart healthy:

- **Eat healthful foods.** Eat a variety of fresh fruits and vegetables, whole-grain cereals, and lean sources of protein.

- **Participate in regular physical activity.** Regular physical activity strengthens the muscle tissue in your heart. Being active also helps you manage stress and maintain a healthy body weight.

- **Maintain a healthy BMI. Body Mass Index (BMI)** is *a formula you can use to determine if your weight is appropriate for you.* Your heart works best if your BMI is within a healthy range. Ask a health care provider to help you find the right range for you.

- **Manage stress.** Constant stress can lead to high blood pressure. Learn how to relax and reduce stress.

- **Stay tobacco free.** The chemicals in tobacco can lead to heart disease, heart attacks, hypertension, and even strokes.

Reading Check **Describe** How can you lower your risk of heart disease?

Health Online

Visit **health.glencoe.com** and complete the Interactive Study Guide for Lesson 3.

Lesson 3 Review

 After You Read

Review this lesson for new terms, major headings, and Reading Checks.

What I Learned

1. *Vocabulary* Define *hypertension.*

2. *Identify* Name two types of heart disease. How are they similar? How are they different?

3. *Explain* What are some ways to reduce the risk of heart disease?

4. *Give Examples* What are three medical procedures to help people with heart disease?

Thinking Critically

5. *Analyze* Why is it a good idea to have your blood pressure checked regularly by a health care professional?

6. *Apply* What questions would you ask a health care provider if you want the provider to help you set up a plan to reduce your risk of heart disease?

Applying Health Skills

7. *Practicing Healthy Behaviors* Both of Tyler's grandfathers died of heart disease. Tyler wants to reduce his own risk of heart disease. Make a list of positive health behaviors Tyler can do to reduce his risk of heart disease.

Diabetes and Arthritis

Guide to Reading

Building Vocabulary
Fold a sheet of paper in half to form two columns. Write each term on the left side of the fold and its definition on the other side. Fold the sheet in half again. Look at each term and quiz yourself on its definition. Flip over the paper and check the definition.

- diabetes (p. 522)
- insulin (p. 522)
- type 1 diabetes (p. 523)
- type 2 diabetes (p. 523)
- arthritis (p. 524)
- osteoarthritis (p. 524)
- rheumatoid arthritis (p. 525)

Focusing on the Main Ideas
In this lesson you will learn to

- **describe** the different types of diabetes.
- **identify** different types of arthritis.
- **explain** how to manage diabetes and arthritis.

Reading Strategy
Organizing Information Using the diagram below as a guide, create a table that helps you sort the information about diabetes and arthritis that appears in this lesson.

Diabetes	Arthritis
Types	Types
Ways to Manage	Ways to Manage

Quick Write

Write two facts that you already know about diabetes.

What Is Diabetes?

Diabetes (dy·uh·BEE·teez) is *a disease that prevents the body from converting food into energy.* People with diabetes are referred to as *diabetics.* Their bodies do not produce or properly use insulin. **Insulin** (IN·suh·lin) is *a protein made in the pancreas that regulates the level of glucose in the blood.* The body uses insulin to convert the food you eat into the energy that your body's cells need.

How does it work? Your body breaks down the food you eat into glucose, a simple sugar. The pancreas, sensing that you have eaten, releases insulin. The insulin allows glucose from the blood to enter the cells throughout the body. Diabetics either do not produce enough natural insulin, or cannot properly use their insulin to move the glucose into their cells. Instead, the glucose stays in the bloodstream and can cause many health problems. If not treated properly, diabetes can cause kidney problems, blindness, and heart disease.

▶ Getting regular physical activity can lower your risk of getting type 2 diabetes. **What is the difference between type 1 and type 2 diabetes?**

Types of Diabetes

There are two main types of diabetes: type 1 and type 2. **Type 1 diabetes** is *a condition in which the immune system attacks insulin-producing cells in the pancreas.* When the cells that produce insulin are killed, the body cannot control how much glucose is in the bloodstream. Type 1 diabetes often starts in childhood, but it may also begin in adulthood. Somewhere between 5 and 10 percent of diabetics have type 1 diabetes.

Type 2 diabetes is *a condition in which the body cannot effectively use the insulin it produces.* In type 2 diabetes, the cells in the pancreas still make insulin but the body does not use it well. Between 90 and 95 percent of diabetics have type 2 diabetes, which usually begins in adulthood. Obese people and physically inactive people are especially at risk. Type 2 diabetes is also becoming more and more common among children and teens.

Reading Check **Recall** How does the body use insulin?

Managing Diabetes

Although there is no cure for diabetes, people with the disease can keep it under control and lead normal lives. Type 1 diabetics usually need to regularly inject insulin into their bodies. Or, they may receive insulin from a pump attached to their bodies. Even children with type 1 diabetes can learn to manage their condition. Type 2 diabetics may also need insulin or other medications. People with either type of diabetes can help control their disease by making healthy food choices, managing their weight, and being physically active. **Figure 19.4** on page 524 shows ways people manage this condition.

Reading Check **Describe** How can diabetes be managed?

Connect To... Science

Monitoring Glucose Levels

Today's technology provides portable blood glucose monitors that can be used anywhere. Several models give voice instructions—in a choice of languages—to guide the user through the test procedure. The machine then announces the test results.

Who might benefit most from one of these "talking" blood glucose monitors?

MANAGING DIABETES

People with diabetes can successfully learn to manage their condition. **What are some ways that people can use the following strategies in their daily lives?**

Healthful Food Plan	Medical professionals can help people with diabetes create a food plan that helps keep blood glucose levels within a healthy range.
Weight Management	To maintain a healthy weight, people with diabetes should engage in regular physical activity.
Insulin Injections	People with Type 1 diabetes and some with Type 2 diabetes usually inject insulin through a syringe or pump.
Medical Care	Diabetics should be under the care of a health care professional. He or she can monitor the diabetic's health and watch for problems.

What Is Arthritis?

Arthritis (ar·THRY·tus) is *a disease of the joints marked by painful swelling and stiffness.* More than 40 million people in the United States have arthritis. This disease is usually linked to older adults, but even children can get arthritis. The two most common types of arthritis are osteoarthritis and rheumatoid arthritis.

Osteoarthritis

Osteoarthritis (ahs·tee·oh·ahr·THRY·tuhs) is *a chronic disease that results from a breakdown in cartilage in the joints.* Cartilage cushions the place where bones meet in a joint. Osteoarthritis most often affects the knees and hips. When cartilage wears down, the bones in the joints rub against each other. This rubbing creates pain in the joint, swelling, and morning stiffness. Risk factors for osteoarthritis include age, heredity, and excess weight.

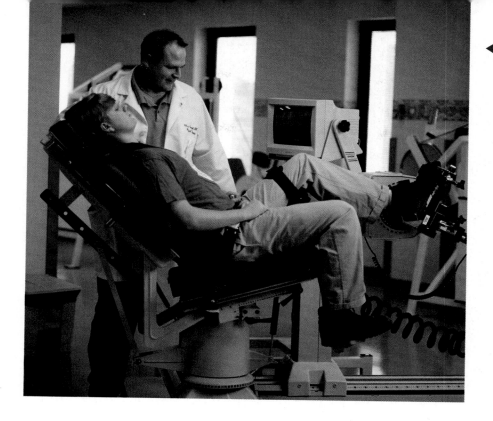

This teen has juvenile rheumatoid arthritis (JRA), which causes joint pain and can limit movement. **What types of challenges might a teen with arthritis face?**

Rheumatoid Arthritis

Rheumatoid arthritis (ROO·muh·toyd) is *a chronic disease characterized by pain, inflammation, swelling, and stiffness of the joints.* This type of arthritis is more serious than osteoarthritis. People can develop rheumatoid arthritis when their immune system attacks healthy joint tissue, leading to painful swelling. Rheumatoid arthritis can affect any joint in the body, including joints in the shoulders, elbows, hands, hips, and feet. The joints affected by rheumatoid arthritis often become deformed and no longer function normally. Symptoms include soreness, joint pain and stiffness, body aches, and fatigue.

Reading Check

Name What are two of the most common types of arthritis?

Managing Arthritis

Unfortunately, there is no cure for arthritis. However, people with this disease can develop a plan to reduce their symptoms and improve their personal health. Many plans involve a combination of the following healthy behaviors:

- **Physical activity and rest.** A key to managing arthritis is to develop a good balance between low-impact physical activity (such as walking and swimming) and rest. Physical activity can reduce swelling and help increase flexibility in the joints. When people with arthritis get enough rest it helps them cope with the fatigue they often experience.

- **A balanced eating plan.** Eating healthy foods helps maintain overall health and keeps weight under control.
- **Joint protection.** Braces and splints can sometimes be used to help support the joints.
- **Heat and cold treatments.** Hot baths can ease the pain of some kinds of arthritis. Cold treatments can help decrease the swelling.
- **Medication.** Some people who have arthritis take medicine to help ease the pain and swelling and to slow the inflammatory process.
- **Massage.** When given by a properly trained massage therapist, a very mild massage can help relax the joints and increase blood flow to sore areas.
- **Surgery and joint replacement.** Sometimes in extreme cases, surgeons can operate to repair or realign a joint. A joint may even be replaced with an artificial one.

Health Online

Visit **health.glencoe.com** and complete the Interactive Study Guide for Lesson 4.

Reading Check **Give Examples** What are four ways to manage arthritis?

Lesson 4 Review

After You Read

Review this lesson for new terms, major headings, and Reading Checks.

What I Learned

1. *Vocabulary* What is *arthritis*?

2. *Describe* Describe the two different types of diabetes.

3. *Explain* What often happens to a joint affected by rheumatoid arthritis?

Thinking Critically

4. *Analysis* What do type 1 diabetes and rheumatoid arthritis have in common?

5. *Evaluation* Based on what you know about arthritis, how can you help someone with arthritis manage the disease?

Applying Health Skills

6. *Practicing Healthful Behaviors* Participating in regular physical activity can help reduce your risk of developing type 2 diabetes. If you enjoy what you do, you are more likely to participate in the activity on a regular basis. List ten physical activities you enjoy or might enjoy doing. Make a check mark beside three activities you will participate in during the next month. Make a commitment to do each of these activities at least once a week.

Allergies and Asthma

Guide to Reading

Building Vocabulary
As you read this lesson, write each term below and its definition in your notebook.

- allergy (p. 527)
- allergens (p. 527)
- pollen (p. 527)
- histamines (p. 528)
- hives (p. 528)
- antihistamines (p. 529)
- asthma (p. 530)
- bronchodilators (p. 531)

Focusing on the Main Ideas
In this lesson you will learn to

- **describe** how to manage an allergic reaction.
- **explain** what happens during an asthma attack.
- **identify** ways to manage asthma.

Reading Strategy
Comparing and Contrasting Identify the similarities and differences between the symptoms and treatments of allergies and asthma.

Quick Write

List three allergy symptoms. How can they be managed?

What Are Allergies?

Your immune system reacts to foreign substances in your body by trying to weaken or eliminate them. As it reacts, it releases antibodies that fight the foreign substances. Sometimes, however, your immune system reacts to a fairly harmless substance. This reaction is an allergic response. An **allergy** is *an extreme sensitivity to a substance.*

A person can be allergic to a number of different substances in the environment. *Substances that cause allergic responses* are called **allergens.** Allergens are very small. **Figure 19.5** on page 528 illustrates some common allergens. When an allergen enters or comes in contact with a person's body, the immune system reacts as though it were harmful. When people are allergic to cats, for example, their allergic response is usually caused by dander on the cat's skin or fur. When people are allergic to ragweed, it is the tiny pollen grains from the plant that cause the allergic reaction, not the plant as a whole. **Pollen** is *a powdery substance released by the flowers of some plants.* Every day, the U.S. Environmental Protection Agency measures the amount of pollen in the air, which is reported in newspapers and on radio and television.

COMMON ALLERGENS

Some allergens are easier to avoid than others. What kind of difficulties do people who suffer from allergies face?

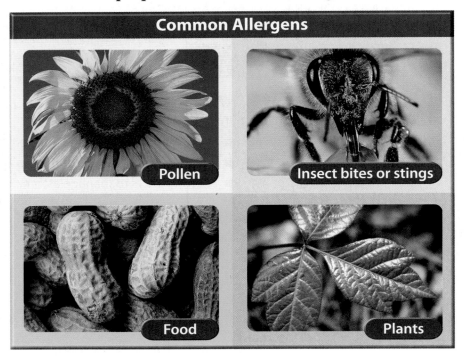

Common Allergens

Pollen

Insect bites or stings

Food

Plants

Allergic Reactions

When someone comes into contact with an allergen, the allergen binds to white blood cells called lymphocytes. These lymphocytes then release proteins called **histamines** (HIS·tuh·meenz). These are *the chemicals in the body that cause the symptoms of the allergic reaction.* **Figure 19.6** on page 529 shows some of the symptoms a person may experience during an allergic reaction. Allergic reactions can range from minor irritations to severe problems. For example, some people get hives as a reaction to an allergen. **Hives** are *raised bumps on the skin that are very itchy.* Most allergic reactions happen within seconds or minutes of the time the allergen enters the body.

Some people are at risk for severe allergic reactions, including throat swelling or extreme difficulty breathing. Because they might die if they are not treated immediately, these people may need to carry medicine called *epinephrine.* Epinephrine slows down or stops the allergic reaction by preventing the body from releasing histamines.

Reading Check **List** What are five ways that the body responds to allergens?

How to Manage Allergies

Although there is no cure for allergies, there are three basic ways to manage them.

- **Avoid the allergen.** If you have a food allergy, learn to read ingredient labels. Ask about the ingredients of foods in restaurants. Avoid plants or animals that you are allergic to.

- **Take medication.** People with allergies often take medicines that help reduce allergy symptoms. **Antihistamines** are *medicines that help control the effects triggered by histamines.* For example, antihistamines may relieve itching and redness around the eyes and nose.

- **Get injections.** In severe cases, a long-term series of injections is needed. The injections contain a tiny amount of the allergen to help the body build up immunity.

Reading Check **Describe** What are three methods that people can use to manage allergies?

▼ **FIGURE 19.6**

THE BODY'S RESPONSES TO ALLERGENS

Allergic reactions vary depending on the allergen. Different people sometimes even react differently to the same allergen. **Which allergic reaction do you think has the most dangerous health consequences?**

Body Responses to Allergens

Eyes
redden, itch, water, eyelids swell

Respiratory System
runny nose, sneezing, coughing, difficulty breathing

Throat
difficulty swallowing

Skin
redness, rash, hives, itching

Digestive System
pain, cramps, diarrhea, nausea

▲ Many people with asthma carry inhalers that contain bronchodilators. **What are some other ways to manage asthma?**

What Is Asthma?

Asthma is *a condition in which the small airways in the lungs narrow, making breathing difficult.* More than 20 million people in the United States have asthma. About one-third of these people are under 18 years old. Some people outgrow their asthma, while others develop this disease in adulthood.

Asthma attacks can be triggered by many substances and conditions. A substance that triggers an attack in one person may have no effect on someone else. Common triggers include tobacco smoke, air pollution, and animal dander. Cold air, strenuous physical activity, strong emotions, and stress can also trigger an asthma attack. **Figure 19.7** explains what happens during an asthma attack.

Reading Check **Recall** What are some common triggers of asthma attacks?

▼ **FIGURE 19.7**

ASTHMA ATTACK

During an asthma attack, air passages become constricted and clogged with mucus. **What are some symptoms of an asthma attack?**

A Healthy bronchial tubes are clear and open. Air passes easily through them to fill tiny air sacs in the lungs.

B During an asthma attack, muscles around the bronchial tubes tighten. The tubes narrow and their inner lining swells. Excess mucus clogs airways, making breathing difficult.

Swelling

Mucus

Normal, clear airways

Tightened airways

How to Manage Asthma

Since there is no cure for asthma, most people with the disease learn to manage it and lead active lives. Managing asthma is often a team effort. Parents or trusted guardians, health care professionals, and friends can help people with asthma stay healthy. Here are some strategies that people with asthma can use to help avoid asthma attacks:

- **Manage the environment.** Avoid triggers that can cause asthma attacks.

- **Manage stress.** Stress is a major cause of asthma attacks. Learn to manage stress in healthful ways.

- **Take medication.** Relievers and controllers are two kinds of asthma medicines. **Bronchodilators** are *reliever medications used to relax the muscles around the air passages.* They help reduce symptoms during an asthma attack. Controller medications are often taken daily and help prevent asthma attacks from occuring.

Reading Check **Describe** How can a teen with asthma reduce triggers in the surrounding environment?

Health Online

Visit **health.glencoe.com** and complete the Interactive Study Guide for Lesson 5.

Lesson 5 Review

After You Read

Review this lesson for new terms, major headings, and Reading Checks.

What I Learned

1. *Vocabulary* Define *allergy* and *asthma*.

2. *Give Examples* What are three ways to manage an asthma attack?

3. *Describe* What are some common symptoms of an allergic reaction?

4. *Identify* Name four common types of allergens.

Thinking Critically

5. *Synthesize* If your friend is having an asthma attack, what are two ways you could help?

6. *Hypothesize* If someone has a food allergy, why do you think it is important for that person to be careful eating in restaurants?

Applying Health Skills

7. *Communication Skills* Alisha tried out for the cheerleading team and made it! She has asthma, however, and is too embarrassed to tell anyone about it. Write a short letter to Alisha and tell her why you think she should tell her coach and teammates that she has asthma.

Lifelong Good Health Habits

DIRECTIONS

Goal Setting involves setting positive goals and taking steps to achieve them. This activity will give you the opportunity to develop and master this important health skill. Here's a guide to the different parts of this activity:

❶ In the **Model** section, you will read about a teen who performs the health skill successfully. This "model" scenario will show you how the skill is done.

❷ The **Practice** section will help guide you in practicing the skill.

❸ In the **Apply** section, you will have a chance to perform the skill on your own. You can use the Self-Check to check your work.

To complete this activity, first read the scenario presented in the Model. Then move on to the Practice. Finally, go ahead and try the Apply.

❶ Model

Sasha is excited about the upcoming 10-mile race. The race is a fundraiser to support diabetes research. Sasha has diabetes and has kept herself physically fit. She wants to participate in the event, although she has never jogged 10 miles.

Sasha decides to set a goal of participating in the race. First, she writes down her goal—jogging in the race. Next, she gets help from her doctor. Her doctor outlines a program that she can follow to prepare her for the 10-mile run. Her doctor schedules an appointment two weeks from now to evaluate Sasha's health. Sasha also decides she will reward herself with a new pair of walking shoes when she reaches her goal. She follows the steps, raises $350 through sponsorships, and ends up having a lot of fun.

② Practice

Sasha's friend Becca has been diagnosed with type 1 diabetes. Becca wants to go with Sasha and her other classmates to Washington, D.C., for a school-sponsored trip. Becca would like to learn how to manage her diabetes well enough so that she can go on the school trip and have a good time.

1. What is Becca's goal?
2. What are the steps Becca needs to take to reach her goal?
3. Whom can Becca go to for help?
4. How can Becca evaluate her progress?
5. What is Becca's reward?

Skill Summary
GOAL SETTING

- Set a specific goal and write it down.
- List the steps to reach your goal.
- Get help and support from others.
- Evaluate your progress.
- Reward yourself once you reach your goal.

③ Apply

Think of a physical activity that you want to try, such as in-line skating or rock climbing. Set a goal to do this activity. Use the goal setting process to help you develop a plan to achieve your goal.

1. Identify your goal and write it down.
2. Make a list of what you will need to get started.
3. Think of people who could help you achieve your goal.
4. How will you know when you have achieved your goal?
5. Think of a way to reward yourself when you reach your goal.

Self-Check

- Did I set a specific goal?
- Did I make a list of what I will need to get started?
- Did I identify someone who could help me reach my goal?

The Eber family bikes around the world to help fight asthma.

The Road to A CURE

The Ebers in Germany

Recently, the four members of the Eber family rode their bikes to the U.S. Capitol in Washington, D.C. It was no lazy Saturday-morning outing. It was the last leg of a 16-month bike trip around the world. Paula, Lorenz, Anya, and Yvonne Eber pedaled more than 9,300 miles and visited 24 countries. Their mission: to raise awareness of—and money for—asthma.

"Asthma is a big problem," Anya, 15, said. The disease makes it hard for as many as 150 million people

Paula, 45, knows how hard having asthma can be. As a child, her severe case forced her to spend months in bed. Medications that enabled her to participate in sports weren't available until she was a teenager. "A lot of kids [with asthma] today still don't get to live an active life," Paula explains.

The Ebers have taken many bike trips, but nothing like this one! Highlights included eating a Christmas dinner of Chinese duck in Hong Kong and celebrating Yvonne's 12th birthday with coconut-and-mango cake in Tonga, which is located in the Pacific Ocean. On most of the journey, the family slept in tents. The hardest part, Yvonne says, was braving the heat, wind, rain, and bugs.

While on the road to help find a cure, the Ebers furthered their love of nature. Returning to life at their home in Bainbridge Island, Washington, wasn't easy. "I've had school outdoors for months," Anya says. "It will be so weird to sit at a desk!"

The Ebers in Holland

throughout the world to breathe. The Ebers hope to collect donations for World Bike for Breath, the organization that they began. The money will be spent on asthma research and programs for kids who have the illness.

ASTHMA BY THE NUMBERS

With today's treatments, experts say most kids with asthma shouldn't experience too many symptoms. A 2004 study of the six million kids in the U.S. who have asthma, however, showed that in one year...

54 percent had a severe asthma attack

23 percent made at least one trip to the emergency room

54 percent missed some school or day care

62 percent had to limit their activities as a result of their condition

Source: TIME

Reading Review

FOLDABLES™ Study Organizer

Foldables™ and Other Study Aids Take out the Foldable™ you created for Lesson 1 and any graphic organizers that you created for Lessons 1–5. Find a partner and quiz each other using these study aids.

Lesson 1) Causes of Noncommunicable Diseases

Key Ideas

- Noncommunicable diseases cannot be spread from one person to another.
- Risk factors include heredity, age, gender, lifestyle choices, and environmental factors.

Vocabulary

- noncommunicable diseases (p. 508)
- chronic diseases (p. 508)
- degenerative disease (p. 508)
- congenital disorder (p. 508)
- heredity (p. 509)

Lesson 2) Cancer

Key Ideas

- Cancer is characterized by the rapid and uncontrolled growth of abnormal cells.
- Three common cancer treatments are radiation therapy, chemotherapy, and surgery.

Vocabulary

- cancer (p. 511)
- tumor (p. 511)
- benign (p. 512)
- malignant (p. 512)
- risk factors (p. 513)
- carcinogens (p. 513)
- biopsy (p. 513)
- radiation therapy (p. 514)
- chemotherapy (p. 514)
- remission (p. 515)
- recurrence (p. 515)

Lesson 3) Heart and Circulatory Problems

Key Idea

- Heart disease is any condition that weakens the heart or impairs the way it functions.

Vocabulary

- arteriosclerosis (p. 518)
- atherosclerosis (p. 518)
- hypertension (p. 519)
- stroke (p. 519)
- heart attack (p. 519)
- angioplasty (p. 519)
- body mass index (BMI) (p. 521)

Lesson 4) Diabetes and Arthritis

Key Ideas

- Diabetes is a disease that prevents the body from converting food into energy.
- A disease of the joints marked by painful swelling and stiffness is called arthritis.

Vocabulary

- diabetes (p. 522)
- insulin (p. 522)
- type 1 diabetes (p. 523)
- type 2 diabetes (p. 523)
- arthritis (p. 524)
- osteoarthritis (p. 524)
- rheumatoid arthritis (p. 525)

Lesson 5) Allergies and Asthma

Key Idea

- Allergies and asthma can both be managed with medicine, and by avoiding known allergens.

Vocabulary

- allergy (p. 527)
- allergens (p. 527)
- pollen (p. 527)
- histamines (p. 528)
- hives (p. 528)
- antihistamines (p. 529)
- asthma (p. 530)
- bronchodilators (p. 531)

After You Read

HEALTH INVENTORY

Now that you have read the chapter, look back at your answers to the Health Inventory in the chapter opener. Is there anything you should do differently?

Reviewing Vocabulary and Main Ideas

On a sheet of paper, write the numbers 1–8. After each number, write the term from the list that best completes each statement.

- chronic
- heredity
- degenerative
- arteriosclerosis
- heart attack
- stroke
- tumor
- benign
- malignant
- risk factors

Lesson 1 Causes of Noncommunicable Diseases

1. _____ disease symptoms are present continuously or off and on over a long period of time.

2. Some noncommunicable diseases can be the result of _____.

Lesson 2 Cancer

3. A group of abnormal cells in the body is called a(n) _____.

4. When tumors are cancerous, they are called _____.

5. _____ are behaviors that increase the likelihood of developing a medical disorder or disease.

Lesson 3 Heart and Circulatory Problems

6. _____ is a group of disorders in which arteries harden and become more rigid.

7. When the blood supply to the heart slows or stops and the heart muscle is damaged, a(n) _____ can happen.

8. When an artery of the brain breaks or becomes blocked, the person may have a(n) _____.

*On a sheet of paper, write the numbers 9–14. Write **True** or **False** for each statement below. If the statement is false, change the underlined word or phrase to make it true.*

Lesson 4 Diabetes and Arthritis

9. Arthritis is a disease of the joints marked by painful swelling and stiffness.

10. Type 1 diabetes is the most common form of the disease.

11. Keeping physically active helps manage diabetes.

Lesson 5 Allergies and Asthma

12. Hives are a powdery substance released by the flowers of some plants.

13. Chemicals in the body that cause the symptoms of an allergic reaction are called allergens.

14. A serious chronic condition that causes air passages in the respiratory system to become narrow or blocked is asthma.

Thinking Critically

Using complete sentences, answer the following questions on a sheet of paper.

15. **Apply** If someone has arthritis, why might swimming be helpful?

16. **Hypothesize** Why might people who are allergic to flower pollen experience fewer symptoms in places with cold winters?

Write About It

17. **Practicing Healthful Behaviors** Interview someone you know who is a diabetic. Write a paragraph describing how diabetes has affected this person's life. Include the healthy ways he or she manages the disease.

Career Corner

Family Practice Physicians Would you like to be a physician who takes care of common health problems? One type of doctor who provides basic care for a variety of illnesses and injuries is called a "family practioner." If you were this type of doctor, you would provide general health care for people of all ages. However, if a patient has a specific medical problem, you might refer them to a specialist. To become a family practitioner, you need a bachelor's degree, four years of medical school, and several years of medical residency. Read more about this career and other medical health careers by visiting *Career Corner* at **health.glencoe.com**.

Standardized Test Practice

Math

Acute lymphoblastic leukemia (A.L.L.) is a serious disease that affects the white blood cells in the body. This table shows the survival rates of patients with A.L.L.

Use the table to answer the questions.

Survival Rates for A.L.L. Patients	
Year	% of Patients Surviving at Least 5 Years
1965	5
2000	85

TEST-TAKING TIP

When you are trying to find trends by studying the data from a chart, it often helps to sketch a line graph of the data.

1. What is a *false* statement about the disease, according to the table?
   A. A greater percentage of the patients survived in 2000 than in 1965.
   B. A lower percentage of the patients survived in 1965 than in 2000.
   C. 85% of patients survived A.L.L. for at least 5 years in 1965.
   D. 5% of patients survived A.L.L. for at least 5 years in 1965.

2. The percentage of patients who survived A.L.L. for 5 years or more
   A. stayed the same from 1965 to 2000.
   B. increased between 1965 and 2000.
   C. decreased between 1965 and 2000.
   D. cannot be determined by the table.

20 Safety and Emergencies

Chapter Preview

▲ *Working With the Photo*

Safety includes planning ahead and being prepared for emergencies. **Do you or your family have a plan in place to handle emergencies?**

Start-Up Activities

Before You Read   Do you know how to stay safe at home? Take the short quiz on this page. Keep a record of your answers.

HEALTH QUIZ Answer *true* or *false* for each of the following statements:

1. You should put out a grease fire by throwing water on it.
2. Fires cause the most common type of injury in the home.
3. The batteries in smoke alarms should be changed regularly.
4. First-aid supplies in the home can come in handy for minor injuries such as scrapes, minor cuts, sprains, and minor burns.

ANSWERS: 1. false; 2. false; 3. true; 4. true.

FOLDABLES™ Study Organizer

As You Read   Make this Foldable™ to organize what you learn in Lesson 1 about safety at home and at school. Begin with two sheets of notebook paper.

1 Fold one sheet in half from top to bottom. Cut about 1" along the fold at both ends, stopping at the margin lines.

2 Fold the second sheet in half from top to bottom. Cut or shave off the fold *between* the margin lines.

3 Insert the first sheet through the second sheet and align folds.

4 Fold the bound pages in half to make a booklet, and label the cover as shown. Then label each page as instructed by your teacher.

Safety in the Home and at School

Take notes, define terms, and give examples of home and school safety on the appropriate page of your Foldable.

Health Online   Visit **health.glencoe.com** and complete the Chapter 20 crossword puzzle.

Safety in the Home and at School

Guide to Reading

● Building Vocabulary
As you read this lesson, write each new highlighted term and its definition in your notebook.

- accident (p. 540)
- accidental injuries (p. 540)
- accident chain (p. 541)

● Focusing on the Main Ideas
In this lesson, you will learn to

- **explain** how to stay safe in the home and at school.
- **identify** the parts of an accident chain.
- **develop** safe habits.

● Reading Strategy
Predicting Quickly look over the headings in this lesson. For each heading, write a sentence describing what information you think will be covered in that section.

FOLDABLES Study Organizer Use the Foldable™ on p. 539 as you read this lesson.

***Q**uick Write*

Write a short paragraph that completes this sentence opener: "I practice safe habits when I . . . _____."

Developing Safe Habits

An **accident** is *any event that was not intended to happen.* Accidents kill at least one person between the ages of 10 and 19 in the United States every hour of every day. About 60 percent of those deaths result from **accidental injuries,** which are *injuries that result from an accident.* Falling on an icy sidewalk in front of your home and injuring yourself is an example of an accidental injury. Most accidental injuries can be prevented by developing safe habits.

► When engaging in physical activity, stay safe by sticking to your level of skill. **What are some other safety precautions you should take?**

Injuries often occur as a result of an **accident chain.** This is *a series of events that include a situation, an unsafe habit, and an unsafe action.* Understanding accident chains, such as the one illustrated in **Figure 20.1,** can help you avoid injuries. Here are some guidelines:

- **Concentrate on your actions.** Be extra careful when you are tired, excited, upset, sad, or in a hurry.

- **Recognize your limits.** For example, do not mountain bike down a steep hill if you are just learning how to ride a mountain bike.

- **Think ahead.** Plan ahead by thinking of possible risks before it is too late.

Safety in the Home

The most common type of home injury involves falls. Other injuries result from poisonings, electrical shocks, and guns. Fires are the third leading cause of unintentional injury and death in the home. Many home injuries and deaths can be prevented.

▼ **FIGURE 20.1**

THE ACCIDENT CHAIN

Many injuries can be prevented by breaking the accident chain. What strategies could Margo have used to prevent the accidental injury shown here?

The Situation

1. Margo arrives home from school and rushes to answer the phone.

The Unsafe Habit

2. Margo often leaves her things scattered on the floor of her room.

The Unsafe Action

3. After talking on the phone, Margo goes to get ready for her soccer game and trips over a pile of belongings on the floor.

The Accident and the Injury

4. Margo falls and hurts her ankle. Now she can't go to her soccer game.

▲ Keep young children safe from poisonous products by storing them where they cannot be reached. **Do you know who to call if a poisoning does occur?**

Preventing Falls

Most injuries from falling occur in the kitchen, the bathroom, and on stairs. To help prevent falls, wipe up spills right away. Use non-skid rugs, or place a rubber pad under loose rugs. Keep stairways well lit and free of clutter.

Preventing Poisonings

Poisoning can happen by ingestion (swallowing), absorption (through the skin), injection (from a syringe), or inhalation (breathing). Store cleaning products, insecticides, and other potential poisons out of reach of young children.

Preventing Electrical Shocks

Electrical items found in the home can cause serious injury or death if they are misused. Unplug any appliance that is not working properly. Replace broken or frayed electrical cords, and avoid running cords under rugs. Never use electrical appliances near water.

Preventing Gun Accidents

The best way to prevent a gun accident in the home is to not have guns in the home. If a gun must be kept in the home, use the following safety precautions:

- Guns should have trigger locks and be stored unloaded in a locked cabinet.
- Ammunition should be stored in a separate locked cabinet.
- Anyone who handles a gun should be trained in gun safety.
- All guns should be handled as if they are loaded.
- Guns should *never* be pointed at anyone.

Fire Safety

A fire needs three elements to start—fuel, heat, and air. A cigarette, match, or electrical wire are sources of heat. If these sources come in contact with household chemicals, rags, wood, or newspapers, a fire can result.

Here are some safety guidelines to help you prevent fires in the home:

- Keep stoves and ovens clean to prevent pieces of food or grease from catching fire.
- Keep flammable objects at least 3 feet away from portable heaters.
- Remind adults who smoke never to smoke in bed or on overstuffed furniture.

- Regularly inspect electrical wires, outlets, and appliances to make sure they are in proper working order.
- Discard old newspapers, oily rags, and other materials that burn easily.
- Use and store matches and lighters properly. Keep them out of reach of young children.
- Install smoke alarms on each level of the home, including the basement. They should be located in hallways outside bedrooms. Remember to check the batteries regularly.

Reducing Risk of Injury in a Fire

Knowing what to do if there is a fire in your home can reduce your risk of injury. Follow these guidelines:

- Leave the house immediately if possible. Call the fire department from a nearby house or a cellular phone.
- While you are in the house, stay as close to the floor as you can below the smoke. Try to keep your mouth and nose covered to avoid breathing in smoke.
- Before you open a closed door, feel it. If it is hot, find another way to leave the room.
- If your clothing catches fire, *stop, drop,* and *roll*. Stop. Don't run. Drop to the ground. Roll on the ground to put out the fire.

Reading Check **Give Examples** What are three ways to prevent fires in the home?

▲ Prevent electrical shock by using the proper number of cords per outlet. **Why might an overloaded electrical outlet cause a problem?**

Connect To... Science

Grease Fires

If a grease fire starts in a pan on the stove, do not throw water on it. If you do, the flames may actually spread because oil and grease float on water. Your best bet is to carefully slide a lid over the pan and turn off the burner. You can also smother the flames with baking soda. Let the pan cool completely before moving it or taking off the lid.

Health Online

Visit **health.glencoe.com** and complete the Interactive Study Guide for Lesson 1.

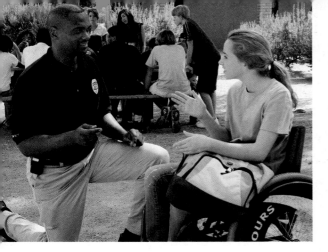

Safety at School

Your school probably has rules in place to keep students and teachers safe. Many accidental injuries at school can be avoided. Follow these strategies to protect the health and safety of students and teachers.

- **Play by the rules.** Rules are made to protect you and others. The cafeteria, classrooms, halls, gym, and auditorium may all have important safety rules to follow.

- **Report weapons or unsafe activities.** It's essential to follow rules prohibiting weapon possession at school. If you think that someone has brought a gun or other weapon to school, report it immediately to a teacher or principal.

- **Wear necessary safety gear.** Working in a science lab or playing sports are two places where appropriate gear will help keep you safe.

▲ Some schools have security guards patrolling campus to help keep students safe. **What should you do if you suspect that someone is planning to bring a weapon to school?**

Reading Check

Recall What strategies can you use to stay safe at school?

Lesson 1 Review

After You Read

Review this lesson for new terms, major headings, and Reading Checks.

What I Learned

1. *Vocabulary* Define *accident*. Use the word in an original sentence.

2. *Identify* Name the sequence of events in an accident chain.

3. *Recall* What are two strategies for preventing falls at home?

Thinking Critically

4. *Apply* Molly's older sister was frying food on their stove last night. Some of the oil she was using spilled onto the stovetop. This morning Molly noticed that the oil was still there. What advice would you give Molly?

5. *Evaluate* What is your family's fire safety plan? How could it be improved?

Applying Health Skills

6. *Advocacy* Kyle is babysitting for a family that has just moved into town. Both of the children are under age 5 and cannot read yet. Kyle notices several bottles of cleaning products, including ammonia, under the kitchen sink. None of the bottles have childproof caps. What can Kyle do to advocate for the safety of the children?

Health *Online* For more review questions for Lesson 1, go to **health.glencoe.com**.

Safety on the Road and Outdoors

Guide to Reading

Building Vocabulary
Write the highlighted word and its definition in your notebook.

■ defensive driving (p. 546)

Focusing on the Main Ideas
In this lesson, you will learn to

■ **describe** ways to avoid injuries in the water and outdoors.
■ **explain** how to stay safe as a pedestrian.
■ **identify** do's and don'ts of pedestrian safety.
■ **name** safety and traffic rules for bicycles, skates, skateboards, and scooters.

Reading Strategy
Finding the Main Idea For each major heading in this lesson, write one sentence that states the main idea.

Quick Write

Make a list of five basic safety rules you should follow while riding a bicycle, skateboard, or scooter.

Traffic Safety

The behavior of the passengers riding in a car can be just as important as the driver's behavior. Using good decision-making skills while you are a passenger in a car will reduce your risk of injury. Here are some safety rules to follow:

• Follow the rules of the road.

• Always buckle your safety belt.

• Never get in a car with a driver who has been drinking alcohol or using drugs.

• Don't distract the driver.

Safety on Wheels and Motorized Vehicles

Riding bicycles and using skates, skateboards, scooters, and motorized vehicles are activities many teens enjoy. One way to prevent injury while participating in these activities is to learn about the risks and then follow rules to avoid them.

▶ Buckling up every time you ride in a car is a simple action that could save your life. **What are some other precautions you could take to ensure your safety on the road?**

Bicycle Safety

The number-one way to stay safe while riding a bicycle is to always wear a bike helmet. Head injuries cause 70 to 80 percent of the deaths from bicycle accidents. Wearing a helmet every time you get on your bike can reduce your risk of head injury by 85 percent.

It is also important for bicycle riders to obey traffic signs and signals. Bicyclists and drivers must practice **defensive driving,** which means *watching out for other people on the road and anticipating unsafe acts*. To stay safe, do not ride at night or in bad weather.

Skates, Skateboards, and Scooters

Skates, skateboards, and scooters can be a lot of fun, but only when they are used safely. Here are some guidelines for having fun while staying injury free.

- Wear protective gear, including a hard-shell helmet, wrist guards, gloves, elbow pads, and knee pads.
- Do not let your speed get out of control.
- Do not skate or ride in parking lots, streets, and other areas with traffic.
- Before you head downhill, practice a safe way to fall on a soft surface.

Reading Check **List** Name three rules of bicycle safety.

▶ Bicycle riders need to obey the same traffic rules as drivers. **What else should bicycle riders do to stay safe?**

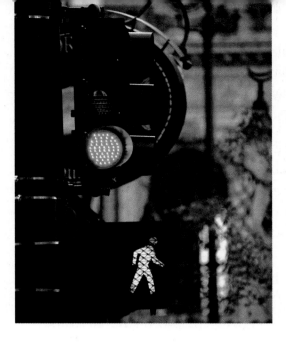

◄ Even if a traffic signal tells you that it's okay to cross, don't forget to look both ways beforehand. **What other safety precautions should you take as a pedestrian?**

Pedestrian Safety

Each year thousands of pedestrians are injured or killed in traffic accidents. A pedestrian is a person traveling on foot. The following guidelines will help you reduce your risk of injury while walking or running.

- Cross streets only at crosswalks. Don't jaywalk, or cross the street in the middle of the block.

- Obey all traffic signals.

- During the day, wear bright clothing. At night, wear reflective gear and carry a flashlight.

- Walk on the sidewalk if there is one. If there is no sidewalk, walk facing oncoming traffic, staying to the left side of the road.

Reading Check **Name** What are two safety guidelines for pedestrians?

Recreational Safety

There are a lot of risks associated with outdoor activities. If you know these risks ahead of time, you can take preventive actions to stay safe. When enjoying an outdoor activity, use common sense and follow these two rules:

- **Be attentive to the weather.** A major risk present during outdoor activities is an electrical storm. If you are caught outdoors during an electrical storm, try to find shelter in a building or car. On a hot day, drink plenty of water, stay in the shade if possible, and do not do any strenuous exercise. On a very cold day, dress in warm layers and stay dry.

- **Use the buddy system.** Agree to stay with at least one other person. With a buddy, you can help each other avoid or cope with a potentially dangerous situation.

Water Safety

Thousands of Americans die each year from drowning, including many children. You can protect yourself and others by following these water safety rules:

- Learn to swim if you don't know how.

- Never swim alone.

- Always use a life jacket when boating or waterskiing. If you fall in cold water, use the survival techniques shown in **Figure 20.2.**

- If you get caught in a strong current, swim parallel to the shore. When the current lessens, swim to shore.

- Never dive into water unless you know it is at least 9 feet deep and free of obstacles.

Hiking and Camping Safety

Preparation is the first step in a safe and enjoyable hike or camping trip. First, check the weather forecast, and take the necessary clothing and equipment. Always let an adult know where you will be and when you plan to return. Some additional safety guidelines are provided on the next page.

▼ FIGURE 20.2

SURVIVAL IN COLD WATER

Hypothermia is a dangerous drop in body temperature which can be life threatening to people in cold water. Use these techniques to help you survive until help arrives. **Why should you always wear a life jacket while boating?**

Reduce heat loss by drawing your knees up to your chest and keeping your upper arms close to the sides of your body. About 50 percent of heat loss is from your head, so try to keep it out of the water.

If you are with other people, huddle close together in a circle to preserve body heat. A child or smaller person who loses heat faster should be placed in the center of the circle.

- **Wear protective clothing.** Dress in layers and wear long pants to protect yourself against ticks.
- **Bring equipment and supplies.** You should have a map, compass, first aid kit, flashlight, extra batteries, and an adequate supply of drinking water.
- **Follow fire safety rules.** Light campfires only where allowed. To put out your campfire, drown it with water or bury it with dirt that is free of debris.
- **Be able to identify poisonous plants and animals.** Learn first aid to treat reactions to poisonous plants, insects, and snakebites.
- **Stay with a buddy.**

Outdoor Sports

Whether you like summer or winter sports, you should always wear appropriate safety gear and stay within your ability level. In the summer, you need to protect yourself against sunburn and heatstroke. Wear sunscreen with a sun protection factor (SPF) of at least 15, sunglasses, a hat, and appropriate clothing. Avoid direct sunlight during the hottest times of the day (10 A.M. to 4 P.M.), if possible, and drink plenty of water. Also, pay attention to your body's signals. If you feel tired or overheated, take a break.

In the winter, protect yourself against cold weather by wearing layers of clothing, a hat, mittens or gloves, and proper footwear.

Health Online

Visit **health.glencoe.com** and complete the Interactive Study Guide for Lesson 2.

Lesson 2 Review

After You Read

Review this lesson for new terms, major headings, and Reading Checks.

What I Learned

1. *Vocabulary* What is *defensive driving*? Use it in an original sentence.

2. *List* What are four safety rules that can reduce your risk of traffic injuries?

3. *Identify* Name three ways to stay safe while in the water.

Thinking Critically

4. *Analyze* How does practicing the buddy system help keep you safe outdoors?

5. *Explain* Why is it important to learn how to fall when skating or riding a bike?

Applying Health Skills

6. *Accessing Information* Think about an outdoor sport or activity you would like to try. Using reliable print or online sources, research what safety equipment you would need and what safety rules you should follow.

Safety in Weather Emergencies

Quick Write

List several weather emergencies that might occur where you live. Write two emergency preparations for each.

Hazardous Weather and Natural Disasters

You have been learning about ways to prevent emergencies. There are some emergencies, however, that even the most careful planning and best safety habits cannot prevent. These include weather emergencies and natural disasters. Perhaps you live in an area where tornadoes, hurricanes, earthquakes, or blizzards occur. Tornadoes are often found in the central states. Hurricanes commonly turn up along the Atlantic Coast and the Gulf of Mexico. Earthquakes typically occur on the West Coast and in southern Alaska. These emergencies can cause serious health problems.

▶ Knowing what to do when a tornado strikes is the key to staying safe. **Why are tornadoes so dangerous?**

Tornadoes

A **tornado** is *a whirling, funnel-shaped windstorm that may drop from the sky to the ground.* Tornadoes are extremely dangerous storms, often destroying everything in their path. If a tornado is headed your way, take the following steps to help reduce your risk of injury:

- **Stay clear of windows.** Go to an inner hallway or any central, windowless room such as a bathroom or closet.

- **Take cover.** A basement or cellar that has no windows is the safest place to wait out a tornado.

- **Get low.** Lie down in a ditch if you are outside or other low-lying area.

Reading Check **Explain** What are some precautions to take in the event of a tornado?

Hurricanes

A **hurricane** is *a strong windstorm with driving rain that originates at sea.* The storm clouds of a hurricane can extend over hundreds of miles and revolve around a calm center called an eye. Hurricanes occur most often in late summer and early fall.

The National Weather Service tracks tornadoes and hurricanes. **Figure 20.3** shows one hurricane's path. To prepare for a hurricane, secure your home by boarding up windows. Close storm shutters before the winds start blowing. Then, leave the area and head inland, away from the hurricane.

Blizzards

A **blizzard** is *a very heavy snowstorm with winds up to 45 miles per hour.* Visibility usually is reduced to less than 500 feet, making it easy to get lost or disoriented. You can protect yourself during blizzards and winter storms by following these precautions:

- **Stay indoors.** The safest place during a blizzard is inside.

- **Bundle up.** If you must go out, wear layers of loose-fitting lightweight clothing under layers of outerwear that is both wind- and waterproof. Add a scarf, hat, gloves and boots.

- **Don't wander.** Use landmarks to avoid getting lost, or stay put until help arrives.

MediaWatch

Storm Tracking

Satellite images and computers help forecasters gather information on the directions in which storms are headed. The newest weather satellites are the GOES series, or Geostationary Operational Environmental Satellite.

Where can you get up-to-date hurricane forecast information?

▼ **FIGURE 20.3**

TRACKING A HURRICANE

Weather experts track the path of a hurricane by recording the coordinates of its location at regular intervals. How might hurricane tracking help people who live in coastal areas?

Frances 2004

▶ Schools have drills to prepare for weather emergencies. **Does your school have drills to practice safety strategies?**

Health *Online*

Topic: Be Prepared!

Visit **health.glencoe.com** for Student Web Activities to learn about the various kinds of natural disasters and how to prepare for them.

Activity: Using the information provided at the link above, write a script for a public radio announcement that educates listeners about how to prepare for one of the disasters you studied.

Health *Online*

Visit **health.glencoe.com** and complete the Interactive Study Guide for Lesson 3.

Floods

In the event of a flood, head to high ground and stay away from the water. Never swim, walk, bike, or ride in a car through floodwaters. Drowning and electrocution from downed power lines pose a serious risk.

Flash floods are responsible for the majority of flood fatalities. Water can rise so fast and move so swiftly that people, cars, and even homes can be swept away. During a flood, pay attention to bulletins from the National Weather Service and follow their advice.

Earthquakes

An **earthquake** is *a violent shaking movement of the earth's surface.* Earthquakes can occur anywhere in the United States, but happen most often west of the Rocky Mountains. Collapsing walls and falling debris are responsible for causing most injuries in an earthquake. To reduce your risk of injury, follow these precautions:

- **Stay indoors.** Crouch under a sturdy piece of furniture, against an interior wall, or in a strongly supported doorway. Stay away from objects that might fall, shatter, or cave in. Use your arms or a pillow to cover your head.

- **Get in the open if outdoors.** Avoid buildings, trees, telephone and electric lines, streetlights, and overpasses. Drivers should stop their cars and both the driver and passengers should stay inside the car.

- **Be careful afterward.** After the shaking stops, stay out of damaged buildings. Electrical and gas lines could be damaged and may be hazardous. Small quakes called aftershocks often occur after the main earthquake.

Reading Check

Recall What are three ways to stay safe during a blizzard?

Health Skills Activity

Practicing Healthful Behaviors

Preparing for Weather Emergencies

Follow these tips to plan ahead for weather emergencies:

- Identify which weather emergencies are likely to affect your area.
- Check with a reliable source about precautions to take during these types of weather emergencies.
- Develop and maintain a personal and family emergency plan.
- Prepare and maintain an emergency supplies kit that includes a battery-operated radio and flashlight, extra batteries, canned and ready-to-eat foods, a can opener, water (one gallon per person per day), a first-aid kit, and blankets.
- Identify emergency evacuation routes in your local area.

With a Group

In small groups, choose a weather emergency that occurs in your area. Prepare information sheets on preparing for and staying safe during this type of emergency. Post these at home, with your parents' permission.

Lesson 3 Review

After You Read

Review this lesson for new terms, major headings, and Reading Checks.

What I Learned

1. **Vocabulary** Define *hurricane,* and use it in a sentence.

2. **Describe** Describe how to protect yourself during a flood.

3. **Identify** What are four kinds of weather emergencies?

Thinking Critically

4. **Analyze** Why is it dangerous to be outside during a blizzard?

5. **Synthesize** After a major earthquake, your friend wants you go with him or her to inspect a damaged building. How would you respond? Explain your answer.

Applying Health Skills

6. **Communication Skills** With a partner, choose a weather emergency from this lesson. Write and perform a skit to demonstrate strategies for staying safe during that event.

Basic First Aid

Guide to Reading

Building Vocabulary
As you read this lesson, write each new highlighted term and its definition in your notebook.

- first aid (p. 554)
- universal precautions (p. 555)

Focusing on the Main Ideas
In this lesson, you will learn to

- **explain** universal precautions.
- **identify** the steps to take in an emergency.
- **assemble** your own first-aid kit.

Reading Strategy
Predicting Look over the lesson, including the headings and pictures. Then write a sentence predicting what information you think the lesson will provide.

*Q*uick Write

Imagine that you and a friend are skating and your friend falls and injures his or her leg. Write a paragraph describing what you would do to help your friend.

First Aid

First aid is *the immediate temporary care given to an injured or ill person until he or she can get professional help.* You can prevent further injury and may even speed recovery if you know what to do in an emergency. Knowing what *not* to do is equally important. Administering the proper first aid sometimes means the difference between life and death. Staying calm allows you to better help the victim. In this lesson you will learn what supplies are needed for a basic first-aid kit. You will also learn how to respond in an emergency and how to protect yourself when providing first aid.

Emergency Phone # List

Emergency Medical Services	911
Family Doctor	444-211-0000
Poison Control Center	1-800-222-1222
Police	444-211-0001
Fire Dept.	444-211-0002
Parents Work #	444-211-0003
Mom's Cell	444-211-0004
Dad's Cell	444-211-0005
Uncle Jimmy	444-211-0006
Our neighbors the Smiths	444-211-0007

◀ Keeping an emergency phone list handy can save time during an emergency. **What numbers should be on an emergency phone list?**

Being Prepared

Without warning, at any time or place, you might find yourself in a position where you need to give first aid. Learning basic skills will help you handle most common emergencies. Keeping a list of emergency numbers near all phones is one simple way to be prepared. Make sure all family members know where everyone's health records are. If your sister and brother have certain allergies, that information will be important in an emergency.

Both the home and car should be stocked with first-aid supplies and everyone should learn their use. First-aid kits come pre-packaged, or you can assemble your own. **Figure 20.4** lists some basic first-aid supplies. You may need to add specific medicines if someone in your family has a medical condition.

Reading Check **Identify** What is one way to be prepared for an emergency at home?

Taking Universal Precautions

Viruses such as HIV and hepatitis B and C can be spread through contact with an infected person's blood. As a result, steps should be taken to minimize contact with another person's blood. To protect yourself when giving first aid, follow **universal precautions.** These are *actions taken to prevent the spread of disease by treating all blood as if it were contaminated.* Wear protective

▼ **FIGURE 20.4**

First-Aid Supplies

Keeping a first-aid kit in your home will help your family be prepared for emergencies. *What other supplies might you add to this kit?*

Instruments:	Equipment:	Medications:	Dressings:	Miscellaneous:
tweezers, scissors	thermometer, cotton swabs, blanket, cold pack	antiseptic ointment, sterile eyewash, activated charcoal, syrup of ipecac	gauze pads, adhesive tape, adhesive bandages, triangular bandage	small flashlight, tissues, hand cleanser, disposable gloves, face mask, plastic bags

When you call 911 and report an emergency, be prepared to tell the operator as much as you know about the situation. **Why is stress management an important skill to have when responding to an emergency?**

Citizenship

A good neighbor and citizen is prepared to report accidents, fires, serious illnesses, injuries, and crimes. Familiarize yourself with emergency phone numbers to call in your community. Make a list to keep handy by the telephone.

gloves while treating a victim. Use a face mask or shield when giving first aid for breathing emergencies. Cover any open wounds on your body with sterile dressings. Avoid touching any object that was in contact with the victim's blood. Always wash hands thoroughly after giving first aid.

The First Steps

Although every emergency situation is unique, there are four steps to take for most emergencies. Recognize the signs of an emergency, decide to act, call for help, and provide care until help arrives.

Identifying the Signs of an Emergency

Often something you see, hear, or smell will alert you to an emergency. Is someone calling out in trouble? Have you heard glass shattering? Do you smell smoke or anything unusual that makes your eyes sting or causes you to cough or have difficulty breathing? These sensations can signal a chemical spill or toxic gas release.

Taking Action

Decide what action to take by evaluating the situation. Before acting, consider your strengths and limitations. Do not dive into a lake to rescue someone who's drowning unless you are trained in lifesaving. Instead, you might throw a life preserver or something else that floats. Protect your own safety first. Putting yourself in danger can harm both you and the person who needs help. One action that never hurts is calling for help. Getting help can save a life and is sometimes the best and only action for you to take.

Calling for Help

Dial 911 for all emergencies in most of the United States. In some small towns, dialing zero (for operator) is an option. When making a call for help, stay calm. Describe the emergency to the operator and give a street address or describe the location by using landmarks. The operator will notify the police, fire, or emergency medical service departments. Stay on the phone until the operator tells you to hang up.

Providing Care Until Help Arrives

Having called for help, stay with the victim until help arrives. Carefully loosen any tight clothing. Offer a coat or blanket for cover or provide shade to help the person maintain a normal body temperature.

◀ While you wait for medical help to arrive, help the victim stay calm by providing comfort and reassurance. **Why should you avoid moving an injured person?**

Avoid moving the victim to prevent further pain or injury. Only move the victim if he or she is in danger, such as in the path of traffic.

Cardiopulmonary resuscitation (CPR) may be necessary if the victim is unconscious and unresponsive. This lifesaving technique is described in Lesson 6 of this chapter.

 Reading Check **Explain** What are some signs of an emergency?

 Health Online

Visit **health.glencoe.com** and complete the Interactive Study Guide for Lesson 4.

Lesson 4 Review

After You Read

Review this lesson for new terms, major headings, and Reading Checks.

What I Learned

1. *Vocabulary* Define *first aid*. Use the term in a sentence.

2. *Recall* Name four universal precautions to take when administering first aid.

3. *List* Give two examples of ways you can help an injured person until professional help arrives.

Thinking Critically

4. *Analyze* Why is it important to know basic first-aid strategies?

5. *Apply* If you come upon an injured person on a hiking trail, should you try to move the person off the trail? Why or why not?

Applying Health Skills

6. *Goal Setting* Gather your family to discuss your preparedness for emergencies. Set a goal to become better prepared. Develop a plan to achieve your goal.

First Aid for Common Emergencies

Guide to Reading

● **Building Vocabulary**
As you read this lesson, write each new highlighted term and its definition in your notebook.

- sprain (p. 559)
- fracture (p. 559)
- heat cramps (p. 562)
- heat exhaustion (p. 562)
- heatstroke (p. 562)

● **Focusing on the Main Ideas**
In this lesson, you will learn to

- **describe** the different types of common emergencies.
- **explain** first-aid treatments for common emergencies.
- **identify** when it is time to call for medical assistance.

● **Reading Strategy**
Organizing Information Create a chart listing the common emergencies discussed in this lesson and the first-aid techniques used to treat them.

Quick Write

Make a list of common emergencies in which you feel capable of providing help.

Common Emergencies

Common emergencies include insect bites, burns, poisoning, foreign objects in the eye, nosebleed, and fainting. Others include heat cramps and heatstroke as well as sprains, bruises, and broken bones. In this chapter you will learn how to treat these minor conditions and recognize more serious conditions that need professional medical assistance.

▶ Treating a sprained ankle can include elevating it above the level of the heart. **How does this help the injury?**

Sprains

A **sprain** is *a condition in which the ligaments that hold the joints in position are stretched or torn.* Sprains often result from a sudden force such as a twisting movement. The most commonly sprained joints are ankles and knees. Symptoms of sprains include swelling and bruising. While a doctor should evaluate serious sprains, minor sprains can be treated using the P.R.I.C.E. method:

- **Protect** the injured part by keeping it still. Moving it could cause further injury.
- **Rest** the affected joint for 24 to 48 hours.
- **Ice** the injured part to reduce swelling and pain. A cloth between the skin and ice bag will reduce discomfort.
- **Compress** the injured area by wrapping it in an elastic bandage.
- **Elevate** the injured part above the level of the heart to reduce swelling.

Broken Bones

A **fracture** is *a break in the bone.* An open fracture is a complete break with one or both sides of the bone piercing the skin. A closed fracture does not break the skin and may be difficult to identify. Pain, swelling and a misshapen appearance are typical symptoms of a closed fracture. However, not all broken bones cause immediate pain. An X ray is the only way to be sure if a bone is broken.

Insect Bites and Stings

Insect bites and stings can be serious and even life-threatening for people with certain allergies. Professional help should be called if a person is known to be allergic, develops a rash, has difficulty breathing, or shows signs of shock.

Wash the area of the bite and then apply a special lotion for relief. You can remove an insect's stinger by scraping against the affected area with a fingernail. Apply ice or a cold pack to relieve pain and prevent swelling once the stinger is out. Tick bites require the careful removal of the entire insect if it has burrowed under the skin.

Burns

First-aid techniques for treating burns vary depending on the location and the severity of the burn. Third-degree and some second-degree burns are very serious and require immediate medical help. **Figure 20.5** on page 560 explains how to recognize and treat three classifications of burns.

▼ If you have a fracture, your doctor will look at an X ray of your bone to determine where the fracture is located. **What are the two different types of fractures?**

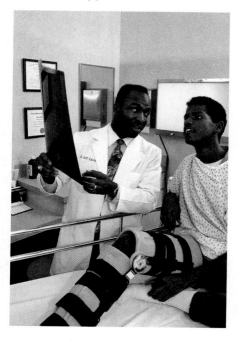

THREE DEGREES OF BURNS

Treatment for burns depends on the severity of the burn. **Which type of burns require immediate medical help?**

Three Degrees of Burns		
Type of Burn	**Description**	**Treatment**
First-Degree	Affects only the outer layer of the skin. The skin is usually red, but the outer layer has not been burned through. There may be swelling and pain.	Cool the burn with running water, immerse the burn in cold water, or apply cold compresses for at least 15 minutes. Cover the burn with a sterile bandage.
Second-Degree	Burns through the first layer of skin and burns the second layer of skin. Blisters develop, and the skin looks red and splotchy. Usually there is severe pain and swelling.	A burn no longer than 2 to 3 inches in diameter can be treated as a first-degree burn. If the burn is larger, or is on the hands, feet, face, groin, buttocks, or a major joint, get medical help immediately.
Third-Degree	Involves all layers of skin and may affect fat, muscle, and bone. The burned area may be charred black or appear dry and white. There may be little or no pain felt at this stage. If the burn is deeper than the skin, then it is called fourth degree.	Call for medical help. While you are waiting, treat the victim for shock as described in Lesson 6. Do not remove burned clothing. Apply cold water to the burn, then cover with a sterile bandage or clean cloth. Keep the victim still and help him or her to sip fluids.

Poisoning

A poison is a substance that causes harm when swallowed, inhaled, absorbed by the skin, or injected into the body. Medicines and household products play a role in about half of all poisonings. All poisonings require immediate treatment. In the event of a poisoning, call the nearest poison control center, a 24-hour hot line providing medical information about treating poisoning victims. Be ready to provide information about the victim and the suspected poison. The poison control center will advise you about how to proceed. The victim might need to drink water or milk to dilute the poison, or a dose of syrup of ipecac, a medication that causes vomiting.

If a poisonous chemical such as a pesticide or household cleaning agent has made contact with someone's skin, first remove all clothing that has touched the chemical and then wash the surface of the skin with water for 15 minutes. Call the poison control center while the skin is being washed.

Foreign Object in the Eye

Do not rub your eye if there is a foreign object in it. Use clean water to flush the object out. Hold the rim of a small, clean glass filled with water against the base of your eye socket. Gently pour the water into the open eye. Repeat the process until the object washes out, or get assistance if you cannot clear your eye.

If someone else has a foreign object in the eye, locate the object by gently pulling the lower lid downward while the person looks up and then holding the upper lid open while the person looks down. If it is floating on the surface of the eye, lightly touch the object with a moistened cotton swab or corner of a clean cloth. Call for medical assistance if you cannot remove the object.

▲ If you feel faint, sit down and put your head between your knees. This will let blood flow into your head. **What should you do if you are with someone who faints?**

Nosebleed

An injury or even a cold can cause a nosebleed. It can also be caused by being in a very dry place. To stop a nosebleed, pinch shut the bleeding nose between the thumb and index finger and breath through your mouth for 5 to 10 minutes. If the bleeding is heavy and it continues for more than 15 minutes, get medical help.

Fainting

Fainting is a brief loss of consciousness that occurs when the blood supply to the brain is cut off for a short amount of time. If you feel faint you should lie or sit down, placing your head between your knees. If someone else faints, here's how to help:

- Leave the person lying down and check the airway. Raise the legs above the level of the head if the person is breathing.

- Loosen any tight clothing.

- Call for help if the person does not regain consciousness in a minute or so. Call for help and start CPR if the person is not breathing. CPR is discussed in Lesson 6.

- Losing consciousness as a result of a head injury is not fainting. If this occurs, call for help immediately. Begin CPR if the person is not breathing.

Heat-Related Illnesses

Heat cramps, heat exhaustion and heatstroke are heat-related illnesses. **Heat cramps** are *painful, involuntary muscle spasms that usually occur during strenuous exercise in hot weather.* Resting, cooling down, and drinking water or a sports drink containing electrolytes should help to relieve heat cramps. Gentle stretching exercises and massage also may help.

Heat exhaustion is *characterized by faintness, nausea, rapid heartbeat and hot, red, dry, or sweaty skin.* Anyone with these symptoms needs to lie down in a shady or air-conditioned place and elevate his or her feet. Loosen the victim's clothing and offer cold, but not iced, water to drink. Fan the person while spraying them with cool water. Watch the victim carefully. Heat exhaustion can quickly become heatstroke, the most serious of heat illnesses.

Heatstroke is *the most serious form of heat illness.* A heatstroke occurs because the body has stopped sweating. Sweating is the body's way of releasing heat. Heatstroke can be life-threatening. The primary symptoms are a significant increase in body temperature—generally higher than 104° F—and rapid heartbeat and shallow breathing. Call immediately for medical assistance while treating the victim for heat exhaustion as described above.

Health Online

Visit **health.glencoe.com** and complete the Interactive Study Guide for Lesson 5.

Reading Check

Explain How do you treat a person with heat exhaustion?

Lesson 5 Review

After You Read

Review this lesson for new terms, major headings, and Reading Checks.

What I Learned

1. *Vocabulary* Define *sprain* and *fracture.* Use both terms in a sentence that demonstrates their meanings.

2. *Name* What are the different types of common emergencies?

3. *List* Name two symptoms of heatstroke.

Thinking Critically

4. *Compare and Contrast* How does the treatment for insect stings differ from that for insect bites?

5. *Analyze* How would you respond to this accidental injury: a burn on the elbow of about $1^1/_2$ inches in diameter that has burned through the first and second layer of skin.

Applying Health Skills

6. *Practicing Healthful Behaviors* With a partner, write a scenario for dealing with a common emergency. Demonstrate strategies for responding to accidental injury by acting out your scenario for the class.

562 Chapter 20: Safety and Emergencies

Health Online For more review questions for Lesson 5, go to **health.glencoe.com**.

Life-Threatening Emergencies

Guide to Reading

Building Vocabulary
Make a word diagram that shows the relationship among the terms below. Decide which term is the one the others relate to.
- abdominal thrusts (p. 564)
- cardiopulmonary resuscitation (CPR) (p. 566)
- shock (p. 567)

Focusing on the Main Ideas
In this lesson, you will learn to
- **explain** different kinds of life-threatening emergencies.
- **describe** how to perform rescue breathing.
- **identify** the symptoms of shock.
- **explain** how to help someone who is choking.

Reading Strategy
Finding the Main Idea For each major heading in this lesson, write one sentence that states the main idea.

When Emergency Strikes

Unless the proper treatment is given, a person may have only minutes to live in a life-threatening emergency. You could help save someone's life if you stay calm, call for help, and provide appropriate first aid.

Choking

Choking kills more than 3,000 people every year in the United States. When a piece of food or some other object blocks a person's airway, oxygen cannot reach the lungs. If a person is clutching his or her throat, that is the universal sign for choking. Other symptoms include gasping or wheezing, a reddish-purple coloration, bulging eyes, and an inability to speak. If a person can speak or cough, it is not a choking emergency.

Quick Write
Make a list of life-threatening emergencies in which you feel capable of helping and write what actions you'd take.

▶ This teen is demonstrating the universal sign for choking—grabbing the throat with thumbs and fingers extended. **How would you respond to someone showing this sign?**

A choking person could die if the object is not removed quickly. If an adult or older child is choking, use the abdominal thrusts maneuver shown in **Figure 20.6.** The **abdominal thrusts** maneuver *involves quick upward pulls into the diaphragm to force out an obstruction blocking the airway.* Choking infants require a different first-aid procedure. Check with a first-aid manual to learn how to help babies and small children.

If you are alone and choking, there are two ways to give yourself an abdominal thrust. First, make a fist and position it slightly above your navel. With your other hand, grasp your fist and thrust inward and upward into your abdomen until the object dislodges. Another technique is to lean over the back of a chair, or any firm object, pressing your abdomen into it.

Reading Check **Recall** What are some signs that a person may be choking?

▼**FIGURE 20.6**

FIRST AID FOR A CHOKING ADULT OR OLDER CHILD

Before you perform abdominal thrusts, ask the person if he or she is choking. How can asking this question help you determine if a person is choking?

A Stand behind the person who is choking. Wrap your arms around the person's waist and tip the person slightly forward. Make a fist. Place the fist just above the person's navel but below the breastbone. Position the fist so the thumb side is against the victim's abdomen. Grab your fist with your other hand.

B Quickly, thrust inward and upward. The motion is similar to one you would use if you were trying to lift the person off the ground. Repeat thrusts until the food or object is dislodged. If the person becomes unresponsive, call for medical help and begin CPR.

Severe Bleeding

To stop severe bleeding, have the person lie down and, if possible, elevate the site of the bleeding above the level of the heart. Take precautions to minimize contact with another person's blood. Wear protective gloves, if possible, and always wash your hands afterwards. Apply direct pressure to the wound using a clean cloth. If the bleeding continues, apply pressure to that artery supplying blood to the area of the wound. **Figure 20.7** shows the areas on the body that can be pressed to control bleeding. Once the bleeding has stopped, cover the wound with a clean cloth to reduce the risk of infection. Leave the bandages in place and seek professional medical help as soon as possible.

▼ FIGURE 20.7

PRESSURE POINT BLEEDING CONTROL

This illustration shows the areas on arms and legs that can be pressed against a bone to stop blood flow to the injured area. **Once the bleeding has stopped, what should you do next?**

Arm
Use your fingers to press on the inside of the upper arm at the area circled in the diagram. You will press the artery at this point against the arm bone. To find the artery, feel for the pulse below the round muscle of the biceps.

Leg
Keeping your arm straight, use the heel of your hand to press the groin at the area shown in the diagram. You will press the artery at this point against the pelvic bone. You may need to use both hands to apply enough pressure.

CPR

Imagine being in an emergency situation when someone loses consciousness. The person does not respond when gently shaken and when asked, "Are you okay?" If this happens, call 911 or the local emergency number. While waiting for help to arrive, a trained person should begin administering **cardiopulmonary resuscitation (CPR)**—*a first aid procedure that combines rescue breathing with chest compressions to restore breathing and circulation.* The steps used for adults and children over the age of 12 are shown in **Figure 20.8.** A first-aid manual will explain the ways in which to administer CPR to younger children and infants.

▼ FIGURE 20.8

The Steps of CPR

The first steps of CPR involve checking for breathing and rescue breaths. If you have an available breathing mask, follow the directions that come with the mask. **In what type of situation should you use CPR?**

1. Check Breathing. Look inside the victim's mouth. If you see anything blocking the airway, remove it. Lay the person flat on a firm surface. Gently tilt the head back with one hand and lift the chin with the other. Look, listen, and feel to find out if the victim is breathing normally. *Look* for chest movement. *Listen* at the victim's mouth for breathing sounds. *Feel* for exhaled air on your cheek.

2. Rescue Breaths. If the victim is not breathing normally, begin rescue breathing. Pinch the person's nostrils shut, take a normal breath and place your mouth over the victim's, forming a seal. Give two breaths, each about one second long. The victim's chest should rise with each breath.

3. Chest Compressions. Immediately after giving two rescue breaths, begin chest compressions. Place the heel of one hand on the center of the victim's chest between the nipples. Place the heel of the second hand on top of the first so that the hands are overlapped. Press straight down quickly and firmly at a rate of about 100 compressions per minute. Allow the victim's chest to spring back between compressions. After every 30 compressions, give two rescue breaths.

Shock

Shock is *a life threatening condition in which the circulatory system fails to deliver enough blood to vital tissues and organs.* Injury, burns, and severe infection can cause a person to go into shock, as can heat, poisoning, blood loss and heart attack. Always look for the signs of shock when providing first aid because it can result from a medical emergency.

Signs to watch for include cool, clammy, pale or gray skin; weak and rapid pulse; and slow, shallow breathing. The eyes may have a dull look with the pupils dilated. The victim, if conscious, may feel faint, weak, confused, and anxious.

If you think someone is in shock or about to go into shock, call for medical help and take these precautions:

- Help the person to lie down quietly on his or her back with feet raised slightly higher than the head. Try to keep the person as still as possible.

- Loosen tight clothing.

- Use a blanket, coat or any available cover to help keep the person warm.

- Do not give the person anything to drink.

- Roll the person onto his or her side to help prevent choking in the event of vomiting or bleeding from the mouth.

Health Online

Visit **health.glencoe.com** and complete the Interactive Study Guide for Lesson 6.

Lesson 6 Review

After You Read

Review this lesson for new terms, major headings, and Reading Checks.

What I Learned

1. *Vocabulary* Define *shock*. Use the term in a sentence.

2. *Recall* What is the universal sign for choking? What is the first thing you should do if an adult is choking?

3. *List* Name two symptoms of shock.

Thinking Critically

4. *Compare and Contrast* How does the treatment for shock differ from that of choking?

5. *Apply* A friend has fallen while hiking. His leg is bleeding severely. You have brought a first-aid kit with you. What will you do?

Applying Health Skills

6. *Advocacy* Research where first-aid procedures are taught in your community. Develop a flyer encouraging teens to complete a first-aid class. Include information on the cost, location, requirements, and certifications issued after completion of the course.

Building Health Skills

PRACTICING HEALTHFUL BEHAVIORS

Complete a House Inspection

DIRECTIONS

Practicing Healthful Behaviors involves taking specific actions to stay healthy and avoid risky behaviors. This activity will give you the opportunity to develop and master this important health skill. Here's a guide to the different parts of this activity:

❶ In the **Model** section, you will read about a teen who performs the health skill successfully. This "model" scenario will show you how the skill is done.

❷ The **Practice** section will help guide you in practicing the skill.

❸ In the **Apply** section, you will have a chance to perform the skill on your own. You can use the Self-Check to check your work.

To complete this activity, first read the scenario presented in the Model. Then move on to the Practice. Finally, go ahead and try the Apply.

❶ Model

Many fires in the home can be prevented. One effective way to keep your family safe is to regularly inspect your home for possible fire dangers. Read about two teens who made sure that their home was safe.

Shawna and Aaron decided to complete a home inspection for fire dangers after a fire-fighter came to their school and spoke about the importance of fire prevention. As the teens went through each room in their home, they made notes of possible fire hazards. Some risks, like *piles of old newspapers,* needed to be removed. Others, like an *appliance with a frayed cord,* needed to be repaired. Shawna and Aaron showed the list to their parents. The family made a plan to address each fire hazard the teens identified.

❷ Practice

Below is a list of possible hazards to check for in your home. Use the list to create a Home Inspection Check-Off List that you can use to inspect your home for potential fire hazards.

- Are all kitchen appliances in good working order?
- Is the stove clean?
- Are all electrical wires and outlets working properly?
- Have you thrown out all piles of newspapers or other materials that burn easily?
- Are all flammable objects at least 3 feet away from portable heaters?
- Is there a smoke alarm on each level of your home?
- Does each smoke alarm have working batteries?
- Are matches and cigarette lighters stored out of reach of young children?

Skill Summary
PRACTICING HEALTHFUL BEHAVIORS

Fire safety in the home includes the following behaviors:

- Change smoke alarm batteries regularly. Check alarms often.
- Make sure all kitchen appliances are in good working order.
- Keep matches out of reach of young children.

❸ Apply

Using the Home Inspection Check-Off List you created, complete an inspection of your home. Write down any items on the list that indicate a possible fire danger. Then write down what steps you can take to eliminate each possible fire danger. Be prepared to share your findings with the class.

Self-Check

- Did I identify any possible fire dangers in my home?
- Did I list the steps I need to take to eliminate each possible danger?

A Home Emergency Kit

Weather emergencies and natural disasters are situations that no one can prevent. You can, however, be prepared. Creating a home emergency kit for your family can help keep you safe and secure until the emergency is over.

What You Will Need

- one piece of poster board
- marker
- paper
- pencil or pen

What You Will Do

1 Working in a small group, brainstorm all of the supplies you would include in a home emergency kit. Your kit should include enough items to last for three days.

2 Have one member of the group write all the items on the poster board.

3 Discuss why you feel certain items should or should not be included.

4 Make your list final. Then, compare your list with other groups in the class. Are your lists similar? How are they different?

Wrapping It Up

Write down the final list on a piece of paper. At home, discuss creating a home emergency kit with your family using the list you created.

FOLDABLES™ Study Organizer

Foldables™ and Other Study Aids Take out the Foldable™ that you created for Lesson 1 and any other study aids you created for Lessons 1–6. Find a partner and quiz each other using these study aids.

Lesson 1 Safety in the Home and at School

Key Idea
- Accident chains include a situation, an unsafe habit, an unsafe action, and the resulting injury.

Vocabulary
- accidental injuries (p. 540)
- accident (p. 540)
- accident chain (p. 541)

Lesson 2 Safety on the Road and Outdoors

Key Ideas
- The behavior of passengers riding in a car can be just as important as the driver's behavior.
- Two important behaviors to keep you safe during outdoor activities are being prepared and using the buddy system.

Vocabulary
- defensive driving (p. 546)

Lesson 3 Safety in Weather Emergencies

Key Idea
- Weather emergencies and natural disasters include tornadoes, hurricanes, floods, blizzards, and earthquakes.

Vocabulary
- tornado (p. 551)
- hurricane (p. 551)
- blizzard (p. 551)
- earthquake (p. 552)

Lesson 4 Basic First Aid

Key Idea
- There are four steps to take for most emergencies: recognize the signs, decide to act, call for help, and provide care until help arrives.

Vocabulary
- first aid (p. 554)
- universal precautions (p. 555)

Lesson 5 First Aid for Common Emergencies

Key Idea
- Sprains require the P.R.I.C.E. method to treat them: Protect, Rest, Ice, Compress, and Elevate.

Vocabulary
- sprain (p. 559)
- fracture (p. 559)
- heat cramps (p. 562)
- heat exhaustion (p. 562)
- heatstroke (p. 562)

Lesson 6 Life-Threatening Emergencies

Key Idea
- During a life-threatening emergency, staying calm, calling for help, and providing first aid can save a person's life.

Vocabulary
- abdominal thrusts (p. 564)
- cardiopulmonary resuscitation (CPR) (p. 566)
- shock (p. 567)

After You Read

HEALTH QUIZ

Now that you have read the chapter, look back at your answers to the Health Quiz on the chapter opener. Would you answer any of the questions differently?

Reviewing Vocabulary and Main Ideas

On a sheet of paper, write the numbers 1–6. After each number, write the term from the list that best completes each sentence.

- poisonings
- blizzards
- helmet
- accident
- defensive driving
- earthquake

Lesson 1 Safety in the Home and at School

1. A(n) _____ is any event that was not intended to happen.
2. Cleaning products and medicines are the most common causes of _____ among children.

Lesson 2 Safety on the Road and Outdoors

3. _____ involves watching out for other people on the road and anticipating unsafe acts.
4. Cyclists can reduce the risk of head injury by wearing a(n) _____.

Lesson 3 Safety in Weather Emergencies

5. If you are indoors when a(n) _____ starts, crouch under sturdy furniture.
6. People can easily become disoriented and lost during _____.

*On a sheet of paper, write the numbers 7–12. Write **True** or **False** for each statement below. If the statement is false, change the underlined word or phrase to make it true.*

Lesson 4 Basic First Aid

7. Universal <u>precautions</u> are steps taken to prevent disease by treating all blood as if it was contaminated.
8. <u>Taking action</u> is your first step in any emergency situation.

Lesson 5 First Aid for Common Emergencies

9. A <u>sprain</u> is an invisible break in a bone.
10. A marked increase in body temperature is a main symptom of <u>heat exhaustion</u>.

Lesson 6 Life-Threatening Emergencies

11. The abdominal thrusts maneuver is used to help a victim of <u>shock</u>.
12. <u>Gasping</u> is the universal sign for choking.

Health Online Visit health.glencoe.com and take the Online Quiz for Chapter 20.

Thinking Critically

Using complete sentences, answer the following questions on a sheet of paper.

13. Evaluate How would you assess whether a victim needed CPR?

14. Analyze How does an understanding of accident chains help prevent injuries?

Write About It

15. Practicing Healthful Behaviors Write a short story about a teen involved in a situation that leads to an accident. Describe the situation and the events that make up the accident chain. Then, write an alternate ending describing how the teen used strategies to prevent the accident from happening.

16. Stress Management Write a paragraph describing ways to manage stress during an emergency.

Standardized Test Practice

Reading and Writing

Read the passage and then answer the questions.

A severe lightning storm hit Baltimore yesterday evening, causing a power outage in the northern section of town. One bolt struck a tree branch that fell and injured a Mini Mart employee. The lightning struck when the Mart was crowded with customers. Power was out for more than two hours after the storm.

When the lightning hit, Mini Mart owner Mike Wojer told customers and employees to stay inside and away from the doors and windows. He turned off the lights and appliances and asked customers to not make any phone calls.

"Thankfully, no one in the store was injured by lightning," said Wojer.

The injured employee, however, was outside the store when lightning struck. He was hit by a tree branch that had been struck by lighting, witnesses said. Thankfully, he is now in good condition at the hospital.

1. What is this news article about?
   A. the events of lightning striking near a store
   B. the store owner's bravery
   C. the damage lightning can cause
   D. the injuries caused by lightning

2. A reader can conclude that
   A. lightning is not dangerous.
   B. it's safer to be indoors when lightning strikes.
   C. lightning strikes only trees.
   D. all thunderstorms have lightning.

Chapter Preview

▲ *Working With the Photo*
Our earth's natural resources are limited. **What can you do to conserve resources and advocate for a healthy environment?**

Start-Up Activities

Before You Read Look at the Instant message below. What would you say to zurlatch4? Keep a record of your answers.

IM Express

zurlatch4: come to the beach with me tomorrow! I'm meeting Jenn and Brad

mustApha_Mond_ZarDanian: but what about the warning signs on the beach? there was some chemical spill last week

FOLDABLES™ Study Organizer

As You Read Make this Foldable™ to help you organize the information about air, water, and land pollution in Lesson 1. Begin with a plain sheet of 11" × 17" paper.

1 Fold the short sides of a sheet of paper along the long axis, leaving a 1" tab along the side.

2 Turn the paper and fold it into thirds.

3 Unfold and cut the top layer along both fold lines. This makes three tabs.

4 Label the tabs as shown.

Pollution

| Air | Water | Land |

Under the appropriate tabs, define terms and summarize main ideas about air, water and land pollution.

Health Online Visit health.glencoe.com and complete the Health Inventory for Chapter 21.

Pollution and Health

Guide to Reading

● Building Vocabulary
As you read this lesson, write each new highlighted term and its definition in your notebook.

- pollution (p. 577)
- pesticides (p. 577)
- acid rain (p. 577)
- smog (p. 578)
- ozone layer (p. 578)
- greenhouse effect (p. 578)
- global warming (p. 578)
- landfills (p. 579)
- hazardous wastes (p. 580)

● Focusing on the Main Ideas
In this lesson, you will learn to
- **explain** what pollution is.
- **identify** what contributes to air, water, and land pollution.
- **develop** strategies to reduce the ways you contribute to pollution.
- **recognize** how pollution affects the environment.

● Reading Strategy
Skimming Quickly look over the headings in this lesson. For each heading, write a sentence describing what information you think will be covered in that section.

FOLDABLES Study Organizer Use the Foldable™ on p. 575 as you read this lesson.

Quick Write
Give three examples of types of pollution that affect your local community.

Your Environment

Everything surrounding you makes up your environment. Locally, your environment includes your home, school, and community. Your environment, however, is also the air you breathe, the water you drink, the plants and animals that live nearby, and the climate you live in. It is all the living and nonliving elements that make up your world.

▶ The health of our natural environment has an effect on many aspects of life. **What steps can you take to preserve the beauty and health of your surroundings?**

DANGER
SEWAGE CONTAMINATED
BEACH AND WATER

AVOID SHELLFISH HARVESTING, SWIMMING, BEACH COMBING, OR OTHER CONTACT ACTIVITIES

Air, water, and land make life on earth possible. However, people pollute all these resources. **Pollution** includes *any dirty or harmful substance in the environment*. It affects both the living and nonliving things in your environment. It can also affect the decisions you make. For example, on days when air pollution is heavy, you may have to limit the time you spend outside. Your health—everyone's health, even the health of future generations—depends upon us taking action now to protect the environment.

Air Pollution

Some air pollution is natural, caused by events such as forest fires and erupting volcanoes. However, most air pollution results from human activities that release gases, dust, soot, and other substances into the air. The major sources of air pollution are described below:

- **Burning fossil fuels.** Burning oil, coal, and natural gas provides the energy that people depend on to run motor vehicles, heat and cool buildings, and carry out countless daily tasks at home and work. Burning these fossil fuels also releases toxic gases that harm the atmosphere. These include carbon monoxide, sulfur dioxide, and nitrogen oxides. Tiny particles of soot, ash and other substances, known as particulates, remain in the air for a long time.

- **Chemicals.** Many chemicals also pollute the air. Among them are **pesticides,** which are *products used on crops to control insects and other pests*. Chlorofluorocarbons (CFCs) are chemicals traditionally used in air conditioners and refrigerators. These have damaged the layer of the earth's atmosphere that shields us from dangerous solar radiation. CFC use is being phased out because of an international agreement signed in 1987 by more than 150 countries.

- **Other sources.** Natural sources, such as forest fires, release carbon monoxide and other gases into the atmosphere. Natural sources add to man-made pollution, increasing the overall amount of air pollution.

Reading Check **Define** What are *pesticides*?

Effects of Air Pollution

The environment is suffering because of air pollution. Some of the effects are described below:

- **Acid rain.** *Rain that is far more acidic than normal* is known as **acid rain.** Sulfur dioxides and nitrogen oxides—gases that mix with water vapor to form weak acids—are produced

Connect To...
Science

Pesticide Perils

Prolonged exposure to pesticides has been linked to many serious health problems.

Research the health hazards of exposure to pesticides and ways to avoid this potentially harmful environmental condition.

when fossil fuels are burned. The acid in the rain can hurt everything from trees to amphibians and fish.

- **Smog.** *A yellow-brown haze that forms when sunlight reacts with air pollution* is known as **smog.** When smog levels are high, people with respiratory problems are advised to stay indoors.

- **Destruction of the ozone layer.** The **ozone layer,** located miles above the earth's surface, acts as *a shield that protects living things from ultraviolet (UV) radiation.* Air pollution causes the deterioration of the ozone layer, allowing excessive UV radiation to reach the earth's surface. Too much UV radiation can cause skin cancer.

- **Global warming.** *The trapping of heat by carbon dioxide and other gases in the air* is known as the **greenhouse effect** (see **Figure 21.1**). The earth would be too cold to support life if there were no greenhouse effect. However, air pollution intensifies the greenhouse effect and may be causing increased **global warming,** *a rise in the earth's temperatures.* This could affect weather patterns as well as ocean water levels.

▼ FIGURE 21.1

THE GREENHOUSE EFFECT

The heating of the earth by gases in our atmosphere is similar to how a greenhouse warms. **What can be done to stop the greenhouse effect from causing an overall rise in temperatures?**

1 Light energy from the sun reaches the earth's lower atmosphere and is converted to heat.

2 A layer of carbon dioxide and other gases surrounding the earth traps the heat.

3 The surface of the earth and the lower atmosphere become warmer because of the trapped heat.

▶ Litter is one cause of land pollution. **What happens to all the trash that is produced?**

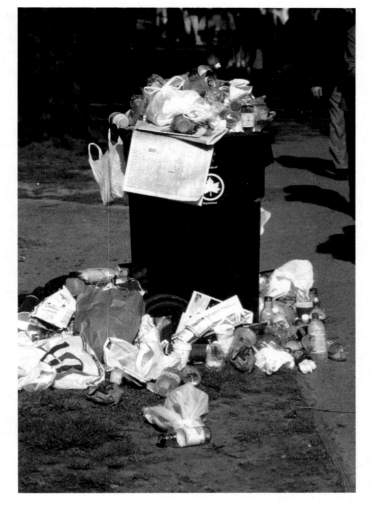

Water Pollution

Water is vital to all forms of life. However, various kinds of wastes, chemicals, and other harmful substances pollute the earth's water. One type of pollution is sewage—garbage, detergents, and other household wastes washed down drains. Sewage in the United States is treated, but many countries lack the education, money, and facilities needed to properly treat water. Industrial chemicals also contribute to water pollution. Some enter the water from factories. Agriculture also contributes pesticides, herbicides, and fertilizers that run off the land and into the water supply.

Oil spills from large tanker ships have far-reaching effects, killing plants and animals and ravaging delicate habitats. When spilled on land, oil runs off into nearby lakes, rivers, and wetlands.

Water polluted with sewage can spread horrible diseases such as typhoid fever and cholera. Eating shellfish from polluted water can cause hepatitis, a disease of the liver. Drinking water contaminated by heavy metals such as lead or mercury can damage the liver, kidneys, and the brain. It can also cause birth defects.

Land Pollution

Land pollution results from littering and the careless disposal of household and industrial garbage. This affects not only the soil but also the water and air. Two forms of land pollution are solid waste and hazardous wastes.

Solid Waste

The average U.S. citizen produces about 4.4 pounds of trash, or solid waste, daily. The solid waste produced by households and businesses usually ends up in **landfills**—*huge pits where wastes are dumped and buried.* Landfills are lined with a protective barrier that prevents wastes from seeping into the surrounding soil and into groundwater.

Topic: Caring for the Environment

Visit **health.glencoe.com** for Student Web Activities to learn about a variety of environmental groups that teens can take part in.

Activity: Using the information provided at the link above, choose an environmental issue that appeals to you. Then, create a flyer that tells other teens about the issue and what they can do to help.

◄ The household products shown in this picture are all hazardous materials and need to be disposed of safely. **How can you find out how to safely dispose of hazardous wastes in your community?**

Hazardous Wastes

With each new industry and each new product, there is the potential of a new waste problem. **Hazardous wastes** are *human-made liquid or solid wastes that may endanger human health or the environment.* When hazardous wastes pollute the soil, water, or air, they can cause injury, illness, and even death. All hazardous wastes require careful handling and special disposal.

Many products we use daily—and discard—contain hazardous materials: batteries, bleach, insecticides, motor oil, antifreeze, paint, and certain cleaning fluids. These materials should not be discarded in your regular trash can. Your local health department or environmental agency can advise you about how to dispose of them safely.

Health Online

Visit **health.glencoe.com** and complete the Interactive Study Guide for Lesson 1.

Reading Check **Recall** What are two forms of land pollution?

Lesson 1 Review

After You Read

Review this lesson for new terms, major headings, and Reading Checks.

What I Learned

1. *Vocabulary* Define *pollution*. Use the word in an original sentence.

2. *Identify* Name five common products that contain hazardous materials that contribute to pollution.

3. *Recall* Name two sources of air pollution and two sources of water pollution.

Thinking Critically

4. *Explain* How do fossil fuels contribute to global warming?

5. *Evaluate* Why do hazardous wastes pose a greater problem today than they did a century ago?

Applying Health Skills

6. *Accessing Information* Use reliable sources to research the dangers of exposure to lead paint and explain how to avoid this potentially harmful substance. Report your findings to the class.

Preventing and Reducing Pollution

Guide to Reading

● Building Vocabulary
Make a word diagram that shows the relationship among the terms below. Decide which term is the most general and the one all the others relate to.

- Environmental Protection Agency (EPA) (p. 581)
- biodegradable (p. 582)
- nonrenewable resources (p. 582)
- conservation (p. 582)
- precycling (p. 584)

● Focusing on the Main Ideas
In this lesson, you will learn to
- **describe** the three Rs: reduce, reuse, and recycle.
- **explain** actions individuals can take to protect the environment.
- **identify** nonrenewable resources.
- **communicate** your concerns about the environment.

● Reading Strategy
Finding the Main Idea For each major heading in this lesson, write one sentence that states the main idea.

Reduce, Reuse, Recycle

Governments around the world are committed to reducing and preventing pollution. Here, in the United States, the **Environmental Protection Agency (EPA)** is *the governmental agency that is committed to protecting the environment.* In addition, many states and countries maintain air and water quality by applying waste management strategies and controlling emissions (the gases, including exhaust, that vehicles release into the air). Waste management involves efforts to dispose of wastes in a way that protects the health of the environment and the people.

Quick Write

Make a list of actions you already take to protect the environment.

▶ Some communities provide bins for collecting different kinds of recyclable materials. **What does your community do to encourage recycling?**

You can help protect the environment by practicing the three Rs: reduce, reuse, and recycle. *Reduce* your consumption of energy and other resources. *Reuse* items by repairing, selling, or donating them. *Recycle* materials so they can be used again.

Many communities have introduced collection programs that make recycling convenient for people. These programs are only effective if citizens participate.

Protecting the Air and Water

Anytime you use an electrical appliance, drive a car, or run a power lawn mower, you are burning fossil fuels to produce energy. You are also contributing to air pollution. If you want cleaner air, try these strategies:

- **Walk or pedal your bike instead of having someone drive you.** You can help cut down on air pollution while getting the benefit of some physical activity.

- **Use public transportation or carpool.** Carpooling, or taking a bus, train, or subway cuts down on the number of cars producing exhaust fumes.

- **Don't burn trash, leaves, and brush.** Let the local waste management facility dispose of your trash.

To keep from polluting the water, use detergents that are **biodegradable**—*broken down easily in the environment.* Discard all waste materials properly. Take hazardous waste materials to the appropriate collection sites.

Conservation

Fossil fuels are natural materials known as **non-renewable resources**—*substances that cannot be replaced once they are used.* A barrel of oil burned is a barrel of oil gone forever.

Conservation is *the saving of resources.* Using less of a resource is the best way to conserve it. Your own home offers lots of opportunities for you to save energy. When you save energy you are also saving fossil fuels. **Figure 21.2** on the next page shows some ways to reduce your energy and water use at home.

Recycling and Precycling

When you change an item in some way in order to use it again, that is recycling. Recycling conserves energy and natural resources while it helps reduce solid waste. Paper, aluminum, glass, plastics and yard waste are the most commonly collected recycling materials.

▼ There are many alternate forms of transportation available that can cut down the amount of air pollution. **What can you do to promote cleaner air?**

FIGURE 21.2

CONSERVATION IN THE HOUSE

The best way to conserve a resource is to use less of it. What are some ways to save energy and water at home?

Heating and Cooling

- Seal air leaks around doors, windows, and electric sockets to prevent heat from escaping.
- Keep doors and windows closed during the air-conditioning season, and keep air-conditioning at about 78°F.
- Buy an energy-efficient heating/cooling system that features a thermostat with a timer.

Water

- Never let water run unnecessarily.
- Wash clothes in warm or cold water, which uses less energy than hot water.
- Run the washing machine or dishwasher only when you have a full load, and use the short cycle when appropriate.
- If you have an older toilet, place a one-liter bottle filled with water inside your toilet tank. This will reduce the amount of water used for flushing. Another option is to replace an older toilet with a newer model that requires less water per flush.

Lighting and Appliances

- Turn off lights when you are not using them.
- Replace traditional lightbulbs with compact fluorescent bulbs. They use less energy and last longer.
- Turn off televisions, computers, fans, and other electric appliances when you are not using them.

Cooking

- Don't preheat a conventional oven for longer than necessary.
- Avoid opening the oven while cooking. Instead, use a timer and the oven door window to check if food is done.
- Heat small quantities of food in a microwave, toaster oven, or slow cooker.

To understand how recycling conserves energy and natural resources, think about aluminum soda cans. It takes energy to mine the ore used to make the aluminum, to process the ore, and to manufacture the cans. When aluminum cans are recycled, they are changed back into sheets of aluminum that can be used to make new cans or other products. When less ore is taken from the ground, less energy is needed.

A symbol with three curved arrows appears on many kinds of products. It indicates that an item can be recycled, or that it is made of recycled materials. A number appears in the center of the symbol on plastic items. This is a code identifying the specific type of material. Plastic objects are sorted according to number at recycling facilities.

More and more people are becoming involved in recycling through drop off centers and curbside programs. However, plastics have not kept pace with other recycling efforts (**Figure 21.3**). Most recycling programs accept plastics, but not necessarily all types of plastics.

▼ FIGURE 21.3

RESULTS OF RECYCLING EFFORTS

As awareness of environmental health grows, people take a more active role in recycling. **What else can you infer from this graph?**

Aluminum 3.1 0.9 **28%**

Steel 12.4 4.3 **35%**

Glass 12.5 3.2 **25%**

Plastics 22.4 1.2 **5%**

Yard Trimmings 27.7 12.6 **45%**

Paper/Paperboard 84.1 35.0 **45%**

■ **Amount Discarded** (in metric tons)

■ **Amount Recycled**

% **Percentage Recycled**

Source: U.S. Environmental Protection Agency, 2000.

Precycling—*reducing waste before it occurs*—is another way to put the brakes on consumption of resources. Below are some basic guidelines for precycling:

- Buy products in packages made of glass, metal, or paper (all materials that can be reused or recycled).
- Look for products in refillable containers.
- Carry store-bought purchases home in your own reusable cloth sack or plastic bags.

Protecting the Environment

Everyone needs to play a part in protecting the environment. Here are some suggestions:

- **Lead your family's recycling effort.** Find out which recyclables are collected in your community and set up a system that your family can follow.
- **Practice environmental awareness.** Evaluate advertising, labels, contents, and packaging to determine their environmental friendliness.
- **Support a conservation organization.** Request information about current environmental issues, attend meetings, and help to make a difference.

Health Online

Visit **health.glencoe.com** and complete the Interactive Study Guide for Lesson 2.

Health Skills Activity

Practicing Healthful Behaviors

Environment-Friendly Shopping

You have an opportunity to help the environment every time you shop. Below are some tips on how to be an environmentally friendly consumer.

- **Plan.** Make a shopping list and buy only what you need.
- **Buy in bulk.** Select larger packages of foods such as cereals and snacks. Buying in larger quantities cuts down on the amount of packaging that you'll ultimately discard.
- **Be aware of packaging.** Choose products packaged in materials that easily break down or are recyclable. For example, buy beverages in glass or aluminum containers.
- **Read labels carefully.** Some common household products such as oven cleaners and paint thinners contain substances harmful to humans. Look for safer commercial products or research alternatives.

In a Group

List all the ways you can think of to save energy, packaging, and waste. Combine the ideas on one list and post it on a bulletin board.

Lesson 2 Review

After You Read

Review this lesson for new terms, major headings, and Reading Checks.

What I Learned

1. *Vocabulary* What is a *nonrenewable resource*?

2. *List* What are three ways that you can conserve energy and water at home?

3. *Identify* Name the three Rs and tell how they are related to your health.

Thinking Critically

4. *Synthesize* Explain why recycling and precycling are keys to a cleaner environment.

5. *Apply* Briefly describe how each of the following strategies helps protect the environment: emission control, monitoring water quality, and waste management.

Applying Health Skills

6. *Goal Setting* Working with family members, analyze your current approach to the three Rs and set specific goals to improve your household record for reducing, reusing, and recycling.

Building Health Skills

Make the Most of It

DIRECTIONS

Practicing Healthful Behaviors involves taking specific actions to stay healthy and avoid risky behaviors. This activity will give you the opportunity to develop and master this important health skill. Here's a guide to the different parts of this activity:

❶ In the **Model** section, you will read about a teen who performs the health skill successfully. This "model" scenario will show you how the skill is done.

❷ The **Practice** section will help guide you in practicing the skill.

❸ In the **Apply** section, you will have a chance to perform the skill on your own. You can use the Self-Check to check your work.

To complete this activity, first read the scenario presented in the Model. Then move on to the Practice. Finally, go ahead and try the Apply.

❶ Model

Josh and his family care about the environment. They look for alternatives to always buying new items at the store. They are aware that the manufacturing and packaging of new products uses natural resources that may not be renewable. Whenever possible, they **reuse** items such as grocery bags. Josh cuts up paper bags to cover his schoolbooks, and his family lines their wastebaskets with used plastic bags.

The family **reduces** waste in other ways, too. They use cloth napkins instead of paper and clean up spills with sponges instead of paper towels. Josh carries his lunch in a reusable sack instead of using disposable paper bags. Josh and his family **recycle** items as well. They recycle aluminum cans, newspapers, water bottles, and many other items. All these choices help protect the environment.

② Practice

Form small groups. Choose three items from this list and discuss creative ways to reduce, reuse, or recycle them.

- Paper and plastic bags
- Cardboard boxes
- Metal cans
- Old clothes
- Paper goods
- Old tires
- Plastic milk containers

Share your group's ideas with the class. Then, as a class, come up with a master list of at least three ideas for each item. With your teacher's permission, post the master list in the hallway of your school.

Skill Summary
PRACTICING HEALTHFUL BEHAVIORS

You can reduce waste by

- reusing items.
- reducing the number of items used.
- repairing broken items.
- recycling items.

③ Apply

Create a chart with your ideas for ways to reduce waste. Divide it into three columns. Label the first column "Items We Throw Away." List all of the items you throw out.

Label the second column "Ways to Reduce, Reuse, and Recycle." Here, list the changes you can make so that you would reduce, reuse, or recycle the items you are throwing away. Finally, label the third column "Why It Matters," and list the advantages of reducing, reusing, and recycling items.

Self-Check

- Did I identify items that I throw away?
- Did I describe ways to reduce, reuse, and recycle these items?
- Did I explain the benefits of reducing, reusing, and recycling?

Pitch In for the PLANET

Five ways for you to be an Earth Day hero.

When then Wisconsin Senator Gaylord Nelson developed the idea for the first Earth Day in 1970, little did he know how that idea would take root and bloom. Earth Day was meant to draw attention to environmental problems. America's enthusiasm for Earth Day helped persuade lawmakers to pass the 1970 Clean Air Act and to create the Environmental Protection Agency.

More than 30 years after the first Earth Day, people around the world gather to show that they care about our planet. Earth Day is celebrated on April 22, but you can celebrate Earth Day every day. Here are some easy things you can do to protect the air, water, and soil:

1. RECYCLE BATTERIES

The batteries used in toys, cell phones, and other devices can be harmful to the environment. If your batteries contain cadmium, nickel, lead, or mercury, don't throw them in the garbage. Take used batteries to a recycling or collection center in your community.

2. CUT DOWN ON GARBAGE

Prevention is the best way to fight pollution! If you don't create garbage then no one has to clean it up. Buy products that don't have a lot of packaging. Reuse containers instead of throwing them out. Try to make Earth Day a garbage-free day.

3. AVOID CHEMICALS

Plant marigolds, mint, garlic, or onions in a garden instead of spraying pesticides. Insects don't like these plants and will stay away. Use natural ingredients like vinegar, baking soda, and salt to make cleaners in place of store-bought chemical cleansers.

4. DON'T WASTE ENERGY

Just think how much electricity you could save if you always turned off lights and appliances when not using them. Remind your parents and friends to conserve energy.

Is the heat in your classroom on high with the window open? Do you let the faucet or shower run longer than needed? It takes energy to make hot water. Use less and you'll save precious resources.

5. GET INVOLVED

Is there a place in your community that needs to be cleaned up? Get the job done by organizing an event. Working with others is fun, and teamwork will get it done faster.

Reading Review

FOLDABLES Study Organizer

Foldables™ and Other Study Aids Take out the Foldable™ that you created for Lesson 1 and any other study guide you created. Find a partner and quiz each other using these study aids.

Lesson 1 Pollution and Health

Key Ideas

- Your environment is all the living and nonliving elements that make up your world.

- Although natural events such as forest fires and volcanoes cause air pollution, it's human activities that contribute the most by allowing gases, dust, soot, and other substances to be released into the air.

- Land pollution, resulting from littering and the careless disposal of household and industrial garbage, impacts not only the soil, but also the water and air.

Vocabulary

- pollution (p. 577)
- pesticides (p. 577)
- acid rain (p. 577)
- smog (p. 578)
- ozone layer (p. 578)
- greenhouse effect (p. 578)
- global warming (p. 578)
- landfills (p. 579)
- hazardous wastes (p. 580)

Lesson 2 Preventing and Reducing Pollution

Key Ideas

- Individuals can make a difference in the health of their environment by committing to the three Rs: reducing consumption of energy and other resources, reusing items by repairing, selling, or donating them, and recycling materials to be used again.

- Many natural materials such as oil cannot be replaced once they are used. These are known as nonrenewable resources.

- Recycling not only conserves energy and natural resources, it also helps to reduce the amount of solid waste discarded into landfills.

Vocabulary

- Environmental Protection Agency (EPA) (p. 581)
- biodegradable (p. 582)
- nonrenewable resources (p. 582)
- conservation (p. 582)
- precycling (p. 584)

Reviewing Vocabulary and Main Ideas

On a sheet of paper, write the numbers 1–10. After each number, write the term from the list that best completes each sentence.

- precycling
- fossil fuels
- greenhouse effect
- hazardous wastes
- biodegradable
- smog
- pollution
- conservation
- nonrenewable resources
- global warming

Lesson 1 Pollution and Health

1. The _____ is the trapping of heat near the earth's surface.

2. _____ is a yellow-brown haze formed when sunlight reacts with air pollution.

3. The burning of _____ contributes greatly to air pollution.

4. _____ is any dirty or harmful substance in the environment.

5. _____ is a rise in the earth's temperatures.

Lesson 2 Preventing and Reducing Pollution

6. You can help keep the water clean by using detergents that are _____.

7. The practice of reducing waste before it occurs is called _____.

8. Advances in science and technology have led to the problem of _____, or waste products that can cause illness, injury, or death.

9. _____ are substances that cannot be replaced once they are used.

10. The saving of resources is _____.

Thinking Critically

Using complete sentences, answer the following questions on a sheet of paper.

11. **Apply** What changes could you make in your life to conserve energy and reduce air pollution?

12. **Analyze** Why is the disposal of hazardous wastes more of a challenge than the disposal of other solid wastes?

13. **Evaluate** Why is it important for people to become actively involved in protecting the environment? What might happen if people ignore environmental problems?

Write About It

14. Communication Skills Imagine that you are writing an article for a newsletter of the Environmental Protection Agency (EPA). In your article, define and discuss the different forms of pollution. Tell what factors contribute to each form of pollution. Explain how pollution affects the health of our environment.

15. Advocacy Write a public service announcement (PSA) that encourages teens to recycle and conserve resources. In your PSA, state facts about the need to recycle and conserve, and opinions about the benefits of taking these actions. Give examples that show how teens can recycle and conserve resources and how they, too, can advocate for environmental health.

16. Goal Setting Choose one action that you could take that would improve the health of the environment. Set a goal to make this behavior part of your weekly routine. Develop a plan to achieve your goal.

Standardized Test Practice

Reading & Writing

Read the passage and then answer the questions.

Air, water, and land pollution affects your health and that of your environment. Air pollution can worsen symptoms in people with respiratory problems. Water pollution can contaminate the water we drink, swim, and fish in, causing health problems and negatively affecting aquatic life. When discarded improperly, hazardous substances in common products such as batteries can leak into the surrounding soil. These facts make it clear that it is worth your while to work to reduce pollution.

There are, however, ways to reduce pollution. Use mass transit when it's available and properly dispose of household products, such as bleach and motor oil.

1. Which sentence from the passage represents the author's opinion?

  A. Air, water, and land pollution affects your health and that of your environment.

  B. Air pollution can worsen symptoms in people with respiratory problems.

  C. These facts make it clear that it is worth your while to work to reduce pollution.

  D. Water pollution can contaminate the water we drink, swim, and fish in, making us ill and killing aquatic life.

2. The author probably wrote the editorial

  A. to explain why pollution occurs.

  B. to criticize people who litter.

  C. to describe the steps he or she takes to reduce pollution.

  D. to persuade readers to take steps to reduce pollution.

Glossary

The Glossary contains all the important terms used throughout the text. It includes the **boldfaced** terms listed in the "Vocabulary" lists at the beginning of each lesson and which appear in text and art.

The Glossary lists the term, the pronunciation (in the case of difficult terms), the definition, and the page on which the term is defined. The pronunciations here and in the text follow the system outlined below. The column headed "Symbol" shows the spelling used in this book to represent the appropriate method.

Pronunciation Key

Sound	As In	Symbol	Example
ă	hat, map	a	abscess (AB·ses)
ā	age, face	ay	atrium (AY·tree·uhm)
a	care, their	eh	capillaries (KAP·uh·lehr·eez)
ä, ŏ	father, hot	ah	biopsy (BY·ahp·See)
ar	far	ar	cardiac (KAR·dee·ak)
ch	child, much	ch	barbiturate (bar·BI·chuh·ruht)
ĕ	let, best	e	vessel (VE·suhl)
ē	beat, See, city	ee	acne (AK·nee)
er	term, stir, purr	er	nuclear (NOO·klee·er)
g	grow	g	malignant (muh·LIG·nuhnt)
ĭ	it, hymn	i	bacteria (bak·TIR·ee·uh)
ī	ice, five	y	benign (bi·NYN)
		eye	iris (EYE·ris)
j	page, fungi	j	cartilage (KAR·tuhl·ij)
k	coat, look, chorus	k	defect (DEE·fekt)
ō	open, coat, grow	oh	aerobic (ehr·OH·bik)
ô	order	or	organ (OR·guhn)
ȯ	flaw, all	aw	palsy (PAWL·zee)
oi	voice	oy	goiter (GOY·ter)
ou	out	ow	fountain (FOWN·tuhn)
s	say, rice	s	dermis (DER·mis)
sh	she, attention	sh	conservation (kahn·ser·VAY·shuhn)
ŭ	cup, flood	uh	bunion (BUHN·yuhn)
u	put, wood, could	u	pulmonary (PUL·muh·nehr·ee)
ü	rule, move, you	oo	attitudes (AT·i·toodz)
w	win	w	warranty (WAWR·uhn·tee)
y	your	yu	urethra (yu·REE·thruh)
z	says	z	hormones (HOR·mohnz)
zh	pleasure	zh	transfusion (trans·FYOO·zhuhn)
ə	about, collide	uh	addiction (uh·DIK·shuhn)

A

Abdominal thrusts Quick, upward pulls into the diaphragm to force out an obstruction blocking the airway. (page 564)

Abstinence The conscious, active choice not to participate in high-risk behaviors. (pages 16 and 119)

Abuse The physical, emotional, or mental mistreatment of one person by another. (page 188)

Accident Any event that was not intended to happen. (page 540)

Accident chain A series of events that include a situation, an unsafe habit, and an unsafe action. (page 541)

Accidental injuries Injuries resulting from an accident. (page 540)

Accountability A willingness to answer for your actions and decisions. (page 35)

Acid rain Rain that is far more acidic than normal. (page 577)

Active listening Hearing, thinking about, and responding to another person's message. (page 110)

Adapt To adjust to new situations. (page 52)

Addiction A physical or psychological need for a drug. (page 291)

Addictive Capable of causing a user to develop intense cravings. (page 309)

Adolescence The stage of life between childhood and adulthood. (page 8)

Adrenaline A hormone that gives the body extra energy. (page 65)

Advocacy Informing others about health practices and encouraging healthful behaviors. (page 43)

Aerobic exercise Rhythmic, nonstop, moderate to vigorous activity that requires large amounts of oxygen. (page 207)

Affection Feelings of love for another person. (page 120)

Aggressive Overly forceful, pushy, hostile, or otherwise attacking in approach. (page 116)

AIDS (Acquired Immunodeficiency Syndrome) A deadly disease that interferes with the body's natural ability to fight infection. (page 496)

Air Quality Index (AQI) A measure of ozone, sulfur dioxide, carbon monoxide, and fine particles close to the ground. (page 421)

Alcohol A drug that is produced by a chemical reaction in fruits, vegetables, and grains. (page 278)

Alcohol abuse A pattern of drinking that results in one or more well-defined behaviors within a twelve-month period. (page 295)

Alcohol poisoning A dangerous condition that results when a person drinks excessive amounts of alcohol over a short time period. (page 283)

Alcoholism A progressive, chronic disease involving a mental and physical need for alcohol. (page 291)

Allergen (AL·er·juhn) A substance that causes an allergic reaction. (page 527)

Allergy An extreme sensitivity to a substance. (page 527)

Allied health professionals Medical professionals who perform duties which would otherwise have to be performed by doctors or nurses. (page 389)

Alternatives Other ways of thinking or acting. (page 281)

Alveoli (al·VEE·uh·ly) Tiny air sacs in the lungs where carbon dioxide is exchanged with oxygen. (page 420)

Amino acids Small units that make up protein. (page 240)

Amnesia Partial or total loss of memory. (page 341)

Amphetamine (am·FE·tuh·meen) A drug that stimulates the central nervous system. (page 348)

Anabolic steroids A synthetic substance related to the male sex hormones. (page 343)

Anaerobic exercise Intense physical activity that requires little oxygen but uses short bursts of energy. (page 208)

Angioplasty A surgical procedure in which an instrument with a tiny balloon, drill bit, or laser attached is inserted into a blocked artery to clear a blockage. (page 519)

Anorexia nervosa An eating disorder characterized by self-starvation leading to extreme weight loss. (page 267)

Antibiotics (an·ti·by·AH·tiks) Medicines that reduce or kill harmful bacteria in the body. (page 385)

Antibodies Proteins that attach to antigens, keeping them from harming the body. (page 486)

Antigen Substances released by invading pathogens. (page 486)

Antihistamines Medicines that help control the effects triggered by histamines. (page 529)

Anxiety A state of uneasiness, usually associated with a future uncertainty. (page 58)

Anxiety disorder A disorder in which intense anxiety or fear keeps a person from functioning normally. (page 81)

Appetite The psychological desire for food. (page 236)

Appropriate weight The weight that is best for your body. (page 261)

Arteries Blood vessels that carry blood away from the heart to other parts of the body. (page 415)

Arteriosclerosis (ar·tir·ee·oh·skluh·ROH·sis) A group of disorders in which arteries harden and become more rigid. (page 518)

Arthritis (ar·THRY·tuhs) A disease of the joints marked by pain and swelling in body joints. (page 524)

Assault An unlawful threat or attempt to do bodily injury to another person. (page 181)

Assertive Behaving with confidence and clearly stating your intentions. (page 116)

Asthma (AZ·muh) A condition in which the small airways in the lungs narrow, making breathing difficult. (pages 420 and 530)

Atherosclerosis (a·thuh·roh·skluh·ROH·sis) A form of arteriosclerosis in which fatty substances in the blood build up on the walls of the arteries. (page 518)

Attitude A personal feeling or belief. (page 17)

Autonomic (aw·tuh·NAH·mik) **system** The part of the nervous system that deals with actions you do not usually control. (page 424)

B

Bacteria Tiny one-celled organisms that live nearly everywhere. (page 479)

Balance A feeling of stability and control over your body. (page 205)

Battery The unlawful beating, hitting, or kicking of another person. (page 181)

Benign (bi·NYN) Not cancerous. (page 512)

Binge When a drug is taken repeatedly and at increasingly high doses. (page 348)

Binge drinking The consumption of a large quantity of alcohol in a very short period of time. (page 289)

Binge eating disorder Compulsive overeating. (page 267)

Biodegradable Broken down easily in the environment. (page 582)

Biological age Age determined by how well various body parts are working. (page 468)

Biopsy The removal of a tissue sample from a person for examination. (page 513)

Birth defects Abnormalities present at birth that causes physical or mental disability or death. (page 458)

Blended family A family that consists of a parent, a stepparent, and the children of one or both parents. (page 137)

Blizzard A very heavy snowstorm with winds up to 45 miles per hour. (page 551)

Blood alcohol content (BAC) A measure of the amount of alcohol present in a person's blood. (page 283)

Body composition The ratio of body fat to lean body tissue, such as bone, muscle, and fluid. (page 213)

Body image The way you see and feel about your body. (page 260)

Body language The use of visual cues to communicate a message. (page 108)

Body mass index (BMI) A formula you can use to determine if your weight is appropriate for you. (pages 262 and 521)

Bronchi (BRONG·ky) Passages through which air enters and spreads through the lungs. (pages 309 and 420)

Bronchodilators (brahn·ko·DY·lay·terz) Medicines used to relax the muscles that have tightened around the airways. (page 531)

Bulimia nervosa A condition in which a person eats large amounts of food and then secretly purges. (page 268)

Bully Someone who picks on individuals who are smaller or weaker. (page 157)

C

Calorie A unit of heat that measures the energy available in food. (pages 205 and 245)

Cancer A disease characterized by the rapid and uncontrolled growth of abnormal cells. (page 511)

Capillaries Tiny blood vessels that connect the veins and arteries to the body's cells. (page 415)

Carbohydrates The sugars and starches that occur naturally in foods, mainly in plants. (page 238)

Carbon monoxide A colorless, odorless, poisonous gas. (page 309)

Carcinogens (kar·SIN·uh·juhn) Substances that cause cancer. (page 513)

Cardiac muscles Muscles found in the walls of your heart. (page 410)

Cardiopulmonary resuscitation (CPR) A first aid procedure that combines rescue breathing with chest compressions to restore breathing and circulation. (page 566)

Cardiovascular disease A disease of the heart and blood vessels. (page 313)

Cardiovascular (KAR·dee·oh·VAS·kyoo·ler) **system** Organs and tissues that transport essential materials to body cells and remove their waste products. (page 413)

Carrier A person who is infected with a virus and who can pass it on to others. (page 496)

Cartilage (KAHR·tuhl·ij) Strong, flexible tissue that provides cushioning at the joints. (page 406)

Cell respiration Process in which the body's cells are nourished and energized. (page 414)

Central nervous system (CNS) The brain and spinal cord. (page 423)

Cervix The entrance of the uterus. (page 454)

Character The way in which a person thinks, feels, and acts. (page 32)

Character trait A quality that demonstrates how a person thinks, feels, and acts. (page 32)

Chemotherapy The use of powerful medicines to destroy cancer cells. (page 514)

Chlamydia (kluh·MI·dee·uh) A bacterial STD that may affect the reproductive organs, urethra, and anus. (page 492)

Chromosomes (KROH·muh·sohmz) The threadlike structures found within the nucleus of a cell that carry the codes for inherited traits. (page 456)

Chronic diseases Diseases that are present either continuously or off and on over a long time. (page 508)

Chronic obstructive pulmonary disease (COPD) A condition in which passages in the lungs become swollen and irritated, eventually losing their elasticity. (page 313)

Chronological (krah·nuh·LAH·ji·kuhl) **age** Age measured in years. (page 468)

Circulatory (SER·kyuh·luh·tohr·ee) **system** Organs and tissues that transport essential materials to body cells and remove their waste products. (page 413)

Cirrhosis (suh·ROH·sis) A disease characterized by scarring and eventual destruction of the liver. (page 287)

Citizenship The way you conduct yourself as a member of a community. (page 36)

Clinical social worker (CSW) A licensed, certified mental health professional with a master's degree in social work. (page 93)

Clique A group of friends who hang out together and act in similar ways. (page 105)

CNS depressants Substances that slow down normal brain function. (page 350)

Cold turkey Term used to describe quitting a habit, such as smoking, all at once. (page 317)

Colon (KOH·luhn) The large intestine. (page 430)

Commitment A pledge or a promise. (page 140)

Communicable (kuh·MYOO·ni·kuh·buhl) **disease** A disease that can be passed to a person from another person, animal, or object. (page 478)

Communication The exchange of thoughts, feelings, and beliefs between two or more people. (pages 39 and 108)

Community service Volunteer programs whose goal is to improve the community and the life of its residents. (page 12)

Comparison shopping A method of judging the benefits of different products and services by measuring and comparing several factors, such as quality, effectiveness, safety, and cost. (page 381)

Compromise An arrangement in which each side gives up something to reach a satisfactory solution. (page 166)

Conditioning Regular activity and exercise that prepare a person for a sport. (page 222)

Conflict A disagreement between people with opposing viewpoints, ideas, or goals. (page 154)

Conflict resolution Solving a disagreement in a way that satisfies both sides. (pages 40 and 164)

Congenital disorders All disorders that are present when the baby is born. (page 508)

Consequences Outcomes or effects that may occur as a result of a decision or an action. (page 119)

Conservation The saving of resources. (page 582)

Consumer Anyone who purchases products or services. (page 379)

Consumer skills Techniques that enable you to make wise, informed purchases. (page 379)

Contagious period The length of time that a disease can spread from person to person. (page 489)

Cool-down A period of low to moderate exercise to prepare your body to end a workout session. (page 220)

Coordination The smooth and effective working together of your muscles and bones. (page 205)

Coping strategies Ways of dealing with the sense of loss people feel when someone close to them dies. (page 70)

Cornea A clear protective structure of the eye that lets in light. (page 377)

Crisis hot line A toll-free telephone service where abuse victims can get help and information. (page 193)

Cross-training Switching between different forms of physical exercise on different days. (page 215)

Cumulative risks Related risks that increase in effect with each added risk. (page 15)

Cuticle (KYOO·ti·kuhl) A fold of epidermis around the fingernails and toenails. (page 374)

Cycle of abuse Pattern of repeating abuse from one generation to the next. (page 193)

D

Dandruff A flaking of the outer layer of dead skin cells. (page 374)

Decibel A measure of the loudness of sound. (page 377)

Decision making The process of making a choice or finding a solution. (page 27)

Defensive driving Watching out for other people on the road and anticipating unsafe acts. (page 546)

Degenerative diseases Diseases that cause further breakdown in body cells, tissues, and organs as they progress. (page 508)

Dehydration Condition caused by excessive water loss. (page 225)

Depressants Substances that slow down body functions and reactions. (page 278)

Dermatologist (DER·muh·TAHL·uh·jist) A physician who treats skin disorders. (page 373)

Dermis (DER·mis) The thick inner layer of skin. (page 373)

Detoxification (dee·tahk·si·fi·KAY·shuhn) The physical process of freeing the body of an addictive substance. (pages 297 and 359)

Developmental tasks Events that need to happen in order for you to continue growing toward becoming a healthy, mature adult. (page 460)

Diabetes A disease that prevents the body from converting food into energy. (page 522)

Diaphragm (DY·uh·fram) A dome-shaped muscle that separates the chest from the abdomen. (page 420)

Digestion (dy·JES·chuhn) The changing of food you eat into substances your body can use. (page 428)

Digestive system The body system that converts food to a form useful to the body. (page 427)

Disease Any condition that interferes with the proper functioning of the body or mind. (page 478)

Disorder A disturbance in the normal function of a part of the body. (page 80)

Divorce A legal end to a marriage contract. (page 142)

Domestic violence Physical abuse that occurs within a family. (page 189)

Driving while intoxicated (DWI) A driver with a blood alcohol concentration (BAC) of 0.08% or greater. (page 288)

Drug A substance other than food that changes the structure or function of the body or mind. (page 334)

Drug abuse The intentional use of drugs in a way that is unhealthy or illegal. (page 336)

Drug free A characteristic of a person not taking illegal drugs or of a place where no illegal drugs are used. (page 361)

Drug misuse Taking or using medicine in a way that is not intended. (page 335)

Drug trafficking The buying or selling of drugs. (page 177)

E

Earthquake A violent, shaking movement of the earth's surface. (page 552)

Eating disorder Extreme and damaging eating behavior that can lead to sickness and even death. (page 266)

Egg cell The reproductive cell from the female that joins with a sperm cell to make a new life. (page 450)

Embryo A developing organism from the time of fertilization to about the eighth week of development. (page 452)

Emotional needs Needs that affect a person's feelings and sense of well-being. (page 61)

Emotions Feelings that arise in response to thoughts, remarks, and events. (page 57)

Empathy The ability to understand and show concern for another person's feelings. (page 36)

Empty-calorie foods Foods that offer few, if any, nutrients but do supply calories. (page 249)

Enablers Persons who create an atmosphere in which the alcoholic can comfortably continue his or her unacceptable behavior. (page 294)

Endocrine (EN·duh·krin) **system** The body's chemical communication system that regulates many functions. (page 433)

Environment The sum total of a person's surroundings. (page 456)

Environmental Protection Agency (EPA) The agency of the United States government that is committed to protecting the environment. (page 581)

Enzymes Proteins that affect the many body processes. (page 428)

Epidermis (e·puh·DER·mis) The outermost layer of the skin. (page 373)

Epiglottis (e·puh·GLAH·tis) A flap of tissue that closes over the trachea when you swallow. (page 419)

Escalate To become more serious. (page 159)

Euphoria A feeling of well-being or elation. (page 346)

Excretion (ek·SKREE·shuhn) The process of removing wastes from the body. (page 430)

Excretory system The body system that removes wastes from the body. (page 430)

Exercise Planned physical activity done regularly to build or maintain one's fitness. (page 207)

Extended family A person's immediate family plus other relatives such as grandparents, aunts, uncles, and cousins. (page 135)

F

Family The basic unit of society, and includes two or more people brought together by blood, marriage, adoption, or a desire for mutual support. (page 134)

Family therapy Counseling that seeks to improve troubled family relationships. (page 92)

Famine A widespread shortage of food. (page 395)

Fatty liver A condition in which fats build up in the liver and cannot be broken down. (page 287)

Fertilization The joining together of a male sperm cell and a female egg cell. (pages 439 and 450)

Fetal alcohol syndrome (FAS) A group of alcohol-related birth defects that include both physical and mental problems. (page 290)

Fetus A developing organism from the end of the eighth week of the mother's pregnancy until birth. (page 452)

Fiber The part of fruits, vegetables, grains, and beans that your body cannot digest. (page 239)

Fight-or-flight response The process by which the body prepares to deal with a stressor. (page 64)

First aid The immediate temporary care given to an injured or ill person until professional help is available. (page 554)

FITT principle A method for safely increasing aspects of your workout without injuring yourself. (page 218)

Flexibility The ability of your body's joints to move easily through a full range of motion. (page 212)

Foodborne illness Sickness that results from eating food that is not safe to eat. (page 247)

Fracture A break in a bone. (page 559)

Fraud Deliberate deceit or trickery. (page 381)

Fungi (FUHN·jy) Organisms that are more complex than bacteria, but cannot make their own food. (page 479)

G

Gallbladder A small, saclike organ that stores bile. (page 429)

Gang A group of people whose members often use violence or take part in criminal activity. (page 177)

Gender discrimination Singling out or excluding a person based on gender. (page 186)

Genes The basic units of heredity. (page 456)

Genetic (juh·NE·tik) **disorder** A disorder that is caused partly or completely by a defect in genes. (page 456)

Genital herpes (HER·peez) A viral STD that produces painful blisters on the genital area. (page 493)

Genital warts Growths or bumps in the genital area caused by certain types of the human papillomavirus (HPV). (page 493)

Germs Organisms that cause disease and that are so small they can only be seen through a microscope. (page 478)

Gingivitis (jin·juh·VY·tis) A common disorder in which the gums are red and sore and bleed easily. (page 375)

Gland A group of cells, or an organ, that secretes a chemical substance. (page 434)

Global warming A rise in the earth's temperatures. (page 578)

Goal setting The process of working toward something you want to accomplish. (page 29)

Gonorrhea (gah·nuh·REE·uh) A bacterial STD that affects the mucous membranes of the body, particularly in the genital area. (page 494)

Greenhouse effect The trapping of heat by carbon dioxide and other gases in the air. (page 578)

Grief The sorrow caused by loss of a loved one. (page 69)

Grief reaction The process of dealing with strong feelings following any loss. (page 69)

H

Hallucinogens (huh·LOO·suhn·uh·jenz) Drugs that distort moods, thoughts, and senses. (page 352)

Hangnail A split in the cuticle along the edge of a fingernail. (page 374)

Harassment (huh-RAS-muhnt) Ongoing conduct that offends another person by criticizing his or her race, color, religion, physical disability, or gender. (page 186)

Hazardous wastes Human-made liquid or solid wastes that may endanger human health or the environment. (page 580)

Health A combination of physical, mental/emotional, and social well-being. (page 4)

Health care system All the medical care available to a nation's people, the way they receive the care, and the way the care is paid for. (page 388)

Health fraud The selling of products or services to prevent diseases or cure health problems which have not been scientifically proven safe or effective for such purposes. (page 381)

Health insurance A contract between an insurance company and a person which requires the person to pay a monthly fee. (page 391)

Heart and lung endurance A measure of how efficiently your heart and lungs work when you exercise and how quickly they return to normal when you stop. (page 210)

Heart attack A condition in which blood flow to a part of the heart is greatly reduced or blocked. (page 519)

Heat cramps Painful, involuntary muscle spasms that may occur during strenuous exercise in hot weather. (page 562)

Heat exhaustion An overheating of the body that can result from dehydration. (pages 225 and 562)

Heatstroke A serious form of heat illness in which the body's normal processes for dealing with heat close down. (page 562)

Hepatitis (hep·uh·TYT·uhs) A viral disease of the liver characterized by yellowing of the skin and the whites of the eyes. (page 490)

Heredity The passing of traits from parents to their children. (pages 214, 455, and 509)

Hernia An internal organ pushing against or through a surrounding cavity wall. (page 439)

High blood pressure A condition in which a person's blood pressure stays at a level that is higher than normal. (page 519)

Histamines Chemicals in the body that cause the symptoms of an allergic reaction. (page 528)

HIV (human immunodeficiency virus) The virus that causes AIDS. (page 496)

Hives Raised bumps on the skin that are very itchy. (page 528)

Homicide The killing of one human being by another. (page 176)

Hormones Chemical substances, produced in glands, that help to regulate many body functions. (page 9)

Hospice care Care provided to the terminally ill that focuses on comfort, not cure. (page 390)

Hunger The physical need for food. (page 236)

Hurricane A strong windstorm with driving rain that originates at sea. (page 551)

Hygiene Cleanliness. (page 480)

Hypertension A condition in which the pressure of the blood on the walls of the blood vessels stays at a level that is higher than normal. (page 519)

I

"I" message A statement that presents a situation from the speaker's personal viewpoint. (page 110)

Immune system A combination of body defenses made up of cells, tissues, and organs that fight off pathogens and disease. (page 483)

Immunity Your body's ability to resist the pathogens that cause a particular disease. (page 483)

Infancy The first year of life. (page 462)

Infection A condition that occurs when pathogens get inside the body, multiply, and damage body cells. (page 478)

Inflammation The body's response to injury or disease, resulting in a condition of swelling, pain, heat, and redness. (page 484)

Ingrown toenail A condition in which the nail pushes into the skin on the side of the toe. (page 374)

Inhalant Any substance whose fumes are sniffed and inhaled to produce mind-altering sensations. (page 354)

Inhibition A conscious or unconscious restraint on his or her behaviors or actions. (page 289)

Insulin (IN·suh·lin) A protein made in the pancreas that regulates the level of glucose in the blood. (page 522)

Integrity The quality of doing what you know is right. (page 33)

Intervention A gathering in which family and friends get the problem drinker to agree to seek help. (page 296)

Intimidation Purposely frightening another person through threatening words, looks, or body language. (page 185)

Intoxication Physically and mentally impaired by the use of alcohol. (page 283)

Iris The colored part of the eye. (page 377)

J

Joint The point at which two bones meet. (page 406)

K

Kidneys Organs that filter water and dissolved wastes from the blood and help maintain proper levels of water and salts in the body. (page 430)

L

Labeling Name-calling. (page 158)

Landfills Huge pits where wastes are dumped and buried. (page 579)

Larynx (LA·ringks) The upper part of the respiratory system, which contains the vocal cords. (page 419)

Lens A clear flexible structure of the eye that focuses light on the retina. (page 377)

Lifestyle factors Behaviors and habits that help determine a person's level of health and wellness. (page 13)

Ligaments (LI·guh·ments) Strong cords of tissue that connect the bones in each joint. (page 406)

Limits Invisible boundaries that protect you. (page 118)

Liver A large gland that has many digestive functions. (page 429)

Lymphatic (lim·FA·tik) **system** A secondary circulatory system that helps the body fight pathogens and maintain its fluid balance. (page 485)

Lymphocytes (LIM·fuh·sytes) White blood cells in the lymphatic system. (page 485)

M

Mainstream smoke Smoke that is exhaled by a smoker. (page 320)

Major depression A very serious mood disorder in which people lose interest in life and can no longer find enjoyment in anything. (page 83)

Malignant (muh·LIG·nuhnt) Cancerous. (page 512)

Malnutrition A condition in which the body doesn't get the nutrients it needs to grow and function properly. (page 285)

Managed care An arrangement that saves money by limiting the choice of doctors to patients who are members. (page 391)

Marijuana Dried leaves and flowers of the hemp plant, called cannabis sativa. (page 338)

Marrow A soft tissue in the center of some bones. (page 405)

Media Various methods for communicating information. (page 41)

Mediation A process in which a third person, a mediator, helps those in conflict find a solution. (page 165)

Medicines Drugs that are used to treat or prevent diseases and other conditions. (page 383)

Menstrual (MEN·stroo·uhl) **cycle** Hormonal changes that occur in females from the beginning of one menstruation to the next. (page 439)

Menstruation (men·stroo·AY·shuhn) Lining material, the unfertilized egg, and some blood flow out of the body. (page 439)

Mental and emotional health The ability to accept oneself and others, adapt to and cope with emotions, and deal with the problems and challenges one meets in life. (page 6)

Methamphetamine A stimulant similar to amphetamine. (page 349)

Minerals Elements needed in small quantities for forming healthy bones and teeth, and for regulating certain body processes. (page 240)

Mixed message A situation in which your words say one thing but your body language says another. (page 109)

Mob mentality Acting or behaving in a certain and often negative manner because others are doing it. (page 162)

Mononucleosis (mahn·oh·noo·klee·OH·sis) A viral disease characterized by a severe sore throat and swelling of the lymph glands in the neck and around the throat area. (page 489)

Mood disorder A disorder in which a person undergoes changes in mood that seem inappropriate or extreme. (page 83)

Muscle endurance The measure of a muscle's ability to repeatedly exert a force over a prolonged period of time. (page 211)

Muscle strength The most weight you can lift or the most force you can exert at one time. (page 211)

Muscular system The group of structures that make your body parts move. (page 409)

MyPyramid food guidance system A system designed to help Americans make healthful food choices. (page 243)

N

Narcotics Specific drugs that are obtainable only by prescription and are used to relieve pain. (page 345)

Negative peer pressure Pressure you feel to go along with harmful behaviors or beliefs of others your age. (page 323)

Neglect The failure to meet a person's basic physical and emotional needs. (page 190)

Nervous system The body's message and control center. (page 422)

Neurons (NOO·rahnz) Specialized nerve cells. (page 423)

Nicotine An addictive drug found in tobacco leaves and in all tobacco products. (page 308)

Nicotine replacement therapies (NRT) Products that assist a person in breaking a tobacco habit. (page 317)

Noncommunicable diseases Diseases that are not spread from person to person. (page 508)

Nonrenewable resources Substances that cannot be replaced once they are used. (page 582)

Nutrient deficiency A shortage of a nutrient. (page 236)

Nutrient density The amount of nutrients relative to the number of calories they provide. (page 250)

Nutrients Substances in food that your body needs. (page 235)

Nutrition The study of nutrients and how the body uses them. (page 235)

O

Obese Weighing more than 20 percent higher than what is appropriate for their height, age, and body frame. (page 267)

Obstetrician (ahb·stuh·TRI·shuhn) Doctor who specializes in the care of a pregnant female and her developing fetus, and who is present at the birth of the baby. (page 457)

Opium A liquid from the poppy plant containing substances that numb the body. (page 345)

Opportunistic infection An infection that rarely occurs in a healthy person. (page 496)

Organ Body part that performs a particular function. (page 451)

Orthodontist (or·thuh·DAHN·tist) A dentist who prevents or corrects problems with the alignment or spacing of teeth. (page 376)

Osteoarthritis (ahs·tee·oh·ahr·THRY·tuhs) A chronic disease that is characterized by the breakdown of the cartilage in joints. (page 524)

Over-the-counter (OTC) medicines Medicines that are safe enough to be taken without a written order from a physician. (pages 335 and 384)

Overweight More than the appropriate weight for gender, height, age, body frame, and growth pattern. (page 263)

Ovulation The release of one mature egg cell each month. (page 439)

Ozone layer A shield above the earth's surface that protects living things from ultraviolet (UV) radiation. (page 578)

Pacemaker A small device that sends steady electrical impulses to the heart to make it beat regularly. (page 520)

Pancreas An organ that produces enzymes that assist in digestion. (page 429)

Panic A feeling of sudden, intense fear. (page 59)

Passive A tendency to give up, give in, or back down without standing up for your rights and needs. (page 116)

Passive smoker A nonsmoker who breathes in secondhand smoke. (page 320)

Pathogens Disease-causing organisms that are so small they can only be seen through a microscope. (page 478)

Peers People in the same age group. (page 11)

Peer pressure The influence to go along with the beliefs and actions of other people of your age. (page 105)

Peripheral nervous system (PNS) The nerves that connect the central nervous system to all parts of the body. (page 423)

Personality The unique combination of feelings, thoughts, and behavior that makes one person different from everyone else. (page 53)

Personality disorder A psychological condition that affects a person's ability to interact normally with others. (page 82)

Pesticides Products used on crops to control insects and other pests. (page 577)

Phobia Intense and exaggerated fear of a specific situation or object. (page 81)

Physical activity Any kind of movement that uses up energy. (page 204)

Physical dependence A type of addiction in which the body feels a direct need for a drug. (pages 292 and 316)

Physical fitness The ability to handle the physical demands of everyday life without becoming overly tired. (page 206)

Pituitary gland A gland that signals other endocrine glands to produce hormones when needed. (page 434)

Placenta (pluh·SEN·tuh) A thick, rich tissue that lines the walls of the uterus during pregnancy and that nourishes the fetus. (page 453)

Plaque (PLAK) A soft, colorless, sticky film containing bacteria that forms on teeth. (page 375)

Pneumonia A serious inflammation of the lungs. (page 491)

Point-of-sale promotion Advertising campaigns in which a product is promoted at a store's checkout counter. (page 324)

Pollen A powdery substance released by the flowers of some plants. (page 527)

Pollution Any dirty or harmful substance in the environment. (page 577)

Precautions Planned actions taken before an event to increase the chances of a safe outcome. (page 15)

Precycling Reducing waste before it occurs. (page 584)

Prejudice An opinion or fear formed without having facts or firsthand knowledge. (page 34)

Prenatal (pree·NAY·tuhl) **care** Steps taken to provide for the health of a pregnant female and her baby. (page 457)

Preschoolers Children between the ages of three and five. (page 462)

Prescription medicines Medicines that can be sold only with a written order from a physician. (pages 335 and 383)

Prevention Taking steps to keep something from happening or getting worse. (page 15)

Preventive care Steps taken to keep disease or injury from happening or getting worse. (page 388)

PRICE formula Protect, rest, ice, compress, and elevate. (page 224)

Proteins Nutrients your body uses to build, repair, and maintain cells and tissues. (page 240)

Protozoa (proh·tuh·ZOH·uh) Single-celled organisms that are more complex than bacteria. (page 479)

Psychiatrist (sy·KY·uh·trist) A medical doctor who treats mental health problems. (page 93)

Psychological dependence An addiction in which the mind sends the body a message that it needs more of a drug. (page 316)

Psychologist (sy·KAH·luh·jist) A mental health professional who is trained and licensed by the state to perform therapy. (page 93)

Puberty The time when you start developing physical characteristics of adults of your gender. (pages 9 and 463)

Public health Involves efforts to monitor and promote the welfare of the population. (page 392)

Pupil The dark opening in the center of the iris. (page 377)

R

Radiation therapy A treatment that uses X rays or other forms of radiation to kill cancer cells. (page 514)

Rape Any kind of sexual intercourse against a person's will. (page 181)

Reaction time The ability of the body to respond quickly and appropriately to situations. (page 282)

Recall An announcement that informs the public that a product has been determined unsafe. (page 392)

Recovery The process of learning to live an alcohol-free life. (page 297)

Recurrence The return of cancer after a remission. (page 515)

Refusal skills Communication strategies that help you say no effectively. (pages 40 and 115)

Relapse A return to the use of a drug after attempting to stop. (pages 296 and 318)

Relationships The connections you have with other people and groups in your life. (pages 10 and 102)

Remission A period during which cancer signs and symptoms disappear. (page 515)

Reproductive (ree·pruh·DUHK·tiv) **system** The organs that make possible the production of offspring. (page 437)

Resilience The ability to bounce back from disappointment. (page 55)

Respiration The exchange of gases between your body and the air. (page 418)

Respiratory system The organs that provide the body with a continuous supply of oxygen and rid the body of carbon dioxide. (page 418)

Resting heart rate The number of times your heart beats per minute when you are relaxing. (page 219)

Retina (RE·tin·uh) A thin layer of nerve cells in the eye that absorb light. (page 377)

Revenge Punishment, injury, or insult to the person seen as the cause of the strong emotion. (page 161)

Rheumatoid (ROO·muh·toyd) **arthritis** A chronic disease characterized by pain, inflammation, swelling, and stiffness of the joints. (page 525)

Risk behaviors Actions or behaviors that might cause injury or harm to yourself or others. (page 14)

Risk factors Characteristics or behaviors that increase a person's chances of developing a disease. (page 513)

Role A part you play when you interact with another person. (page 131)

S

Saliva (suh·LY·vuh) Fluid produced by the salivary glands. (page 428)

Saturated fats Fats that are solid at room temperature. (page 240)

Schizophrenia (skit·zoh·FREE·nee·uh) A severe mental disorder in which a person loses contact with reality. (page 85)

Secondhand smoke Environmental tobacco smoke (ETS). (page 320)

Sedentary lifestyle A way of life that includes little physical activity. (page 15)

Self-concept The view you have of yourself. (page 54)

Self-esteem The way you feel about yourself, and how you value yourself. (page 55)

Sexual abuse When a person forces another person to participate in a sexual act against his or her will. (page 190)

Sexual harassment Uninvited and unwelcome sexual conduct directed at another person. (page 191)

Sexually transmitted diseases (STDs) Infections spread from person to person through sexual contact. (page 492)

Shock A life-threatening condition in which the circulatory system fails to deliver enough blood to vital tissues and organs. (page 567)

Side effect Any effect of a medicine other than the one intended. (pages 335 and 386)

Sidestream smoke Smoke given off by the burning end of a cigarette, cigar, or pipe. (page 320)

Single-parent family A family made up of one parent plus a child or children. (page 135)

Skeletal muscles Muscle attached to bones that enables you to move your body. (page 410)

Skeletal system An internal body system made up of bones, joints, and connective tissue. (page 404)

Small intestine A coiled, tubelike digestive organ that is about 20 feet long. (page 429)

Smog A yellow-brown haze that forms when sunlight reacts with air pollution. (page 578)

Smokeless tobacco Ground tobacco that is chewed or inhaled through the nose. (page 310)

Smooth muscles The muscles found in organs, blood vessels, and glands. (page 410)

Social age Age measured by your lifestyle and the connections you have with others. (page 468)

Social health Your ability to get along with the people around you. (page 131)

Sodium A nutrient that helps control the amount of fluid in your body. (page 246)

Somatic (soh·MA·tik) **system** The part of the nervous system that deals with actions that you control. (page 424)

Specialist Doctor trained to handle particular kinds of patients or medical conditions. (page 389)

Sperm Male sex cells. (page 437)

Sperm cell The cell from the male that enters the egg cell during fertilization. (page 450)

Sprain A condition in which the ligaments that hold the joints in position are stretched or torn. (page 559)

Stimulants (STIM·yuh·luhnts) Drugs that speed up activity in the human brain and spinal cord. (page 348)

Strep throat A sore throat caused by streptococcal bacteria. (page 491)

Stress Your body's response to change. (pages 43 and 63)

Stressor Anything that causes stress. (page 64)

Stroke A condition in which a blood vessel bringing oxygen to the brain bursts or is blocked. (page 519)

Subcutaneous (suhb·kyoo·TAY·nee·uhs) **layer** The innermost layer of skin. (page 373)

Suicide The intentional taking of one's own life. (page 86)

Sympathetic (simp·uh·THET·ik) Aware of how you may be feeling at a given moment. (page 103)

Syphilis (SIH·fuh·luhs) A bacterial STD that can affect many parts of the body. It is a very serious STD. (page 494)

Tar A dark, thick, oily liquid that forms when tobacco burns. (page 309)

Target heart rate The range of numbers between which your heart and lungs receive the most benefit from a workout. (page 219)

Tartar A hard coating on the teeth that is difficult to remove. (page 375)

Tendons Tough bands of tissue that attach muscles to bones. (page 406)

THC The main active chemical in marijuana. (page 338)

Therapy An approach that teaches you different ways of thinking or behaving. (page 91)

Time management Strategies for using time efficiently. (page 67)

Tissues Groups of similar cells that perform a specific function. (page 451)

Toddlers Children between the ages of one and three who are learning to walk and talk. (page 462)

Tolerance The ability to accept other people as they are. (pages 34 and 132)

Tolerance A condition in which a person's body becomes used to the effect of a medicine or drug, and needs greater amounts of it in order for it to be effective. (pages 292, 316, and 335)

Tornado A whirling, funnel-shaped windstorm that may drop from the sky to the ground. (page 551)

Trachea (TRAY·kee·uh) Windpipe that directs air to the lungs. (page 419)

Traumatic brain injury (TBI) A condition caused by the brain being jarred and striking the inside of the skull. (page 425)

Trichomoniasis (TREE·koh·moh·NI·ah·sis) An STD caused by the protozoan *Trichomonas vaginalis*. (page 493)

Tuberculosis (too·ber·kyuh·LOH·sis) **(TB)** A bacterial disease that usually affects the lungs. (page 491)

Tumor A mass of abnormal cells. (page 511)

Type 1 diabetes A condition in which the immune system attacks insulin-producing cells in the pancreas. (page 523)

Type 2 diabetes A condition in which the body cannot effectively use the insulin it produces. (page 523)

Umbilical (uhm·BIL·i·kuhl) **cord** A tube that connects the fetus and the mother's placenta. (page 453)

Unconditional love Love without limitation or qualification. (page 143)

Underweight Less than the appropriate weight for gender, height, age, body frame, and growth pattern. (page 263)

Universal precautions Actions taken to prevent the spread of disease by treating all blood as if it were contaminated. (page 555)

Unsaturated fats Fats that remain liquid at room temperature. (page 240)

Uterus (YOO·tuh·ruhs) A pear-shaped organ inside a female's body where a fetus is protected and nourished. (page 452)

V

Vaccine A preparation of dead or weakened germs that causes the immune system to produce antibodies. (pages 384 and 486)

Values The beliefs and principles that guide the way a person lives. (page 28)

Vector An organism, such as an insect, that transmits a pathogen. (page 480)

Veins Blood vessels that carry blood from the body back to the heart. (page 415)

Victim Any individual who suffers injury, loss, or death due to violence. (page 180)

Violence Any act that causes physical or psychological harm to a person or damage to property. (page 176)

Viruses The smallest pathogens. (page 479)

Vitamins Substances that help your body fight infections and use other nutrients, among other jobs. (page 240)

W

Warm-up A period of low to moderate exercise to prepare your body for more vigorous activity. (page 219)

Warranty A written promise to refund your money if a product fails to work as claimed. (page 381)

Wellness A state of well-being, or total health. (page 6)

Win-win solution An agreement that gives each party something they want. (page 165)

Withdrawal The physical and psychological reactions that occur when someone stops using an addictive substance. (pages 297 and 317)

Withdrawal symptoms Symptoms that occur after chronic use of a drug is reduced or stopped. (page 346)

Zero tolerance policy A policy that makes no exceptions for anybody for any reason. (page 178)

A

Abdominal thrusts/presiones abdominales
Presiones rápidas y hacia arriba que se hacen sobre el diafragma para forzar la salida de algo que esté bloqueando la vía respiratoria.

Abstinence/abstinencia Opción activa y consciente de no participar in comportamientos de alto riesgo.

Abuse/abuso Maltrato físico, emocional o mental de una persona a otra.

Accident/accidente Suceso que ocurre de manera no intencional.

Accident chain/accidente en cadena Serie de sucesos que incluye una situación, un hábito peligroso y un acto peligroso.

Accidental injuries/lesiones accidentales
Lesiones que resultan de un accidente.

Accountability/responsabilidad Voluntad de responder de tus acciones y decisiones.

Acid rain/lluvia ácida Lluvia que es mucho más ácida de lo normal.

Acquired immunodeficiency syndrome (AIDS)/ síndrome de inmunodeficiencia adquirida (SIDA) Enfermedad mortal que interfiere con la habilidad natural del cuerpo de combatir infecciones.

Active listening/audición activa Oír el mensaje de otra persona, pensar en el mensaje y responder.

Adapt/adaptar Acostumbrarse a nuevas situaciones.

Addiction/adicción Necesidad física o psicológica de una droga.

Addictive/adictivo Capaz de ocasionar que el consumidor desarrolle una necesidad repentina intensa.

Adolescence/adolescencia Etapa de la vida entre la niñez y la edad adulta.

Adrenaline/adrenalina Hormona que proporciona energía adicional al cuerpo.

Advocacy/promoción Informa a otros sobre prácticas de salud y anima a comportamientos saludables.

Aerobic exercise/ejercicio aeróbico Actividad rítmica ininterrumpida de intensidad moderada a vigorosa que requiere grandes cantidades de oxígeno y hace que el corazón trabaje.

Affection/afecto Sentimiento de amor hacia otra persona.

Aggressive/agresivo(a) Excesivamente forzoso, hostil o de otra manera, que ataca durante el acercamiento.

Air Quality Index (AQI)/índice de calidad del aire Medida de ozono, dióxido de sulfuro, monoxido de carbono y finas partículas que hay cerca de a la tierra.

Alcohol/alcohol Droga producida por una reacción química en frutas, verduras y granos.

Alcohol abuse/abuso de alcohol Forma de consumo de alcohol que resulta en uno o más episodios en un periodo de doce meses.

Alcohol poisoning/intoxicación con alcohol
Condición peligrosa que ocurre cuando una persona consume cantidades de alcohol excesivas en un corto periodo de tiempo.

Alcoholism/alcoholismo Enfermedad progresiva y crónica caracterizada por una necesidad mental y física de consumir alcohol.

Allergen/alergeno Sustancia que causa una reacción alérgica.

Allergy/alergia Sensibilidad extrema hacia una sustancia.

Allied health professionals/profesionales médicos aliados Profesionales médicos que desarrollan deberes que de otra manera serian desarrollados por doctores o enfermeras.

Alternatives/alternativas Diferentes maneras de pensar o actuar.

Alveoli/alvéolos Pequeños sacos de aire de los pulmones donde el dióxido de carbono es intercambiado por oxigeno.

Amino acids/aminoácidos Unidades pequeñas que forman las proteínas.

Amnesia/amnesia Pérdida total o parcial de la memoria.

Amphetamine/anfetamina Droga que estimula el sistema nervioso central.

Anabolic steroids/esteroides anabólicos Sustancia sintética relacionada con las hormonas sexuales masculinas.

Anaerobic exercise/ejercicio anaeróbico Actividad física intensa que requiere poco oxígeno pero exige breves brotes de energía.

Angioplasty/angioplastia Procedimiento quirúrgico en el cual un instrumento con un globo pequeño, un pedacito de taladro, o láser unido es insertado en una arteria bloqueada para limpiar el bloque.

Anorexia nervosa/anorexia nerviosa Trastorno en la alimentación que se caracteriza por autoinanición conducente a una pérdida de peso extrema.

Antibiotics/antibióticos Medicinas que disminuyen o matan bacterias dañinas en el cuerpo.

Antibodies/anticuerpos Proteínas que se adhieren a los antígenos para prevenir que dañen al cuerpo.

Antigens/antígenos Sustancias que liberan los agentes patógenos.

Antihistamines/antihistamínicos Medicinas que ayudan a controlar los efectos que provocan las histaminas.

Anxiety/ansiedad Estado de intranquilidad, usualmente asociado con una incertidumbre futura.

Anxiety disorder/trastorno de ansiedad Trastorno en el cual la ansiedad intensa o el miedo impide que una persona funcione de manera normal

Appetite/apetito Deseo psicológico de alimentarse.

Appropriate weight/peso apropiado Peso más adecuado para tu cuerpo.

Arteries/arterias Vasos sanguíneos que llevan sangre desde el corazón a otras partes del cuerpo.

Arteriosclerosis/arteriosclerosis Conjunto de trastornos por el cual las arterias se endurecen y se tornan rígidas.

Arthritis/artritis Enfermedad de las articulaciones identificada con hinchazón dolorosa y rigidez.

Assault/asalto Amenaza ilegal o intento de lesión corporal hacia otra persona.

Assertive/firme Comportarte con seguridad y declarar claramente tus intenciones.

Asthma/asma Condición en la cual los pequeños pasajes de aire en los pulmones se encogen y dificultan la respiración.

Atherosclerosis/aterosclerosis Un tipo de arteriosclerosis por el cual sustancias grasas en la sangre se acumulan en las paredes de las arterias.

Attitude/actitud Sentimientos y creencias.

Autonomic system/sistema autonómico Sistema que envuelve las acciones que no controlas.

B

Bacteria/bacterias Organismos diminutos unicelulares que viven en casi todas partes.

Balance/equilibrio Sentimiento de estabilidad y control.

Battery/asalto Paliza, golpiza, o pateadura contra una persona ilegalmente.

Benign/benigno No es canceroso.

Binge/consumo compulsivo de drogas Cuando una droga es usada repetitivamente y en altas dosis que se incrementan.

Binge drinking/borrachera Consumo de cantidades grandes de alcohol en un periódo de tiempo muy corto.

Binge eating disorder/trastorno de la alimentación compulsiva Sentirse impulsado a comer demasiado.

Biodegradable/biodegradable Que se descompone fácilmente en el medio ambiente.

Biological age/edad biológica Medida de la edad, determinada según el funcionamiento de varias partes del cuerpo.

Biopsy/biopsia Extirpación de una muestra de tejido de una persona para ser examinado.

Birth defects/defecto de nacimiento Anormalidad presente al momento del nacimiento que causa incapacidad física o mental o la muerte.

Blended family/familia mezclada Familia que consiste en padre o madre, padrastro o madrastra, y los hijos de uno o ambos padres.

Blizzard/ventisca Tormenta de nieve fuerte, con vientos que llegan a 45 millas por hora.

Blood alcohol content (BAC)/ concentración de alcohol en la sangre Cantidad de alcohol presente en el torrente sanguíneo de una persona.

Body composition/composición del cuerpo Proporción entre la grasa del cuerpo y los tejidos magros, tales como huesos, músculos y líquidos.

Body image/autoimagen La manera en que te ves a ti mismo.

Body language/lenguaje corporal Uso de movimientos corporales y gestos para comunicar un mensaje.

Body mass index (BMI)/índice de masa corporal Fórmula que puede ser utilizada para determinar si tu peso es el apropiado.

Bronchi/bronquios Pasajes a través de los cuales entra el aire en los pulmones.

Bronchodilators/broncodilatadores Medicinas que se usan para relajar los músculos que se han tensado alrededor de las vías respiratorias.

Bulimia nervosa/bulimia Condición en la cual una persona come grandes cantidades de comida y purga secretamente.

Bully/intimidar Alguien que molesta a individuos que son más pequeños o más débiles.

Calorie/caloría Unidad de calor que mide la energía disponible en los alimentos.

Cancer/cáncer Enfermedad que se caracteriza por el desarrollo rápido e incontrolable de células anormales.

Capillaries/vasos capilares Conductos minúsculos que llevan sangre desde las arterias a las células del cuerpo, y de regreso a las venas.

Carbohydrates/hidratos de carbono Azúcares y almidones que le proporcionan a tu cuerpo la mayor parte de su energía.

Carbon monoxide/monóxido de carbono Gas incoloro, inodoro y tóxico que se produce al quemarse el tabaco.

Carcinogens/carcinógenos Sustancias que causan el cáncer.

Cardiac muscle/músculo cardiaco Músculo de las paredes del corazón.

Cardiopulmonary resuscitation (CPR)/ resucitación cardiopulmonar Procedimiento de primeros auxilios que combina la respiración de rescate y compresiones sobre el pecho para restaurar la respiración y la circulación.

Cardiovascular disease/enfermedad cardiovascular Enfermedad del corazón y de los vasos sanguíneos.

Cardiovascular system/sistema cardiovascular Órganos y tejidos que transportan materia esencial a las células del cuerpo y eliminan los desechos.

Carrier/portador Persona que parece saludable pero esta infectada con el VIH y puede transmitirlo a otros.

Cartilage/cartílago Tejido fuerte y flexible que amortigua las articulaciones.

Cell respiration/respiración celular Proceso en el cual las células del cuerpo se nutren y energizan.

Central nervous system (CNS)/sistema nervioso central Cerebro y médula espinal.

Cervix/cuello del útero Entrada del útero o matriz.

Character/carácter Manera en la que una persona piensa, siente y actúa.

Character trait/rasgo del carácter Cualidad que demuestra la manera en que una persona piensa, siente y actúa.

Chemotherapy/quimioterapia Uso de medicinas poderosas para destruir células cancerosas.

Chlamydia/clamidia Enfermedad bacteriana trasmitida sexualmente que afecta los organos reproductivos, uretra y ano.

Chromosomes/cromosomas Estructuras filiformes dentro del núcleo de las células que contienen los códigos de las características hereditarias.

Chronic diseases/enfermedades crónicas Enfermedades que están siempre presentes o reaparecen repetidamente durante un largo periodo de tiempo.

Chronic obstructive pulmonary disease (COPD)/inflamación pulmonar crónica Condición en la cual los pasajes de los pulmones se hinchan e irritan, y eventualmente pierden su elasticidad.

Chronological age/edad cronológica Edad medida en años.

Circulatory system/aparato circulatorio Órganos y tejidos que transportan materias esenciales a las células del cuerpo y se llevan sus desechos.

Cirrhosis/cirrosis Enfermedad caracterizada por la cicatrización y eventualmente la destrucción del hígado.

Citizenship/civilidad Forma en que te comportas como miembro de una comunidad.

Clinical social worker (CSW)/trabajador social clínico Profesional en salud mental licenciado y certificado en trabajo social.

Clique/camarilla Grupo de amigos que salen juntos y que se comportan de manera similar.

CNS depressants/depresores del SNC Sustancias que hacen que las funciones corporales sean más lentas, incluyendo al corazón y la respiración.

Cold turkey/parar en seco Expresión que se usa para describir la acción de abandonar un vicio de una vez, por ejemplo el fumar.

Colon/colon Intestino grueso.

Commitment/compromiso Promesa o voto.

Communicable disease/enfermedad contagiosa Enfermedad que se puede propagar de una persona a otra persona, un animal o un objeto.

Communication/comunicación Intercambio de ideas, sentimientos y creencias entre dos o más personas.

Community service/servicio comunitario Programas voluntarios desarrollados con la meta de mejorar la comunidad y la vida de los residentes.

Comparison shopping/comparación de productos Método de evaluar los beneficios de diferentes productos y servicios al medir y comparar varios factores, tales como la calidad, las características y el precio.

Compromise/compromiso Acuerdo en el cual los dos lados renuncian a algo para alcanzar una solución satisfactoria.

Conditioning/acondicionamiento Actividad regular y ejercicios que preparan a una persona para algún deporte.

Conflict/conflicto Desacuerdo entre personas con puntos de vista, ideas o metas opuestos.

Conflict resolution/habilidades de solución de conflictos Habilidad que implica el hecho de resolver un desacuerdo satisfaciendo a los dos lados.

Congenital disorders/desordenes congénitos Todos los desórdenes que se presentan cuando el bebé nace.

Consequences/consecuencias Resultados o efectos que pueden ocurrir como resultado de una decisión o un acto.

Conservation/conservación Ahorro de recursos.

Consumer/consumidor Persona que compra bienes o servicios.

Consumer skills/habilidades del consumidor Técnicas que te permiten hacer compras inteligentes e informadas.

Contagious period/periodo de contagio El periodo de tiempo en que una enfermedad se puede propagar de una persona a otra.

Cool-down/recuperación Un periodo en el que se realizan ejercicios de intensidad baja a moderada a fin de preparar al cuerpo para terminar una serie de ejercicios vigorosos.

Coordination/coordinación El funcionamiento conjunto de los músculos y los huesos de manera eficiente y sin complicaciones.

Coping strategies/estrategias Formas de tratar con el sentido de pérdida que las personas sienten cuando alguien cercano fallece.

Crisis hot line/linea de reporte de crisis Servicio telefónico sin pago en cual las víctimas de abusos pueden recibir ayuda e información.

Cross-training/entrenamiento variado Cambiar de un ejercicio físico a otro.

Cumulative risks/riesgos acumulativos Riesgos relacionados cuyos efectos aumentan con cada uno que se añade.

Cuticle/cutícula Doblez de epidermis alrededor de las uñas de los pies y las manos.

Cycle of abuse/ciclo de abuso Patrón de repetición del abuso de una generación a la siguiente.

D

Dandruff/caspa Escamas de piel muerta en la superficie del cuero cabelludo.

Decibel/decibel Medida del volumen del sonido.

Decision making/toma de decisiones Proceso de hacer una selección o de hallar una solución.

Defensive driving/conducir de manera defensiva Estar atento a las otras personas en la carretera y anticipar acciones peligrosas.

Degenerative diseases/enfermedades degenerativas Enfermedades que causan la destrucción progresiva de las células, tejidos y órganos del cuerpo a medida que avanzan.

Dehydration/deshidratación Condición causada por pérdida excesiva de agua.

Depressants/sedantes Drogas que hacen que las funciones corporales y las reacciones sean lentas.

Dermatologist/dermatólogo Médico que trata trastornos de la piel.

Dermis/dermis Capa gruesa e interna de la piel.

Detoxification/desintoxicación Proceso físico de liberar al cuerpo de una sustancia adictiva.

Developmental tasks/tareas requeridas para el desarrollo Sucesos que deben ocurrir para que continúes desarrollándote hasta llegar a convertirte en un adulto saludable y maduro.

Diabetes/diabetes Enfermedad que impide que el cuerpo convierta los alimentos en energía.

Diaphragm/diafragma Músculo en forma de domo que separa los pulmones del abdomen.

Digestion/digestión Proceso de convertir los alimentos que comes en sustancias que tu cuerpo pueda usar.

Digestive system/aparato digestivo Sistema de órganos que convierten los alimentos en una forma útil para el cuerpo.

Disease/enfermedad Cualquier condición que interfiere con el funcionamiento propio del cuerpo o la mente.

Disorder/desorden Desequilibrio en el funcionamiento normal de una parte del cuerpo.

Divorce/divorcio Fin legal a un contrato matrimonial.

Domestic violence/violencia doméstica Abuso físico que ocurre dentro de una familia.

Driving while intoxicated (DWI)/manejar con intoxicación Persona que maneja un auto con una concentración de alcohol en la sangre de 0/08% o mayor.

Drug/drogas Sustancias, que no sean alimentos, que cambian la estructura o el funcionamiento del cuerpo o la mente.

Drug abuse/abuso de drogas Uso intencional de drogas en forma no saludable o ilegal.

Drug free/libre de drogas Características de una persona que no consume drogas ilícitas, o establecimiento donde no se consumen drogas.

Drug misuse/mal empleo de drogas Tomar o usar medicinas en una forma diferente a la indicada.

Drug trafficking/tráfico de drogas Compra o venta de drogas.

E

Earthquake/terremoto Sacudimiento violento de la superficie de la tierra.

Eating disorder/trastorno alimentación Costumbre en la alimentación por la cual una persona come de manera extrema y nociva y que puede causar enfermedades y aun la muerte.

Egg cell/óvulo La célula reproductora femenina que se une con el espermatozoide para crear una nueva vida.

Embryo/embrión Organismo en desarrollo desde la fecundación hasta aproximadamente la octava semana del desarrollo.

Emotional needs/necesidades emocionales Necesidades que afectan los sentimientos y el bienestar de una persona.

Emotions/emociones Sentimientos que surgen en respuesta a pensamientos, comentarios y sucesos.

Empathy/empatía Habilidad de entender y compartir los sentimientos de otra persona.

Empty-calorie foods/comidas sin valor calórico Comidas que ofrecen pocos nutrientes pero si contienen calorías.

Enablers/habilitadores Personas que crean una atmósfera en la cual el alcohólico puede continuar su comportamiento inaceptable de una forma cómoda.

Endocrine system/sistema endocrino Sistema químico de comunicaciones del cuerpo que regula varias funciones.

Environment/medio Suma total de lo que rodea a una persona.

Environmental Protection Agency (EPA)/ Agencia de Protección Ambiental Agencia del gobierno de Estados Unidos a cargo de la protección del medio ambiente.

Enzymes/enzimas Proteínas que afectan varios procesos corporales.

Epidermis/epidermis Capa visible y más externa de la piel.

Epiglottis/epiglotis Pliegue de tejido que cubre la tráquea cuando tragas.

Escalate/intensificar Llegar a ser más grave.

Euphoria/euforia Sentimiento de bienestar o regocijo.

Excretion/excreción Proceso de eliminar desechos del cuerpo.

Excretory system/sistema excretor Sistema del cuerpo que elimina desechos del cuerpo.

Exercise/ejercicio Actividad física planeada hecha para mantener el estado físico.

Extended family/familia extensa Familia nuclear y otros parientes tales como abuelos, tías, tíos y primos.

F

Family/familia La unidad básica de la sociedad, incluye 2 o más personas relacionadas por sangre, matrimonio, adopción o deseo de apoyo mutuo.

Family therapy/terapia familiar Asesoramiento cuyo propósito es mejorar relaciones problemáticas entre familiares.

Famine/hambre Falta general de alimentos.

Fatty liver/higago adiposo Condición en la cual la grasa se forma en el hígado y no puede ser deshecha.

Fertilization/fertilización Unión de un espermatozoide y un óvulo.

Fetal alcohol syndrome (FAS)/síndrome de alcoholismo fetal Conjunto de defectos de nacimiento causados por el alcohol que incluyen problemas físicos y mentales.

Fetus/feto Organismo en desarrollo desde el final de la octava semana del embarazo hasta el momento del nacimiento.

Fiber/fibra Parte de las frutas, verduras, granos y frijoles que tu cuerpo no puede dirigir.

Fight-or-flight response/respuesta de lucha o huida El proceso mediante el cual el cuerpo se prepara a enfrentarse con un estresante.

First aid/primeros auxilios Cuidado inmediato y temporal que se le proporciona a una persona herida o enferma hasta que reciba ayuda profesional.

FITT principle/principio FITT Método mediante el cual es posible incrementar con seguridad aspectos del ejercicio sin hacerte daño a ti mismo.

Flexibility/flexibilidad Habilidad de mover las articulaciones del cuerpo con facilidad a través del arco completo de movimiento.

Foodborne illness/enfermedad producida por un alimento Enfermedad que proviene de haber comido un alimento no sano.

Fracture/fractura Rotura de un hueso.

Fraud/fraude Engaño o deliberado.

Fungi/fungi Organismos que son más complejos que las bacterias, pero no pueden hacer su propio alimento.

G

Gallbladder/vesícula biliar Pequeño órgano en forma de bolsa que almacena bilis.

Gang/pandilla Grupo en el cual los miembros usan violencia para ser parte de actividades criminales.

Gender discrimination/discriminación sexual Distinguir o excluir a personas de acuerdo a su sexo.

Genes/genes Unidades básicas de la herencia.

Genetic disorder/trastorno genético Trastorno causado parcial o totalmente por defectos en los genes.

Genital herpes/herpes genital Enfermedad viral de transmisión sexual que produce dolorosas heridas en el área genital.

Genital warts/verrugas genitales Crecimiento o hinchazón in el área genital causada por algún tipo de papillomavirus(HPV).

Germs/gérmenes Organismos que causan enfermedades y que son tan pequeños que sólo pueden ser vistos a través de microscopios.

Gingivitis/gingivitis Trastorno común que se caracteriza por el enrojecimiento y dolor de las encías que sangran con facilidad.

Gland/glándula Un grupo de células, o un órgano, que secreta una sustancia química.

Global warming/calentamiento del planeta Aumento en las temperaturas de la Tierra.

Goal setting/establecer metas Proceso de esforzarte para lograr algo que quieres.

Gonorrhea/gonorrea Enfermedad bacteriana transmitida sexualmente que afecta la membrana mucosa del cuerpo, particularmente el área genital.

Greenhouse effect/efecto invernadero Retención del calor por la presencia de dióxido de carbono y otros gases en el aire.

Grief/pena Pesar provocado por la muerte de un ser querido.

Grief reaction/reacción a la desgracia El proceso de tratar con algún sentimientos fuertes que se ocasionan por alguna perdida.

H

Hallucinogens/alucinógenos Drogas que alteran el estado de ánimo, los pensamientos y los sentidos.

Hangnail/padrastro Una grieta en la cutícula al lado del borde de la uña.

Harassment/acoso Conducta frecuente que ofende a otra persona con criticas sobre su raza, color, religión, incapacidad física, o sexo.

Hazardous wastes/desechos peligrosos Desechos líquidos o sólidos generados por los seres humanos, que pueden perjudicar la salud de las personas o el medio ambiente.

Health/salud Una combinación de bienestar físico, mental/emocional y social.

Health care system/sistema de cuidado de la salud Servicios médicos disponiblse para la gente de una nación y las formas en las cuales estos son pagados.

Health fraud/fraude médico Venta de productos o servicios para prevenir enfermedades o curar problemas de salud que no han sido aprobados científicamente o hechos efectivos para ese uso.

Health insurance/seguro medico Plan en el que las compañías privadas o los programas del gobierno pagan una parte de los gastos médicos de una persona.

Heart and lung endurance/resistencia del corazón y los pulmones Medida de qué tan eficientemente trabajan tu corazón y tus pulmones cuando haces ejercicios y qué tan rápido regresan a lo normal cuando paras.

Heart attack/ataque cardiaco Afección en la cual el flujo de sangre a una parte del corazón está considerablemente reducido u obstruido

Heat cramps/calambres debido al calor Dolorosos espasmos involuntarios de los músculos que pueden ocurrir al realizar ejercicio vigoroso cuando hace mucho calor.

Heat exhaustion/agotamiento por calor Recalentamiento del cuerpo que puede dar como resultado una deshidratación.

Heatstroke/insolación Tipo de enfermedad debido al calor grave en que los procesos normales del cuerpo que controlan los efectos del calor dejan de funcionar.

Hepatitis/hepatitis Enfermedad vírica del hígado que se caracteriza por el color amarillo de la piel y del blanco de los ojos.

Heredity/herencia Transferencia de características de los padres a sus hijos.

Hernia/hernia Órgano interno que está empujando contra o a través de una pared de cavidad.

High blood pressure/presión arterial alta Afección en la que la presión arterial de una persona se mantiene a un nivel más alto de lo normal.

Histamines/histaminas Sustancias químicas del cuerpo que provocan los síntomas de una reacción alérgica.

HIV (Human Immunodeficiency Virus)/virus de inmunodeficiencia humana (VIH) Virus que causa el minúscerlas.

Hives/urticaria Granos en la piel que pican mucho.

Homicide/homicidio Acto en que una persona mata a otra.

Hormones/hormonas Sustancias químicas, producidas por glándulas, que ayudan a regular varias funciones del cuerpo.

Hospice care/asistencia para enfermos desahuciados Asistencia para personas con enfermedades incurables que apunta a brindar comodidad, no a la cura.

Hunger/hambre Necesidad física de alimentos.

Hurricane/huracán Tormenta de vientos y lluvia torrencial que se origina en alta mar.

Hygiene/higiene Limpieza.

Hypertension/hipertensión Condición en la cual la presión de la sangre en las paredes de los vasos sanguíneos se mantienen a un nivel mas alto de lo normal.

"I" message Una declaración que presenta una situación desde el punto de vista personal del orador.

Immune system/sistema inmunológico Combinación de las defensas del cuerpo, compuesta de células, tejidos y órganos que combaten que patógenos y enfermedades.

Immunity/inmunidad Habilidad del cuerpo para resistir los agentes patógenos que causan enfermedades particulares.

Infancy/infancia Primer año de vida.

Infection/infección Una afección que se produce cuando agentes patógenos invaden el cuerpo, se multiplican y dañan las células del cuerpo.

Inflammation/inflamación Reacción del cuerpo cuando ocurre un daño o enfermedad, resultando en hinchazón, dolor, calentamiento y enrojecimiento.

Ingrown toenail/uña encarnada Afección en la cual la uña se introduce en la piel al lado del dedo del pie.

Inhalant/inhalante Toda sustancia cuyos gases se aspiran para producir sensaciones alucinantes.

Inhibition/inhibición Reprimir comportamientos o acciones consiente o inconscientemente.

Insulin/insulina Proteína que es producida en el páncreas y que regula el nivel de glucosa en el cuerpo.

Integrity/integridad Cualidad de hacer lo que sabes que es lo correcto.

Intervention/intervención Una reunión en la cual familia y amigos hacen que la persona con problemas alcohólicos busque ayuda.

Intimidation/intimidación Asustar a otra persona a propósito con palabras amenazantes, miradas o lenguaje corporal.

Intoxication/intoxicado Física y mentalmente afectado por el consumo de alcohol.

Iris/iris La parte coloreada del ojo.

Joint/articulacion Lugares en donde se unen los huesos.

K

Kidneys/riñones Órganos que filtran el agua y los desechos disueltos de la sangre y contribuyen a mantener los niveles adecuados de agua y sales en el cuerpo.

L

Labeling/marcar Dar nombre.

Landfills/terraplenes sanitarios Pozos enormes donde se tiran y se entierran desechos.

Larynx/laringe Parte superior del aparato respiratorio que contiene las cuerdas vocales.

Lens/cristalino Estructura transparente y flexible del ojo que enfoca la luz en la retina.

Lifestyle factors/factores del estilo de vida Conductas y hábitos que ayudan a determinar el nivel de salud de una persona.

Ligaments/ligamentos Tejidos que parecen cables que conectan los huesos con cada articulación.

Limits/límites Barreras invisibles que te protegen.

Liver/hígado Glándula grande que tiene varias funciones digestivas.

Lymphatic system/sistema linfático Aparato circulatorio secundario que le ayuda al cuerpo a combatir los agentes patógenos y a mantener el equilibrio de los líquidos.

Lymphocytes/linfocito Células blancas del sistema linfático.

M

Mainstream smoke/humo directo Humo que es inhalado por el fumador.

Major depression/depresión mayor Serio desorden del estado deánimo en el cual las personas pierden interes en su vida y no encuentran placer en nada.

Malignant/maligno Tumor canceroso.

Malnutrition/Desnutrición La cual es una affección en la que el cuerpo no recibe los nutrients que necesita para crecer y funcionar de forma adecuada.

Managed care/cuidado controlado Arreglo que ahorra dinero limitando las opciones de los doctores a pacientes que son miembros.

Marijuana/mariguana Hojas y flores secas de la planta de cáñamo, llamada cannabis sativa.

Marrow/médula Un tejido en el centro de algunos huesos.

Media/medios de difusión Diversos métodos de comunicar información.

Mediation/mediación Proceso en el cual una tercera persona, un mediador, ayuda a otros a encontrar una solución al conflicto entre ellos.

Medicines/medicinas Drogas que se usan para curar o prevenir enfermedades u otras afecciones.

Menstrual cycle/ciclo menstrual Cambio hormonal que ocurre en las mujeres desde el comienzo de una menstruación hasta el siguiente.

Menstruation/menstruación Material de forro, óvulos no fertilizados y sangre que fluyen fuera del cuerpo.

Mental and emotional health/salud mental y emocional Capacidad de aceptarse a sí mismo y a otros, de adaptarse a las emociones y sobrellevarlas y de superar los problemas y retos de la vida.

Methamphetamine/metanfetamina Estimulantes parecidos a las anfetaminas.

Minerals/minerales Elementos que se necesitan en cantidades pequeñas para la formación de dientes y huesos saludables y para regular determinados procesos corporales.

Mixed message/mensaje contradictorio Una situación en que tus palabras expresan algo pero tu lenguaje corporal lo contradice.

Mob mentality/mentalidad de movimiento Actua o comportarse de cierta manera, normalmente maneras negativas, sólo porque otros lo están haciendo.

Mononucleosis/mononucleosis Enfermedad vírica cuyos síntomas incluyen hinchazón y dolor en áreas del cuello y dolor de garganta.

Mood disorder/trastorno del ánimo humor Trastorno en que la persona cambia de humor de manera aparentemente inapropiada o extrema.

Muscle endurance/resistencia muscular Capacidad que tiene un músculo de ejercer una fuerza repetidamente durante un largo periodo de tiempo.

Muscle strength/fuerza muscular Medida del peso máximo que puedes cargar o la fuerza máxima que puedes emplear a un mismo tiempo.

Muscular system/sistema muscular Grupo de estructuras que permiten el movimiento de las partes de tu cuerpo.

MyPyramid Food Guidance System/pirámide alimenticia Ayuda visual diseñada para ayudar a los Americanos sin mayúscula a tomar decisiones alimenticias saludables.

Narcotics/narcóticos Ciertas drogas específicas que se pueden obtener únicamente con receta médica y que se usan para aliviar el dolor.

Negative peer pressure/presión negativa de compañeros Presión que sientes de seguir comportamientos malos o creencias de otras personas de tu misma edad.

Neglect/abandono El no satisfacer las necesidades básicas físicas y emocionales de una persona.

Nervous system/sistema nervioso Centro de mensajes y control del cuerpo.

Neurons/neuronas Células especializadas que componen el sistema nervioso.

Nicotine/nicotina Droga adictiva que se encuentra en las hojas del tabaco y en todos los productos del tabaco.

Nicotine replacement therapies (NRT)/terapias para remplazar la nicotina Productos que ayudan a las personas a romper el hábito del tabaco.

Noncommunicable diseases/enfermedades no contagiosas Enfermedades que no pueden ser pasadas de una persona a la otra.

Nonrenewable resources/recursos no renovables Sustancias que no se pueden reemplazar una vez que se han usado.

Nutrient deficiency/deficiencia nutricional Escasez de un nutriente.

Nutrient density/densidad de los nutrientes La cantidad de nutrientes comparados con las calorías que proporcionan.

Nutrients/nutrientes Sustancias de los alimentos que tu cuerpo necesita.

Nutrition/nutrición Ciencia que estudia las sustancias presentes en los alimentos y el modo en que el cuerpo las utilice.

Obese/obeso(a) Más del 20 por ciento del peso que es adecuado para tu estatura, edad y tipo de cuerpo.

Obstetrician/obstetra Médico especialista en el cuidado de la mujer embarazada y el feto en desarrollo y que está presente durante el nacimiento del bebé.

Opium/opio Líquido extraído de la planta de amapola que contiene sustancias que adormecen el cuerpo.

Opportunistic infection/infección oportunista Infección que ocurre raramente en personas saludables.

Organs/órganos Partes del cuerpo que cumplen funciones determinadas.

Orthodontist/ortodoncista Dentista que previene o corrige problemas del alineamiento o del espacio entre los dientes.

Osteoarthritis/osteoartritis Enfermedad que se caracteriza por el deterioro del cartílago de las articulaciones.

Over-the-counter (OTC) medicines/medicinas sin receta Medicinas inofensivas que se pueden consumir sin receta médica.

Overweight/sobrepeso Más del peso apropiado de acuerdo al sexo, estatura, edad, estructura corporal y ritmo de crecimiento.

Ovulation/ovulación Desprendimiento de un óvulo maduro cada mes.

Ozone layer/capa de ozono Capa protectora sobre la superficie de la Tierra que protege a los seres vivos de la radiación ultravioleta.

Pacemaker/marcapasos Pequeño aparato que envía pulsaciones eléctricas constantes al corazón, para que los latidos sean regulares.

Pancreas/páncreas Órgano que produce enzimas que ayudan en la digestión.

Panic/pánico Sentimiento repentino de miedo intenso.

Passive/pasivo Tendencia a renunciar, dejar de lado, o hacerse atrás sin reclamar derechos o necesidades.

Passive smoker/fumador pasivo Una persona no fumadora que respira el humo de segunda mano.

Pathogens/agentes patógenos Organismos microscópicos que causan enfermedades contagiosas.

Peers/compañeros Personas en grupos de la misma edad.

Peer pressure/presión de pares Influencia que personas de tu misma edad tienen sobre ti para que adoptes sus creeencias y forma de actuar.

Peripheral nervous system (PNS)/sistema nervioso periférico Nervios que conectan al sistema nervioso central con todas partes del cuerpo.

Personality/personalidad Combinación singular de sentimientos, pensamientos y conducta que hacen a una persona diferente de todas las demás.

Personality disorder/desorden de personalidad Condición sicológica que afecta la habilidad de una persona de actuar normalmente con otras.

Pesticides/pesticida Producto que se usa en las cosechas para matar insectos y otras plagas.

Phobia/fobia Miedo exagerado hacia una situación o objeto específico.

Physical activity/actividad física Todo movimiento que usa energía.

Physical dependence/dependencia física Adicción en que el cuerpo siente una necesidad directa de una droga.

Physical fitness/buen estado físico Capacidad de cumplir con las exigencias físicas de la vida diaria sin cansarse demasiado.

Pituitary gland/hipófisis Glándula que indica a otras glándulas endocrinas la necesidad de producir hormonas.

Placenta/placenta Tejido espeso y rico que cubre las paredes del útero o matriz durante el embarazo y que nutre al feto.

Plaque/placa bacteriana Película blanda, incolora y pegajosa que contiene bacterias y que se acumula en los dientes.

Pneumonia/neumonía Inflamación seria de los pulmones.

Point-of-sale promotion/punto de promoción de venta Campañas de publicidad en las cuales un producto puede adquirirse en la caja .

Pollen/polen Sustancia en polvo descargada por flores y otras plantas.

Pollution/contaminación Toda sustancia sucia o nociva en el medio ambiente.

Precautions/precauciones Acciones planeadas que son tomadas antes de un evento para incrementar seguridad.

Precycling/preciclaje Proceso de reducir los desechos antes de que se produzcan.

Prejudice/prejuicio Opinión negativa e injusta, generalmente en contra de personas de otro grupo racial, religioso o cultural.

Prenatal care/cuidado prenatal Medidas que se toman para cuidar de la salud de una mujer embarazada y su feto.

Preschoolers/niño en edad preescolar Niños de entre tres y cinco años de edad.

Prescription medicines/medicinas bajo receta Medicinas que sólo se pueden vender con receta de un médico.

Prevention/prevención Tomar acción para hacer que algo no pase o sea peor.

Preventive care/cuidado preventivo Medidas que se toman para evitar que ocurran enfermedades o daños o que empeoren.

PRICE Protege, descansa, hiela, comprime, y eleva.

Proteins/proteínas Nutrientes que el cuerpo usa para crear, reparar y mantener células y tejidos.

Protozoa/protozarios Organismos de una célula que son mas complejos que las bacterias.

Psychiatrist/psiquiatra Médico que trata trastornos de la salud mental.

Psychological dependence/dependencia psicológica Adicción por la cual la mente envía un mensaje al cuerpo indicando que necesita mayor cantidad de una droga.

Psychologist/psicólogo Profesional de la salud mental que está licenciado por el estado para hacer terapias.

Puberty/pubertad Tiempo en el cual empiezas a desarrollar características físicas de adultos de los mismo sexo.

Public health/salud pública Esfuerzos para comprobar y promover el bienestar de la población.

Pupil/pupila Abertura oscura en el centro del iris.

R

Radiation therapy/terapia de radiación Tratamiento que usa rayos X u otra forma de radiación para matar células cancerosas.

Rape/violación Todo tipo de relación sexual contra la voluntad de la persona.

Reaction time/tiempo de reacción Habilidad del cuerpo de responder rápidamente y apropiadamente a diferentes situaciones.

Recall/retirar del mercado La solicitud publica de un fabricante de devolver todos los productos que puedan tener defectos o estén contaminados.

Recovery/recuperación Proceso del aprender a vivir una vida libre de alcohol.

Recurrence/reaparición Regreso de cáncer después de una remisión.

Refusal skills/habilidades de rechazo Estrategias de la comunicación para ayudarte a decir que no de manera eficaz.

Relapse/recaída regresar al uso de la droga después de haber intentado parar.

Relationships/relaciones Conexiones que tienes con otras personas o grupos en tu vida.

Remission/remisión Periodo durante el cual desaparecen las señales y síntomas del cáncer.

Reproductive system/aparato reproductor Órganos que posibilitan la producción de hijos.

Resilience/capacidad de recuperación Habilidad para adaptarse y recuperarse después de una decepción, dificultad o crisis.

Respiration/respiración Intercambio de gases entre el cuerpo y el aire.

Respiratory system/aparato respiratorio Órganos que proporcionan oxígeno continuamente al cuerpo y que eliminan el bióxido de carbono.

Resting heart rate/ritmo cardiaco de descanso Número de veces el corazón late por minuto cuando estás relajado.

Retina/retina Capa delgada de neuronas en el ojo que absorben la luz.

Revenge/venganza Castigo, daño, o insulto hacia una persona por causa de una emoción fuerte.

Rheumatoid arthritis/artritis reumatoide Enfermedad crónica que se caracteriza por dolor, inflamación, hinchazón y anquilosamiento de las articulaciones.

Risk behavior/conducta arriesgada Acto o conducta que puede causarte daño o perjudicarte a ti o a otros.

Risk factors/factores de riesgo Características o comportamientos que incrementan la posibilidad de desarrollar un desorden médico o enfermedad.

Role/papel Parte que tú desempeñas cuando actúas con otra persona.

S

Saliva/saliva Líquido producido por las glándulas salivales de la boca.

Saturated fats/grasas saturadas Grasas que son sólidas a la temperatura ambiente.

Schizophrenia/esquizofrenia Trastorno mental grave por el cual una persona pierde contacto con la realidad.

Secondhand smoke/humo secundario Humo de tabaco en el ambiente.

Sedentary lifestyle/estilo de vida sedentario Forma de vida que incluye poca actividad física.

Self-concept/autoconcepto Manera en que te ves a ti mismo.

Self-esteem/autoestima Opinión que tienes de ti mismo y cuánto te valoras.

Sexual abuse/abuso sexual una persona fuerza a otra persona a participar en actos sexuales en contra de su voluntad.

Sexual harassment/acoso sexual Conducta sexual no solicitada y fuera de lugar dirigida a otra persona.

Sexually transmitted diseases (STDs)/enfermedades de transmisión sexual (ETS) Enfermedades que se propagan de una persona a otra a través del contacto sexual.

Shock/choque Una afección que puede causar la muerte en la cual el aparato circulatorio no lleva la suficiente cantidad de sangre a los tejidos y órganos vitales.

Side effect/efecto secundario Todo efecto o reacción inesperada de una medicina.

Sidestream smoke/humo indirecto El humo producido por la colilla encendida de un cigarrillo, puro o pipa.

Single-parent family/familia de un solo padre Una familia constituida por sólo uno de los padres y un niño o más.

Skeletal muscles/músculo del sistema osteoarticular Músculo ligado a huesos que te permiten mover el cuerpo.

Skeletal system/sistema osteoarticular Sistema corporal interno compuesto de huesos, articulaciones y tejidos conjuntivos.

Small intestine/intestino delgado Órgano digestivo enrollado y semejante a un tubo que mide unos 20 pies de largo.

Smog/smog Neblina de color amarillo-café que se forma cuando la luz solar reacciona con la contaminación del aire.

Smokeless tobacco/rapé Tabaco molido que es masticado o inhalado a través de la nariz.

Smooth muscles/músculo liso Tipo de músculo que se encuentra en los órganos, los vasos sanguíneos y las glándulas.

Social age/edad social Edad calculada de acuerdo con tu estilo de vida y las conexiones que tienes con los demás.

Social health/salud social Habilidad para llevarte bien con las personas que te rodean.

Sodium/sodio Nutriente que ayuda a controlar la cantidad de fluidos en el cuerpo.

Somatic system/sistema somático Parte del sistema nervioso relacionada con las acciones que tú controlas.

Specialist/especialista Médico que está capacitado para tratar determinada clase de pacientes o problemas de salud.

Sperm/espermatozoides Células reproductoras masculinas.

Sperm cell/espermatozoides Célula del padre que entra en el óvulo durante la fertilización.

Sprain/torcedura Una afección en que los ligamentos que mantienen las articulaciones en su lugar están distendidos o quebrados.

Stimulants/estimulantes Drogas que aceleran la actividad en el cerebro humano y la médula espinal.

Strep throat/amigdalitis estreptocócica Dolor de garganta causado por estreptococos.

Stress/estrés Reacción de tu cuerpo a cambios.

Stressor/factor estresante Todo lo que provoca el estrés.

Stroke/apoplejía Afección que ocurre cuando un vaso sanguíneo que lleva oxígeno al cerebro estalla o se obstruye.

Subcutaneous layer/capa subcutánea Capa de grasa debajo de la piel.

Suicide/suicidio Quitarse la vida intencionalmente.

Sympathetic/solidaro Estar consciente que como te puedes estar sintiendo en un momento indicado.

Syphilis/sífilis Enfermedad bacteriana transmitida sexualmente que puede afectar varias partes del cuerpo. Es una enfermedad transmitida sexualmente muy seria.

T

Tar/alquitrán Líquido espeso, oscuro y pegajoso que se forma al quemarse el tabaco.

Target heart rate/ meta ritmo cardiaco Distancia de numeros entre los cuales tu corazón y los pulmones reciben el mayor beneficio por el ejercicio.

Tartar/sarro Placa endurecida que se forma en la superficie de los dientes y que es difícil de quitar.

Tendons/tendones Bandas de tejidos fuertes que unen los músculos y los huesos.

THC Principio activo de la mariguana.

Therapy/terapia Enfoque que enseña una manera diferente de pensar o de comportarse.

Time management/organización del tiempo Estrategias para usar el tiempo eficazmente.

Tissues/tejidos Masa de células similares que desempeñan una función específica.

Toddlers/niño que empieza a andar Niño de entre uno y tres años de edad que está aprendiendo a caminar y a hablar.

Tolerance/tolerancia Habilidad de aceptar a otras personas de la forma que son.

Tolerance/tolerancia Afección por la cual el cuerpo de una persona se acostumbra a los efectos de una medicina y necesita mayor cantidad para que ésta sea eficaz.

Tornado/tornado Tormenta de viento en torbellino, con forma de embudo, que gira en grandes círculos y que puede caer del cielo a la tierra.

Trachea/tráquea Vía respiratoria que dirige el aire a los pulmones.

Traumatic brain injury (TBI)/daño cerebral traumático Condición causada por irritación de cerebro y es notable en el interior del cráneo.

Trichomoniasis/tricomoniasis Enfermedad transmitida sexualmente causada por tricomonas vaginalis.

Tuberculosis/tuberculosis (TB) Una enfermedad bacteriana que normalmente afecta a los pulmones.

Tumor/tumor Una masa de células anormales.

Type 1 diabetes/diabetes tipo 1 Afección por la cual el sistema inmunológico ataca las células productoras de insulina en el páncreas.

Type 2 diabetes/diabetes tipo 2 Afección que se caracteriza por la inhabilidad del cuerpo para usar de manera eficaz la insulina que produce.

U

Umbilical cord/cordón umbilical Conducto que conecta el feto con la placenta de la madre.

Unconditional love/amor incondicional Amor sin restricciones ni reservas.

Underweight/de peso insuficiente Por debajo del peso apropiado de acuerdo con el sexo, estatura, edad, estructura corporal y ritmo de crecimiento.

Universal precautions/precauciones universales Medidas para prevenir la propagación de enfermedades al tratar toda la sangre como si estuviera contaminada.

Unsaturated fats/grasas no saturadas Grasas que permanecen líquidas a la temperatura ambiente.

Uterus/útero Matriz órgano en forma de pera que se encuentra dentro del cuerpo de una mujer donde el embrión es protegido y alimentado.

V

Vaccine/vacuna Preparado de gérmenes muertos o debilitados que se inyecta en el cuerpo para hacer que el sistema immunólogico produzca anticuerpos.

Values/valores Creencias y principios que guían la vida de las personas.

Vector/vector Órganismo, por ejemplo un insecto, que transmite un agente patógeno.

Veins/venas Vasos sanguíneos que llevan la sangre desde el cuerpo de regreso al corazón.

Victim/víctima Cualquier individuo que sufre algún daño, pérdida o muerte debido a la violencia.

Violence/violencia Cualquier comportamiento que cause daño físico o psicológico a una persona o daño a la propiedad.

Virus/virus El organismo más pequeño causante de enfermedades.

Vitamins/vitaminas Sustancias que ayudan al cuerpo a combatir infecciones y aportan otros nutrientes, entre otras funcíones.

Warm-up/precalentamiento Período de ejercicio suave que se hace para preparar al cuerpo para actividad más vigorosa.

Warranty/garantía Promesa de rembolsar el dinero pagado si es que el producto no funciona como lo anunciado.

Wellness/bienestar Estado de bienestar total.

Win-win solution/solución de ganancia doble Un acuerdo o resultado que da algo de lo que quieren a cada lado.

Withdrawal symptoms/síndrome de abstinencia Síntomas que ocurren después del uso crónico de una droga es reducido o suprimido.

Withdrawal/abstinencia Las reacciones físicas y psicológicas que ocurren cuando una persona deja de usar una sustancia adictiva.

Zero tolerance policy/normativa de tolerancia nula Una normativa en que no hay excepciones para nadie por ninguna razón.

Index

Photo Credits

Cover: Getty Images (bl), Picturequest (t, br)

Photo Credits (continued)

Photography; **308:** Richard Hutchings/PhotoEdit; **309:** Brand X/SuperStock; **311:** Michael Newman/PhotoEdit; **313 (both):** SIU/Visuals Unlimited; **315:** Sheila Terry/Science Photo Library; **317:** Don Hammond/Design Pics Inc; **319:** Masterfile Royalty-Free; **320:** Bruce Ayres/Getty Images; **323:** Randy Faris/Corbis; **325:** Pixland/age fotostock; **326:** Martin Riedl/Getty Images; **328:** Stone/Getty Images; **332–333:** Tim Fuller Photography; **334:** Stockbyte/SuperStock; **335:** Dion Ogust/The Image Works; **337:** Myrleen Ferguson Cate/PhotoEdit; **338:** Richard T. Nowitz/Corbis; **340:** Syracuse Newspapers/Danielle Austen/The Image Works; **342:** Phototake Inc./Alamy; **343:** Nicolas Russell/Getty Images; **344:** Royalty-Free/Corbis; **345:** Jose Luis Pelaez, Inc./Getty Images; **346, 347:** Royalty-Free/Corbis; **350:** Andreas Kuehn/Getty Images; **352:** Jonathan Nourok/PhotoEdit; **355:** Jennie Woodcock-Reflections Photolibrary/Corbis; **356:** Ryan McVay/Getty Images; **357:** Nancy Richmond/The Image Works; **358:** Michael Newman/PhotoEdit; **360:** Ariel Skelley/Corbis; **361:** Charles Gupton/Corbis; **362:** Royalty-Free/Corbis; **363:** Robert Llewellyn/Corbis; **364:** Tim Fuller Photography; **366:** Bob Daemmrich/The Image Works; **370–371:** Tim Fuller Photography; **372:** Myrleen Ferguson Cate/PhotoEdit; **373:** David Young-Wolff/PhotoEdit; **374:** Bill Aron/PhotoEdit; **376:** Royalty-Free/Corbis; **379:** Cindy Charles/PhotoEdit; **381:** Don Smetzer/Getty Images; **384:** Angela Maynard/Life File/Getty Images; **386:** Tim Fuller Photography; **388:** Ron Chapple/Getty Images; **390:** Tim Pannell/Corbis; **392:** Christina Kennedy/Getty Images; **396:** LWA-Dann Tardif/Corbis; **398 (top):** K.Lounatmaa/Photo Researchers; **398 (bottom):** Image Source/PunchStock; **402–403:** Tim Fuller Photography; **404:** Jeff Greenberg/PhotoEdit; **406:** Index Stock; **408:** Royalty-Free/Corbis; **409:** Panorama/The Image Works; **413:** Lawrence M. Sawyer/Getty Images; **416:** Momentum Creative Group/Alamy; **420:** Mary Kate Denny/PhotoEdit; **422:** Royalty-Free/Corbis; **423:** Mike Powell/Getty Images; **425:** Index Stock; **427:** Michael Newman/PhotoEdit; **429:** Index Stock; **431, 433:** David Young-Wolff/PhotoEdit; **435:** Paul Windsor/Getty Images; **439:** Ariel Skelley/Corbis; **442:** Bonnie Kamin/PhotoEdit; **444, 448–449:** Tim Fuller Photography; **452:** BananaStock/Alamy; **454:** Fisher/Thatcher/Getty Images; **455:** Rommel/Masterfile; **456:** Neil Bromhall/Science Photo Library; **458:** Stock Solution/Index Stock; **459:** Robert Brenner/PhotoEdit; **460:** Index Stock; **461 (top):** Gareth Brown/Corbis; **461 (center):** David Stoecklein/Corbis; **461 (bottom):** George Shelley/Masterfile; **462:** Laura Dwight/Corbis; **463:** Yellow Dog Productions/Getty Images; **466:** Randy Faris/Corbis; **467:** Bluestone Productions/SuperStock; **468:** Tom Stewart/zefa/Corbis; **469:** Index Stock; **470:** David Young-Wolff/Alamy; **472:** Steve Liss for Time; **476–477:** Tim Fuller Photography; **479:** Kwame Zikomo/SuperStock; **480, 481:** David Young-Wolff/PhotoEdit; **484:** Photodisc; **486:** Taylor Kennedy/Alamy; **488:** age fotostock/SuperStock; **489:** Michael Newman/PhotoEdit; **491:** Tom McCarthy/PhotoEdit; **494:** Digital Vision Ltd./SuperStock; **495, 498:** Tim Fuller Photography; **499:** David Kelly Crow/PhotoEdit; **500:** Michael Newman/PhotoEdit; **502:** Myrleen Ferguson Cate/PhotoEdit; **506–507:** Tim Fuller Photography; **509:** Myrleen Ferguson Cate/PhotoEdit; **510:** Steve Starr/Corbis; **513 (top):** Dr. David M. Phillips/Visuals Unlimited; **513 (bottom):** Steve Gschmeissner/Science Photo Library; **515:** Gabe Palmer/Corbis; **517:** Janine Wiedel Photolibrary/Alamy; **519:** Photodisc Collection/Getty Images; **523:** Pete Saloutos/Corbis; **524:** David Kelly Crow/PhotoEdit; **525:** Jerry Atnip/SuperStock; **528 (top left):** David Fraizer/The Image Works; **528 (top right):** F. Rauschenbach/zefa/Corbis; **528 (bottom left):** bildagentur-online.com/Alamy; **528 (bottom right):** Townsend P. Dickinson/The Image Works; **529 (both):** Lester Bergman; **530:** Stockbyte; **532:** Dennis MacDonald/PhotoEdit; **534 (both):** Courtesy The Eber Family; **538–539:** Tim Fuller Photography; **540:** Steve Mason/Getty Images; **541:** Tim Fuller Photography; **542:** Michelle D. Bridwell/PhotoEdit; **543:** David Young-Wolff/PhotoEdit; **544:** Tim Fuller Photography; **545:** Photodisc Collection/Getty Images; **546:** David Young-Wolff/PhotoEdit; **547:** Altrendo Images/Getty Images; **550:** Aaron Horowitz/Corbis; **552:** Davis Barber/PhotoEdit; **555:** Superstock; **556:** Bob Daemmrich/PhotoEdit; **557, 558:** Tim Fuller Photography; **559:** Bob Daemmrich/The Image Works; **561:** Design Pics Inc./Alamy; **563:** Custom Medical Stock Photos; **568:** Tony Freeman/Photoedit; **570:** Jeff Smith/Fotosmith; **574–575:** Tim Fuller Photography; **576:** Jeff Greenberg/PhotoEdit; **579:** Robert Brenner/PhotoEdit; **580, 581:** Tony Freeman/PhotoEdit; **582:** David Young-Wolff/PhotoEdit; **583:** Dana White/PhotoEdit; **588:** Peter Beck/Corbis